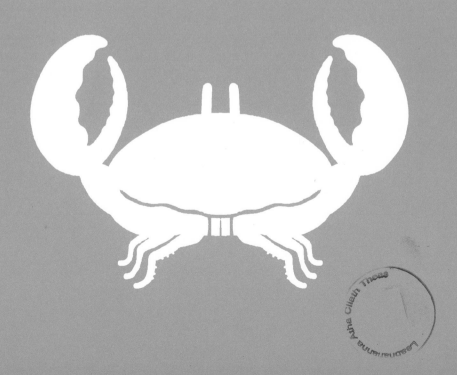

Ceux qui savent manger sont comparativement de dix ans plus jeunes que ceux à qui cette science est étrangère.

♦ ♦ ♦

People who know how to eat are ten years younger than those to whom that science is a mystery.

Jean-Anthelme Brillat-Savarin, *Physiologie du goût* (*The Physiology of Taste*), 1825

RECIPES

FOREWORD

The cuisine of France is among the richest and most diverse in the world, and the techniques and traditions it is built on have had a long-standing influence on chefs everywhere. However, this considerable reputation sometimes overshadows the profound appeal of *cuisine ménagère*, or French home cooking, which is anything but intimidating. It is a style of cooking based on resourcefulness and simplicity, on a wealth of national classics and regional flavours, as fit for everyday meals as for celebrations.

Ginette Mathiot's *Je sais cuisiner* (*I Know How To Cook*) is the perfect illustration of this. In it, she equips her readers with the building blocks for good cooking, educates them about the ingredients they'll encounter and the skills they'll need, and conveys the philosophy that's at the heart of the French kitchen: creating maximum flavour out of a small set of ingredients, and making the most of one's resources through an ingenious use of leftovers and simple preserving techniques. Written in the early thirties, the book reflects the mind-set of an era when the lady of the house spent a good deal of her time at the stove, yet Ginette Mathiot's teachings are no less relevant today: the modern cook is just as concerned as she was about letting well-chosen ingredients shine through, and adopting an economical approach to cooking.

When I got to work on this project and started telling friends that I would help revise and update the book, family stories flew in left and right. Many remembered the battered volume that lived on top of their mother's refrigerator, and had themselves received a copy as a gift when they flew the coop. They told me they had turned to the book to make their first soufflé or their first coq au vin, and referred to it still when they needed guidance on a French classic. I myself own my grandmother's copy of *Je sais cuisiner*. The cover is missing so I don't know which edition it is, but my grandmother got married in 1933 and she must have acquired the book shortly thereafter. The pages have become so fragile they must be turned with care, lest they leave a sprinkle of yellowed paper crumbs in your lap, but I cherish it as the heirloom that it is, and for what it represents.

When *Je sais cuisiner* was first published in 1932, Geneviève Mathiot (Ginette is a nickname) was just twenty-five. As a young home economics teacher, she had been contacted by a French publisher to put together a comprehensive collection of recipes for the home cook, one that would be more practical and exacting than ever before. It would also include — and this was a novel idea at the time — dietary considerations. Mademoiselle Mathiot got to work, enrolled her students to help with the testing, and delivered a manuscript that contained some 1,900 recipes, covering everything a homemaker needed to know about cooking, baking and preserving. The quality, simplicity and breadth of the recipes, as well as the author's sensible voice, made the book an instantaneous success, and a lasting one, too. Seventy-seven years and multiple editions later, the book has sold many millions of copies. Although Ms. Mathiot is no longer here to see it — she passed away in 1998 — her work has stood the test of time like no other.

Initially written with the young bride in mind, to guide her first steps in the kitchen and help her feed her family, *Je sais cuisiner* transcended this pattern as French society evolved. It is not insignificant that the author herself, a strong-headed woman whose dreams of becoming a doctor were thwarted by her conservative family, never married, and instead carved a successful career for herself in the French education system, leading up to her final position as a general inspector. Her book is now used by men and women alike, regardless of their age or situation. They listen to Ginette as they would a knowledgeable relative they can call on for tips when they have a leg of lamb to roast, and future in-laws to impress. Her recipes are dependable, blissfully free of trendy antics, and it is this old-school charm that explains why *Je sais cuisiner* remains, to this day, the best-loved reference on classic French home cooking.

The challenge of the book was this: to offer international editions of *Je sais cuisiner*, and also to make necessary adaptations for the contemporary kitchen. The recipes in the original version are often laconic, in the typical style of French cookbooks, and we opted to fill in the blanks, detailing this or that step and breaking down some of the techniques, to make them accessible to those who haven't learned to cook at their French mother's knee. Additionally, we took the liberty of adjusting some of the recipes to suit the modern palate — by making a more reasoned use of oil and butter, for example, or cooking vegetables and fish more briefly. Such decisions were never made lightly, as our utmost concern was to remain true to the spirit of the original book. Ours was a collaborative effort, involving a team of cookery editors, recipe testers and myself. Batches of recipes travelled back and forth between all of us, to be reworded, augmented, annotated or corrected.

The result is the book you now hold in your hands. Some of the recipes you'll want to make exactly as Ms. Mathiot intended, without changing an iota, while you may adjust others to your taste or your circumstances; all will teach and inspire. We hope *I Know How To Cook* becomes a trusted companion in your kitchen, and serves you as well as it has millions of French cooks since 1932.

Clotilde Dusoulier

Dear Friends,

You want to prepare food that is not too complicated and that will turn out successfully. And isn't this because you want to please the people you are cooking for? So you have chosen this book, which has a long-standing, reliable reputation behind it.

I Know How To Cook will be extremely useful to those men and women who want to cook. This is because a good cookery book must only offer useful information. It will avoid second-rate recipes or those that are too complicated for the way we live now. This is why I am very pleased to be introducing a well-organized work based on sound cooking principles. It must be practical and useful at a time when the need to save time and money is at the forefront of everyone's thoughts. Finally, to keep up-to-date, I have kept in mind those who would like to prepare modern dishes as well as traditional ones.

In creating the recipes and menus, I have always been careful to follow the rules of a nutritious diet. You will also find dishes from the different regions of France. The explanations are given in the simplest possible way, and recipes always serve six. Naturally, the time given for preparation will vary with the experience of the person who is making the dish. But at least the cook will know that some dishes are quicker to make than others. The cooking times are given accurately, from the time it comes to the boil or is put in the (preheated) oven. The oven temperature is always stated. This means that you can follow the recipes without fear of failure.

The many letters that I have received from readers of this book since the first edition appeared have helped me supplement and make improvements to each new edition. I hope that this simple book of family food will remain my readers' favourite adviser.

Ginette Mathiot

GINETTE'S COOKING FUNDAMENTALS

WHY DO WE EAT?

Everyone more or less knows the answer: we have to eat to live. But how should we eat? This is what most people don't know and don't want to find out, despite the vast amount of information and advice given in books and magazines. In modern times, as the science behind food becomes better known — sometimes to the exclusion of simple pleasures — our diet is too often left to habit and prejudice, or depends on chance or whim. But knowing how to provide food for yourself is a science that cannot be neglected without harming your health and your family budget.

Food fulfils two essential needs for our bodies: the need for energy (provided by carbohydrates, fats and proteins), and the need for building, repairing and keeping the body in working order (for which proteins, vitamins, minerals, fibre and water are useful). The French are appreciative and fond of their food; they won't refuse to heed dietary advice, but above all the food must be delicious.

We should therefore make every effort to satisfy these needs, and create harmony between the various courses of a meal so that the palate is stimulated. The main course should be a climax of flavour without dominating the meal; its impact will be toned down by the dessert, which will create a satisfying end to the meal. Each dish should have its own special flavour, not masked by intense aromas, but rather combining them with the food to provide a background of secondary flavours or half-tones that enhance the main ingredient: the backdrop to its true flavour.

Everyone's life would certainly be much simpler if the meal pills promised by scientists became available. But then life would lose one of its main attractions. What is more pleasant than a properly conducted meal or a well-presented dish with an aroma so good that just smelling it makes your mouth water? Fortunately, it is still necessary to prepare most foods by cooking them to make them fit to eat. It is an opportunity to give full rein to your imagination, for cooking is an art. But the cook must also obey the rules of the kitchen, because it should not be forgotten that cooking is also a science.

COOKING UTENSILS

Although it is tempting to buy a lot of kitchen utensils, it is far better to buy a small quantity of well-made items, rather than cluttering the kitchen with too many utensils.

However, it is not possible to limit oneself to a single item. Ideal cooking utensils are sturdy, rust-proof, have an internal lining that will not be damaged in use, are good conductors of heat and easy to clean. To make sweets and preserves, a copper pan is essential; for stews, cast iron is ideal; but for heating water a stainless steel pan is best. A set of stainless steel pans with thick bases and firm insulated handles offers many advantages: they are easy to clean, durable, and affordable. Aluminium pans are also practical.

Cheap pans have many disadvantages: they are not robust, the metal is of poor quality, is too thin and the shape is not practical. Ovenproof glass cookware is perfectly functional, but it is at the mercy of accident: once cracked or broken, it is unusable.

UTENSILS FOR FOOD PREPARATION

- Mechanical or digital scales
- 2 measuring jugs, 1 litre (1¾ pints) and ¼ litre (8 fl oz)
- Clock and timer
- Stockpot or large pan, 24 x 24 cm (9½ x 9½ inches)
- 1 heavy-based pan, 28 cm (11¼ inches) in diameter
- 1 set of 5 pans with lids
- 2 cast-iron casseroles
- 2 non-stick frying pans, 24 and 28 cm (9½ and 11¼ inches) in diameter
- 1 electric deep-fryer
- 2 oval roasting dishes
- 2 gratin dishes
- 1 funnel
- 1 large pan with double base for steaming
- 2 terrines of different sizes
- 1 blender
- 1 food processor
- 1 vegetable mill or mouli
- 1 mini-mouli (herb chopper)
- 2 colanders, with different-sized holes
- 1 mechanical mincer
- 1 cleaver
- 1 pestle and mortar
- 2 spatulas
- 1 ladle
- 1 slotted spoon
- 1 conical sieve (chinois)
- 1 grater
- 1 chopping board
- 4 table mats
- 1 set of cooking knives (including paring knife, filleting knife, chopping knife, sharpening steel and potato peeler)

UTENSILS FOR CAKES AND PASTRIES

- 1 board for kneading and rolling out doughs and pastries
- 1 scraper for removing the mixture from the board
- 1 rolling pin
- 1 manual or electric whisk
- 1 piping bag with nozzles
- 1 pastry brush
- 1 wooden spoon
- 1 wire rack for cooling cakes
- Cookie cutters in various shapes and sizes
- Various cake tins and moulds, 20–25 cm (8–10 inches) in diameter:
  loaf tins
  rum baba tins
  tart tins
  charlotte moulds
  cake tins
  sandwich tins
  high sided tins
  12-hole muffin tins
  flan dishes
  round and oval tartlet tins
- 1 baking tray

UTENSILS FOR CONFECTIONERY

- 1 preserving pan
- 1 slotted spoon
- 1 copper pan
- 1 mortar and pestle
- 1 sweet cutter

LA PELOTE
★★★

COOKING METHODS

BOILING AND POACHING

Boiling or poaching in water are good methods for cooking very dense foods such as pasta and pulses. Flavours can pass from the liquid into the food itself, such as in a court-bouillon, or they can pass from the ingredients into the liquid covering them, such as in a stock.

When food is added directly to boiling water, the flavours are less likely to seep into the water, so this method is suitable for preserving maximum flavour through rapid cooking, such as for green vegetables. However, during prolonged cooking, soluble substances will eventually pass into the liquid.

When food is added to cold water which is gradually heated, the juices are slowly released into the liquid, so the flavour and nutritional value of the liquid is increased at the same time as it is lost from the food. This is how meat and vegetable stocks are prepared.

STEAMING

A steamer is composed of two pans placed one above the other. The base of the upper container, in which the food to be cooked is placed, is pierced with holes. The lower container holds the boiling water. If a steamer is not available, a colander placed over a pan of boiling water may be used. There are also many kinds of small perforated baskets with collapsible sides, which can be used in pans of different sizes, as they can be adjusted to fit.

DEEP-FRYING

The fats most often used for deep-frying are a combination of vegetable oils and animal fats, which can be heated to high temperatures. Groundnut oil gives high quality fried food. Sunflower, corn and rapeseed oils are more easily damaged by heat and should be used for shallow frying. Any fat used for frying should be brought to a high temperature (180°C/350°F) before the food is added, so that the outer layer cooks rapidly.

Oil should never be allowed to smoke: it goes brown and takes on an unpleasant taste. The food to be cooked should be added carefully in small batches to the hot fat. If the food contains starch it will turn golden brown and crisp, which is why fried foods are often coated in breadcrumbs, batter or flour. The heat of the fat caramelizes this outside layer and the inside cooks in its own juices (such as in vegetable fritters). To achieve this, the fat must be very hot, and the food must be dry with no moisture clinging to it, and must be cut into small pieces.

ROASTING

Roasting involves cooking food in a hot oven with very little fat. The cooking temperature depends on the kind of meat and how well-done it should be. Red meat is browned at 220–240°C/425–475°F/Gas Mark 7–8 to brown the surface, then the temperature is reduced to 200°C/400°F/Gas Mark 6 to complete the cooking. White meat and poultry are roasted at this lower temperature throughout, so that the meat browns and cooks through at the same time.

GRILLING

The process for grilling is always the same: raw ingredients are lightly brushed with oil and exposed to direct heat from a burner. The grill must be heated before beginning the operation. If food is grilled over a wood fire, the smoke permeates it and it takes on a delicious flavour. When cooking red meat on a grill, turn it with tongs or a spatula. Do not prick it with a fork, or the juices will run out.

SPIT-ROASTING

Grills are suitable for small pieces of meat, but a spit is needed for large joints. The spit must be constantly turned (some spits rotate automatically) so that the same surface area is not left exposed to the heat for too long. The joint must be basted frequently during cooking with the fat and juices that run from the meat.

POT-ROASTING

Pot-roasting involves cooking a joint of meat in a covered casserole (or heavy-based pan) on the stove, with a little fat, such as butter, on a bed of sliced carrots, onions or other aromatic vegetables. This cooking technique is used mainly for large joints of veal and large birds such as chickens, capons, or turkeys, which risk drying out if roasted in an oven. During cooking, the aromatic vegetables release steam and this reduces the risk of the joint drying out. Start by browning the roast on all sides, salt it lightly and continue cooking, tightly covered, turning the meat about every 15 minutes.

BRAISING

Braising is the cooking method of the classic meat and vege-table dish estouffade, which was once the boast of French cuisine. It is a very slow cooking process that requires the heat to be evenly distributed. For best results, braised meat should be cooked with the heat coming from above and below. The cooking vessel, a casserole or heavy-based pan with a lid, should be tightly sealed. The dish should be seasoned at the beginning of cooking and the exact time needed for cooking should be calculated.

The steam condenses on the lid and falls onto the meat during cooking, which eventually becomes infused with the flavours of the food, giving the gravy its special flavour. The meat (usually large joints such as top rump of beef) is larded (or studded with bacon) and often marinated the day before cooking. It is browned and braised slowly, covered in a slightly thickened, highly flavoured sauce with aromatic vegetables.

STEWING

Stewing is a cooking method that offers the same advantages and disadvantages as braising. The meat and vegetables cook together in a sauce thickened with flour in a tightly covered casserole or heavy-based pan. A stew does not need a lot of attention. The food becomes deliciously infused with the flavourings, such as spices, wine and stock, with which it is cooked. The cooking must be slow and even. Stews can be white or brown. For a white stew, or blanquette, the pieces of meat or poultry are not browned and the sauce is made with a white stock. Cream may be added, such as for a chicken fricassée. For a brown stew, the pieces of meat or of poultry are well browned first, then a liquid such as red wine or brown stock is added, such as for a navarin or coq au vin.

SAUTÉING (SHALLOW-FRYING)

Sautéing should be done quickly. The food, cut into small pieces, is placed in hot fat or oil in a deep frying pan or sauté pan. Brown the food on one side; when it is half cooked, turn it over to brown the other side. This method is suitable for escalopes, steaks and fish à la meunière. Always remove the fat before deglazing the frying pan.

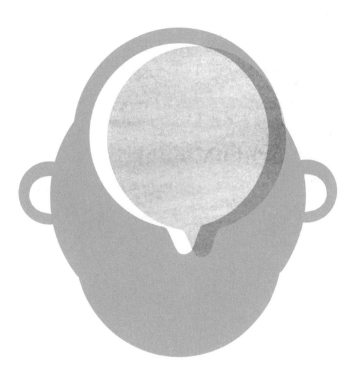

WINE

SELECTING WINES

Brillat-Savarin, the eighteenth-century French gastronome, advised drinking wines in order of strength, from the weakest to the strongest. The selection of wines to accompany a meal must be done very carefully: mild-flavoured food requires a light young wine that can be served cool. Spicy food and dishes with sauces require more full-bodied wines with stronger flavours. It is also important to serve each type of wine at the right temperature to enhance its bouquet.

TEMPERATURE

WHITE AND ROSÉ WINES
These should be served very cool at 6–12°C/43–54°F, if they are dry.

CHAMPAGNE
Chill in the refrigerator, then place in a wine bucket filled with ice cubes.

RED WINES
Red wines are served at room temperature, around 22°C/72°F. Burgundies are often served cooler, around 16°C/60°F. Bordeaux should be served at a slightly higher temperature (18°C/64°F) to be fully appreciated.

SERVING WINES

Table wines can be poured into carafes. Some older wines should be decanted. AOC (*Appellation d'origine contrôlée*) wines are served in the original bottle: if there is a lot of sediment, the bottle can be placed on its side in a special basket to allow it to settle. Very old bottles should not be wiped clean. In general, avoid serving wine with soup or anything with a vinaigrette dressing, such as salad or asparagus. The flavour of wine is spoiled if it is served with chocolate desserts or fruit, especially oranges.

HORS-D'ŒUVRES
Dry or medium-dry white or rosé wine, as long as it is light: try Chablis, Pouilly-Fumé, Sylvaner, Arbois, Muscadet, Rosé des Riceys, Montlouis, Côtes de Provence and Sancerre.

OYSTERS AND CRUSTACEANS
Dry white wine: Muscadet, white Burgundy and Traminer.

FISH STARTERS
Dry or medium-dry white wines are best with fish starters (see the suggestions for hors-d'œuvres).

Sweet wines go well with fish in rich cream and butter sauces: try white Bordeaux such as Barsac, Graves, Château Suduiraut, Château d'Yquem and Château Filhot. White Burgundy is also perfect, such as Meursault and Montrachet, or Alsace wines such as Riesling and Gewürtzraminer. It is better to serve a red or rosé wine with fish that has been cooked in red wine.

MEAT & VEGETABLE STARTERS

These are so varied that it is difficult to give precise instructions on which wine to serve. If the dish contains pastry and offal, such as croustades, vol-au-vents, bouchées, calves' sweetbreads, quenelles and so on, the wine should be white or rosé, dry or medium-dry (see the suggestions for fish starters). If it contains poultry, it may be accompanied with a red wine as long as it is light, supple, and low in tannin. Try red Bordeaux such as Château Lafite, Château Margaux, Saint-Émilion, Saint-Estèphe and Saint-Julien.

ROAST MEAT AND GAME

Red wines for roast meat must be high quality and should be full-bodied for red meat and lighter-bodied for white meat.

Bordeaux: Pomerol, Château-Lafite, Château-Margaux, Saint-Émilion, Saint-Estèphe and Saint-Julien.

Red Burgundy: Gevrey-Chambertin, Closes-Vougeot, La Tâche, Vosne-Romanée, Nuits-Saint-Georges, Corton, Côte de Beaune and Pommard.

FOIE GRAS

In general, slightly sweet white wines or wines from the regions of foie gras production are recommended. Try Sauternes, Monbazillac, Montrachet, Jurançon and Gewürztraminer.

CHEESE

Red wine is usually served with cheese. But the wine should be chosen to suit the cheese. So, for example, Gruyère and Brie require a less full-bodied wine than Roquefort. Goat's milk cheese goes well with a dry white wine such as Sancerre.

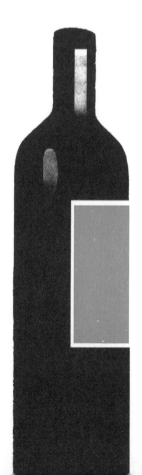

DESSERTS

Champagne is often served with desserts, and medium-dry is the best type to choose. However it should be borne in mind that Champagne is only really appreciated when it is served alone, either at certain points during the meal (in which case it should be dry), or independently of the meal, when the guests' tastes should be taken into account and both medium-dry and dry Champagne should be served. It is usual to end the meal with the same type. Other wines suitable for desserts are white Bordeaux such as Sauternes, Barsac, Loupiac and Monbazillac.

Mention should also be made of some other highly prized wines, such as Vouvray, Saumur and Vin de Paille from the Jura, and fortified wines such as sherry, Banyuls and Muscat.

Grand cru wines can be expensive, but for simple meals there are excellent simpler wines that are more easily available. Whites include Mâcon, Chablis and Zwicker; rosés include Rosé d'Anjou, Tavel and Bourgueil; reds, Bourgueil, Fleurie and Juliénas. There is an increasing trend to serve a single kind of wine throughout the meal; in this case, it should be light, young and served cool.

SEASONAL FOOD

One of the most important factors in devising a menu is whether the ingredients are in season. Now that most fruit and vegetables are available all year round, it is very tempting to use them out of season. However, it is important to remember that things are generally more expensive out of season, and do not have as much flavour. The table on the following pages shows the seasons for the principal meats, fish, cheeses, vegetables and fruit.

	MEAT & FISH	CHEESE	VEGETABLES	FRUIT
JANUARY	Beef Lamb Mutton Rabbit Turkey Wild boar Oysters Snails	Brie Camembert Cantal Goat's milk cheese Livarot Maroilles Munster Parmesan	Cardoons Carrots Celery and celeriac Cabbage Brussels sprouts Crosnes Chicory Leeks Pumpkins	Bananas Clementines Dates Chestnuts Walnuts Oranges Pears Apples
FEBRUARY	Lamb Wild boar Venison Frogs' legs Snails Lemon sole Oysters Salmon Salt cod Whiting	Brie Camembert Bleu de Gex Livarot Parmesan	Barbe-de-Capucin Broccoli Celery and celeriac Cabbage Crosnes Lamb's lettuce Mixed salad leaves Dandelions Salsify Jerusalem artichokes	Pineapples Lemons Dates Oranges Pears Apples
MARCH	Kid Lamb Veal Snails Bream Carp Oysters Perch Salt cod Whitebait Whiting	Bondon Brie Camembert Coulommiers Gorgonzola Swiss cheese	Asparagus Carrots Celery and celeriac Brussels sprouts Cauliflower Spinach Lamb's lettuce Turnips Cos lettuce Salsify	Pineapples Bananas Kiwis Oranges Pears Apples

	MEAT & FISH	CHEESE	VEGETABLES	FRUIT
APRIL	Duckling	Brie	Asparagus	Pineapples
	Grain-fed chicken	Coulommiers	Cauliflower	Bananas
	Kid	Gournay	Cucumbers	Strawberries
	Lamb	Neufchâtel	Lettuce	Oranges
	Pigeon	Roquefort	Morel mushrooms	Kiwis
	Mackerel		Sorrel	
	Salmon		Peas	
	Shad		New potatoes	
	Whiting		Radishes	
			Cos lettuce	
MAY	Chicken	Goat's milk cheese	Artichokes	Almonds
	Kid	Coulommiers	Asparagus	Bananas
	Pigeon	Gournay	Carrots	Cherries
	Rabbit	Neufchâtel	Cucumbers	Strawberries
	Frogs' legs	Roquefort	Watercress	Kiwis
	Cod		Spinach	Melons
	Ling		Broad beans	
	Mackerel		French beans	
	Sea bream		Lettuce	
	Shad		Turnips	
			Sorrel	
			Peas	
			Radishes	
			Cos lettuce	
JUNE	Chicken	Bel Paese	Asparagus	Apricots
	Duck	Bondon	Aubergines	Cherries
	Kid	Coulommiers	Carrots	Strawberries
	Lamb	Gorgonzola	Cucumbers	Raspberries
	Pigeon	Gournay	Courgettes	Redcurrants
	Turkey	Edam	Broad beans	Melons
	Conger eel	Parmesan	Lettuce	Peaches
	Mackerel	Pont-l'Évêque	Turnips	
	Skate		Peas	
	Trout		Potatoes	
	Whiting		Cos lettuce	
			Tomatoes	

	MEAT & FISH	CHEESE	VEGETABLES	FRUIT
JULY	Beef Mutton Pigeon Veal Conger eel Crayfish John Dory Sole Spiny lobster Turbot	Edam Gournay Gruyère Pont-l'Évêque Port-Salut Reblochon	Artichokes Butterhead lettuce Carrots Cauliflower Cucumbers Courgettes Beans Lettuce Turnips Custard marrows Peas Sweet peppers Cos lettuce Tomatoes	Apricots Almonds Bananas Nectarines Cherries Strawberries Raspberries Redcurrants Melons Peaches Plums
AUGUST	Chicken Turkey Carp Crayfish Lobster Spiny lobster Trout	Bel Paese Gournay Gruyère Edam Neufchâtel Pont-l'Évêque Port-Salut Reblochon	Aubergines Carrots Courgettes Beans Turnips Custard marrows Peas Sweet peppers Tomatoes	Apricots Cherries Figs Melons Mirabelle plums Hazelnuts Peaches Apples Grapes Greengages
SEPTEMBER	Hare Partridge Poultry Rabbit Mussels Young partridge Mackerel Oysters	Bleu de Gex Gorgonzola Gruyère Livarot Mont-d'Or Port-Salut Saint-Marcellin	Aubergines Cauliflower Wax beans Fresh haricot beans Lettuce Cos lettuce Tomatoes Truffles	Pineapples Bananas Figs Raspberries Melons Mirabelle plums Blackberries Walnut William pears Apples Red plums Greengages

	MEAT & FISH	CHEESE	VEGETABLES	FRUIT
OCTOBER	Beef Hare Mutton Partridge Pheasant Pork Veal Venison Wild boar Rock salmon Sole Whiting	Brie Camembert Cheddar Livarot Pont-l'Évêque	Aubergines Broccoli Carrots Celery and celeriac Flageolet beans Mixed salad leaves Turnips Tomatoes	Quinces Figs Kiwis Walnuts Apples Red plums Grapes
NOVEMBER	Beef Goose Hare Mutton Partridge Pork Rabbit Mussels Oysters Sardines Tuna	Brie Camembert Cantal Cheddar Livarot Maroilles Parmesan	Broccoli Endive Brussels sprouts Chicory Beans Lentils Mixed salad leaves Cos lettuce Salsify Jerusalem artichokes	Dates Kiwis Chestnuts Medlars Oranges Pears Apples Grapes
DECEMBER	Beef Goose Hare Mutton Pork Rabbit Turkey Haddock Monkfish Skate Sea bass Sea bream	Brie Camembert Cantal Livarot Maroilles Munster Parmesan Pont-l'Évêque	Wild chicory Broccoli Brussels sprouts Savoy cabbage Chicory Dried pulses Chestnuts Mixed salad leaves Salsify	Bananas Clementines Dates Persimmons Chestnuts Hazelnuts Walnuts Pears Apples

FLAVOURINGS

A wide range of ingredients can be added to dishes to give them flavour. Some are ingredients in their own right, and as well as altering the flavour of the dish, they can improve its nutritional value. Flavourings are an essential part of the art of cooking, both for stimulating the appetite, adding depth of flavour and, often, for garnishing dishes. The immense variety of flavourings is like an artist's palette for anyone who loves to cook. Flavourings can basically be divided into four types: aromatic vegetables, herbs, spices and souring agents.

AROMATIC VEGETABLES

These include garlic, shallot and various other members of the onion family, as well as celery.

CELERY
The stalk and leaves are used in cooking, as is the root (celeriac). Celery is frequently used to flavour stock, pot-au-feu and purées. Celery salt is used in tomato juice.

ONIONS
These are very widely used in cooking and form the base of a large number of dishes. To avoid tears when peeling an onion, do it under cold running water or put it in the refrigerator beforehand. The pungent flavour is moderated by cooking and the naturally sweet flavour develops.

GARLIC
Garlic cloves are covered in a fine skin; to remove this, crush each clove under the wide part of the blade of a knife, pressing it hard. The skin will then be easily removed. Pink garlic is milder in flavour.

SHALLOTS
Shallots are similar to garlic and onion, although their taste is generally not as strong. Their subtle flavour forms the base of a great number of sauces.

HERBS

Herbs play a starring role in many dishes. Some form an essential part of traditional dishes, while others offer an opportunity to discover unfamiliar flavours. You can try all sorts of combinations, but aromatic herbs should be used sensibly and in moderation. Most herbs are associated with particular regions, so it is best to use them in dishes that come from the same part of the world, or have sympathetic ingredients.

Generally it is better to use fresh herbs for a fuller flavour, but some herbs, notably the 'woody' plants such as thyme, rosemary and oregano, retain a good flavour when dried, and are better suited to long, slow cooking. Some leafy herbs, notably chervil, basil and chives, have a delicate flavour that can be lost if they are cooked for too long, so it is best to add them towards the end of the cooking process.

BASIL

The tender leaves of this plant have a very subtle flavour that spoils easily. Do not put it through the blender to chop it. In fact, it is often just torn and added at the very end of cooking. It works well in salads and with summer vegetables. Basil is the main ingredient of pesto and the French equivalent, *pistou*.

BAY LEAVES

The leaves of the bay tree have a particularly strong flavour, so should be used in moderation or they may impart bitterness. They can be empolyed fresh or dried, and they are often used in long, slow cooking. They are essential in the making of stock, court-bouillons and in meat stews. Bay is an essential element in a bouquet garni.

BOUQUET GARNI

A bouquet garni is a bunch of herbs tied together or gathered in a muslin bag and used to flavour soups and stews. They are then removed before serving. A bouquet garni can be varied to taste, but almost always includes a bay leaf, some parsley stalks and thyme, but can also feature many other sturdier herbs.

CHERVIL

The delicate leaves of this herb have a subtle aniseed flavour that is useful in soups, some sauces and mixed salads. To retain the full flavour, take the leaves off the stalks. Chervil is one of the classic *fines herbes*.

CHIVES

A member of the onion family, the stalks of this fragrant herb resemble the green tops of very young spring onions. With a delicate and elusive flavour similar to that of the onion, but less pungent, they are best used raw or added at the end of cooking. Chives are another of the classic *fines herbes*.

DILL

An umbelliferous plant with a strong aniseed flavour, dill may be used to enhance a wide variety of dishes, but is particularly good with fish and in pickles.

FENNEL

Another umbelliferous plant, fennel is related to Florence or bulb fennel. The very fine leaves of fennel may be used in place of dill, although it is sweeter and more subtle in flavour. Fennel stalks are often used to flavour grilled, barbecued and flambéed fish. Fennel seeds are common in the cooking of the south of France.

FINES HERBES

This mixture of finely chopped fresh herbs, including chervil, parsley, tarragon and chives, is a classic addition to many French sauces and meat and cheese dishes. It is also well known as an omelette filling. Nowadays, other herbs can be added to the classic quartet, such as thyme.

LEMON BALM

This mint-like herb has a pleasant lemon flavour and is often used in salads and to flavour meat and poultry dishes.

LEMON GRASS

An aromatic herb used in Oriental cooking, notably in Thai cuisine and the cooking of other parts of South-East Asia.

LEMON VERBENA

This herb, native to South America, has a very powerful lemon aroma and flavour that needs to be used with caution. It is primarily used in sweet dishes such as fruit salads.

MARJORAM

Milder in flavour than oregano, marjoram is used in salads, in a wide variety of cooked dishes and with raw vegetables, notably carrots and cucumber. It is best used raw or added late in the cooking process.

MINT

Mint is often used in savoury preparations such as mint sauce and is good with peas and potatoes. Mint is also one of the few herbs used in sweet dishes.

OREGANO

This Mediterranean herb, closely related to marjoram, is strongly flavoured and rarely used raw. It is common in pasta sauces and in Greece it is often used with meat, especially lamb.

PARSLEY

Parsley is commonly used as a garnish for savoury dishes of all kinds. Flat-leaf parsley is more strongly flavoured and peppery than the curly-leaved variety. Parsley is another of the classic *fines herbes* and forms part of a bouquet garni.

ROSEMARY

Rosemary is good for flavouring vegetables and meats, especially suckling pig, veal, lamb and game. It keeps its pungency well when dried. Use this herb with moderation, as it has a very strong aroma and flavour.

SAGE

There are several varieties of this perennial, all with a very distinctive (rather camphor-like) aroma, which does not go well with other aromatic herbs.

SAVORY

Savory can be used in soups, salads and with certain vegetables and pulses.

TARRAGON

One of the herbs essential in the classic *fines herbes* mixture, this fragrant herb is available all year round. It is used chopped or as whole leaves. Its anise-like flavour is powerful and should be used sparingly.

THYME

Thyme is considered by some to be the secret of French cooking. It forms part of a bouquet garni, and suits every sort of dish, but should not be used too regularly. It can be added to *fines herbes*.

SPICES

Spices are becoming increasingly common in French cooking. Ever since the great voyages of exploration, many of these unusual and tasty ingredients have been finding their place in the French culinary repertoire. Today spices are used to make the flavour of a recipe 'sing'.

ANISE
An umbellifer originating in Asia Minor. The seeds are commonly used in pastries and confectionery. In cooking, it is used to flavour some shellfish and mussel dishes.

CHINESE OR STAR ANISE
Used in Chinese food and in making spirits and liqueurs.

CINNAMON
This spice comes in the form of small rolled sticks taken from the bark of a tree, and also as a powder. Since early antiquity, it has been used to spice game, duck, pork and many milk and egg puddings, desserts, cakes and pastries.

CARDAMOM
A spice known in Europe for two millennia. It comes in small pods or as a powder. It has a bitter, peppery taste and is used in processed pork products and in pastries. It is one of the ingredients of curry powder.

CARAWAY
The seeds are dark brown and crescent-shaped, and are often used in processed pork products and sauerkraut. It can be used to flavour any dish, according to taste.

CAYENNE PEPPER
A variety of hot pepper that comes in the form of a reddish powder. It has a hot flavour that is essential in certain shellfish recipes and fish soups.

CHILLI
A hot pepper originating in Mexico, with a pungent flavour. There are many varieties with different degrees of strength.

CLOVES
Cloves were already being used in cooking 800 years ago. The leaves and stalks can be used, but they are most commonly found whole or as a powder. Cloves are very useful when stuck into an onion or shallot, which is then simmered in a pot-au-feu or court-bouillon, or with game.

CORIANDER

An umbellifer whose leaves are used in soups and its seeds in marinades and with fish and vegetables.

CUMIN

Frequently used in Arabic cooking, cumin has a warm flavour.

CURRY POWDER

Curry powder is a mixture of twelve or fifteen different spices. It is used in many curry recipes.

JUNIPER

The fruit of a small evergreen shrub, juniper is used in sauerkraut, marinades and with some game. It is sold as dried berries or as a powder.

GINGER

A very ancient spice, known to the Roman writer Pliny. It comes in the form of a rhizome, and is sold as such, as a powder, or preserved in syrup. It is a strong flavouring that tastes hot, and is widely used to spice white meats, and even fish.

HARISSA

A very strongly flavoured paste prepared from dried hot peppers, crushed and marinated in oil with garlic, coriander, caraway and salt. Accompanies barbecued meats and enhances strong sauces.

MIXED SPICE

A mixture of spices in powder form, including pepper, nutmeg, cloves and ginger. Frequently used in processed pork products and in slowly cooked dishes such as stews and civets.

NUTMEG

Whole nutmeg is grated to flavour many dishes, such as spinach, mashed potato, omelettes, soufflés and chopped meats.

PAPRIKA

A red powder obtained by crushing small hot Hungarian or Spanish peppers. Paprika may be strong, smoked, mild or semi-mild. It is used to flavour shellfish, sauces, eggs, risotto, fish and chicken.

PEPPER

This spice comes in several forms: pink, green, grey, white, and black. Several types can be used together to add variety. White pepper comes in the form of ripe, shelled seeds. Black pepper is the berry, dried before it ripens. Avoid using powdered pepper; use only freshly ground pepper from a pepper mill.

SAFFRON

A powder obtained from the stigma of a variety of crocus, saffron is traditionally used in dishes such as paella and bouillabaisse. It also enhances rice and white meats.

TABASCO

A very hot bottled sauce. A few drops are enough to spice a mild dish, such as stuffed avocados or prawn cocktail.

SOURING AGENTS

Acidic flavourings can enliven some delicately flavoured dishes, but they should not be added to all sauces. Too much acidity in cooking is undesirable and bad for the digestion.

CAPERS

Capers are the flower buds of the caper bush. They are pickled, either in vinegar or in brine; the latter method preserves them better. They can be used to flavour sauces, fish and meats such as rabbit and veal, according to your tastes.

LEMON

Lemon has many culinary uses, as a seasoning and in cakes and pastries, both in the form of the grated zest and the juice.

GHERKIN

A variety of small cucumber. The flesh is firm and the surface rough. They can be bought raw when in season, to be pickled in vinegar, which is how they are usually sold in the shops. Gherkins often accompany processed pork products and other meats, and are the base of many sauces.

MUSTARD

A condiment prepared from powdered mustard seeds, herbs, vinegar or wine. There are a very wide variety of mustards, sometimes with additions such as ginger or coriander, or with sherry, raspberry or tarragon vinegar.

VINEGAR

A product of the acidification of wine by an aerobic bacterium. Food can be enlivened with vinegar, as long as it is well chosen. It is used in court-bouillons, sauces and sweet-and-sour dishes. Vinegar can be made from wine, cider, sherry, raspberries, and many other ingredients.

GLOSSARY

ACIDULATE

To add lemon juice or vinegar to water (or another liquid) to prevent vegetables such as globe artichokes from turning black.

AL DENTE

The point during cooking at which pasta or vegetables are tender, but retain some bite.

ASPIC

A clear jelly made from clarified meat or fish stock.

BAIN-MARIE

The vessel used for a gentle method of heating in which the dish to be cooked is placed in, or over, a pan of hot water, which is then placed in the oven or simmered very gently on the stove.

BARD

To cover a joint of meat or line a pan with strips of bacon or bacon rind, known as bards, to prevent it from drying out.

BIND

To add egg yolks or other thickening agents to a sauce, stuffing or other preparation to thicken it and help it cohere.

BLANCH

To cook food briefly in boiling water, often vegetables. Usually followed by 'refreshing', or plunging straight into cold water to stop the cooking. It is sometimes done to help remove the skin more easily.

BOUQUET GARNI

A small bunch of herbs, including flat-leaf parsley, thyme and bay leaf tied together with string. It is added to sauces and stocks.

BRAISE

To cook gently in a sealed pan with stock or thickened sauce.

BROWN

To fry ingredients in very hot fat in order to colour the surface.

CANAPÉ

Originally a slice of bread fried in butter and covered with a variety of fillings or forcemeats. Now it can mean any bite-sized piece of food.

CAUL

The fatty membrane enclosing the paunch of mammals, especially calves, used in cooking to wrap roast meat.

CHARLOTTE MOULD

A deep circular mould, usually made from non-reactive metal, used for many French cakes and puddings. It tapers towards the bottom and is sometimes gently fluted. A deep round dish can usually be substituted.

CHINOIS

A fine-meshed conical sieve.

CLARIFY

To pass a liquid through a fine-meshed strainer or heat it with egg whites to remove any solid particles and leave a perfectly clear liquid.

CLARIFIED BUTTER

Butter from which the white milk solids have been removed, usually by heating and skimming.

COAT

To cover a dish with a substance, such as a sauce.

CREAM

To beat egg yolks or butter and sugar together with a whisk or wooden spoon until they become thick and pale in colour.

DECANT

To gently transfer a liquid (usually wine) that contains sediment into another container, so that the deposit is left behind.

DECOCTION

A substance boiled in a liquid to extract the soluble elements.

DUXELLES

A mixture of chopped mushrooms, shallots and parsley used as a forcemeat or stuffing.

EMULSIFY

To mix liquids of different densities together to form a thicker liquid, often with the help of an emulsifier, such as mustard.

FARCE

A fine-textured meat or fish-based purée, used on its own or to stuff other dishes.

FLAMBÉ

To pour an alcoholic liquid, such as brandy, over food and ignite it to burn off the alcohol, while keeping the flavour.

GIBLETS

The feet, wings, neck, head, liver and gizzard of poultry. They are often used in making stocks.

GLAZE

To brush the surface of food with a liquid, usually pastry, with a mixture of water and egg yolk. Or, to coat a dish with a thick sauce or syrup before serving.

GRATIN

A dish that has been sprinkled with dried breadcrumbs or grated cheese and browned in a hot oven.

INFUSION

A liquid obtained by pouring boiling water over parts of a plant to extract the flavour.

JULIENNE

To cut vegetables such as carrots, turnips, celery or the white part of leeks into very thin strips.

KNEAD

To work a dough against a work surface with the palm of the hand, until smooth.

LARD

To insert strips of fat bacon into meat at even intervals in the direction of the grain, using a larding needle.

MACÉDOINE

A mixture of vegetables or fruit cut into dice.

MACERATE

To leave food in prolonged contact with a liquid, such as a spirit or liqueur, to flavour and tenderize it.

MARINATE

To place raw meat or other foods in an aromatic liquid to tenderize it prior to cooking, or to add extra flavour.

MIREPOIX

Diced vegetables and herbs fried until brown. Used to intensify the flavour of gravies and sauces.

MOISTEN

To add a liquid, such as water, milk or stock, to a sauce.

MUSLIN

A very fine cloth used to strain sauces and jellies.

POACH

To cook gently in a liquid such as stock, water, milk or sugar syrup.

PURÉE

To reduce ingredients to a smooth paste in a food processor or blender. Also, the name given to the paste itself.

QUENELLE

Small dumplings, often in a characteristic oval shape, poached in water or stock.

REDUCE

To boil or simmer a liquid to evaporate the water it contains, thereby concentrating the flavour and thickening it.

REFRESH

To plunge cooked food into cold water to stop the cooking process quickly.

ROUX

A paste made from melted butter and flour, which forms the basis of many thickened sauces. Also sometimes used to describe the sauce itself.

SAUTÉ

To cook food in a high-sided frying pan or sauté pan with very little fat over a high heat.

SCALD

To heat a liquid, usually milk, to just below boiling point.

SIMMER

To cook slowly over a gentle heat. Simmering point is the point at which a liquid is about to boil, with just a few bubbles breaking the surface.

SINGE

To pass plucked poultry or game birds over an open flame to remove any small feathers.

SLASH

To make a diagonal cut in a piece of fish to prevent it bursting during cooking.

STEAM

To cook in a perforated container set over boiling water with a tightly fitting lid.

STOCK

A flavoured cooking liquid obtained by simmering beef, veal, or poultry with vegetables and aromatics for 2–3 hours. Skim off the fat before use. For speed, a meat stock cube can be dissolved in hot water, and good liquid stocks are also available.

STUD

To insert small strips of fat bacon into the surface of a white meat (such as veal medallions, calves' sweet-breads, poultry breasts) using a larding needle so that the surface does not dry out.

STUFF

To fill the inside of a piece of meat or a vegetable with stuffing.

THICKEN

To add ingredients, such as egg yolks, to make a sauce or soup thicker.

TRIM

To remove all the inedible or blemished parts from food.

TRUSS

To fasten a piece of meat, often a bird, with kitchen string passed though the wings and legs with a trussing needle to keep it in place during cooking.

TURN

To trim a vegetable to a rounded shape while peeling it.

WELL

A hole hollowed out of a mound of flour, into which liquids are added.

ZEST

The thin outer layer of a citrus fruit, on top of the white pith. Usually grated.

- 1 -
SAUCES
&
BASIC RECIPES

SAUCES

There are many sauces in French cuisine, and they can be categorized according to the preparation method. They can coat or surround the dish they accompany, or can be served separately in a sauce boat. Sauces are usually highly flavoured, and are often rich in fat. However, with careful adjustment, some sauces can be included in a healthy diet to help add variety. There are so many sauces that the flavour and appearance of the dishes they are served with can take on infinite variations. Depending on what is available, and the number of guests they are entertaining, French cooks judiciously adapt existing sauce recipes and create new ones when necessary.

For roux-based sauces, home-made beef or veal stock is best, but good quality shop-bought liquid stock or stock powder can be substituted. The recipes in this chapter yield around 500 ml (18 fl oz) sauce, which is normally enough for six people.

JUS

FROM ROAST MEAT
During basting, the fat slides over the joint and gradually accumulates the savoury matter and proteins adhering to it. This mixture forms the *jus*, or natural juices, of the roast.

FROM BRAISED MEAT
The gravy that forms naturally when meat is braised comes from the juices extracted from the meat by the application of heat. The more flavour there is in the juices, the less the meat will retain its own flavour. However, if the cooking process is long enough, the meat takes on the flavour of the juices in which it is braised, and the flavours mingle. Vegetables can also produce delicious juices.

THICKENED SAUCES

When a sauce lacks body or smoothness, it can be improved by adding an ingredient to thicken it. Some starchy ingredients, such as flour, potato or rice flour or breadcrumbs, simply give the sauce body; others, such as cream, egg yolks, butter or blood, also improve the flavour.

THICKENINGS BASED ON STARCH
Mix the starch (flour, potato or rice flour, or cornflour) in a small quantity of cold liquid and pour into the boiling sauce, stirring constantly. Allow to boil for a few moments. It is a simple procedure but should be done with care.

THICKENINGS BASED ON PROTEIN
To thicken sauces with protein, use blood or egg yolks. Slowly and carefully add the hot sauce to the yolks, stirring briskly with a whisk. Then put the sauce on a gentle heat and stir constantly until it thickens; stop before it coagulates completely. The sauce must not boil.

THICKENINGS BASED ON FAT
Fats, carefully added to a liquid, form an emulsion which gives the sauce flavour and consistency. Beat butter or cream into a liquid that is hot but not boiling. Boiling destroys the emulsion and spoils the sauce's delicate flavour.

ROUX

A roux is a sauce made with flour cooked in fat, usually butter, then made into a paste by adding a hot liquid. Depending on how long the flour is cooked, the colour and flavour of the sauce will be more or less pronounced. Roux can be white, blond or brown. They can be mixed with a wide variety of liquids, such as water, milk, stock, wine, or the liquid in which the dishes with which they are to be served have been cooked.

The principle is the same for all types of roux. Put the butter in a pan and melt it (without letting it change colour, if making a white roux). Add the flour. Cook, stirring with a wooden spoon, until the mixture becomes frothy. Allow the flour to cook until it turns light fawn for a blond roux, or brown for a brown roux. Once the flour is cooked to the right stage, gradually pour in the hot liquid, stirring briskly and steadily, over a fairly high heat. However, do not let a brown roux get too dark, because the resulting sauce will be too brown and have a bitter, acrid taste.

EMULSIFIED SAUCES

Emulsified sauces are unstable, delicate preparations, in which an ingredient is vigorously stirred in contact with a liquid, forms fine droplets in suspension, and becomes thick and smooth in appearance. The substance to be emulsified is usually a fat such as cream, butter or oil. The liquid may be oil, water or vinegar. Nowadays the most familiar of these sauces are vinaigrette and mayonnaise. Béarnaise sauce and hollandaise sauce are also widely used. To make an emulsified sauce, beat the fat steadily, slowly adding the liquid; it may be either cold or hot, but it must be kept at an even temperature. If the emulsion separates it is often because the heat has not been evenly distributed. Making an emulsified sauce always requires care.

COULIS, REDUCTIONS & STOCKS

There is a wide range of preparations such as coulis, reductions and stocks (or *fumets*), which form the basis of many sauces, and can be added to improve their colour and flavour. They generally consist of a concentration of the flavours of ingredients such as mushrooms, shellfish or herbs.

BASIC PREPARATIONS FOR SAUCES

BÉARNAISE ESSENCE
ESSENCE BÉARNAISE

- 1 litre (1¾ pints) white
  wine vinegar
- 300 ml (½ pint) dry white wine
- 500 g (1 lb 2 oz) onions,
  chopped
- 375 g (13 oz) shallots, chopped
- 1 large handful of tarragon,
  chopped
- Pepper

Preparation time: 20 minutes
Cooking time: 2 hours
Makes 500 ml (18 fl oz)

This flavouring essence forms the basis of béarnaise sauce (p.75) and the many other sauces derived from it. It keeps well in the refrigerator.

Put all the ingredients in a large pan, bring to a simmer and allow the liquid to evaporate gently over a low heat for about 2 hours, or until reduced in volume by about three-quarters. Strain and discard the solids. Store the liquid in an airtight container in the refrigerator.

GREEN SPINACH PURÉE
VERT D'ÉPINARDS

- 125 g (4¼ oz) spinach
- 125 g (4¼ oz) fresh tarragon
- 100 g (3½ oz) fresh chervil

Preparation time: 5 minutes
Cooking time: 1 minute
Makes 350 ml (12 fl oz)

Bring a large pan of water to the boil and blanch the spinach and herbs in it for 1 minute. Drain and immediately place in a bowl of very cold water to cool completely. Drain again, then purée in a blender or by pushing through a sieve. Use promptly, as the colour will darken to brown very rapidly. Use this vivid green purée to colour sauces.

MIREPOIX

MIREPOIX

Melt the butter in a frying pan over a medium heat and fry the vegetables and ham gently for 5–10 minutes, or until softened. Remove from the heat and stir in the herbs. Use to add flavour to a wide range of sauces.

- **50 g (1¾ oz) butter**
- **100 g (3½ oz) carrots, diced**
- **5 g (1 teaspoon) diced shallot**
- **50 g (1¾ oz) onion, diced**
- **100 g (3½ oz) lean raw ham, diced**
- **1 handful of thyme, finely chopped**
- **1 handful of flat-leaf parsley, finely chopped**
- **1 bay leaf**

Preparation time: 15 minutes
Cooking time: 5 minutes
Makes 250 g (9 oz)

FISH GLAZE

GLACE DE POISSONS

Put all the ingredients except the salt and pepper in a large pan with 1 litre (1¾ pints) water, bring slowly a simmer and cook gently for 30 minutes. Strain, discard the solids, return the liquid to the pan, bring back to a simmer and cook gently for a further 1½ hours, or until reduced by about three-quarters. Season with salt and pepper, leave to cool in a shallow dish, then transfer to an airtight container and store in the refrigerator.

- **500 ml (18 fl oz) white wine**
- **1 kg (2¼ lb) bones and trimmings from whiting, gurnard or other white fish**
- **60 g (2 oz) turnip, chopped**
- **60 g (2 oz) carrot, chopped**
- **50 g (1¾ oz) onion, chopped**
- **1 bouquet garni**
- **1 handful of flat-leaf parsley, chopped**
- **Salt and pepper**

Preparation time: 20 minutes
Cooking time: 2 hours
Makes 500 ml (18 fl oz)

MEAT GLAZE

GLACE DE VIANDE

- 1 kg (2¼ lb) veal or beef bones
- 1 piece of bacon rind
- 1 kg (2¼ lb) lean raw ham, chopped
- 60 g (2 oz) turnip, chopped
- 60 g (2 oz) carrot, chopped
- 50 g (1¾ oz) onion, chopped
- 1 handful of flat-leaf parsley, chopped
- 1 bouquet garni

Preparation time: 30 minutes
Cooking time: 3 hours
Makes 500 ml (18 fl oz)

A meat glaze is a concentrated stock used to add flavour and colour to meat dishes and sauces.

Put the bones, bacon rind and ham in a large pan with 2.5 litres (4½ pints) water. Bring to the boil, reduce the heat and simmer for 15 minutes. Skim, and add the vegetables and herbs. Do not add salt. Bring back to the boil, then simmer over a low heat for 3 hours. Strain, then return the liquid to the pan and continue to simmer until reduced to a glaze-like consistency. Strain the finished reduction, leave it to cool in a shallow dish, then transfer to an airtight container and store in the refrigerator.

MEAT JELLY OR ASPIC

GELÉE DE VIANDE

- 1 kg (2¼ lb) veal knuckle
- 500 g (1 lb 2 oz) beef silverside
- 150 g (5 oz) bacon rind, fat removed
- 2 onions, chopped
- 1 carrot, chopped
- 1 bouquet garni
- Salt and pepper
- 3–4 gelatine leaves (if needed)
- 2 egg whites, to clarify
- 100 ml (3½ fl oz) Madeira, port or sherry, to flavour (optional)

Preparation time: 25 minutes
Cooking time: 4 hours
Makes 500 ml (18 fl oz)

Meat jelly and aspic are made from reduced stocks, which set naturally due to the gelatine in the meat and bones. For aspic, the stock is first clarified so that the jelly will be clear and suitable for its many roles in glazing and garnishing meats and terrines.

Put all the ingredients except the gelatine, egg whites and alcohol, if using, in a large pan with 2.5 litres (4½ pints) water and bring to the boil. Skim and allow to simmer on a steady heat for about 4 hours. Carefully strain through a sieve lined with muslin and allow to cool completely. Remove the fat, which will solidify on the top. When the stock is cold, check the consistency: if it has not set, warm it up and add 3–4 gelatine leaves soaked in cold water.

To clarify the jelly for aspic, beat the egg whites lightly. Put the stock in a pan, stir in the egg whites and gently beat all the liquid, without stopping, so that the egg whites turn frothy, while heating very gradually until the liquid just comes to the boil. If desired, add Madeira, port or sherry to flavour it. Pour the clarified liquid through a sieve lined with damp muslin, discard the solids and leave to set in the refrigerator.

MUSHROOM STOCK

FUMET DE CHAMPIGNONS

Wipe the mushrooms with a damp cloth (do not peel them) and chop them. Melt the butter gently in a pan with a tight-fitting lid, add the lemon juice, 120 ml (4 fl oz) water, and the mushrooms, cover and cook gently for about 10 minutes. Strain and reserve the liquid, which can be reduced further to intensify the flavour if required. Use the liquid to flavour sauces. The cooked mushrooms can be reserved and used as a garnish.

- **250 g (9 oz) mushrooms**
- **60 g (2 oz) butter**
- **1 tablespoon lemon juice**

Preparation time: 10 minutes
Cooking time: 10 minutes
Makes 120 ml (4 fl oz)

FISH STOCK

FUMET DE POISSON

Melt the butter in a large pan and cook the onion and fish bones and trimmings gently for about 8 minutes, or until the onion has softened. Add the wine and just enough water to cover. Add the lemon juice and parsley stalks and season lightly with salt. Cover and cook gently for 20–25 minutes. Strain and leave to cool, then store in the refrigerator. The stock can be used for sauces or fish soups.

- **50 g (1¾ oz) butter**
- **50 g (1¾ oz) onion, sliced**
- **500–600 g (1 lb 2 oz–1 lb 5 oz) bones and trimmings from fish such as sole, whiting or brill**
- **200 ml (7 fl oz) dry white wine**
- **2 teaspoons lemon juice**
- **4 parsley stalks**
- **Salt**

Preparation time: 10 minutes
Cooking time: 20–25 minutes
Makes 500 ml (18 fl oz)

ROAST MEAT JUS

JUS DE RÔTI

A jus, or gravy, for roast meat can be made by dissolving the caramelized sediment at the bottom of the roasting tin in a hot liquid (wine, stock or water) while the meat is resting. It is important to scrape hard with a wooden spoon to free as much of the flavourful residue as possible, and if wine is used, the gravy should be simmered for a few minutes to evaporate the alcohol. The gravy should be strained and the fat removed if necessary, then seasoned with salt and pepper.

If the gravy is too pale, thin or lacking in flavour, it may be reduced very slightly on a high heat. Those who prefer a thickened gravy can add a little cornflour dissolved in a tablespoon or so of water. The gravy should then be brought to the boil, and simmered for a minute or two to thicken and remove any floury taste. If required, add an extra flavouring to the finished gravy, such as Madeira, port, sherry or tomato purée. A little added butter gives it a nice sheen.

'POOR MAN'S' SAUCE

SAUCE SANS CORPS GRAS 'PAUVRE HOMME'

- 3 shallots, chopped
- 1 large handful of flat-leaf parsley, chopped
- 1 bouquet garni
- 500 ml (18 fl oz) pork or game stock
- 1 tablespoon white wine vinegar or lemon juice
- Salt and pepper

Preparation time: 5 minutes
Cooking time: 5 minutes
Makes 500 ml (18 fl oz)

Put the shallots, parsley and bouquet garni in a pan with the stock and vinegar or lemon juice. Season with salt and pepper, bring to the boil, then reduce the heat and simmer for 5 minutes, or until the shallots are tender. Excellent for serving with very fatty or rich meats, like pork and some game.

MAÎTRE D'HÔTEL BUTTER

MAÎTRE D'HÔTEL

 p.83

Beat the butter with the parsley and lemon juice, and season with salt and pepper. Put the mixture in the centre of a small sheet of greaseproof paper or foil and use this to roll the mixture into a log. Chill until required. When ready to serve, unwrap the butter, cut it across into coin shapes and place one on top of each serving. The butter will melt immediately to provide a rich sauce and goes particularly well with grilled meats such as steaks.

- **80 g (2¾ oz) butter, softened**
- **1 small handful of flat-leaf parsley, chopped**
- **1 teaspoon lemon juice**
- **Salt and pepper**

Preparation time: 15 minutes
Makes 90 g (3¼ oz)

RAVIGOTE BUTTER

BEURRE RAVIGOTE

Bring a pan of water to the boil and put the herbs into the boiling water for about 3 minutes. Drain well and chop the herbs finely. Knead them well into the butter, then pass the butter through a sieve to remove the solids. Put the butter in the centre of a small sheet of greaseproof paper or foil and use this to roll the butter into a log. Chill until required. When ready to serve, unwrap the butter, cut it across into coin shapes and place one on top of each serving. Ravigote butter goes well with fish dishes.

- **1 large handful of mixed herbs, such as chervil, chives, tarragon and watercress**
- **80 g (2¾ oz) butter, softened**
- **Salt and pepper**

Preparation time: 5 minutes
Makes 90 g (3¼ oz)

BLACK BUTTER

BEURRE NOIR

p.84

Melt the butter carefully in a small frying pan, stirring continuously, and cook until the milk solids turn deep brown, but not black. If they turn black the butter should be discarded. Pour the butter into a dish. Remove the pan from the heat, add the vinegar and stir for a moment, then pour it over the butter and mix well. Serve with grilled or fried fish, as well as egg and vegetable dishes.

- **60 g (2 oz) butter**
- **1 tablespoon white wine vinegar**

Preparation time: 5 minutes
Makes 75 ml (3 fl oz)

BEURRE BLANC
BEURRE BLANC

- 100 g (3½ oz) shallots, chopped
- 20 g (¾ oz) tarragon
- 100 ml (3½ fl oz) white wine
- 50 ml (2 fl oz) white wine vinegar
- 50 ml (2 fl oz) double cream
- 250 g (9 oz) butter, slightly softened
- Salt and pepper

Preparation time: 15 minutes
Cooking time: 20 minutes
Makes 500 ml (18 fl oz)

In a small dry pan, gently heat the shallots with a few tarragon leaves for a few minutes. Stir in the wine and all but a little of the vinegar. Simmer over a low heat for about 10 minutes to reduce. Add the cream and bring to the boil. Add the butter in small pieces, beating vigorously with a whisk. Process in a blender and add the remaining vinegar to make the sauce smoother. Season with salt and pepper. A little chopped tarragon may be added at the last moment.

COLBERT SAUCE
SAUCE COLBERT

- 200 ml (7 fl oz) meat jelly (p.45)
- 70 g (2½ oz) butter
- 1 tablespoon lemon juice
- 1 handful of flat-leaf parsley, chopped

Preparation time: 10 minutes
Cooking time: 10 minutes
Makes 250 ml (8 fl oz)

Heat the meat jelly in a small pan and, off the heat, add the butter in small pieces, stirring all the time. Finish by adding the lemon juice and parsley. This sauce is often served with fish, especially sole, but it can also be served with grilled meat or vegetables. It can also be flavoured with tarragon, nutmeg, cayenne pepper or Madeira, depending on what it is to be served with.

BERCY SAUCE (FOR MEAT)
SAUCE BERCY (POUR VIANDES)

- 3 shallots, finely chopped
- 200 ml (7 fl oz) white wine
- 50 g (1¾ oz) meat glaze (p.45)
- 50 g (1¾ oz) butter
- Salt and pepper
- 50 g (1¾ oz) beef marrow, finely diced
- 1 large handful of chopped parsley

Preparation time: 10 minutes
Cooking time: 25 minutes
Makes 150 ml (¼ pint)

Named after a part of Paris with a very large wine market, the classic Bercy sauce contains fish stock and is often served with poached fish. This version is suitable for meat and often accompanies grilled entrecôte.

Put the shallots in a small pan and add the wine. Bring to a simmer and reduce the liquid by half over a gentle heat, stirring regularly. This will take around 15–20 minutes. Add the meat glaze, then add the butter in small pieces, beating the mixture constantly. Season with salt and pepper, then stir in the beef marrow and parsley, and cook for a few more minutes.

ROUX-BASED SAUCES

WHITE SAUCE
SAUCE BLANCHE

This basic flour-thickened white sauce is the foundation of many other everyday preparations, such as cream, béchamel and cheese sauces.

METHOD 1
Melt the butter in a pan. Stir in the flour and cook for 2–3 minutes to form a paste. Gradually add the hot water, stirring all the time to prevent lumps forming, and simmer for 10 minutes. Since the absorbency of different flours can vary, it is difficult to specify the exact quantity of liquid needed, so add just enough water to achieve the required consistency. Season with salt and pepper.

- 30 g (1¼ oz) butter
- 40 g (1½ oz) flour
- 500 ml (18 fl oz) hot water
- Salt and pepper

Preparation time: 10 minutes
Cooking time: 20 minutes
Makes 500 ml (18 fl oz)

METHOD 2
This alternative method produces a sauce with a lighter flavour. Put the flour in a pan and gradually add 100 ml (3½ fl oz) cold water to make a paste. In another pan, heat 500 ml (18 fl oz) water and, as soon as that comes to the boil, pour it into the flour paste, stirring continuously. Season with salt and pepper and simmer to reduce to the desired consistency. Add the butter in small pieces just before serving.

- 40 g (1½ oz) flour
- Salt and pepper
- 50 g (1¾ oz) butter

Preparation time: 5 minutes
Cooking time: 20 minutes
Makes 500 ml (18 fl oz)

VARIATIONS

. . . .

BÉCHAMEL SAUCE
SAUCE BÉCHAMEL

 p.85

Widely used in egg, vegetable and gratin dishes, béchamel is made in exactly the same way, following either method above, but with milk instead of water. Depending on how it is to be used, it is also often flavoured with freshly grated nutmeg.

· ·

CHEESE SAUCE

SAUCE MORNAY

Stir 100 g (3½ oz) grated Gruyère or Parmesan cheese into the white or béchamel sauce. The cheese thickens the sauce.

· ·

CREAM SAUCE

SAUCE À LA CRÈME

Over medium-low heat, stir 90 ml (3¼ fl oz) double cream into the white sauce, then whisk in an egg yolk. Do not allow the sauce to boil. Serve with eggs, fish, poultry and vegetables.

NORMANDY CREAM SAUCE

SAUCE À LA CRÈME NORMANDE

- 300 ml (½ pint) thick white sauce (p.50)
- 100 ml (3½ fl oz) fish stock (p.46)
- 100 ml (3½ fl oz) mushroom stock (p.46)
- 1 egg yolk
- 90 ml (3¼ fl oz) double cream

Preparation time: 10 minutes
Cooking time: 20 minutes
Makes 500 ml (18 fl oz)

Prepare the white sauce and just before serving, while it is still hot, whisk in the fish stock, mushroom stock, egg yolk and cream over a medium-low heat, without allowing the mixture to boil. Stir well and serve immediately. This is often served with fish but also goes with chicken and game birds, in which case Calvados replaces the fish stock.

BUTTER SAUCE

SAUCE BÂTARDE

- 1 quantity white sauce (p.50)
- 40 g (1½ oz) butter
- 2 egg yolks, beaten
- 1 tablespoon lemon juice

Preparation time: 15 minutes
Cooking time: 20 minutes
Makes 500 ml (18 fl oz)

Prepare the white sauce and, while it is still hot, put it in a heatproof bowl set over a pan of barely simmering water, over a very gentle heat. Add the butter and egg yolks to the sauce and allow it to thicken, stirring frequently. Do not overheat. Stir in the lemon juice just before serving. Good with poached fish and vegetables.

POULETTE SAUCE
SAUCE POULETTE

Prepare the white sauce, add the onions and simmer for 10–15 minutes, or until the onions are tender. Just before serving, remove and discard the onions (or use them as garnish), stir in the lemon juice and wine, turn down the heat to its lowest setting and stir in the butter and egg yolk. Continue stirring until the sauce thickens. Do not overheat. Originally served with chicken, this sauce is now more often served with snails, seafood and mushrooms. It has a delicate flavour and normally has no seasoning.

- 300 ml (½ pint) white sauce (p.50)
- 100 g (3½ oz) onions, quartered
- 1 tablespoon lemon juice
- 100 ml (3½ fl oz) dry white wine
- 50 g (1¾ oz) butter
- 1 egg yolk

  Preparation time: 10 minutes
  Cooking time: 20 minutes
  Makes 500 ml (18 fl oz)

SUPREME SAUCE
SAUCE SUPRÊME

Prepare the white sauce, add the mushrooms and simmer for 30 minutes. Finish by stirring in the cream. Serve with fried or poached poultry.

- 300 ml (½ pint) white sauce (p.50), made with chicken stock
- 125 g (4¼ oz) mushrooms or mushroom peelings, wiped and cut into pieces
- 100 ml (3½ fl oz) double cream

  Preparation time: 25 minutes
  Cooking time: 30 minutes
  Makes 500 ml (18 fl oz)

NANTUA SAUCE
SAUCE NANTUA

Named after the town of Nantua in the historic Bugey region on the Rhône River, which is famed for its crayfish, this rich sauce is sometimes enhanced with black truffles.

Prepare the béchamel sauce, add half the cream and heat gently. Stir in the remaining cream, the butter and the crayfish tails.

- 300 ml (½ pint) béchamel sauce (p.50)
- 200 ml (7 fl oz) double cream
- 60 g (2 oz) prawn butter (p.99) or ordinary butter
- 10 crayfish tails, shelled and cooked (p.286)

  Preparation time: 1 hour
  Cooking time: 25 minutes
  Makes 500 ml (18 fl oz)

SOUBISE SAUCE

SAUCE SOUBISE

Cook the onions in boiling water for 10 minutes. Drain and put them in a pan with the butter, wine, stock and any meat juices. Allow to simmer for a further 20 minutes, then strain the liquid. Add the liquid and cream to the white sauce at the same time. Season with salt and pepper and do not allow the sauce to cook any longer. Often served with cooked eggs, meat and vegetables.

- 350 g (12 oz) onions, coarsely chopped
- 30 g (1¼ oz) butter
- 100 ml (3½ fl oz) white wine
- 100 ml (3½ fl oz) meat or vegetable stock
- Meat juices (if the sauce is to be served with cooked meat)
- 100 ml (3½ fl oz) double cream
- 300 ml (½ pint) white sauce (p.50)
- Salt and pepper

Preparation time: 10 minutes
Cooking time: 35 minutes
Makes 500 ml (18 fl oz)

HORSERADISH SAUCE

SAUCE AU RAIFORT

Prepare the béchamel sauce. Add the wine and horseradish to the hot sauce and simmer gently for a further 5 minutes. Good with beef, potatoes, pork and smoked fish.

- 1 quantity béchamel sauce (p.50)
- 50 ml (2 fl oz) white wine
- 1 tablespoon grated fresh horseradish

Preparation time: 10 minutes
Cooking time: 25 minutes
Makes 500 ml (18 fl oz)

PRINTANIÈRE OR CHIVRY SAUCE

SAUCE PRINTANIÈRE OU CHIVRY

Prepare the white sauce. Bring a pan of water to the boil and blanch the herbs for 1 minute. Drain well, chop and knead with the butter. Stir the herbed butter into the hot white sauce. Good with fish, poultry and eggs.

- 1 quantity white sauce (p.50)
- 80g (2¾ oz) herbs, including tarragon, chervil, chives and parsley
- 125 g (4¼ oz) butter

Preparation time: 20 minutes
Cooking time: 20 minutes
Makes 500 ml (18 fl oz)

ANCHOVY SAUCE
SAUCE AUX ANCHOIS

- **1 quantity white sauce (p.50)**
- **60 g (2 oz) anchovy butter (p.100)**
- **A few anchovy fillets (optional)**

Preparation time: 15 minutes
Cooking time: 20 minutes
Makes 500 ml (18 fl oz)

Prepare the white sauce and stir in the anchovy butter while the sauce is hot. A few anchovy fillets, sliced very thinly, may be added. Good with poached fish and eggs.

PRAWN SAUCE
SAUCE AUX CREVETTES

- **1 quantity white sauce (p.50) made with court-bouillon (p.82) or fish stock (p.46)**
- **100 g (3½ oz) prawn butter (p.99)**

Preparation time: 1 hour
Cooking time: 20 minutes
Makes 500 ml (18 fl oz)

Prepare the white sauce using the court-bouillon or fish stock and stir in the prawn butter while the sauce is still hot.

MUSSEL SAUCE
SAUCE AUX MOULES

- **1 litre (1¾ pints) mussels, well cleaned**
- **1 quantity white sauce (p.50) made with court-bouillon (p.82) or fish stock (p.46)**
- **1 egg yolk, beaten**

Preparation time: 30 minutes
Cooking time: 20 minutes
Makes 500 ml (18 fl oz)

Discard any mussels that stay open when tapped sharply. Pour a little water in a large pan with a tight-fitting lid, add the mussels and cook over a high heat, covered, for a few minutes, shaking the pan from time to time, until all the mussels have opened. (Discard any that do not open.) Strain and reserve the cooking liquid, shell the mussels (discarding the shells) and keep both cooking liquid and mussels warm. Prepare the white sauce and add the mussels and their cooking liquid. Over a low heat, whisk in the egg yolk until the sauce thickens slightly; do not overheat. Good with fillets of fish.

JOINVILLE SAUCE

SAUCE JOINVILLE

Prepare the white sauce and keep it warm while preparing the hollandaise sauce. Stir the white sauce into the freshly made hollandaise sauce, along with the prawn butter, prawns and truffle, if using. Joinville sauce is usually served with elaborate fish dishes.

- **3 tablespoons white sauce (p.50)**
- **500 ml (18 fl oz) hollandaise sauce (p.74)**
- **50 g (1¾ oz) prawn butter (p.99)**
- **100 g (3½ oz) cooked peeled prawns**
- **10 g (¼ oz) black truffle, cut into julienne strips (optional)**

Preparation time: 30 minutes
Cooking time: 30 minutes
Makes 500 ml (18 fl oz)

CAPER SAUCE

SAUCE AUX CÂPRES

Prepare the béchamel sauce and add the capers while the sauce is still hot. Do not allow it to boil. Serve with poached fish or mutton dishes.

- **1 quantity béchamel sauce (p.50)**
- **125 g (4¼ oz) capers, drained**

Preparation time: 10 minutes
Cooking time: 20 minutes
Makes 500 ml (18 fl oz)

RAVIGOTE SAUCE

SAUCE RAVIGOTE

Prepare the white sauce. In a small pan over a gentle heat, bring the vinegar, wine and shallot to the boil. Simmer to reduce until only 50 ml (2 fl oz) of liquid remains (about 10 minutes) and stir into the white sauce. Simmer for 6 minutes, then strain and keep warm. Just before serving, add the herbs and butter. Do not overheat. This delicate sauce is often served with poached chicken or offal such as calves' heads and brains.

- **1 quantity white sauce (p.50) made with poultry or veal stock**
- **50 ml (2 fl oz) white wine vinegar**
- **50 ml (2 fl oz) white wine**
- **1 shallot, chopped**
- **1 teaspoon chopped chervil**
- **1 teaspoon chopped tarragon**
- **1 teaspoon chopped chives**
- **40 g (1½ oz) butter**

Preparation time: 20 minutes
Cooking time: 15 minutes
Makes 500 ml (18 fl oz)

BLOND ROUX
ROUX BLOND

- **50 g (1¾ oz) butter**
- **60 g (2 oz) flour**
- **500 ml (18 fl oz) stock or water**
- **Salt and white pepper**

Preparation time: 10 minutes
Cooking time: 20 minutes
Makes 500 ml (18 fl oz)

Melt the butter in a heavy-based pan over a moderate heat. When it is hot, on the point of smoking, add the flour and cook, stirring with a wooden spoon, until the roux is light fawn in colour and still sandy in texture. Take the roux off the heat and gradually add the stock or water, stirring constantly to avoid lumps. Return to the heat and slowly bring to the boil, stirring all the time. Once boiling, reduce the heat to a simmer and cook gently for 2 minutes to cook out the taste of flour. Season to taste with salt and pepper.

TOMATO SAUCE
SAUCE TOMATE

- **750 g (1 lb 10 oz) tomatoes, quartered**
- **60 g (2 oz) butter**
- **30 g (1¼ oz) flour**
- **120 ml (4 fl oz) vegetable stock**
- **1 carrot, diced**
- **1 onion, diced**
- **1 sprig of parsley, chopped**
- **1 sprig of thyme, chopped**
- **1 bay leaf**
- **Salt and pepper**

Preparation time: 10 minutes
Cooking time: 30 minutes
Makes 500 ml (18 fl oz)

Put the tomatoes in a pan, with no oil or butter, and cook for 5 minutes over a moderate heat, stirring from time to time. Make a purée by pushing them through a sieve. Prepare a blond roux (see above) with 30 g (1¼ oz) of the butter and the flour, and stir in the sieved tomato pulp. Add the stock, and the carrot, onion, parsley, thyme, bay leaf, salt and pepper. Allow to simmer for 30 minutes. Just before serving, stir in the remaining butter.

FINANCIÈRE SAUCE
SAUCE FINANCIÈRE

- **1 quantity blond roux (above), made with chicken stock**
- **Juice of 1 lemon or 100 ml (3½ fl oz) Madeira**
- **A few truffle slices, chopped (optional)**
- **Salt and pepper**

Preparation time: 25 minutes
Cooking time: 25 minutes
Makes 500 ml (18 fl oz)

Prepare the sauce and add the lemon juice or Madeira and the truffle, if using. Allow to simmer for a few minutes. Season with salt and pepper. Serve with calves' sweetbreads (p.370), poultry quenelles (p.104), or mix with chopped mushrooms as a filling for vol-au-vents or bouchées.

RICHELIEU SAUCE

SAUCE RICHELIEU

Prepare the blond roux and add the truffle and mushrooms. Allow to simmer for 5 minutes, then stir in the butter just before serving. This sauce is often served with roast beef, duck and game.

- 1 quantity blond roux (p.57) made with chicken stock
- Truffle shavings, to taste
- 125 g (4¼ oz) mushrooms, chopped
- 10 g (¼ oz) butter

Preparation time: 15 minutes
Cooking time: 25 minutes
Makes 500 ml (18 fl oz)

BORDELAISE SAUCE

SAUCE BORDELAISE

Prepare the blond roux and set aside. Melt half the butter in a medium pan, add the shallot and cook for 8 minutes, or until translucent. Add the pepper, bay leaf, thyme and wine, and simmer to reduce this mixture by half. Stir it into the blond roux. Simmer gently for 25 minutes, then strain. Finally, stir the rest of the butter, and the beef marrow (if using), into the sauce. Bordelaise sauce is usually served with grilled meat and, if made with white wine, fish.

- 1 quantity blond roux (p.57)
- 40 g (1½ oz) butter
- 30 g (1¼ oz) finely chopped shallot
- Pepper
- 1 bay leaf
- 1 sprig of thyme
- 200 ml (7 fl oz) red Bordeaux wine
- Beef marrow, poached in salted water, drained and cut into cubes (optional)

Preparation time: 15 minutes
Cooking time: 30 minutes
Makes 500 ml (18 fl oz)

MARINIÈRE SAUCE

SAUCE MARINIÈRE

Prepare a blond roux (p.57) using the butter, flour, court-bouillon and wine. Season with salt and pepper and serve with fish.

- 50 g (1¼ oz) butter
- 50 g (1¼ oz) flour
- 100 ml (3½ fl oz) court-bouillon with white wine (p.82)
- 200 ml (7 fl oz) dry white wine
- Salt and pepper

Preparation time: 10 minutes
Cooking time: 20 minutes
Makes 500 ml (18 fl oz)

VELOUTÉ SAUCE
SAUCE POUR VELOUTÉ

- **50 g (1¾ oz) butter**
- **60 g (2 oz) flour**
- **750 ml (1¼ pints) any stock**

  Preparation time: 10 minutes
  Cooking time: 30 minutes
  Makes 500 ml (18 fl oz)

From the French for 'velvet', velouté is a reduced white sauce made from a blond roux and stock, and is one of the most commonly used basic French white sauces.

Make a blond roux (p.57), using the butter, flour and stock. Allow it to reduce for about 30 minutes over a very gentle heat to give it a better consistency and more flavour. (The stock can be replaced with 500 ml (18 fl oz) of concentrated stock to shorten the cooking time.)

VARIATION

. . . .

IVORY VELOUTÉ
VELOUTÉ IVOIRE

Whisk 200 ml (7 fl oz) double cream into the velouté sauce and serve immediately. When made with chicken stock, this is often used with poultry dishes.

CHAUD-FROID SAUCE
CHAUD-FROID

- **1 quantity ivory velouté (see above)**
- **100 ml (3½ fl oz) meat jelly or aspic (p.45)**
- **100 ml (3½ fl oz) double cream**
- **4 egg yolks**

  Preparation time: 15 minutes
  Cooking time: 40 minutes
  Makes 500 ml (18 fl oz)

Chaud-froid dishes are prepared like hot cooked dishes, but served cold. Used to coat pieces of white meat and poultry, the chaud-froid sauce sets as it cools. For game, make a velouté sauce using a brown roux and proceed as below, omitting the cream.

Prepare the ivory velouté, gently add the meat jelly or aspic and simmer over a gentle heat for 20 minutes, stirring frequently. Strain, return the sauce to the pan and add the cream and egg yolks. Stir the sauce continuously, over a low heat, until the sauce has thickened.

BROWN SAUCE

SAUCE BRUNE

This basic brown sauce is the basis of many classic sauces for meat, game and offal. It is based on a brown roux.

Melt the butter in a large heavy-based pan. Add the onion and bacon and cook over a moderate heat until browned. Remove the onion and bacon, set them aside, and increase the heat slightly. When the butter begins to smoke, add the flour to the pan, all at once. Stir with a wooden spoon until the butter and flour mixture browns. Stirring all the time, gradually add the stock, then season with salt and pepper. Return the onion and bacon to the pan with the bouquet garni and cook gently for 20 minutes. Remove them before serving.

- **50 g (1¾ oz) butter**
- **60 g (2 oz) onion, quartered**
- **60 g (2 oz) lean bacon, diced**
- **60 g (2 oz) flour**
- **300 ml (½ pint) water or any stock**
- **Salt and pepper**
- **1 bouquet garni**

Preparation time: 10 minutes
Cooking time: 20 minutes
Makes 300 ml (½ pint)

PIQUANT SAUCE

SAUCE PIQUANTE

Put the vinegar and shallot in a small pan. Simmer over a gentle heat to reduce the liquid until about 3 tablespoons remain. Stir the liquid into the brown sauce and cook gently for about 5 minutes. Stir in the gherkins. Good with beef and pork chops, and boiled tongue.

- **150 ml (¼ pint) white wine vinegar**
- **10 g (¼ oz) finely chopped shallot**
- **1 quantity brown sauce (see above)**
- **80 g (2¾ oz) gherkins, sliced or finely chopped**

Preparation time: 10 minutes
Cooking time: 25 minutes
Makes 500 ml (18 fl oz)

MADEIRA SAUCE

SAUCE MADÈRE

- 1 quantity brown sauce (p.60)
- 2 tablespoons very good
  Madeira

  Preparation time: 5 minutes
  Cooking time: 20 minutes
  Makes 330 ml (11 fl oz)

Prepare the brown sauce and simmer over a low heat for 20 minutes. Add the Madeira just before serving. This sauce is good with most kinds of meat, especially veal and tongue.

VARIATION

. . . .

PÉRIGUEUX SAUCE

SAUCE PÉRIGUEUX

Add 25 g (1 oz) diced black truffle and a drop of truffle essence or oil to the Madeira sauce. Cook just below simmering point for 2 minutes. Do not allow to boil.

MUSHROOM SAUCE

SAUCE AUX CHAMPIGNONS

- 1 quantity Madeira sauce
  (see above)
- 150 g (5 oz) small mushrooms,
  peeled but left whole
- Salt and pepper
- 1 tablespoon Madeira

  Preparation time: 15 minutes
  Cooking time: 20 minutes
  Makes 500 ml (18 fl oz)

Prepare the Madeira sauce. Add the mushrooms to the sauce, season with salt and pepper, and cook gently for about 15 minutes. Add the Madeira and cook for a further 5 minutes. This sauce goes well with chicken and sweetbreads.

NOTE

For an olive sauce to dress pasta or accompany duck, replace the mushrooms with stoned olives.

CHATEAUBRIAND SAUCE

SAUCE CHATEAUBRIAND

Prepare the brown sauce and keep it hot. Melt 30 g (1 oz) of the butter in a pan and stir in the shallots. Simmer over a gentle heat for 10 minutes. Add the mushrooms and wine, and continue to simmer for a further 10 minutes. Strain, discard the solids and stir the liquid into the hot brown sauce with the rest of the butter, and the tarragon and parsley. Good with grilled meat.

- **1 quantity brown sauce (p.60)**
- **50 g (1¾ oz) butter**
- **25 g (1 oz) finely chopped shallots**
- **60 g (2 oz) mushrooms, peeled and finely chopped**
- **100 ml (3½ fl oz) white wine**
- **1 tablespoon chopped tarragon**
- **1 tablespoon chopped flat-leaf parsley**

Preparation time: 15 minutes
Cooking time: 25 minutes
Makes 500 ml (18 fl oz)

PORTUGUESE SAUCE

SAUCE PORTUGAISE

Prepare the brown sauce, stir in the Madeira and tomato purée, and boil for 1 minute. Serve with delicate fish dishes such as mousses or terrines.

- **1 quantity brown sauce (p.60)**
- **200 ml (7 fl oz) Madeira**
- **2 tablespoons tomato purée**

Preparation time: 15 minutes
Cooking time: 2 minutes
Makes 500 ml (18 fl oz)

POIVRADE SAUCE
SAUCE POIVRADE

- 100 ml (3½ fl oz) white
  wine vinegar
- 1 bay leaf
- 1 sprig of thyme
- 1 carrot, sliced
- 1 shallot, chopped
- 1 onion, chopped
- Pepper
- 1 quantity brown sauce (p.60)
- 100 ml (3½ fl oz) dry white wine
- 200 ml (7 fl oz) any stock

Preparation time: 15 minutes
Cooking time: 40 minutes
Makes 500 ml (18 fl oz)

Put the vinegar, bay leaf, thyme, carrot, shallot and onion in a pan with a pinch of pepper. Simmer over a low heat for about 20 minutes, or until reduced by half. Strain and discard the solids. Add this reduction to the brown sauce with the wine and stock, bring to a simmer and cook for 15 minutes. Pass through a fine strainer and add more pepper to taste. Serve with meat or game.

ROBERT SAUCE
SAUCE ROBERT

- 50 g (1¾ oz) butter
- 60 g (2 oz) onion,
  finely chopped
- 60 g (2 oz) flour
- 500 ml (18 fl oz) any stock
- 50 ml (2 fl oz) dry white wine
- Salt and pepper
- ½ tablespoon white
  wine vinegar
- 1 tablespoon mustard
- 1 tablespoon tomato purée

Preparation time: 10 minutes
Cooking time: 25 minutes
Makes 500 ml (18 fl oz)

This classic sauce is served with a wide range of dishes, including grilled pork chops and other meats, rabbit, duck, poached and fried eggs, fried fish and salt cod.

Melt the butter in a pan, add the onion and cook over a medium-high heat until the onion is brown. Add the flour. Allow to colour, while stirring frequently, and gradually add the stock and wine. Season with salt and pepper. Simmer for 20 minutes. Just before serving, stir in the vinegar, mustard and tomato purée.

VARIATION

. . . .

CHARCUTERIE SAUCE
SAUCE CHARCUTIÈRE

To accompany pork and charcuterie, add 80 g (2¾ oz) gherkins, cut into thin strips, to the Robert sauce.

GENEVOISE SAUCE

SAUCE GENEVOISE

Prepare the brown sauce and add the parsley, shallot, mushrooms, salt and pepper. Add the wine and cook gently for 20 minutes. Strain. Just before serving, stir in the butter and, if wished, the anchovy butter. Serve with strongly flavoured poached fish, and if possible make the brown sauce with the liquid in which the fish was cooked.

- 500 ml (18 fl oz) brown sauce (p.60)
- 1 small handful of flat-leaf parsley, chopped
- 1 shallot, chopped
- 125 g (4¼ oz) mushrooms, chopped
- Salt and pepper
- 100 ml (3½ fl oz) red wine
- 50 g (1¾ oz) butter
- 1 knob of anchovy butter (p.100), optional

Preparation time: 15 minutes
Cooking time: 20 minutes
Makes 500 ml (18 fl oz)

MATELOTE SAUCE

SAUCE MATELOTE

Put the wine, 200 ml (7 fl oz) water, the bouquet garni, salt, pepper, garlic and shallots in a pan. Bring to a simmer and cook over a low heat for 20 minutes. Strain the liquid and discard the solids. Make a brown sauce (p.60) with the flour and half the butter and stir in the strained liquid. Just before serving, add the Cognac and the remaining butter. Good with salmon, crustaceans and rabbit.

- 100 ml (3½ fl oz) red wine
- 1 bouquet garni
- Salt and pepper
- 2 garlic cloves, chopped
- 2 shallots, chopped
- 40 g (1½ oz) flour
- 80 g (2¾ oz) butter, chilled
- 50 ml (2 fl oz) Cognac

Preparation time: 10 minutes
Cooking time: 30 minutes
Makes 500 ml (18 fl oz)

BLOOD SAUCE

SAUCE AU SANG

- **Liver and blood from a game animal**
- **50 g (1¾ oz) butter**
- **60 g (2 oz) flour**
- **85 g (3 oz) bacon, finely chopped**
- **50 g (1¾ oz) onion, finely chopped**
- **100 ml (3½ fl oz) any stock**
- **300 ml (½ pint) red wine**
- **1 bouquet garni**
- **Salt and pepper**

Preparation time: 10 minutes
Cooking time: 30 minutes
Makes 500 ml (18 fl oz)

Sauces for game, and game stews, are often thickened with the blood of the animal being cooked, most commonly hare. Stews thickened this way are termed civets.

In a pan, cook the animal's liver in its blood gently for about 10 minutes. Mash the cooked liver to a purée with the blood. Make the roux for a brown sauce (p.60) with the butter, flour, bacon and onion and add the stock, wine, bouquet garni, salt and pepper. Just before serving, pour the sauce into the liver purée. Stir well until the sauce thickens.

CHASSEUR SAUCE

SAUCE CHASSEUR

- **1 litre (1¾ pints) marinade used for meat or game**
- **60 g (2 oz) butter**
- **50 g (1¾ oz) flour**
- **2 tablespoons redcurrant jelly**

Preparation time: 10 minutes
Cooking time: 1 hour 30 minutes
Makes 500 ml (18 fl oz)

Pour the marinade into a pan, bring to the boil, then lower the heat and simmer to reduce the liquid to two-thirds of its volume. Make a brown roux (p.60) with the butter and flour, and stir in enough marinade to create a strongly flavoured sauce. To finish, add the juices scraped from the roasting tin and the redcurrant jelly. Serve with roast meat or game.

EMULSIFIED SAUCES

VINAIGRETTE
SAUCE VINAIGRETTE

This classic dressing for green salads can also be used to dress a wide range of other cold dishes, from vegetables, such as asparagus, leeks and artichokes, to boiled beef and even some fish dishes.

Dissolve the salt in the vinegar, then mix everything together well, either by whisking them in a small bowl or by putting them in a clean jar with a tight-fitting lid and shaking vigorously. Taste the vinaigrette and, if it seems too oily, add a little more salt or vinegar, and whisk or shake it again. Depending on the food the vinaigrette is to dress, the vinegar can be replaced with an acidic fruit juice, such as lemon or orange.

NOTE
The basic vinaigrette can be enhanced in many ways with added ingredients. Try adding a teaspoon of Dijon or other mustard for a mustard vinaigrette (the mustard will also help the ingredients emulsify), a small handful of chopped herbs such as chives, chervil, parsley, tarragon or basil (or a mixture) for a herb vinaigrette, and 1 or 2 crushed or chopped garlic cloves for a garlic vinaigrette.

- Salt
- 1 tablespoon white wine vinegar
- 3 tablespoons good quality olive, groundnut or rapeseed oil, or a combination

Preparation time: 5 minutes
Makes 4 tablespoons

YOGHURT SAUCE
SAUCE AU YAOURT

In a bowl, mix the mustard with the vinegar. Season with salt and pepper, stir in the yoghurt and mix carefully. This low-fat version of vinaigrette is good with most salads and vegetables, as well as with salmon, and game birds such as duck and quail.

- 1–2 teaspoons mild mustard
- 2 tablespoons white wine vinegar
- Salt and pepper
- 4 tablespoons fat-free yoghurt

Preparation time: 5 minutes
Makes 100 ml (3½ fl oz)

MUSTARD SAUCE
SAUCE MOUTARDE

Put the mustard in a heatproof bowl and set the bowl over a pan of barely simmering water on a very gentle heat. Add the butter, stirring continuously. When all the butter is mixed in, add the cornflour and hot water, and continue to stir until thickened. Season with salt and pepper. Serve with oily fish, such as herring or mackerel.

+ **2 tablespoons Dijon mustard**
+ **100 g (3½ oz) butter, diced and at room temperature**
+ **1 teaspoon cornflour**
+ **100 ml (3½ fl oz) hot water**
+ **Salt and pepper**

Preparation time: 10 minutes
Makes 100 ml (3½ fl oz)

RÉMOULADE SAUCE
SAUCE RÉMOULADE

Make sure all the ingredients and utensils to be used are at room temperature. Put the mustard in a bowl and gradually stir in the oil in a thin steady stream as if making mayonnaise (p.70). Season with salt and pepper, and stir in the shallot. This is the classic dressing for grated celeriac. Finely chopped gherkins, capers, parsley, chives or tarragon, or a little anchovy essence can also be added. In this form it may be served with cold meats, fish and shellfish.

+ **2 tablespoons Dijon mustard**
+ **200 ml (7 fl oz) olive, groundnut or sunflower oil, or a combination**
+ **Salt and pepper**
+ **1 shallot, finely chopped**

Preparation time: 10 minutes
Makes 200 ml (7 fl oz)

ROQUEFORT SAUCE
SAUCE AU ROQUEFORT

In a bowl, mash the Roquefort with a fork until smooth. Stir in the lemon juice and cream, and whisk to form an emulsion. Stir in the basil or sage, and serve with salad leaves or as a dip with crudités.

+ **60 g (2 oz) Roquefort cheese**
+ **Juice of ½ lemon**
+ **3 tablespoons double cream**
+ **Several basil leaves, torn, or 2 sage leaves, finely chopped**

Preparation time: 10 minutes
Makes 120 ml (4 fl oz)

GRIBICHE SAUCE

SAUCE GRIBICHE

- 3 eggs
- 1 teaspoon Dijon mustard
- 250 ml (8 fl oz) olive, groundnut or sunflower oil, or a combination
- 2 tablespoons white wine vinegar
- 30 g (1¼ oz) gherkins, finely chopped
- 1 tablespoon chopped herbs, such as parsley, chervil or tarragon, or a mixture
- Salt and pepper

Preparation time: 10 minutes
Makes 300 ml (½ pint)

Hard boil the eggs (about 10 minutes), cool them quickly, shell them and separate the yolks from the whites. Chop the whites finely. Separately, mash the yolks to a smooth paste with the mustard. Gradually add the oil, a little at a time, as if making mayonnaise (p.70), then add the vinegar. Finish by adding the gherkins, chopped egg whites and herbs. Season with salt and pepper. Gribiche sauce is the classic accompaniment to calf's head, and is also used with cold fish dishes.

MAYONNAISE
SAUCE MAYONNAISE

COLD

In a large bowl, beat the egg yolk until creamy, using a wooden spoon or mechanical whisk. Add the oil gradually in small quantities, adding more only when the mixture is completely emulsified. When the mayonnaise is thick, add salt, pepper and vinegar. For the sauce to emulsify successfully, it is important to ensure that all the ingredients and utensils are at room temperature.

HOT

Put the egg yolk and 1 tablespoon vinegar in a heatproof bowl and season with salt and pepper. Set the bowl over a pan of barely simmering water on a gentle heat. Whisk until the mixture thickens. Add the oil gradually, as for the cold method. The temperature of the bain-marie must not reach boiling point.

VARIATIONS

. . . .

GREEN MAYONNAISE
MAYONNAISE AU VERT

Blanch 20 g (¾ oz) each of flat-leaf parsley and chervil with 100 g (3½ oz) sorrel and 300 g (11 oz) spinach in boiling water for 30 seconds. Drain and refresh in cold water, then pass through a sieve to obtain a fine purée. Stir into the mayonnaise and add 20 g (¾ oz) each of finely chopped chives and basil.

. . . .

ANCHOVY MAYONNAISE
MAYONNAISE AUX ANCHOIS

Proceed as for green mayonnaise, and add 6 chopped anchovies and 1 chopped shallot. This makes an excellent dip, and is also very good with fried fish and seafood.

- 1 egg yolk
- 180 ml (6 fl oz) olive, groundnut or sunflower oil, or a combination, at room temperature
- Salt and pepper
- 20 ml (¾ fl oz) white wine vinegar

Preparation time: 10 minutes
Makes about 200 ml (7 fl oz)

 p.86

MOUSSELINE MAYONNAISE
MAYONNAISE MOUSSELINE

- 1 egg, separated
- 180 ml (6 fl oz) olive, groundnut
  or sunflower oil,
  or a combination
- 20 ml (¾ fl oz) white
  wine vinegar
- Salt and pepper

Preparation time: 12 minutes
Makes 225 ml (7½ fl oz)

Make mayonnaise (p.70) using the egg yolk, oil and vinegar. Beat the egg white until very stiff and fold it into the sauce. Season with salt and pepper. This produces a smoother, light-textured mayonnaise that is often served with asparagus.

NORWEGIAN SAUCE
SAUCE NORVÉGIENNE

- 8 anchovy fillets, mashed
- 100 g (3½ oz) shelled
  walnuts, chopped
- 1 garlic clove, crushed
  and finely chopped
- 2 tablespoons mustard
- 250 ml (8 fl oz) olive, groundnut
  or sunflower oil, or a mixture
- 2 tablespoons white wine
  vinegar
- Pepper

Preparation time: 20 minutes
Makes 400 ml (14 fl oz)

Put the anchovies, walnuts, garlic and mustard in a bowl and beat the mixture, gradually adding the oil, then the vinegar, in the same way as for mayonnaise (p.70). Add pepper to taste. Good with smoked salmon, eggs and pastry-based fish dishes.

TARTARE SAUCE

SAUCE TARTARE

Prepare the mayonnaise and stir in the onion, gherkins (if using) herbs, mustard, capers, lemon juice (if using) and cayenne pepper. Taste and season with salt and pepper. The sauce should be highly seasoned.

- 250 ml (8 fl oz) mayonnaise (p.70)
- 1 small onion, finely chopped
- 2 tablespoons finely chopped, rinsed and drained gherkins (optional)
- 1 small handful of chives, finely chopped
- 1 small handful of chervil, finely chopped
- 1 small handful of tarragon, finely chopped
- 1 small handful of flat-leaf parsley, finely chopped
- 2 teaspoons Dijon mustard
- 2 teaspoons rinsed and drained capers, finely chopped
- 1 tablespoon lemon juice (optional)
- Cayenne pepper, to taste
- Salt and pepper

Preparation time: 20 minutes
Makes 500 ml (18 fl oz)

'ANGRY' SAUCE

SAUCE ENRAGÉE

Mash the egg yolks with the oil using a pestle and mortar or in a bowl. Gradually stir in the chillies. Add the vinegar and saffron, and season with salt and pepper. Transfer to a pan and heat the sauce over a gentle heat, stirring constantly, for 10 minutes. Serve in a sauce boat.

- Yolks of 6 hard-boiled eggs
- 100 ml (3½ fl oz) olive oil
- 6 small bird's-eye, pinhead or any other hot chilli peppers, de-seeded (if a milder sauce is preferred) and finely chopped
- 3 tablespoons white wine vinegar
- 1 pinch of saffron threads
- Salt and pepper

Preparation time: 20 minutes
Cooking time: 10 minutes
Makes 150 ml (¼ pint)

AIOLI

AÏOLI

 p.87

This is the classic garlic sauce of Provence, traditionally served with fish stew (*bourride*) and with snails, and with salt cod and vegetables on Fridays.

Boil the potato in its skin until just tender, and peel while still hot. Crush the garlic cloves using a pestle and mortar or in a bowl, add the potato and pound it to a purée with the garlic. Stir in the egg yolks, salt and pepper. Gradually add the olive oil, stirring constantly as when making mayonnaise (p.70), and finish by adding the lemon juice. The potato can be replaced with a piece of stale bread soaked in milk. (Squeeze out the milk when the bread has softened.)

+ **1 floury potato, unpeeled, about 100 g (3½ oz)**
+ **4–6 garlic cloves**
+ **2 egg yolks**
+ **Salt and pepper**
+ **250 ml (8 fl oz) olive oil**
+ **2 teaspoons lemon juice**

Preparation time: 20 minutes
Makes 300 ml (½ pint)

HOLLANDAISE SAUCE

SAUCE HOLLANDAISE

 p.88

One of the classic French sauces, this hot emulsion of egg yolks and butter is also the base for many other sauces, such as mousseline sauce (p.75). Hollandaise is usually served with grilled steaks and fish, eggs and boiled or steamed vegetables.

Put the egg yolks and salt in a heatproof bowl with 1 tablespoon water and set over a pan of barely simmering water on a very gentle heat. Stir vigorously to mix thoroughly. Take the pan off the heat and stir the butter into the yolks in small pieces. When all the butter is stirred in, put the pan back on the heat and stir until the sauce thickens (this is a delicate procedure, so it may be necessary to remove the pan from the heat from time to time if it looks as though the sauce may separate, or turn into scrambled eggs). Pour in the lemon juice, and add salt and pepper. Serve immediately.

+ **3 egg yolks**
+ **Salt and pepper**
+ **175 g (6 oz) butter**
+ **2 teaspoons lemon juice, warmed**

Preparation time: 10 minutes
Cooking time: 10 minutes
Makes 250 ml (8 fl oz)

MOUSSELINE SAUCE
SAUCE MOUSSELINE

- 10 g (¼ oz) cornflour
- 2 egg yolks
- 150 g (5 oz) butter
- 60 ml (2 fl oz) double cream, whipped to stiff peaks
- Salt

Preparation time: 15 minutes
Cooking time: 10 minutes
Makes 250 ml (8 fl oz)

 p.89

Mousseline is the term for an egg emulsion sauce that has a mousse-like texture due to added whipped cream.

Proceed as for hollandaise sauce (p.74), but add the cornflour to the egg yolks and 1 tablespoon water before stirring in the butter. When the sauce has thickened, add the cream and season with salt. Keep the sauce hot in the bain-marie or roasting tin, but whisk it lightly before serving. This sauce is traditionally served with fine-textured fish and asparagus.

BÉARNAISE SAUCE
SAUCE BÉARNAISE

- 100 ml (3½ fl oz) white wine vinegar
- 2 shallots, finely chopped
- ½ garlic clove, finely chopped
- 1 sprig of tarragon, finely chopped
- 3 egg yolks
- 150 g (5 oz) butter

Preparation time: 15 minutes
Cooking time: 1 hour
Makes 300 ml (½ pint)

In a pan, simmer the vinegar with the shallots, garlic and a little of the tarragon over a very low heat for 20–30 minutes. Strain the reduced liquid. Put the egg yolks and the reduction in a heatproof bowl set over a pan of barely simmering water, and place it on a very gentle heat. Stirring constantly, add the butter in small pieces. Add the rest of the chopped tarragon. The reduction can be replaced with 1 tablespoon béarnaise essence (p.43). Good with grilled steaks and lamb fillet.

CRAPAUDINE SAUCE
SAUCE CRAPAUDINE

- 100 ml (3½ fl oz) white wine vinegar
- 2 shallots, finely chopped
- ½ garlic clove, finely chopped
- 1 sprig of tarragon, finely chopped
- 150 g (5 oz) meat glaze (p.45)
- 1 tablespoon lemon juice

Preparation time: 10 minutes
Cooking time: 8 minutes
Makes 250 ml (8 fl oz)

Put the vinegar, shallots, garlic and tarragon in a pan, bring to the boil and simmer to reduce by half (about 8 minutes). Strain. Whisk in the meat glaze and lemon juice. This sauce accompanies chicken, pigeon and rabbit served *à la crapaudine*, or spatchcocked (split down the backbone and flattened, so it looks like a toad, or *crapaud*), coated in breadcrumbs and grilled.

DEVILLED SAUCE
SAUCE À LA DIABLE

Put the wine, vinegar and shallots in a small pan. Bring to the boil and reduce by half (about 8 minutes). Stir in the stock and simmer for 8–10 minutes. Knead the butter with the flour and add it to the mixture, beating with a whisk until the sauce thickens. Just before serving, add the herbs, and the cayenne pepper, if using. This sauce is normally served with food that has been devilled (prepared *à la diable*), or coated with hot mustard, dipped in egg and breadcrumbs, and deep-fried.

- 100 ml (3½ fl oz) white wine
- 100 ml (3½ fl oz) white wine vinegar
- 2 shallots, chopped
- 200 ml (7 fl oz) any stock
- 60 g (2 oz) butter
- 40 g (1½ oz) flour
- 1 small handful of chervil, chopped
- 1 small handful of tarragon, chopped
- 1 pinch of cayenne pepper (optional)

Preparation time: 15 minutes
Cooking time: 20 minutes
Makes 500 ml (18 fl oz)

MARINADES & STUFFINGS

INSTANT MARINADE
FOR SMALL PIECES OF MEAT
MARINADE INSTANTANÉE POUR PETITES PIÈCES

Mix all the ingredients in a large bowl. Marinate pieces of meat in the mixture for about 2 hours, turning frequently.

- 100 ml (3½ fl oz) white wine
- 2–3 sprigs of thyme
- 2–3 sprigs of flat-leaf parsley
- 1 tablespoon olive or sunflower oil
- Juice of 1 lemon
- Pepper

Preparation time: 5 minutes
Makes 150 ml (¼ pint)

COOKED MARINADE
WITH WHITE OR RED WINE

MARINADE CUITE, AU VIN BLANC OU ROUGE

- 750 ml (1¼ pints) white
  or red wine
- 50 ml (2 fl oz) red or white
  wine vinegar
- 40 g (1½ oz) carrot, sliced
- 50 g (1¾ oz) onion, sliced
- Pepper
- 1–2 cloves
- 2–3 sprigs of thyme
- 1 bay leaf
- 1 garlic clove, chopped

Preparation time: 5 minutes
Cooking time: 3–5 minutes
Makes about 900 ml (1½ pints)

Put all the ingredients in a pan and bring to a simmer. Cook for a few minutes, then allow to cool before adding the meat. Store in the refrigerator, turning the meat occasionally.

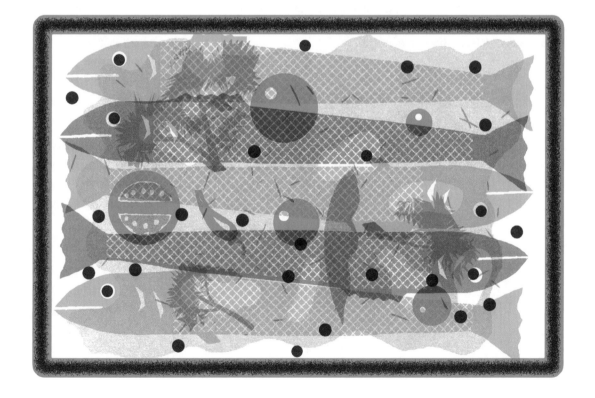

UNCOOKED MARINADE

MARINADE CRUE

Cover the meat or fish to be marinated with the carrot, onion, shallot and garlic, then sprinkle with the cloves, salt, pepper, bay leaf and thyme. Pour over the wine, vinegar and oil. Marinate in the refrigerator for up to 3 days for meat (depending on the type and freshness), or 2–3 hours for fish, turning it regularly.

- 100 g (3½ oz) carrot, sliced
- 100 g (3½ oz) onion, sliced
- 10 g (¼ oz) sliced shallot
- 1–2 garlic cloves, sliced
- 1–2 cloves, ground
- Salt and pepper
- 1 bay leaf, broken up
- 2–3 sprigs of thyme, chopped
- 750 ml (1¼ pints) white wine
- 175 ml (6 fl oz) white wine vinegar
- 2 tablespoons olive or sunflower oil

Preparation time: 10 minutes
Makes 1.5 litres (2½ pints)

SWEET MARINADE

MARINADE DOUCE

Chop the bacon, onion, shallot, garlic, parsley and chervil, and mix them with the oil, vinegar, salt and pepper. Use to marinate meats with a delicate flavour, such as veal.

- 100 g (3½ oz) smoked bacon
- 30 g (1¼ oz) onion
- 10 g (¼ oz) shallot
- 1 small garlic clove
- A few sprigs of flat-leaf parsley
- A few sprigs of chervil
- 1 tablespoon olive or sunflower oil
- 50 ml (2 fl oz) white wine vinegar
- Salt and pepper

Preparation time: 10 minutes
Makes 200 ml (7 fl oz)

STUFFING FOR POULTRY: PIGEON, CHICKEN, GOOSE

FARCE POUR VOLAILLES: PIGEON, POULET, OIE

Chop together the liver, heart and stomach of the bird, if available. Add white bread soaked in hot milk and then drained, mushrooms cooked in butter, parsley, salt and pepper. To increase the quantity of stuffing, add a little finely mashed sausage meat. Fill the inside of the bird.

STUFFING FOR TURKEY

FARCE POUR DINDE

- 125 g (4¼ oz) veal
- The bird's liver (if possible)
- 60 g (2 oz) truffle peelings
- 125 g (4¼ oz) unsmoked bacon
- 500 g (1 lb 2 oz) unsweetened chestnuts
- Salt and pepper

Preparation time: 10 minutes
Makes 800 g (1¾ lb)

Place all the ingredients in a food processor and process to make a coarse paste. Use to stuff the turkey's cavities.

STUFFING FOR PHEASANT

FARCE POUR FAISAN

- 250 g (9 oz) veal
- 100 g (3½ oz) pork
- 500 g (1 lb 2 oz) unsweetened chestnuts
- 2 tablespoons Madeira
- Salt and pepper

Preparation time: 10 minutes
Makes 850 g (2 lb)

Place all the ingredients in a food processor and process to make a coarse paste. Use to stuff the pheasant's cavities.

STUFFING FOR RED MEATS

FARCE POUR VIANDE

Mix all the ingredients in a bowl. For uses for leftover meat (meatballs, pâté and so on), refer to the end of each section on meat.

- ◆ **100 g (3½ oz) unsmoked bacon, finely chopped**
- ◆ **100 g (3½ oz) pork, finely chopped**
- ◆ **1 handful of flat-leaf parsley, finely chopped**
- ◆ **1 tablespoon Cognac**
- ◆ **Salt and pepper**

  Preparation time: 10 minutes
  Makes 200 g (7 oz)

STUFFING FOR FISH

FARCE POUR POISSON

Bring the court-bouillon to the boil, add the fish and simmer gently for 5 minutes. Prepare the white sauce. Remove and discard the head and bones and mash the flesh into the white sauce. If using the mushrooms, cook them in the butter for 10 minutes. Season the sauce with salt and pepper and add the hard-boiled eggs and mushrooms or truffle.

- ◆ **Court-bouillon with vinegar (p.82)**
- ◆ **500 g (1 lb 2 oz) fish (preferably whiting or hake)**
- ◆ **1 quantity white sauce (p.50)**
- ◆ **Truffle peelings or chopped mushrooms**
- ◆ **10 g (¼ oz) butter (optional)**
- ◆ **Salt and pepper**
- ◆ **2 hard-boiled eggs, chopped**

  Preparation time: 10 minutes
  Cooking time: 15 minutes
  Makes 500 g (1 lb 2 oz)

DUXELLES

DUXELLES

- 30 g (1¼ oz) butter
- 1 tablespoon oil
- 60 g (2 oz) onion, finely chopped
- 1 teaspoon finely chopped shallot
- 125 g (4¼ oz) mushrooms, finely chopped
- Freshly grated nutmeg
- 1 tablespoon brown sauce (p.60) or 1 tablespoon dried breadcrumbs mixed with 1 tablespoon tomato purée (optional)
- Salt and pepper
- 1 garlic clove, finely chopped (optional)
- 1 tablespoon chopped flat-leaf parsley (optional)

Preparation time: 10 minutes
Cooking time: 15 minutes
Makes 200 g (7 oz)

Heat the butter and oil in a pan and fry the onion, shallot and mushrooms until the onion is translucent. Add the nutmeg and cook gently until the mixture thickens. To give it more body, add the brown sauce or dried breadcrumbs and tomato purée. Season with salt and pepper, and add the garlic and flat-leaf parsley, if using. Duxelles is used in many meat and vegetable dishes.

FRIED PARSLEY

PERSIL FRIT

Choose fresh green sprigs of flat-leaf or curly parsley and wash them, then dry them carefully with kitchen paper. Heat vegetable oil in a deep-fryer to 190°C/375°F, or until a cube of bread browns in 20 seconds. Blanch the parsley for a few seconds in the hot oil, then remove and drain immediately. The parsley should retain its bright green colour.

COURT-BOUILLON

A court-bouillon is a highly seasoned liquid used for cooking fish and seafood. The fish should be completely covered by the court-bouillon, so adjust the quantity according to the shape and size of the fish and the pan. To prepare a court-bouillon, combine all the ingredients in a pan, bring to the boil and simmer gently for 1 hour, stirring from time to time.

COURT-BOUILLON WITH SALT
COURT-BOUILLON AU SEL

To poach mackerel, sea bream and grey mullet, use 1 litre (1¾ pints) water and 15 g (½ oz) salt.

COURT-BOUILLON WITH VINEGAR
COURT-BOUILLON AU VINAIGRE

To poach hake, pike and carp, use 3 litres (5¼ pints) water, 200 ml (7 fl oz) white wine vinegar, 50 g (1¾ oz) sliced carrot, 50 g (1¾ oz) onion, 1 clove, 1 sprig of flat-leaf parsley, and salt and pepper.

COURT-BOUILLON WITH WHITE WINE
COURT-BOUILLON AU VIN BLANC

To poach salmon and trout, use 2 litres (3½ pints) water, 1 litre (1¾ pints) dry white wine, 50 g (1¾ oz) carrot, 50 g (1¾ oz) onion, 1 large sprig of thyme, 1 large bay leaf, several stalks of flat-leaf parsley, and salt and pepper. For a red wine court-bouillon (for pike, carp and trout), simply replace the white wine with red wine.

COURT-BOUILLON WITH MILK
COURT-BOUILLON AU LAIT

To poach turbot, brill and sole, use 3 litres (5¼ pints) water, 500 ml (18 fl oz) milk, 1 sliced lemon and salt and pepper.

Maître d'hôtel butter   (p.48)

Black butter (p.48)

Béchamel sauce   (p.50)

Green mayonnaise (p.70)

Aioli (p.74)

Hollandaise sauce   (p.74)

Béarnaise sauce   (p.75)

- 2 -
HORS-D'ŒUVRES

HORS-D'ŒUVRES

Hors-d'œuvres are served at the beginning of a meal in order to stimulate the appetite. In addition to fresh vegetable crudités, they can include salted and smoked meats, fish preserved in oil and marinated fish. Butter curls are sometimes served alongside hors-d'œuvres.

HOT HORS-D'ŒUVRES
- Fish, poultry and meat croquettes
- Turnovers or eggs prepared in a variety of ways
- Gnocchi
- Shellfish
- Vol-au-vents
- Spinach and ham tartlets
- Croque-monsieur
- Cheese savouries
- Mushroom pastries
- Poultry croquettes
- Fried eggs

COLD HORS-D'ŒUVRES
- Processed pork products:
  Ham (raw, cooked or smoked), sausage, Mortadella, liver pâté, rillettes
- Fish:
  Sardines, tuna, salmon, mackerel, marinated herrings, herring fillets, anchovies
- Shellfish and molluscs:
  Prawns, mussels, snails, oysters, large and small clams, winkles, crayfish, crabs

ARTICHOKES WITH VINAIGRETTE
ARTICHAUTS 'POIVRADE' À LA VINAIGRETTE

Wash 6 very tender young artichokes (ones that have not yet developed a hairy inner choke). Trim off the tips of the leaves and the stalks, and serve with vinaigrette dressing (p.66).

Preparation time: 15 minutes
Serves 6

AVOCADO COCKTAIL
COCKTAIL À L'AVOCAT

- 6 tablespoons crushed ice
- 4–6 avocados, depending on size, peeled, stoned and diced at the last minute
- 4–6 juicy ripe tomatoes, diced
- 1 tablespoon lemon juice
- Salt and pepper
- Tabasco sauce

Preparation time: 10 minutes
Serves 6

The fruit of the avocado tree is rich in fat and carbohydrates. However, its fat is predominantly the healthy mono-unsaturated type found in olive oil. Avocados are generally eaten raw, mostly in salads.

Put 1 tablespoon of the crushed ice in the bottom of each of 6 cocktail glasses. Divide the avocado dice between the glasses, followed by the tomato dice. Sprinkle with lemon juice. Add salt and pepper and a few drops of Tabasco to each glass.

STUFFED AVOCADOS
AVOCATS FARCIS

- 3 avocados
- 1 large celery stick, thinly sliced
- 20 dried walnut halves, sliced
- 2 teaspoons tomato sauce (p.57)
- 2 teaspoons white wine vinegar
- Salt

Preparation time: 10 minutes
Serves 6

Cut the avocados in half lengthways and remove the stones. Combine the celery slices and walnut halves to make the stuffing. Season with the tomato sauce, vinegar and salt. Fill the hollows of the halved avocados with the stuffing and place in the refrigerator for 1 hour before serving.

STUFFED AVOCADOS WITH PRAWNS
AVOCATS FARCIS AUX CREVETTES

- 3 avocados
- Salt
- Juice of ½ lemon
- 1 celery stick, thinly sliced
- 6 large cooked prawns, shelled and each cut into 3–4 pieces
- Paprika
- Tomato sauce (p.57)

Preparation time: 20 minutes
Serves 6

Cut the avocados in half lengthways and remove the stones. Scoop out the pulp (keeping the skins intact), cut it into cubes and sprinkle with a little fine salt and the lemon juice. Mix the celery slices, prawn pieces and a little paprika in a bowl, and add the cubed avocado pulp. Stir in the tomato sauce. Fill the avocado skins with this salad. Place in the refrigerator until ready to serve.

NOTE
The prawns may be replaced by crab, lobster, spiny lobster or crayfish meat.

RADISHES

RADIS ROSES

Choose radishes that are firm, with straight stalks: this shows they have grown fast, and their flesh will usually be tender. Cut off part of the green leaves and remove the roots. Wash in cold water. Radishes are often served with bread, butter and salt.

BLACK RADISHES

RADIS NOIRS

Peel the radishes and cut them into very thin slices. Sprinkle with salt and leave to drain in a colander. Serve on a small shallow dish.

BEETROOT SALAD

BETTERAVES

Beetroot is generally sold cooked. If bought raw, simmer it in salted water for 3 hours. Allow to cool. Peel and cut into slices. Season with salt and pepper and add sliced onions, cloves, a bay leaf and vinaigrette dressing (p.66). Marinate for 24 hours.

TOMATO SALAD

TOMATES EN SALADE

Skin the tomatoes before slicing them. This is made easier by plunging them into boiling water for 1 minute, then refreshing them in cold water before skinning. Cut the tomatoes into thin slices. Just before serving, pour over a strongly seasoned vinaigrette dressing (p.66).

CUCUMBER

CONCOMBRE

About 3 hours before serving, peel the cucumber and cut it into thin slices. Sprinkle with salt, toss to combine and leave to drain in a colander. Rinse in cold water if the cucumber is too salty. Add a vinaigrette dressing (p.66) or crème fraîche to serve.

RED CABBAGE SALAD

SALADE DE CHOU ROUGE

Cut the cabbage into fine strips, put in a bowl and cover with coarse salt. Leave for 4 hours. Drain, rinse well and toss with a vinaigrette dressing (p.66).

RAW MUSHROOM SALAD WITH CREAM

SALADE DE CHAMPIGNONS CRUS À LA CRÈME

- 250 g (9 oz) mushrooms
- 2 tablespoons lemon juice
- 100 g (3½ oz) crème fraîche
- Salt and pepper
- 1 large handful of flat-leaf parsley, chopped

Preparation time: 15 minutes
Serves 6

Cut off and discard the mushroom stalks and clean the mushrooms carefully with a damp cloth. Cut them into fine strips and sprinkle with 1 tablespoon of the lemon juice to prevent them turning black. Dilute the crème fraîche with the remaining lemon juice and season with salt and pepper. In a bowl, carefully mix the mushroom strips, without breaking them, into the cream sauce. Arrange on a serving dish and sprinkle with the parsley.

NOTE
This recipe should be made shortly before serving, no more than 30 minutes in advance.

MUSHROOMS À LA GRECQUE

CHAMPIGNONS À LA GRECQUE

- 500 g (1 lb 2 oz) mushrooms, preferably button
- 50 ml (2 fl oz) oil
- 1 tablespoon lemon juice
- 100 ml (3½ fl oz) dry white wine
- 10 g (¼ oz) coriander seeds, crushed
- 1 tablespoon tomato purée
- 1 bouquet garni
- Salt and pepper

Preparation time: 10 minutes
Cooking time: 8 minutes
Serves 6

Wipe the mushrooms well. Heat the oil in a frying pan and add the mushrooms. Add the lemon juice, wine, coriander seeds, tomato purée, bouquet garni and salt and pepper. Cook on a very high heat, uncovered, for 8 minutes. Allow to cool in the cooking juices. Serve very cold.

MACÉDOINE
MACÉDOINE

A macédoine is a mixture of diced or sliced vegetables or meats arranged decoratively and seasoned with a vinaigrette (p.66), mayonnaise (p.70) or ravigote sauce (p.56).

VARIATION 1
. . . .

Boil potatoes, cut them into dice and arrange them in a pyramid on a serving dish. Arrange beetroot salad (p.94) round them in a ring, and garnish each slice of beetroot with a little chopped meat. Season with a vinaigrette (p.66) made with chopped herbs, mustard, oil, vinegar, pepper and salt.

VARIATION 2
. . . .

Cut tomatoes into thin slices and arrange them on a serving dish. Cover with slices of hard-boiled egg and lastly add a layer of peeled prawns. Dot with mayonnaise (p.70).

VARIATION 3
. . . .

Boil mixed vegetables (carrots, beans and potatoes), cut them into small dice and arrange in a pyramid on a serving dish. Surround the vegetables with halved hard-boiled eggs dressed with mayonnaise (p.70).

VARIATION 4
. . . .

Cut cabbage, celery and small onions into fine strips. Grate 1–2 carrots and add these, along with cubes of avocado. Dress with a vinaigrette (p.66) or mayonnaise (p.70).

MIXED SALAD LEAVES
SALADE MÉLANGÉE

Mixing 2 or 3 kinds of salad leaf on each plate, or in the same salad bowl, means both soft and crunchy leaves can be enjoyed at the same time. Combine the different leaves imaginatively, for example:

Lamb's lettuce + mixed young salad leaves + Cos lettuce

Loose-leaf lettuce + watercress + radicchio

Chicory (cut in thin slices) + lamb's lettuce + loose-leaf lettuce

Cucumber, sliced tomatoes, beetroot or hard-boiled eggs can also be added. Once the ingredients are chosen, allow 100 g (3½ oz) per person. Clean and carefully wash the salad leaves, and dry in a clean cloth. Choose from many different dressings: vinaigrette (p.66); yoghurt sauce (p.66); Roquefort sauce (p.68); rémoulade sauce (p.68); lemon juice and crème fraîche. Complete the dressing with chopped herbs (a single herb, or several mixed together, such as chervil, tarragon, chives) and chopped shallots. The oil can also be varied (try olive, groundnut, walnut or sunflower oil), as can the vinegar.

PEPPERS IN OIL
POIVRONS À L'HUILE

 p.112

- 4 red peppers
- 4 green peppers
- Olive oil, for greasing
- Salt and white pepper
- 1 quantity vinaigrette (p.66)

Preparation time: 10 minutes
Cooking time: 10 minutes
Serves 6

Preheat the oven to 240°C/475°F/Gas Mark 8. Grease a baking sheet with oil and arrange the peppers on it. Season with salt and pepper. Place in the oven for 8–10 minutes, until the skin blisters and blackens. Remove and leave to cool. Remove the skins, stem and seeds, cut into thin strips and arrange on a dish. Dress with the vinaigrette.

BUTTER

To enjoy butter at its best, take it out of the refrigerator and put it in a dish a little ahead of serving it, to allow it to soften gently and develop its full flavour.

UNPASTEURIZED BUTTER
Made from raw, untreated cream.

RAW CREAM BUTTER
Made from cream or crème fraîche, which may be pasteurized or unpasteurized, but has not been frozen.

OTHER BUTTERS
Called 'fine' or 'cooking' butters, these are made from frozen or pasteurized cream. ·

'LOW-FAT' BUTTER
Made from pasteurized cream and whey, emulsified with gelatine or other vegetable thickeners.

All these butters may be salted or unsalted.

FLAVOURED BUTTERS
There are hundreds of different types of flavoured butter, and the variety of their seasoning, decoration and flavours is a product of the cook's ingenuity, imagination and taste.

BUTTER VERMICELLI
BEURRE EN VERMICELLI

This is a simple way to make butter more attractive for the table. Put the chilled butter into a potato ricer and squeeze it into a small dish or, using a moistened wooden pestle, squeeze the butter through a medium-fine colander.

PRAWN BUTTER

BEURRE DE CREVETTE

Mash some cooked peeled prawns and mix with an equal weight of butter, or mash the butter with whole prawns. Soften in a heatproof bowl set over a pan of barely simmering water and place over a very gentle heat. Press though moistened muslin or a fine-meshed sieve and leave to cool in the refrigerator.

VARIATIONS

. . . .

CORAL BUTTER

BEURRE CORAIL

Poach the roe (or coral) from a lobster in a court-bouillon, mash it with a fork and mix well into the softened butter.

. . . .

CRAYFISH BUTTER

BEURRE D'ÉCREVISSES

Replace the prawns with crayfish and proceed as above.

BUTTER CURLS

BEURRE EN COQUILLES

This way of presenting butter demands a little more work. Use a special knife, or butter curler, dipped in warm water and then drawn over the surface of very cold butter. To do it more simply, use the blade of an ordinary knife to scrape the surface of the butter. Chill the resulting pieces in iced or cold water, and shape into curls by hand.

SARDINE OR ANCHOVY BUTTER

BEURRE DE SARDINE, D'ANCHOIS

Remove the skin and bones of the sardines or anchovies. Pound the sardine flesh with chopped flat-leaf parsley, chopped chervil and Dijon mustard to taste with a pestle and mortar to make a paste. Mix thoroughly with the same weight of softened butter.

HERB BUTTER

BEURRE AUX HERBES

Bring a large pan of salted water to the boil, add the herbs and spinach and cook for 2 minutes. At the same time, cook the shallot in a separate pan of boiling water for 2 minutes. Drain everything thoroughly, pressing out as much water as possible. Pound all the greens with a pestle and mortar or in a bowl and gradually incorporate the butter. The resulting mixture should be smooth.

- 20 g (¾ oz) chives
- 10 g (¼ oz) chervil
- 10 g (¼ oz) tarragon
- 10 g (¼ oz) flat-leaf parsley
- 6 spinach leaves
- 20 g (¾ oz) shallot, chopped
- 100 g (3½ oz) butter, softened

Preparation time: 5 minutes
Cooking time: 5 minutes
Serves 6

CHEESE BUTTER

BEURRE AUX FROMAGES

Remove the rinds from the Brie and the Camembert. Mix the cheeses with the butter and blend with a knife until the mixture is perfectly smooth.

- 80 g (2¾ oz) ripe Brie cheese
- 80 g (2¾ oz) ripe Camembert cheese
- 80 g (2¾ oz) butter, softened

Preparation time: 10 minutes
Serves 6

ROQUEFORT BUTTER

BEURRE AU ROQUEFORT

- **130 g (4½ oz) butter, softened**
- **200 g (7 oz) Roquefort cheese**
- **1 tablespoon Armagnac**

Preparation time: 10 minutes

Serves 6

Carefully blend the butter and Roquefort, using a spoon. Stir in the Armagnac. The mixture should be smooth.

CANAPÉS

The term 'canapé' is nowadays used very loosely to describe a wide range of nibbles to be served before a meal, or as party food. In France, however, it has a much more precise meaning: a thin slice of crustless white bread, often fried in butter, which is then spread with a flavoured butter, such as anchovy butter, or various toppings, such as diced tomato, ham, anchovy or smoked salmon. Canapés come in a wide variety of shapes, but are often triangular.

ANCHOVY CANAPÉS
CANAPÉS À L'ANCHOIS

Cover one half of each slice of bread with chopped hard-boiled egg white, and the other half with mashed egg yolk. Place half an anchovy fillet in the middle.

HERRING CANAPÉS
CANAPÉS DE HARENG

Spread each slice of bread with fromage frais or cream cheese. Arrange half a herring rollmop in the middle and decorate with chopped hard-boiled egg and diced tomato.

RADISH CANAPÉS
CANAPÉS AUX RADIS

Put a little mayonnaise (p.70) in the middle of each slice of bread. Cover with a ring of radish slices, and finish with slices of gherkin.

TARRAGON CANAPÉS
CANAPÉS À L'ESTRAGON OU VIEVILLE

p.113

Beat softened butter with chopped tarragon and spread it onto the slices of bread. Put a slice of ham on top of each one. Garnish with a tarragon leaf.

'NO-NO-NANETTE' CANAPÉS

CANAPÉS NO-NO-NANETTE

Spread each slice of bread with anchovy butter (p.100). Place a slice of hard-boiled egg in the middle and surround with a ring of cooked shelled shrimps, arranged piggy-back. Coat each slice of egg with a little mayonnaise (p.70), and put a few chopped herbs in the centre.

SARDINE CANAPÉS

CANAPÉS À LA SARDINE

De-seed and slice some tomatoes and fry in butter until all the water has evaporated. Butter each slice of bread. Place some fried tomato on each half and some sardine butter (p.100) in the middle.

PRAWN CANAPÉS

CANAPÉS À LA CREVETTE

Split small brioches lengthways and remove some of the interior dough to hollow them out. Fill with a layer of mayonnaise (p.70), and put a small lettuce leaf in the middle and a cooked peeled prawn on either side of it.

NORWEGIAN CANAPÉS
CANAPÉS NORVÉGIENS

Place a piece of smoked ox tongue in the centre of a slice of buttered brown bread and surround it with shredded celeriac in a rémoulade dressing (p.68).

QUENELLES

Quenelles are light dumplings, often made with a purée of left-over meat (such as veal, poultry or liver) or with fish (especially pike, or any leftover, usually oily, fish). They may also be based on bread, flour or mashed potatoes. The meat and fish varieties are often used to fill vol-au-vents or bouchées, and the bread, flour and potato versions are used to top blanquettes and stews. Quenelles are often served with a sauce as a first course. In northern France, very small, ball-shaped quenelles are added to soups. They are known as *fricadelles.*

VEAL QUENELLES
PÂTE À QUENELLES

First make a choux pastry dough (p.774) using 150 ml (¼ pint) water, and the butter and flour. Once cool, return it to the pan and beat in the egg and yolks until the dough is smooth and shiny. Chop the veal in a food processor, season with salt and pepper, and stir it into the well-beaten choux pastry dough, until smooth. Add nutmeg to taste. Grease a plate with butter, spread the dough out on the plate and leave to cool. Mould tablespoons of the dough into small finger-shaped quenelles and roll in flour. Gently poach the quenelles a few at a time, in simmering salted water for 5–8 minutes. Remove carefully with a slotted spoon and drain on kitchen paper.

- 30 g (1¼ oz) butter, plus extra for greasing
- 80 g (2¾ oz) flour, plus extra for rolling
- 1 whole egg, plus 2 extra egg yolks
- 200 g (7 oz) veal, cut into pieces
- Salt and pepper
- Freshly grated nutmeg

Preparation time: 40 minute
Cooking time: 10 minutes
Serves 6

VARIATIONS

· ·

LIVER QUENELLES
QUENELLES DE FOIE

Replace the veal in the above recipe with 300 g (11 oz) chicken or calves' liver.

QUENELLES IN SAUCE
QUENELLES EN SAUCE

Fish or meat quenelles can be served with supreme sauce (p.52), ivory velouté (p.59) or Périgueux sauce (p.61), along with any juices from the meat or fish from which the quenelles have been made.

. . . .

TRUFFLE QUENELLES
QUENELLES AUX TRUFFES

Preheat the oven to 200°C/400°F/Gas Mark 6. Shape the quenelles into slightly flattened batons and garnish them with small, evenly sized pieces of truffle. Slide them carefully into an ovenproof dish of hot stock and cook in the oven for 20 minutes.

FISH QUENELLES
QUENELLES DE POISSON

- 500 g (1 lb 2 oz) fish fillets, skinned and pin bones removed
- 250 g (9 oz) butter
- 200 g (7 oz) breadcrumbs soaked in milk
- 4 eggs
- Salt and pepper

Preparation time: 30 minutes
Cooking time: 15 minutes
Serves 6

Mash the fish in a bowl, and add the butter. Drain the breadcrumbs and add to the mixture. Work the mixture to produce a firm, smooth dough and add the eggs one by one. Season with salt and pepper. Leave to rest for a few hours in the refrigerator. Shape the dough into rolls and poach the quenelles, a few at a time, in simmering salted water for 5 minutes. Remove and drain.

PIKE QUENELLES
QUENELLES DE BROCHET

 p.114

Mash the pike finely. Drain the breadcrumbs thoroughly. Put the breadcrumbs in a bowl or mortar and, in turn, mix in the butter, pike and eggs. Season with salt, pepper and nutmeg. The mixture must be perfectly homogeneous. Leave to rest for a few hours in the refrigerator. Shape the dough into oblong quenelles at least 10 cm (4 inches) long. Poach the quenelles, a few at a time, in simmering water for 3–5 minutes. Serve with a sauce of your choice.

VARIATION

. . . .

NANTUA QUENELLES
QUENELLES À LA NANTUA

Prepare pike quenelles as above. To make the sauce, simmer trimmings from the fish with 200 ml (7 fl oz) dry white wine, 100 ml (3½ fl oz) water, 15 g (½ oz) chopped onion, 1 bouquet garni and salt and pepper, for 1 hour. Strain and reserve the liquid. Prepare a blond roux (p.57) with 50 g (1¾ oz) flour and 40 g (1½ oz) butter, add the the strained liquid, and bring to a simmer. Bind with 60 ml (2 fl oz) double cream and add 5 shelled crayfish tails, cut into small pieces. Put the pike quenelles in the sauce and simmer for 15 minutes. Serve hot.

- **200 g (7 oz) pike fillets, skinned and any pin bones removed**
- **200 g (7 oz) breadcrumbs soaked in milk**
- **200 g (7 oz) butter**
- **4 eggs**
- **Salt and pepper**
- **Freshly grated nutmeg**

Preparation time: 40 minutes
Cooking time: 15 minutes
Serves 6

BREADCRUMB QUENELLES
QUENELLES DE MIE DE PAIN

Drain the breadcrumbs, put them in a bowl and add the eggs and herbs. Mix thoroughly until smooth and season with salt and pepper. Form into small finger-shaped quenelles and roll in flour. Poach the quenelles, a few at a time, in simmering salted water for 10 minutes. Remove and drain.

- **500 g (1 lb 2 oz) stale breadcrumbs soaked in milk**
- **4 eggs**
- **1 large handful of mixed herbs, such as flat-leaf parsley, chives, chervil and tarragon, chopped**
- **Salt and pepper**
- **Flour, for rolling**

Preparation time: 30 minutes
Cooking time: 20 minutes
Serves 6

FLOUR QUENELLES
QUENELLES DE FARINE

- **250 g (9 oz) flour**
- **5 eggs**
- **50 g (1¾ oz) butter, at room temperature**
- **2 tablespoons milk**
- **Salt and pepper**

Preparation time: 10 minutes
Cooking time: 20 minutes
Serves 6

Sift the flour into a large bowl, make a well in the centre of the flour and add the eggs. Slowly incorporate the eggs into the flour with a fork until a dough forms. Cream the butter with the fork and add this and the milk to the dough. Season with salt and pepper and mix well until smooth. Form the dough into round quenelles and poach the quenelles, a few at a time, in simmering salted water for 10 minutes. Remove and drain.

POTATO QUENELLES
QUENELLES DE POMMES DE TERRE

- **350 g (12 oz) waxy yellow potatoes**
- **5 eggs, separated**
- **Salt and pepper**
- **80 g (2¾ oz) crème fraîche**

Preparation time: 15 minutes
Cooking time: 20 minutes
Serves 6

Boil the potatoes until tender then push them through a sieve to make a purée. Beat the egg whites to stiff peaks. Add the egg yolks to the potato purée, season with salt and pepper, and add the beaten egg whites and the crème fraîche. Shape into round quenelles and poach the quenelles, a few at a time, in simmering salted water for 10 minutes. Remove and drain.

FROGS' LEGS & SNAILS

Frogs' legs are at their most succulent from May to July. Only the back legs are eaten. They are usually sold ready-prepared, skinned and threaded on a skewer, twelve at a time. Allow one skewer per person and slide them off the skewer before cooking.

p.115

SAUTÉED FROGS' LEGS

GRENOUILLES SAUTÉES

- **6 skewers of frogs' legs (72 legs)**
- **50 g (1¾ oz) flour**
- **100 g (3½ oz) butter**
- **Salt and pepper**
- **3–4 tablespoons finely chopped shallot or garlic**

Preparation time: 8 minutes
Cooking time: 10 minutes
Serves 6

Sprinkle the frogs' legs with the flour. Melt the butter in a large sauté or frying pan and sauté the legs for 8–10 minutes, or until browned all over. Season with salt and pepper, and sprinkle with the shallot or garlic.

VARIATIONS

FRIED FROGS' LEGS

GRENOUILLES FRITES

Marinate the frogs' legs in the instant marinade for small pieces of meat (p.76) for 30 minutes. Prepare a batter (p.724) and drain the legs. Heat the oil in a deep-fryer to 180°C/350°F, or until a cube of bread browns in 30 seconds. Dip the legs in the batter, and carefully place in the hot oil in batches. Cook for 3–5 minutes, or until golden brown.

FROGS' LEGS IN SAUCE

GRENOUILLES EN SAUCE

Fry the frogs' legs in butter for 5 minutes, then put them into a pan with poulette sauce (p.52) and simmer for 10 minutes.

FROGS' LEGS WITH CREAM

GRENOUILLES À LA CRÈME

- **50 g (1¾ oz) butter**
- **1 onion, thinly sliced**
- **10 g (¼ oz) flour**
- **100 ml (3½ fl oz) white Burgundy**
- **6 skewers of frogs' legs (72 legs)**
- **Salt and pepper**
- **50 ml (2 fl oz) double cream**
- **1 small handful of flat-leaf parsley, finely chopped**
- **1 teaspoon lemon juice**

Preparation time: 10 minutes
Cooking time: 20 minutes
Serves 6

Melt the butter in a pan, add the onion and cook over a gentle heat until softened. Add the flour, and cook briefly without allowing the flour to brown. Stir in the wine, then add the frogs' legs and season with salt and pepper. Simmer for 15 minutes. Add the cream, parsley and lemon juice to the sauce.

SNAILS
ESCARGOTS

Preparation time: 20 minutes,
plus 1 week fasting of the snails
Cooking time: 2 hours
Serves 6

Fast the snails for a week, then purge them by feeding them salt mixed with flour and a dash of white wine vinegar. Wash them carefully and blanch in boiling salted water for 5 minutes. Take each snail out of its shell and remove the black part of the tail. Wash the snails again in plenty of water, then boil them for 2 hours in a well-seasoned court-bouillon with white wine (p.82). Leave to cool in the liquid. Wash each shell carefully and drain on a napkin. Make the stuffing (see below). Preheat the oven to 200°C/400°F/Gas Mark 6. Put a little stuffing in each shell, replace the snail and add more stuffing. Place the snails in a snail dish and bake in the oven for 8 minutes.

 p.116

STUFFING FOR SNAILS
FARCE POUR ESCARGOTS

* **60 g (2 oz) butter**
* **1 teaspoon finely chopped shallot**
* **½ garlic clove, finely chopped**
* **10 g (¼ oz) finely chopped flat-leaf parsley**
* **Salt and pepper**

Preparation time: 15 minutes
Makes enough for 12 snails

Mix all the ingredients together to prepare the stuffing.

NOTE
Tinned or bottled snails, and their shells, can be found in some specialist shops.

 p.117

SNAILS WITH CHABLIS
CASSOLETTES D'ESCARGOTS AU CHABLIS

* **20 g (¾ oz) shallot, finely chopped**
* **1½ teaspoons finely chopped garlic**
* **200 ml (7 fl oz) Chablis**
* **250 ml (8 fl oz) double cream**
* **90 prepared snails (see above)**
* **Salt and pepper**
* **100 g (3½ oz) grated Parmesan cheese**

Preparation time: 15 minutes
Cooking time: 25 minutes
Serves 7–8

Put the shallot and garlic in a pan with the Chablis and simmer over a gentle heat for 15 minutes. Add the cream and reduce the liquid over a gentle heat for another 15 minutes. Stir in the snails, add salt and pepper, and reheat the snails very rapidly. Divide the snails and sauce between 7 or 8 small ramekins. Sprinkle with the Parmesan and brown under the grill for 5 minutes.

NOTE
The dish can be varied by adding 100 g (3½ oz) mushrooms, well wiped and cut into sticks, to the garlic and shallot mixture.

Peppers in oil (p.97)

Tarragon canapés   (p.102)

Pike quenelles (p.106)

Sautéed frogs' legs (p.109)

Stuffing for snails   (p.111)

Snails with Chablis   (p.111)

- 3 -
MILK, EGGS & CHEESE

MILK

Milk supplies the body with many of its nutritional needs, including nitrogen, fat, sugar, minerals, calcium and vitamins. It can be consumed in several kinds of dish, such as in soups and mashed potatoes. Many desserts are based on milk, mainly in the form of cream. People who do not like milk on its own often enjoy sweet or savoury dishes based on dairy products. Milk combines well with many substances that alter its flavour, such as chocolate, coffee, caramel, orange-flower water and vanilla.

The milk sold in shops is usually pasteurized, which involves using various methods to eradicate any harmful bacteria it may contain. UHT sterilized milk, one of the other main types of milk, is sterile and safe, and lasts for two to three days once opened, but the ultra-heat treatment affects its flavour, which is preserved less well than in fresh pasteurized milk. Concentrated or condensed milk can be sweetened or unsweetened. If covered it will keep for two to three days at most in the refrigerator. Powdered milk, whole or skimmed, is very easy to use because it dissolves instantly.

It is sometimes possible to find unpasteurized milk in dairies and farm shops. This is simply chilled after milking, and packed on site. It goes off very quickly and it is therefore advisable to heat it for a moment or two to allow it to reach 100°C (212°F). This does not destroy all the vitamins — only vitamin C is affected. After the milk has come to the boil, cool it quickly by plunging the pan into cold water, then store it in the refrigerator.

Curd cheese (*caillebotte*) is made with milk that has been curdled with the help of a plant-based substance. Different plants are used in different regions. In southern France, a twig from a fig tree, bent to form a cross, is used to whisk boiled milk while it is still hot. In western France, wild thistle flowers are used; a few grams wrapped in muslin are whisked through unpasteurized milk while it is heated slowly. In central France, cooks mainly use the flower heads of *Galium verum*, or Lady's bedstraw, the popular French name of which is *caille-lait*, meaning 'curdle milk'.

p.162

YOGHURT
YAOURT

- **1.5 litres (2½ pints) whole milk**
- **Starter culture, or
  1 heaped tablespoon good, live
  commercial yoghurt**

Preparation time: 12½ hours
Serves 6

Place the milk in a pan, bring to a simmer and cook until the milk has reduced to 1 litre (1¾ pints). Leave to cool slightly. Add the starter culture to the warm milk. Pour into small pots and leave to rest in a warmish place for 12 hours. An electric yoghurt-maker can also be used, which keeps the mixture at exactly the right temperature to encourage the growth of beneficial bacteria.

EGGNOG
LAIT DE POULE

- **500 ml (18 fl oz) milk**
- **60 g (2 oz) caster sugar**
- **2 egg yolks**
- **10 ml–100 ml (2 teaspoons
  –3½ fl oz) orange-flower water**

Preparation time: 2 minutes
Cooking time: 5 minutes
Serves 6

Mix the milk and sugar in a pan, place over a moderate heat and bring to the boil, stirring frequently. Put the egg yolks into a large heatproof bowl. Take the milk off the heat and leave to cool a little, then gradually stir it into the egg yolks. Add orange-flower water to taste, return to the pan and heat gently for a few minutes, stirring regularly until the eggnog thickens slightly. Do not allow it to boil again.

MILK JAM
CONFITURE DE LAIT

- **2 litres (3½ pints) milk**
- **100 g (3½ oz) caster sugar**

Preparation time: 2 minutes
Cooking time: 2 hours
Serves 6

Mix the milk and sugar in a heavy-based pan and simmer over a very low heat for about 2 hours until the mixture has reduced by about two-thirds, stirring frequently to prevent a skin forming. The milk will thicken and turn a pale brownish colour. Serve hot with ice cream or chilled as a dessert in its own right.

SWEETENED WHIPPED CREAM
CRÈME CHANTILLY

- **250 ml (8 fl oz) chilled thick
  double cream, diluted with
  100 ml (3½ fl oz) milk, or 330 ml
  (11 fl oz) whipping cream**
- **Caster sugar, to taste**
- **Vanilla extract, to taste**

Preparation time: 10 minutes
Serves: 6

Whisk the cream, which should be very cold, until the mixture is stiff, frothy and light. Take care not to over-whip it. Add sugar and vanilla to taste. Do not allow the mixture to become too warm, as the cream may turn to butter.

CHEESE

The flavour of cheese develops while it is stored, so it is best enjoyed when mature. The maturation process varies from one cheese to another, as well as from one season to another. It is important to buy and eat cheese when it is at its peak of ripeness. Cheese can be eaten at the end of a substantial meal, and serving it is also a convenient way to end a light meal. Cheese forms part of many dishes, making them tasty and more nutritious. Fresh cheeses include Brousse and Saint-Florentin. Matured cheeses are usually divided into the following categories:

- Soft cheeses:
  Brie, Coulommiers, Livarot and Munster
- Semi-soft cheeses:
  Reblochon, Saint-Nectaire, Cantal and Mimolette
- Firm cheeses:
  Gruyère, Emmenthal and Parmesan
- Blue cheeses:
  Roquefort and Fourme d'Ambert
- Goat's milk cheeses:
  Sainte-Maure, Picodon and Crottin de Chavignol

CREAM CHEESE

FROMAGE À LA CRÈME

Warm the milk in a pan over a gentle heat. Stir and put in a pea-sized piece of rennet (a few drops if using liquid rennet) or, better still, a little milk, curdled the day before. Allow the milk to set, keeping it at a temperature of about 25°C (77°F) for several hours. Then put the milk in a sieve lined with muslin and set over a bowl, or in a special wicker strainer designed for the purpose, to allow it to drain for 4–5 hours. Mix the crème fraîche thoroughly into the cheese before serving, and add sugar to taste.

NOTE
The crème fraîche can be replaced with a little milk and 1 egg yolk to make a very smooth mixture.

- **1 litre (1¾ pints) milk**
- **Rennet or curdled milk**
- **125 g (4¼ oz) crème fraîche**
- **About 150 g (5 oz) caster sugar, to taste**

  Preparation time: 10 minutes, plus draining time
  Serves 6

EXTRA-RICH CREAM CHEESE
FROMAGE À LA CRÈME SURFIN

- **500 g (1 lb 2 oz) fromage frais**
- **500 ml (18 fl oz) crème fraîche**
- **3 egg whites**
- **Single cream, to serve**

  Preparation time: 15 minutes,
  plus draining time
  Serves 6

Drain the fromage frais through a sieve lined with muslin and set over a bowl, until it is very thick. Turn it out into a bowl and mix it with the crème fraîche. Beat for 10 minutes. Whisk the egg whites to soft peaks, stir them into the cheese mixture and strain through a sieve lined with muslin and set over a bowl. Leave to drain for 6 hours in the refrigerator. Turn out and serve cold, with a few spoons of single cream.

SOFT CHEESE BALLS
BOULETTES DE FROMAGE BLANC

Mix together the quark, eggs, sugar, flour and bicarbonate of soda. Stir to obtain a very smooth mixture. Heat the oil in a deep-fryer to 180°C/350°F, or until a cube of bread browns in 30 seconds. Form the quark mixture into balls, coat them with the flour or breadcrumbs and carefully place them, a few at a time, in the hot oil. Fry for 1–2 minutes, until golden, crisp and puffed. The balls are cooked when the blade of a knife inserted into one of the balls comes out clean. Remove from the oil with a slotted spoon and drain on kitchen paper. Sprinkle with sugar and serve immediately.

NOTE
In France, fromage blanc (a soft, fresh cream cheese) is used for this dish. Quark, or fromage frais that has been drained in a muslin-lined sieve until thick, make good substitutes.

- **350 g (12 oz) quark or fromage frais (see note)**
- **2 eggs**
- **80 g (2¾ oz) caster sugar, plus extra for sprinkling**
- **200 g (7 oz) flour**
- **1 teaspoon bicarbonate of soda**
- **Vegetable oil, for deep-frying**
- **Dried breadcrumbs or flour, for coating**

Preparation time: 10 minutes
Cooking time: 5 minutes
Serves 6

CHEESE SAVOURIES
DÉLICIEUSES DE FROMAGE

Beat the egg whites until very stiff and quickly fold in the cheese. Season with salt and pepper. Without squeezing the mixture too much, make egg-sized balls and coat them with the breadcrumbs. Heat the oil in a deep-fryer to 180°C/350°F, or until a cube of bread browns in 30 seconds. Carefully drop the balls into the hot oil, a few at a time, and cook until brown, about 1–2 minutes. Remove the balls from the oil with a slotted spoon and drain on kitchen paper. Garnish with fried parsley.

- **4 egg whites**
- **200 g (7 oz) Gruyère cheese, grated**
- **Salt and pepper**
- **Dried breadcrumbs, for coating**
- **Vegetable oil, for deep-frying**
- **Fried parsley (p.81)**

Preparation time: 10 minutes
Cooking time: 3 minutes
Serves 6

p.163

CHEESE FRITTERS

BEIGNETS AU FROMAGE

- 50 g (1¾ oz) butter
- 200 g (7 oz) flour
- 250 g (9 oz) Gruyère cheese, grated
- 2 eggs, lightly beaten
- Salt and pepper
- Vegetable oil, for deep-frying

Preparation time: 15 minutes
Cooking time: 6 minutes
Serves 6

Put the butter and 300 ml (½ pint) water in a pan and bring to the boil. Add the flour all at once and stir vigorously to make a smooth batter. Mix in the cheese. Leave to cool. Add the eggs and season with salt and pepper. Heat the oil in a deep-fryer to 180°C/350°F, or until a cube of bread browns in 30 seconds. Drop the batter into the hot oil, a spoonful at a time. Cook each spoonful for 1–2 minutes or until nicely browned. Remove the fritters from the oil with a slotted spoon and drain on kitchen paper.

SIMPLE CROQUE-MONSIEUR

CROQUE-MONSIEUR ÉCONOMIQUE

- 250 g (9 oz) crustless white bread, preferably stale
- 125 g (4¼ oz) butter
- 60 g (2 oz) Gruyère cheese, grated

Preparation time: 15 minutes
Cooking time: 16 minutes
Serves 6

Cut the bread into thin, evenly shaped slices and spread all the slices lightly with some of the butter. Sprinkle the cheese over half of them. Cover each of these slices with another slice. Press firmly so that the two slices stick together. Melt the remaining butter in a frying pan over a moderate heat. Add the croque-monsieurs and brown for 4 minutes on each side. Serve piping hot.

p.164

CROQUE-MONSIEUR WITH HAM

CROQUE-MONSIEUR AU JAMBON

- 250 g (9 oz) crustless white bread, preferably stale
- 100 g (3½ oz) butter
- 60 g (2 oz) Gruyère cheese, grated
- 85 g (3 oz) ham, sliced

Preparation time: 15 minutes
Cooking time: 8 minutes
Serves 6

Cut the bread into thin, evenly shaped slices. Spread all the slices with some of the butter and sprinkle with the cheese. Put a piece of ham on half the bread slices. Cover each one with a buttered slice. Tie together with kitchen string. Melt the remaining butter in a frying pan over a moderate heat. Add the croque-monsieurs and brown for 4 minutes on each side. Remove the string to serve.

CHEESE CROQUETTES

CROQUETTES AU FROMAGE

Make a very thick béchamel sauce with the butter, flour and milk (p.50). Mix in the cheese and egg yolks. Shape into thumb-sized croquettes and coat with the breadcrumbs. Heat the oil in a deep-fryer to 180°C/350°F, or until a cube of bread browns in 30 seconds. Add the croquettes, a few at a time, and cook for 1–2 minutes, or until browned. Lift out of the oil with a slotted spoon and drain on kitchen paper.

- **80 g (2¾ oz) butter**
- **90 g (3¼ oz) flour**
- **500 ml (18 fl oz) milk**
- **150 g (5 oz) Gruyère cheese, grated**
- **2 egg yolks**
- **Dried breadcrumbs, for coating**
- **Vegetable oil, for deep-frying**

Preparation time: 25 minutes
Cooking time: 5 minutes
Serves 6

FRENCH TOAST WITH GRUYÈRE CHEESE

PAIN PERDU AU GRUYÈRE

Bring the milk to the boil and remove from the heat. Add the eggs and season with salt. Spread the butter on the slices of bread, then soak the slices in the warm milk mixture for 15 minutes. Preheat the oven to 220°C/425°F/Gas Mark 7 and grease an ovenproof dish. Place the slices of bread on the dish. Sprinkle generously with the cheese. Brown in the oven for 25 minutes.

- **500 ml (18 fl oz) milk**
- **3 eggs, lightly beaten**
- **Salt**
- **50 g (1¾ oz) butter, plus extra for greasing**
- **200 g (7 oz) stale bread, thinly sliced**
- **100 g (3½ oz) Gruyère cheese, grated**

Preparation time: 20 minutes
Cooking time: 25 minutes
Serves 6

CHEESE GNOCCHI

GNOCCHIS AU FROMAGE

Preheat the oven to 250°C/500°F/Gas Mark 9. Shape the choux pastry dough into finger-thick rolls. Cut into small pieces 1.5 cm (¾ inch) long to make gnocchi. Bring a large pan of salted water to the boil. Carefully drop the gnocchi in and simmer gently for 10 minutes. Drain. Arrange the gnocchi in an ovenproof dish and sprinkle with the cheese. Season with salt and pepper. Brush with the butter and bake for 10 minutes.

- **300 g (11 oz) choux pastry dough (p.774)**
- **125 g (4¼ oz) Gruyère cheese, grated**
- **Salt and pepper**
- **60 g (2 oz) butter, melted**

Preparation time: 20 minutes
Cooking time: 20 minutes
Serves 6

BREAD BOURGUIGNON

PAIN BOURGUIGNON

- 100 g (3½ oz) butter
- 70 g (2½ oz) flour
- 250 ml (8 fl oz) milk
- 6 eggs
- 125 g (4¼ oz) Gruyère cheese, grated
- Salt and pepper
- 1 quantity tomato sauce (p.57) or mushroom sauce (p.61), to serve

Preparation time: 15 minutes
Cooking time: 1¾ hours
Serves 6

Preheat the oven to 140°C/275°F/Gas Mark 1. Make a béchamel sauce (p.50) with the butter (reserve a knob to grease the ring mould), flour and milk. Beat in the eggs one by one, followed by the cheese. Season with salt and pepper. Butter a ring mould, pour in the mixture and set the mould in a deep roasting tin half-filled with hot water. Cook in the oven for 1¾ hours. Remove the bread Bourguignon from the mould and serve with tomato or mushroom sauce.

HAM & EGG GRATIN

BOUCHÉES GRATINÉES

- 25 g (1 oz) butter
- 80 g (2¾ oz) cooked ham, diced
- 2 eggs, beaten
- 250 ml (8 fl oz) boiling milk
- Salt and pepper
- Freshly grated nutmeg
- 80 g (2¾ oz) Gruyère cheese, grated

Preparation time: 10 minutes
Cooking time: 25 minutes
Serves 6

Preheat the oven to 200°C/400°F/Gas Mark 6 and grease 6 ramekins with the butter. In a heatproof mixing bowl, add the ham to the eggs, then gradually add the milk, stirring the mixture constantly. Season with salt and pepper and a pinch of nutmeg. Pour the mixture into the ramekins, sprinkle each with the cheese, and cook in the oven for 25 minutes or until set.

CHEESE SOUFFLÉ

SOUFFLÉ AU FROMAGE

 p.165

Preheat the oven to 180°C/350°F/Gas Mark 4 and grease a soufflé dish or 6 individual ramekins right to the top. Make a very thick béchamel sauce (p.50) with the butter, flour and milk. Add the cheese. Leave to cool, then add the egg yolks. Whisk the egg whites to stiff peaks and fold into the cheese mixture. Season with salt and pepper, and pour into the prepared dishes. If using a soufflé dish, bake in the oven for 30 minutes, then turn the heat up to 220°C/425°F/Gas Mark 7 and cook for a further 15 minutes. If using individual ramekins, cook for 10 minutes, then turn up the heat and cook for a further 5–10 minutes, or until the soufflé is golden and just set.

- 100 g (3½ oz) butter, plus extra for greasing
- 100 g (3½ oz) flour
- 500 ml (18 fl oz) milk
- 125 g (4¼ oz) Gruyère cheese, grated
- 5 eggs, separated
- Salt and pepper

Preparation time: 25 minutes
Cooking time: 45 minutes
Serves 6

GOUGÈRE

GOUGÈRE

 p.166

This delicious cheese pastry comes from the Burgundy region in eastern France.

Preheat the oven to 200°C/400°F/Gas Mark 6 and grease a baking tray with the butter. Make the choux pastry dough, omitting the sugar and adding the cheese. Pipe or spoon the pastry dough in a ring shape, or place individual, well-spaced spoonfuls, on the prepared baking tray. Sprinkle with extra cheese. Bake for 25–30 minutes (or 15–20 minutes for individual gougères), until risen and golden brown.

- 10 g (¼ oz) butter
- 300 g (11 oz) choux pastry dough (p.774)
- 125 g (4¼ oz) Gruyère cheese, grated or cut into thin strips, plus extra for sprinkling

Preparation time: 15 minutes
Cooking time: 15–30 minutes
Serves 6

CHEESE TART

TARTE AU FROMAGE

Preheat the oven to 220°C/425°F/Gas Mark 7. Roll out the shortcrust pastry dough on a surface dusted with flour and line a deep 23-cm (9-inch) loose-bottomed tart tin. Bake blind (p.784), then remove from the oven and lower the heat to 180°C/350°F/Gas Mark 4. Beat the eggs and add the milk, crème fraîche and cheese. Season with salt and pepper. Pour the mixture into the pastry case and bake in the oven for 30 minutes.

- 300 g (11 oz) shortcrust pastry dough (p.784)
- Flour, for dusting
- 3 eggs
- 250 ml (8 fl oz) milk
- 125 g (4¼ oz) crème fraîche
- 125 g (4¼ oz) Gruyère cheese, grated
- Salt and pepper

Preparation time: 20 minutes
Cooking time: 30 minutes
Serves 6

COMTÉ CHEESE SAVOURY

ENTRÉE COMTOISE

- **6 day-old croissants**
- **1 quantity white sauce (p.50)**
- **100 g (3½ oz) Comté cheese, grated**
- **50 g (1¼ oz) butter, softened**

Preparation time: 20 minutes
Cooking time: 10–15 minutes
Serves 6

Preheat the oven to 240ºC/475ºF/Gas Mark 8. Cut the croissants in half horizontally and hollow out each half. Mix the white sauce with the cheese and fill the hollows with this mixture. Spread with the butter and brown in the oven for 10–15 minutes.

FROMAGE BLANC & SULTANA TART

TARTE AU FROMAGE BLANC ET AUX RAISINS

Prepare the shortbread or shortcrust pastry dough. Preheat the oven to 200°C/400°F/Gas Mark 6. Roll the dough out on a surface dusted with flour, and line a deep 23-cm (9-inch) loose-bottomed tart tin. Sprinkle the breadcrumbs and the currants or sultanas over the base. Cream the butter with the sugar and stir in 3 egg yolks, and the flour, lemon zest and juice, fromage frais and crème fraîche. Whisk all the egg whites until stiff and carefully fold into the mixture. Pour the mixture into the pastry case. Brush with the remaining egg yolk to glaze. Bake in the oven for 45 minutes. This tart is delicious served cold.

- 1 quantity sablé biscuit dough (p.761) or shortcrust pastry dough (p.784)
- 50 g (1¾ oz) dried breadcrumbs
- 100 g (3½ oz) currants or sultanas
- 50 g (1¾ oz) butter, softened
- 125 g (4¼ oz) caster sugar
- 4 eggs, separated
- 30 g (1¼ oz) flour, plus extra for dusting
- Grated zest and juice of ½ lemon
- 500 g (1 lb 2 oz) quark or other cream cheese
- 100 g (3½ oz) crème fraîche

Preparation time: 30 minutes
Cooking time: 45 minutes
Serves 6

QUICHE LORRAINE

QUICHE LORRAINE

 p.167

Prepare the shortcut pastry dough. Preheat the oven to 200°C/400°F/Gas Mark 6. Roll the dough out on a surface dusted with flour and line a solid-based 23-cm (9-inch) tart tin. Sprinkle the bacon over the base. Beat the eggs in a bowl, add the crème fraîche, or crème fraîche and milk, and season with salt and pepper. Pour the mixture into the pastry case. Bake for 40 minutes, or until golden and set.

- 200 g (7 oz) shortcrust pastry dough (p.784)
- Flour, for dusting
- 125 g (4¼ oz) smoked bacon, diced
- 4 eggs
- 500 ml (18 fl oz) crème fraîche, or 250 ml (8 fl oz) milk mixed with 250 ml (8 fl oz) crème fraîche
- Salt and pepper

Preparation time: 20 minutes
Cooking time: 40 minutes
Serves 6

p.168

HOT CHAVIGNOL CROTTINS
CROTTINS DE CHAVIGNOL CHAUDS

- **6 slices of crustless white bread**
- **Salad leaves of your choice**
- **3 Crottin de Chavignol goat's milk cheeses**

Preparation time: 10 minutes
Cooking time: 7–10 minutes
Serves 6

Preheat the grill. Brown the slices of bread on both sides under the hot grill. Place some salad leaves on each of 6 plates. Cut each cheese horizontally into 2 pieces. Place each piece of cheese on a slice of bread and return to the grill. Cook until soft and golden. Place the cheese on top of the salad leaves and serve immediately.

CHEESE FONDUE FROM FRANCHE-COMTÉ
FONDUE FRANC-COMTOISE

- **1 garlic clove**
- **100 ml (3½ fl oz) dry white wine**
- **130 g (4½ oz) Comté cheese, grated**
- **6 eggs, beaten**
- **65 g (2¼ oz) butter**
- **Salt and pepper**
- **Freshly grated nutmeg**
- **Bread, sliced, to serve**

Preparation time: 5 minutes
Cooking time: 20 minutes
Serves 6

Rub the bottom of a heavy-based pan with the garlic until the clove disintegrates. Pour in the wine and bring to a simmer. Add the cheese and cook over a gentle heat, stirring constantly as it melts, until it has the consistency of cream. Add the eggs and butter. Continue to cook gently for 7–8 minutes until the mixture thickens, stirring constantly. Season with salt, pepper and nutmeg, and serve on slices of bread.

EGGS

Eggs are a rich source of nutrients, including vitamins, iron and sulphur. They should be eaten when very fresh. Check the date on which they were laid, as well as the use-by date. Eggs are graded for size and quality, and most of the eggs available in shops and supermarkets are good quality. It is a good idea to take eggs out of the refrigerator 1–2 hours before use to bring them to room temperature before cooking.

SOFT-BOILED EGGS IN THE SHELL
OEUFS À LA COQUE

There are 3 methods for cooking soft-boiled eggs:

Cooking time: 2–3 minutes

METHOD 1
Bring a small pan of water to the boil, then gently lower the eggs into it. Boil for 2 minutes, or 3 minutes at the most, then remove and serve.

METHOD 2
Bring a small pan of water to the boil, add a pinch of salt and gently lower the eggs into it. Cover, remove the pan from the heat and leave to stand for 4–5 minutes, then remove and serve.

METHOD 3
Put the eggs into a small pan, pour in cold water to cover and set over the heat. As soon as the water boils, remove the eggs and serve. Soft-boiled eggs are served wrapped in a napkin, with salt and butter.

SHELLED SOFT-BOILED EGGS
OEUFS MOLLETS

Bring a small pan of water to the boil, add a pinch of salt and gently lower the eggs into it. Boil for 5 minutes, then remove with a spoon and plunge into cold water. Peel and discard the shells. Serve the eggs with vegetables or a sauce.

Cooking time: 5 minutes

HARD-BOILED EGGS
OEUFS DURS

Bring a small pan of water to the boil, add a pinch of salt and gently lower the eggs into it. Boil for 10 minutes, then remove with a spoon. If you want the yolk to stay in the centre of the white, stir constantly for a few minutes after lowering the eggs into the water. To shell hard-boiled eggs easily, pour cold water over them after cooking. Older eggs are easier to shell than freshly laid eggs. Hard-boiled eggs can be used to garnish salads, a vegetable macédoine or cold fish.

Cooking time: 10 minutes

VARIATIONS

. . . .

HARD- OR SOFT-BOILED EGGS IN A SAUCE
OEUFS DURS OU MOLLETS EN SAUCE

Hard-boiled eggs, halved lengthways, and whole soft-boiled eggs may be served coated in various sauces. Serve hot with white sauce (p.50), béchamel sauce (p.50), cheese sauce (p.51), tomato sauce (p.57) or Robert sauce (p.63).

. . . .

HARD-BOILED EGGS IN MAYONNAISE
OEUFS DURS MAYONNAISE

Shelled hard-boiled eggs may be halved or sliced when cold, then coated with mayonnaise (p.70) and garnished with lettuce leaves, capers or slices of tomato. Use as a garnish for cold salads, fish or macédoines, and hot spinach or cooked salads.

. . . .

HARD-BOILED EGGS WITH SPINACH
OEUFS DURS ÉPINARDS

Cut hot hard-boiled eggs in half lengthways and arrange on a bed of cooked spinach.

. . . .

HARD-BOILED EGG SALAD
OEUFS DURS EN SALADE

Shell and dice cooled hard-boiled eggs and dress with a vinaigrette (p.66) or ravigote sauce (p.56). Capers, gherkins, sliced tomatoes, cucumbers (de-seeded), cold boiled beef, herring fillets or anchovy fillets, can also be added.

EGGS MIMOSA

OEUFS MIMOSA

- **6 eggs**
- **1 quantity mayonnaise (p.70)**
- **Chopped parsley, to garnish**

Preparation time: 30 minutes
Cooking time: 10 minutes
Serves 6

Hard boil the eggs (p.134), then cool and shell them. Cut them in half lengthways, carefully remove the yolks with a teaspoon and put them in a bowl. Mash the yolks and stir two-thirds of them into the mayonnaise. Arrange the white halves on a serving dish and fill with the egg and mayonnaise mixture. Pass the remaining yolks through a coarse sieve and sprinkle over the filled egg whites to cover the mayonnaise. Garnish with chopped parsley.

PLAIN STUFFED EGGS

OEUFS FARCIS AU MAIGRE

- **1 quantity white sauce (p.50) or béchamel sauce (p.50)**
- **6 eggs**
- **25 g (1 oz) breadcrumbs**
- **50 ml (2 fl oz) milk**
- **15 g (½ oz) butter**
- **1 bunch of mixed herbs, such as chives, flat-leaf parsley, tarragon and chervil**
- **Salt and pepper**

Preparation time: 20 minutes
Cooking time: 20 minutes
Serves 6

Prepare the white or béchamel sauce. Hard boil the eggs (p.134), then cool and shell them. Cut them in half lengthways, carefully remove the yolks with a teaspoon and put them into a bowl. Place the white halves in an ovenproof dish. Preheat the oven to 240°C/475°F/Gas Mark 8. Put the breadcrumbs into another bowl, pour in the milk and leave to soak.

Meanwhile, melt the butter in a frying pan. Add the herbs and cook over a low heat, stirring frequently, for 2–3 minutes. Remove from the heat, chop the herbs and mix with the egg yolks. Drain the breadcrumbs, add them to the egg yolk mixture and season with salt and pepper. Mash well until thoroughly combined. Fill the egg white halves with the mixture. Pour the sauce over them and bake for 10 minutes. Serve immediately.

NOTE
The stuffing can be flavoured by adding other ingredients, such as truffles, prawns or mushrooms.

EGGS WITH ANCHOVY STUFFING

OEUFS FARCIS AUX ANCHOIS

Preheat the oven to its highest setting and grease an oven-proof dish with the butter. Hard boil the eggs (p.134), then cool and shell them. Cut them in half lengthways, carefully remove the yolks with a teaspoon and put them into a bowl. Add the anchovy fillets and parsley, season with salt and pepper and mash well until thoroughly combined and smooth. Stir in the lemon juice and fill the egg white halves with the mixture. Put the eggs into the prepared dish, pour the crème fraîche over them and bake for 10–15 minutes, or until lightly browned.

- 15 g (½ oz) butter
- 6 eggs
- 6 canned anchovy fillets, drained and chopped
- 2 tablespoons chopped flat-leaf parsley
- Salt and pepper
- 1 teaspoon lemon juice
- 5 tablespoons crème fraîche

Preparation time: 35 minutes
Cooking time: 10–15 minutes
Serves 6

EGGS À LA ROYALE

OEUFS À LA ROYALE

Hard boil the eggs (p.134), then cool and shell them. Cut them in half lengthways, carefully remove the yolks with a teaspoon and pass them through a sieve. Make a béchamel sauce (p.50) with the butter, flour, milk and a pinch of nutmeg, and season with salt and pepper. Put a ring of egg white halves on a serving dish, and fill the centre with the sieved yolks, then coat with the béchamel sauce. In a pan, heat the tomato passata, pour it onto the eggs and serve immediately.

- 100 g (3½ oz) tomato passata
- 6 eggs
- 50 g (1¾ oz) butter
- 25 g (1 oz) flour
- 200 ml (7 fl oz) milk
- Freshly grated nutmeg
- Salt and pepper

Preparation time: 15 minutes
Cooking time: 20 minutes
Serves 6

EGGS À LA TRIPE

OEUFS À LA TRIPE

Hard boil the eggs (p.134) and leave to cool. Melt the butter in a pan. Add the onions and cook over a low heat, stirring occasionally, for 5 minutes, until softened. Stir in the flour and cook, stirring constantly, for a few minutes, but do not allow the flour to brown. Gradually stir in the stock. Shell the eggs and cut into thick slices. Add them to the pan, season with salt and pepper, and simmer, stirring frequently, for 20 minutes.

- 6 eggs
- 20 g (¾ oz) butter
- 2 onions, finely chopped
- 20 g (¾ oz) flour
- 250 ml (8 fl oz) any stock
- Salt and pepper

Preparation time: 15 minutes
Cooking time: 20 minutes
Serves 6

BRUSSELS-STYLE EGGS
OEUFS BRUXELLOIS

- **50 g (1¾ oz) butter**
- **3 eggs**
- **500 g (1 lb 2 oz) Brussels sprouts**
- **100 g (3½ oz) Gruyère cheese, grated**
- **30 g (1¼ oz) flour**
- **500 ml (18 fl oz) milk**
- **Freshly grated nutmeg**
- **Salt and pepper**

Preparation time: 40 minutes
Cooking time: 10 minutes
Serves 6

Preheat the oven to its highest setting and grease an oven-proof dish with a little of the butter. Hard boil the eggs (p.134). Cook the Brussels sprouts in salted boiling water for 8–10 minutes, or until tender. Drain and pass through a fine sieve into a bowl. Stir in half the cheese and spread out the mixture in the prepared dish. Shell and coarsely chop the eggs. Make a thick béchamel sauce (p.50) with the remaining butter, and the flour, milk and a pinch of nutmeg, and season with salt and pepper. Mix the eggs with the béchamel sauce and pour the mixture over the Brussels sprouts. Sprinkle with the remaining cheese and bake for 10 minutes, or until lightly browned.

ITALIAN-STYLE EGGS
OEUFS À L'ITALIENNE

- **100 g (3½ oz) tomato sauce (p.57)**
- **6 eggs**
- **15 g (½ oz) butter**
- **150 g (5 oz) ribbon pasta or small macaroni**
- **50 g (1¾ oz) Gruyère cheese, grated**
- **4 tablespoons dried breadcrumbs**
- **Salt and pepper**

Preparation time: 15 minutes
Cooking time: 30 minutes
Serves 6

Prepare the tomato sauce and keep it warm. Meanwhile, hard boil the eggs (p.134), then cool and shell them. Cut into thick slices. Preheat the oven to 250°C/500°F/Gas Mark 9 and grease an ovenproof dish with the butter. Cook the pasta in a large pan of salted boiling water for 8–12 minutes or until al dente, then drain and spoon on to the prepared dish to form a ring. Fill the centre with the egg slices. Spoon the tomato sauce over the eggs and pasta and sprinkle with the cheese and breadcrumbs. Season with salt and pepper and bake for 10 minutes, or until lightly browned.

CINDERELLA EGGS

OEUFS CENDRILLON

Hard boil the eggs (p.134), then cool and shell them. Cut them in half lengthways and carefully remove the yolks with a teaspoon. Mix the ham, foie gras, crème fraîche and butter in a bowl until thoroughly combined, and season with salt and pepper. Fill the egg white halves with the mixture and put them on a serving dish. Pass the egg yolks through a sieve, and sprinkle over the top. If desired, garnish the eggs with aspic.

- 6 eggs
- 125 g (4¼ oz) lean ham, finely chopped
- 125 g (4¼ oz) foie gras mousse
- 5 tablespoons crème fraîche
- 25 g (1 oz) butter
- Salt and pepper
- Aspic (p.45), chopped, to serve (optional)

Preparation time: 25 minutes
Cooking time: 10 minutes
Serves 6

EGGS WITH TRUFFLES

OEUFS AUX TRUFFES

 p.169

Hard boil the eggs (p.134), then cool and shell them. Cut them in half lengthways, carefully remove the yolks with a teaspoon and pass them through a sieve into a bowl. Preheat the oven to 250°C/500°F/Gas Mark 9 and grease an ovenproof dish with a little of the melted butter. Pour the cream and brandy into a pan, add a pinch of nutmeg, season with salt and pepper and simmer for 10 minutes. Remove the pan from the heat and stir in the egg yolks and truffle shavings, mixing to a paste. Fill the egg white halves with the mixture and put them in the prepared dish. Pour the rest of the melted butter over them and bake for 5 minutes, or until lightly browned.

- 6 eggs
- 50 g (1¾ oz) butter, melted
- 200 ml (7 fl oz) double cream
- 175 ml (6 fl oz) brandy
- Freshly grated nutmeg
- Salt and pepper
- 80 g (2¾ oz) truffle shavings

Preparation time: 20 minutes
Cooking time: 15 minutes
Serves 6

EGGS CHIMAY

OEUFS CHIMAY

- Butter, for greasing
- 1 quantity cheese sauce (p.51)
- 6 eggs
- 150 g (5 oz) duxelles (p.81)
- 1 sprig of flat-leaf parsley, finely chopped
- Salt and pepper
- 50 g (1¾ oz) Gruyère cheese, grated

Preparation time: 25 minutes
Cooking time: 10 minutes
Serves 6

Preheat the oven to 250°C/500°F/Gas Mark 9 and grease an ovenproof dish with butter. Prepare the cheese sauce and keep hot. Meanwhile, hard boil the eggs (p.134), then cool and shell them. Cut them in half lengthways and carefully remove the yolks with a teaspoon. Put them into a bowl and mash, gradually incorporating the duxelles, with 1 tablespoon of the cheese sauce and the parsley. Season with salt and pepper. Fill the egg white halves with the mixture, put them into the prepared dish and pour the remaining sauce over them. Sprinkle with the cheese and bake for 10 minutes, or until lightly browned.

EGGS À L'AURORE

OEUFS À L'AURORE

- 50 g (1¾ oz) butter, plus extra for greasing
- 20 g (¾ oz) flour
- 250 ml (8 fl oz) milk
- 30 g (1¾ oz) Gruyère cheese, grated
- 6 eggs
- Salt and pepper

Preparation time: 15 minutes
Cooking time: 25 minutes
Serves 6

Make a béchamel sauce (p.50), with the butter, flour and milk, and stir in the cheese. Preheat the oven to 240°C/475°F/Gas Mark 8 and grease 6 ramekins with butter. Hard boil the eggs (p.134), then cool and shell them. Cut them in half lengthways and carefully remove the yolks with a teaspoon. Chop the egg whites and stir them into the sauce. Season with salt and pepper. Pass the yolks through a fine sieve into a bowl. Make alternate layers of the sauce mixture and the egg yolks in the prepared ramekins, ending with a layer of yolks. Bake for 10–15 minutes, or until lightly browned.

NEAPOLITAN-STYLE EGGS

OEUFS À LA NAPOLITAINE

Hard boil the eggs (p.134), then cool and shell them. Cut them in half lengthways. Cook the rice in a pan of salted boiling water for 20 minutes, or until tender, then drain. Meanwhile, preheat the oven to 250°C/500°F/Gas Mark 9 and grease an ovenproof dish with butter. Mix the rice with half the cheese and spoon into the prepared dish. Put the eggs on top and sprinkle with the remaining cheese and the herbs. Dot with the butter and bake for 5 minutes. Do not bake any longer, as this spoils the whites.

- 6 eggs
- 150 g (5 oz) long-grain rice
- 25 g (1 oz) butter, plus extra for greasing
- 75 g (2½ oz) Gruyère cheese, grated
- 1 tablespoon finely chopped mixed herbs, such as flat-leaf parsley, chives, tarragon and chervil
- Salt

Preparation time: 10 minutes
Cooking time: 5 minutes
Serves 6

BASQUE EGGS

OEUFS BASQUAISE

Hard boil the eggs (p.134), then cool. Peel the prawns, reserving the shells, and chop finely. Put the mushrooms and half the butter into a pan, pour in 300 ml (½ pint) water and the lemon juice and simmer for 10 minutes. Remove the mushrooms with a slotted spoon, set them aside, and add the prawn shells to the pan. Bring to the boil then reduce the heat and simmer for 10 minutes. Remove from the heat and strain the stock into a bowl. Make a fairly thin white sauce (p.50) with the remaining butter, flour and prawn stock.

Meanwhile, preheat the oven to 250°C/500°F/Gas Mark 9. Shell the hard-boiled eggs, cut them in half lengthways and carefully remove the yolks with a teaspoon. Put the yolks into a bowl, add the prawns, mushrooms and herbs, season with salt and pepper, and mash well with a fork until thoroughly combined. Fill the egg white halves with the mixture, put them into an ovenproof dish and pour the sauce over them. Bake for 5 minutes and serve.

- 6 eggs
- 125 g (4¼ oz) cooked unpeeled prawns
- 125 g (4¼ oz) mushrooms, chopped
- 50 g (1¾ oz) butter
- Juice of 1 lemon
- 25 g (1 oz) flour
- 1 tablespoon finely chopped mixed herbs, such as such as flat-leaf parsley, chives, tarragon and chervil
- Salt and pepper

Preparation time: 25 minutes
Cooking time: 5 minutes
Serves 6

EGGS GUITTE
OEUFS GUITTE

- 20 g (¾ oz) butter
- 6 very fresh eggs
- Salt and pepper
- 250 ml (8 fl oz) mayonnaise (p.70)
- 2 tablespoons chopped mixed herbs, such as such as flat-leaf parsley, chives, tarragon and chervil

Preparation time: 5 minutes
Cooking time: 15 minutes
Serves 6

Preheat the oven to 200°C/400°F/Gas Mark 6 and grease 6 small ramekins with the butter. Carefully break an egg into each one and season with salt and pepper. Put the ramekins in a roasting tin and pour in boiling water to come about halfway up the sides. Bake for about 15 minutes, or until the eggs are set. Remove the roasting tin from the oven, lift out the ramekins and leave to cool completely. Turn out the eggs onto an oval serving dish and top each one with 1 teaspoon of the mayonnaise. Surround the eggs with the remaining mayonnaise, and garnish with the herbs. Serve cold.

TSARINA EGGS
OEUFS À LA TSARINE

- 6 eggs
- 15 g (½ oz) butter
- 3 large tomatoes, skinned and chopped
- 1 onion, chopped
- 1 bouquet garni
- Salt and pepper
- 1 quantity béchamel sauce (p.50) or hollandaise sauce (p.74)
- 60 g (2 oz) mushrooms

Preparation time: 20 minutes
Cooking time: 10 minutes
Serves 6

Hard boil the eggs (p.134), shell them and put them in a bowl of hot water. Melt half the butter in a pan, add the tomatoes, onion and bouquet garni, season with salt and pepper and cook over a low heat, stirring occasionally, for 20 minutes. Remove and discard the bouquet garni, transfer the mixture to a food processor or blender and process until combined, then scrape into a bowl.

Prepare the béchamel sauce, if using, and preheat the grill. Blanch the mushrooms in a pan of salted boiling water for 5 minutes, then drain and chop. Add them to the tomato mixture and mix in the remaining butter. Cut the eggs in half lengthways and carefully remove the yolks with a teaspoon. Stir them into the tomato and mushroom mixture and season with salt and pepper. Fill the egg white halves with this mixture. Prepare the hollandaise sauce, if using. Arrange the eggs in an ovenproof dish and pour the béchamel or hollandaise over them. If using béchamel sauce, grill for 10 minutes until lightly browned, then serve. If using hollandaise sauce, serve immediately.

TURKISH-STYLE EGGS

OEUFS À LA TURQUE

Hard boil the eggs (p.134), then cool and shell them. Carefully remove the egg whites, leaving the yolks intact. Cut the egg whites into thin strips. Melt the butter in a pan. Add the onions and bouquet garni, season with salt and pepper and cook over a low heat, stirring occasionally, for 5 minutes. Add the flour all at once and cook, stirring constantly, for 1 minute. Stir in the wine and stock and season with salt and pepper. Stir in the strips of egg white, add the whole egg yolks and briefly heat through, but do not allow the mixture to boil. Serve immediately.

- **6 eggs**
- **50 g (1¾ oz) butter**
- **2 large onions, chopped**
- **1 bouquet garni**
- **Salt and pepper**
- **2 tablespoons flour**
- **100 ml (3½ fl oz) white wine**
- **100 ml (3½ fl oz) veal stock**

Preparation time: 25 minutes
Cooking time: 15 minutes
Serves 6

EGGS IN MEURETTE SAUCE

OEUFS EN MEURETTE

Cook the eggs; they can be hard-boiled (p.134) or soft-boiled (p.132), and then shelled, or poached (p.143). Put the wine, onion, shallot, thyme, bay leaf and parsley in a pan. Bring to a boil then reduce the heat and simmer until reduced by half. Work 25 g (1 oz) of the butter into the flour to make a smooth paste and whisk this into the wine. Boil for 1 minute to thicken. Whisk in the remaining butter and strain the sauce through a sieve, discarding the solids. Season the sauce with salt and pepper. Melt a little butter in a frying pan and fry the bread, then rub the slices with the garlic clove. Peel the eggs if necessary, place them on top of the fried bread and coat with the sauce.

- **6 eggs**
- **750 ml (1¼ pints) red wine**
- **1 small onion, finely chopped**
- **1 shallot, finely chopped**
- **1 sprig of thyme**
- **1 bay leaf**
- **2 sprigs of flat-leaf parsley**
- **70 g (2½ oz) butter,
  plus extra for frying**
- **15 g (½ oz) flour**
- **Salt and pepper**
- **6 slices bread**
- **½ garlic clove**

Preparation time: 10 minutes
Cooking time: 25 minutes
Serves 6

EGGS À LA DIEPPOISE

OEUFS À LA DIEPPOISE

- **6 eggs**
- **60 g (2 oz) butter, softened**
- **2 tablespoons flat-leaf parsley, chopped**
- **500 ml (18 fl oz) crème fraîche**
- **Salt and pepper**
- **250 ml (8 fl oz) mayonnaise (p.70)**
- **100 g (3½ oz) cooked peeled prawns, diced**

Preparation time: 15 minutes
Cooking time: 12 minutes
Serves 6

Hard boil the eggs (p.134) then cool and shell them. Cut them in half widthways. Carefully remove the yolks with a teaspoon and mash them in a small bowl with the butter, parsley and 250 ml (8 fl oz) of the crème fraîche. Season with salt and pepper. Fill the halved egg whites with the mixture. Mix the mayonnaise with the prawns and remaining crème fraîche and coat the eggs with the mixture.

POACHED EGGS

OEUFS POCHÉS

- **6 eggs**
- **3 tablespoons white wine vinegar**

Preparation time: 2 minutes
Cooking time: 3½ minutes per egg
Serves 6

Use very fresh eggs. It is important to use the correct amount of water for the number of eggs to be cooked: use 500 ml (18 fl oz) per egg. Pour the water and vinegar into a pan and bring to the boil, then reduce to a gentle simmer. Crack each egg into a cup or ramekin, then let it slide into the water so that it is just covered. If necessary, spoon the white back over the yolk. Simmer gently for 3½ minutes. Remove the egg with a slotted spoon and drain on a clean tea towel. Repeat with the remaining eggs. Put the eggs on a serving dish and coat with your choice of sauce (see below). Poached eggs can be kept hot in a bowl of warm water containing 1 teaspoon salt per litre (1¾ pints).

VARIATION

. . . .

POACHED EGGS IN A SAUCE

OEUFS POCHÉS EN SAUCE

Poached eggs can be served with white sauce (p.50), béchamel sauce (p.50), Robert sauce (p.63), tomato sauce (p.57), piquant sauce (p.60), or with black butter (p.48).

POACHED EGGS MORNAY

OEUFS POCHÉS À LA MORNAY

Preheat the oven to 240ºC/475ºF/Gas Mark 8 and grease an ovenproof dish with butter. Pour 3 litres (5¼ pints) water and the vinegar into a pan, bring to the boil, reduce to a gentle simmer and poach the eggs (p.143), then remove and drain. Make a cheese sauce with the remaining ingredients (p.51). Spoon a layer of the sauce into the prepared dish, add the eggs and pour the remaining sauce over them. Bake for 10 minutes, or until golden brown.

- **40 g (1½ oz) butter, plus extra for greasing**
- **3 tablespoons white wine vinegar**
- **6 eggs**
- **25 g (1 oz) flour**
- **500 ml (18 fl oz) milk**
- **60 g (2 oz) Gruyère cheese, grated**

Preparation time: 25 minutes
Cooking time: 30 minutes
Serves 6

STRASBOURG TOASTS

TARTINES STRASBOURGEOISES

Prepare the Périgueux sauce and keep it hot. Pour 3 litres (5¼ pints) water and the vinegar into a pan and bring to the boil, then reduce to a gentle simmer. Poach the eggs (p.143), then remove and drain them. Meanwhile, melt the butter in a frying pan, add the bread and fry for a few minutes on both sides until golden. Using a fish slice, transfer to a serving dish. Top each slice of fried bread with a slice of foie gras and put a poached egg on top. Spoon over the Périgueux sauce, garnish with truffle shavings and serve immediately.

- **500 ml (18 fl oz) Périgueux sauce (p.61)**
- **3 tablespoons white wine vinegar**
- **6 eggs**
- **50 g (1¾ oz) butter**
- **6 slices white bread, crusts removed**
- **6 slices foie gras**
- **Truffle shavings, to garnish**

Preparation time: 15 minutes
Cooking time: 5 minutes
Serves 6

EGGS IN A NEST

OEUFS AU NID

- 6 globe artichokes,
  trimmed (p.510)
- 500 ml (18 fl oz)
  Bordelaise sauce (p.58)
- 3 tablespoons
  white wine vinegar
- 6 eggs

Preparation time: 1 hour
Cooking time: 45 minutes
Serves 6

Cook the artichokes in a pan of salted boiling water for 30–45 minutes, or until tender. Prepare the Bordelaise sauce and keep hot. Pour 3 litres (5¼ pints) water and the vinegar into a pan and bring to the boil, then reduce to a gentle simmer. Poach the eggs (p.143), then remove and drain them. Drain the artichokes, remove and discard the leaves and chokes and put the hearts in a dish. Put a poached egg on each artichoke heart and pour the Bordelaise sauce around them. Serve immediately.

POACHED EGGS WITH ASPARAGUS

OEUFS POCHÉS AUX ASPERGES

- 3 tablespoons white
  wine vinegar
- 6 eggs
- 18 asparagus spears, trimmed
  to 10 cm (4 inches) if green or
  5 cm (2 inches) if white
- 4 tablespoons crème fraîche
- 20 g (¾ oz) butter
- Salt and pepper

Preparation time: 15 minutes
Cooking time: 20 minutes
Serves 6

Pour 3 litres (5¼ pints) water and the vinegar into a pan and bring to the boil, then reduce to a gentle simmer. Poach the eggs (p.143), then remove and keep warm in salted warm water. Cook the asparagus in a pan of salted boiling water for 5 minutes, or until just tender, then drain. Return the asparagus to the pan with the crème fraîche and butter and cook over a low heat for 10 minutes. Season with salt and pepper. Drain the eggs, put them on a dish and spoon the asparagus mixture over them.

VARIATION

. . . .

POACHED EGGS WITH MUSHROOMS

OEUFS POCHÉS AUX CHAMPIGNONS

Proceed as above, substituting 60 g (2 oz) sliced mushrooms for the asparagus. Cook them in 4 tablespoons crème fraîche and 30 g (1¼ oz) butter.

EGGS MATELOTE

OEUFS EN MATELOTE

Put the bouquet garni and onion into a pan, pour in the wine and 500 ml (18 fl oz) water and bring to the boil, then reduce the heat and simmer for 20 minutes. Remove and discard the bouquet garni and onion. Poach the eggs (p.143) in the flavoured liquid, then remove and keep warm in salted warm water. Strain the cooking liquid into a bowl.

Melt half the butter in a pan. Stir in the flour and cook, stirring constantly, for 2 minutes. Season with salt and pepper and gradually stir in the reserved cooking liquid. Cook, stirring constantly, for 15–20 minutes, until thickened. Melt the remaining butter in a frying pan, add the bread and fry for a few minutes on each side until golden. Remove with a fish slice and rub the slices with the cut sides of the garlic clove. Put the fried bread rounds on a serving dish, drain the eggs and put them on top. Pour the sauce over them and serve.

* **1 bouquet garni**
* **1 large onion, halved**
* **500 ml (18 fl oz) red wine**
* **6 eggs**
* **40 g (1½ oz) butter**
* **15 g (½ oz) flour**
* **Salt and pepper**
* **6 slices bread, crusts removed, cut into 5-cm (2-inch) rounds**
* **1 garlic clove, halved**

Preparation time: 15 minutes
Cooking time: 45 minutes
Serves 6

EGGS DUCHESSE

OEUFS DUCHESSE

Cook the asparagus in a pan of salted boiling water for 4–8 minutes, or until just tender. Meanwhile, melt half the butter in a frying pan. Add the chicken and a pinch of nutmeg, season with salt and pepper and cook over a low heat, stirring occasionally, for 5–8 minutes until heated through. Spoon the rice on to a serving dish and put the chicken in the centre. Melt the remaining butter. Drain the asparagus, dip in the melted butter and arrange the spears around the chicken. Keep it warm while poaching the eggs. Pour 3 litres (5¼ pints) water and the vinegar into a pan and bring to the boil, then reduce to a gentle simmer. Poach the eggs (p.143), then remove and drain them. Transfer to the serving dish and serve.

* **150 g (5 oz) asparagus spears, trimmed to 10 cm (4 inches) if green or 5 cm (2 inches) if white**
* **50 g (1¾ oz) butter**
* **225–275 g (8–10 oz) cooked chicken, minced**
* **Freshly grated nutmeg**
* **Salt and pepper**
* **¾ quantity freshly cooked rich rice (p.618)**
* **3 tablespoons white wine vinegar**
* **6 eggs**

Preparation time: 10 minutes
Cooking time: 15 minutes
Serves 6

EGGS VERT-PRÉ

OEUFS VERT-PRÉ

- 6 evenly sized waxy
  yellow potatoes
- 75 g (2½ oz) butter
- 2 tablespoons flour
- 200 ml (7 fl oz) milk
- Freshly grated nutmeg
- Salt and pepper
- 50 g (1¾ oz) Gruyère
  cheese, grated
- 125 g (4¼ oz) spinach,
  coarse stalks removed,
  coarsely chopped
- 3 tablespoons white
  wine vinegar
- 6 eggs

Preparation time: 35–40 minutes
Cooking time: 40 minutes
Serves 6

Preheat the oven to its highest setting. Bake the potatoes, unpeeled, turning frequently, for 30 minutes, or until tender. Meanwhile, make a béchamel sauce (p.50) with 20 g (¾ oz) of the butter and the flour and milk. Add a pinch of nutmeg, season with salt and pepper, stir in half the cheese and cook for a further 5 minutes. Melt 20 g (¾ oz) of the remaining butter in a frying pan. Add the spinach and cook over a high heat, stirring constantly, for a few minutes until wilted, then remove the pan from the heat. Pour 3 litres (5¼ pints) water and the vinegar into a pan and bring to the boil, then reduce to a gentle simmer. Poach the eggs (p.143), then remove them and keep warm in salted warm water.

Preheat the grill. Remove the potatoes from the oven, make a small hole in the skins and scoop out the flesh. Mash the flesh in a bowl, beat in 20 g (¾ oz) of the remaining butter and season with salt and pepper. Garnish the potato skins with a little of this mixture and put the potatoes into a flame-proof dish. Put a poached egg on each potato and surround with the spinach. Pour the béchamel sauce over the potatoes and spinach, sprinkle with the remaining cheese, dot with the remaining butter and cook under the grill for 2–3 minutes, until browned.

EGGS IN JELLY

OEUFS EN GELÉE

- Meat jelly or aspic (p.45)
- 3 tablespoons white
  wine vinegar
- 6 eggs
- 6 tarragon leaves
- 1 small truffle,
  cut into 6 slices
- 125 g (4¼ oz) cooked
  peeled prawns
- 2 tablespoons chopped mixed
  herbs, such as flat-leaf parsley,
  chives, tarragon and chervil

Preparation time: 20 minutes,
plus setting time
Cooking time: 10 minutes
Serves 6

Prepare the jelly, and spoon a layer into the base of each of 6 small round moulds or ramekins while it is still slightly warm. Set the remaining jelly aside. Put the moulds in the refrigerator to set. Meanwhile, pour 3 litres (5¼ pints) water and the vinegar into a pan and bring to the boil, then reduce to a gentle simmer. Poach the eggs (p.143), then remove and drain them. When the jelly in the moulds has set, garnish each layer with a tarragon leaf and a slice of truffle. Carefully put a poached egg into each mould and spoon in some of the reserved jelly to fill it. Chill the moulds and the remaining jelly in the refrigerator for 3 hours, or until set. Run the blade of a knife around the edge of each mould and turn out on a serving dish. Chop the remaining jelly. Garnish the moulded jellies with the chopped jelly, prawns and herbs.

POACHED-EGG GRATIN

OEUFS POCHÉS GRATINÉS

Preheat the oven to 180°C/350°F/Gas Mark 4. Roll out the pastry on a lightly floured surface, cut out 6 x 12-cm (5-inch) rounds and use to line 6 x 10-cm (4-inch) tartlet tins. Prick the bases with a fork and bake for 20 minutes. Meanwhile, pour 3 litres (5¼ pints) water and the vinegar into a pan and bring to the boil, then reduce to a gentle simmer. Poach the eggs (p.143), then remove them and keep warm in salted warm water.

Remove the tartlet tins from the oven and increase the oven temperature to 250°C/500°F/Gas Mark 9. Take the tartlets out of the tins and put them on a baking sheet. Put a half-slice of ham into each, then drain a poached egg and place it on the ham. Spoon the cream over the eggs, season with salt and pepper, sprinkle with the cheese and bake for 5 minutes, until golden.

- 400 g (14 oz) shortcrust pastry dough (p.784)
- Flour, for dusting
- 3 tablespoons white wine vinegar
- 6 eggs
- 3 slices ham, halved
- 4 tablespoons double cream
- Salt and pepper
- 30 g (1¼ oz) Gruyère cheese, grated

Preparation time: 45 minutes
Cooking time: 5 minutes
Serves 6

EGGS WITH CHEESE

OEUFS AU FROMAGE

Put the butter, cheese and parsley into a small, round flame-proof dish or pan and heat gently until the butter and cheese have melted. Gently break the eggs into it and cook over a low heat for 2–3 minutes. Season with salt and serve. To serve more people, cook 2 eggs per person in separate dishes.

- 15 g (½ oz) butter
- 3 tablespoons Gruyère cheese, grated
- 1 tablespoon chopped flat-leaf parsley
- 2 eggs
- Salt

Preparation time: 4 minutes
Cooking time: 3 minutes
Serves 1

EGGS WITH CREAM

OEUFS À LA CRÈME

Preheat the oven to 180–190°C/350–375°F/Gas Mark 4–5. Pour the crème fraîche into a small cast-iron dish or pan. Bring to the boil over a very low heat. Immediately break the eggs into it and cook for a few seconds, then transfer to the oven and bake until the whites set. Season with salt and pepper and serve.

- 125 ml (4½ fl oz) crème fraîche
- 6 eggs
- Salt and pepper

Preparation time: 3 minutes
Cooking time: 5 minutes
Serves 6

MIRRORED EGGS

OEUFS MIROIR

- **10 g (¼ oz) butter, plus extra melted butter for the yolks**
- **2 eggs**
- **Salt**

  Preparation time: 2 minutes
  Cooking time: 3 minutes
  Serves 1

Preheat the oven to 180°C/350°F/Gas Mark 4. Melt the butter in a small, round flameproof dish or pan. Gently break the eggs into it and cook over a low heat for 2–3 minutes. Put 2–3 drops of melted butter on each yolk, season only the whites with salt and transfer to the oven until the eggs have set, then serve. To serve more people, cook 2 eggs per person in separate dishes.

EGGS WITH HAM OR BACON

OEUFS AU JAMBON ET AU BACON

Melt the butter in a frying pan. Add the ham or bacon and cook briefly over a medium heat, until browned on both sides. Break an egg on to each slice, increase the heat to high and cook for a few minutes until the whites have set. Season with pepper and serve.

- **30 g (1¼ oz) butter**
- **6 slices ham or bacon**
- **6 eggs**
- **Pepper**

Preparation time: 4 minutes
Cooking time: 5 minutes
Serves 6

EGGS À LA CHANOINESSE

OEUFS À LA CHANOINESSE

Preheat the oven to 250°C/500°F/Gas Mark 9. Melt the butter in a frying pan. Add the onions and cook over a low heat, stirring occasionally, for 15 minutes until golden brown. Spoon them into an ovenproof dish and cover with the chestnut purée. Break the eggs into the centre, sprinkle with the cheese and bake for 5 minutes until golden brown. Season with salt and pepper and serve.

- **30 g (1¼ oz) butter**
- **2 onions, sliced**
- **500 g (1 lb 2 oz) chestnut purée (p.559)**
- **6 eggs**
- **30 g (1¼ oz) Gruyère cheese, grated**
- **Salt and pepper**

Preparation time: 45 minutes
Cooking time: 5 minutes
Serves 6

ARDENNES-STYLE EGGS

OEUFS À L'ARDENNAISE

Preheat the oven to 220°C/425°F/Gas Mark 7 and generously grease an ovenproof dish with the butter. Whisk the egg whites to stiff peaks in a grease-free bowl, then spoon them into the prepared dish, spreading them out evenly. Spoon the crème fraîche in an even layer over the egg whites, slide the yolks on top and season with salt and pepper. Bake for 10 minutes, then serve.

- **15 g (½ oz) butter**
- **6 eggs, separated**
- **150 ml (¼ pint) crème fraîche**
- **Salt and pepper**

Preparation time: 10 minutes
Cooking time: 10 minutes
Serves 6

EGGS À LA ROSSINI

OEUFS À LA ROSSINI

- 30 g (1¼ oz) butter
- 6 eggs, separated
- 75 g (2½ oz) Parmesan cheese, grated
- 100 ml (3½ fl oz) crème fraîche
- Salt and pepper

Preparation time: 10 minutes
Cooking time: 6 minutes
Serves 6

Preheat the oven to 220°C/425°F/Gas Mark 7 and grease an ovenproof dish with half the butter. Whisk the egg whites to stiff peaks in a grease-free bowl, then spoon them into the prepared dish, spreading them out evenly. Sprinkle with half the cheese, slide the whole yolks on top, sprinkle with the remaining cheese and dot with the remaining butter. Bake for 6 minutes, spoon the crème fraîche on top, season with salt and pepper and serve.

EGGS À LA MEYERBEER

OEUFS À LA MEYERBEER

- 50 g (1¾ oz) butter
- 3 lambs' kidneys, skinned, halved and cored
- 6 eggs
- Salt and pepper

Preparation time: 10 minutes
Cooking time: 10 minutes
Serves 6

Preheat the oven to 240°C/475°F/Gas Mark 8 and generously grease an ovenproof dish with a little of the butter. Melt the remaining butter in a frying pan. Add the kidneys and cook over a medium-high heat for 4 minutes. Transfer the kidneys to the prepared dish, break the eggs over them, season with salt and pepper and bake for 5 minutes. Serve immediately.

EGGS PONTAILLAC

OEUFS PONTAILLAC

 p.170

- 1 quantity tomato sauce (p.57)
- 20 g (¾ oz) butter
- 6 chipolata sausages
- 6 eggs
- Salt and pepper
- 2 tablespoons chopped mixed herbs, such as flat-leaf parsley, chives, tarragon and chervil

Preparation time: 20 minutes
Cooking time: 12 minutes
Serves 6

Prepare the tomato sauce and keep it hot. Melt the butter in an enamelled cast-iron dish or pan. Add the sausages and cook, turning occasionally, for 7–8 minutes, until browned. Push them to the edge of the dish, gently break the eggs into the centre and cook for 3–4 minutes. Season with salt and pepper. Stir the herbs into the tomato sauce and pour it over the eggs. Serve immediately, straight from the dish.

EGGS EN CAISSE

OEUFS EN CAISSE

Preheat the oven to 200°C/400°F/Gas Mark 6. Divide the butter among 6 ramekins and season with salt and pepper. Heat in the oven until the butter has melted, then remove and break 1 egg into each ramekin. Sprinkle with the cheese, herbs and breadcrumbs, return to the oven and bake for 10 minutes, or until golden brown.

- **60 g (2 oz) butter**
- **Salt and pepper**
- **6 eggs**
- **30 g (1¼ oz) Parmesan cheese, grated**
- **2 tablespoons chopped mixed herbs, such as flat-leaf parsley, chives, tarragon and chervil**
- **2 tablespoons dried breadcrumbs**

Preparation time: 10 minutes
Cooking time: 10 minutes
Serves 6

EGGS IN COCOTTES

OEUFS COCOTTE

📷 p.171

Preheat the oven to 220°C/425°F/Gas Mark 7. Half-fill a roasting tin with boiling water. Put 2 teaspoons of the crème fraîche into each of 6 ceramic cocottes or ramekins, put the ramekins into the roasting tin and heat in the oven for 2 minutes. Break 1 egg into each cocotte, divide the remaining crème fraîche among them and season with salt and pepper. Return the roasting tin to the oven and bake for 6–8 minutes or until set, then serve.

- **125 ml (4½ fl oz) crème fraîche**
- **6 eggs**
- **Salt and pepper**

Preparation time: 5 minutes
Cooking time: 10 minutes
Serves 6

EGGS IN TOMATOES

OEUFS EN TOMATE

Preheat the oven to 180°C/350°F/Gas Mark 4 and brush an ovenproof dish with the oil. Cut a large hole in the stalk end of each tomato and scoop out the seeds, but do not remove the skin. Break 1 egg into each tomato, season with salt and pepper and sprinkle with the garlic. Put into the prepared dish and bake for 25 minutes. Sprinkle with the herbs and serve immediately.

- **1 tablespoon olive oil**
- **6 large round tomatoes**
- **6 eggs**
- **Salt and pepper**
- **½ clove garlic, finely chopped**
- **2 tablespoons chopped mixed herbs, such as chives, chervil, tarragon and flat-leaf parsley**

Preparation time: 10 minutes
Cooking time: 25 minutes
Serves 6

SCRAMBLED EGGS

OEUFS BROUILLÉS

- **6 eggs**
- **50 ml (2 fl oz) milk**
- **Salt and pepper**
- **60 g (2 oz) softened butter, diced**

Preparation time: 5 minutes
Cooking time: 12 minutes
Serves 6

Beat together the eggs and milk in a bowl, season with salt and pepper and gradually beat in half the butter. Melt the remaining butter in a heavy-based pan over a low heat. Pour in the egg mixture and cook, stirring constantly, for 12 minutes, or until creamy. Serve immediately.

NOTE
Grated cheese, asparagus tips, mushrooms or truffles braised in butter for 10 minutes, croutons fried in butter, or peeled prawns can be added to the egg mixture.

SCRAMBLED EGG RING

COURONNE D'ŒUFS BROUILLÉS

- **500 ml (18 fl oz) tomato sauce (p.57)**
- **180 g (6¼ oz) freshly cooked Indian rice (p.616)**
- **6 eggs**
- **50 ml (2 fl oz) milk**
- **Salt and pepper**
- **50 g (1¾ oz) butter**

Preparation time: 15 minutes
Cooking time: 1 hour
Serves 6

Prepare the tomato sauce and keep it hot. Cook the scrambled eggs with the eggs, milk, salt and pepper and butter (see above). Spoon the rice into a ring on a round serving dish and put the eggs in the centre. Spoon the tomato sauce around the ring and serve immediately.

NEW YORK-STYLE EGGS

OEUFS NEW-YORKAIS

- **50 g (1¾ oz) butter**
- **6 eggs**
- **50 g (1¾ oz) tomato sauce (p.57), or passata**
- **50 g (1¾ oz) ham, diced**
- **100 ml (3½ fl oz) single cream**
- **Salt and pepper**

Preparation time: 5 minutes
Cooking time: 12 minutes
Serves 6

Melt the butter in a pan over low heat. Break the eggs into the pan, stirring constantly. Add the tomato sauce or passata and the ham. Gradually, stir in the cream, a little at a time, until the mixture is creamy and the eggs have set. Season with salt and pepper, then serve in ramekins.

BELGIAN-STYLE EGGS

OEUFS BELGES

Mix the cheese and egg yolks in a bowl until thoroughly combined into a paste. Spread the paste on one side of each slice of bread. Top with a slice of ham, cut to the same size. Whisk the egg whites to stiff peaks in a grease-free bowl and spoon them over the ham. Heat the oil in a frying pan and preheat the grill. Add the slices, plain side down, and cook for 5 minutes over a low heat until the bottom of the bread is crisp and golden, and the cheese paste is melting. Lift the slices on to a baking tray and grill for 1–2 minutes, until the egg whites are just cooked and beginning to turn golden. Season with salt and pepper and serve immediately.

- 150 g (5 oz) Gruyère cheese, grated
- 3 eggs, separated
- 6 slices white bread, 1 cm (½ inch) thick, crusts removed
- 6 slices lean ham
- 3 tablespoons oil
- Salt and pepper

Preparation time: 25 minutes
Cooking time: 5 minutes
Serves 6

FRIED EGGS

OEUFS FRITS

Melt the fat or heat the oil in a frying pan. Break 1 egg into a ladle or cup and slide it gently into the pan. Fold the white over the yolk, turn the egg over and remove from the pan with a fish slice. Cook the remaining eggs, one at a time, in the same way. Serve garnished with fried parsley and croutons.

- 60 g (2 oz) butter, lard or goose fat or 2 tablespoons olive oil
- 6 eggs
- Fried parsley (p.81), to serve
- Croutons (p.183), to serve

Preparation time: 2 minutes
Cooking time: 3 minutes
Serves 6

VARIATIONS

· ·

FRIED EGGS IN A SAUCE

OEUFS FRITS EN SAUCE

Proceed as above. When the eggs are cooked, put them on to a dish of croutons (p.183) and cover with hot black butter (p.48), tomato sauce (p.57) or chasseur sauce (p.65).

· ·

FRIED EGGS WITH CELERIAC

OEUFS FRITS AU CÉLERI

Proceed as above, and serve the fried eggs on a bed of celeriac purée (p.524).

ORIENTAL-STYLE EGGS
OEUFS À L'ORIENTALE

- 4 tablespoons olive oil
- 3 tomatoes, chopped
- 1 aubergine, chopped
- 2 garlic cloves, finely chopped
- 2 large onions, chopped
- 2 red peppers, de-seeded and chopped
- 1 teaspoon paprika
- 1 tablespoon chopped flat-leaf parsley
- Salt and pepper
- ¾ quantity freshly cooked Indian rice (p.616)
- 6 eggs

Preparation time: 15 minutes
Cooking time: 25 minutes
Serves 6

Heat 2 tablespoons of the oil in a pan. Add the tomatoes, aubergine, garlic, onions, peppers, paprika and parsley, cover and cook over a low heat, stirring occasionally, for 20–25 minutes. Season with salt and pepper. Spoon the Indian rice into a ring on a serving dish. Spoon the vegetable mixture into the centre of the ring and keep warm. Heat the remaining oil in a frying pan and fry the eggs, one at a time (p.154). Put them on top of the vegetable mixture and serve immediately.

EGGS WITH PAPRIKA
OEUFS AU PAPRIKA

- 2 tomatoes, diced
- 1 aubergine, diced
- 1 onion, diced
- 2 red peppers, de-seeded and diced
- 1 courgette, diced
- 5 tablespoons olive oil
- Salt and pepper
- 150 g (5 oz) freshly cooked Indian rice (p.616)
- 6 eggs
- 350 ml (12 fl oz) cream sauce (p.51)
- 10 g (¼ oz) best Hungarian paprika

Preparation time: 45 minutes
Cooking time: 30 minutes
Serves 6

Put all the vegetables into a colander, sprinkling each layer with salt, and leave to drain for 20 minutes, then rinse and drain. Heat 3 tablespoons of the oil in a pan. Add the vegetables and cook over a low heat, stirring occasionally, for about 10 minutes, then season with salt and pepper. Spoon the Indian rice into a serving dish and pour the vegetable mixture over it. Keep warm. Heat the remaining oil and fry the eggs (p.154), then put them on the top of the vegetables. Make the cream sauce, add the paprika when it comes to the boil, and pour it over the eggs. Serve immediately.

EGG MOULD

TURBAN D'OEUFS

Preheat the oven to 180°C/350°F/Gas Mark 4 and grease a ring mould with butter. Pour the milk into a pan, season with salt and pepper and bring just to the boil. Beat the eggs in a bowl and gradually beat in the hot milk. Pour the mixture into the prepared mould and stand the mould in a roasting tin. Pour in boiling water to come about halfway up the sides of the mould and bake for 45 minutes, or until set. Meanwhile, prepare the tomato sauce. Turn the mould out on to a serving dish, pour the tomato sauce into the centre of the ring and serve.

- **Butter, for greasing**
- **1 litre (1¾ pints) milk**
- **Salt and pepper**
- **6 eggs**
- **500 ml (18 fl oz) tomato sauce (p.57)**

Preparation time: 10 minutes
Cooking time: 45 minutes
Serves 6

EGG CROQUETTES

CROQUETTES D'OEUFS

Hard boil 7 eggs (p.134) and separate the remaining 2. Make a very thick white sauce (p.50) with the butter, flour and milk. Stir in 2 raw egg yolks, season with salt and pepper and leave to cool. Whisk the egg whites to soft peaks in a grease-free bowl. Heat the oil in a deep-fryer to 180°C/350°F, or until a cube of bread browns in 30 seconds. Shell and dice the hard-boiled eggs and stir them into the sauce. Shape thumb-sized croquettes from the mixture and roll them in the whisked egg whites, then in the breadcrumbs. Add the croquettes, in batches if necessary, and fry for 2–3 minutes, or until golden brown. Remove and drain, then serve.

- **9 eggs**
- **50 g (1¾ oz) butter**
- **3 tablespoons flour**
- **250 ml (8 fl oz) milk**
- **Salt and pepper**
- **Dried breadcrumbs, for coating**
- **Vegetable oil, for deep-frying**

Preparation time: 25 minutes
Cooking time: 35 minutes
Serves 6

CHEESE TARTS

GNOCCHIS RAMEQUINS

Preheat the oven to 180°C/350°F/Gas Mark 4. Roll out the pastry dough on a lightly floured surface, stamp out 6 x 12-cm (5-inch) rounds and use to line 6 x 10-cm (4-inch) tartlet tins. Whisk the egg whites to stiff peaks in a grease-free bowl. Beat together the egg yolks, cheese and crème fraîche in a another bowl, then gently fold into the egg whites. Season with salt and pepper and spoon the mixture into the pastry cases. Bake for 35 minutes.

- **400 g (14 oz) shortcrust pastry dough (p.784)**
- **Flour, for dusting**
- **3 egg whites**
- **6 egg yolks**
- **100 g (3½ oz) Parmesan cheese, grated**
- **5½ tablespoons crème fraîche**
- **Salt and pepper**

Preparation time: 30 minutes
Cooking time: 35 minutes
Serves 6

PLAIN OMELETTE

OMELETTE AU NATUREL

- **6 eggs**
- **Salt and pepper**
- **30 g (1¼ oz) butter**

Preparation time: 5 minutes
Cooking time: 5 minutes
Serves 6

 p.172

Beat the eggs with salt and pepper in a bowl. Heat a frying pan or omelette pan and melt the butter in it. When the butter is very hot and nut-coloured, pour the eggs into the pan. When the eggs are set and small bubbles have formed around the edge, bring the edges of the omelette towards the centre with a fork while shaking the frying pan. Fold the half of the omelette nearest to the handle of the pan towards the outside edge and quickly slide on to a hot dish. A good omelette should be slightly runny in the centre.

VARIATIONS

. . . .

HERB OMELETTE

OMELETTE AUX FINES HERBES

Chop fresh herbs, such as flat-leaf parsley, chervil, chives and tarragon, and add to the egg mixture before it is cooked, and sprinkle more over once cooked, if liked.

. . . .

CHEESE OMELETTE

OMELETTE AUX FROMAGE

A few seconds before folding the omelette, add 75 g (2½ oz) grated cheese.

. . . .

MUSHROOM OR TRUFFLE OMELETTE

OMELETTE AUX CHAMPIGNONS OU AUX TRUFFES

Fry sliced mushrooms or truffles for a few minutes in butter and add to the omelette just before folding it.

. . . .

ASPARAGUS OMELETTE

OMELETTE AUX POINTES D'ASPERGES

Cook trimmed asparagus spears in salted boiling water for 4−8 minutes, or until tender, then drain. Slice, then add to the omelette just before folding it.

SEAFOOD OMELETTE
OMELETTE AUX FRUITS DE MERS

Use canned anchovies, herring fillets or fish roe; cooked prawns or mussels; or fish quenelles (p.105) cut into pieces. Add to the omelette just before folding it.

. . . .

OMELETTE WITH KIDNEYS, CROUTONS OR POTATOES
OMELETTE AUX ROGNONS, AUX CROUTONS, AUX POMMES DE TERRE

Prepare some calves' kidneys (p.363), croutons (p.183) or sauté potatoes (p.574). Fry them in hot butter and fill the omelette just before folding it.

. . . .

OMELETTE WITH PASTA OR RICE
OMELETTE AU RIZ, AUX MACARONIS, AUX NOUILLES

Cook the pasta according to the instructions on the packet, or prepare some Indian rice (p.616), and drain. Add to the omelette just before folding it.

. . . .

BACON, HAM OR ONION OMELETTE
OMELETTE AU LARD, AU JAMBON, À L'OIGNON

Dice the meat or onion and fry in hot butter, then add the beaten egg mixture and cook as usual.

. . . .

TOMATO, SORREL OR SPINACH OMELETTE
OMELETTE À LA TOMATE, À L'OSEILLE, AUX ÉPINARDS

Chop and soften the tomato, sorrel or spinach in melted butter for 2–3 minutes and fill the omelette just before folding it.

. . . .

PROVENÇALE OMELETTE
OMELETTE PROVENÇALE

Prepare some brandade (p.258), and add to the omelette just before folding it.

RAINBOW OMELETTES

OMELETTES EN ARC-EN-CIEL

Make small 2-egg omelettes using different ingredients of different colours (such as spinach or tomato) and arrange in a circle on a dish so that they overlap slightly. You can make a white omelette by using only the egg whites, or a yellow one using only the yolks. Fill the centre of the circle with hot tomato sauce (p.57).

GERMAN OMELETTE

OMELETTE ALLEMANDE

- 75 g (2½ oz) flour
- 350 ml (12 fl oz) milk
- 6 eggs, separated
- 60 g (2 oz) grated cheese or chopped herbs
- Salt and pepper
- 25 g (1 oz) butter

Preparation time: 8 minutes
Cooking time: 10 minutes
Serves 6

Put the flour in a bowl and add the milk gradually, whisking to combine, then add the egg yolks. Whisk the egg whites to stiff peaks in a grease-free bowl and fold into the yolk mixture, then fold in the cheese or herbs. Season with salt and pepper. Heat a frying pan and melt the butter in it. Pour the egg mixture into the pan and cook until small bubbles form around the edge. Bring the edges of the omelette towards the centre with a fork held in one hand while shaking the frying pan with the other. Flip the omelette over with a palette knife and cook the second side until lightly browned, then slide out of the pan.

POTATO OMELETTE

CRIQUE À L'ANCIENNE

- 6 eggs
- Salt and pepper
- 50 ml (2 fl oz) milk
- 4 waxy yellow potatoes, grated
- 30 g (1¼ oz) butter

Preparation time: 10 minutes
Cooking time: 15 minutes
Serves 6

Beat the eggs with salt and pepper in a bowl, then add the milk and potatoes. Melt the butter in a frying pan, pour in the egg mixture, cover and cook over a medium heat for 10 minutes until golden and crisp. Flip the omelette over with a palette knife, re-cover the pan and cook for a further 5 minutes. Slide the omelette out of the pan and serve.

ANGEVINE OMELETTE

OMELETTE ANGEVINE

Preheat the oven to 220°C/425°F/Gas Mark 7. Put the lardons and potato into a frying pan and cook over a medium heat until golden. Meanwhile, melt half the butter in a pan. Add the leek and cook over a low heat, stirring occasionally, for 5 minutes until softened. Beat the eggs with salt and pepper in a bowl and add all the other ingredients, except the remaining butter. Melt this in an ovenproof frying pan. Pour in the mixture and cook until small bubbles form around the edge. Bring the edges of the omelette towards the centre with a fork held in one hand while shaking the frying pan with the other. Transfer the frying pan to the oven and bake for 5 minutes, or until the top has set. Turn out on a dish and serve.

- ½ tablespoon lardons
- 1 large potato, diced
- 50 g (1¾ oz) butter
- 1 leek, white part only, chopped
- 6 eggs
- Salt and pepper
- 60 g (2 oz) Gruyère cheese, grated
- 1 tablespoon chopped flat-leaf parsley

Preparation time: 10 minutes
Cooking time: 10 minutes
Serves 6

PIPERADE

PIPERADE

 p.173

Heat the oil in a large pan and fry the onion, peppers and tomatoes until the onions have softened. Add the garlic and season with salt and pepper. Simmer over a low heat to thicken and reduce the liquid. Fry the ham separately in another pan and keep hot. Beat the eggs in a bowl and stir them into the vegetables. Continue to cook gently until the eggs are scrambled. Season with salt and pepper. Serve in a hot dish garnished with the ham.

- 4 tablespoons oil
- 1 onion, chopped
- 1 kg (2¼ lb) green peppers, de-seeded and chopped
- 1 kg (2¼ lb) tomatoes, skinned and chopped
- 1 garlic clove, crushed
- Salt and pepper
- 3 slices raw ham
- 6 eggs

Preparation time: 25 minutes
Cooking time: 45-60 minutes
Serves 6

CASSE-MUSEAU

CASSE-MUSEAU

- 1 litre (1¾ pints) ewe's milk
- A few drops of rennet
- 3 eggs, beaten
- 400 g (14 oz) flour
- Salt
- Sweet chestnut leaves, washed

Preparation time: 25 minutes,
plus draining time
Cooking time: 20 minutes
Serves 6

The name of these crunchy biscuits from the Poitou region of France literally means 'muzzle-breakers'.

Put the milk in a pan, heat until just lukewarm and add a few drops of rennet. When it curdles, leave to drain in a muslin-lined sieve set over a bowl in the refrigerator for 12 hours. Preheat the oven to 180°C/350°F/Gas Mark 4. Place the curd cheese in a bowl and beat in the eggs, flour and a pinch of salt. Wrap walnut-sized pieces of the mixture in freshly picked chestnut leaves, place on a baking tray and bake for 20 minutes.

TUTSCHE

TUTSCHE

- 300 ml (½ pint) milk
- 25 g (1 oz) fresh yeast, or 15 g (½ oz) dried yeast
- 500 g (1 lb 2 oz) flour
- 150 g (5 oz) butter, plus extra for greasing
- 1 teaspoon salt
- 300 ml (½ pint) crème fraîche
- 2 eggs

Preparation time: 20 minutes
Cooking time: 30 minutes
Serves 6

Prepare 2 hours in advance. Warm the milk to blood heat. Whisk in the fresh or dried yeast and set aside for 5 minutes. Put the flour in a bowl with 100 g (3½ oz) of the butter, the warm milk and ½ teaspoon of the salt. Mix, then knead to a smooth dough. Cover and set aside to rise for 2 hours. Preheat the oven to 200°C/400°F/Gas Mark 6 and grease a large flan dish with butter. Roll out the dough to a thickness of 1 cm (½ inch) and line the prepared dish. Beat the crème fraîche, eggs and remaining salt together and pour into the flan case. Dot with the remaining butter. Bake for 30 minutes.

MILLAS FROM TOULOUSE

MILLAS DE TOULOUSE

- 250 g (9 oz) cornmeal
- 500 ml (18 fl oz) milk
- 3 eggs, beaten
- 125 g (4¼ oz) butter
- 100 ml (3½ fl oz) crème fraîche
- Salt

Preparation time: 10 minutes
Cooking time: 40 minutes
Serves 6

Mix the cornmeal to a paste with a little cold water. Bring the 500 ml (18 fl oz) water to the boil in a large pan and add the cornmeal paste. Simmer for 20 minutes, stirring constantly. Add the milk and cook for a further 10 minutes, stirring frequently. Remove from the heat and add the eggs, half the butter and the crème fraîche. Season with salt. Return the mixture to the heat to thicken, stirring constantly, without allowing it to boil. Spread the mixture on a dish to a thickness of 1–2 cm (½–¾ inch) and leave to cool. Once set, cut into circles with a glass or cookie cutter, melt the remaining butter in a frying pan and fry the circles until golden on both sides, as for crêpes.

Yoghurt (p.121)

Cheese fritters (p.125)

Crôque-monsieur with ham (p.125)

Cheese soufflé (p.128)

Gougère (p.128)

Quiche Lorraine (p.130)

Hot Chavignol crottins (p.131)

Eggs with truffles   (p.138)

Eggs Pontaillac   (p.151)

Eggs in cocottes   (p.152)

Herb omelette (p.157)

Piperade (p.160)

- 4 -
SOUPS

SOUPS

Soups are usually served as a first course at the beginning of a meal. With their great variety – from clear soups such as bouillons and consommés, to thicker ones such as vegetable purées, cream soups and veloutés – they are an area in which cooks can easily vary the seasoning and combine different vegetables or meats. They can be transformed into a dish for a special occasion, or serve just as well as an everyday first course. Soups should always be served piping hot; the only exceptions are chilled summer soups and certain consommés.

Around 300–400 ml (½ pint–14 fl oz) soup is enough for one person. To this the following quantities of additional ingredients can be added per person: 125 g (4¼ oz) fresh vegetables, 10g (¼ oz) pasta or 40 g (1½ oz) dried pulses. To season, add 1¼ teaspoons salt per litre (1¾ pints) of soup. A thickening made from egg, flour or potato flour improves the consistency of the soup and means that smaller quantities of additional vegetables or pasta are needed.

RICH BEEF STOCK (POT-AU-FEU)

BOUILLON GRAS (POT-AU-FEU)

Put the beef with its bones in a large pan with the salt. Cover with water. Bring to the boil, then reduce the heat and simmer for 15 minutes. Skim to remove the scum, and add the vegetables. Bring back to the boil, then simmer over a low heat for 3 hours. Just before serving, skim off the fat and put the toast in the bottom of a soup tureen. Strain the soup into the tureen over the toast.

- 800 g (1¾ lb) stewing beef on the bone
- 30 g (1¼ oz) salt
- 200 g (7 oz) carrots, diced
- 125 g (4¼ oz) turnips, diced
- 100 g (3½ oz) leeks, coarsely chopped
- 60 g (2 oz) parsnips, diced
- 1 celery stick, diced
- Slices of toast, to serve

Preparation time: 25 minutes
Cooking time: 3½ hours
Serves 6

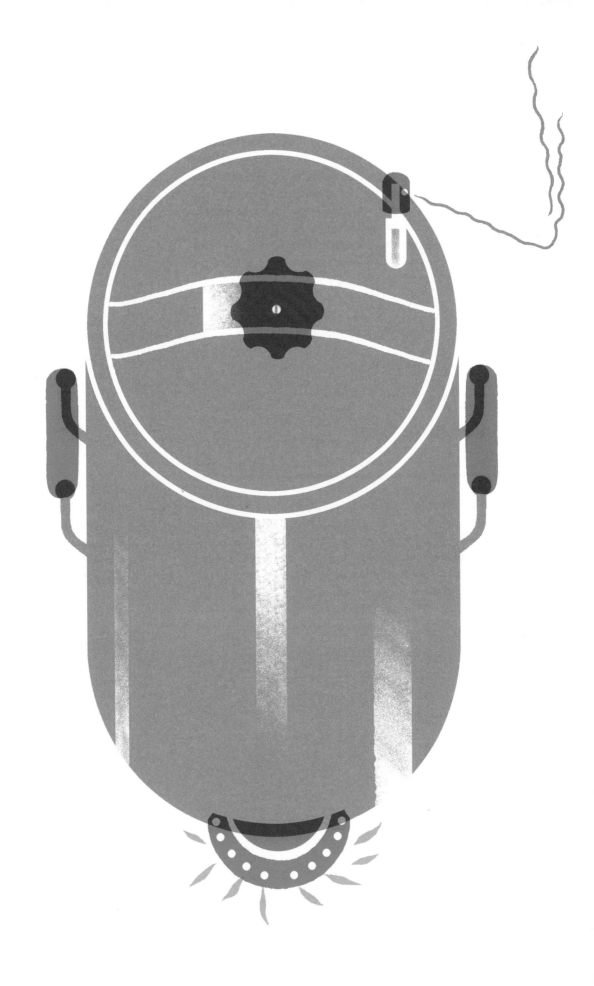

CONSOMMÉ

CONSOMMÉ

Put 4 litres (7 pints) water, the beef and giblets into a large pan. Gently bring to the boil. Skim to remove the scum. Add the vegetables and salt to taste, and simmer for 3½ hours over a low heat. Leave to cool, then skim the fat. To clarify, beat the egg whites lightly. Pour the consommé into a pan, stir in the egg whites and gently beat the liquid without stopping, while heating very gradually until it comes to the boil. Pour the liquid through a sieve lined with damp muslin, discard the solids and serve hot or cold.

- 1 kg (2¼ lb) beef
  (any inexpensive cut)
- Giblets of 6 chickens
  or game birds
- 200 g (7 oz) carrots, diced
- 125 g (4¼ oz) turnips, diced
- 100 g (3½ oz) leeks,
  coarsely chopped
- 60 g (2 oz) parsnips, diced
- 1 celery stick, diced
- Salt
- 2 egg whites

Preparation time: 25 minutes
Cooking time: 4 hours
Serves 6

VELVET SOUP

POTAGE VELOURS

Bring the stock to the boil in a large pan and pour in the tapioca all at once. Simmer for 10 minutes over a low heat, stirring frequently to prevent lumps forming. In a cup, make a thickening mixture by blending the egg yolk, butter and a little of the hot soup. Stir this mixture back into the pan and stir until the soup has thickened. Pour into a soup tureen, stirring constantly.

- 2 litres (3½ pints) rich beef
  stock (p.176), strained
- 100 g (3½ oz) tapioca
- 1 egg yolk
- 50 g (1¾ oz) butter

Preparation time: 15 minutes
Cooking time: 15 minutes
Serves 6

SOUPS BASED ON STOCK

VERMICELLI SOUP

POTAGE AU VERMICELLE

- 2 litres (3½ pints) rich beef stock (p.176), strained
- 100 g (3½ oz) vermicelli

Preparation time: 2 minutes
Cooking time: 6 minutes
Serves 6

Bring the stock to the boil in a large pan, add the vermicelli and cook for 6 minutes, or until just al dente. Serve hot.

NOODLE SOUP

POTAGE AUX PETITES PÂTES

- 2 litres (3½ pints) rich beef stock (p.176), strained
- 100 g (3½ oz) small noodles or pasta shapes

Preparation time: 2 minutes
Cooking time: 8 minutes
Serves 6

Bring the stock to the boil in a large pan, add the noodles and cook for 8 minutes, or until just al dente. Skim to remove any scum before serving.

SOUP À L'AURORE

POTAGE À L'AURORE

- 3 hard-boiled eggs (p.134), shelled
- 1 large handful of croutons (p.183)
- 2 litres (3½ pints) rich beef stock (p.176), strained
- 200 ml (7 fl oz) Madeira

Preparation time: 10 minutes
Cooking time: 15 minutes
Serves 6

Mash the eggs thoroughly with a fork. Put the croutons in the bottom of a soup tureen and sprinkle with the mashed eggs. In a large pan, bring the stock to the boil and add the Madeira. Pour over the eggs and croutons in the tureen, and serve hot.

MACARONI SOUP
POTAGE AUX MACARONIS

Bring a pan of salted water to the boil, add the macaroni and cook for half the time indicated on the packet. Put the stock in another, large pan. Drain the macaroni and add to the stock. Bring to a simmer and cook for a further 4–5 minutes, or until the macaroni is al dente. Put the cheese in a soup tureen and pour the soup over. Serve hot.

- **180 g (6¼ oz) macaroni**
- **2 litres (3½ pints) rich beef stock (p.176), strained**
- **60 g (2 oz) Gruyère cheese, grated**

Preparation time: 5 minutes
Cooking time: 20 minutes
Serves 6

HERB SOUPS

WATERCRESS SOUP
POTAGE AU CRESSON OU POTAGE SANTÉ

Set aside a few watercress leaves to garnish the soup; chop the rest. Heat the butter in a large pan, add the watercress and soften it over a gentle heat. Add 1.75 litres (3 pints) boiling water and cook for 5 minutes. Add the rice, salt and pepper, and cook for a further 20 minutes, or until the rice is tender. Just before serving, add the egg yolk to the soup and stir until thickened. Add the reserved watercress leaves and serve hot.

- **1 bunch of watercress**
- **30 g (1¼ oz) butter**
- **80 g (2¾ oz) rice**
- **Salt and pepper**
- **1 egg yolk, beaten**

Preparation time: 20 minutes
Cooking time: 25 minutes
Serves 6

SORREL SOUP
POTAGE À L'OSEILLE

Melt the butter in a large pan over a low heat, add the sorrel, and cook, stirring, for 2 minutes, or until wilted. Pour in 2 litres (3½ pints) water. Add the potatoes and season with salt and pepper. Bring to the boil and cook over a low heat for 30 minutes. Just before serving, transfer the mixture to a food processor or blender and process until smooth. Beat the egg yolk in a large bowl or tureen and add the hot soup, stirring until thickened.

- **30 g (1¼ oz) butter**
- **250 g (9 oz) sorrel, chopped**
- **500 g (1 lb 2 oz) potatoes, cut into pieces**
- **Salt and pepper**
- **1 egg yolk, beaten**

Preparation time: 20 minutes
Cooking time: 30 minutes
Serves 6

PARSLEY SOUP

POTAGE AU PERSIL OU CHOISY

- 100 g (3½ oz) flat-leaf parsley
- Salt
- 1 bunch of watercress
- 500 g (1 lb 2 oz) potatoes
- 30 g (1¼ oz) butter

Preparation time: 20 minutes
Cooking time: 30 minutes
Serves 6

Set aside a few sprigs of parsley to garnish the soup. Bring 1.75 litres (3 pints) water to the boil in a large pan. Add salt and the parsley, watercress and potatoes. Simmer for 30 minutes over a low heat. Just before serving, transfer the mixture to a food processor or blender and process until smooth, then pour into a tureen and add the butter. Chop the reserved parsley finely and sprinkle it over the soup.

VARIATION

. . . .

CHERVIL SOUP

POTAGE AU CERFEUIL

Replace the parsley and watercress with chervil and proceed as above.

 p.211

PISTOU SOUP

SOUPE AU PISTOU

- 50 ml (2 fl oz) olive oil
- 150 g (5 oz) carrots, diced
- 150 g (5 oz) turnips, diced
- 60 g (2 oz) onions, diced
- Salt and pepper
- 100 g (3½ oz) very ripe tomatoes, cut into wedges
- 1 garlic clove, crushed
- 1 good sprig of fresh basil, finely chopped
- Grated Gruyère cheese, to serve (optional)

Preparation time: 25 minutes
Cooking time: 40 minutes
Serves 6

Heat half the oil in a large pan and add the diced vegetables. Cook over a gentle heat for 10 minutes, then add 1.75 litres (3 pints) water. Add salt and pepper to taste, bring to a simmer and cook gently for 10 minutes. Meanwhile, in a frying pan, fry the tomato wedges and garlic gently in the rest of the oil for a few minutes. Add to the vegetable stock and cook for a further 20 minutes. A few minutes before serving, add the basil. Serve very hot, with grated Gruyère if desired.

HERB SOUP

POTAGE AUX FINES HERBES

Melt half the butter in a large pan over a gentle heat. Add the sorrel and lettuce and soften gently in the butter for a few minutes. When they are softened, cover with 2 litres (3½ pints) water, bring to a simmer and season with salt and pepper. After 10 minutes, pour in the tapioca all at once, then continue to simmer for 20 minutes, or until tender. Stir in the rest of the butter and the chives, and serve in a soup tureen.

- 30 g (1¼ oz) butter
- 125 g (4¼ oz) sorrel, finely chopped
- 250 g (9 oz) lettuce, finely chopped
- Salt and pepper
- 60 g (2 oz) tapioca
- 60 g (2 oz) chives, finely chopped

Preparation time: 20 minutes
Cooking time: 30 minutes
Serves 6

LIÉGEOISE SOUP

POTAGE À LA LIÉGEOISE

Melt the butter in a large pan over a medium-high heat. Add the leeks, celery and sorrel, and cook, stirring frequently, until they are softened. Add 2 litres (3½ pints) boiling water, and the bay leaf and chervil, and season with salt and pepper. Bring back to the boil and add the potatoes. Reduce to a simmer and cook for 30 minutes. Remove the bay leaf, strain the soup and add the tomatoes. Bring back to a simmer, stirring well, and serve.

- 40 g (1½ oz) butter
- 2 leeks, chopped
- 1 celery stick, chopped
- 125 g (4¼ oz) sorrel, chopped
- 1 bay leaf
- 1 large sprig of chervil, chopped
- Salt and pepper
- 500 g (1 lb 2 oz) potatoes, diced
- 200 g (7 oz) tomatoes, puréed with a hand-held blender or ricer

Preparation time: 20 minutes
Cooking time: 45 minutes
Serves 6

VEGETABLE SOUPS

ASPARAGUS SOUP
POTAGE AUX ASPERGES

- 500 g (1 lb 2 oz) asparagus spears, stalks scraped and diced, tips reserved
- 40 g (1½ oz) butter
- 125 ml (4½ fl oz) double cream or 2 egg yolks

Preparation time: 25 minutes
Cooking time: 45 minutes
Serves 6

Bring 1.5 litres (2½ pints) salted water to the boil in a large pan. Blanch the asparagus stalks for 2 minutes. Drain and reserve the cooking liquid. In another large pan, melt 20 g (¾ oz) of the butter, add the drained asparagus and cook gently for 10 minutes until softened. Pour in the reserved cooking liquid, bring to a simmer and cook gently for another 30 minutes, then transfer the mixture to a food processor or blender and process until smooth. About 10 minutes before serving, add the asparagus tips and reheat the soup. Add the cream or egg yolks with the remaining butter, and stir until thickened slightly.

CARROT SOUP
POTAGE AUX CAROTTES OU PURÉE CRÉCY

- 500 g (1 lb 2 oz) carrots, cut into small dice
- 125 g (4¼ oz) turnips, cut into small dice
- 500 g (1 lb 2 oz) potatoes, cut into small dice
- 150 g (5 oz) onions, chopped
- 10 g (¼ oz) butter
- Salt and pepper

For the croutons:
- 15 g (½ oz) butter
- 1 garlic clove, finely chopped (optional)
- 2–3 thick slices fairly dry stale bread, crusts removed, cut into dice

Preparation time: 20 minutes
Cooking time: 1 hour
Serves 6

Put all the vegetables, except the onions, in a large pan with 2 litres (3½ pints) water, bring to a simmer and cook gently for 40 minutes. Meanwhile, in a frying pan, fry the onions very gently in the butter for 30 minutes, stirring from time to time. Season the vegetable mixture with salt and pepper then transfer it to a food processor or blender and process until smooth. Add the onions to the blended soup and simmer for 20 minutes.

Meanwhile, make the croutons. Heat the butter in a frying pan and gently cook the garlic, if using, for 3–4 minutes, or until softened, then add the bread cubes. Increase the heat to moderate and cook, stirring frequently, for 3–5 minutes until nicely browned. Scatter the croutons on the bottom of a tureen and pour the soup over them.

BONNE FEMME SOUP

POTAGE BONNE FEMME

 p.212

Melt 20 g (¾ oz) of the butter in a large pan. Add the vegetables and cook over a medium heat for a few minutes, stirring occasionally and without letting them brown. Add 1.5 litres (2½ pints) boiling water and the bay leaf and cloves and season with salt and pepper. Bring to a simmer and cook for 30 minutes. Serve the soup with the vegetable pieces left whole. Add the remaining butter or a little double cream if desired, just before serving.

- 40 g (1½ oz) butter
- 250 g (9 oz) carrots, cut into small dice
- 250 g (9 oz) leeks, finely chopped
- 500 g (1 lb 2 oz) potatoes, cut into small dice
- 1 bay leaf
- 1–2 cloves
- Salt and pepper
- Double cream, to serve (optional)

Preparation time: 20 minutes
Cooking time: 30 minutes
Serves 6

CELERIAC SOUP

POTAGE AU CÉLERI OU CRÈME MARIA

Bring the stock to the boil in a large pan, add the celeriac and simmer for 30 minutes, until tender. Transfer to a food processor or blender and process to a purée. Return the purée to the pan and bring to the boil. Mix the rice flour with a little water to make a paste, then add the paste to the pan and cook for 5 minutes. Just before serving, stir in the egg yolk to thicken the soup slightly.

- 1.5 litres (2½ pints) any stock
- 1 celeriac, about 1 kg (2¼ lb), sliced
- 60 g (2 oz) rice flour
- 1 egg yolk

Preparation time: 15 minutes
Cooking time: 35 minutes
Serves 6

MUSHROOM SOUP

POTAGE AUX CHAMPIGNONS

- **250 g (9 oz) mushrooms, well wiped and stalks removed**
- **1 sprig of thyme**
- **25 g (1 oz) butter**
- **60 g (2 oz) rice flour**
- **Salt and pepper**
- **Double cream, to taste**

Preparation time: 30 minutes
Cooking time: 40 minutes
Serves 6

Cut two-thirds of the mushrooms into fine strips. Put them in a large pan with 1.5 litres (2½ pints) water and bring to a simmer. Add the thyme and cook for 20 minutes. Remove and discard the thyme. Transfer the mixture to a food processor or blender and process until smooth, then return it to the pan and bring to the boil. Meanwhile, chop the remaining mushrooms and cook them gently in the butter in a frying pan for a few minutes until softened. Mix the rice flour with a little water to make a paste, and add the paste to the soup along with the mushrooms. Season with salt and pepper, add the cream and cook for a further 10 minutes. Serve piping hot.

CAULIFLOWER SOUP

POTAGE AU CHOU-FLEUR OU CRÈME DUBARRY

- **1 medium cauliflower**
- **30 g (1¼ oz) cornflour**
- **2 egg yolks**
- **30 g (1¼ oz) butter**
- **Salt, to taste**

Preparation time: 30 minutes
Cooking time: 30 minutes
Serves 6

Separate the cauliflower into florets. Bring 1.5 litres (2½ pints) salted water to the boil in a large pan, add the cauliflower and cook for 15 minutes, or until tender. Drain well, reserving the cooking liquid. Set aside a few very small florets to be added to the soup just before serving. Purée the rest in a food processor or blender and mix with the cornflour. Thin to a good soup consistency with the cooking liquid, return to the pan and simmer for 10 minutes. Just before serving, thicken by stirring in the egg yolks, then add the butter and reserved cauliflower florets. Season with salt, if necessary.

RED CABBAGE SOUP

POTAGE AU CHOU ROUGE

Bring 2.25 litres (4 pints) water to the boil in a large pan, add the cabbage and simmer for 10 minutes. Drain (reserving the cooking liquid), return the cabbage to the pan, add enough of the reserved cooking liquid to cover, and add the potatoes and the onions. Season with salt and simmer for 30 minutes. Transfer the mixture to a food processor or blender and process until smooth. Add the wine, if using, and reheat to serve.

- 1 red cabbage, coarsely chopped
- 500 g (1 lb 2 oz) potatoes, cut into large dice
- 60 g (2 oz) onion, chopped
- Salt
- 100 ml (3½ fl oz) red Bordeaux wine (optional)

Preparation time: 10 minutes
Cooking time: 40 minutes
Serves 6

BRUSSELS SPROUT SOUP

SOUPE AUX CHOUX DE BRUXELLES OU POTAGE BELGE

Bring a large pan of salted water to the boil, add the sprouts and cook for 15 minutes, or until just tender. Drain. Heat the butter in a large pan and fry the sprouts until lightly browned, then sprinkle them with the flour. Pour in the hot water or stock. Season with salt and pepper, and cook for 30 minutes. Transfer the mixture to a food processor or blender and process until smooth. Place the croutons in a tureen, pour the soup over them and serve.

- 500 g (1 lb 2 oz) Brussels sprouts
- 50 g (1¾ oz) butter
- 30 g (1¼ oz) flour
- 1.5 litres (2½ pints) hot water or any stock
- Salt and pepper
- 1 quantity croutons (p.183)

Preparation time: 20 minutes
Cooking time: 1 hour
Serves 6

CABBAGE SOUP

SOUPE AUX CHOUX

- 250 g (9 oz) smoked bacon, in one piece
- 250 g (9 oz) streaky bacon, in one piece
- 500 g (1 lb 2 oz) pork knuckle
- 1 medium cabbage, halved
- 200 g (7 oz) potatoes, diced
- 200 g (7 oz) turnips, diced
- 200 g (7 oz) carrots, diced
- 50 g (1¾ oz) onion, chopped
- Salt and pepper
- Thin slices bread, to serve

Preparation time: 20 minutes
Cooking time: 2½ hours
Serves 6

Put the bacon and pork knuckle into a large pan with 4 litres (7 pints) water. Bring to the boil, skim to remove the scum and cook gently for 1 hour. Add the vegetables and season with salt and pepper. Continue to cook for 1 hour. Remove the meat, leave to cool slightly, then cut into pieces. Return the meat to the soup and pour over slices of bread placed in warmed soup bowls.

SPINACH SOUP

SOUPE AUX ÉPINARDS OU POTAGE FLORENTINE

- 30 g (1¼ oz) butter
- 40 g (1½ oz) flour
- 2 litres (3½ pints) any stock
- 500 g (1 lb 2 oz) spinach, finely chopped
- Salt and pepper
- Freshly grated nutmeg
- 1 quantity croutons (p.183), to serve

Preparation time: 30 minutes
Cooking time: 45 minutes
Serves 6

In a large pan, make a white sauce (p.50) with the butter and flour, then mix in the stock. Bring to the boil, reduce the heat and simmer for 5 minutes. Add the spinach and season with salt and pepper and nutmeg. Simmer for 30 minutes. Place the croutons in a tureen, pour the soup over them and serve.

CREAM OF BROAD BEAN SOUP

CRÈME DE FÈVES

Bring 1.5 litres (2½ pints) water to the boil in a large pan. Add a pinch of salt, the beans and savory or thyme and cook for 10 minutes, or until tender. Drain the beans, and return the cooking liquid to the pan. Set aside any beans that are still whole. Put the remainder into a food processor or blender and process to a purée. Stir the purée into the liquid in the pan, add half the milk and return to the heat. Mix the flour with the remaining milk in a bowl, then stir into the soup and cook, stirring frequently, for a further 5 minutes, until thickened. Stir in the whole beans and the butter, season with salt and pepper and serve.

- 750 g (1 lb 10 oz) shelled broad beans
- 2 sprigs of savory or fresh thyme
- 500 ml (18 fl oz) milk
- 10 g (¼ oz) flour
- 30 g (1¼ oz) butter
- Salt and pepper

Preparation time: 20 minutes
Cooking time: 35 minutes
Serves 6

GARBURE

GARBURE

Select the vegetables according to the time of year. Bring 3 litres (5¼ pints) water to the boil in a large pan. Add the chosen vegetables, beans (if using), herbs and garlic, and season with salt and pepper. Simmer gently for 2–2½ hours, topping up with boiling water if necessary during cooking. An hour before serving, add the cabbage, if using. Half an hour before serving add the goose confit. Put the bread in a tureen, pour in the soup and serve the goose separately. The soup should be very thick: the spoon should stand upright in the tureen. If the soup is too liquid, thicken it with a purée of cooked haricot beans.

In summer:
- 250 g (9 oz) French beans
- 250 g (9 oz) broad beans, shelled
- 250 g (9 oz) peas
- 300 g (11 oz) potatoes, cut into pieces
- 1 small green cabbage, shredded

In winter:
- 250 g (9 oz) carrots, chopped
- 1 onion, chopped
- 100 g (3½ oz) turnips, chopped
- 500 g (1 lb 2 oz) dried haricot beans, soaked overnight

- 1 handful of chopped herbs, such as flat-leaf parsley, marjoram or thyme
- 3 garlic cloves, crushed
- Salt and pepper
- 1 piece of goose confit
- 6 slices of bread
- Cooked haricot beans, puréed, to thicken (optional)

Preparation time: 40 minutes
Cooking time: 3–3½ hours
Serves 6

FRENCH BEAN SOUP

POTAGE AUX HARICOTS VERTS OU CRÈME MIMOSA

- 250 g (9 oz) French beans, trimmed
- 1 litre (1¾ pints) vegetable stock
- 30 g (1¼ oz) rice flour
- 3 hard-boiled eggs (p.134)
- 30 g (1¼ oz) butter
- Salt and pepper

Preparation time: 45 minutes
Cooking time: 30 minutes
Serves 6

Bring 750 ml (1¼ pints) water to the boil in a large pan. Add a pinch of salt and the beans and cook for 10–15 minutes, or until tender. Meanwhile, pour the stock into another pan and heat. Drain the beans, reserving the cooking liquid, and cut into fine strips. Mix the rice flour to a paste with 3–4 tablespoons water in a bowl and stir into the hot stock. Add the reserved cooking liquid and simmer for 5 minutes to thicken. Halve the eggs and gently scoop out the yolks with a teaspoon, then pass them through a coarse sieve into a tureen (reserve the whites for another use). Add the beans and butter to the tureen, pour in the stock and season to taste with salt and pepper, then serve.

CREAM OF FRENCH BEAN SOUP

CRÈME DE HARICOTS VERTS

- 400 g (14 oz) French beans, trimmed
- 1 quantity béchamel sauce (p.50)
- Salt and pepper
- 1.5 litres (2½ pints) any stock, hot
- 100 ml (3½ fl oz) crème fraîche
- 30 g (1¼ oz) butter

Preparation time: 1 hour
Cooking time: 20 minutes
Serves 6

Blanch the beans in a pan of boiling water for 5 minutes, then drain. Set aside a good handful for the garnish, add the remainder to the béchamel sauce and cook over a low heat for 15 minutes. Meanwhile, cut the reserved beans into diamond shapes. Season the béchamel mixture with salt and pepper, ladle into a food processor or blender and process to a purée. Add the stock and process briefly to mix, then pour into a tureen. Stir in the crème fraîche and butter to thicken, then garnish with the reserved beans and serve.

CHESTNUT SOUP

POTAGE AUX MARRONS

- **500 g (1 lb 2 oz) chestnuts**
- **2 litres (3½ pints) any stock**
- **Salt and pepper**
- **60 g (2 oz) butter**
- **1 quantity croutons (p.183)**

Preparation time: 35 minutes
Cooking time: 45 minutes
Serves 6

Slit the chestnuts, put them in a heatproof bowl, pour in boiling water to cover and leave to soak for 5 minutes. Drain and carefully remove the shells and skins. Put them into a pan, add the stock and bring to the boil, then reduce the heat and simmer for 30 minutes. Season with salt and pepper, transfer to a food processor or blender and process until smooth. Return to the pan, add the butter and cook for a further 10 minutes. Place the croutons in a tureen, pour the soup over them and serve.

ONION SOUP

SOUPE À L'OIGNON OU POTAGE PARISIEN

- **60 g (2 oz) butter**
- **250 g (9 oz) onions, finely chopped**
- **80 g (2¾ oz) flour**
- **1.5 litres (2½ pints) any stock, hot**
- **Salt and pepper**
- **6 slices bread or 50 g (1¾ oz) vermicelli**

Preparation time: 10 minutes
Cooking time: 20 minutes
Serves 6

 p.214

Melt the butter in a large pan. Add the onions and cook over a low heat, stirring occasionally, for 10 minutes until golden brown. Sprinkle with the flour and cook, stirring constantly, for a few minutes until browned. Pour in the stock and simmer for 10 minutes. Season with salt and pepper. Place the bread, if using, in a tureen, then strain the soup to remove the onion and pour it over the bread. Alternatively, return the strained soup to the pan, add the vermicelli and cook briefly until the pasta is tender.

VARIATION

. . . .

ONION SOUP GRATIN

SOUPE GRATINÉE

Make the onion soup as above, then pour it into an ovenproof tureen. Sprinkle with grated Gruyère cheese and brown in an oven preheated to 240°C/475°F/Gas Mark 8 for 10 minutes.

JULIENNE SOUP

POTAGE JULIENNE

 p.213

Put the carrots, turnips, leeks, celery, cabbage and potatoes into a large pan, pour in 2 litres (3½ pints) water and bring to the boil, then reduce the heat, cover and simmer for 30 minutes. Season with salt and pepper, add the peas, chervil and lettuce and simmer for a further 15 minutes. Ladle into a tureen, stir in the butter and serve immediately.

- 150 g (5 oz) carrots, cut into julienne strips
- 150 g (5 oz) turnips, cut into julienne strips
- 2 leeks, cut into julienne strips
- 100 g (3½ oz) celery, cut into julienne strips
- 100 g (3½ oz) cabbage, cut into julienne strips
- 200 g (7 oz) potatoes, cut into julienne strips
- Salt and pepper
- 100 g (3½ oz) shelled peas
- 2 sprigs of chervil, finely chopped
- 1 lettuce, finely chopped
- 30 g (1¼ oz) butter

Preparation time: 45 minutes
Cooking time: 45 minutes
Serves 6

TURNIP SOUP

POTAGE AUX NAVETS OU CRÈME FLAMANDE

Put the bread, turnips and potatoes into a large pan, pour in 1.75 litres (3 pints) water, season with salt and pepper and bring to the boil. Reduce the heat, cover and simmer for 30–40 minutes or until tender. Ladle the mixture into a food processor or blender and process until smooth. Return to the pan and reheat gently. Just before serving, stir in the crème fraîche and parsley.

- 200 g (7 oz) day-old bread, cut into pieces
- 500 g (1 lb 2 oz) turnips, cut into pieces
- 500 g (1 lb 2 oz) potatoes, cut into pieces
- Salt and pepper
- 100 ml (3½ fl oz) crème fraîche
- 3 tablespoons finely chopped flat-leaf parsley

Preparation time: 20 minutes
Cooking time: 40 minutes
Serves 6

CREAM OF ONION SOUP

PURÉE D'OIGNONS OU POTAGE SOUBISE

- **50 g (1¾ oz) butter**
- **500 g (1 lb 2 oz) onions, sliced**
- **50 g (1¾ oz) flour**
- **500 ml (18 fl oz) hot milk**
- **Salt and pepper**
- **1 litre (1¾ pints) any stock**
- **1 egg yolk**

Preparation time: 20 minutes
Cooking time: 35 minutes
Serves 6

Melt 30 g (1¼ oz) of the butter in a pan, add the onions and cook, stirring frequently, for 10 minutes, or until translucent. Sprinkle with the flour and cook, stirring constantly, for 2 minutes, then stir in the hot milk, season with salt and pepper and simmer for 20 minutes. Transfer the mixture to a food processor or blender and process until smooth. Return to the pan, add the stock and simmer for a further 10 minutes. Beat the egg yolk with the remaining butter in a tureen, then pour in the soup, stirring constantly, and serve.

PARMENTIÈRE SOUP
POTAGE PARMENTIÈRE

Bring a pan of salted water to the boil, add the unpeeled potatoes and cook for 20 minutes until tender. Drain, peel and mash until smooth. Melt the butter in a large pan. Add the onions and parsley and cook over a low heat, stirring occasionally, for 15 minutes until golden brown. Add the mashed potatoes, hot water and enough milk to give the soup a creamy consistency. Season with salt and pepper and simmer for a further 10 minutes, then serve.

- 1 kg (2¼ lb) potatoes, unpeeled
- 50 g (1¾ oz) butter
- 100 g (3½ oz) onions, chopped
- 2 sprigs of flat-leaf parsley, chopped
- 1 litre (1¾ pints) hot water
- 1 litre (1¾ pints) milk
- Salt and pepper

Preparation time: 10 minutes
Cooking time: 45 minutes
Serves 6

PUMPKIN SOUP
POTAGE AU POTIRON OU CRÈME D'OR

Put the pumpkin in a large pan, pour in 1.5 litres (2½ pints) water and bring to the boil. Reduce the heat and simmer for 25 minutes, or until tender. Transfer the mixture to a food processor or blender and process until smooth. Return to the pan, stir in the milk, season with salt and pepper and simmer for a further 5 minutes. Put the butter and croutons into a tureen, pour the soup over them and serve.

- 1.5 kg (3¼ lb) pumpkin, peeled, de-seeded and diced
- 1 litre (1¾ pints) milk
- 30 g (1¼ oz) butter
- Salt and pepper
- 1 quantity croutons (p.183)

Preparation time: 15 minutes
Cooking time: 30 minutes
Serves 6

AURORE SOUP
POTAGE AURORE

 p.215

Melt the butter in a large pan. Add the pumpkin and tomatoes and cook over a low heat for 5 minutes. Pour in 2 litres (3½ pints) boiling water, season with salt and pepper and add the potatoes, then cover and simmer for 40 minutes. Transfer the mixture to a food processor or blender and process until smooth. Return to the pan and cook for a further 5 minutes, then pour into a tureen. Beat the egg yolk with the crème fraîche in a bowl, then stir into the soup to thicken. Serve immediately.

- 60 g (2 oz) butter
- 500 g (1 lb 2 oz) pumpkin, peeled, de-seeded and sliced
- 250 g (9 oz) tomatoes, sliced
- Salt and pepper
- 250 g (9 oz) potatoes
- 1 egg yolk
- 50 ml (2 fl oz) crème fraîche

Preparation time: 15 minutes
Cooking time: 45 minutes
Serves 6

LEEK SOUP

SOUPE AUX POIREAUX

- **500 g (1 lb 2 oz) leeks, diced**
- **500 g (1 lb 2 oz) potatoes, diced**
- **Salt and pepper**
- **500 ml (18 fl oz) hot milk**
- **30 g (1¼ oz) butter**

Preparation time: 20 minutes
Cooking time: 45 minutes
Serves 6

Put the leeks and potatoes in a large pan, pour in 1.25 litres (2 pints) water, season with salt and pepper and bring to the boil. Reduce the heat, cover and simmer gently for 30 minutes, or until tender. Transfer the mixture to a food processor or blender and process until smooth. Add the hot milk and process briefly to mix. Put the butter in a tureen, pour the soup over it and serve.

NOTE
As a variation, replace the potatoes with 100 g (3½ oz) long-grain rice.

THRIFTY SOUP

SOUPE ÉCONOMIQUE

- **1.5 litres (2½ pints) any stock**
- **500 g (1 lb 2 oz) potatoes**
- **30 g (1¼ oz) butter**
- **Salt and pepper**

Preparation time: 20 minutes
Cooking time: 10 minutes
Serves 6

Bring the stock to the boil in a pan and grate the raw potatoes into it, then simmer for 10 minutes. Put the butter in a tureen, pour the soup over it, season with salt and pepper and serve.

PORTUGUESE TOMATO SOUP

POTAGE AUX TOMATES OU PORTUGAIS

- **250 g (9 oz) potatoes,**
  cut into pieces
- **500 g (1 lb 2 oz) tomatoes,**
  cut into pieces
- **1.5 litres (2½ pints) any stock**
- **3 tablespoons finely**
  chopped chervil
- **1 quantity croutons (p.183)**

Preparation time: 10 minutes
Cooking time: 30 minutes
Serves 6

Put the potatoes and tomatoes in a large pan, pour in the stock and bring to the boil. Reduce the heat, cover and simmer for 30 minutes. Put the chervil and croutons in a soup tureen, pour the soup over them and serve.

ITALIAN TOMATO SOUP

POTAGE AUX TOMATES OU ITALIEN

Melt the butter in a large pan. Add the onions and tomatoes and cook over a low heat, stirring occasionally, for 10 minutes, until golden. Pour in the hot stock, season with salt and pepper, add the rice and cook for 30 minutes. Put the cheese in a tureen, pour the soup over it and serve.

- 50 g (1¾ oz) butter
- 150 g (5 oz) onions, sliced
- 500 g (1 lb 2 oz) tomatoes, cut into pieces
- 2 litres (3½ pints) any stock, hot
- Salt and pepper
- 100 g (3½ oz) long-grain rice
- 60 g (2 oz) Gruyère cheese, grated

Preparation time: 10 minutes
Cooking time: 40 minutes
Serves 6

GARLIC SOUP

SOUPE À L'AIL

Heat the oil in a large pan. Add the tomatoes, garlic, onions, thyme, parsley and saffron and season with salt and pepper. Cover and cook over a low heat, stirring occasionally, for 20 minutes. Pass the mixture through a sieve into a bowl or transfer to a food processor or blender and process to a purée. Return the purée to the pan, stir in the hot water and reheat gently for 15 minutes. Put the egg yolk and croutons in a tureen, pour in the soup, stirring constantly, and serve.

- 2 tablespoons olive oil
- 500 g (1 lb 2 oz) tomatoes, diced
- 15 g (½ oz) garlic, finely chopped
- 100 g (3½ oz) onion, chopped
- 1 sprig of thyme
- 1 sprig of flat-leaf parsley
- Pinch of saffron threads
- Salt and pepper
- 1.75 litres (3 pints) hot water
- 1 egg yolk
- 1 quantity croutons (p.183)

Preparation time: 35 minutes
Cooking time: 35 minutes
Serves 6

CHAMPENOIS SOUP

POTAGE CHAMPENOIS

- 30 g (1¼ oz) butter
- 125 g (4¼ oz) leeks, chopped
- 750 g (1 lb 10 oz) potatoes, diced
- Salt and pepper
- 4 tablespoons olive oil
- 125 g (4¼ oz) bread, cut into cubes
- 50 g (1¾ oz) Gruyère cheese, grated
- 30 g (1¼ oz) short macaroni

Preparation time: 25 minutes
Cooking time: 50 minutes
Serves 6

Melt the butter in a large pan. Add the leeks and cook over a low heat, stirring occasionally, for 5 minutes. Add the potatoes, pour in 3 litres (5¼ pints) water, season with salt and pepper and bring to the boil. Reduce the heat, cover and simmer for 30 minutes.

Meanwhile, preheat the oven to 180°C/350°F/Gas Mark 4. Heat the oil in a frying pan, add the bread and cook over a medium heat, turning frequently, for a few minutes until golden brown all over. Remove from the heat, transfer to a baking sheet, sprinkle with the cheese and bake for about 5 minutes until the cheese has melted. Transfer the cheese croutons to a tureen. Add the macaroni to the soup and simmer for a further 15 minutes. Pour the soup into the tureen and serve.

SPLIT PEA SOUP

POTAGE AUX POIS CASSÉS

- 300 g (11 oz) green or yellow split peas, soaked in 1 litre (1¾ pints) water for 1 hour and drained
- 1 tablespoon chopped sorrel
- Salt
- 30 g (1¼ oz) butter
- 1 quantity croutons (p.183)

Preparation time: 10 minutes, plus soaking time
Cooking time: 2¼ hours
Serves 6

Put the peas in a large pan, pour in 2 litres (3½ pints) water, add the sorrel and bring to the boil. Reduce the heat, cover and simmer gently for 2 hours, or until very tender. Season with salt and simmer for a further 15 minutes. Put the butter and croutons in a soup tureen, pour the soup over them and serve.

PEA SOUP

POTAGE AUX PETITS POIS OU CRÈME CLAMART

Put the peas in a large pan, pour in the stock and bring to the boil. Reduce the heat, cover and simmer for 10 minutes. Pass the soup through a sieve into a tureen, season with salt and pepper and serve with the crème fraîche and croutons.

- ◆ **750 g (1 lb 10 oz) shelled peas**
- ◆ **1.5 litres (2½ pints) any stock**
- ◆ **125 ml (4¼ fl oz) crème fraîche**
- ◆ **Salt and pepper**
- ◆ **1 quantity croutons (p.183)**

  Preparation time: 30 minutes
  Cooking time: 10 minutes
  Serves 6

SAINT-GERMAIN SOUP

POTAGE SAINT-GERMAIN

Put the leeks and lettuce in a large pan, pour in 1.5 litres (2½ pints) water, add a pinch of salt and bring to the boil. Reduce the heat, cover and simmer for 10 minutes. Add the peas and continue to simmer for 10 minutes, or until tender. Beat the egg yolk with the crème fraîche in a tureen and add the butter. Mash the vegetables in their cooking liquid, pour the soup into the tureen, stirring constantly, and serve.

- ◆ **60 g (2 oz) leeks, chopped**
- ◆ **1 lettuce, shredded**
- ◆ **Salt**
- ◆ **500 g (1 lb 2 oz) shelled peas**
- ◆ **1 egg yolk**
- ◆ **4 tablespoons crème fraîche**
- ◆ **30 g (1¼ oz) butter**

  Preparation time: 30 minutes
  Cooking time: 20 minutes
  Serves 6

FAUBONNE SOUP

POTAGE À LA FAUBONNE

Put the peas in a large pan, pour in 1.75 litres (3 pints) water and bring to the boil. Reduce the heat, cover and simmer for 2 hours, or until very tender. Blanch the onions in a pan of boiling water for 5 minutes, then drain. Add the onions, sorrel, leeks and celery to the peas and cook for a further 20 minutes. Put the croutons in a tureen. Season the soup with salt and pepper, pass through a fine sieve into the tureen, and serve.

- ◆ **350 g (12 oz) green or yellow split peas, soaked in 1 litre (1¼ pints) water for 1 hour and drained**
- ◆ **60 g (2 oz) onions, chopped**
- ◆ **125 g (4¼ oz) sorrel, chopped**
- ◆ **60 g (2 oz) leeks, chopped**
- ◆ **100 g (3½ oz) celery, chopped**
- ◆ **1 quantity croutons (p.183)**
- ◆ **Salt and pepper**

  Preparation time: 25 minutes, plus soaking time
  Cooking time: 2½ hours
  Serves 6

COMBES SOUP

POTAGE COMBES

- 250 g (9 oz) green or yellow split peas, soaked in 1 litre (1¾ pints) water for 1 hour and drained
- 1 onion
- Salt
- 4 tablespoons long-grain rice
- 50 g (1¾ oz) butter or 50 ml (2 fl oz) crème fraîche

Preparation time: 10 minutes, plus soaking time
Cooking time: 2 hours 20 minutes
Serves 6

Put the peas and onion in a large pan, pour in 2 litres (3½ pints) water and bring to the boil. Reduce the heat, cover and simmer for 2 hours, or until very tender. Transfer the mixture to a food processor or blender and process until smooth. Return to the pan and season with salt. Return the pan to the heat and bring to the boil, then add the rice and cook for a further 20 minutes. Put the butter or crème fraîche in a tureen, pour in the soup and serve.

RED KIDNEY BEAN SOUP

POTAGE AUX HARICOTS ROUGES OU POTAGE CONDÉ

- 800 g (1¾ lb) dried red kidney beans, soaked in 1 litre (1¾ pints) water for 3–4 hours or overnight and drained
- 30 g (1¾ oz) butter
- 150 g (5 oz) onions, sliced
- Salt
- 1 quantity croutons (p.183)
- 60 g (2 oz) Gruyère cheese, grated, to serve

Preparation time: 10 minutes, plus soaking time
Cooking time: 2½ hours
Serves 6

Put the beans in a large pan, pour in water to cover and bring to the boil, then boil vigorously for 15 minutes. Drain, rinse and return to the pan. Meanwhile, melt the butter in a small pan. Add the onions and cook over a low heat, stirring occasionally, for 10 minutes, until golden. Add the onions to the beans, pour in 2.5 litres (4½ pints) water and bring to the boil. Reduce the heat, cover and simmer for 2¼ hours, or until very tender, seasoning with salt halfway through the cooking time. Put the croutons in a tureen and pass the soup through a sieve over the croutons. Serve immediately, handing the cheese separately.

VARIATION

. . . .

RED KIDNEY BEAN & SORREL SOUP
POTAGE AUX HARICOTS ROUGES ET À L'OSEILLE

Proceed as above. Meanwhile, cook 200 g (7 oz) chopped sorrel in 40 g (1½ oz) butter over a low heat for a few minutes until wilted. Add to the soup shortly before the end of the cooking time, once the beans have disintegrated.

RUSSIAN SOUP
POTAGE RUSSE

Put the beans and potatoes in a large pan, pour in 1.5 litres (2½ pints) water and bring to the boil. Reduce the heat, cover and simmer for 1½ hours, or until very tender. Transfer the mixture to a food processor or blender and process until smooth. Return to the pan, season with salt and stir in the sorrel, chervil and lettuce. Return to the heat and simmer for a further 15 minutes. Put the butter and the croutons, if using, into a tureen, pour the soup over them and serve.

- 350 g (12 oz) dried haricot beans, soaked in 1 litre (1¾ pints) water for 3–4 hours or overnight, and drained
- 250 g (9 oz) potatoes, cut into quarters
- Salt
- 125 g (4¼ oz) sorrel, finely chopped
- 1 sprig of chervil, finely chopped
- 1 lettuce, finely chopped
- 50 g (1¾ oz) butter
- 1 quantity croutons (p.183), optional

Preparation time: 15 minutes, plus soaking time
Cooking time: 1¾ hours
Serves 6

LENTIL COULIS
COULIS AUX LENTILLES

Put the lentils, onion and carrots in a large pan, pour in 2.5 litres (4½ pints) water and bring to the boil. Reduce the heat, cover and simmer, stirring frequently, for 1 hour, or until very tender. Season with salt and pepper, transfer the mixture to a food processor or blender and process until smooth. If the coulis is too thick, stir in a little hot stock; if it is too runny, return it to the pan and cook for a further 10 minutes until reduced.

- 500 g (1 lb 2 oz) green or brown lentils
- 50 g (1¾ oz) onion
- 250 g (9 oz) carrots
- Salt and pepper
- 4–5 tablespoons hot vegetable stock (optional)

Preparation time: 10 minutes
Cooking time: 1 hour
Serves 6

SIMPLE RICE SOUP

POTAGE SIMPLE AU RIZ

- 125 g (4¼ oz) long-grain rice
- 30 g (1¼ oz) butter
- 1.5 litres (2½ pints)
  boiling water
- Salt
- 2 egg yolks
- 100 ml (3½ fl oz) crème fraîche

Preparation time: 5 minutes
Cooking time: 25 minutes
Serves 6

Put the rice and butter into a pan, pour in the boiling water, and add a pinch of salt. Bring to the boil and cook for 25 minutes. Beat the egg yolks with the crème fraîche in a tureen, pour in the soup, stirring constantly, and serve.

RICE SOUP

POTAGE AU RIZ

- 100 g (3½ oz) onions, chopped
- 100 g (3½ oz) carrots,
  cut in pieces
- 100 g (3½ oz) turnips,
  cut in pieces
- 100 g (3½ oz) sorrel, chopped
- Salt and pepper
- 60 g (2 oz) long-grain rice
- 30 g (1¼ oz) butter

Preparation time: 25 minutes
Cooking time: 55 minutes
Serves 6

Put the onions, carrots, turnips and sorrel in a pan, pour in 2 litres (3½ pints) water and bring to the boil. Reduce the heat and simmer for 30 minutes. Season with salt and pepper, transfer the mixture to a food processor or blender and process until smooth. Return to the pan, add the rice and cook over a low heat for 25 minutes. Put the butter in a tureen, pour in the soup and serve.

BRAZILIAN SOUP

POTAGE À LA BRÉSILIENNE

Melt the butter in a large pan. Add the carrots, turnips, onions, leeks and celery, season with salt and pepper, cover and cook over a low heat, stirring occasionally, for 30 minutes. Add the tomatoes, pour in the consommé and simmer for 10 minutes. Stir in the bean purée. Put the Creole rice in a tureen, pour the soup over it and serve.

NOTE

To make the black bean purée, soak dried black beans overnight, drain, rinse and cook in boiling water for 2 hours, or until very tender. Drain and purée in a food processor. Alternatively, drain and rinse canned black beans and purée in a food processor.

- 50 g (1¾ oz) butter
- 100 g (3½ oz) carrots, cut into thin strips
- 100 g (3½ oz) turnips, cut into thin strips
- 60 g (2 oz) onions, cut into thin strips
- 100 g (3½ oz) leeks, cut into thin strips
- 40 g (1½ oz) celery, cut into thin strips
- Salt and pepper
- 200 g (7 oz) tomatoes, skinned, de-seeded and diced
- 1.5 litres (2½ pints) consommé (p.178)
- 3 tablespoons black bean purée (see note)
- 60 g (2 oz) Creole rice (p.617)

Preparation time: 30 minutes
Cooking time: 40 minutes
Serves 6

IMPERIAL CONSOMMÉ

CONSOMMÉ IMPÉRIAL

Bring the consommé to the boil in a large pan, then tip in all the tapioca at once and cook for 5–8 minutes, or until tender. Put the peas and chervil leaves in a tureen. Pour in the soup and serve immediately.

- 1.5 litres (2½ pints) consommé (p.178)
- 80 g (2¾ oz) tapioca
- 4 tablespoons cooked peas
- 6 chervil leaves

Preparation time: 10 minutes
Cooking time: 10 minutes
Serves 6

PETITE MARMITE

PETITE MARMITE

 p.216

Use a melon baller to cut the carrots and turnips into small balls. Melt the butter in a large pan. Add the carrots, turnips, leeks and cabbage, cover and cook over a low heat, stirring occasionally, for 30 minutes. Season with salt and pepper, pour in the consommé and cook for a further 5 minutes. Divide the chicken, beef and vegetable balls between 6 soup bowls and ladle the soup over them. Serve immediately, handing the toast separately.

- 100 g (3½ oz) carrots
- 100 g (3½ oz) turnips
- 60 g (2 oz) butter
- 100 g (3½ oz) leeks, white parts only, diced
- 100 g (3½ oz) cabbage, shredded
- Salt and pepper
- 1.5 litres (2½ pints) consommé (p.178)
- 100 g (3½ oz) cooked chicken, diced
- 100 g (3½ oz) cooked beef, diced
- 18–20 small slices toast, to serve

Preparation time: 25 minutes
Cooking time: 40 minutes
Serves 6

OXTAIL SOUP

POTAGE OX-TAIL OU QUEUES DE BŒUF

Prepare the rich stock, adding the oxtails with the rest of the meat, and simmer for 3 hours. Strain the stock into a clean pan, return to the heat and add the Madeira, tomato purée and quenelles. Simmer for 10 minutes, then serve.

- 1.5 litres (2½ pints) rich beef stock (p.176)
- 3 oxtails, cut into pieces
- 4 tablespoons Madeira
- 1½ teaspoons tomato purée
- 125 g (4¼ oz) veal quenelles (p.104), diced
- Salt and pepper

Preparation time: 40 minutes
Cooking time: 3 hours 10 minutes
Serves 6

PROVENÇALE FISH SOUP

SOUPE DE POISSONS

- 1 onion, sliced
- 2 leeks, white parts only, sliced
- 50 ml (2 fl oz) olive oil
- 2 garlic cloves
- 100 g (3½ oz) tomatoes, chopped
- 1 tablespoon fennel fronds, snipped
- 1 bay leaf
- ½ teaspoon cayenne pepper
- 1 pinch of saffron threads
- 1 kg (2¼ lb) rock fish, cleaned, such as red scorpion fish, John Dory, small conger eels, wrasse
- Salt
- 6 slices bread
- 50 g (1¾ oz) Gruyère cheese, grated, to serve

Preparation time: 20 minutes
Cooking time: 20 minutes
Serves 6

In a large pan, fry the onion and leeks in the oil until softened, without allowing them to brown. Crush 1 garlic clove and halve the other. Add the tomatoes and crushed garlic, fennel, bay leaf, cayenne pepper and saffron. Add the fish. Season with salt and add 2.5 litres (4½ pints) water. Bring to the boil and simmer for 20 minutes. Strain through a fine sieve and press the fish through. Toast the bread and rub each slice with the garlic halves. Serve the soup very hot, on the toast if you wish, and hand the cheese separately.

 p.217

LOBSTER BISQUE

POTAGE À LA BISQUE DE HOMARD

- Tail and claw meat from 1 freshly cooked lobster (p.280), head and shell reserved
- 100 ml (3½ fl oz) crème fraîche
- 90 g (3¼ oz) butter
- 50 g (1¾ oz) rice flour or 1 tablespoon cornflour
- 1.5 litres (2½ pints) any stock
- 2 egg yolks

Preparation time: 1½ hours
Cooking time: 55 minutes
Serves 6

Dice half the lobster meat and set aside, then finely chop the remainder. Put the reserved head and shell into a chinois (conical sieve) or other fine-meshed strainer, and pound with a pestle over a bowl. Mix the resulting paste with the finely chopped lobster flesh. Gently heat the crème fraîche in a small pan, but do not allow it to boil. Meanwhile, melt 60 g (2 oz) of the butter in a large pan. Stir in the rice flour or cornflour and cook, stirring constantly, for a few minutes, then gradually stir in the stock. Cook, stirring constantly, until thickened. Stir in the warm crème fraîche and the lobster paste. Beat the egg yolks with the remaining butter in a bowl and stir into the soup. Just before serving, add the diced lobster meat.

CRAYFISH BISQUE

POTAGE À LA BISQUE D'ÉCREVISSES

Melt the butter in a large pan. Add the onion, carrot, parsley, thyme and bay leaf and cook over a low heat, stirring occasionally, for 10 minutes until golden brown. Increase the heat to high, add the crayfish and cook over a high heat until the shells turn red. Add the brandy and cook for 1–2 minutes to evaporate the alcohol. Pour in the wine and season with salt and pepper. Lower the heat, cover and simmer for 12 minutes, then remove the pan from the heat.

Cook the rice in salted boiling water or stock, according to the instructions on the packet, then drain. Remove the crayfish from the pan with a slotted spoon, peel off and reserve the heads and shells. Dice the tails and set aside. Put the heads and shells into a chinois (conical sieve) and pound with a pestle over a bowl, reserving the liquid. Bring the consommé to a simmer in a large pan and add the liquid from the crayfish shells. Meanwhile, using a slotted spoon, transfer the cooked vegetables to a bowl, remove the bay leaf, add the cooked rice and mash well. Stir the rice mixture into the consommé and add any leftover cooking liquid from the crayfish pan. Add the crayfish tails and crème fraîche and serve.

- 50 g (1¾ oz) butter
- 30 g (1¼ oz) onion, finely chopped
- 30 g (1¼ oz) carrot, finely chopped
- 1 sprig of parsley, finely chopped
- 1 sprig of thyme, finely chopped
- 1 bay leaf
- 18 crayfish, deveined (p.286)
- 50 ml (2 fl oz) brandy
- 100 ml (3½ fl oz) white wine
- Salt and pepper
- 75 g (2½ oz) long-grain rice
- Fish stock, for cooking the rice (optional)
- 1.5 litres (2½ pints) consommé (p.178)
- 100 ml (3½ fl oz) crème fraîche

Preparation time: 1 hour
Cooking time: 25 minutes
Serves 6

FISH VELOUTÉ

VELOUTÉ DE POISSON

Fillet the sole (p.262), reserving the bones, and set aside. Cut the other fish into pieces and put them into a large pan with the reserved bones and the onions. Pour in the wine and 2.5 litres (4½ pints) water, season with salt and pepper and bring to the boil over a low heat. Simmer gently for 25–30 minutes, then remove the pan from the heat. Strain the stock through a fine-meshed sieve into a clean pan. Add the sole fillets, return to the heat and poach gently for 3 minutes. Remove the fillets with a fish slice and reserve the stock. Cook the quenelles. Cut the sole fillets into thin strips and dice the quenelles. Reheat the stock and beat in the egg yolks. Add the quenelles, crayfish tails and strips of sole and serve immediately. Use the flesh from the remaining white fish to make croquettes or a fish loaf.

- 1 kg (2¼ lb) white fish, including 1 sole, cleaned
- 100 g (3½ oz) onions, thinly sliced
- 100 ml (3½ fl oz) dry white wine
- Salt and pepper
- 2 egg yolks

For the garnish:
- 100 g (3½ oz) fish quenelles (p.105)
- 3 cooked crayfish tails, cut into small strips

Preparation time: 30 minutes
Cooking time: 35 minutes
Serves 6

DIEPPOISE SOUP

POTAGE À LA DIEPPOISE

- ◆ **1 kg (2¼ lb) live mussels, scrubbed**
- ◆ **50 g (1¾ oz) butter**
- ◆ **125 g (4¼ oz) leek, white part only, chopped**
- ◆ **125 g (4¼ oz) mushrooms, chopped**
- ◆ **1.5 litres (2½ pints) fish stock**
- ◆ **Salt and pepper (optional)**
- ◆ **100 g (3½ oz) cooked prawns, peeled and deveined**
- ◆ **1 egg**
- ◆ **50 ml (2 fl oz) crème fraîche**

Preparation time: 30 minutes
Cooking time: 30 minutes
Serves 6

Cook the mussels (p.271) and drain, reserving the cooking liquid. Discard any mussels that remain closed and remove the remainder from their shells. Strain the cooking liquid through a chinois (conical sieve) or muslin-lined strainer into a clean pan and set aside. Melt the butter in a large pan. Add the leek and mushrooms and cook over a low heat, stirring occasionally, for 5 minutes until softened. Pour in the fish stock and bring to the boil, then reduce the heat and simmer for 20 minutes. Strain the stock into the reserved mussel cooking liquid and reheat briefly. Taste and season with salt and pepper if necessary. Put the prawns and shelled mussels into a tureen. Beat the egg with the crème fraîche in a bowl and add to the tureen. Pour in the piping hot soup, stirring constantly, and serve immediately.

MARINE SOUP

CRÈME MARINE

- ◆ **1 kg (2¼ lb) live mussels, scrubbed**
- ◆ **12 oysters**
- ◆ **Juice of 1 lemon**
- ◆ **Pepper**
- ◆ **125 g (4¼ oz) mushrooms, cut into thin strips**
- ◆ **1 sprig of thyme**
- ◆ **1 bay leaf**
- ◆ **2 egg yolks**

Preparation time: 45 minutes
Cooking time: 20 minutes
Serves 6

Cook the mussels (p.271) and drain, reserving the cooking liquid. Discard any mussels that remain closed and remove the remainder from their shells. Strain the cooking liquid through a chinois (conical sieve) or muslin-lined strainer into a measuring jug and set aside. Shuck the oysters: wrap one hand in a tea towel to protect it and hold the oyster, flat shell uppermost. Insert an oyster knife into the hinged edge and twist to prise the shells apart. Slide the blade of the knife along the inside of the upper shell to sever the ligament. Carefully lift off the upper shell without spilling the oyster juices. Slide the blade of the knife underneath the oyster to sever the second ligament.

Leave the opened oysters on their half shells until all the oysters have been shucked. Tip the oyster juices into a pan, add the lemon juice, season with pepper and bring to the boil. Add the oysters and cook for 3 minutes, then drain, reserving the cooking liquid. Mix with the reserved mussel cooking liquid, measure and make up to 1.5 litres (2½ pints) with water. Pour the liquid into a pan, add the mushrooms, thyme and bay leaf and cook for 15 minutes, then remove and discard the herbs. Pour the soup into a tureen and whisk in the egg yolks. Add the mussels and oysters and serve.

FISHERMAN'S SOUP

POTAGE DU PÊCHEUR

Heat the oil in a large pan. Add the leek, onion and garlic and cook over a low heat, stirring occasionally, for 5 minutes. Increase the heat, add the tomatoes, herbs and hot water and bring to the boil. Reduce the heat, cover and simmer for 20 minutes. Increase the heat to high, plunge the crabs into the pan and boil for 30 minutes. Season with salt and pepper, remove the pan from the heat and strain the cooking liquid into a clean pan. Reserve the crabs and discard the flavourings. Mix the rice flour to a paste with 4 tablespoons water in a bowl. Return the cooking liquid to the heat, stir in the rice flour paste and simmer, stirring frequently, for 10 minutes. Shell the crabs and cut the flesh into small pieces. Add the crab meat to the soup and stir in the crème fraîche. Serve immediately.

- 3 tablespoons olive oil
- 60 g (2 oz) leek, finely chopped
- 50 g (1¾ oz) onion, finely chopped
- 1 garlic clove, finely chopped
- 125 g (4¼ oz) tomatoes,
  cut into pieces
- 1 sprig of thyme
- 1 bay leaf
- 1.5 litres (2½ pints) hot water
- 10 live velvet or other small crabs
- Salt and pepper
- 40 g (1½ oz) rice flour
- 5 tablespoons crème fraîche

Preparation time: 25 minutes
Cooking time: 1 hour
Serves 6

FISHERMAN'S BROTH

NAGE DES PÊCHEURS

- 1 kg (2¼ lb) live mussels, scrubbed
- 1 kg (2¼ lb) live shellfish, such as clams, cockles or razor shells
- 50 g (1¾ oz) butter
- 30 g (1¼ oz) onion, cut into julienne strips
- 100 g (3½ oz) carrots, cut into julienne strips
- 100 g (3½ oz) leek, cut into julienne strips
- 20 g (¾ oz) fresh root ginger, cut into julienne strips
- 100 ml (3½ fl oz) dry white wine
- Juice of 3 oranges
- 2 litres (3½ pints) fish stock
- 1 bouquet garni

Preparation time: 25 minutes
Cooking time: 1 hour
Serves 6

Cook the mussels and other shellfish (p.271) and drain, reserving the cooking liquid. Discard any mussels that remain closed and remove the remainder from their shells. Strain the cooking liquid through a chinois (conical sieve) or muslin-lined strainer into a bowl and set aside. Melt the butter in a large pan. Add the onion, carrots, leek and ginger, cover and cook over a low heat, stirring occasionally, for 20 minutes. Pour in the wine and cook, stirring and scraping up any sediment from the base of the pan, for a few minutes. Pour in the orange juice, stock and reserved cooking juices and add the bouquet garni. Bring to the boil, then reduce the heat, cover and simmer for 30–40 minutes. Just before serving, add the mussels and other shellfish to the pan and reheat gently. Remove the bouquet garni and serve.

FISH SOUP

SOUPE DE POISSONS

- Fish heads from white fish, such as whiting, sea bream or red mullet (serve the rest as the main course)
- 60 g (2 oz) onion
- 1 teaspoon chopped garlic
- 30 g (1¼ oz) butter
- 40 g (1½ oz) flour
- 500 ml (18 fl oz) milk
- 200 ml (7 fl oz) crème fraîche
- 6 slices of bread
- 1 garlic clove, halved
- Salt and pepper

Preparation time: 25 minutes
Cooking time: 40 minutes
Serves 6

Cut out and discard the gills from the fish heads. Put the heads in a large pan, add the onion, chopped garlic and 1 litre (1¾ pints) water. Bring to the boil, then reduce the heat, cover and simmer for 20 minutes, then drain, pressing the fish heads to extract as much flavour as possible, and reserving the stock. Melt the butter in another pan. Stir in the flour and cook over a low heat, stirring constantly, for 1–2 minutes, but do not allow the flour to brown. Gradually stir in the reserved stock and then the milk and bring to the boil, stirring constantly. Season with salt and pepper and simmer, stirring frequently, for 20 minutes. Toast each slice of bread on one side, then rub the untoasted side with the cut side of a garlic half, and toast. Put the garlic toasts into 6 serving dishes. Stir the crème fraîche into the soup and pour the soup over the garlic toasts. Serve immediately.

NOTE

If desired, omit the garlic toasts and poach 12 shucked oysters in boiling water for 2 minutes, then add them to the soup just before serving.

PANADE

PANADE

Put the bread in a large pan and pour in 2 litres (3½ pints) water. Bring to the boil, then reduce the heat and simmer gently for 1 hour. Remove from the heat and mash the bread until very smooth. Stir in the salt and milk or cream. (You may not need all the liquid, depending on the type of bread and how dry it is.) Serve hot.

* **250 g (9 oz) day-old bread, torn into pieces**
* **20 g (¾ oz) salt**
* **100 ml (3½ fl oz) milk or double cream**

Preparation time: 5 minutes
Cooking time: 1¼ hours
Serves 6

MONACO SOUP

POTAGE À LA MONACO

Cut the bread into 18 squares, measuring 3 cm x 3 cm (1¼ x 1¼ inches). Melt a knob of butter in a pan and fry the squares until golden on both sides. Sprinkle them with a little of the sugar on both sides and place in a tureen. Pour the milk into a pan, stir in the remaining sugar and bring just to the boil. Pour the milk over the toasts. Whisk in the egg yolks and serve.

VARIATION

* **Butter, for frying**
* **6 slices white bread, crusts removed**
* **100 g (3½ oz) caster sugar**
* **1 litre (1¾ pints) milk**
* **2 egg yolks**

Preparation time: 15 minutes
Cooking time: 10 minutes
Serves 6

. . . .

MILK SOUP

SOUPE AU LAIT

Spread 18 slices bread (crusts removed) with 100 g (3½ oz) butter. Toast, then put the slices in a tureen. Pour 1.5 litres (2½ pints) milk into a pan, season with salt and bring just to the boil. Pour the milk over the toasts and serve immediately.

Pistou soup (p.181)

Bonne femme soup (p.184)

Julienne soup   (p.192)

Onion soup gratin   (p.191)

Aurore soup   (p.194)

Petite marmite   (p.204)

Lobster bisque (p.205)

FISH

FISH

Fish has an important role to play in home cooking, as it is rich in protein and minerals and leaner than meat. Do not be deterred if you are unsure how to prepare it; the fishmonger can usually scale, clean and fillet the fish before you buy. Although fish has become scarce and expensive, there are still many species, such as mackerel and gurnard, which are very affordable.

PREPARATION

FRESHNESS
To check if a fish is fresh, look for bright, light-coloured eyes and undamaged fins, a firm belly, shiny skin and red gills. When fish is not fresh the eyes are hollow, the fins damaged, the belly sunken and blotchy; the flesh is no longer firm and retains an imprint when pressed.

SCALING
Hold the fish by the tail and scrape from the tail to the head with a flat knife or a fish-scaler. This is best done in cold running water or in a bag to catch the scales.

SKINNING
For sole and eel, make a slit and cut the skin just above the tail. Take hold of the skin using a cloth and pull hard from top to bottom. For other fish it is better to skin after filleting.

CLEANING
Insert your index finger into the gill-slit and pull out the innards and the gills. With large fish, make a slit in the belly and pull out all the insides. Rinse the fish in cold water.

TRIMMING
Cut off the fins with kitchen scissors.

SCORING
Make diagonal cuts on the back of the fish, 2 mm (⅛ inch) deep and evenly spaced.

FILLETING

For flat fish, cut off the fins all round the fish with kitchen scissors. Make a cut down the middle from the tail to the head to detach the flesh from the bones. Slide the blade of a filleting knife (or other knife with a thin, flexible blade) between the fillet and the bones. Remove all 4 fillets. For round fish, make a cut along the backbone of the fish from the head to the tail. Cut off the head and immediately remove the fillets with a filleting knife.

COOKING METHODS

POACHING IN WATER OR A COURT-BOUILLON

Choose the appropriate court-bouillon (p.82) and heat in a large pan or fish kettle, ideally one with a removable rack. Plunge the cleaned and prepared fish into the pan. Bring to the boil, then reduce the heat so that the water barely bubbles. If it is fresh, fish cooked in a court-bouillon should not give off any smell in the kitchen.

Cooking times are counted from the moment the liquid starts to simmer. For large fish, allow 10 minutes per 500 g (1 lb 2 oz); for flat fish or fillets, 8 minutes per 500 g (1 lb 2 oz); for small fish weighing 200 g (7 oz), 12 minutes in total. Fish that is to be served cold, such as poached salmon, should be left to cool in the court-bouillon.

DEEP-FRYING

Pat the fish dry with kitchen paper, roll it in flour to coat it completely and cook in oil in a deep-fryer preheated to 180–190°C/350–375°F, or until a cube of bread browns in 30 seconds. To deep-fry tiny fish, do not gut them first. Pat dry, roll in flour and fry for 5 minutes. To deep-fry a large fish, clean it and score the skin. Pat dry, roll in flour and deep-fry for 10 minutes. Large fish may be cooked in two stages: first deep-fry for 6 minutes. Remove the fish and increase the temperature to 190°C/375°F. Return the fish to the deep-fryer and cook until lightly browned. Season with salt and serve garnished with parsley and slices of lemon.

GRILLING

Grilling is best for flat fish. Preheat the grill. Pat the fish dry with kitchen paper, brush with oil and put on the grill rack. Cook for 15 minutes per 500 g (1 lb 2 oz), turning once. Season with salt and serve with melted butter, maître d'hôtel butter (p.48) or béarnaise sauce (p.75).

ROASTING

Preheat the oven to 220°C/425°F/Gas Mark 7. Cook in the same way as roast meat, basting with the juices given off during cooking, for 15 minutes per 500 g (1 lb 2 oz). Season with salt and serve with maître d'hôtel butter (p.48).

SHALLOW-FRYING

Shallow-frying is suitable for fish weighing 120–200 g (4–7 oz). Clean the fish and pat dry, dip it in milk, then roll in flour. Melt enough butter to coat the bottom of a frying pan. Add the fish and cook until browned on one side. Turn, season the browned side with salt and cook the other side. Season again with salt and pepper.

SAUCES

HOT

Anchovy (p.55); béarnaise (p.75); beurre blanc (p.49); maître d'hôtel butter (p.48); black butter (p.48); ravigote butter (p.48); caper (p.56); scallop coulis (p.89); prawn (p.55); Genevoise (p.64); hollandaise (p.74); Joinville (p.56); hot mayonnaise (p.70); matelote (p.64); cheese (p.51); mussel (p.55); mousse-line (p.75); Nantua (p.52); tomato (p.57).

COLD

Ravigote butter (p.48); aioli (p.74); devilled (p.76); gribiche (p.69); mayonnaise (p.70); mustard (p.68); ravigote (p.56); rémoulade (p.68); vinaigrette (p.66).

PRESENTATION

LARGE POACHED FISH

Serve on a very long dish or on a board covered with a white napkin. To serve, skin the fish and cut the fillets diagonally into portions. Garnish with flat-leaf parsley, anchovies, capers, sliced tomatoes, hard-boiled eggs or lemon. Serve with a sauce in a sauce boat.

FISH IN ASPIC

Serve on a large dish garnished with chopped jelly and tarragon.

GRILLED OR ROAST FISH

Serve on a dish garnished with lemon slices or quarters, with a sauce in a sauce boat.

DEEP-FRIED

Serve on a dish lined with a warm napkin, garnished with lemon slices or quarters.

FISH MEUNIÈRE

Serve on a dish, coated with the sauce in which it was cooked, garnished with lemon slices or quarters.

FRESHWATER FISH

Freshwater fish provide a good (and sometimes more sustainable) alternative to sea fish, and they are becoming increasingly popular. If the fish specified in the recipe is unavailable, ask your fishmonger to suggest alternatives.

SHAD

Shad can be cooked in a court-bouillon with salt (p.82) and served hot with hollandaise sauce (p.74) or prawn sauce (p.55). It can also be grilled (p.221) and served with braised sorrel (p.562).

STUFFED SHAD

ALOSE FARCIE

- 1 quantity stuffing for fish (p.80)
- 1 kg (2¼ lb) shad, scaled and cleaned
- 1 quantity court-bouillon with salt (p.82)
- 1 quantity marinière sauce (p.58)

Preparation time: 15 minutes
Cooking time: 20 minutes
Serves 6

Make the stuffing. Stuff the shad and secure the opening with trussing thread, then wrap the fish in a piece of muslin. Cook in the court-bouillon for 10 minutes per 500 g (1 lb 2 oz) and serve with the marinière sauce.

SHAD À LA PORTUGAISE

ALOSE À LA PORTUGAISE

Preheat the oven to 200°C/400°F/Gas Mark 6. Spread out half the tomatoes in the base of a flameproof dish. Sprinkle with the parsley and half the onions and lay the shad on top. Cover with the remaining tomatoes, remaining onions and the mushrooms. Pour in the wine, dot with the butter and season with salt and pepper. Cook over a low heat for 10 minutes, then transfer to the oven and bake for 30 minutes.

- 750 g (1 lb 10 oz) tomatoes, cut into wedges
- 2 tablespoons chopped flat-leaf parsley
- 125 g (4¼ oz) onions, chopped
- 1 kg (2¼ lb) shad, scaled and cleaned
- 125 g (4¼ oz) mushrooms, coarsely chopped
- 100 ml (3½ fl oz) white wine
- 60 g (2 oz) butter
- Salt and pepper

Preparation time: 20 minutes
Cooking time: 40 minutes
Serves 6

SHAD À LA CHARTREUSE

ALOSE À LA CHARTREUSE

Put the carrots, lettuce, tomatoes, sorrel and onions into a heavy-based pan, pour in 100 ml (3½ fl oz) water, season with salt and pepper and mix well. Cover and simmer over a low heat for 30 minutes until almost reduced to a purée. Put the shad on top of the vegetables, cover with the slices of ham and add the bay leaf. Pour in the wine, cover and cook for a further 30 minutes. Remove and discard the bay leaf before serving.

- 250 g (9 oz) carrots, chopped
- 1 lettuce, shredded
- 500 g (1 lb 2 oz) tomatoes, skinned, de-seeded and chopped
- 250 g (9 oz) sorrel, chopped
- 200 g (7 oz) onions, chopped
- Salt and pepper
- 1 kg (2¼ lb) shad, scaled and cleaned
- 4–5 thin slices cured ham
- 1 bay leaf
- 100 ml (3½ fl oz) white wine

Preparation time: 45 minutes
Cooking time: 1 hour
Serves 6

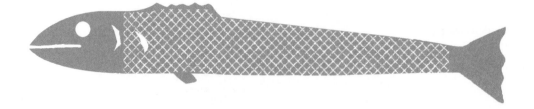

SHAD MONTAGNARDE

ALOSE MONTAGNARDE

- 500 ml (18 fl oz) white wine
- 600 g (1 lb 5 oz) shad
- 125 g (4¼ oz) mushrooms
- 10–12 button onions or shallots, diced
- 3 artichoke hearts, diced
- 75 g (2½ oz) butter
- Salt and pepper
- 1 lemon, sliced, to garnish

Preparation time: 25 minutes
Cooking time: 1¾ hours
Serves 6

Prepare a court-bouillon using the wine (p.82). Clean, trim and scale the shad and cut into thick slices. Clean the mushrooms and cut them into into dice. Melt the butter in a heavy-based pan and fry the fish and vegetables. Strain the court-bouillon. When the fish and vegetables are golden brown, add the strained court-bouillon. Simmer over a very low heat for 45 minutes. Check the seasoning and add salt and pepper if necessary. Place on a warmed serving dish and garnish with the slices of lemon.

EEL

Conger eel is purplish-grey on the back. For preference, choose a large specimen; the small ones contain too many bones. Eel can be cooked in a court-bouillon with salt (p.82), following the instructions on p.221, and served with a sauce of your choice.

For roast eel, skin the eel and follow the instructions on p.222. Serve with marinière sauce (p.58), poulette sauce (p.52) or tartare sauce (p.72).

For grilled eel, skin the eel and follow the instructions on p.221. Serve with braised sorrel (p.562). For fried eel, skin the eel and follow the instructions on p.222. Serve with tomato sauce (p.57).

EEL MATELOTE

ANGUILLE À LA MATELOTE

 p.293

Melt half the butter in a large pan. Add the onion and bacon and cook over a low heat, stirring occasionally, for 10–15 minutes until golden brown, then remove with a slotted spoon and set aside. Stir the flour into the pan and cook, stirring constantly, for a few minutes until browned, then gradually stir in the stock and wine. Return the onion and bacon to the pan, add the mushrooms and bouquet garni and season with salt and pepper, then cover and simmer for 30 minutes. Add the eel, cover the pan and simmer gently for 45 minutes.

Melt the remaining butter in a frying pan, add the bread and fry on both sides until golden brown. Place the fried bread on a serving dish. Carefully lift the eel out of the pan with a fish slice and place on top of the fried bread. Remove and discard the bouquet garni and ladle the sauce over the fish. Serve immediately.

- 60 g (2 oz) butter
- 60 g (2 oz) onion, chopped
- 125 g (4¼ oz) streaky bacon, diced
- 40 g (1½ oz) flour
- 100 ml (3½ fl oz) any stock, hot
- 100 ml (3½ fl oz) red wine
- 125 g (4¼ oz) mushrooms, sliced
- 1 bouquet garni
- Salt and pepper
- 1 kg (2¼ lb) eel, skinned and sliced
- 6 slices white bread, crusts removed

Preparation time: 40 minutes
Cooking time: 1½ hours
Serves 6

EEL IN ASPIC

ASPIC D'ANGUILLE

Put a sprig of tarragon and a slice of tomato in the base of each of 6 small terrines. Cut the eel into 6 pieces and add a piece of eel to each terrine. Cover with a slice of egg. Prepare the aspic and use it to fill each terrine, then season with salt and pepper. Leave in the refrigerator to set for 12 hours. Turn out to serve.

- 6 sprigs of tarragon
- 150 g (5 oz) tomatoes, sliced
- 300 g (11 oz) cooked eel
- 1 hard-boiled egg, sliced
- 1 sachet instant aspic jelly or 1 quantity aspic (p.45)
- Salt and pepper

Preparation time: 20 minutes, plus setting time
Serves 6

EEL IN WHITE WINE

ANGUILLE AU VIN BLANC

- 100 g (3½ oz) butter
- 125 g (4¼ oz) button onions or shallots
- 1 kg (2¼ lb) eel, skinned and cut into pieces
- 5 garlic cloves
- 1 bouquet garni
- Salt and pepper
- 500 ml (18 fl oz) white wine
- 50 g (1¾ oz) flour

Preparation time: 20 minutes
Cooking time: 30 minutes
Serves 6

Melt 20 g (¾ oz) of the butter in a large pan. Add the onions or shallots and cook over a low heat, stirring occasionally, for 10 minutes, until browned. Add the eel, garlic and bouquet garni, season with salt and pepper, pour in the wine and bring to the boil. Reduce the heat, cover and simmer for 30 minutes.

Meanwhile, mix the flour with the remaining butter to a paste in a bowl. Remove the pieces of eel with a slotted spoon and put them on a serving dish. Strain the cooking juices into a clean pan and bring to the boil. Stir in small pieces of the flour and butter paste, only adding the next piece when the previous one has been fully incorporated. Ladle the sauce into a sauce boat and serve with the fish.

MEURETTE

MEURETTE

- 250 g (9 oz) eel
- 250 g (9 oz) carp
- 250 g (9 oz) pike
- 1 bottle of aged red Burgundy
- 1 onion, chopped
- 1 garlic clove, crushed
- 1 bouquet garni
- 100 g (3½ oz) butter
- Salt and pepper
- 100 ml (3½ fl oz) brandy
- 30 g (1¼ oz) flour

Preparation time: 15 minutes
Cooking time: 30 minutes
Serves 6

Scale and clean the eel and fish and cut into slices. Bring the wine to the boil in a large pan. Add the fish and the onion, garlic, bouquet garni and half the butter. Season with salt and pepper. After 10 minutes, pour in the brandy and boil for 1–2 minutes to evaporate the alcohol. Reduce the heat and simmer gently for 15 minutes. Work the remaining butter into the flour to make a smooth paste. Stir small knobs of the paste into the fish stew and cook for a further 5 minutes, until thickened. Remove and discard the bouquet garni. Serve the dish with more of the same Burgundy wine.

NOTE

Pauchouse is a fish stew similar to *meurette*. To make it, proceed as above, replacing the red wine with white. Once cooked, thicken the liquid with 150 ml (¼ pint) crème fraîche, 100 g (3½ oz) butter and 2 egg yolks.

BARBEL & FRESHWATER BREAM

Barbel and bream can be cooked in a court-bouillon with salt (p.82), following the instructions on p.221, and served with a jardinière of vegetables (p.555).

STUFFED BARBEL

BARBEAU FARCI

 p.294

Preheat the oven to 190°C/375°F/Gas Mark 5. Prepare the stuffing and spoon it into the cavity of the barbel. Put half the onion into the base of an ovenproof dish, lay the fish on top and cover with the remaining onion. Season with salt and pepper, sprinkle with the breadcrumbs, dot with the butter and pour in the wine. Bake for 30 minutes. Using a fish slice, transfer the fish to a serving dish. Bring the cooking juices to the boil and boil until reduced. Strain, pour over the fish and serve.

- **1 quantity stuffing for fish (p.80)**
- **1 x 1-kg (2¼-lb) barbel or bream, scaled and cleaned**
- **100 g (3½ oz) onions, chopped**
- **Salt and pepper**
- **4 tablespoons dried breadcrumbs**
- **30 g (1¼ oz) butter**
- **200 ml (7 fl oz) white wine**

Preparation time: 20 minutes
Cooking time: 30 minutes
Serves 6

PIKE

Pike can be cooked in a court-bouillon with salt (p.82), following the instructions on p.221, and served with hollandaise sauce (p.74), béchamel sauce (p.50) or green mayonnaise (p.70). Remove and discard any roe (eggs) before poaching.

For roast pike, preheat the oven to 220°C/425°F/Gas Mark 7. Cut the pike into slices and thread on skewers, alternating with strips of bacon. Roast in the oven for 15 minutes per 500 g (1 lb 2 oz). Serve with lemon, capers and black olives.

ROAST PIKE WITH ORANGE

BROCHET RÔTI À L'ORANGE

- 1 bunch of flat-leaf parsley, chopped, plus extra sprigs to garnish
- ½ bunch of thyme, chopped
- 2 bay leaves
- 1 small shallot, chopped
- 1 tablespoon chopped chives
- 2 garlic cloves, sliced
- 6 cloves
- 1 x 1.5-kg (3¼-lb) pike, scaled and cleaned
- 100 ml (3½ fl oz) oil
- Salt and pepper
- 200 ml (7 fl oz) white wine
- Juice of 1 orange
- Orange slices, to garnish

Preparation time: 20 minutes, plus marinating time
Cooking time: 30 minutes
Serves 6

Start the day before. Mix together the parsley, thyme, bay leaves, shallot, chives and garlic in the base of a long, deep dish. Stick the cloves into the pike and place it on top. Pour the oil over it, season with salt and pepper and leave to marinate in the refrigerator, turning the fish 2–3 times, for 24 hours. The next day, drain the fish and discard the marinade. Put the fish into an ovenproof dish. Preheat the oven to 220°C/425°F/Gas Mark 7. Pour the wine and orange juice over the fish and roast for 30 minutes. Using a fish slice, transfer the fish to a serving dish and garnish with parsley sprigs and orange slices. Pour the cooking juices into a sauce boat. Serve immediately, handing the sauce separately.

PIKE AU BLEU

BROCHET AU BLEU

- 1 litre (1¾ pints) white wine vinegar
- 1 pike, scaled and cleaned
- 1 quantity court-bouillon with red wine or vinegar (p.82)
- Oil, for brushing (optional)
- Maître d'hôtel butter (p.48) or tartare sauce (p.72), to serve

Preparation time: 15 minutes
Cooking time: About 30 minutes
Serves 6

Pour the vinegar into a wide pan and bring to the boil. Add the pike and cook for 5 minutes. Heat the court-bouillon in another pan or fish kettle and carefully transfer the fish to it. Bring to a simmer and poach for 15 minutes per 500 g (1 lb 2 oz). Remove the fish from the pan and serve hot with maître d'hôtel butter. Alternatively, leave to cool, brush with oil to glaze and serve with tartare sauce.

NOTE
Carp can be cooked in the same way.

PIKE WITH CRÈME FRAÎCHE

BROCHET À LA CRÈME

Preheat the oven to 220°C/425°F/Gas Mark 7. Beat 60 g (2 oz) of the butter with the parsley until thoroughly combined, then stuff the cavity of the pike with this mixture. Put it into an ovenproof dish, dot with the remaining butter, season with salt and pepper and bake for 10 minutes. Pour 3 tablespoons of the crème fraîche over the fish and return to the oven for a further 5 minutes. Repeat every 5 minutes until the fish is cooked. Sprinkle it with the breadcrumbs and extra chopped parsley after the final addition of crème fraîche.

- 80 g (2¾ oz) butter
- 3 tablespoons finely chopped flat-leaf parsley, plus extra to garnish
- 1 x 1-kg (2¼-lb) pike, scaled and cleaned
- Salt and pepper
- 180 ml (6¼ fl oz) crème fraîche
- 4 tablespoons dried breadcrumbs

Preparation time: 15 minutes
Cooking time: 30 minutes
Serves 6

SMALL PIKE IN WHITE WINE

BROCHETONS AU VIN BLANC

Preheat the oven to 190°C/375°F/Gas Mark 5 and grease a gratin dish with 30 g (1¼ oz) of the butter. Put the pike into the prepared dish and cover with the onion. Pour in the wine, season with salt and pepper, add the thyme and bay leaf and bake for 15–20 minutes, or until cooked. Transfer the fish to a serving dish and keep warm. Strain the cooking juices into a pan and set over a low heat. Mix together the egg yolk and lemon juice in a bowl, stir in 1 tablespoon of the cooking juices, then stir the mixture into the pan. Gradually stir in the remaining butter. Pour the sauce over the fish and serve immediately.

- 90 g (3¼ oz) butter
- 2 small pike, scaled and cleaned
- 60 g (2 oz) onion, sliced
- 100 ml (3½ fl oz) white wine
- Salt and pepper
- 1 sprig of thyme
- 1 bay leaf
- 1 egg yolk
- Juice of 1 lemon

Preparation time: 30 minutes
Cooking time: 30 minutes
Serves 6

PIKE WITH BEURRE BLANC
BROCHET AU BEURRE BLANC

- **1 pike, around 1 kg (2¼ lb),
  scaled and cleaned**
- **1 quantity court-bouillon
  with vinegar (p.82)**
- **60 g (2 oz) shallots**
- **100 ml (3½ fl oz) Muscadet
  wine**
- **150 g (5 oz) butter, diced**
- **Salt and pepper**

Preparation time: 20 minutes
Cooking time: 35 minutes
Serves 6

Place the pike in a fish kettle or large pan and cover with the court-bouillon. Bring to the boil, reduce the heat and simmer very gently for 25 minutes. Chop the shallots finely and place in a small pan with the wine. Simmer for 20–25 minutes, or until the liquid has reduced by three-quarters. Gradually whisk in the butter and season with salt and pepper. The reduction should emulsify with the butter, and turn creamy and white. Serve immediately in a sauce boat with the fish.

CARP

Carp can be cooked in a court-bouillon with salt (p.82), following the instructions on p.221, and served with a hot or cold sauce (p.222). It can also be cooked *au bleu* (p.229).

For fried carp, deep-fry following the instructions on p.221 and serve with piquant sauce (p.60) or caper sauce (p.56). Tench can be prepared in the same ways as carp.

CARP CUTLETS
CÔTELETTES DE CARPES

- **1 x 1-kg (2¼-lb) carp,
  scaled and cleaned**
- **Salt and pepper**
- **Flour, for rolling**
- **85 g (3 oz) butter**
- **1 quantity Madeira sauce,
  mushroom sauce or
  Périgueux sauce (p.61)**

Preparation time: 20 minutes
Cooking time: 15 minutes
Serves 6

Separate the carp into fillets. Season with salt and pepper and roll in flour. Melt the butter in a frying pan, add the fish and cook over a medium heat, turning once, until golden brown. Serve with the chosen sauce.

CARP IN ASPIC

CARPE EN GELÉE

Prepare the day before. Cut the carp into slices, reserving the head and tail. Put the slices into a pan of warm court-bouillon and poach for 30 minutes. Lift out the fish with a fish slice and remove the skin. Arrange the slices of fish on a deep serving dish to reassemble the fish. Bring the court-bouillon to the boil, add the reserved head and tail and the basil and cook until the liquid is reduced by half. Dissolve the gelatine in 2 tablespoons hot water and add to the liquid. Clarify the liquid (p.45), strain it into a jug and pour it over the carp. Chill in the refrigerator overnight, or until set.

- 1 x 1-kg (2¼-lb) carp, scaled and cleaned
- 1 quantity court-bouillon with white wine (p.82)
- 1–2 sprigs of basil
- 10 g (¼ oz) powdered gelatine

Preparation time: 20 minutes, plus setting time
Cooking time: 30 minutes
Serves 6

STUFFED CARP

CARPE FARCIE

Put the carp into a dish, pour in the oil, add the thyme, bay leaf and parsley, season with salt and pepper and turn to coat. Leave to marinate for 45 minutes. Preheat the oven to 190°C/375°F/ Gas Mark 5. Drain the fish, reserving the marinade, spoon the stuffing into the cavity and put the fish into an ovenproof dish. Pour the marinade over it and bake for 45 minutes.

- 1 x 1-kg (2¼-lb) carp, scaled and cleaned
- 250 ml (8 fl oz) oil
- 1 sprig of thyme, chopped
- 1 bay leaf
- 1 sprig of flat-leaf parsley, chopped
- Salt and pepper
- 250 g (9 oz) stuffing for fish (p.80)

Preparation time: 10 minutes, plus marinating time
Cooking time: 45 minutes
Serves 6

STURGEON

The meat of cooked sturgeon is very similar to veal and can be prepared in the same ways. Sturgeon steaks can be fried and served in the same way as cod steaks (p.243).

BRAISED STURGEON
ESTURGEON BRAISÉ

- 1 kg (2¼ lb) sturgeon
- 80 g (2¾ oz) butter
- 60 g (2 oz) onion, chopped
- 1 carrot, sliced
- 200 ml (7 fl oz) white wine
- Salt and pepper
- 1 quantity peas à la française (p.564), to serve

Preparation time: 10 minutes
Cooking time: 40 minutes
Serves 6

Truss the sturgeon with kitchen string, like a roast, and set aside. Melt the butter in a large pan. Add the onion and cook over a low heat, stirring occasionally, for 5 minutes, until softened. Add the fish and carrot, pour in the wine and season with salt and pepper. Cover and cook over a low heat for 30–40 minutes. Transfer the fish and sauce to a serving dish, remove and discard the trussing string, and serve with the peas.

LAKE TROUT

LAKE TROUT WITH CRÈME FRAÎCHE
LAVARET À LA CRÈME

- 800 g (1¾ lb) lake trout fillets
- 30 g (1¼ oz) flour
- Salt and pepper
- 30 g (1¼ oz) butter
- 50 ml (2 fl oz) dry white wine
- 30 g (1¼ oz) shallot, finely chopped
- 100 g (3½ oz) mushrooms, chopped
- 150 ml (¼ pint) crème fraîche
- Chopped flat-leaf parsley, to garnish (optional)

Preparation time: 25 minutes
Cooking time: 10 minutes
Serves 6

Cut the fillets into 100-g (3½-oz) pieces, coat with the flour and season with salt and pepper. Melt the butter in a frying pan, add the fish and cook over a low heat, turning once, until lightly browned. Pour in the wine, sprinkle with the shallot and mushrooms and spoon the crème fraîche on top. Simmer for 10 minutes. Transfer the fish to a serving dish. Bring the sauce to the boil and spoon it over the fish. Garnish with chopped parsley, if desired, and serve.

PERCH

Perch can be deep-fried following the instructions on p.221. Take care when preparing perch: their bones can be very sharp.

PERCH MEUNIÈRE

PERCHE À LA MEUNIÈRE

Season the perch with salt and pepper, dip it in the milk, then roll in the flour. Melt 50 g (1¾ oz) of the butter in a frying pan. Add the fish and cook over a high heat, turning once, for 15 minutes, or until browned. Transfer the fish to a serving dish and sprinkle with the parsley. Heat the remaining butter in a pan until it is nut-brown, stir it into the frying pan and then pour over the fish. Serve immediately.

- 1 x 1.2-kg (2½-lb) perch, scaled and cleaned
- Salt and pepper
- 120 ml (4 fl oz) milk
- 40 g (1½ oz) flour
- 80 g (2¾ oz) butter
- 2 tablespoons chopped flat-leaf parsley

Preparation time: 15 minutes
Cooking time: 15 minutes
Serves 6

PIKE-PERCH WITH VINAIGRETTE DRESSING

SANDRE À LA VINAIGRETTE

Bring a pan of salted water to the boil, add the onions and cook for 10–15 minutes. Add the broccoli and cook for 5 minutes, then drain. Preheat the grill and brush a flameproof dish with oil. Cut the pike-perch into strips, put them into the prepared dish, brush with oil and season with salt and pepper. Grill for 6–10 minutes.

Meanwhile, put the onions, broccoli and prawns into a pan and heat gently. Pour the vinegar into a small pan and heat gently until warm. Pour into a bowl, add the oil, season with salt and pepper and whisk together. When the fish is cooked, transfer it to a serving dish. Garnish with the warm prawn mixture and the tomatoes. Pour the warm vinaigrette over it, sprinkle with the shallots and herbs, season lightly with salt and pepper and serve.

- 250 g (9 oz) button onions
- 100 g (3½ oz) broccoli
- 100 ml (3½ fl oz) oil, plus extra for brushing
- 1 x 1.2-kg (2½-lb) pike-perch (zander), scaled and filleted
- Salt and pepper
- 250 g (9 oz) peeled cooked prawns
- 50 ml (2 fl oz) sherry vinegar
- 250 g (9 oz) cherry tomatoes, skinned
- 50 g (1¾ oz) shallot, finely chopped
- 50 g (1¾ oz) mixed chopped chives and chervil

Preparation time: 45 minutes
Cooking time: 15 minutes
Serves 6

SALMON

Fresh salmon is a large fish that is rarely served whole, and is usually sold in the form of steaks or slices. Salmon can be poached in salted water. Cut it into 2-cm (¾-inch) thick slices and poach for 12 minutes, or poach it whole for 10 minutes per 500g (1 lb 2 oz).

To poach in a court-bouillon with salt (p.82), follow the instructions on p.221. Serve with hollandaise sauce (p.74), mussel sauce (p.55), caper sauce (p.56), maître d'hôtel butter (p.48), mayonnaise (p.70), prawn sauce (p.55) or béarnaise sauce (p.75). Serve hot with boiled potatoes, or cold with a garnish of anchovies and parsley. In both cases, remove and discard the skin and brush the fish with oil to make it glossy.

To grill salmon, follow the instructions on p.221. Serve with hollandaise sauce (p.74), béarnaise sauce (p.75), ravigote sauce (p.56) or tartare sauce (p.72).

GALANTINE OF SALMON

GALANTINE DE SAUMON

 p.295

Put the breadcrumbs into a bowl, pour in the milk and leave to soak. Meanwhile, cut the salmon in half along the backbone and remove and discard the central bone. Put the fish on a piece of muslin and stud each side of each piece with the anchovies, mushrooms and gherkins. To make the stuffing, put the whiting, soaked breadcrumbs and herbs in a food processor or blender and process until smooth, then season with salt and pepper. Sandwich the salmon halves together with the mixture, tie with string and wrap securely in the muslin. Put the parcel into a pan of warm court-bouillon and simmer for 30–35 minutes. Remove from the heat leave to cool in the court-bouillon. Refrigerate and serve cold the next day.

* 100 g (3½ oz) fresh breadcrumbs
* 4 tablespoons milk
* 500 g (1 lb 2 oz) salmon in 1 piece
* 6 canned anchovy fillets, drained and chopped
* 100 g (3½ oz) mushrooms, peeled and chopped
* 50 g (1¾ oz) pickled gherkins, chopped
* 100 g (3½ oz) cooked whiting
* 2 tablespoons mixed herbs, such as dill, flat-leaf parsley, chervil and chives
* Salt and pepper
* 1 quantity warm court-bouillon with white wine (p.82)

Preparation time: 25 minutes, plus cooling time
Cooking time: 35 minutes
Serves 6

SALMON MARINATED IN DILL

SAUMON MARINÉ À L'ANETH

- 1.2 kg (2½ lb) salmon
  or salmon-trout fillet
- 400 g (14 oz) caster sugar
- 300 g (11 oz) coarse salt
- 30 g (1¼ oz) coarsely ground
  pepper
- 1 small bunch of dill, chopped
- 500 g (1 lb 2 oz) potatoes
- 3 tablespoons Dijon mustard
- 6 tablespoons mayonnaise
  (p.70)
- 6 slices white bread, crusts
  removed, toasted
- 100 ml (3½ fl oz) vinaigrette
  (p.66)

Preparation time: 1 hour,
plus marinating time
Cooking time: 20 minutes
Serves 6

Prepare 3 days in advance. If using salmon trout, remove and discard the skin and backbone. Put the fish, skin side down if using salmon, in a deep dish. Mix together the sugar and salt in a bowl and sprinkle the mixture over the fish to cover it, then sprinkle with the pepper. Leave to marinate in the refrigerator for 48 hours. Two days later, remove the fish from the dish, rinse and pat dry. Put it on a serving dish, sprinkle with three-quarters of the dill and return to the refrigerator for 24 hours. The next day, boil the potatoes until tender, leave to cool and slice. Shortly before serving, stir the mustard and remaining dill into the mayonnaise. Serve the fish thinly sliced, with the toast, potatoes, the mayonnaise in a sauce boat and the vinaigrette.

SALMON IN SCALLOP SHELLS

SAUMON EN COQUILLE

- 500 g (1 lb 2 oz) cooked salmon
  fillet or drained canned salmon,
  skinned
- 400 ml (14 fl oz) white sauce
  (p.50)
- Salt and pepper
- 6 tablespoons dried
  breadcrumbs
- 50 g (1¾ oz) butter, melted

Preparation time: 20 minutes
Cooking time: 30 minutes
Serves 6

Preheat the oven to 220°C/425°F/Gas Mark 7. Flake the salmon and mix it with the sauce. Season with salt and pepper. Divide the mixture among 6 cleaned scallop shells, sprinkle with the breadcrumbs and pour the butter over the top. Put the shells on a baking tray and bake for 10 minutes, or until the topping is lightly browned.

SALMON LOAF

PAIN DE SAUMON

Boil the potatoes for 20–25 minutes or bake in the oven for 45–60 minutes, then drain, if necessary, peel and pass through a sieve into a bowl. Flake the fish and stir it into the potatoes with the herbs and butter. Season with salt and pepper and mix well. Grease a charlotte mould with butter and spoon in the mixture. Leave to stand in the refrigerator for 24 hours. To serve, plunge the base of the mould into hot water and turn out onto a serving dish. Cover with the mayonnaise and garnish with the hard-boiled eggs.

- 200 g (7 oz) potatoes, unpeeled
- 500 g (1 lb 2 oz) cooked salmon fillet or drained canned salmon, skinned
- 3 tablespoons chopped mixed herbs, such as parsley, chervil, tarragon and chives
- 60 g (2 oz) butter, plus extra for greasing
- Salt and pepper
- 1 quantity mayonnaise (p.70)
- 2 hard-boiled eggs, chopped, to garnish

Preparation time: 30 minutes, plus standing time
Cooking time: 20 minutes
Serves 6

TROUT

Trout can be cooked in a court-bouillon with salt (p.82), following the instructions on p.221. It can also be cooked *au bleu* (p.229), or fried following the instructions on p.222.

TROUT WITH ALMONDS

TRUITES AUX AMANDES

 p.296

Dip the trout first in the milk and then in the flour. Melt half the butter with the oil in a large frying pan. Cook the trout over a medium heat, turning once, for 10–15 minutes, until browned on both sides. Season with salt and pepper and drain off the fat. Melt the remaining butter in a small pan. Add the almonds and cook over a low heat, stirring frequently, for a few minutes until lightly browned. Transfer the trout to a dish, sprinkle with the almonds and garnish with slices or small wedges of lemon. Serve immediately.

- 6 trout, cleaned
- 100 ml (3½ fl oz) milk
- 60 g (2 oz) flour
- 50 g (1¾ oz) butter
- 50 ml (2 fl oz) oil
- Salt and pepper
- 100 g (3½ oz) flaked almonds
- Lemon slices or wedges, to garnish

Preparation time: 20 minutes
Cooking time: 10–15 minutes
Serves 6

TROUT GRATIN WITH CREAM

TRUITES GRATINÉES À LA CRÈME

- 60 g (2 oz) shallots, finely chopped
- 6 trout, cleaned
- Salt and pepper
- Juice of ½ lemon
- 200 ml (7 fl oz) dry white wine or equal quantities white wine and dry white vermouth
- 100 ml (3½ fl oz) fish stock (p.46)
- 250 ml (8 fl oz) hollandaise sauce (p.74)
- 4 tablespoons crème fraîche
- 1 pinch of cayenne pepper
- 30 g (1¼ oz) Gruyère cheese, grated

Preparation time: 40 minutes
Cooking time: 40 minutes
Serves 6

Preheat the oven to 190°C/375°F/Gas Mark 5. Make a bed of the shallots in a gratin dish, put the trout on top, season with salt and pepper and pour in the lemon juice and the wine or wine mixture. Cover and bake for 20 minutes. Transfer the trout to an ovenproof serving dish and keep warm. Increase the oven temperature to 250°C/500°F/Gas Mark 9.

To make the sauce, strain the cooking juices into a pan, bring to the boil and cook until reduced by half. Stir in the stock, hollandaise sauce and crème fraîche and cook over a low heat, stirring constantly, for a few minutes, but do not let the mixture boil. Stir in the cayenne pepper and pour the sauce over the fish. Sprinkle with the cheese and return to the oven for 3 minutes, or until lightly browned. Serve immediately.

TROUT À LA SUPRÊME

TRUITES À LA SUPRÊME

- 1 egg
- 4 tablespoons oil
- 6 small trout
- 80 g (2¾ oz) dried breadcrumbs
- Vegetable oil, for deep-frying
- 175 g (6 oz) anchovy butter (p.100)

Preparation time: 30 minutes
Cooking time: 30 minutes
Serves 6

Beat together the egg and oil in a shallow dish. Split the trout along the backbone, remove the large bones and clean the fish. Dip the fish in the egg and oil mixture and roll them in the breadcrumbs. Heat the oil in a deep-fryer to 180°C/350°F, or until a cube of bread browns in 30 seconds. Add the trout and cook, in batches if necessary, for 10 minutes, or until lightly browned all over. Remove, drain and keep warm. Warm the anchovy butter in a small pan, then divide it among the cavities in the backs of the trout. Serve immediately.

TROUT WITH CREAM

TRUITES À LA CRÈME

Preheat the oven to 200°C/400°F/Gas Mark 6. Melt half the butter in a large frying pan and fry the trout over a medium heat until browned, about 2–3 minutes each side. Transfer carefully to an ovenproof dish. Fry the mushrooms in the same pan for 5–10 minutes, then cover the fish with them. Beat the crème fraîche and egg yolks together in a bowl. Coat the fish and mushrooms with the mixture and bake for 10 minutes. Fry the slices of bread in the remaining butter and serve the fish on the bread.

- 125 g (4¼ oz) butter
- 6 small trout, cleaned
- 250 g (9 oz) mushrooms, finely chopped
- 150 ml (¼ pint) crème fraîche
- 2 egg yolks
- 6 slices bread, crusts removed

Preparation time: 15 minutes
Cooking time: 25 minutes
Serves 6

SALMON TROUT IN ASPIC

TRUITE SAUMONÉE EN GELÉE

Mix together the court-bouillon and wine in a fish kettle or large pan and heat gently. Add the trout, cover and poach gently for 12–15 minutes. Remove from the heat and leave the fish to cool in the court-bouillon. When it is cold, transfer it to a plate, cover and store in the refrigerator until required. Reserve the cooking liquid. Put the fish trimmings and bones, white fish, mushrooms and parsley in a pan, add the reserved cooking liquid and bring to the boil. Reduce the heat and simmer for 45 minutes. Strain the liquid into a bowl and clarify it (see p.45). Put the trout on a serving dish, remove and discard the skin and coat the fish with the juices. Chill in the refrigerator to set. Serve with green mayonnaise.

- 1 quantity court-bouillon with white wine (p.82)
- 1 litre (1¾ pints) white Burgundy wine
- 1 x 1.5-kg (3¼–lb) salmon trout, cleaned
- 500 g (1 lb 2 oz) white fish trimmings and bones
- 300 g (11 oz) white fish, such as whiting or cod
- 75 g (2½ oz) mushrooms, peeled
- 4 sprigs of flat-leaf parsley
- Green mayonnaise (p.70), to serve

Preparation time: 1 hour, plus cooling time
Cooking time: 1 hour
Serves 6

SEA FISH

Many sea fish species are now threatened by overfishing, and availability varies in different regions. It is best to ask your fishmonger for advice on sustainable alternatives.

SEA BASS

Small sea bass can be cooked *à la meunière* (p.234), or fried following the instructions on p.222.

SEA BASS IN A SEAWEED COURT-BOUILLON

BAR, COURT-BOUILLON AUX ALGUES

- 3-cm (1¼- inch) piece of kombu seaweed, soaked in 3 litres (5¼ pints) water for 30–60 minutes
- 30 g (1¼ oz) salt
- 1 x 1.2–1.5-kg (2½–3¼-lb) sea bass, fins trimmed, scaled and cleaned
- 1 quantity mayonnaise (p.70), hollandaise sauce (p.74) or mousseline sauce (p.75), to serve

Preparation time: 10 minutes, plus cooling time
Cooking time: 20 minutes
Serves 6

Pour the kombu and its soaking water into a pan and bring just to the boil. Remove the pan from the heat and discard the kombu. Make a court-bouillon with the seaweed-flavoured water and the salt in a fish kettle or large pan (p.82). Add the fish to the pan and poach, allowing 10–15 minutes per 500 g (1 lb 2 oz). Remove from the heat and leave to cool in the cooking liquid. Remove from the pan and serve cold with mayonnaise. Alternatively, reheat briefly in the court-bouillon and serve hot with the chosen sauce.

NOTE
If using mousseline sauce, 20 g (¾ oz) flaked nori seaweed can be added to the court-bouillon when reheating, without soaking it first.

MONKFISH

Monkfish is a highly prized fish with a huge head, and it can be prepared in the same way as eel. Only the tail fillet of this fish is edible. Cut it into slices and cook it in a court-bouillon with salt (p.82), following the instructions on p.221, with the sauce of your choice, or *à la Portugaise* (p.224), or *à la crème* (p.240), replacing the butter with 80 ml (3 fl oz) crème fraîche.

MONKFISH GRATIN
LOTTE EN GRATIN

Preheat the oven to 220°C/425°F/Gas Mark 7. Mix together the onion and half the parsley in the base of an ovenproof dish. Score the skin of the monkfish. Put the fish into the dish and cover with the butter and remaining parsley. Season with salt and pepper, pour in the wine and 100 ml (3½ fl oz) water and sprinkle with the breadcrumbs. Bake, basting with the cooking juices every 5 minutes, for 20 minutes.

NOTE
Sea bream and gurnard can be cooked in the same way.

- 50 g (1¾ oz) onion, chopped
- 1 bunch of flat-leaf parsley, chopped
- 1 x 1.2-kg (2½-lb) monkfish
- 50 g (1¾ oz) butter
- Salt and pepper
- 100 ml (3½ fl oz) white wine
- 4 tablespoons dried breadcrumbs

Preparation time: 20 minutes
Cooking time: 20 minutes
Serves 6

MONKFISH À L'AMERICAINE
LOTTE À L'AMÉRICAINE

Bone the monkfish tail and cut it into pieces. Dust the pieces in flour. Heat the oil in a frying pan. Add the monkfish pieces and cook over a medium heat, stirring and turning carefully, for 5 minutes, until lightly browned. Pour 50 ml (2 fl oz) of the brandy into a metal ladle and heat it gently, then pour it into the pan. Ensuring the pan is well away from anything flammable, and standing well back, carefully touch a lighted match to the edge of the pan to ignite. When the flames have died down, remove the fish and pour the cooking liquid into a pan. Add the wine, remaining brandy, onion, garlic, tomato purée, clove, nutmeg and stock and simmer for 30 minutes. Season with salt and pepper. Return the pieces of monkfish to the pan and simmer for a further 15 minutes. Serve hot.

- 750 g (1 lb 10 oz) monkfish tail
- Flour, for dusting
- 100 ml (3½ fl oz) oil
- 150 ml (¼ pint) brandy
- 500 ml (18 fl oz) white wine
- 1 onion, chopped
- 1 garlic clove, finely chopped
- 2 tablespoons tomato purée
- 1 clove
- 1 pinch of grated nutmeg
- 50 ml (2 fl oz) any stock
- Salt and pepper

Preparation time: 10 minutes
Cooking time: 50 minutes
Serves 6

COD

Cod can be cooked in a court-bouillon with salt (p.82), following the instructions on p.221. Serve with a sauce of your choice, such as hollandaise sauce (p.74), white sauce (p.50), or caper sauce (p.56). Haddock can be cooked in the same ways as cod, but will need slightly longer.

COD STEAKS
CÔTELETTES DE CABILLAUD

- 6 cod steaks
- 1 egg, lightly beaten
- 6 tablespoons dried breadcrumbs
- Salt and pepper
- 60 g (2 oz) butter
- 2 sprigs of flat-leaf parsley, chopped
- Juice of 1 lemon

Preparation time: 25 minutes
Cooking time: 10 minutes
Serves 6

Pat the steaks dry with kitchen paper, then dip first into the beaten egg, then into the breadcrumbs. Season with salt and pepper. Melt the butter in a frying pan. Add the fish and cook over a medium heat, turning once, for 10 minutes, until lightly browned on both sides. Add the parsley and lemon juice and serve immediately.

SAUTÉED COD
SAUTÉ DE CABILLAUD

- 60 g (2 oz) butter
- 6 cod steaks
- 2 tablespoons chopped flat-leaf parsley
- 1 bouquet garni
- Juice of 1 lemon
- Salt and pepper
- 1 tablespoon flour
- Chopped chervil, to garnish

Preparation time: 10 minutes
Cooking time: 15 minutes
Serves 6

Melt the butter in a frying pan. Add the cod steaks, parsley, bouquet garni and lemon juice and season with salt and pepper. Cook over a low heat for 15 minutes, until the flesh flakes easily. Transfer the fish to a warmed serving dish. Bring the cooking juices to the boil, stir in the flour and cook, stirring constantly, until thickened. Taste and adjust the seasoning if necessary, and pour the sauce over the fish. Garnish with chopped chervil and serve immediately.

PLAICE

Plaice can be fried following the instructions on p.222, or prepared *à la meunière* (p.234).

PLAICE IN WHITE WINE

CARRELETS AU VIN BLANC

Melt the butter in a frying pan. Add the onion and cook over a low heat, stirring occasionally, for about 8 minutes, until lightly browned. Add the plaice, season with salt and pepper and pour in the wine. Increase the heat to high and cook for 5 minutes, then reduce the heat and simmer gently for a further 15 minutes. Stir in the flour and egg yolks and cook, stirring constantly, until thickened. Sprinkle with chopped parsley and serve.

- 30 g (1¼ oz) butter
- 60 g (2 oz) onion, chopped
- 500 g (1 lb 2 oz) large plaice, cleaned and cut into pieces
- Salt and pepper
- 300 ml (½ pint) white wine
- 20 g (¾ oz) flour
- 2 egg yolks
- Chopped flat-leaf parsley, to garnish

Preparation time: 25 minutes
Cooking time: 20 minutes
Serves 6

POLLACK

Pollack can be cooked in a court-bouillon with salt (p.82), following the instructions on p.221, and served with the sauce of your choice. Whole pollack can be roasted following the instructions on p.222, or prepared *à la meunière* (p.234).

Slices of pollack can be grilled following the instructions on p.221, and served with a hot or cold sauce.

POLLACK À LA BRETONNE

COLIN À LA BRETONNE

- 1 quantity warm court-bouillon with salt (p.82)
- 1 kg (2¼ lb) pollack fillets
- 125 g (4¼ oz) Gruyère cheese, grated
- 100 ml (3½ fl oz) cheese sauce (p.50)

Preparation time: 25 minutes
Cooking time: 30 minutes
Serves 6

Pour the court-bouillon into a pan, add the pollack and poach gently for 20 minutes. Meanwhile, preheat the oven to 240°C/475°F/Gas Mark 8. Remove the pollack with a fish slice and remove and discard the skin. Put the fillets into an oven-proof dish, sprinkle with the cheese and spoon the cheese sauce over them. Bake for 10 minutes, or until lightly browned, and serve immediately.

POLLACK OR HAKE MOULD

TURBAN DE COLIN OU DE MERLU

- 200 g (7 oz) fresh breadcrumbs
- 200 ml (7 fl oz) milk
- 1 quantity warm court-bouillon with salt (p.82)
- 500 g (1 lb 2 oz) hake or pollack, cleaned
- Butter, for greasing
- 3 eggs, separated
- Salt and pepper
- 4 tablespoons crème fraîche
- 1 quantity prawn sauce (p.55) or mussel sauce (p.55)

Preparation time: 30 minutes
Cooking time: 1 hour
Serves 6

Put the breadcrumbs into a bowl, pour in the milk and leave to soak. Pour the court-bouillon into a pan, add the pollack or hake, bring to the boil and poach for 10 minutes. Meanwhile, preheat the oven to 190°C/375°F/Gas Mark 5 and grease a mould with butter. Lift out the fish with a fish slice and remove and discard the skin and bones. Flake the flesh in a bowl and stir in the breadcrumbs, then stir in the egg yolks. Whisk the egg whites to stiff peaks in a grease-free bowl, then fold into the fish mixture and season with salt and pepper.

Spoon the mixture into the prepared mould and put the mould into a roasting tin. Pour in boiling water to come about half-way up the side and bake for 1 hour. Meanwhile, mix the crème fraîche with the chosen sauce. Remove the fish from the oven and turn out onto a serving dish. Serve immediately with the sauce.

SEA BREAM

Sea bream can be prepared and served *au gratin* (p.242). It can also be cooked in a court-bouillon with salt (p.82), following the instructions on p.221, and served with a hot or cold sauce.

SEA BREAM WITH HERBS

DORADE AUX HERBES

 p.297

Preheat the oven to 190°C/375°F/Gas Mark 5 and brush a gratin dish with oil. Make 3–4 slashes on each side of the bream and put it into the prepared dish. Scatter the onion over the bream. Put the tomatoes around the fish, sprinkle it with the fennel, chives and parsley and add the thyme and bay leaf. Pour the wine over the fish and dot with the butter. Sprinkle with the nutmeg and season with salt and pepper. Bake for 30 minutes. Remove and discard the thyme and bay leaf and serve immediately.

- Oil, for brushing
- 1 x 1.2-kg (2½-lb) sea bream, scaled and cleaned
- 60 g (2 oz) onion, sliced
- 350 g (12 oz) tomatoes, quartered
- 1 sprig of fennel, chopped
- ½ tablespoon chopped chives
- 1 sprig of flat-leaf parsley, chopped
- 1 sprig of thyme
- 1 bay leaf
- 40 g (1½ oz) butter
- 200 ml (7 fl oz) white wine
- Freshly grated nutmeg
- Salt and pepper

Preparation time: 20 minutes
Cooking time: 30 minutes
Serves 6

SEA BREAM WITH SEAWEED

DORADE AUX ALGUES

Preheat the oven to 180°C/350°F/Gas Mark 4 and brush a gratin dish with the oil. Put the dulse into another dish, add the lemon juice and leave to soak for a few minutes. Make 3–4 small slashes on each side of the bream. Drain the dulse, reserving the lemon juice, wrap the fish in it and put into the prepared dish. Season with salt and pepper, pour in the wine and dot with the butter. Bake, occasionally basting with the reserved lemon juice, for 30–35 minutes. Serve immediately.

- 50 ml (2 fl oz) oil
- 10 sheets of dulse seaweed
- Juice of 2 lemons
- 2.5 kg (5½ lb) sea bream, scaled and cleaned
- Salt and pepper
- 200 ml (7 fl oz) white wine
- 40 g (1½ oz) butter

Preparation time: 15 minutes
Cooking time: 30–35 minutes
Serves 6

SEA BREAM À LA MONACO

DORADE À LA MONACO

- 100 ml (3½ fl oz) oil
- 1 garlic clove, finely chopped
- 2 tablespoons chopped flat-leaf parsley
- 1 x 1.2-kg (2½-lb) sea bream, scaled, cleaned and cut into pieces
- 400 g (14 oz) tomatoes
- 100 ml (3½ fl oz) white wine
- Salt and pepper

Preparation time: 20 minutes
Cooking time: 30 minutes
Serves 6

Skin, de-seed and chop the tomatoes. Heat the oil in a large pan, add the garlic and parsley and cook over a low heat, stirring frequently, for a few minutes, then add the bream. Cover with the tomatoes, pour in the wine and season well with salt and pepper. Cover and simmer for 30 minutes, then serve.

GURNARD

Gurnard should be prepared carefully because it has very large fins. It is served belly-side down. It can be cooked in a court-bouillon with salt (p.82), following the instructions on p.221, with a sauce of your choice, or *au gratin* (p.242).

GURNARD À L'ORIENTALE

GRONDIN À L'ORIENTALE

- 6 gurnard, cleaned
- 1 tablespoon oil
- 400 ml (14 fl oz) white wine
- 400 g (14 oz) tomatoes, chopped
- 1 garlic clove, finely chopped
- 1 sprig of thyme, chopped
- 1 bay leaf
- 1 pinch of saffron threads
- Salt and pepper

Preparation time: 25 minutes
Cooking time: 12 minutes
Serves 6

Put each gurnard, belly-side down, on a chopping board and make a shallow cut between the spiny dorsal fin and the head with a sharp knife. Holding the dorsal fin with one hand, run the knife horizontally just under the skin along the length of the fish. Cut almost all the way through the backbone behind the head. Grasp the head with one hand and the body with the other, then pull the head down towards the belly. As the head and skin become free, continue pulling until all the skin comes away. Pour the oil into a wide pan and add the fish, making sure that they are lying flat. Pour in the wine, add the tomatoes, garlic, thyme, bay leaf and saffron and season with salt and pepper. Bring to the boil, then reduce the heat, cover and simmer for 12 minutes. Remove from the heat and leave to cool in the cooking liquid. When cold, remove and discard the thyme and bay leaf and serve the fish with the cooled cooking liquid.

HADDOCK

Haddock can be prepared in many of the same ways as cod (p.243) or pollack (p.244). Smoked haddock can be cooked in a court-bouillon made with vinegar or milk (p.82), following the instructions on p.221.

GRILLED SMOKED HADDOCK
ÉGLEFIN FUMÉ GRILLÉ

Preheat the grill. Poach the haddock fillets in a wide pan of very gently boiling water for 5 minutes. Drain, pat the fillets dry with kitchen paper and brush with oil or melted butter, then grill for 8–10 minutes on each side, or until opaque in the centre. Serve with the cream sauce or maître d'hôtel butter.

- 6 smoked haddock fillets
- Oil or melted butter, for brushing
- 1 quantity cream sauce (p.51) or maître d'hôtel butter (p.48)

Preparation time: 5 minutes
Cooking time: 20 minutes
Serves 6

HADDOCK IN RAMEKINS
ÉGLEFIN EN RAMEQUINS

Blanch the cabbage in a pan of boiling water for 10 minutes. Drain, refresh under cold running water and drain again. Melt 40 g (1½ oz) of the butter in a flameproof heavy-based pan. Add the onions and cook over a low heat, stirring occasionally, for 5 minutes, until softened. Add the cabbage, season lightly with pepper, cover and cook, stirring occasionally, for 20 minutes, or until just tender.

Preheat the oven to 180°C/350°F/Gas Mark 4 and grease 6 ramekins with some of the remaining butter. Line the ramekins with the slices of haddock. Drain the cabbage and onions, squeeze out as much water as possible from the cabbage and chop it finely. Divide the cabbage and onions among the ramekins. Cut out circles of greaseproof paper to fit the ramekins and butter them with the remaining butter. Cover the ramekins with the circles and bake for 10 minutes. Alternatively, cover the ramekins with heatsafe clingfilm and steam for 10 minutes. Meanwhile, prepare the beurre blanc and stir the salmon roe and chives into it. Remove the ramekins from the oven or steamer, uncover them and turn out onto individual plates. Spoon the beurre blanc over the moulds and serve.

- 1 kg (2¼ lb) green cabbage, cut into quarters
- 60 g (2 oz) butter
- 150 g (5 oz) onions, chopped
- Pepper
- 500 g (1 lb 2 oz) haddock fillets, cut into thin strips
- 125 g (4¼ oz) salmon roe
- 50 g (1¾ oz) chives, chopped
- 150 ml (¼ pint) beurre blanc (p.49)

Preparation time: 30 minutes
Cooking time: 45 minutes
Serves 6

HERRINGS

Herrings are eaten in three different forms: fresh, salted and smoked. Smoked herrings are also known as kippers.

TO GRILL HERRINGS
Slash the fish twice on each side. Cut the fish in half length-ways and brush each half with oil. Cook under a preheated grill, turning once, for 15 minutes. Serve with a strongly flavoured sauce, such as mustard sauce (p.68).

TO FRY HERRINGS
Scale and clean the fish, removing the heads, dip in flour and fry in hot oil. Serve with lemon and fried parsley (p.81), or mustard sauce (p.68). They can also be served *à la meunière* (p.234).

TO COOK STUFFED HERRINGS
Scale and clean the fish and pat dry. Remove the bones and stuff with a layer of stuffing (p.80). Grill or fry following the instructions on pp.221–2.

TO COOK SALTED HERRINGS
Rinse the herrings and soak in milk for 3 hours. Remove the heads and skin and separate the fillets. Cook in court-bouillon with salt (p.82), following the instructions on p.221.

MARINATED HERRING FILLETS
FILETS DE HARENGS MARINÉS

- 6 herrings with soft roe, cleaned and filleted
- 1 quantity court-bouillon (p.82)
- 100 ml (3½ fl oz) white wine vinegar
- 100 ml (3½ fl oz) oil
- Pepper
- Chervil or flat-leaf parsley, chopped
- 1 bouquet garni (optional)
- 1 carrot, sliced
- 1 lemon, sliced
- 1 small onion, sliced

Preparation time: 20 minutes, plus marinating time

Serves 6

Prepare 4 days in advance. Bring the court-bouillon to the boil in a large pan and poach the herring fillets for 8 minutes per 500 g (1 lb 2 oz). There are 2 alternative ways to prepare the roe: either mash it well, mix with the vinegar and oil, season with pepper and add the chervil or parsley. Or, alternatively, heat the vinegar with the bouquet garni and pepper. Bring to the boil and cook for 2 minutes. Remove the bouquet garni, allow to cool slightly and add to the roe, mashing well, then add the oil and the chervil or parsley. Put the herring fillets on a dish and cover with the carrot, lemon and onion slices. Pour the roe mixture over them. Leave to marinate in the refrigerator for 4 days.

ROLLMOPS

HARENGS ROLLMOPS

Prepare 2–3 days ahead. Bring the vinegar to the boil with the bouquet garni and pepper and simmer for 2 minutes. Remove the bouquet garni. Roll up the herring fillets, putting a gherkin in the middle of each one if desired, and secure with a wooden cocktail stick. Pack them into a terrine, pour in the vinegar to cover, and add the onion and carrot. Leave to marinate for 2–3 days.

- 300 ml (½ pint) white wine vinegar
- 1 bouquet garni
- Pepper, to taste
- 12 herring fillets, halved
- Pickled gherkins (optional)
- 1 onion, sliced
- 1 carrot, sliced

Preparation time: 15 minutes, plus marinating time

Serves 6

KIPPERS

Choose plump kippers. Remove and discard the skin and soak them in a mixture of milk and water for 3 hours to remove excess salt. Drain and pat dry. They are now ready for use in any recipe.

Kippers can be grilled following the instructions on p.221, and served with mustard sauce (p.68). For devilled kippers, brush the fillets with mustard, then with oil. Sprinkle with dried bread-crumbs and shallow-fry following the instructions on p.222.

KIPPER SALAD

SALADE DE HARENGS SAURS

Prepare the kippers (see above), then cut them into small squares. Cut the celery into thin strips and mix with the kippers in a bowl. Stir in the ravigote sauce.

- 125 g (4¼ oz) kippers
- 100 g (3½ oz) celery
- 1 quantity ravigote sauce (p.56)

Preparation time: 20 minutes, plus soaking time

Serves 6

MACKEREL

Mackerel can be cooked in a court-bouillon with red wine (p.82) following the instructions on p.221, and served hot with a strongly flavoured sauce.

For grilled mackerel, preheat the grill and cut the fish in half lengthways. Brush the halves with oil and grill, turning once, for 15 minutes. Serve with maître d'hôtel butter (p.48) or mustard sauce (p.68).

STUFFED MACKEREL
MAQUEREAUX FARCIS

📷 p.298

- 60 g (2 oz) fresh breadcrumbs
- 120 g (4 oz) cooked peeled prawns, chopped
- 120 g (4 oz) mushrooms, chopped
- 60 g (2 oz) onion, chopped
- 3 tablespoons chopped flat-leaf parsley
- Salt and pepper
- 6 mackerel, scaled and cleaned
- 175 g (6 oz) butter, melted
- 6 tablespoons dried breadcrumbs

Preparation time: 30 minutes
Cooking time: 25 minutes
Serves 6

Put the fresh breadcrumbs into a bowl, add 4 tablespoons water and leave to soak for 10 minutes. Mix together the prawns, mushrooms, onion, parsley and soaked breadcrumbs in a bowl and season with salt and pepper. Preheat the oven to 190°C/375°F/Gas Mark 5. Divide the stuffing among the mackerel, filling them through the gills. Put the fish into an ovenproof dish, brush with the butter, sprinkle with the dried breadcrumbs and bake for 25 minutes. The mackerel can also be grilled, in which case omit the dried breadcrumbs.

MACKEREL PARCELS
MACKEREL EN PAPILLOTES

- 6 mackerel, scaled and cleaned
- 1 quantity stuffing for fish (p.80)
- Salt and pepper
- Butter, for dotting

Preparation time: 30 minutes
Cooking time: 25 minutes
Serves 6

Preheat the oven to 200°C/400°F/Gas Mark 6. Stuff the mackerel with the stuffing. Season with salt and pepper and dot with butter. Wrap each mackerel in a piece of foil, put onto a baking tray and bake for 20 minutes. Unwrap the fish, put them onto a serving dish and pour the cooking juices over them.

MACKEREL WITH GOOSEBERRIES

MAQUEREAUX AUX GROSEILLES

First, make the stuffing. Cook the gooseberries in a pan of salt-ed boiling water for 10 minutes, then drain and chop. Mix together the butter, gooseberries and hard-boiled eggs in a bowl. Cut along the back of each mackerel, cut off the head and remove the backbone. Divide the gooseberry stuffing among the fish, spooning it into the cavities along the backs.

Wrap each fish in a piece of muslin, put into a fish kettle or large pan, pour in the court-bouillon, bring to a simmer and poach the fish for 15–20 minutes. Meanwhile, make the sauce. Bring the cream to the boil and boil for a few minutes, then stir in the gooseberries and season with salt and pepper. Remove the fish from the pan, unwrap and transfer to a serving dish. Pour the sauce over them and serve.

- 6 mackerel, scaled and cleaned
- 1 quantity warm court-bouillon with salt (p.82)

For the stuffing:
- 350 g (12 oz) gooseberries, topped and tailed
- 90 g (3¼ oz) butter, diced
- 3 hard-boiled eggs, shelled and chopped

For the sauce:
- 200 ml (7 fl oz) double cream
- 125 g (4¼ oz) gooseberries
- Salt and pepper

Preparation time: 20 minutes
Cooking time: 15–20 minutes
Serves 6

MARINATED MACKEREL

MAQUEREAUX MARINÉS

Prepare the day before. Cut off and discard the mackerel heads, if this has not already been done, and put the fish into a non-metallic dish. Pour in water to cover, add the salt and vinegar and leave to soak for 5 minutes. Drain the fish and put them into a flameproof terrine. Pour in the hot marinade to cover, add the oil and bring to the boil. Remove from the heat, and seal tightly. Leave to cool, then transfer to the refrigerator and leave to marinate for 12 hours. Serve cold with slices of lemon.

- 6 small mackerel, scaled and cleaned
- 1 teaspoon salt
- 2 tablespoons white wine vinegar
- 1 quantity cooked marinade (p.77)
- 100 ml (3½ fl oz) oil
- 1 lemon, sliced, to serve

Preparation time: 15 minutes, plus marinating time
Cooking time: 15 minutes
Serves 6

MACKEREL IN WHITE WINE

MAQUEREAUX AU VIN BLANC

- 100 ml (3½ fl oz) white wine vinegar
- 200 ml (7 fl oz) white wine
- 50 ml (2 fl oz) oil, plus extra for brushing
- 1 sprig of thyme
- 1 sprig of flat-leaf parsley
- 1 bay leaf
- 1 teaspoon ground coriander
- 1 carrot, sliced
- 1 onion, sliced
- Salt and pepper
- 6 mackerel, scaled and cleaned
- 1 lemon, sliced

Preparation time: 15 minutes, plus marinating time
Cooking time: 30 minutes
Serves 6

Prepare 2–3 days ahead. Pour the vinegar, wine and oil into a pan, add the thyme, parsley, bay leaf, coriander, carrot and onion, season with salt and pepper and bring to the boil. Reduce the heat, cover and simmer for 10 minutes. Meanwhile, preheat the oven to 190°C/375°F/Gas Mark 5 and brush a flameproof heavy-based pan with oil. Put the mackerel into the pan in a single layer and pour in the marinade. Garnish each fish with a slice of lemon. Cover with greaseproof paper and bring to the boil over a medium heat. Transfer the pan to the oven and bake for 15 minutes. Transfer the fish to a serving dish and leave to cool, then store in the refrigerator for 2–3 days.

WHITING

Whiting can be cooked in a court-bouillon with salt (p.82) following the instructions on p.221, and served hot with a sauce of your choice. For fried or grilled whiting, follow the instructions on pp.221–2. It can also be prepared *à la meunière* (p.234), or cooked in white wine (p.230).

CHAUDRÉE

CHAUDRÉE

- 1.5 kg (3¼ lb) whiting, scaled and cleaned
- 300 ml (½ pint) white wine
- Salt and pepper
- 100 g (3½ oz) butter, softened
- 40 g (1½ oz) flour

Preparation time: 30 minutes
Cooking time: 20 minutes
Serves 6

This traditional fish stew comes from the Charente region in western France.

Cut the whiting in pieces and put in a large pan. Cover with 300 ml (½ pint) water and the wine. Season with salt and pepper. Rapidly bring to the boil and boil briskly for 10 minutes, then reduce the heat and simmer for a further 5 minutes. Work the butter and flour together in a small bowl to make a smooth paste, then add this to the fish to thicken the pan juices. Cook for a further 5 minutes and serve.

WHITING DUGLÉRÉ

MERLANS À LA DUGLÉRÉ

Preheat the oven to 220°C/425°F/Gas Mark 7 and grease a flameproof dish with butter. Mix together the onion, shallot, parsley and tomatoes in a bowl, spoon into the prepared dish and season with salt and pepper. Put the whiting on top and pour the wine over them. Bring to the boil over a high heat, then cover with buttered greaseproof paper, transfer to the oven and bake for 15 minutes. Meanwhile, mix the butter with the flour to a paste in a bowl. Transfer the fish to a serving dish and keep warm. Bring the cooking juices to the boil and boil until reduced, then gradually stir in pieces of the flour and butter paste, making sure that each piece is fully incorporated before adding the next. Stir in lemon juice to taste and the crème fraîche, then taste and adjust the seasoning. Pour the sauce over the fish, garnish with parsley and serve.

- 50 g (1¾ oz) butter, plus extra for greasing
- 50 g (1¾ oz) onion, chopped
- 20 g (¾ oz) shallot, chopped
- 1 tablespoon chopped flat-leaf parsley, plus extra to garnish
- 250 g (9 oz) tomatoes, skinned, de-seeded and crushed
- Salt and pepper
- 6 whiting, scaled and cleaned
- 400 ml (14 fl oz) white wine
- 30 g (1¼ oz) flour
- Juice of 1 lemon
- 2 tablespoons crème fraîche

Preparation time: 20 minutes
Cooking time: 30 minutes
Serves 6

POUPETON

POUPETON

Preheat the oven to 180°C/350°F/Gas Mark 4 and grease a loaf tin with oil. Bring a large pan of salted water to the boil, then reduce the heat and simmer the whiting and lampreys for 15 minutes, or until tender. Soak the bread in the milk. Remove the skin and bones from the fish and pound the flesh in a mortar, adding the crème fraîche, bread and cheese a little at a time. Add the egg yolks. Whisk the egg whites to stiff peaks and fold into the fish mixture. Season with nutmeg, salt and pepper. Pour the mixture into the prepared loaf tin and bake for 40 minutes. Turn out, slice and serve hot.

- Oil, for greasing
- 1 whiting, scaled and cleaned
- 250 g (9 oz) lampreys
- 100 g (3½ oz) crustless white bread
- 100 ml (3½ fl oz) milk
- 125 ml (4½ fl oz) crème fraîche
- 60 g (2 oz) Parmesan cheese, grated
- 4 eggs, separated
- Freshly grated nutmeg
- Salt and pepper

Preparation time: 25 minutes
Cooking time: 50 minutes
Serves 6

SALT COD

Salt cod should be thick, and the flesh should glisten. Canned salt cod, most frequently sold as fillets, is often of excellent quality. Before cooking, the excess salt must be removed: put the fish, skin side up (to allow the salt to fall to the bottom), into a colander in a bowl of water and leave to soak for 12–24 hours, changing the water 2–3 times.

To poach salt cod, put the fillets into a pan, pour in plenty of cold water or court-bouillon with white wine (p.82) to cover. Bring just to the boil over a high heat, then immediately remove the pan from the heat, cover and leave to stand for 10–15 minutes. Never allow salt cod to boil. Drain the pieces of fish and serve with a garnish. Serve hot with maître d'hôtel butter (p.48), black butter (p.48) or béchamel sauce (p.50). To serve cold, flake the cooked fish and put onto a serving dish with lettuce, capers, pickled gherkins and mayonnaise (p.70).

Salt cod can be deep-fried or grilled. To grill, cut fillets of soaked and poached salt cod (above) into slices. Pat dry with kitchen paper, and dip in beaten egg then in dried breadcrumbs. Lightly brush each slice with oil and grill for 5 minutes. Serve with mustard sauce (p.68) or tartare sauce (p.72). To deep-fry, cut the soaked fillets into slices. Pat dry with kitchen paper, then dip them in milk, roll in flour and deep-fry in very hot oil (180°C/350°F, or until a cube of bread browns in 30 seconds) until golden brown.

SALT COD FRITTERS

FRITOS DE MORUE

- 1 quantity hot tomato sauce (p.57)
- 300 g (11 oz) salt cod, soaked and poached (above)
- Juice of 1 lemon
- Pepper
- 1 quantity batter (p.725)
- Vegetable oil, for deep-frying

Preparation time: 20 minutes
Cooking time: 20 minutes
Serves 6

Prepare the tomato sauce and keep warm. Break the salt cod into small pieces, sprinkle with the lemon juice and season with pepper. Coat each piece of cod in batter. Heat the oil in a deep-fryer to 180–190°C/350–375°F, or until a cube of bread browns in 30 seconds. Add the fritters in batches and fry until golden brown. Remove with a slotted spoon, drain and serve with the tomato sauce.

SALT COD WITH CRÈME FRAÎCHE

MORUE À LA CRÈME

Prepare the béchamel sauce in a large pan, then stir the crème fraîche into it. Flake the salt cod into the pan and warm it through over a low heat for 5 minutes, but do not allow the mixture to boil. Transfer to a serving dish and serve.

- 250 ml (8 fl oz) hot béchamel sauce (p.50)
- 100 ml (3½ fl oz) crème fraîche
- 500 g (1 lb 2 oz) salt cod, soaked and poached (p.255)

Preparation time: 20 minutes
Cooking time: 20 minutes
Serves 6

SALT COD À LA PROVENÇALE

MORUE À LA PROVENÇALE

 p.299

Heat the oil in a pan. Add the onions, garlic and tomatoes and cook over a low heat, stirring occasionally, for 5 minutes. Add the olives and parsley, season with pepper and cook for a further 5 minutes. Flake the salt cod, add it to the pan and simmer gently for 10 minutes, then serve.

- 2 tablespoons oil
- 100 g (3½ oz) onions, chopped
- 5 garlic cloves, chopped
- 500 g (1 lb 2 oz) tomatoes, coarsely chopped
- 125 g (4¼ oz) black olives
- 2 tablespoons chopped flat-leaf parsley
- Pepper
- 500 g (1 lb 2 oz) salt cod, soaked and poached (p.255)

Preparation time: 20 minutes
Cooking time: 20 minutes
Serves 6

ICELANDIC SALT COD

MORUE ISLANDAISE

Put the salt cod and potatoes into a pan, sprinkle with the onions, pour in the wine, dot with the butter and season with pepper. Cover and cook over a low heat for 45 minutes.

- 500 g (1 lb 2 oz) salt cod, soaked
- 600 g (1 lb 5 oz) potatoes, cut into quarters
- 100 g (3½ oz) onions, chopped
- 300 ml (½ pint) white wine
- 150 g (5 oz) butter
- Pepper

Preparation time: 25 minutes
Cooking time: 45 minutes
Serves 6

SALT COD WITH MILK

MORUE AU LAIT

- 500 g (1 lb 2 oz) salt cod, soaked
- 600 g (1 lb 5 oz) potatoes, sliced
- 50 g (1¾ oz) onion, chopped
- 1 litre (1¾ pints) milk
- Pepper

Preparation time: 20 minutes
Cooking time: 45 minutes
Serves 6

Preheat the oven to 200°C/400°F/Gas Mark 6. Put the salt cod into an ovenproof dish and cover it with the potatoes and onion. Pour in the milk, season with pepper and bake for 45 minutes.

SALT COD PARMENTIER

MORUE À LA PARMENTIER

- 1 kg (2¼ lb) potatoes
- Salt
- 50 g (1¾ oz) butter
- 500 ml (18 fl oz) milk
- 1 quantity salt cod with crème fraîche (p.256)
- 100 g (3½ oz) Gruyère cheese, grated

Preparation time: 20 minutes
Cooking time: 30 minutes
Serves 6

Put the potatoes into a pan, pour in water to cover and add a little salt. Bring to the boil, cover and cook for 20 minutes. Meanwhile, preheat the oven to 220°C/425°F/Gas Mark 7. Drain the potatoes and pass through a sieve or potato ricer into a bowl while they are still hot. Beat in the butter and milk with a wooden spoon, then make a ring of mashed potatoes around the edge of an ovenproof dish. Pour the salt cod into the centre, sprinkle with the cheese and bake for 10 minutes, or until lightly browned. Serve immediately.

VARIATION

. . . .

SALT COD WITH NOODLES

MORUE AUX NOUILLES

Proceed as above, substituting cooked noodles, which have been drained and fried in butter, for the mashed potatoes.

SALT COD FLORENTINE

MORUE À LA FLORENTINE

Preheat the oven to 220°C/425°F/Gas Mark 7. Blanch the spinach in a pan of salted boiling water for a few minutes, then drain, squeezing out as much water as possible, and chop coarsely. Melt the butter in a frying pan. Add the spinach and cook over a medium-low heat, stirring occasionally, for a few minutes. Season with salt and pepper, stir in the nutmeg and remove the pan from the heat. Put the spinach into a gratin dish, flake the cod over it and cover with the béchamel sauce. Sprinkle with the cheese and bake for 10 minutes, until lightly browned.

- 1 kg (2¼ lb) spinach, coarse stalks removed
- 40 g (1½ oz) butter
- Salt and pepper
- 1 pinch of freshly grated nutmeg
- 500 g (1 lb 2 oz) salt cod, soaked and poached (p.255)
- 250 ml (8 fl oz) béchamel sauce (p.50)
- 30 g (1¼ oz) Gruyère cheese, grated

Preparation time: 20 minutes
Cooking time: 30 minutes
Serves 6

BRANDADE

BRANDADE

Soak the salt cod overnight in cold water. Next day, poach it in fresh simmering water for about 8 minutes. Drain the fish, remove any skin and bones, and flake the flesh. Crush the garlic in a mortar with the fish, adding the oil a little at a time, until the mixture becomes creamy. Place in a pan over a very low heat, and, stirring constantly, add the crème fraîche a little at a time. Season with pepper and the lemon juice. Serve cold.

- 500 g (1 lb 2 oz) salt cod
- 2 garlic cloves
- 250 ml (8 fl oz) olive oil
- 75 ml (3 fl oz) crème fraîche
- Pepper
- Juice of 1 lemon

Preparation time: 25 minutes, plus soaking time
Cooking time: 10 minutes
Serves 6

GREY MULLET

Large grey mullet can be cooked in a court-bouillon with salt (p.82) following the instructions on p.221, and served hot with a hot or cold sauce of your choice. For fried or grilled grey mullet, follow the instructions on pp.221–2.

BOTTARGA

BOUTARGUE

Preparation time: 5 minutes,
plus salting and drying time

Cover grey mullet roes with coarse salt. Cover with a clean cloth and chill in the refrigerator for 2 days. Press the roes between 2 boards and place a weight on top for 2 hours. Wash thoroughly. Leave to dry in the sun for 2 hours. Pour over some olive oil and serve sliced as an hors-d'oeuvre with slices of lemon.

SKATE

To prepare, rinse several times in cold water. It can be cooked in a court-bouillon with salt (p.82) following the instructions on p.221. Small skate are cooked whole, but large ones should be cut into pieces. Serve with maître d'hôtel butter (p.48).

FLAKED SKATE WITH HERBS

EFFILOCHÉE DE RAIE AUX AROMATES

- 1 quantity warm court-bouillon with salt (p.82)
- 1.4 kg (3 lb) skate wings
- 80 g (2¾ oz) garlic, separated into cloves
- 1 egg
- 100 ml (3½ fl oz) oil
- 50 ml (2 fl oz) sherry vinegar
- 1 tablespoon Dijon mustard
- Salt and pepper
- 700 g (1 lb 8½ oz) tomatoes, skinned, de-seeded and diced
- 50 g (1¾ oz) chervil, chopped
- 60 g (2 oz) chives, snipped
- 100 g (3½ oz) shallots, very finely chopped
- 60 g (2 oz) capers
- Boiled potatoes, sliced, to serve (optional)
- 1 quantity vinaigrette made with sherry vinegar (p.66)

Preparation time: 45 minutes
Cooking time: 15 minutes
Serves 6

Pour the court-bouillon into a large pan and add the skate. Bring to a simmer and poach gently for 20 minutes. Remove from the heat and keep warm. Blanch the garlic in a pan of boiling water for 2 minutes, drain and blanch in fresh boiling water twice more, then drain and slice thinly. Make a mayonnaise (p.70) with the egg, oil, vinegar and mustard in a large heatproof bowl and season with salt and pepper. Set the bowl over a pan of simmering water and heat until warm. Drain the skate.

Remove and discard the skin and flake the flesh, taking care to remove all the cartilage. Transfer the fish to a serving dish. Remove the mayonnaise from the heat and stir in the garlic, tomatoes, chervil, chives, shallots and capers, then pour it over the fish. Serve immediately. If desired, serve with sliced boiled potatoes, seasoned with a sherry vinaigrette dressing.

SAUTÉED SKATE

RAIE SAUTÉE

 p.300

Preheat the oven to 160°C/325°F/Gas Mark 3. Put the pieces of skate into a dish, pour in the marinade and leave to soak for 5 minutes. Drain and dip into the flour to coat. Melt the butter in an ovenproof pan. Add the pieces of fish and cook over a low heat for 5 minutes on each side. Transfer the pan to the oven and bake for 15 minutes. Season with salt and pepper, garnish with the lemon wedges and serve.

- 1 kg (2¼ lb) skate wings, cut into pieces
- 1 quantity uncooked marinade (p.78)
- 50 g (1¾ oz) flour
- 50 g (1¾ oz) butter
- Salt and pepper
- 1 lemon, cut into wedges, to garnish

Preparation time: 10 minutes
Cooking time: 25 minutes
Serves 6

RED MULLET

Red mullet can be cooked in a court-bouillon with salt (p.82) following the instructions on p.221, and served hot with a sauce of your choice. For fried mullet, follow the instructions on p.222. For grilled red mullet, marinate first in an uncooked marinade (p.78) before following the instructions on p.221.

RED MULLET WITH TOMATOES

ROUGETS AUX TOMATES

Heat the oil in a large pan and cut the tomatoes into quarters. Add the onion, garlic, shallot and tomatoes and cook over a low heat, stirring occasionally, for 5 minutes. Add the bouquet garni, season with salt and pepper, pour in the wine, cover and simmer for 15 minutes. Add the red mullet, cover the pan and simmer for a further 15 minutes. Remove the bouquet garni and add the parsley. Cut the fish into pieces and serve in the sauce.

- 2 tablespoons olive oil
- 1 onion, chopped
- 1 garlic clove, chopped
- 1 shallot, chopped
- 500 g (1 lb 2 oz) tomatoes
- 1 bouquet garni
- Salt and pepper
- 200 ml (7 fl oz) dry white wine
- 1.2 kg (2½ lb) red mullet, scaled and cleaned
- 2 tablespoons chopped flat-leaf parsley

Preparation time: 20 minutes
Cooking time: 30 minutes
Serves 6

SARDINES

To prepare sardines, scale them, cut off the heads, and gut and clean them (or buy them ready prepared). To fry them, roll in flour and fry for 5 minutes on each side in hot butter in a frying pan. To grill them, brush with oil and grill for 5 minutes on each side. Serve with maître d'hôtel butter (p.48).

SARDINES WITH HERBS

SARDINES AUX FINES HERBES

 p.301

Preheat the oven to 200°C/400°F/Gas Mark 6. Put the sardines into an ovenproof dish, sprinkle with the breadcrumbs and herbs, season with salt and pepper and pour the oil over them. Bake for 20 minutes.

- 12–18 sardines, scaled and cleaned
- 40 g (1½ oz) dried breadcrumbs
- 60 g (2 oz) finely chopped mixed herbs, such as flat-leaf parsley, chives and tarragon
- Salt and pepper
- 50 ml (2 fl oz) oil

Preparation time: 10 minutes
Cooking time: 20 minutes
Serves 6

SOLE

To prepare Dover sole, clean and trim off the frills and fins with kitchen scissors. Scrape the skin on the white underside. Remove the skin from the grey upper side by making a cut at the tail end. Lift this skin with the tip of a knife, grasp it with a tea towel and pull it towards you, while holding the end of the tail with your other hand. The skin will come off up to the head. To fillet the sole, make a cut along the backbone, slide the tip of the knife between the bones and the flesh and lift it away.

Lemon sole is not as highly regarded as Dover sole and is less delicate. It can be prepared and cooked in the same ways.

Sole can be cooked in a court-bouillon with white wine (p.82) or milk (p.82) following the instructions on p.221, and served hot with maître d'hôtel butter (p.48) or hollandaise sauce (p.74). For fried sole, prepare the fish as above and follow the instructions on p.222. If using oil, dip the prepared fish in milk, then flour. If using butter, dip in flour only and serve with lemon wedges.

p.302

SOLE MEUNIÈRE

SOLE À LA MEUNIÈRE

* 3 Dover or lemon sole, cleaned and skinned
* Salt and pepper
* 120 ml (4 fl oz) milk
* 40 g (1½ oz) flour
* 100 g (3½ oz) butter
* 2 tablespoons chopped flat-leaf parsley

Preparation time: 15 minutes
Cooking time: 15 minutes
Serves 6

Season each sole with salt and pepper, dip it in the milk, then roll in the flour. Melt 60 g (2 oz) of the butter in a frying pan. Add the fish and cook over a high heat, turning once, for 10–15 minutes, until browned. Transfer the fish to a serving dish and sprinkle with the parsley. Heat the remaining butter in another pan until it is nut-brown, stir it into the frying pan and then pour the mixture over the fish. Serve immediately.

SOLE À LA NORMANDE

SOLE À LA NORMANDE

* 1 kg (2¼ lb) live mussels, scrubbed and debearded
* 6 langoustines (Dublin Bay prawns)
* 200 g (7 oz) mushrooms
* 3 Dover or lemon sole, cleaned and skinned
* 200 ml (7 fl oz) white wine
* 80 g (2¾ oz) butter
* 20 g (¾ oz) flour
* 2 egg yolks
* 6 oysters, shucked

Preparation time: 1½ hours
Cooking time: 35 minutes
Serves 6

Cook the mussels (p.271) and the langoustines (p.286), reserving the cooking juices. Melt 10 g (¼ oz) of the butter in a pan, add the mushrooms and fry for 5–10 minutes. Put the sole in a wide, shallow pan and pour in the wine and 200 ml (7 fl oz) of the reserved cooking juices. Dice 20 g (¾ oz) of the butter and add to the pan. Set the pan over a medium-low heat and bring to the boil, then reduce the heat and simmer gently for 15 minutes.

Transfer the sole to a warmed serving dish, pour the cooking juices over them and keep warm. Make a white sauce (p.50) with 30 g (1¼ oz) of the remaining butter, the flour and 500 ml (18 fl oz) liquid, including any remaining reserved cooking liquid. Beat the egg yolks with the remaining butter in a bowl, stir in a ladleful of the sauce, then stir the mixture back into the sauce. Garnish the fish with the oysters, mussels and mushrooms, spoon the sauce over them and put the langoustines on top.

SOLE À LA BASQUAISE

SOLE À LA BASQUAISE

Preheat the oven to 200°C/400°F/Gas Mark 6. Cut along the centre of the sole to remove and discard the central bones, and put the fish into an ovenproof dish. Pour in the wine and bake for 10 minutes. Meanwhile, mix together the chives, parsley, shallot, mushrooms and butter in a bowl to make a stuffing. Remove the fish from the oven and fill the cavities left by removing the bones with the stuffing, pour in the stock and season with salt and pepper. Reduce the oven temperature to 160°C/325°F/Gas Mark 3, return the dish to the oven and bake for a further 10 minutes. Serve sprinkled with the lemon juice.

- 3 Dover or lemon sole, cleaned and skinned
- 100 ml (3½ fl oz) white wine
- 1 tablespoon chopped chives
- 2 tablespoons chopped flat-leaf parsley
- 1 shallot, chopped
- 100 g (3½ oz) mushrooms, chopped
- 50 g (1¾ oz) butter
- 200 ml (7 fl oz) any stock
- Salt and pepper
- Juice of 1 lemon

Preparation time: 30 minutes
Cooking time: 20 minutes
Serves 6

FILLETS OF SOLE WITH TOMATO

FILETS DE SOLE À LA TOMATE

Chop the sole heads and bones and put them into a pan with the lemon juice and 1 parsley sprig. Pour in 200 ml (7 fl oz) of the wine and 200 ml (7 fl oz) water, season with salt and pepper and bring to the boil. Reduce the heat, cover and simmer for 20 minutes, then strain the stock into a bowl.

Meanwhile, chop the remaining parsley. Grease a flameproof dish with a little of the butter, put the fish fillets into it and pour in 100 ml (3½ fl oz) of the fish stock and the remaining wine. Season with salt and pepper, sprinkle with the chopped parsley, shallot and tomatoes and cook over a medium heat for 12–15 minutes. Using a fish slice, transfer the sole fillets to a warmed serving dish. Reduce the heat and gradually stir the remaining butter into the cooking juices. Taste and adjust the seasoning, if necessary, then pour the sauce over the fish and serve.

- 3 Dover or lemon sole, filleted, heads and bones reserved
- Juice of 1 lemon
- ½ bunch of flat-leaf parsley
- 300 ml (½ pint) white wine
- Salt and pepper
- 50 g (1¾ oz) butter
- 15 g (½ oz) shallot, finely chopped
- 200 g (7 oz) tomatoes, de-seeded and coarsely chopped

Preparation time: 12 minutes
Cooking time: 35 minutes
Serves 6

FILLETS OF SOLE ORLY
FILETS DE SOLE À LA ORLY

- 3 Dover or lemon sole, filleted and skinned
- 1 carrot, sliced
- 1 onion, sliced
- 1 lemon, sliced
- Salt and pepper
- 2 tablespoons olive oil
- 500 ml (18 fl oz) hot tomato sauce (p.57)
- Vegetable oil, for deep-frying
- 1 egg, lightly beaten
- 120 g (4 oz) dried breadcrumbs
- 400 g (14 oz) cooked peas (p.563)

Preparation time: 45 minutes
Cooking time: 10–15 minutes
Serves 6

Put the sole fillets, carrot, onion and lemon into a bowl, season with salt and pepper, pour in the olive oil and leave to marinate for 30 minutes. Prepare the tomato sauce and keep warm. Drain the fish fillets, roll up and secure each one with a wooden cocktail stick. Heat the vegetable oil in a deep-fryer to 180°C/350°F, or until a cube of bread browns in 30 seconds. Dip the fish rolls first in the egg, then in the breadcrumbs, and deep-fry for 5 minutes, in batches if necessary, until the fish is cooked through but not browned. Remove the fish rolls and increase the temperature of the oil. Return the fish rolls and fry until lightly browned. Remove the rolls and drain, then remove and discard the cocktail sticks. Put the fish in a ring on a round dish, spoon the peas into the centre and pour the tomato sauce over the rolls.

FRICASSÉE OF SOLE WITH ASPARAGUS
FRICASSÉE DE SOLES AUX ASPERGES

- 300 g (11 oz) white asparagus, trimmed and peeled
- 1.5 kg (3¼ lb) Dover or lemon sole, filleted
- 500 g (1 lb 2 oz) live clams, scrubbed
- 60 g (2 oz) butter
- 50 g (1¾ oz) shallot, finely chopped
- Salt and pepper
- 60 ml (2 fl oz) dry white wine
- 150 ml (¼ pint) crème fraîche
- 40 g (1½ oz) chervil

Preparation time: 1 hour
Cooking time: 35 minutes
Serves 6

Cook the asparagus in a pan of salted boiling water for 4–8 minutes, or until tender, then drain and refresh in cold water. Cut the spears into 3-cm (1¼-inch) pieces and set aside. Cut the sole fillets into 4–5-cm (1½–2-inch) long pieces. Put the clams into a pan, cover and cook over a high heat, shaking the pan occasionally, for about 5 minutes until opened. Lift out the clams with a slotted spoon and reserve the liquid they have produced. Discard any clams that remain closed, remove the remainder from the shells and set aside.

Melt 40 g (1½ oz) of the butter in a frying pan. Add the fish and cook for 5 minutes on each side. Sprinkle with the shallot, season with salt and pepper and pour in the wine and reserved clam juices. Stir in the clams and the pieces of asparagus. Drain the cooking liquid into a bowl. Keep the fish, clams and asparagus warm. Stir the crème fraîche into the cooking liquid, pour into a food processor or blender and process for 2 minutes. Pour the mixture into a pan and heat gently. Cut the remaining butter into small pieces and gradually stir into the sauce. Put the sole, asparagus and clam mixture onto a serving dish, spoon the sauce over them and garnish with sprigs of chervil.

TIMBALE OF SOLE

TIMBALE DE FILETS DE SOLE

Put the fish heads and bones into a pan, pour in the wine and 200 ml (7 fl oz) water and bring to the boil. Reduce the heat, cover and simmer for 30 minutes, then strain into a bowl. Melt 50 g (1¾ oz) of the butter in a pan. Stir in the flour and cook over a low heat, stirring constantly, for 1 minute. Do not allow the flour to colour. Gradually stir in the fish stock and bring to the boil, stirring constantly, then simmer, stirring frequently, until thickened.

Meanwhile, in a large pan, poach the sole fillets in the court-bouillon for 3 minutes, then remove from the heat and keep warm. Melt the remaining butter in a small frying pan. Add the mushrooms and cook over a low heat, stirring occasionally, for 5–8 minutes. Stir the mushrooms, prawns and mussels into the sauce, then add the fish fillets, season with salt and pepper and heat through before serving.

- 4 Dover or lemon sole, filleted, heads and bones reserved
- 200 ml (7 fl oz) white wine
- 70 g (2½ oz) butter
- 50 g (1¾ oz) flour
- 1 quantity warm court-bouillon with white wine or milk (p.82)
- 185 g (6½ oz) mushrooms, sliced
- 125 g (4¼ oz) cooked peeled prawns
- 125 g (4¼ oz) shelled cooked mussels (p.271)
- Salt and pepper

Preparation time: 1½ hours
Cooking time: 45 minutes
Serves 6

TUNA

Since it is a large fish, tuna is usually sold in the form of slices or steaks. It can be cooked in a court-bouillon with salt (p.82) following the instructions on p.221, and served hot with a sauce of your choice.

For grilled tuna, marinate slices of tuna in an uncooked marinade (p.78). Put the slices in a hot grill pan and cook under a medium-hot grill for 10 minutes on each side. Tuna can also be prepared *à la Chartreuse* (p.224).

CASSEROLED TUNA
THON À LA CASSEROLE

- 1 quantity uncooked marinade (p.78)
- 600 g (1 lb 5 oz) tuna
- 250 g (9 oz) bacon rashers
- 2 tablespoons oil
- 350 ml (12 fl oz) vegetable stock
- Salt and pepper
- 1 garlic clove, chopped
- 1 shallot, chopped
- 30 g (1¼ oz) butter

Preparation time: 10 minutes, plus marinating time
Cooking time: 1 hour
Serves 6

Put the marinade in a bowl, cut the tuna into thick slices and add to the marinade. Leave to marinate in the refrigerator for 2 hours, turning occasionally. Drain, reserving the marinade, and wrap the tuna in the bacon rashers. Heat the oil in a large pan, add the tuna parcels and cook over a medium heat, turning once, for 8 minutes. Pour in 150 ml (¼ pint) of the reserved marinade and the stock, season with salt and pepper, add the garlic and shallot and dot with the butter. Reduce the heat, cover and simmer for 1 hour, turning every 15 minutes.

TUNA WITH OLIVES
THON AUX OLIVES

- 400 g (14 oz) canned tuna in brine, drained
- 100 g (3½ oz) butter, softened
- 1 quantity mayonnaise (p.70)
- Salt and pepper
- Bread slices, to serve (optional)
- 125 g (4¼ oz) stoned olives

Preparation time: 25 minutes
Serves 6

Mash together the tuna and the butter in a bowl until smooth. Season the mayonnaise with salt and pepper and stir into the fish mixture. Spoon onto a dish in a dome shape, or onto slices of bread. Garnish with the olives.

TUNA ESCALOPES
ESCALOPES DE THON

Beat the egg with the milk in a bowl. Dip the tuna slices into the egg mixture and then into the flour. Heat the oil in a frying pan. Add the tuna and cook over a medium heat for 5–6 minutes, until lightly browned. Remove with a fish slice, drain and season with salt and pepper. Serve immediately, garnished with fried parsley, croutons and slices of lemon.

- 1 egg
- 50 ml (2 fl oz) milk
- 750 g (1 lb 10 oz) tuna, cut into 1-cm (½-inch) slices
- 75 g (2½ oz) flour
- 3 tablespoons oil
- Salt and pepper
- Fried flat-leaf parsley (p.81)
- 8–10 croutons
- 1 lemon, sliced

Preparation time: 10 minutes
Cooking time: 10 minutes
Serves 6

TURBOT

Turbot can be cooked in a court-bouillon with milk (p.82). Make an incision all along the backbone, then follow the instructions on p.221, and remove the skin when the fish is cooked. Serve with hollandaise sauce (p.74) or mayonnaise (p.70). For grilled turbot, follow the instructions on p.221 and serve with béarnaise sauce (p.75). Brill can be cooked in the same ways as turbot.

TURBOT GRATIN
TURBOT EN GRATIN

Preheat the oven to 200°C/400°F/Gas Mark 6 and generously grease a flameproof dish with some of the butter. Make a bed of the onion and half the parsley in the base of the dish. Score the skin of the turbot, put the fish on top of the onion and parsley, dark side down, and dot with the remaining butter. Add the remaining parsley and the mushrooms, season with salt and pepper, pour in the wine and 100 ml (3½ fl oz) water and sprinkle with the breadcrumbs. Cook on a high heat for 5 minutes, then transfer to the oven and bake, basting frequently, for 20 minutes.

- 50 g (1¾ oz) butter
- 50 g (1¾ oz) onion, chopped
- 1 bunch of flat-leaf parsley, chopped
- 1 x 1-kg (2¼-lb) turbot
- 125 g (4¼ oz) mushrooms, chopped
- Salt and pepper
- 100 ml (3½ fl oz) white wine
- 50 g (1¾ oz) dried breadcrumbs

Preparation time: 20 minutes
Cooking time: 25 minutes
Serves 6

TURBOT IN SCALLOP SHELLS
TURBOT EN COQUILLES

- **1 quantity court-bouillon (p.82)**
- **300 g (11 oz) turbot**
- **500 ml (18 fl oz) cream sauce (p.51)**
- **60 g (2 oz) Gruyère cheese, grated**

Preparation time: 20 minutes
Cooking time: 20 minutes
Serves 6

Heat the court-bouillon in a large pan, add the turbot and simmer for 8 minutes, or until cooked through. Preheat the oven to 240°C/475°F/Gas Mark 8. Drain the turbot, tip it into a bowl, add the cream sauce and mash together with a fork. Divide the mixture among 6 cleaned scallop shells, sprinkle with the cheese and bake for 10 minutes.

WEEVER

Weever can be cooked in a court-bouillon with salt (p.82), vinegar (p.82), or white wine (p.82), following the instructions on p.221. Serve with the sauce of your choice.

For grilled weever, follow the instructions on p.221 and serve with béarnaise sauce (p.75), mustard sauce (p.68) or tartare sauce (p.72). For fried weever, follow the instructions on p.222 and serve with maître d'hôtel butter (p.48).

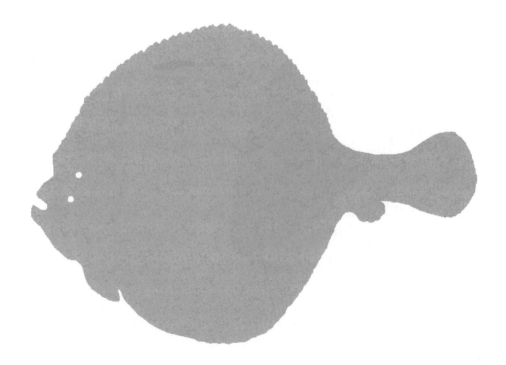

BOUILLABAISSE

BOUILLABAISSE

 p.303

Crush 2 of the garlic cloves. In a large pan, heat the oil and fry the leeks, onions, tomatoes, and crushed garlic. Season with salt and pepper, and add the herbs and saffron. Slice the thicker fish (such as conger eel, weever and monkfish) and add to the pan along with the crustaceans. Cover with 250 ml (8 fl oz) water per person. Rapidly bring to the boil and cook for 7 minutes. Add the more delicate fish. Continue to cook over a high heat for a further 8 minutes, adding the mussels 3 minutes before serving.

Meanwhile, make the rouille. Pound the garlic and pepper to a paste with a pestle and mortar, add the egg yolks and season with salt. Add the olive oil gradually, stirring constantly, until thick and smooth. Add 1 tablespoon of the cooking liquid and set aside. Check the seasoning of the bouillabaisse and add more salt and pepper if necessary. Toast the bread and rub it with the remaining garlic clove. Put the garlic toast in a soup tureen, and pour the fish cooking juices over. Serve the fish, crustaceans and mussels separately on a serving dish, accompanied by the rouille.

- 3 garlic cloves
- 5 tablespoons olive oil
- 100 g (3½ oz) leeks (white part only), chopped
- 100 g (3½ oz) onions, chopped
- 250 g (9 oz) tomatoes, skinned, de-seeded and chopped
- Salt and pepper
- 1 handful of mixed herbs, such as flat-leaf parsley and fennel
- 1 bay leaf
- 1 pinch of saffron threads
- 2.5 kg (4½ lb) fish fillets, such as whiting, weever, conger eel, monkfish, red scorpion fish, gurnard, red mullet or John Dory
- 1 kg (2¼ lb) crustaceans, such as langoustines and spiny lobsters
- 1 litre (1¾ pints) mussels, cleaned
- Slices of bread, for toasting

For the rouille:
- 2 garlic cloves
- 3 small hot peppers, de-seeded
- 2 egg yolks
- 300 ml (½ pint) olive oil

Preparation time: 25 minutes
Cooking time: 20 minutes
Serves 6

BOURRIDE

BOURRIDE

- 800 g (1¾ lb) white fish, such as sea bream, hake, monkfish, eel and skate
- 1 bay leaf
- 1 sprig of thyme
- 2 onions, chopped
- Salt and pepper
- Slices of bread, to serve
- 1 quantity aioli (p.74)
- Crème fraîche, to serve (optional)

Preparation time: 30 minutes
Cooking time: 30 minutes
Serves 6

Place the fish and 2 litres (3½ pints) water in a large pan with the bay leaf, thyme, onions, salt and pepper. Bring to a simmer and cook for 20 minutes. Meanwhile, preheat the oven to 140°C/275°F/Gas Mark 1 and put the slices of bread in the oven for 15 minutes to dry out. Strain the stock, keeping the fish to one side. Mix the stock and aioli gently. Place the bread in a soup tureen, cover with the fish and pour on the aioli to serve. The soup can be finished with the crème fraîche, if desired.

SHELLFISH

Shellfish have a very subtle flavour and soft texture, which is highly prized. Only cook shellfish that are very fresh.

MUSSELS

MUSSELS AU NATUREL

MOULES AU NATUREL

- 3 kg (6½ lb) mussels
- 30 g (1¼ oz) butter
- 50 g (1¾ oz) carrot, chopped
- 30 g (1¼ oz) onion, chopped
- 1 tablespoon chopped flat-leaf parsley
- 1 sprig of thyme
- 1 bay leaf
- Pepper

Preparation time: 20 minutes
Cooking time: 6 minutes
Serves 6

Choose mussels that are firmly closed; discard any that are cracked or that remain open when tapped. Remove the beards, scrape and wash the mussels in several changes of water, then drain. Put the mussels in a large pan with the butter, carrot, onion, parsley, thyme and bay leaf. Season with pepper. Cover and cook over a low heat for about 6 minutes, shaking the pan to mix the mussels when they begin to open. Discard any that remain closed. Serve immediately.

NOTE
Mussels can be served cold. Proceed as above, leave to cool, then remove from their shells and mix with mayonnaise (p.70).

MOULES MARINIÈRES

MOULES MARINIÈRES

 p.304

Prepare and cook the mussels (p.271), discarding the empty half-shells. Transfer the mussels to a warm serving dish and set aside. Strain the cooking liquid and pour it back into the pan, along with the wine, butter, parsley, shallot and onion. Cook over a high heat for 3 minutes. Pour the sauce over the mussels and serve hot.

- 3 kg (6½ lb) mussels
- 200 ml (7 fl oz) dry white wine
- 50 g (1¾ oz) butter
- 1 tablespoon chopped flat-leaf parsley
- 1 shallot, chopped
- 60 g (2 oz) onion, chopped

Preparation time: 20 minutes
Cooking time: 10 minutes
Serves 6

MUSSELS À LA POULETTE

MOULES À LA POULETTE

Make the blond roux. Meanwhile, prepare and cook the mussels (p.271), discarding the empty half-shells. Transfer the mussels to a warm dish and set aside. Strain the cooking liquid and stir it into the blond roux. Just before serving, whisk the egg yolks into the sauce over a low heat until it thickens, then add the lemon juice. Pour the sauce over the mussels and sprinkle with the parsley.

- 250 ml (8 fl oz) blond roux (p.57)
- 2 kg (4½ lb) mussels
- 2 egg yolks
- Juice of 1 lemon
- 1 tablespoon chopped flat-leaf parsley

Preparation time: 20 minutes
Cooking time: 20 minutes
Serves 6

MUSSEL GRATIN WITH BÉCHAMEL SAUCE

MOULES À LA BÉCHAMEL ET AU GRATIN

Preheat the oven to 220°C/425°F/Gas Mark 7. Make the béchamel sauce. Meanwhile, prepare and cook the mussels (p.271), and remove them from their shells. Add the mussels to the sauce and simmer for 5 minutes. Pour the mussels and sauce into a shallow baking dish, sprinkle with the breadcrumbs, dot with the butter and bake for 10 minutes, or until golden brown.

- 1 quantity béchamel sauce (p.50)
- 3 kg (6½ lb) mussels
- Dried breadcrumbs, for sprinkling
- 30 g (1¾ oz) butter, cut into small pieces

Preparation time: 20 minutes
Cooking time: 20 minutes
Serves 6

MUSSELS BAKED IN SHELLS

COQUILLES DE MOULES GRATINÉES

Preheat the oven to 220°C/425°F/Gas Mark 7. Prepare and cook the mussels (p.271), and remove them from their shells. Arrange 6 scallop shells in a shallow baking dish. Mix together the breadcrumbs, butter, chives and parsley. Season with salt and pepper. Put a layer of the breadcrumb mixture in the bottom of each scallop shell, then a layer of mussels, and finish with another layer of the breadcrumb mixture. Bake for 8 minutes.

- 2 kg (4½ lb) mussels
- 6 empty scallop shells, scrubbed and blanched in boiling water
- 60 g (2 oz) dried breadcrumbs
- 60 g (2 oz) butter, softened
- 15 g (½ oz) chopped chives
- 15 g (½ oz) flat-leaf parsley, chopped
- Salt and pepper

Preparation time: 30 minutes
Cooking time: 8 minutes
Serves 6

MOUCLADE

MOUCLADE

 p.305

Wash and scrape the mussels, removing the beard and discarding any that remain open when tapped. Place in a large pan and cook over a moderate heat until they open (about 5 minutes). Strain the mussels through a sieve set over a bowl and reserve the liquid. Remove 1 half-shell from each mussel and keep the mussels hot, covered. Make a white sauce (p.50) with the butter and flour, adding half water and half cooking liquid from the mussels. Stir in the garlic and season with salt and pepper. Simmer the roux gently for 10 minutes, stirring frequently. Add the egg yolk and stir to thicken, then finally add the lemon juice and hot mussels at the last moment. Sprinkle with the parsley and serve.

- 3 kg (6½ lb) mussels
- 50 g (1¾ oz) butter
- 40 g (1½ oz) flour
- 1 garlic clove, finely chopped
- Salt and pepper
- 1 egg yolk
- Juice of ½ lemon
- 3 tablespoons flat-leaf parsley, chopped

Preparation time: 25 minutes
Cooking time: 25 minutes
Serves 6

OYSTERS

Oysters can be cooked like other shellfish, although they are more commonly eaten raw. To open an oyster, wrap a tea towel around the hand that will hold the oyster to protect it. Place an oyster curved side down in the palm of your hand. Wedge a wide-bladed oyster-shucking knife into the hinge that connects the top and bottom shells. Run the knife all the way around the oyster and, using a twisting motion, prise the shells apart, taking care not to spill the liquid inside. Slide the knife under the oyster to sever its base and release the meat. Leave the oyster and its liquor in the half-shell and serve with a slice of lemon or chopped shallots in vinegar.

STUFFED OYSTERS
COQUILLES D'HUÎTRES FARCIES

📷 p.306

- 18 Pacific oysters
- Juice of ½ lemon
- 30 g (1¼ oz) butter, plus extra for dotting
- 100 g (3½ oz) mushrooms, chopped
- 120 ml (4 fl oz) milk
- 25 g (1 oz) fresh breadcrumbs
- 1 hard-boiled egg yolk
- 25 g (1 oz) dried breadcrumbs, plus extra for sprinkling
- Salt and pepper

Preparation time: 15 minutes
Cooking time: 15 minutes
Serves 6

Preheat the oven to 240°C / 475°F / Gas Mark 8. Open the oysters (see above), put them on a plate and sprinkle with the lemon juice. Wash and dry 9 of the bottom shells, arrange them in an ovenproof dish, and put the oysters back in (2 per shell). Melt the butter in a frying pan, add the mushrooms and cook for a few minutes over a medium heat until softened. In a pan over a medium heat, warm the milk, taking care not to let it boil, then add the fresh breadcrumbs and allow them to soak. Mash the egg yolk and add it to the breadcrumb and milk mixture, along with the mushrooms and dried breadcrumbs. Season with salt and pepper. Cover the oysters with this stuffing, sprinkle with more dried breadcrumbs and dot each one with butter. Bake for 10 minutes, or until golden brown.

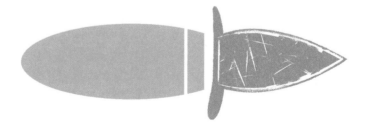

OYSTER GRATIN

HUÎTRES EN GRATIN

Preheat the oven to 190°C/375°F/Gas Mark 5. Melt the butter in a shallow gratin dish. Add 4 tablespoons of the dried breadcrumbs and allow them to absorb the butter. Open the oysters (p.275) and remove from their shells, retaining their liquid. Arrange the oysters on the bed of breadcrumbs and pour over the crème fraîche and 2 tablespoons of the liquid from the oysters. Cover with the remaining dried breadcrumbs and bake for 15 minutes, or until golden brown.

- 60 g (2 oz) butter
- 30 g (1¼ oz) dried breadcrumbs
- 5 dozen oysters
- 90 ml (3¼ fl oz) crème fraîche

Preparation time: 10 minutes
Cooking time: 15 minutes
Serves 6

FRIED OYSTERS

HUÎTRES FRITES

Open the oysters (p.275) and remove from their shells. Season with salt and pepper, dip in the egg, then in the breadcrumbs. Melt the butter in a frying pan over a medium-high heat, add the coated oysters and fry until nicely browned, turning once. Remove the oysters from the pan, arrange on a dish and coat with the tomato sauce.

VARIATION

. . . .

OYSTERS ON TOAST

HUÎTRES SUR CROÛTONS

Fry the oysters as above, and toast 10 slices of bread. Arrange 6 fried oysters on each slice. Drizzle with the butter in which they were cooked and serve hot.

- 5 dozen oysters
- Salt and pepper
- 1 egg, beaten
- Dried breadcrumbs, for dipping
- 100 g (3½ oz) butter
- 1 quantity tomato sauce (p.57)

Preparation time: 10 minutes
Cooking time: 5 minutes
Serves 6

OYSTERS WITH MUSHROOMS

HUÎTRES AUX CHAMPIGNONS

Preheat the oven to 220°C/425°F/Gas Mark 7. Open the oysters (p.275) and remove from their shells. Poach them in the court-bouillon for about 3 minutes, or until their edges begin to curl. Drain, and cut the largest ones in half. Wash and dry the bottom shells and arrange them in an ovenproof dish. Heat half the butter in a frying pan over a medium-high heat, add the mushrooms and cook until softened, then slice thinly. Season with salt and pepper. Mix the oysters and mushrooms together, and stir in the béchamel sauce. Spoon the mixture into the prepared shells, sprinkle with the breadcrumbs, pour on the remaining butter and bake for 5–6 minutes.

- 3 dozen oysters
- 1 litre (1¾ pints) court-bouillon with white wine (p.82)
- 40 g (1½ oz) butter, melted
- 150 g (5 oz) mushrooms, stalks removed, cleaned
- Salt and pepper
- 200 ml (7 fl oz) béchamel sauce (p.50)
- Dried breadcrumbs, for sprinkling

Preparation time: 25 minutes
Cooking time: 25 minutes
Serves 6

SCALLOPS

SCALLOP GRATIN

SAINT-JACQUES EN GRATIN

 p.307

Preheat the oven to 220°C/425°F/Gas Mark 7. Take the scallops out of their shells, remove the black muscle and wash the meat and corals in water. Scrub 6 of the shells to clean them, and blanch them in a pan of boiling water. Allow to cool and dry them. Arrange the cleaned shells in a baking dish. Bring 200 ml (7 fl oz) salted water to the boil; add the scallops and poach for 1 minute. Drain and dry thoroughly and set aside. Heat 20 g (¾ oz) of the butter in a frying pan over a medium-high heat, add the shallot, parsley and mushrooms, and cook until the shallot is softened.

Melt 30 g (1¼ oz) of the remaining butter, and when it is on the point of smoking add the flour and stir until it is light fawn in colour. Gradually add the wine and stock, stirring constantly. Boil for 2 minutes. Whisk in the egg yolk over a low heat to bind everything together, then add the scallops and the shallot, parsley and mushroom mixture. Spoon the mixture into the shells, 3 scallops per shell, sprinkle with the breadcrumbs, dot each shell with some of the remaining butter and bake for 10 minutes.

- 18 scallops
- 70 g (2½ oz) butter
- 1 shallot, chopped
- Small handful flat-leaf parsley, chopped
- 125 g (4¼ oz) mushrooms, chopped
- 30 g (1¼ oz) flour
- 100 ml (3½ fl oz) white wine
- 200 ml (7 fl oz) any stock
- 1 egg yolk
- Dried breadcrumbs, for sprinkling
- Salt

Preparation time: 50 minutes
Cooking time: 15 minutes
Serves 6

SAUTÉED SCALLOPS
SAINT-JACQUES SAUTÉES

- 24 scallops
- 60 g (2 oz) butter
- 1 garlic clove, chopped
- 1 tablespoon flat-leaf parsley, finely chopped
- Salt and pepper

Preparation time: 10 minutes
Cooking time: 4 minutes
Serves 6

Take the scallops out of their shells, remove the black muscle and wash the meat and corals in water. Dry thoroughly. Heat the butter in a frying pan and add the garlic and parsley. Add the scallops and fry over a high heat for 2 minutes on each side without moving them, to allow the formation of a crust. Season with salt and pepper and serve immediately.

SCALLOPS IN CHEESE SAUCE
SAINT-JACQUES SAUCE MORNAY

- 24 scallops
- 1 quantity cheese sauce (p.50)

Preparation time: 10 minutes
Cooking time: 25 minutes
Serves 6

Preheat the oven to 240°C/475°F/Gas Mark 8. Take the scallops out of their shells, remove the black muscle and wash the meat and corals in water. Bring a pan of water almost to the boil, add the scallops and poach for 3 minutes. Remove, drain and leave to cool slightly. Dice the scallops, cover with the cheese sauce, and pour the mixture into an ovenproof dish. Bake for 5 minutes, or until golden brown.

SEA URCHINS

Sea urchins can be eaten raw or cooked. Raw, they are delicious on their own, or with a squeeze of lemon juice. To cook them, wash the urchins carefully, using a cloth as protection from the spines, and boil them in salted water for 5 minutes. Cut off the tops, as with a boiled egg, to find the edible orange ovaries (or corals) inside. Sea urchins are eaten in winter and spring.

CRUSTACEANS

Crustaceans are highly prized creatures, caught in both salt and fresh water. The shell that covers their body turns red during cooking. Their flesh is nourishing and has a subtle, delicate flavour. Crustaceans must be eaten very fresh.

LOBSTERS & SPINY LOBSTERS

It is usually recommended to place lobsters in the freezer for a few hours before cooking them. Cook lobsters in a simmering court-bouillon with salt or vinegar (p.82) for 8 minutes per 400 g (14 oz), or 10 minutes per 1 kg (2¼ lb). Leave them to cool in the court-bouillon. When you take them out, make a small incision in the head to drain out the court-bouillon.

To prepare cooked lobsters, turn them on their back, split the abdominal wall all the way down and remove the tail. Remove the intestines from the middle and cut the flesh into slices. Shell the claws and feet. Spiny lobsters are prepared in the same way as lobsters, but most of the meat is in the tail, as the front legs have no claws.

LOBSTER THERMIDOR
HOMARD THERMIDOR

 p.308

Preheat the oven to 220°C/425°F/Gas Mark 7. Put the court-bouillon in a large pan and bring to the boil. Add the lobster and boil for about 10 minutes. Remove the lobster and allow it to cool slightly. When it is cool enough to handle, remove the meat from the shell and chop into small dice. Melt the butter in a large frying pan, add the diced lobster and cook over a medium heat for 5 minutes. Pour in the crème fraîche then add the Madeira and Cognac. Season with salt and cayenne pepper. Put the mixture into an ovenproof dish and bake for 5 minutes before serving.

- 1 x 500-g (1 lb 2-oz) lobster
- 1 quantity court-bouillon with salt (p.82) or vinegar (p.82)
- 125 g (4¼ oz) butter
- 200 ml (7 fl oz) crème fraîche
- 100 ml (3½ fl oz) Madeira
- 100 ml (3½ fl oz) Cognac
- Salt
- Cayenne pepper

Preparation time: 1 hour
Cooking time: 30 minutes
Serves 6

LOBSTER SALAD

SALADE DE HOMARD

- **1 quantity court-bouillon with salt or vinegar (p.82)**
- **1 x 1-kg (2¼-lb) lobster**
- **Salad leaves, to serve**
- **1 quantity vinaigrette (p.66)**
- **1 quantity mayonnaise (p.70)**

Preparation time: 20 minutes
Cooking time: 10 minutes
Serves 6

Put the court-bouillon in a large pan and bring to the boil. Add the lobster and boil for 10 minutes. Remove the lobster and allow it to cool slightly. When it is cool enough to handle, remove the meat and cut into thin slices. Arrange the slices on some lettuce leaves, dress with the vinaigrette, and serve with the mayonnaise.

LOBSTER À L'AMÉRICAINE

HOMARD À L'AMÉRICAINE

Place the lobster in the freezer for 2 hours. Bring a large pan of salted water to the boil and plunge the lobster, head first and upside down, into the water. Boil for 2 minutes, drain and allow to cool. Heat the ordinary Cognac in a small pan over a high heat and boil for a few minutes to evaporate the alcohol. Set aside.

Flatten the lobster on a work surface, holding the tail where it joins the body. Press the tip of a large chef's knife through the head to the cutting board, then bring the blade down between the eyes to finish the cut. Cut the claws and tail into 6 pieces. Remove and reserve the creamy material (tomalley) and the coral from the body. Heat the oil, add the pieces of lobster and cook for a few minutes, until they turn red. Remove from the pan. Add the shallot, garlic, ordinary Cognac, wine and tomatoes, season with salt and cayenne pepper, and simmer for a few minutes. Remove from the heat, pour in the fine Cognac and boil briskly for a few minutes to evaporate the alcohol. Simmer for 15 minutes. Return the lobster to the pan and simmer for 5 minutes more. Transfer the lobster to a serving dish. Continue simmering to reduce the sauce a little, then add the tomalley, coral, butter and herbs, and stir until thickened. Pour over the lobster and serve hot.

- 1 x 1-kg (2¼-lb) lobster
- 50 ml (2 fl oz) ordinary Cognac
- 3 tablespoons oil
- 20 g (¾ oz) shallot, chopped
- 1 garlic clove, chopped
- 200 ml (7 fl oz) white wine
- 300 g (11 oz) tomatoes, skinned and pulped
- Salt and cayenne pepper
- 50 ml (2 fl oz) fine Cognac
- 60 g (2 oz) butter
- 1 tablespoon chopped chervil
- 1 tablespoon chopped flat-leaf parsley
- 1 tablespoon chopped tarragon

Preparation time: 25 minutes
Cooking time: 20 minutes
Serves 6

SPINY LOBSTER SOUFFLÉ

SOUFFLÉ DE LANGOUSTE

Put the court-bouillon in a large pan and bring to the boil. Add the lobster and cook for 8–9 minutes. When it is cool enough to handle, peel, chop and mash all the meat. Preheat the oven to 190°C/375°F/Gas Mark 5 and grease a soufflé dish with butter. Make the béchamel sauce and stir in the wine, lobster meat, butter and egg yolks. Whisk the egg whites to stiff peaks and fold into the lobster mixture. Stir in the Cognac and season with salt and cayenne pepper. Pour the mixture into the prepared dish and bake for 20 minutes, or until risen and golden brown.

- 1 quantity court-bouillon with salt or vinegar (p.82)
- 1 x 500-g (1 lb 2-oz) spiny lobster
- 50 g (1¾ oz) butter, plus extra for greasing
- 1 quantity béchamel sauce (p.50)
- 50 ml (2 fl oz) white wine
- 3 egg yolks
- 4 egg whites
- 20 ml (¾ fl oz) Cognac
- Salt and cayenne pepper

Preparation time: 1 hour
Cooking time: 20 minutes
Serves 6

SPINY LOBSTER COCKTAIL
COCKTAIL DE LANGOUSTE

- 350 g (12 oz) cooked spiny lobster meat (p.280)
- 3 tablespoons mayonnaise (p.70)
- Salt and pepper
- 100 ml (3½ fl oz) Cognac
- ½ quantity velouté sauce (p.59)
- 50 ml (2 fl oz) mushroom stock (p.46)
- 1 tablespoon Madeira
- 1 teaspoon tomato purée

Preparation time: 25 minutes, plus chilling time
Serves 6

Divide the spiny lobster meat between 6 large cocktail glasses. Season the mayonaise well with salt and pepper, and mix in the Cognac. Combine the velouté sauce with the mushroom stock, Madeira and tomato purée, and add this to the mayonnaise. Top the spiny lobster meat in the glasses with this sauce. Chill before serving.

PRAWNS & SHRIMPS

Cook prawns and shrimps in heavily salted boiling water. Depending on size, prawns will take around 3 minutes, shrimps around 2 minutes. Remove and drain thoroughly immediately after cooking. To remove the meat, separate the head from the tail and open the shell to release the tail.

PRAWN CROQUETTES
CROQUETTES DE CREVETTES

- 500 g (1 lb 2 oz) prawns
- 750 ml (1¼ pints) milk
- 100 g (3½ oz) butter
- 100 g (3½ oz) flour
- Freshly grated nutmeg
- Salt and pepper
- Oil or butter, for frying

Preparation time: 45 minutes
Cooking time: 40 minutes
Serves 6

Cook the prawns (see above) and peel them, reserving the shells. Bring the milk to the boil in a pan, add the shells and simmer gently for 15 minutes. Strain, reserving the liquid, then carefully mash the shells in the sieve and strain again, to obtain more liquid. Make a white sauce (p.50) with the butter, flour, prawn milk and the liquid produced from mashing the shells. Stir in the prawns, season with nutmeg, salt and pepper, cook for 5 minutes until the liquid has evaporated, then cool. The mixture should be very thick. Form the mixture into small balls or patties. Heat oil or butter in a large frying pan, add the croquettes and fry until golden, turning as needed to brown on all sides.

PRAWN SALAD

SALADE DE CREVETTES

Cook the shrimps or prawns (p.283), and peel. Discard the shells. Mix the salmon with the shrimp or prawn tails and season with the vinaigrette dressing or mayonnaise. Chill in the refrigerator for 2 hours before serving.

- 200 g (7 oz) shrimps or prawns
- 60 g (2 oz) smoked salmon, cut into strips
- 1 quantity vinaigrette dressing (p.66) or mayonnaise (p.70)

Preparation time: 20 minutes, plus chilling time
Cooking time: 3 minutes
Serves 6

PRAWN RISSOLES

RISSOLES AUX CREVETTES

Cook the shrimps or prawns (p.283), cool slightly and peel, reserving the shells. Bring 350 ml (12 fl oz) water to the boil in a medium pan, add the shells, then reduce the heat and simmer for 10 minutes. Strain the liquid into a pan and discard the shells. Use the liquid to make a white sauce (p.50) with the flour and butter. Stir in the mustard and add the shrimps or prawns. Roll the pastry out to a thickness of 3 mm (⅛ inch). Cut into rounds 7 cm (3 inches) in diameter. Place a small spoonful of the mixture in the centre of each round and fold over into a crescent shape like a turnover. Seal the edges with a little water. In a deep sauté pan, add oil to a depth of around 2 cm (¾ inch) and heat. Carefully fry the rissoles in the hot oil for a few minutes on each side. Drain on kitchen paper and serve very hot.

- 350 g (12 oz) shrimps or prawns
- 40 g (1½ oz) flour
- 30 g (1¼ oz) butter
- 1 teaspoon mustard
- Shortcrust pastry made with 150 g (5 oz) flour (p.784)
- Oil, for frying

Preparation time: 20 minutes
Cooking time: 10 minutes
Serves 6

PRAWN COCKTAIL
COCKTAIL DE CREVETTES

- Juice of 1 lemon
- 1 tablespoon Cognac
- 1 tablespoon tomato purée
- 150 ml (¼ pint) mayonnaise (p.70)
- Salt and pepper
- Curry powder, to taste
- 6 lettuce leaves
- 200 g (7 oz) cooked peeled shrimps or prawns

Preparation time: 20 minutes
Serves 6

Stir the lemon juice, Cognac and tomato purée into the mayonnaise. Season with salt, pepper and curry powder. Chop the lettuce leaves coarsely and place in the bottom of 6 individual glasses. Mix the shrimps or prawns into the mayonnaise and fill each glass with this mixture.

CRAB

Cook crabs in a boiling court-bouillon with salt (p.82) for 30 minutes per kg (2¼ lb). Leave to cool in the court-bouillon. When you take them out, make a small incision in the head to drain out the court-bouillon.

To prepare cooked crabs, remove the meat and the coral contained in the shell. Shell the legs and claws.

CURRIED CRAB ON THE SHELL
COQUILLES DE CRABES À L'INDIENNE

- 1 quantity court-bouillon with salt (p.82)
- 6 x 450-g (1-lb) crabs
- 100 g (3½ oz) tomato purée
- Cayenne pepper, to taste
- Curry powder, to taste
- 50 g (1¾ oz) butter

Preparation time: 30 minutes
Cooking time: 30–40 minutes
Serves 6

Preheat the oven to 240°C/475°F/Gas Mark 8. Bring the court-bouillon to the boil, add the crabs and boil for about 15 minutes for each crab. Remove from the pan, rinse and allow to cool. Twist off the claws and legs and set aside. Crack and remove the belly shell and discard the stomach sac and soft gills. Reserve and clean out the top shells. Scoop out and reserve the brown meat. Crack the claws and legs and remove the white meat. Finely chop all the meat. Mash the coral, the creamy material contained in the shell and the tomato purée with cayenne pepper and curry powder to taste. Arrange the reserved shells in an ovenproof dish and divide the crab meat mixture between the shells. Dot with the butter and bake for 10 minutes.

ROSCOFF CRAB

TOURTEAUX À LA ROSCOVITE

Cook the crabs in the court-bouillon (p.285) for 15 minutes per crab, remove from the pan, rinse and allow to cool. Extract the meat. Twist off the claws and legs and set aside. Crack and remove the belly shell and discard the stomach sac and soft gills. Reserve and clean out one of the shells. Scoop out and reserve the brown meat. Crack the claws and legs and remove the white meat. Finely chop all of the meat, and mix it with the coral, three-quarters of the egg slices, and the herbs and mayonnaise. Arrange in the reserved shell in a pyramid shape. Garnish with the tomato slices, remaining egg slices and chopped parsley.

- 2 crabs
- 1 quantity court-bouillon with salt (p.82)
- 3 hard-boiled eggs (p.134), peeled and sliced
- 1 handful of mixed herbs, such as flat-leaf parsley, chives, chervil and tarragon, chopped, plus extra parsley to garnish
- 250 ml (8 fl oz) mayonnaise (p.70)
- 2 tomatoes, sliced

Preparation time: 30 minutes
Cooking time: 20 minutes
Serves 6

CRAYFISH & LANGOUSTINES

To cook crayfish and langoustines (also known as Dublin Bay prawns), poach them in court-bouillon made with salt or vinegar (p.82) for 8–10 minutes. Leave to cool in the court-bouillon. After removing them, make a small incision in the shell to allow the court-bouillon to drain out. To devein (or remove the intestinal organs) from each crayfish or langoustine, snap off the fin in the centre of the tail, and the black tube will come away whole.

Serve on a dish, arranged in a pyramid shape and garnished with parsley. Crayfish and langoustines can be served just as they are, or with a vinaigrette dressing (p.66), mayonnaise (p.70) or butter.

CRAYFISH NANTUA
ÉCREVISSES À LA NANTUA

- **40 crayfish**
- **1 quantity court-bouillon with salt or vinegar (p.82)**
- **40 g (1½ oz) butter**
- **185 g (6½ oz) mushrooms**
- **200 ml (7 fl oz) crème fraîche**
- **4 egg yolks**

Preparation time: 1½ hours
Cooking time: 1 hour 10 minutes
Serves 6

Prepare and cook the crayfish (p.286), reserving 1 litre (1¾ pints) of the court-bouillon. Peel the crayfish and set the tail meat aside. Carefully crush all the shells thoroughly, add them to the reserved court-bouillon and cook over a low heat for 1 hour to reduce the liquid by half. Pass the reduction through a sieve to make a sauce.

Meanwhile, melt half the butter in a large frying pan over a medium heat and cook the mushrooms for 10 minutes, then remove the mushrooms and set them aside. Add the remaining butter to the pan and cook the crayfish tails for 10 minutes. Add the sauce and stir in the crème fraîche and the mushrooms. Before serving, whisk the egg yolks into the sauce over a low heat to thicken it.

LANGOUSTINE SALAD
SALADE DE LANGOUSTINES

 p.309

- **300 g (11 oz) curly endive**
- **200 g (7 oz) lamb's lettuce**
- **100 g (3½ oz) purslane**
- **60 g (2 oz) French beans**
- **200 g (7 oz) asparagus**
- **50 small langoustines**
- **25 g (1 oz) mushrooms**
- **1 quantity vinaigrette (p.66)**
- **50 ml (2 fl oz) oil**
- **Salt and pepper**
- **50 g (1¼ oz) chives, chopped**

Preparation time: 30–40 minutes
Cooking time: 10 minutes
Serves 6

Peel, wash, drain and dry the salad leaves. Trim the beans and asparagus, bring a large pan of salted water to the boil and blanch them for 5–8 minutes, or until tender. Peel the langoustine tails and discard the claws. If desired, keep some langoustines whole and unpeeled to garnish the salad. Remove the stalks from the mushrooms and wipe them with a damp cloth, then cut into strips.

Dress the salad leaves with some of the vinaigrette, mix thoroughly and arrange on a dish. Cut the asparagus into slices and the beans into julienne strips. Heat the oil in a frying pan over a high heat, fry the langoustines, then add the asparagus, beans and mushrooms. Moisten with a little vinaigrette, season with salt and pepper and sprinkle with the chives. Arrange the contents of the frying pan on top of the bed of salad and serve immediately.

COOKED FISH & SHELLFISH

SHELLFISH DEBELLEYME
COQUILLES DEBELLEYME

Preheat the oven to 220°C/425°F/Gas Mark 7 and arrange the scallop shells in an ovenproof dish. Melt 30 g (1¼ oz) of the butter in a frying pan and fry the onion over a low heat for 10 minutes, stirring occasionally. Soak the fresh breadcrumbs in the warm milk. Add the mushrooms to the onion, and cook for 8 minutes. Squeeze the excess liquid out of the breadcrumbs and add them and the wine to the onion and mushrooms, and season with salt and pepper. Simmer for 10 minutes. Add the shellfish and coat well with the sauce. Divide the mixture between the scallop shells, sprinkle with the breadcrumbs, dot with the remaining butter and bake for 10 minutes.

- 6 empty scallop shells, scrubbed and blanched in boiling water
- 40 g (1½ oz) butter
- 60 g (2 oz) onion, finely chopped
- 80 g (2¾ oz) fresh breadcrumbs
- 200 ml (7 fl oz) warm milk
- 100 g (3½ oz) mushrooms, chopped
- 100 ml (3½ fl oz) white wine
- Salt and pepper
- 300 g (11 oz) cooked shellfish
- Dried breadcrumbs, for sprinkling

Preparation time: 30 minutes
Cooking time: 40 minutes
Serves 6

SHELLFISH À LA MORNAY
COQUILLES À LA MORNAY

Preheat the oven to 220°C/425°F/Gas Mark 7 and arrange the scallop shells in an ovenproof dish. Divide the shellfish between the shells. Cover with the cheese sauce and bake for 10 minutes.

- 6 empty scallop shells, scrubbed and blanched in boiling water
- 400 g (14 oz) cooked shellfish
- 500 ml (18 fl oz) cheese sauce (p.50)

Preparation time: 15 minutes
Cooking time: 30 minutes
Serves 6

RISSOLES

RISSOLES

- Flour, for dusting
- 300 g (11 oz) ready-made shortcrust or puff pastry
- 200 ml (7 fl oz) white sauce (p.50)
- 250 g (9 oz) cooked fish, skinned and cut into small pieces
- Salt and pepper
- 30 g (1¼ oz) butter
- 100 g (3½ oz) mushrooms, chopped
- 1 egg, beaten

Preparation time: 1 hour
Cooking time: 40 minutes
Serves 6

Preheat the oven to 200°C/400°F/Gas Mark 6. Lightly flour a work surface, roll out the pastry thinly and cut 7-cm (3-inch) circles with a cookie cutter or an inverted drinking glass. Make the white sauce, add the fish and season with salt and pepper. Meanwhile, melt the butter in a frying pan, add the mushrooms and cook for 5 minutes over a medium heat. Add to the fish. Arrange 1 teaspoon of the fish mixture on half of each circle of pastry. Fold over into a crescent shape like a turnover and seal the edges with a little water. Brush both sides with the egg, arrange on a baking tray and bake for 20 minutes.

NOTE
The turnovers can also be deep-fried.

FISH FRITTERS

BEIGNETS DE POISSON

- 250 g (9 oz) cooked fish, skinned and cut into pieces
- 1 quantity batter (p.725)
- Vegetable oil, for deep-frying

Preparation time: 30 minutes
Cooking time: 15 minutes
Serves 6

Stir the fish into the batter. Heat the oil in a deep-fryer to 180°C/350°F, or until a cube of bread browns in 30 seconds. Carefully drop spoonfuls of the battered fish into the hot oil. Fry, in batches, for about 5 minutes, or until brown and crisp. Drain on kitchen paper and serve warm.

FISH CROQUETTES

SUBRICS DE POISSON

Melt the butter in a large frying pan over a medium heat, add the mushrooms and cook for 10 minutes. Make the white sauce, stir in the fish and mushrooms, season with salt and pepper, and allow to cool. Heat the oil in a deep-fryer to 180°C /350°F, or until a cube of bread browns in 30 seconds. Shape the mixture into small oblongs, dip them in the egg and roll in the breadcrumbs to coat, then carefully place in the hot oil and deep-fry, in batches, for about 5 minutes, or until brown and crisp. Drain on kitchen paper and serve with the lemon wedges and fried parsley.

- 50 g (1¾ oz) butter
- 125 g (4¼ oz) mushrooms, chopped
- 250 ml (8 fl oz) white sauce (p.50)
- 250 g (9 oz) cooked fish, skinned and cut into pieces
- Salt and pepper
- Vegetable oil, for deep-frying
- 1 egg, lightly beaten
- Dried breadcrumbs, to coat
- 1 lemon, cut into wedges, to serve
- Fried flat-leaf parsley (p.81), to serve

Preparation time: 15 minutes
Cooking time: 15 minutes
Serves 6

FISH IN ASPIC

ASPIC DE POISSON

Place a slice of tomato on the bottom of each of 6 small dishes or ramekins, cover with a little of the macédoine of vegetables and top with a piece of fish. Prepare the aspic jelly, following the instructions on the packet, and pour it into each dish. Cover with clingfilm and allow to set in the refrigerator for 12 hours. Run a knife carefully around the edge of each dish to loosen, flip onto a serving plate, and shake gently to unmould. Serve cold.

- 6 slices tomato
- 175 g (6 oz) macédoine of vegetables (p.96)
- 250 g (9 oz) cooked fish, skinned and cut into pieces
- 1 packet aspic jelly, or 1 quantity aspic (p.45)

Preparation time: 20 minutes, plus setting time
Serves 6

FISH SOUFFLÉ

SOUFFLÉ DE POISSON

- 50 g (1¾ oz) butter,
  plus extra for greasing
- 70 g (2½ oz) flour
- 300 ml (½ pint) milk
- 200 g (7 oz) cooked fish,
  skinned and cut into
  small pieces
- 4 eggs, separated
- Any sauce, to serve

Preparation time: 20 minutes
Cooking time: 65 minutes
Serves 6

Preheat the oven to 160°C/325°F/Gas Mark 3. Grease a soufflé dish with butter. Make a béchamel sauce (p.50) with the butter, flour and milk. Mix the fish pieces into it and stir in the egg yolks. Whisk the egg whites to stiff peaks and fold into the mixture. Put the mixture into the prepared dish and bake for 45 minutes, then increase the heat to 200°C/400°F/Gas Mark 6 and bake for 20 minutes more, or until risen and brown. Serve with the chosen sauce.

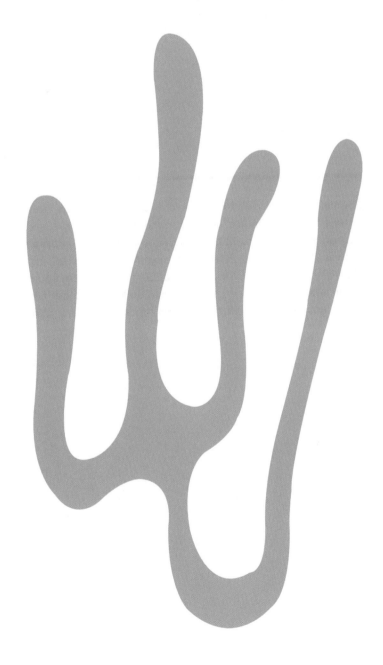

FISH PIE

TIMBALE PARMENTIER

Preheat the oven to 220°C/425°F/Gas Mark 7. Boil the potatoes in salted water until soft, then mash them finely, mix in the
eggs and season with salt and pepper. Arrange the potatoes in
a ring in an ovenproof dish, dot with 30 g (1¼ oz) of the butter
and bake for 20 minutes, until brown. Meanwhile, melt 20 g
(¾ oz) of the butter in a pan, add the mushrooms and cook
for about 10 minutes over gentle heat. Make the white sauce
and stir in the mushrooms, fish and remaining butter. Heat
gently for 10 minutes, then pour the mixture into the centre of
the potato ring. Serve immediately.

- **500 g (1 lb 2 oz) potatoes, quartered**
- **3 eggs, lightly beaten**
- **Salt and pepper**
- **125 g (4¼ oz) mushrooms, chopped**
- **50 g (1¼ oz) butter**
- **500 ml (18 fl oz) white sauce (p.50)**
- **400 g (14 oz) cooked fish, skinned and cut into pieces**

Preparation time: 1 hour
Cooking time: 35 minutes
Serves 6

FISH BALLS

BOULETTES DE POISSON

Boil the potatoes in salted water until soft, then mash them
finely and mix in the fish and eggs, and season with salt and
pepper. Heat the oil to 180°C/350°F, or until a cube of bread
browns in 30 seconds. Shape the mixture into balls and dip
them in the flour to coat. Fry in the hot oil, in batches, for about
5 minutes, or until golden brown. Drain on kitchen paper and
serve, accompanied with the tomato sauce in a sauce boat.

- **400 g (14 oz) potatoes**
- **400 g (14 oz) cooked fish, skinned and mashed**
- **3 eggs, lightly beaten**
- **Salt and pepper**
- **Vegetable oil, for deep-frying**
- **50 g (1¼ oz) flour**
- **1 quantity tomato sauce (p.57), to serve**

Preparation time: 20 minutes
Cooking time: 20 minutes
Serves 6

Eel matelote   (p226)

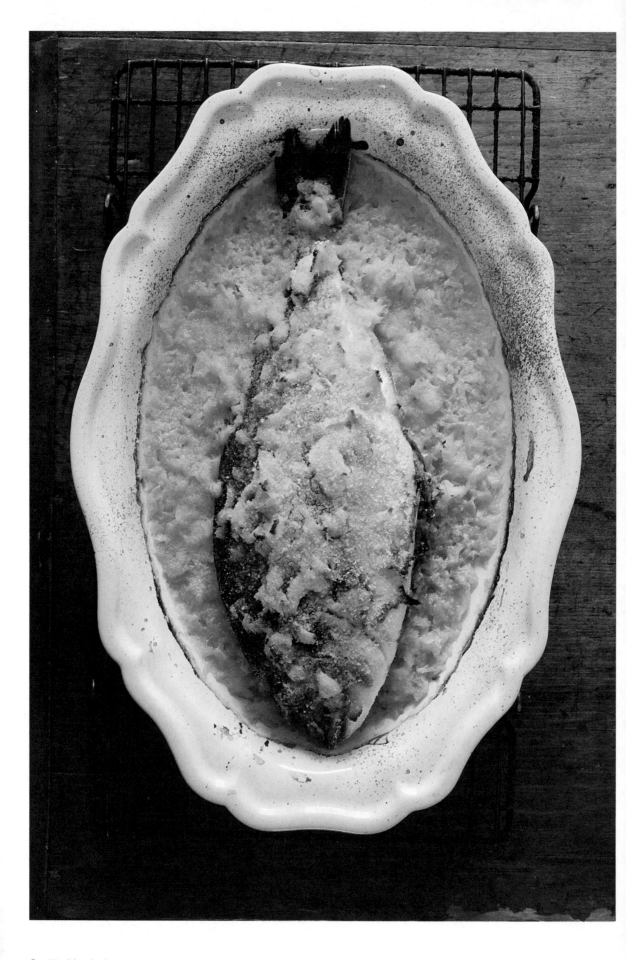

Stuffed barbel   (p.228)

Galantine of salmon   (p.236)

Trout with almonds (p.238)

Sea bream with herbs (p.246)

Stuffed mackerel   (p.251)

Salt cod à la provençale   (p.256)

Sautéed skate (p.260)

Sardines with herbs (p.262)

Sole meunière (p.263)

Bouillabaisse (p.270)

Moules marinière   (p.272)

Mouclade (p.274)

Stuffed oysters (p.275)

Scallop gratin (p.278)

Lobster Thermidor (p.280)

Langoustine salad   (p.287)

MEAT

A distinction is normally made between red meat, such as beef and mutton, and white meat, such as veal, chicken, pork and rabbit. This has nothing to do with their nutritional benefits. It is the specific cut (how fat or lean it is) and the method of cooking that are important. Meat that is simply grilled, roasted or poached will be lighter than meat that has been cooked for a long time and served in a sauce. Frozen meat, if prepared well, often has as fine a flavour as fresh meat, but it must be defrosted very slowly before being cooked. It should be placed in the refrigerator a few hours before you start to cook, and very large pieces should be defrosted overnight.

On average, 120 g (4 oz) meat off the bone and 160 g (5½ oz) on the bone is sufficient for one person. Lastly, bear in mind that about 35 per cent of the weight of a cut of meat is lost in slow cooking, and 20 per cent in rapid cooking.

PREPARATION

Trimming and preparing meat for cooking involves removing parts that are too fatty or are not required, such as skin or tendons. The treatment of meat varies according to the cooking methods used: for grilled meat, oil the grill pan and the piece of meat. For a roast, bard the joint, which means covering it with a thin layer of fat (streaky) bacon, and tie it up with string. For braised meat, lard it, which means threading small pieces of streaky or smoked bacon through it, using a larding needle. All the meat recipes assume that the fat is butter. The butter may be replaced, especially in the case of braised meats and stews, by other fats such as flavourless oils, olive oil or goose or duck fat.

PRESENTATION

COLD MEAT
Cut into thin slices and serve on a long serving dish with gherkins, mustard, mayonnaise and a salad.

GRILLED MEAT
Arrange the meat on a dish decorated with salad leaves or watercress. Grilled meat is often served with fried potatoes or chips.

ROAST MEAT

Slice the meat and arrange it on a serving dish with one or more garnishes of vegetables, and serve the sauce or the roasting juices separately in a sauce boat.

BRAISED MEAT

Arrange the meat on a serving dish, with its garnish, or serve the garnish separately in another dish.

MEAT IN A SAUCE

Serve the meat on a serving dish, coated in some of the sauce, with the rest served separately, in a sauce boat. See below for suggested sauces.

SAUCES

FOR WHITE MEAT

HOT

Butter (p.51); béarnaise (p.75); béchamel (p.50); Bordelaise (p.58); caper (p.56); printanière or chivry (p.54); hot or cold blond roux (p.57); financière (p.57); hollandaise (p.74); poulette (p.52); Richelieu (p.58); soubise (p.54); supreme (p.52); tomato (p.57); velouté (p.59); ivory velouté (p.59).

COLD

Mayonnaise (p.70); green mayonnaise (p.70); tartare (p.72); rémoulade (p.68).

FOR RED MEAT

HOT

Béarnaise (p.75); mushroom (p.61); chasseur (p.65); chateaubriand (p.62); poor man's (p.47); Périgueux (p.61); poivrade (p.63); crapaudine (p.75); Madeira (p.61); mustard (p.68); Portuguese (p.62); horseradish (p.54); Robert (p.63); tomato (p.57).

COLD

Mayonnaise (p.70); ravigote (p.56); Norwegian (p.71); devilled (p.76).

BEEF

The characteristics and cooking quality of beef differ depending on which part of the animal the cut is taken from. A carcass consists of the upper section, from the animal's back, which provides the best, most tender cuts, suitable for rapid cooking. The meat from the lower section, known as the side or flank, is tougher, suitable for braising or boiling. Beef should always be bright red, firm and glossy. The white or pale yellow fat may be near the surface, or it may be spread more deeply throughout the muscle; the meat is then said to be 'marbled'. It is important to know where a piece of meat has come from, so that you can be sure of its quality and choose an appropriate cut for the dish you intend to make.

1 • Neck
2 • Clod
3 • Chuck and blade
4 • Fore rib
5 • Thick rib
6 • Thin rib
7 • Rolled ribs
8 • Sirloin
9 • Rump
10 • Silverside
11 • Topside
12 • Thick flank
13 • Leg
14 • Flank
15 • Brisket
16 • Shin

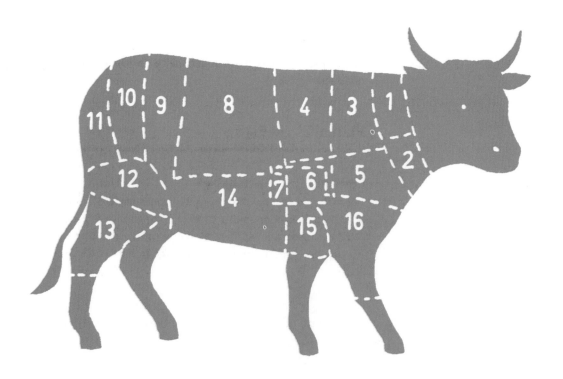

COOKING METHOD	CUTS	COOKING TIMES
POACHING	Thick flank Silverside Leg Thin rib; thick rib Rolled rib Neck Flank Sirloin Cheek Tail	3½ hours per 1 kg (2¼ lb)
GRILLING	Fillet Rump Faux-filet Entrecôte	8–15 minutes, depending on thickness
FRYING (STEAKS)	Cuts listed under grilling, plus: Flank Thick flank Chuck Shank Shoulder	8–15 minutes, depending on thickness
ROASTING	Sirloin Fillet Faux-filet Rump Rolled rib	15–25 minutes per 500 g (1 lb 2 oz) (15 for rare, 25 for well done)
BRAISING	Thick flank Round Chuck roast Arm roast Skirt	3–4 hours per 1 kg (2¼ lb)
STEWING	Breast Thick flank English roast Skirt	3 hours per 1 kg (2¼ lb)

POACHING

BOILED BEEF, OR POT-AU-FEU
BŒUF BOUILLI OR POT-AU-FEU

Put 3 litres (5¼ pints) water and the salt in a large pan over a high heat and bring to the boil. Carefully put the meat and bones into the boiling water, then reduce the heat and simmer for 15 minutes. Skim off the fat, and add the vegetables. Bring back to the boil, then lower the heat and simmer for 3 hours. Just before serving, skim off the fat and pour the soup into a tureen. Serve the beef separately surrounded by its vegetables, with coarse salt, mustard and gherkins.

- 30 g (1¼ oz) salt
- 800 g (1¾ lb) stewing beef on the bone
- 200 g (7 oz) carrots, roughly chopped
- 125 g (4¼ oz) turnips, roughly chopped
- 100 g (3½ oz) leeks, roughly chopped
- 60 g (2 oz) parsnips, chopped
- 1 celery stick, chopped
- Coarse salt, to serve
- Mustard, to serve
- Gherkins, to serve

Preparation time: 25 minutes
Cooking time: 3½ hours
Serves 6

GRIDDLING

STEAK
BIFTECKS

Prepare the maître d'hôtel butter, heat the griddle and brush the steaks with oil. When the griddle is very hot, put on the steaks and brown for 2 minutes on each side to serve them rare. Season with salt and pepper and serve with the maître d'hôtel butter.

NOTE
To cook in a frying pan, use steaks that are no more than 1.5 cm (¾ inch) thick. Melt 20 g (¾ oz) butter in the pan, put the steaks in and brown for 2 minutes on each side. Discard the cooked butter, and season the steaks with salt and pepper before serving.

- 1 quantity maître d'hôtel butter (p.48), to serve
- 6 x 100 g (3½ oz) steaks, such as rump or sirloin 2 cm (¾ inch) thick
- Oil, for brushing
- Salt and pepper

Preparation time: 5 minutes
Cooking time: 4–5 minutes
Serves 6

p.412

ENTRECÔTE STEAK
ENTRECÔTE

- 1 quantity sauce, to serve:
  Maître d'hôtel butter (p.48),
  Bordelaise sauce (p.58),
  or béarnaise sauce (p.75)
- 6 x 100 g (3½ oz)
  entrecôte steaks
- Oil, for brushing
- Salt and pepper

Preparation time: 5 minutes
Cooking time: 9 minutes
Serves 6

Prepare the chosen sauce. Meanwhile, heat the griddle and brush the steaks with oil. As entrecôtes are thicker than other steaks, they need to be cooked longer. When the griddle is hot, put on the steaks and brown for 4 minutes on one side and 5 minutes on the other. Serve with the chosen sauce.

NOTE
Entrecôte steaks are cut from just behind the shoulder, between the ribs. Sirloin and rump steaks can be cooked in the same way.

FRYING

STEAK À L'ALSACIENNE
BIFTECKS À L'ALSACIENNE

- 20 g (¾ oz) butter
- 60 g (2 oz) onion, sliced
- 6 steaks
- 6 eggs
- Salt and pepper

Preparation time: 5 minutes
Cooking time: 7 minutes
Serves 6

Heat the butter in a frying pan over a high heat, add the onion and cook until golden brown. Put the steaks in and cook for 2 minutes. Turn the steaks, crack an egg onto each one, season with salt and pepper, and cook for 5 minutes more. Serve immediately.

STEAK À L'ALLEMANDE

BIFTECKS À L'ALLEMANDE

Heat half the butter in a large frying pan over a medium-high heat. Add the onion and cook until softened but do not allow to brown. Meanwhile, soak the breadcrumbs in the warm milk, then squeeze out the liquid and put them into a bowl. Mix in the beef and the cooked onion. Add the egg, mix well, and season with salt and pepper. Shape into 6 patties of equal size. Heat the remaining butter in a frying pan, put the patties in and cook for 5 minutes on each side. Garnish with parsley.

- 40 g (1½ oz) butter
- 60 g (2 oz) onion, chopped
- 60 g (2 oz) fresh white breadcrumbs
- 200 ml (7 fl oz) warm milk
- 400 g (14 oz) beef, chopped or minced
- 1 egg
- Salt and pepper
- Flat-leaf parsley, chopped, to garnish

Preparation time: 25 minutes
Cooking time: 10 minutes
Serves 6

FILLET STEAK CHÂTELAINE

FILETS MIGNONS CHÂTELAINE

Put the bacon, carrot and onion in the bottom of a heavy-based pan with a lid and place the lettuces on top. Pour in the beef and veal stock, add the bouquet garni, cover and cook over a medium heat for 40 minutes. Turn the lettuces over after 20 minutes. Remove the lettuces and keep warm. Bring the cooking liquid to a fierce boil and reduce to a light syrup consistency. Heat half the butter in a frying pan and cook the fillets for about 2–3 minutes on each side, or until cooked to your liking. Season with salt and pepper. Arrange the steaks on a serving dish, alternating with the lettuces. Strain the reduced cooking liquid into the steak pan and simmer, scraping the base of the pan with the spoon to release any sediment. Whisk in the rest of the butter in small pieces, pour the sauce over the meat and serve immediately.

- 60 g (2 oz) bacon, cut into pieces
- 60 g (2 oz) carrot, sliced
- 30 g (1¼ oz) onion, sliced
- 6 baby or little gem lettuces, washed, outer leaves discarded
- 500 ml (18 fl oz) beef stock
- 100 ml (3½ fl oz) veal stock
- 1 bouquet garni
- 30 g (1¼ oz) butter
- 6 slices fillet steak
- Salt and pepper

Preparation time: 25 minutes
Cooking time: 1 hour
Serves 6

BOURGUIGNON FONDUE

FONDUE BOURGUIGNONNE

First make the chosen dipping sauces. If making mayonnaise, flavour it with Cognac or whisky. Put a portion of meat on each guest's plate. Heat the oil with the garlic in a pan until it is hot enough to brown a cube of bread in 30 seconds, then remove the garlic and carefully pour the oil into a fondue pot, set over a medium-hot table heater. Guests take a cube of meat on a fork or fondue skewer and dip it into the hot oil to cook it for as long as they like. Serve with the dipping sauces in ramekins, and pickled onions and gherkins.

- 1 quantity sauce, such as mayonnaise (p.70), piquant sauce (p.60), horseradish sauce (p.54), or tomato sauce (p.57)
- Cognac or whisky, to taste (optional)
- 700 g (1½ lb) rump steak, cut into 2-cm (¾-inch) cubes
- 1 litre (1¾ pints) oil
- 1 garlic clove, crushed
- Pickled onions, to serve
- Gherkins, to serve

Preparation time: 1 hour
Serves 6

TOURNEDOS

TOURNEDOS

Prepare the béarnaise or Madeira sauce, if using. Heat half the butter in a frying pan, add the bread and brown on both sides. Remove the bread and set aside. Heat the remaining butter in the pan and cook the tournedos for about 3 minutes on each side for medium rare. Season with salt and pepper and place each tournedos on a slice of fried bread. If desired, add the Madeira to the butter in which the meat was cooked, add the mushrooms and sauté for 5 minutes. Serve the tournedos with the mushrooms and the prepared sauce, if using.

NOTE
A tournedos is a steak 1.5 cm (¾ inch) thick and 5–6 cm (2–2½ inches) in diameter, cut from the fillet.

- 1 quantity sauce, such as béarnaise sauce (p.75), or Madeira sauce (p.61) (optional)
- 50 g (1¾ oz) butter
- 6 slices day-old bread
- 6 tournedos steaks
- Salt and pepper
- 3 tablespoons Madeira (optional)
- 250 g (9 oz) mushrooms, sliced (optional)

Preparation time: 10 minutes
Cooking time: 10 minutes
Serves 6

TOURNEDOS ROSSINI
TOURNEDOS ROSSINI

- 90 g (3¼ oz) butter
- 6 slices day-old bread
- 6 tournedos steaks
- Salt and pepper
- 6 slices foie gras
- 1 truffle, sliced

Preparation time: 15 minutes
Cooking time: 15 minutes
Serves 6

Heat half the butter in a frying pan and brown the bread slices on both sides. Heat the remaining butter and cook the tournedos for about 3 minutes on each side for medium rare. Season with salt and pepper and place each tournedos on a slice of fried bread. Heat the pan again and, when it is very hot, sear the foie gras slices for 1–2 minutes on each side until deep golden brown, arrange them on top of the tournedos and put a slice of truffle on each one.

NOTE
The foie gras only needs to be seared if it is raw. Slices of foie gras terrine can also be used, in which case no further cooking is necessary.

FILLET STEAK
FILETS MIGNONS

- 1 quantity maître d'hôtel butter (p.48)
- Oil, for brushing
- 6 fillet steaks, sliced 2-cm (¾-inch) thick

Preparation time: 10 minutes
Cooking time: 4 minutes
Serves 6

Prepare the maître d'hôtel butter and brush the steaks with oil. Heat a griddle or frying pan, add the steaks and cook for 2 minutes on each side. Serve with the maître d'hôtel butter.

STEAK PROVENÇALE
BIFTECKS À LA PROVENÇALE

- 400 g (14 oz) beef, chopped or minced
- 100 g (3½ oz) mushrooms, chopped
- 3 garlic cloves, crushed
- 1 egg
- Salt and pepper
- 3 tablespoons olive oil
- Flour, for dredging

Preparation time: 25 minutes
Cooking time: 5 minutes
Serves 6

Mix the beef, mushrooms and garlic in a bowl, add the egg, mix well, and season with salt and pepper. Heat the oil in a frying pan. Shape the mixture into 6 patties and dredge them in the flour. Brown for about 2 minutes on each side.

ROASTING

ROAST BEEF
RÔTI

Preheat the oven to 240°C/475°F/Gas Mark 8. Cover the joint with the bacon and place on a rack or grid, in a roasting tin. Roast for 12–15 minutes per 450 g (1 lb), removing the bacon for the last 10 minutes of cooking to brown the meat. When the meat is golden brown, sprinkle it with salt. To make a gravy, add a little hot water and stir, scraping to release any sediment. Continue cooking to reduce, then remove from the heat, let the juices settle for a few minutes and remove the fat with a spoon. Stir in the butter and serve the gravy in a sauce boat. Serve the beef with the chosen sauce and a vegetable purée or mashed potatoes.

- 600 g (1 lb 5 oz) beef sirloin, rib roast or rump roast
- Strips of bacon, for barding
- Salt
- 20 g (¾ oz) butter, cut into small pieces
- Madeira sauce (p.61), Soubise sauce (p.54), or mushroom sauce (p.61), to serve
- Carrot, spinach or onion purée (p.560) or mashed potatoes (p.568), to serve

Preparation time: 5 minutes
Cooking time: 25 minutes
Serves 6

BRAISING

BEEF À LA MODE
BŒUF À LA MODE

Preheat the oven to 180°C/350°F/Gas Mark 4. Line an ovenproof heavy-based pan with the bacon rashers and rinds. Lard the beef with the bacon lardons (p.312) and put it and the calf's foot in the pan, then add the onion and carrots. Pour in the hot stock and the wine. Add the bouquet garni, season with salt and pepper, then cover with a tightly fitting lid. Heat the pan on the hob, and as soon as it comes to the boil, transfer it to the oven for 4 hours. It is important that the joint is heated evenly all round. For the last hour, baste every 10 minutes. Remove the lid, leaving the meat exposed to the heat of the oven for 25 minutes. The meat should be golden brown.

- 150 g (5 oz) bacon rashers, for barding
- Bacon rinds, for barding
- 900 g (2 lb) braising beef in one piece
- Bacon lardons, for larding
- 1 calf's foot
- 60 g (2 oz) onion, sliced
- 1 kg (2¼ lb) carrots, sliced
- 200 ml (7 fl oz) any hot stock
- 200 ml (7 fl oz) white wine
- 1 bouquet garni
- Salt and pepper

Preparation time: 30 minutes
Cooking time: 4½ hours
Serves 6

. . . .

COLD BEEF À LA MODE
BŒUF À LA MODE FROID

Prepare and cook the meat (p.332). Put the sliced meat in a terrine, surrounded by the carrots, then pour in the juices. Allow to cool and set to a jelly in the refrigerator. Turn out the next day and serve cold.

. . . .

BEEF CASSEROLE
BŒUF À LA CASSEROLE

If no oven is available, meat can be roasted in a lidded heavy-based pan on the hob. Prepare the ingredients as above, but first heat 40 g (1½ oz) butter and fry the onion for 5 minutes, then brown the meat all over on a high heat. Add the bacon rinds and calf's foot and pour in the stock and wine. Add the bouquet garni and season with salt and pepper. Simmer for 1½ hours. Then add the carrots and cook over a very low heat for 2 hours more.

VENISON-STYLE BEEF
BŒUF EN CHEVREUIL

- 900 g (2 lb) stewing beef in 1 piece
- Bacon lardons, for larding
- Streaky bacon, for barding
- 1 quantity uncooked marinade (p.78)
- 50 g (1¾ oz) butter
- Salt and pepper
- 1 quantity chasseur sauce (p.65)

Preparation time: 10 minutes, plus marinating time
Cooking time: 3 hours
Serves 6

Prepare 24 hours in advance. Lard the beef with the bacon lardons and bard it with the streaky bacon (p.312). Prepare the marinade and marinate the meat for 24 hours. Heat the butter in a heavy-based pan, add the beef and cook for 10 minutes or until browned all over, then cover and cook for 3 hours on a low heat. Season with salt and pepper. Meanwhile, using the marinade, make the chasseur sauce, adding the cooking juices. Serve the sauce in a sauce boat to accompany the beef.

DAUBE OF BEEF

BŒUF EN DAUBE

Prepare 12 hours in advance. Make the marinade and marinate the beef for 12 hours. In a heavy-based pan, heat the butter on a medium-high heat. Pat the slices of meat dry, add them to the butter and brown them on both sides, then lower the heat and cook gently for 15 minutes. Add half the marinade, and the stock, onion, bouquet garni, salt and pepper. Cover and cook on a low heat for 3 hours.

- 1 quantity uncooked or sweet marinade (p.78)
- 900 g (2 lb) stewing beef, cut into 3-cm (1¼-inch) slices
- 30 g (1¼ oz) butter
- 200 ml (7 fl oz) any stock
- 1 onion, chopped
- 1 bouquet garni
- Salt and pepper

Preparation time: 15 minutes, plus marinating time
Cooking time: 3¼ hours
Serves 6

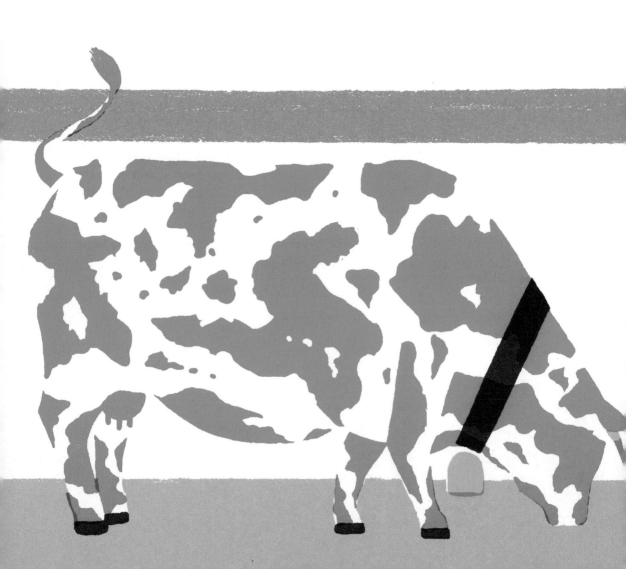

BEEF WITH RICE

BŒUF AU RIZ

- 30 g (1¼ oz) butter
- 900 g (2 lb) stewing beef
  in one piece
- 100 g (3½ oz) onions, chopped
- 1 bouquet garni
- Salt and pepper
- 750 ml (1¼ pints) any stock
- 250 g (9 oz) long-grain rice

Preparation time: 15 minutes
Cooking time: 3½ hours
Serves 6

In a heavy-based pan, heat the butter on a medium-high heat, add the beef and brown it all over. Add the onion and bouquet garni and season with salt and pepper. Pour in the stock and cook on a low heat for 3 hours. Rinse the rice thoroughly, add it to the casserole and cook on a low heat for 30 minutes more.

BRAISED BEEF

ESTOUFFADE DE BŒUF

- 900 g (2 lb) stewing beef
  in one piece
- 100 g (3½ oz) bacon lardons
- 300 g (11 oz) onions, sliced
- 500 ml (18 fl oz) red wine
- 200 ml (7 fl oz) any stock
- 1 large shallot, chopped
- 2 sprigs of flat-leaf parsley
- 2 sprigs of chervil
- 2 sprigs of thyme
- 1 bay leaf
- Salt and pepper

Preparation time: 20 minutes,
plus marinating time
Cooking time: 5 hours
Serves 6

Lard the piece of beef with the bacon lardons (p.312) and cut it into 3-cm (1¼-inch) slices. Arrange alternating layers of the beef and onions in a bowl, pour in the wine and marinate for 6 hours. Preheat the oven to 180°C/350°F/Gas Mark 4. Place the meat and the onions in an ovenproof heavy-based pan with a tight-fitting lid. Pour in the wine and stock. Add the shallot, herbs, and season with salt and pepper. Cover and cook for 5 hours. This dish is served hot or cold, as for beef à la mode (p.322).

BEEF PAUPIETTES
PAUPIETTES DE BOEUF

Lay the beef slices on a work surface and put a small slice of bacon on each one, then sprinkle with the shallot and parsley. Roll each slice into a barrel shape and tie with kitchen string. Melt the butter in a heavy-based pan, add the beef rolls and brown them for a few minutes on all sides. Pour in the stock, season with salt and pepper and simmer for 1½ hours. Skim off any fat from the cooking juices and serve them separately in a sauce boat.

- 500 g (1 lb 2 oz) stewing beef, cut into 6 thin slices
- 250 g (9 oz) smoked bacon, cut into 6 thin slices
- 1 shallot, finely chopped
- 1 tablespoon flat-leaf parsley, chopped
- 30 g (1¼ oz) butter
- 200 ml (7 fl oz) any stock
- Salt and pepper

Preparation time: 40 minutes
Cooking time: 1½ hours
Serves 6

BEEF BOURGUIGNON
BŒUF BOURGUIGNON

 p.413

In a heavy-based pan over a medium-high heat, fry the onions and lardons until browned. Remove them, add the meat and brown it on all sides. Sprinkle with the flour, stir until browned, then add the hot stock. Add the lardons, onions, wine and bouquet garni, and season with salt and pepper. Simmer gently on a low heat for 2 hours, then add the mushrooms and cook for 30 minutes more.

- 60 g (2 oz) button onions or shallots
- 100 g (3½ oz) bacon lardons
- 700 g (1 lb 8½ oz) stewing beef, cut into pieces
- 30 g (1¼ oz) flour
- 300 ml (½ pint) any stock, hot
- 300 ml (½ pint) red wine
- 1 bouquet garni
- Salt and pepper
- 100 g (3½ oz) mushrooms, peeled and chopped

Preparation time: 20 minutes
Cooking time: 2½ hours
Serves 6

CARBONADE WITH HERBS
CARBONADE AUX HERBES

- 1 kg (2¼ lb) chuck, blade or fore rib of beef, cut into 5-cm (2-inch) pieces
- 60 g (2 oz) flour
- 40 g (1½ oz) butter
- 500 ml (18 fl oz) any stock, hot
- 2 sprigs of flat-leaf parsley, chopped
- 2 sprigs of tarragon, chopped
- 2 sprigs of chervil, chopped
- 60 g (2 oz) onion, chopped
- Salt and pepper
- 80 g (2¾ oz) pain d'épice (p.798)
- 200 ml (7 fl oz) beer
- 60 g (2 oz) gherkins, sliced

Preparation time: 15 minutes
Cooking time: 2¼ hours
Serves 6

Roll the beef in the flour. Melt the butter in a heavy-based pan, add the beef in batches and brown it on all sides. Pour in the hot stock and stir, scraping the bottom of the pan to release any sediment. Add the parsley, tarragon, chervil and onion, and season with salt and pepper. Cook gently, covered, for 1½ hours. Crumble the pain d'épice into the beer and add it to the meat, along with the gherkins. Simmer for 45 minutes more, or until the beef is tender.

COOKED BEEF

BEEF IN A SAUCE
BŒUF EN SAUCE

- 1 quantity sauce, such as mushroom sauce (p.61), piquant sauce (p.60) or tomato sauce (p.57)
- 600–700 g (1 lb 5 oz– 1 lb 8½ oz) leftover cooked beef, sliced

Preparation time: 5 minutes
Cooking time: 10 minutes
Serves 6

Prepare the chosen sauce. Add the beef slices and gently reheat them in the sauce for a few minutes, taking care not to let it boil, otherwise the meat will become tough.

BEEF WITH PARSLEY SAUCE

BŒUF À LA PERSILLADE

Marinate the beef slices in the vinegar for 1–2 hours and season with salt and pepper. Make a blond roux with the butter and flour (p.57). Remove the meat from the vinegar and place on a serving dish, reserving the vinegar. Stir the hot stock, reserved vinegar, parsley and mustard into the roux. Pour the sauce over the beef.

- **600–700 g (1 lb 5 oz–1 lb 8½ oz) leftover cooked beef, cut into 12 slices**
- **100 ml (3½ fl oz) white wine vinegar**
- **Salt and pepper**
- **40 g (1½ oz) butter**
- **20 g (¾ oz) flour**
- **200 ml (7 fl oz) any stock, hot**
- **1 handful of flat-leaf parsley, chopped**
- **1 teaspoon mustard**

Preparation time: 20 minutes, plus marinating time
Cooking time: 30 minutes
Serves 6

BEEF MIROTON

BŒUF MIROTON

Preheat the oven to 240°C/475°F/Gas Mark 8. Make the brown sauce and add the tomato purée and gherkins. Put a little of the sauce in a gratin dish, arrange the beef slices on top and coat with the rest of the sauce. Brown in the oven for 15 minutes.

- **500 ml (18 fl oz) brown sauce (p.60)**
- **40 g (1½ oz) tomato purée**
- **8 gherkins, sliced**
- **600–700 g (1 lb 5 oz–1 lb 8½ oz) leftover cooked beef, cut into 12 slices**

Preparation time: 10 minutes
Cooking time: 15 minutes
Serves 6

FRIED BEEF

BŒUF FRIT

- 600–700 g
  (1 lb 5 oz–1 lb 8½ oz)
  leftover cooked beef, cut into
  12 slices
- 100 ml (3½ fl oz) olive oil
- 100 ml (3½ fl oz) white wine
  vinegar
- Salt and pepper
- Vegetable oil, for deep-frying
- 1 quantity batter (p.725)

Preparation time: 10 minutes,
plus marinating time
Cooking time: 15 minutes
Serves 6

Marinate the beef slices in the olive oil and vinegar for 1–2 hours and season with salt and pepper. Heat the vegetable oil in a deep-fryer to 180°C/350°F, or until a cube of bread browns in 30 seconds. Dip the beef slices in the batter and carefully place in the hot oil, in batches if necessary. Cook until browned all over and drain on kitchen paper. Serve hot.

VARIATION

. . . .

SAUTÉED BEEF

BŒUF GRILLÉ

Melt 40 g (1½ oz) butter in a frying pan, and cook the beef slices for 2 minutes on each side.

BEEF SALAD

BŒUF EN SALADE

- 1 quantity vinaigrette (p.66)
- 600–700 g
  (1 lb 5 oz–1 lb 8½ oz)
  leftover cooked beef,
  chopped into small dice
- 1 tablespoon chopped
  flat-leaf parsley
- 1 tablespoon chopped
  chives

Preparation time: 5 minutes
Serves 6

Make the vinaigrette. Sprinkle the beef with the dressing and sprinkle with the parsley and chives.

BEEF CROQUETTES

BŒUF EN CROQUETTES

Heat the butter in a pan over a medium-high heat, add the onion and cook until softened. Soak the breadcrumbs in the hot milk, then squeeze out the excess liquid. Mix together the beef, bacon, onion, breadcrumbs and chopped parsley. Mix in the egg to bind everything together, and season with salt and pepper. Heat the oil in a deep-fryer to 180°C (350°F), or until a cube of bread browns in 30 seconds. Shape the mixture into balls, roll them in the flour, then carefully put them into the hot oil and deep-fry, in batches if necessary, for about 5 minutes or until brown and crisp. Drain on kitchen paper and serve with the fried parsley.

VARIATION

. . . .

BEEF CROQUETTES ON BEAN PURÉE

PALETS DE BŒUF SUR PURÉE DE HARICOTS

Prepare a fresh haricot bean purée (p.553). Prepare the croquttes as above. Melt a knob of butter in a pan and fry the croquettes until brown on both sides. Arrange on a serving dish on top of the haricot bean purée. Drizzle with more melted butter.

- 20 g (¾ oz) butter
- 60 g (2 oz) onion, chopped
- 100 g (3½ oz) fresh breadcrumbs
- 100 ml (3½ fl oz) hot milk
- 300 g (11 oz) leftover cooked beef, chopped
- 100 g (3½ oz) smoked bacon, chopped
- 1 tablespoon chopped flat-leaf parsley
- 1 egg
- Salt and pepper
- 50 g (1¾ oz) flour
- Vegetable oil, for deep-frying
- 1 quantity fried flat-leaf parsley (p.81)

Preparation time: 45 minutes
Cooking time: 15 minutes
Serves 6

SHEPHERD'S PIE

HACHIS PARMENTIER

Preheat the oven to 200°C/400°F/Gas Mark 6. Prepare the mince mixture and make the mashed potatoes. Place a layer of the potato in an ovenproof dish, put the beef mixture on top, then top with the rest of the potatoes. Sprinkle with the breadcrumbs or cheese. Dot with the butter and cook in the oven for 20 minutes, until brown.

- 1 quantity minced beef mixture from beef croquettes (see above)
- 1 quantity mashed potatoes (p.568)
- 60 g (2 oz) dried breadcrumbs or grated Gruyère cheese
- Butter, cut into small pieces, for dotting

Preparation time: 1 hour
Cooking time: 20 minutes
Serves 6

BEEF LOAF

PAIN DE BŒUF

- 40 g (1½ oz) butter, plus extra for greasing
- 40 g (1½ oz) flour
- 200 ml (7 fl oz) milk
- 250 g (9 oz) leftover cooked beef, chopped
- 3 eggs, separated
- Salt and pepper

Preparation time: 30 minutes
Cooking time: 1 hour
Serves 6

Preheat the oven to 190°C/375°F/Gas Mark 5 and grease an ovenproof mould or loaf tin with butter. Make a béchamel sauce (p.50) with the butter, flour and milk, and mix it with the beef. Add the egg yolks. Beat the whites to stiff peaks, and season with salt and pepper. Fold the whites into the beef mixture. Pour the mixture into the prepared mould or tin. Bake for 40 minutes, then leave to stand for 5 minutes before turning out and slicing.

POTTED MEAT

POTTED MEAT

- 250 g (9 oz) leftover cooked beef, finely chopped
- 250 g (9 oz) butter, softened
- 2 tablespoons anchovy sauce (p.55)
- Freshly grated nutmeg
- Salt and pepper
- Lard or goose fat, to cover

Preparation time: 20 minutes
Serves 6

Work the beef into the butter until it is very smooth (this can be done in a food processor). Add the anchovy sauce, nutmeg, salt and pepper. Melt the lard or goose fat over a gentle heat. Put the mixture in a terrine or 6 individual ramekins and cover with a layer of fat. It will keep in the refrigerator for 5–6 days.

ROAST MINCED BEEF

HACHIS RÔTI

- 1 piece of pig's caul
- 1 quantity minced beef mixture from beef croquettes (p.330), made with 400 g (14 oz) beef
- 75 g (2½ oz) streaky bacon
- 20 g (¾ oz) butter
- 1 bunch of watercress, to serve

Preparation time: 30 minutes, plus soaking time
Cooking time: 1 hour
Serves 6

Soak the pig's caul in water for about 3 hours before use, then gently pat dry with kitchen paper. Preheat the oven to 220°C/425°F/Gas Mark 7. Make the minced beef mixture and wrap it in the pig's caul in the shape of a long joint of meat. Cover it with the streaky bacon, spread it with the butter and place it in a baking dish with 1 tablespoon water. Brown in the oven for 10 minutes, turn, then reduce the heat to 200°C/400°F/Gas Mark 6 and cook for about 45 minutes. Serve like a roast, on a bed of watercress, with the cooking juices in a sauce boat.

USING LEFTOVER ROAST BEEF
UTILISATION DES RESTES DE RÔTI

Prepare the tartare sauce or mayonnaise. Arrange the beef slices on a dish, garnish with the watercress and serve with the chosen sauce in a sauce boat.

NOTE
Leftover roast beef can be served cut into thin slices and reheated in a sauce, as for beef in a sauce (p.327).

- 1 quantity sauce, such as tartare sauce (p.72) or mayonnaise (p.70)
- Leftover roast beef, sliced
- 1 bunch of watercress, to garnish

Preparation time: 10–20 minutes
Serves 6

BEEF OFFAL

Offal should be absolutely fresh and it is important to be sure of its origin. The regulations controlling the sale of offal, and its availability, vary from country to country, so it is best to ask your butcher for advice.

PREPARATION

HEART
Stud the heart with lardons or thread it with fat using a larding needle. Alternatively, bard it with streaky bacon, tie it with string and treat it like beef à la mode (p.322) or beef casserole (p.323).

LIVER
Remove the gall bladder and cut away the thin membranes. Slice the liver if the method of cooking (grilling or frying) requires it, or leave it whole, studded with lardons if it is going to be cooked slowly.

TRIPE
Wash, brush and scrape the tripe and soak it for about 4 hours in water. To cook, place in a large pan filled with plenty of salted water. For flavouring add carrots, onions, white wine, pepper or cloves. Cover and bring to a simmer, then cook for at least 5 hours. Cut cooked tripe into strips and cover with a vinaigrette (p.66), ravigote sauce (p.56) or devilled sauce (p.76).

TONGUE

Soak the tongue in water for 12 hours, changing the water 2–3 times. Remove the fat and then plunge the tongue into boiling water and simmer for 20 minutes. Rinse in cold water, then remove the rough skin and bony part by cutting the skin at the base of the tongue and pulling it towards the tip. Wash and sponge dry.

KIDNEYS

Beef kidneys require special care, because they smell strongly of ammonia. Split the kidneys into two and remove the thin outer membrane, the fat and the small internal membranes. Dry with kitchen paper, cut into slices and blanch for 5 minutes in boiling water.

BEEF HEART MATELOTE

CŒUR DE BŒUF EN MATELOTE

- 60 g (2 oz) butter
- 1 onion, sliced
- 2 beef hearts
- 20 g (¾ oz) flour
- 100 ml (3½ fl oz) red wine
- 500 ml (18 fl oz) any stock
- 1 bouquet garni
- Salt and pepper
- 2 thick slices bread, cut into cubes

Preparation time: 20 minutes
Cooking time: 2½ hours
Serves 6

Heat half the butter in a heavy-based pan, add the onion and cook until browned. Add the hearts, brown them all over and sprinkle with the flour, stirring to combine. Add the wine, stock and bouquet garni, and season with salt and pepper. Simmer for 2 hours, then strain the cooking liquid and return it to the pan. Cut the hearts into thin slices, put them back in the pan and simmer for 20 minutes more. Meanwhile, heat the remaining butter in a frying pan, add the bread and fry until golden brown and crisp. Serve the heart slices with the sauce and croutons.

 p.414

GRILLED LIVER

FOIE GRILLÉ

- 1 quantity sauce, such as maître d'hôtel butter (p.48), black butter (p.48), or ravigote sauce (p.56)
- 500 g (1 lb 2 oz) liver, cut in thin slices
- Oil, for brushing

Preparation time: 5 minutes
Cooking time: 10 minutes
Serves 6

Prepare the chosen sauce. Brush the liver slices with oil. Heat a griddle and cook for 5 minutes on each side. Serve with the prepared sauce.

CASSEROLED LIVER

FOIE À LA CASSEROLE

Heat the butter in a heavy-based pan, add the onion and cook until golden brown. Remove the onion. Stud the liver with the lardons, put it in the pan and fry for about 5 minutes on each side. Remove the liver and sprinkle the flour onto the fat, stirring to combine. Pour in the wine, stirring constantly, add the thyme, bay leaf and cooked onions, and season with salt and pepper. Return the liver to the pan and cook gently for 40 minutes, basting it from time to time. Just before serving, strain the juices and coat the liver with them.

- 40 g (1½ oz) butter
- 50 g (1¾ oz) onion, sliced
- 500 g (1 lb 2 oz) liver
- Bacon lardons, for studding
- 30 g (1¼ oz) flour
- 300 ml (½ pint) white wine
- 2 sprigs of thyme
- 1 bay leaf
- Salt and pepper

Preparation time: 5 minutes
Cooking time: 50 minutes
Serves 6

TRIPE IN A SAUCE

GRAS-DOUBLE EN SAUCE

Prepare the chosen sauce. Add the tripe to the sauce and simmer for 20 minutes to heat through.

- 1 quantity sauce, such as béchamel sauce (p.50), poulette sauce (p.52), piquant sauce (p.60), or tomato sauce (p.57)
- 500 g (1 lb 2 oz) cooked tripe (p.332), cut in 1-cm (½-inch) strips

Preparation time:
30–50 minutes
Cooking time: 20 minutes
Serves 6

TRIPE PARCELS PROVENÇALE

PIEDS PAQUETS À LA PROVENÇALE

- 500 g (1 lb 2 oz) cooked tripe (p.332)
- 125 g (4¼ oz) streaky bacon, cut into strips
- 60 g (2 oz) garlic
- Chopped mixed herbs, such as parsley, chives, tarragon and chervil
- White pepper
- Freshly grated nutmeg
- 100 g (3½ oz) pork rind
- 1 clove
- 1 onion
- 150 ml (¼ pint) tomato purée
- 200 ml (7 fl oz) dry white wine
- Salt and pepper
- 1 small calf's foot, quartered
- Stock, to cover
- 1 quantity potatoes à l'anglaise (p.567)

Preparation time: 30 minutes
Cooking time: 2 hours
Serves 6

Cut the tripe into rectangles measuring about 15 x 10 cm (6 x 4 inches). Place 1 bacon strip on each piece of tripe, along with 1 garlic clove and a large pinch of herbs. Season with the pepper and nutmeg. Roll each piece to make a parcel and tie tightly with kitchen string.

Line a heavy-based pan with the pork rind. Stick the clove into the onion and put the onion into the pan, along with the tripe parcels, then add the tomato purée, wine, salt and pepper and calf's foot. Pour in enough stock to cover the parcels, cover and bring to the boil, then lower the heat and simmer over a gentle, steady heat for 2 hours. Meanwhile, prepare the potatoes à l'anglaise. Remove the strings from the tripe parcels and pass the sauce through a sieve. Serve the tripe with the sauce and the potatoes.

TRIPE À LA LYONNAISE

GRAS-DOUBLE À LA LYONNAISE

Prepare and cook the tripe (p.332) and cut it into strips. Heat the butter in a frying pan, add the onions and cook for about 5 minutes, or until browned. Add the tripe and cook for 15 minutes. Just before serving, stir in the vinegar and sprinkle with the parsley.

- 500 g (1 lb 2 oz) tripe
- 30 g (1¼ oz) butter
- 150 g (5 oz) onions, chopped
- 100 ml (3½ fl oz) white wine vinegar
- 2 tablespoons chopped flat-leaf parsley

Preparation time: 5 minutes
Cooking time: 20 minutes
Serves 6

TRIPE À LA MODE

TRIPES À LA MODE

 p.415

Preheat the oven to 150°C/300°F/Gas Mark 2. Arrange a layer of the tripe and a layer of the onions, shallot, chives, parsley and breadcrumbs in an ovenproof dish. Season with salt and pepper and continue to add alternating layers until all the tripe is used up. Pour in the wine, dot with the butter, cover and cook for 6–8 hours.

- 1 kg (2¼ lb) cooked tripe (p.332)
- 200 g (7 oz) onions, chopped
- 1 shallot, chopped
- 2 tablespoons chopped chives
- 2 tablespoons chopped flat-leaf parsley
- 100 g (3½ oz) fresh white breadcrumbs
- Salt and pepper
- 400 ml (14 fl oz) white wine
- 40 g (1½ oz) butter, cut into small pieces

Preparation time: 35 minutes
Cooking time: 8 hours
Serves 6

TRIPE COOKED IN CIDER

TRIPES À LA MODE DE CAEN

- 1 kg (2¼ lb) cooked tripe (p.332)
- 1 calf's foot
- 1 ox foot
- 100 g (3½ oz) pork rinds
- 2 carrots, halved
- 1 onion, quartered
- 1 garlic clove, crushed
- 1 bouquet garni
- 3 cloves
- Salt and pepper
- 1 litre (1¾ pints) dry cider
- Calvados, to taste
- 3 tablespoons flour

Preparation time: 30 minutes
Cooking time: 8 hours
Serves 6

Place the tripe in a large heavy-based pan with a lid. Cut up the calf's and ox feet and add to the pan with the pork rinds, carrots, onion and garlic. Add the bouquet garni and cloves and season with salt and pepper. Add enough cider to cover the vegetables and meat, then add the Calvados. Cover the pan. Make a paste with the flour and 3 tablespoons water, and use it to seal the edges of the lid. Bring to the boil, then reduce the heat and simmer gently for 8 hours. Remove the bones, vegetables and bouquet garni and serve the meat on warmed plates.

BOILED TONGUE

LANGUE BOUILLIE

- 1 quantity court-bouillon with vinegar or white wine (p.82)
- 1 ox tongue, prepared (p.333)
- 1 quantity sauce, such as caper sauce (p.56), soubise sauce (p.54), piquant sauce (p.60), or tomato sauce (p.57)

Preparation time: 40 minutes
Cooking time: 3 hours
Serves 6

Make the court-bouillon and allow it to cool. Put the tongue in the court-bouillon and cook for 3 hours over a low heat. Meanwhile, prepare the chosen sauce. Cut the tongue lengthways or diagonally into slices 1 cm (½ inch) thick, and serve with the prepared sauce.

NOTE
The tongue can be served on a purée of vegetables such as chestnut purée (p.559), braised sorrel (p.562), lentil purée (p.614) or mushroom purée (p.525).

CASSEROLED TONGUE

LANGUE À LA CASSEROLE

Prepare the court-bouillon, put it in a large pan and add the tongue. Bring to the boil, then reduce the heat and simmer for 2 hours. Drain and dry the tongue. Melt the butter in a heavy-based pan and add the onion and tongue. Brown on both sides. Sprinkle with the flour, stir in the wine, season with salt and pepper and simmer gently for 1 hour. Cut into slices to serve.

- **1 quantity court-bouillon with vinegar (p.82)**
- **1 ox tongue, prepared (p.333)**
- **60 g (2 oz) butter**
- **60 g (2 oz) onion, chopped**
- **20 g (¾ oz) flour**
- **200 ml (7 fl oz) white wine**
- **Salt and pepper**

Preparation time: 40 minutes
Cooking time: 3 hours
Serves 6

TONGUE À L'ITALIENNE

LANGUE À L'ITALIENNE

Prepare the court-bouillon, put it in a large pan and add the tongue. Cook for 1½ hours over a low heat, then drain and dry the tongue. Preheat the oven to 150°C/300°F/Gas Mark 2. Put the bacon, onion and carrot in a heavy-based ovenproof dish. Place the tongue on top and pour in the wine and stock. Season with salt and pepper and bring to the boil. Cover tightly and cook in the oven for 2½ hours.

Meanwhile, make the stuffed tomatoes and cook the macaroni in salted boiling water for 8–10 minutes, or until al dente. Shortly before serving, stir the macaroni into the dish containing the tongue. Just before serving, stir in the cheese. Cut the tongue into diagonal slices 1 cm (½ inch) thick and place on a serving dish with the macaroni and stuffed tomatoes. Skim the fat from the juices in the dish, strain and serve the juices in a sauce boat.

- **1 quantity court-bouillon with vinegar (p.82)**
- **1 ox tongue, prepared (p.333)**
- **100 g (3½ oz) bacon rashers**
- **60 g (2 oz) onion, sliced**
- **60 g (2 oz) carrot, sliced**
- **200 ml (7 fl oz) white wine**
- **200 ml (7 fl oz) any stock**
- **Salt and pepper**
- **6 small tomatoes stuffed with rice (p.580)**
- **200 g (7 oz) macaroni**
- **150 g (5 oz) Gruyère cheese, grated**

Preparation time: 1 hour
Cooking time: 2½ hours
Serves 6

FRIED KIDNEYS

ROGNONS SAUTÉS

- 30 g (1¼ oz) butter
- 500 g (1 lb 2 oz) kidneys, prepared (p.333)
- Salt
- 20 g (¾ oz) flour
- 25 g (1 oz) chopped shallot
- Any stock, for the sauce

  Preparation time: 15 minutes
  Cooking time: 30 minutes
  Serves 6

Heat the butter in a frying pan, add the kidneys and brown on both sides. Season with salt, sprinkle with the flour and add the shallot. Gradually add enough stock to produce a well-thickened sauce and simmer for 30 minutes, stirring occasionally.

NOTE
Kidneys can be served with a Bordelaise sauce (p.58), poivrade sauce (p.63) or Robert sauce (p.63).

KIDNEYS WITH MUSHROOMS

ROGNONS AUX CHAMPIGNONS

- 60 g (2 oz) butter, plus extra for frying
- 200 g (7 oz) mushrooms
- 700 g (1 lb 8½ oz) kidneys (p.333)
- 30 g (1¼ oz) flour
- 200 ml (7 fl oz) Madeira
- 100 ml (3½ fl oz) tomato purée
- Salt and pepper
- 1 tablespoon chopped flat-leaf parsley
- 6 slices day-old bread, cubed

  Preparation time: 25 minutes
  Cooking time: 35 minutes
  Serves 6

Melt 20 g (¾ oz) of the butter in a pan, add the mushrooms and cook for 10 minutes. Set aside, reserving both the mushrooms and the pan juices. Cut the kidneys into diagonal slices 1 cm (½ inch) thick. Melt 20 g (¾ oz) butter and fry the kidneys in it for 4 minutes, then remove them. Mix the flour with the pan juices from the mushrooms and add to the pan juices from the kidneys, along with the Madeira and tomato purée. Simmer to reduce and thicken the sauce, then add the kidneys and cook for 20 minutes more.

Meanwhile, heat the remaining butter in another pan, add the bread cubes and fry until golden brown and crisp. Shortly before serving, add the mushrooms to the kidneys. Season with salt and pepper and sprinkle with the parsley. Serve with the croutons.

VEAL

Veal is the meat from a calf, usually less than six months old. There are two kinds of calves: firstly, those that are fed exclusively on their mother's milk, or sometimes the milk of other cows. Their meat is tender and very pale in colour, and its firm white fat never marbles the meat. Secondly, there are calves reared in small groups and fed on powdered milk. Their meat tends to be of a lower quality, but can still be good if they are raised with care.

1 • Head
2 • Scrag end
3 • Middle neck
4 • Best end
5 • Loin
6 • Rump
7 • Leg, silverside, topside
8 • Knuckle, shin
9 • Breast
10 • Shoulder

COOKING METHOD	CUTS	COOKING TIMES
POACHING	Shoulder Middle neck Breast Scrag end of neck Knuckle (shank)	2 hours per 1 kg (2¼ lb)
GRILLING AND FRYING (ESCALOPES & CUTLETS)	Thick flank or Rump Cushion Loin Round (from the leg) Chops	10–15 minutes depending on thickness
ROASTING	Rump Best end of neck Round (from the leg) Loin Kidney	30 minutes per 500 g (1 lb 2 oz)
BRAISING	Cushion Best end of neck Middle neck Shoulder	2–3 hours per 1 kg (2¼ lb)
STEWING	Best end of neck Scrag end of neck Middle neck Breast	2 hours per 1 kg (2¼ lb)

POACHING

VEAL BLANQUETTE
BLANQUETTE

Put the veal pieces in a heavy-based pan and pour in enough water to just cover the meat. Add the wine, carrot, onion and bouquet garni. Season with salt and pepper, bring to the boil, skim, then reduce the heat and simmer gently for 1½–2 hours, until tender. Drain the meat and keep it warm, and strain the stock in which it was cooked. Make a blond roux (p.57), with the butter and flour and strained stock. Simmer for 10 minutes, stirring frequently. Just before serving, whisk the egg yolk into the sauce over a low heat until it thickens. Pour the sauce over the veal and serve.

- 500 g (1 lb 2 oz) breast of veal, cut into pieces
- 500 g (1 lb 2 oz) veal shoulder, cut into pieces
- 200 ml (7 fl oz) dry white wine
- 60 g (2 oz) carrot
- 1 onion, sliced
- 1 bouquet garni
- Salt and pepper
- 40 g (1½ oz) butter
- 40 g (1½ oz) flour
- 1 egg yolk

Preparation time: 15 minutes
Cooking time: 2½ hours
Serves 6

VARIATION

. . . .

VEAL WITH MUSHROOMS
BLANQUETTE AUX CHAMPIGNONS

Cook the veal blanquette as above. Meanwhile, in a frying pan, heat 40 g (1½ oz) butter, add 100 g (3½ oz) chopped onions and 125 g (4¼ oz) chopped mushrooms, and cook over a low heat for 25 minutes or until softened and golden brown. Add the mushrooms and onions to the blanquette sauce, pour the sauce over the veal pieces and serve.

BREAST OF VEAL MÉNAGÈRE
POITRINE DE VEAU MÉNAGÈRE

Put the veal pieces in a large pan with the bacon. Cover with 3.5 litres (6 pints) water, bring to the boil and simmer gently for 1½ hours. Add the vegetables and cook for 1 hour more. Arrange the veal in the centre of a serving dish with the vegetables in a ring round it. Slice the bacon and use to garnish the veal.

- 1 kg (2¼ lb) breast of veal, cut into pieces
- 250 g (9 oz) salted bacon
- 1 small cabbage, trimmed and quartered
- 200 g (7 oz) carrots
- 200 g (7 oz) turnips, quartered

Preparation time: 25 minutes
Cooking time: 2½ hours
Serves 6

GRIDDLING

[📷] p.417

VEAL CHOPS
CÔTES DE VEAU

- 60 g (2 oz) maître d'hôtel butter (p.48)
- 6 veal chops
- Oil, for brushing
- Salt and pepper

Preparation time: 5 minutes
Cooking time: 10 minutes
Serves 6

Prepare the maître d'hôtel butter, heat the griddle and brush the chops with oil. Put the chops on the very hot griddle and brown for 5 minutes on each side. Season with salt and pepper and serve with the maître d'hôtel butter.

FRYING

PLAIN ESCALOPES
ESCALOPES NATURE

- 40 g (1½ oz) butter
- 6 veal escalopes
- Salt
- Juice of 1 lemon
- ½ handful of flat-leaf parsley, chopped

Preparation time: 6 minutes
Cooking time: 10 minutes
Serves 6

Flatten the veal escalopes by placing them between 2 pieces of clingfilm and beating them with a meat mallet to about 5 mm (¼ inch) thick. Heat the butter in a frying pan over a high heat, add the escalopes and brown them for 5 minutes on each side. Arrange on a warm serving dish and season with a little salt. Add 1 tablespoon water to the pan and stir, scraping the base of the pan to release any sediment. Turn up the heat, add the lemon juice, season with salt and pour over the meat. Sprinkle the escalopes with the parsley.

NOTE
Serve with mushroom purée (p.525) or onion purée (p.560).

ESCALOPES IN BREADCRUMBS

ESCALOPES PANÉES

Dip the escalopes in the beaten eggs, then dredge them in the breadcrumbs. Heat the butter in a frying pan over a high heat, add the escalopes, and cook for 5 minutes on each side, or until golden. Season with salt and pepper, and sprinkle with the parsley.

NOTE
The escalopes can be served with tomato sauce (p.57) in a sauce boat.

- 6 veal escalopes, flattened to about 5 mm (¼ inch) thick (p.343)
- 2 eggs, beaten
- 150 g (5 oz) dried breadcrumbs
- 60 g (2 oz) butter
- Salt and pepper
- ½ handful of flat-leaf parsley, chopped

Preparation time: 10 minutes
Cooking time: 10 minutes
Serves 6

VIENNESE ESCALOPES

ESCALOPES À LA VIENNOISE

First, prepare the garnish. Roll each anchovy fillet around an olive and place in the centre of a lemon slice; set aside. Dredge each escalope in the flour, then in the beaten egg. Season with salt and pepper, and roll in the breadcrumbs, making sure that the breadcrumbs stick to the meat. Add oil to a depth of around 2 cm (¾ inch) to a deep sauté pan and heat until almost smoking. Carefully slide in the escalopes (2 at a time if there is room in the pan). Cook on each side for 3–4 minutes. Arrange the escalopes on a serving dish and garnish each with a slice of lemon topped with an anchovy-wrapped olive. Serve very hot.

- 6 anchovy fillets
- 6 olives, stoned
- 6 slices of lemon
- 6 veal escalopes, flattened to about 5 mm (¼ inch) thick (p.343)
- 30 g (1¼ oz) flour
- 1 egg, beaten
- Salt and pepper
- 150 g (5 oz) dried breadcrumbs
- Vegetable oil, for deep-frying

Preparation time: 20 minutes
Cooking time: 20 minutes
Serves 6

ESCALOPES IN BREADCRUMBS À LA MILANAISE
ESCALOPES PANÉES À LA MILANAISE

- 100 g (3½ oz) Comté cheese, grated
- 150 g (5 oz) dried breadcrumbs
- 6 veal escalopes, flattened to about 5 mm (¼ inch) thick (p.343)
- 2 eggs, beaten
- 30 g (1¼ oz) butter
- 2 tablespoons oil
- Salt and pepper
- 1 lemon

Preparation time: 15 minutes
Cooking time: 10 minutes
Serves 6

Mix the cheese with the breadcrumbs. Dip each escalope in the beaten eggs, then dredge in the cheese and breadcrumb mixture. Heat the butter and oil in a frying pan over a high heat, add the escalopes and cook for 5 minutes on each side, or until golden. Season with salt and pepper. Squeeze some lemon juice into the cooking juices, and serve with the escalopes.

ZEPHYR ESCALOPES
ESCALOPES ZEPHYR

- 30 g (1¼ oz) butter
- 6 veal escalopes, flattened to about 5 mm (¼ inch) thick (p.343)
- 300 ml (½ pint) crème fraîche
- Salt and pepper
- Lemon slices, to garnish

Preparation time: 5 minutes
Cooking time: 15 minutes
Serves 6

Heat the butter in a frying pan over a high heat, add the escalopes and cook for 5 minutes on each side, or until golden. Remove them from the pan and arrange on a warm serving dish, reserving the cooking juices in the pan. Add the crème fraîche to the juices and bring to a simmer, stirring constantly. Season with salt and pepper and pour over the escalopes. Garnish with slices of lemon.

ESCALOPES AU GRATIN
ESCALOPES GRATINÉES

Preheat the oven to 220°C/425°F/Gas Mark 7. Melt 40 g (1½ oz) of the butter in a frying pan, add the escalopes and cook over a medium heat for 5 minutes on each side, or until golden. Remove them from the pan and place in an ovenproof dish. Meanwhile, make a béchamel sauce (p.50) with the remaining butter and the flour and milk. Add the mushrooms and cook for 10 minutes. Stir in the crème fraîche. Cover the escalopes with the sauce, sprinkle with the cheese and bake for 10 minutes, or until the cheese is nicely browned.

- 70 g (2½ oz) butter
- 6 veal escalopes, flattened to about 5 mm (¼ inch) thick (p.343)
- 40 g (1½ oz) flour
- 100 ml (3½ fl oz) milk
- 150 g (5 oz) mushrooms, sliced
- 150 ml (¼ pint) crème fraîche
- 50 g (1¾ oz) Gruyère cheese, grated

Preparation time: 10 minutes
Cooking time: 30 minutes
Serves 6

FRIED VEAL CHOPS
CÔTES DE VEAU SAUTÉES

Melt the butter in a frying pan, add the chops and cook over a medium heat for 5 minutes on each side, or until golden. For thicker chops, cook for 2–3 minutes more. Serve on a bed of vegetables, such as mashed potatoes (p.568), mushroom purée (p.525), spinach or onion purée (p.560), or braised sorrel (p.562) with a tomato (p.57) or Madeira sauce (p.61) in a sauce boat.

- 60 g (2 oz) butter
- 6 veal chops

Preparation time: 6 minutes
Cooking time: 10–15 minutes
Serves 6

VEAL CHOPS À LA VERT-PRÉ
CÔTES DE VEAU À LA VERT-PRÉ

Melt half the butter in a frying pan, add the chops and brown over a medium heat for 6 minutes on each side. Remove from the heat and cover. Mix the rest of the butter with the chervil and put some of the mixture on each chop. Season with salt and pepper and serve immediately.

- 80 g (2¾ oz) butter, softened
- 6 veal chops
- 1 bunch of chervil, chopped
- Salt and pepper

Preparation time: 5 minutes
Cooking time: 15 minutes
Serves 6

VEAL CHOPS WITH TRUFFLES

CÔTES DE VEAU AUX TRUFFES

- 50 g (1¾ oz) butter
- 6 veal chops
- Salt
- 200 ml (7 fl oz) Madeira
- Truffle peelings, or chopped truffle, to taste

Preparation time: 5 minutes
Cooking time: 15 minutes
Serves 6

Melt the butter in a frying pan, add the chops and brown over a medium heat for 6 minutes on each side. Season with salt. Remove the chops and keep them hot. Add the Madeira and truffle to the cooking juices in the pan and cook, stirring, for 3 minutes. Coat the chops with this sauce and serve immediately.

VEAL CHOPS IN PARCELS

CÔTES DE VEAU EN PAPILLOTES

- 80 g (2¾ oz) butter
- ½ onion, chopped
- 2 shallots, chopped
- 100 g (3½ oz) mushrooms, chopped
- 50 g (1¾ oz) streaky bacon, finely chopped, plus 6 rashers for barding
- 50 g (1¾ oz) ham, finely chopped
- ½ handful of flat-leaf parsley, finely chopped
- Salt and pepper
- 6 veal chops
- Oil, for greasing
- Juice of 2 lemons

Preparation time: 45 minutes
Cooking time: 30 minutes
Serves 6

Preheat the oven to 200°C/400°F/Gas Mark 6. Melt 30 g (1¼ oz) of the butter in a large frying pan, add the onion and shallots and cook over medium heat for 5 minutes. Stir in the mushrooms and cook for 5 minutes more. Stir in the bacon, ham and parsley and cook for 5 minutes more, then season with salt and pepper. Heat the remaining butter in another frying pan over a high heat and brown the chops for 2 minutes on each side.

To make the parcels, cut a large piece of greaseproof paper or aluminium foil and fold it in half to make a square of double thickness, taking care to make it 5 cm (2 inches) larger on all sides than the veal chop. Oil the paper thoroughly. Lay a bacon rasher across the centre, place 1 teaspoon of the bacon mixture in the centre of the rasher, place a veal chop on the mixture, then top with another teaspoon of the mixture. Wrap the ends of the bacon rasher around the chop to bard it, then wrap each chop in the paper or foil, rolling the edges together so that the parcel is closed, and tying with kitchen string if necessary. Place the parcels in an ovenproof dish and bake for 30 minutes. Just before serving, open the parcels and squeeze the lemon juice over the chops.

ROASTING

ROAST VEAL
RÔTI DE VEAU

 p.416

Preheat the oven to 220°C/425°F/Gas Mark 7. Bard the joint with the bacon rashers (p.312), tie it with string and place on a rack in a roasting tin. Roast for 30 minutes per 500 g (1 lb 2 oz) veal, or until the juices run clear. When the meat is golden brown, season with salt and baste with the cooking juices. To serve, untie the joint, pour a little water or stock into the tin and cook, stirring to release any sediment on the base of the tin. Skim the fat from the cooking juices and pour them into a sauce boat. Serve the veal with the chosen sauce and vegetable garnish, and the juices.

NOTE
Leftover veal can be served sliced, cold or hot. To serve cold, arrange the slices on a dish garnished with parsley and gherkins. Serve with mayonnaise (p.70) in a sauce boat. To serve hot, make a sauce, such as tomato (p.57), Richelieu (p.58), poulette (p.52), or soubise (p.54). About 10 minutes before serving, add the veal slices to the sauce in the pan and heat through over a low heat, taking care not to boil. Serve in a deep serving dish.

- 1 x 1-kg (2¼-lb) veal joint, such as rump, best end, round or loin
- Bacon rashers, for barding
- Salt
- Any stock or water, for deglazing
- 1 quantity sauce, such as tomato sauce (p.57), mushroom sauce (p.61), or Périgueux sauce (p.61)
- 1 quantity vegetables, such as jardinière of vegetables (p.555), macédoine (p.96), onion purée (p.560) or mashed potatoes (p.568)

Preparation time: 10 minutes
Cooking time: 1–2 hours
Serves 6

ROAST VEAL WITH MUSTARD
RÔTI DE VEAU À LA MOUTARDE

Prepare the day before serving. Place the veal in a roasting tin. Carefully spread the mustard all over the joint, then coat with the crème fraîche. Marinate in the refrigerator for 24 hours. Preheat the oven to 220°C/425°C/Gas Mark 7. Remove the crème fraîche and mustard from the veal, and put them in a small pan. Roast the veal in the oven for 45 minutes. Pour off the cooking juices and mix them into the mustard and crème fraîche. Bring to the boil and simmer over a low heat for 5 minutes. Season with salt and pepper. Return the veal to the oven and continue roasting for 15–20 minutes more, or until the juices run clear. Serve the sauce in a sauce boat.

- 1 x 1-kg (2¼-lb) veal joint, such as leg or fillet
- 60 g (2 oz) strong mustard
- 100 ml (3½ fl oz) crème fraîche
- Salt and pepper

Preparation time: 15 minutes, plus marinating time
Cooking time: 1 hour
Serves 6

STUFFED BREAST OF VEAL

POITRINE DE VEAU FARCIE

- 200 g (7 oz) unsmoked bacon, finely chopped
- 200 g (7 oz) minced pork
- 1 tablespoon chopped flat-leaf parsley
- 50 ml (2 fl oz) Cognac
- 1 kg (2¼ lb) boned breast of veal
- Bacon rashers, for barding
- Salt and pepper

Preparation time: 30 minutes
Cooking time: 1 hour
Serves 6

Preheat the oven to 220°C/425°F/Gas Mark 7. In a bowl, mix together the chopped bacon, pork, parsley and Cognac to make a stuffing. Cut a large pocket in the side of the veal breast, open the pocket and stuff in the mixture. Cover the breast with the bacon rashers, tie with string and place in a roasting tin. Roast for 1 hour, or until the juices run clear. Season with salt and pepper and baste with the cooking juices.

BRAISING

VEAL CASSEROLE

VEAU À LA CASSEROLE

- 40 g (1½ oz) butter
- 700 g (1 lb 8½ oz) stewing veal
- Bacon rashers, for barding
- Salt and pepper

Preparation time: 15 minutes
Cooking time: 50 minutes
Serves 6

Preheat the oven to 220°C/425°F/Gas Mark 7. In an ovenproof heavy-based pan, heat the butter over a high heat, add the veal and brown it on all sides. Cover the veal with the bacon and tie with kitchen string. Cook in the oven, uncovered, for 45 minutes, or until the juices run clear, turning every 5 minutes. When the meat is golden, season with salt and pepper and baste with the cooking juices. Finish and serve as for roast veal (p.348).

STEWED VEAL

VEAU À L'ÉTOUFFÉE

- 1 x 800-g (1¾-lb) veal joint
- Bacon rashers, for barding
- 40 g (1½ oz) butter
- 1 onion, chopped
- 20 ml (1 fl oz) dry white wine
- 20 ml (1 fl oz) any stock, hot
- Salt and pepper

Preparation time: 5 minutes
Cooking time: 2 hours
Serves 6

Cover the veal with the bacon and tie with kitchen string. Heat the butter in a heavy-based pan over a high heat, add the veal and brown on all sides. Sprinkle with the onion, then pour in the wine and hot stock. Season with salt and pepper, cover and simmer very gently for 2 hours.

BRAISED VEAL

FRICANDEAU

Make slits in the veal joint with a sharp knife at regular intervals and insert the bacon lardons into them. Heat the butter in an ovenproof heavy-based pan over a high heat, add the veal, brown it on all sides, then remove it. Put the bacon rashers and the rinds, if using, into the pan and add the veal, carrot, onion and bouquet garni. Pour in 100 ml (3½ fl oz) of the hot stock and the Cognac, season with salt and pepper and cover. Simmer gently for 1 hour. Preheat the oven to 190°C/375°F/Gas Mark 5. Pour in the rest of the stock. Bring to the boil, cover and transfer the pan to the oven. Cook for 2½ hours. Remove the fat from the cooking juices, strain them and pour them over the meat.

- 1 x 800-g (1¾-lb) veal joint, such as leg or fillet
- 150 g (5 oz) unsmoked bacon lardons
- 30 g (1¼ oz) butter
- 150 g (5 oz) bacon rashers
- Bacon rinds (optional)
- 1 carrot
- 1 onion
- 1 bouquet garni
- 500 ml (18 fl oz) any stock, hot
- 1 tablespoon Cognac
- Salt and pepper

Preparation time: 40 minutes
Cooking time: 3½ hours
Serves 6

VEAL À LA BOURGEOISE

VEAU À LA BOURGEOISE

Make slits in the veal joint with a sharp knife at regular intervals and insert the diced bacon into them. Melt the butter in a heavy-based pan over a high heat, add the veal and brown it on all sides. Add the onions and bouquet garni and season with salt and pepper. Pour in the hot stock, cover and simmer for 1 hour. Add the carrots and cook for 1 hour more.

- 1 x 800-g (1¾-lb) veal joint, such as leg or fillet
- 125 g (4¼ oz) smoked bacon, diced
- 40 g (1½ oz) butter
- 125 g (4¼ oz) onions
- 1 bouquet garni
- Salt and pepper
- 500 ml (18 fl oz) any stock, hot
- 1 kg (2¼ lb) carrots, sliced

Preparation time: 25 minutes
Cooking time: 2 hours
Serves 6

VEAL JARDINIÈRE
VEAU JARDINIÈRE

- 40 g (1½ oz) butter
- 10 button onions or shallots
- 100 g (3½ oz) bacon, diced
- 800 g (1¾ lb) veal joint
- Salt and pepper
- 100 ml (3½ fl oz) any stock, hot
- 250 g (9 oz) baby carrots
- 350 g (12 oz) new potatoes
- 350 g (12 oz) shelled peas
- 1 lettuce
- 250 g (9 oz) French beans, trimmed

Preparation time: 45 minutes
Cooking time: 2¾ hours
Serves 6

Heat the butter in a heavy-based pan, add the onions or shallots and bacon and fry over a medium heat until golden brown. Add the veal, season with salt and pepper and brown on all sides over a high heat. Pour in the hot stock, cover and simmer, turning occasionally, for 1½ hours. Arrange the carrots, potatoes, peas and lettuce around the meat and cook for 1 hour more. Meanwhile, bring a pan of salted water to the boil, add the French beans and cook for 15 minutes. Add them to the meat and vegetables 15 minutes before serving. Serve the veal in a deep dish, with the vegetables and sauce.

VEAL WITH CREAM
VEAU À LA CRÈME

- 800 g (1¾ lb) veal joint
- Bacon rashers, for barding
- 40 g (1½ oz) butter
- 2 onions, chopped
- 30 g (1¼ oz) flour
- 100 ml (3½ fl oz) white wine
- 100 ml (3½ fl oz) any stock, hot
- Salt and pepper
- 2 egg yolks
- 100 ml (3½ fl oz) crème fraîche

Preparation time: 10 minutes
Cooking time: 2 hours
Serves 6

Cover the veal with the bacon rashers and tie with kitchen string. Heat the butter in a heavy-based pan over a high heat, add the veal and brown on all sides. Sprinkle with the onions and flour and cook until browned. Pour in the wine and hot stock. Season with salt and pepper, cover and cook very gently for 2 hours. Remove the veal and keep warm. Strain the cooking juices into a heatproof bowl set over a pan of barely simmering water and whisk the egg yolks and crème fraîche into the juices over a low heat until the sauce thickens. Remove the bacon and string from the veal and dress with the sauce.

VEAL FRANCHARD

VEAU FRANCHARD

Cover the veal with the bacon rashers and tie with kitchen string. Heat the butter in a heavy-based pan over a high heat, add the veal and chopped bacon, and brown the veal on all sides Add the onions or shallots and the tarragon. Pour in the hot stock, season with salt and pepper, and simmer over a very gentle heat for 1 hour. Add the mushrooms and cook for 30 minutes more. Just before serving, remove and discard the tarragon, bacon and string. Serve in a deep dish.

- 1 kg (2¼ lb) veal joint
- Bacon rashers, for barding
- 40 g (1½ oz) butter
- 125 g (4¼ oz) bacon, chopped
- 10 button onions or shallots
- 1 bunch of tarragon
- 100 ml (3½ fl oz) any stock, hot
- Salt and pepper
- 125 g (4¼ oz) mushrooms

Preparation time: 10 minutes
Cooking time: 1½ hours
Serves 6

NECK OF VEAL À LA BÛCHERONNE

CARRÉ DE VEAU À LA BÛCHERONNE

Trim the veal, cover it with the bacon rashers and tie with kitchen string. Heat the butter in a heavy-based pan over a high heat and fry the veal until brown on all sides. Remove the veal from the pan. Add the onions or shallots to the pan, sprinkle with the sugar and cook until golden brown. Return the veal to the pan and pour in the wine. Add the bouquet garni, season with salt and pepper, cover and simmer for 2 hours. Remove the bacon and string from the veal. Add the mushrooms and cook for 30 minutes more. Remove the veal, take the pan off the heat and whisk in the egg yolk to thicken the sauce. Serve the veal in a deep dish.

- 1 kg (2¼ lb) veal , such as middle neck
- Bacon rashers, for barding
- 50 g (1¾ oz) butter
- 12–15 button onions or shallots
- 15 g (½ oz) caster sugar
- 500 ml (18 fl oz) red Bordeaux wine
- 1 bouquet garni
- Salt and pepper
- 125 g (4¼ oz) mushrooms
- 1 egg yolk

Preparation time: 20 minutes
Cooking time: 2½ hours
Serves 6

p.418

VEAL PAUPIETTES
PAUPIETTES DE VEAU

- 30 g (1¼ oz) fresh breadcrumbs
- 1 tablespoon hot milk
- 50 g (1¾ oz) butter
- 1 onion, chopped
- 60 g (2 oz) bacon, diced
- 100 g (3½ oz) mushrooms, chopped
- 1 handful of flat-leaf parsley, chopped
- Salt and pepper
- 6 large veal escalopes, flattened to about 5 mm (¼ inch) thick (p.343)
- 100 ml (3½ fl oz) any stock

Preparation time: 35 minutes
Cooking time: 1¾ hours
Serves 6

In a small bowl, soak the breadcrumbs in the hot milk. Heat half the butter in a heavy-based pan, add the onion and bacon and cook until the onion is lightly browned. Remove from the heat and stir in the mushrooms, parsley and soaked breadcrumbs. Season with salt and pepper. Put 1 teaspoon of this mixture on each escalope, roll it up and tie it with string to keep the stuffing in. Melt the remaining butter in the pan over a high heat, brown the paupiettes on all sides then pour in the hot stock. Cover and simmer gently for 1½ hours. Remove the string to serve. Strain the cooking juices and serve with the paupiettes.

SANDWICHED ESCALOPES
ESCALOPES SANDWICHES

- 6 small, thick veal escalopes
- 3 thin slices cured ham
- 3 thin slices smoked bacon
- 40 g (1½ oz) butter
- 200 ml (7 fl oz) any stock, hot

Preparation time: 20 minutes
Cooking time: 45 minutes
Serves 6

Slice the escalopes in half widthways. Place half a slice of ham and half a slice of bacon between the 2 halves. Tie with kitchen string. Heat the butter in a heavy-based pan over a high heat, add the escalopes and brown on all sides. Pour in the hot stock and cook gently for 45 minutes. Remove the string to serve.

ESCALOPES WITH CHOPPED MUSHROOMS

ESCALOPES AUX CHAMPIGNONS HACHÉS

Make a stuffing by mixing together the mushrooms, bread-crumbs and herbs, and season with salt and pepper. Heat 40 g (1½ oz) of the butter in a heavy-based pan over a high heat, add the escalopes and brown on both sides. Put 1 tablespoon of the stuffing on each one. Pour the stock around them, cover and simmer for 30 minutes. Meanwhile, melt 10 g (¼ oz) of the remaining butter in a frying pan, add 2 of the bread slices and brown on both sides. Repeat with the rest of the butter and the remaining bread slices. To serve, place an escalope on each bread slice and drizzle with some of the lemon juice.

- 200 g (7 oz) mushrooms, chopped
- 50 g (1¾ oz) fresh white breadcrumbs
- 1 teaspoon tarragon leaves, chopped
- ½ handful of flat-leaf parsley, chopped
- Salt and pepper
- 70 g (2½ oz) butter
- 6 small thick veal escalopes
- 200 ml (7 fl oz) any stock
- 6 slices bread
- Juice of 1 lemon

Preparation time: 30 minutes
Cooking time: 40 minutes
Serves 6

VEAL MEDALLIONS

GRENADINS DE VEAU

Heat the butter in a heavy-based pan over a high heat, add the veal medallions and brown on both sides. Pour in the Cognac and simmer for a few minutes to evaporate the alcohol, then pour in the stock. Season with salt and pepper, cover and simmer for 30 minutes. Add the mushrooms and shallot and simmer for 30 minutes more. Just before serving, place the medallions on a serving dish. Add the crème fraîche to the cooking juices and coat the medallions with the sauce.

- 40 g (1½ oz) butter
- 6 veal medallions
- 1 tablespoon Cognac
- 50 ml (2 fl oz) any stock
- Salt and pepper
- 125 g (4¼ oz) mushrooms, chopped
- 1 shallot, chopped
- 100 ml (3½ fl oz) crème fraîche

Preparation time: 20 minutes
Cooking time: 1 hour
Serves 6

VEAL NOISETTES À LA FINANCIÈRE

NOISETTES DE VEAU À LA FINANCIÈRE

- 800 g (1¾ lb) veal, such as leg or fillet
- 120 g (4 oz) unsmoked bacon, cut into strips
- 50 g (1¾ oz) butter
- 1 carrot
- 1 onion, sliced
- Bacon rinds or rashers, for barding
- Salt and pepper
- 400 ml (14 fl oz) any stock, hot
- 1 bouquet garni
- 100 ml (3½ fl oz) Madeira

Preparation time: 30 minutes
Cooking time: 1¼ hours
Serves 6

Cut the veal into 10 round slices, 5 cm (2 inches) in diameter and 2 cm (¾ inch) thick. Make evenly spaced slits with a sharp knife and insert the bacon strips into them. Heat the butter in a large pan over a high heat, add the veal noisettes and brown them on both sides. Remove them and put the carrot, onion and bacon rinds or rashers in the pan. Season with salt and pepper, pour in the hot stock and put the meat back in. Add the bouquet garni and simmer gently, covered, for 1 hour. Remove the veal noisettes and keep warm. Strain the cooking juices, add the Madeira and simmer to reduce to around 200 ml (7 fl oz). Place the veal noisettes on a serving dish and coat with the Madeira sauce.

VEAL IN ASPIC

VEAU EN GELÉE

- 2 shallots, chopped
- 2 tablespoons chopped flat-leaf parsley
- 500 g (1 lb 2 oz) veal shoulder, cut into small thin slices
- 500 g (1 lb 2 oz) pork fillet, cut into small thin slices
- Salt and pepper
- 500 ml (18 fl oz) white wine
- 1 calf's foot, boned and cut into pieces

Preparation time: 30 minutes, plus setting time
Cooking time: 3 hours
Serves 6

Prepare the day before serving. Preheat the oven to 150°C/300°F/Gas Mark 2. Put a little of the chopped shallots on the bottom of a terrine, and arrange some of the sliced meats over them. Add another layer of shallots and parsley, season with salt and pepper, and add another layer of sliced meats. Pour in the wine, then add the calf's foot. Cover and cook in the oven for 3 hours. Remove the calf's foot and place a plate over the terrine, with a 500 g (1 lb 2 oz) weight on top of it. Leave in the refrigerator to set. The next day, turn the meat out of the terrine. Chop the jelly and serve it around the meat.

LEG OF VEAL WITH BACON

ROUELLE DE VEAU À LA COUENNE

Preheat the oven to 200°C/400°F/Gas Mark 6. Make evenly spaced slits with a sharp knife and insert the unsmoked bacon into them. Season with salt and pepper. In a terrine, place alternate layers of streaky bacon, veal slices and back bacon, ending with a layer of streaky bacon. Pour in the stock and Cognac, and sprinkle with the parsley, chives and shallot. Cook in the oven for 2½ hours. Serve hot.

- 500 g (1 lb 2 oz) leg of veal, cut into thick slices
- Unsmoked bacon, cut into strips, for larding
- Salt and pepper
- 200 g (7 oz) streaky bacon rashers
- 200 g (7 oz) back bacon rashers
- 100 ml (3½ fl oz) any stock
- 100 ml (3½ fl oz) Cognac
- ½ handful of flat-leaf parsley, chopped
- 1 tablespoon finely chopped chives
- 1 shallot, finely chopped

Preparation time: 20 minutes
Cooking time: 2½ hours
Serves 6

VEAL LOAF

PAIN DE VEAU

Preheat the oven to 200°C/400°F/Gas Mark 6. Melt the butter in a frying pan, add the mushrooms and cook over a medium heat until softened. In a bowl, mix the mushrooms with the breadcrumbs, eggs, veal and pork. Season with salt and a little nutmeg. Shape into a loaf, place in an ovenproof dish and brush the top with butter. Bake for 1 hour. Serve with the chosen sauce.

- 20 g (¾ oz) butter, plus extra for brushing
- 125 g (4¼ oz) mushrooms, chopped
- 100 g (3½ oz) fresh breadcrumbs
- 2 eggs, lightly beaten
- 350 g (12 oz) veal, such as middle neck, finely chopped
- 150 g (5 oz) pork belly, finely chopped
- Salt
- Freshly grated nutmeg
- 1 quantity strongly flavoured sauce, such as tomato sauce (p.57) or 'poor man's' sauce (p.47)

Preparation time: 30 minutes
Cooking time: 1 hour
Serves 6

MEATBALLS IN BÉCHAMEL SAUCE

BOULETTES À LA BÉCHAMEL

- 25 g (1 oz) butter
- 3 shallots, finely chopped
- 150 g (5 oz) day-old bread,
  torn into pieces
- 500 ml (18 fl oz) milk
- 300 g (11 oz) veal, chopped
- 200 g (7 oz) pork, chopped
- 1 egg, lightly beaten,
  plus 2 egg yolks
- Salt and pepper
- 1 quantity béchamel sauce
  (p.50)

Preparation time: 30 minutes
Cooking time: 45 minutes
Serves 6

Heat the butter in a frying pan, add the shallots and cook over a low heat until softened. Soak the bread in the milk until softened, then squeeze out the milk and mix the bread with the veal and pork, beaten egg and shallots. Season with salt and pepper. Put enough salted water in a heavy-based pan to cover the bottom and bring it to a simmer. Shape the meat mixture into balls and place them in the water. Cook for 25 minutes, rolling the meatballs around occasionally. Meanwhile, make the béchamel sauce and whisk in the egg yolks until the sauce has thickened. Arrange the meatballs in a serving dish and pour the sauce over them.

NOTE
The meatballs can be served with tomato sauce (p.57) instead of béchamel.

LITTLE LETTUCE PARCELS

PETITS PAQUETS À LA SALADE

- 300 g (11 oz) veal, chopped
- 200 g (7 oz) pork, chopped
- 3 tablespoons rice, rinsed
- 1 egg, lightly beaten
- Salt and pepper
- 2 escarole or other
  loose-leafed lettuces
- 25 g (1 oz) butter
- 1 tablespoon olive oil
- 500 ml (18 fl oz) any stock

Preparation time: 30 minutes
Cooking time: 1 hour 20 minutes
Serves 6

In a large bowl, combine the veal, pork, rice and egg. Season with salt and pepper. Bring a pan of salted water to the boil and blanch the lettuces for 30 seconds, then plunge them into cold water and drain. Spread each leaf out flat, place 1 tablespoon of the meat mixture on it and roll it up. Heat the butter and oil in a heavy-based pan, add the lettuce parcels and brown them on all sides. Pour in the stock, cover and simmer for 1 hour, then remove the lid and simmer for 20 minutes more.

VEAL STEW

RAGOÛT DE VEAU

Heat the butter in a heavy-based pan, add the onions or shallots and the veal and cook until they are lightly browned. Sprinkle with the flour and cook, stirring frequently, until it browns. Pour in the hot stock, season with salt and pepper, and add the bouquet garni. Add the wine, if using. Cook gently, covered, for 1 hour. Add the vegetables and cook for 1 hour more.

- 50 g (1¾ oz) butter
- 10 button onions or shallots
- 1 kg (2¼ lb) veal, cut into pieces
- 50 g (1¾ oz) flour
- 400 ml (14 fl oz) any stock, hot
- Salt and pepper
- 1 bouquet garni
- 100 ml (3½ fl oz) white wine (optional)
- Turnips, potatoes, carrots, or a combination, sliced

Preparation time: 10 minutes
Cooking time: 2 hours
Serves 6

VEAL MARENGO

VEAU MARENGO

Heat the oil and butter in a heavy-based pan, add the onion and veal, and cook over a medium heat until the veal is lightly browned. Scatter with the shallot and most of the parsley. Sprinkle with the flour, cook until brown, then pour in the hot stock and the wine. Add the bouquet garni, season with salt and pepper, and simmer for 1½ hours. Add the tomato purée and mushrooms and simmer for 30 minutes more. Remove the bouquet garni and serve the veal sprinkled with the remaining parsley.

- 2 tablespoons oil
- 30 g (1¼ oz) butter
- 1 onion
- 1 kg (2¼ lb) veal, cut into pieces
- 1 shallot, chopped
- 1 handful of flat-leaf parsley, chopped
- 30 g (1¼ oz) flour
- 100 ml (3½ fl oz) any stock, hot
- 100 ml (3½ fl oz) white wine
- 1 bouquet garni
- Salt and pepper
- 25 g (1 oz) tomato purée
- 100 g (3½ oz) mushrooms, chopped

Preparation time: 25 minutes
Cooking time: 2 hours
Serves 6

VEAL MATELOTE

VEAU EN MATELOTE

- 40 g (1½ oz) butter
- 1 kg (2¼ lb) veal,
  cut into pieces
- 1 onion, chopped
- 40 g (1½ oz) flour
- 100 ml (3½ fl oz) any stock,
  hot
- 200 ml (7 fl oz) red wine
- Juice of 1 lemon
- 1 bouquet garni
- Salt and pepper
- 2 tablespoons red wine vinegar

Preparation time: 15 minutes
Cooking time: 2 hours
Serves 6

Heat the butter in a heavy-based pan, add the veal and onion and cook over a medium-high heat until the veal is brown on all sides. Remove the veal and onion from the pan and set aside. Sprinkle the cooking juices with the flour and cook until golden brown. Pour in the hot stock, wine and lemon juice, and add the bouquet garni. Season with salt and pepper. Return the veal and onion to the pan and simmer for 2 hours. Just before serving, stir in the vinegar.

POITOU VEAL STEAK

ROUELLE DE VEAU POITEVINE

- 500 g (1 lb 2 oz) round veal
  steak
- 200 g (7 oz) pork rind
- 1 calf's foot
- 1 bouquet garni
- 1 onion studded with cloves
- Salt and pepper
- 2 teaspoons caster sugar
- 100 ml (3½ fl oz) white wine
- 1 tablespoon Cognac
- 50 g (1¾ oz) butter, softened
- 1 tablespoon flour

Preparation time: 15 minutes
Cooking time: 4 hours
Serves 6

Preheat the oven to 160°C/325°F/Gas Mark 3. Cut the veal and the pork rind into very large dice. Cut the calf's foot into pieces and place in an ovenproof dish with the bouquet garni and the onion. Add the veal and cover with the rind. Add salt, pepper and the sugar. Pour in the wine and Cognac. Cover the dish, put it in the oven and cook for 4 hours. Remove the meat from the dish, arrange it in a serving dish, and keep hot. Blend together the butter and flour to make a paste, then stir the paste into the cooking juices to thicken them. Strain the sauce and pour it over the meat to serve.

COOKED VEAL

VEAL BALLS
BOULETTES DE VEAU

Make a white sauce (p.50) with the butter, flour and stock. Season with salt and pepper. Stir the meat into the sauce and add 2 of the eggs. Heat the mixture over a gentle heat, stirring constantly, but do not let it boil. Allow it to cool. Beat the remaining egg in a bowl and heat the oil in a deep-fryer to 180°C/350°F, or until a cube of bread browns in 30 seconds. Shape the meat mixture into balls, dip them in the beaten egg, then roll them in the breadcrumbs. Cook the balls, in batches, for 5 minutes in the hot oil until brown, then drain on kitchen paper. Serve with the parsley.

- **30 g (1¼ oz) butter**
- **40 g (1½ oz) flour**
- **400 ml (14 fl oz) any stock**
- **Salt and pepper**
- **300 g (11 oz) leftover veal, finely chopped**
- **3 eggs**
- **Vegetable oil, for deep-frying**
- **Dried breadcrumbs, for rolling**
- **1 quantity fried flat-leaf parsley (p.81)**

Preparation time: 30 minutes
Cooking time: 25 minutes
Serves 6

VEAL GRATIN
GRATIN DE VEAU

Preheat the oven to 220°C/425°F/Gas Mark 7. Heat 15 g (½ oz) of the butter in a frying pan, add the mushrooms and cook for a few minutes, until softened. Make a béchamel sauce (p.50) with 30 g (1¼ oz) of the butter and the flour and milk, and season with salt and pepper. In a bowl, mix the veal, ham and sauce with the mushrooms and pour the mixture into an ovenproof dish. Sprinkle with the breadcrumbs and dot with the remaining butter. Bake for 10 minutes, until golden brown.

- **60 g (2 oz) butter**
- **150 g (5 oz) mushrooms, finely chopped**
- **250 g (9 oz) leftover veal, chopped**
- **150 g (5 oz) ham, chopped**
- **40 g (1½ oz) flour**
- **400 ml (14 fl oz) milk**
- **Dried breadcrumbs, for sprinkling**
- **Salt and pepper**

Preparation time: 40 minutes
Cooking time: 30 minutes
Serves 6

VEAL CROQUETTES

CROQUETTES DE VEAU

- 100 g (3½ oz) fresh
  breadcrumbs
- 100 ml (3½ fl oz) hot milk
- 300 g (11 oz) leftover veal,
  finely chopped
- 125 g (4¼ oz) ham, finely
  chopped
- 2 eggs, lightly beaten
- Dried breadcrumbs, for rolling
- 60 g (2 oz) butter

Preparation time: 40 minutes
Cooking time: 15 minutes
Serves 6

Preheat the oven to 220°C/425°F/Gas Mark 7. In a large bowl, soak the fresh breadcrumbs in the hot milk. Add the veal, ham and eggs and stir to combine. Shape this mixture into croquettes 3.5 cm (1½ inches) long. Roll them in the dried breadcrumbs, put them in an ovenproof dish and top with small knobs of butter. Bake for 15 minutes, until golden brown.

VEAL PASTIES

RISSOLES

- 1 quantity shortcrust pastry
  (p.784)
- 100 g (3½ oz) veal
- 100 g (3½ oz) unsmoked bacon
- ½ handful of flat-leaf parsley,
  chopped
- 1 tablespoon Cognac
- Salt and pepper
- 1 egg, beaten with a little water

Preparation time: 1¼ hours
Cooking time: 25 minutes
Serves 6

Preheat the oven to 220°C/425°F/Gas Mark 7. Make the shortcrust pastry. In a food processor, chop the veal, bacon and parsley. Stir in the Cognac and season with salt and pepper. Roll out the pastry and cut into circles about 10 cm (4 inches) in diameter. Place 1 tablespoon of the stuffing on one half of each circle. Fold the pastry over and seal the edges with a little water to form a semicircle. Place the pasties on a baking tray, glaze with the egg and bake for 25 minutes, until golden.

STUFFED CRÊPES

CRÊPES FARCIES

Make the crêpes. Preheat the oven to 220°C/425°F/Gas Mark 7. In a large bowl, soak the breadcrumbs in the hot milk. Add the veal, ham, herbs and mushrooms and stir to combine. Season with salt and pepper. Put 1 tablespoon of the stuffing in the centre of each crêpe. Roll the crêpes up and place them side-by-side in an ovenproof dish. Dot with the butter and bake for 8 minutes.

NOTE
As an alternative, make a béchamel sauce (p.50) and stir in a handful of grated Gruyère cheese. Pour the sauce over the crêpes, then bake for 10 minutes.

- 12 small crêpes (p.722)
- 50 g (1¾ oz) fresh breadcrumbs
- 100 ml (3½ fl oz) hot milk
- 250 g (9 oz) leftover veal, chopped
- 150 g (5 oz) ham, chopped
- 1 handful of chopped mixed herbs, such as chives, chervil, flat-leaf parsley and tarragon
- 125 g (4¼ oz) mushrooms, chopped
- Salt and pepper
- 50 g (1¾ oz) butter, cut into small pieces

Preparation time: 35 minutes
Cooking time: 8 minutes
Serves 6

VEAL OFFAL

Offal should be absolutely fresh and it is important to be sure of its origin. The regulations controlling the sale of offal, and its availability, vary from country to country, so it is best to ask your butcher for advice.

PREPARATION

BRAINS
Wash the brains well and soak them for 1 hour in cold water with a little vinegar, then rinse thoroughly. Remove the outer membrane and any blood spots. Bring a pan of water or court-bouillon to the boil, add the brains and simmer for 15 minutes before using. Pig's brains can be prepared in the same way.

HEART
Split the heart down one side and remove any blood clots. It can be studded with lardons, barded with bacon, tied with kitchen string and cooked in the same way as for beef à la mode (p.322) or beef casserole (p.323).

CAUL

Clean the caul by soaking it in water for 2–3 hours. Remove, drain well and cut in pieces. Simmer for 1½ hours in a court-bouillon with salt (p.82) and serve with a ravigote sauce (p.56).

SWEETBREADS

Clean the sweetbreads by soaking them in water for 5 hours, changing the water several times. Then put them in a large pan, cover with salted water, slowly bring to the boil, simmer gently for 3–5 minutes, and drain. Rinse in water and pat dry. Remove the thin membrane which covers them, and the gristle. Wrap them in a cloth, cover with a chopping board and place a 2-kg (4½-lb) weight on top. Leave to stand for 1 hour in the refrigerator. The sweetbreads are now ready to use. Serve with a cheese sauce (p.51), with a few sliced truffles, or arrange in a deep serving dish and coat with a mushroom (p.61), tomato (p.57) or Madeira (p.61) sauce.

KIDNEYS

Calves' kidneys should not be boiled. Remove the outer membrane and gristle, and cut in diagonal slices. They should be cooked quickly, until they are a pale golden colour. Ox kidneys have a rather strong ammonia smell, which can be eliminated by blanching them in boiling water before cooking.

CALF'S HEAD

Soak the calf's head in water for 24 hours. Bone, tie with string, cover with water in a large pan and boil for 10 minutes, then plunge immediately into cold water. Serve hot with a vinaigrette (p.66) or ravigote sauce (p.56).

CALVES' BRAIN FRITTERS

BEIGNETS DE CERVELLE

- 2 small calves' brains
- 2 eggs, beaten
- 100 g (3½ oz) Gruyère cheese, grated
- 40 g (1½ oz) flour
- Salt and pepper
- 60 g (2 oz) butter
- 1 lemon, sliced, to serve

Preparation time: 25 minutes
Cooking time: 8 minutes
Serves 6

Prepare and cook the brains (p.362). Dice the cooked brains and put them in a bowl. Mix in the eggs, cheese and flour. Season with salt and pepper. Heat the butter in a frying pan and drop the mixture in, a spoonful at a time. Cook over a medium-high heat for about 8 minutes, or until brown, drain on kitchen paper and serve immediately with the lemon slices.

CALVES' BRAIN LOAF

PAIN DE CERVELLE

Prepare and cook the brains (p.362). Preheat the oven to 140°C/275°F/Gas Mark 1. Put the brains in a food processor or blender and process to a purée. Add the eggs, crème fraîche and parsley. Season with salt and pepper. Grease a mould or loaf tin with butter and sprinkle it with the breadcrumbs. Fill with the brains mixture. Place in a roasting tin half-filled with hot water and cook in the oven for 1 hour. Serve hot in the mould or tin, with the tomato sauce.

- 3 calves' brains, prepared (p.362)
- 4 eggs, lightly beaten
- 25 g (1 oz) butter, plus extra for greasing
- 200 ml (7 fl oz) crème fraîche
- 1 tablespoon chopped flat-leaf parsley
- Salt and pepper
- Dried breadcrumbs, for sprinkling
- 1 quantity tomato sauce (p.57), to serve

Preparation time: 25 minutes
Cooking time: 1 hour
Serves 6

CALVES' BRAINS À LA CHIVRY

CERVELLE À LA CHIVRY

Preheat the oven to 180°C/350°F/Gas Mark 4. Mash the brains with a fork. Make a béchamel sauce (p.50) with the butter, flour and milk and stir it, a spoonful at a time, into the brains. Add the eggs and egg yolks. Season with salt and pepper. Grease a mould with butter, pour the mixture into it, and put the mould into a roasting tin half-filled with hot water. Cook, covered, in the oven for 45 minutes. Allow to stand for 10 minutes before serving, then serve with the printanière or Chivry sauce.

- 500 g (1 lb 2 oz) calves' brains, prepared (p.362)
- 35 g (1½ oz) butter, plus extra for greasing
- 30 g (1¼ oz) flour
- 200 ml (7 fl oz) milk
- 3 eggs, lightly beaten
- 3 egg yolks, lightly beaten
- Salt and pepper
- 1 quantity printanière or Chivry sauce (p.54), to serve

Preparation time: 30 minutes
Cooking time: 45 minutes
Serves 6

BRAISED CALVES' HEARTS

CŒUR BRAISÉ

- 35 g (1½ oz) butter
- 2 calves' hearts, prepared (p.362)
- 50 g (1¾ oz) onion, chopped
- 60 g (2 oz) carrot, cut into strips
- 100 ml (3½ fl oz) any stock, hot
- Salt and pepper

Preparation time: 5 minutes
Cooking time: 35 minutes
Serves 6

Heat the butter in a heavy-based pan, add the hearts and onion and cook over a medium heat for about 5 minutes, or until the onion has softened. Add the carrot and hot stock. Season with salt and pepper. Cover and simmer for 30 minutes.

STUFFED CALVES' HEARTS

CŒUR FARCI

- 125 g (4¼ oz) stuffing for red meats (p.80)
- 2 calves' hearts, prepared (p.362)
- 50 g (1¾ oz) butter
- 60 g (2 oz) bacon lardons, chopped
- 400 ml (14 fl oz) any stock
- 100 ml (3½ fl oz) Madeira
- 50 g (1¾ oz) carrot
- 50 g (1¾ oz) onion
- 1 bouquet garni

Preparation time: 30 minutes
Cooking time: 1 hour
Serves 6

Make the stuffing. Put half the stuffing in each heart and tie with kitchen string. Melt the butter in a heavy-based pan and brown the lardons, and then the hearts, over a medium heat. Add the stock, Madeira, carrot, onion and bouquet garni and simmer for 1 hour.

NOTE

As a variation, add blanched haricot beans to the pan for the final 30 minutes of cooking.

FRIED CALVES' HEARTS

CŒUR SAUTÉ

Cut the hearts into 3-cm (1¼-inch) slices. Melt the butter in a frying pan, add the heart slices and brown on both sides. Sprinkle with the flour and parsley and season with salt and pepper. Fry for 10 minutes, then remove from the heat and pour in the Cognac. Return to the heat and cook for 5 minutes more, to evaporate the alcohol.

- 2 calves' hearts, prepared (p.362)
- 50 g (1¾ oz) butter
- 10 g (¼ oz) flour
- ½ handful of flat-leaf parsley, chopped
- Salt and pepper
- 50 ml (2 fl oz) Cognac

Preparation time: 5 minutes
Cooking time: 15 minutes
Serves 6

CALVES' HEARTS IN A SAUCE

CŒUR EN SAUCE

Cut the hearts into 3-cm (1¼-inch) slices. Heat the oil in a heavy-based pan, add the lardons and onions and cook over a medium heat until the onions are soft. Add the heart slices and brown for a few minutes, then pour in the wine and a few tablespoons water. Season with salt and pepper and simmer, covered, for 1½ hours, adding more water if necessary. Add the tomato purée and mushrooms, and cook for 10 minutes more.

- 2 calves' hearts, prepared (p.362)
- 2 tablespoons olive oil
- 125 g (4¼ oz) bacon lardons, chopped
- 100 g (3½ oz) onions, chopped
- 200 ml (7 fl oz) white wine
- Salt and pepper
- 100 ml (3½ fl oz) tomato purée
- 60 g (2 oz) mushrooms, chopped

Preparation time: 15 minutes
Cooking time: 1¾ hours
Serves 6

CALVES' LIVER ON SKEWERS

BROCHETTES DE FOIE DE VEAU

- 150 g (5 oz) bacon, cut into
  4-cm (1½-inch) squares just
  under 1 cm (½ inch) thick
- 80 g (2¾ oz) butter
- 200 g (7 oz) mushrooms,
  stalks removed and discarded
- Salt and pepper
- 400 g (14 oz) calves' liver, cut
  into 4-cm (1½-inch) squares
  2 cm (¾ inch) thick
- 50 g (1¾ oz) dried
  breadcrumbs
- 1 quantity tomato sauce (p.57),
  chilled, or maître d'hôtel
  butter (p.48), to serve

Preparation time: 30 minutes
Cooking time: 8–10 minutes
Serves 6

Bring a pan of water to the boil, add the bacon and cook for 8–10 minutes, then drain. Heat 30 g (1¼ oz) of the butter in a frying pan, add the mushrooms and cook over a medium heat until browned. Season with salt, drain and remove from the pan. Thread pieces of liver, bacon, and mushrooms onto 6 metal skewers. Roll the skewers in the breadcrumbs. Melt the remaining butter and pour it over the skewers, then leave them to rest for 10 minutes. Heat a griddle until very hot and place the skewers on it, turning them regularly until they are golden brown all over. Season with salt and pepper, if necessary. Serve with the tomato sauce, chilled, or the maître d'hôtel butter.

NOTE
To prepare calves' liver see p.332. Ox liver is coarser than calves' liver, but is less expensive and can replace it if necessary.

OX OR CALVES' LIVER LOAF

PAIN DE FOIE DE VEAU OU DE GÉNISSE

- 500 g (1 lb 2 oz) ox or calves'
  liver, prepared (p.332)
- 135 g (4½ oz) butter, softened
- 200 ml (7 fl oz) crème fraîche
- 4 egg yolks
- Salt and pepper
- Dried breadcrumbs,
  for sprinkling

Preparation time: 30 minutes
Cooking time: 2 hours
Serves 6

Preheat the oven to 140°C/275°F/Gas Mark 1. In a blender or food processor, purée the liver. Stir in 125 g (4¼ oz) of the butter and the crème fraîche and egg yolks. Season with salt and pepper. Grease a mould with the remaining butter, sprinkle with dried breadcrumbs, and fill with the liver mixture. Place the mould in a roasting tin half-filled with hot water and bake for 2 hours.

BURGUNDY CALVES' LIVER

FOIE DE VEAU DE BOURGOGNE

Stud the liver with half the lardons. Heat the butter in a frying pan, add the remaining lardons and the onions or shallots, and cook on a medium-low heat until the onions or shallots are softened. Remove from the pan. Put the liver in the pan and brown on all sides. Add the wine. Return the bacon and onions or shallots to the pan, add the bouquet garni, and season with salt and pepper. Cook, covered, on a low heat for 45 minutes, then add the mushrooms and cook for 15 minutes more.

- **600 g (1 lb 5 oz) calves' liver**
- **125 g (4¼ oz) smoked bacon lardons**
- **20 g (¾ oz) butter**
- **125 g (4¼ oz) button onions or shallots, chopped**
- **250 ml (8 fl oz) red Burgundy wine**
- **1 bouquet garni**
- **Salt and pepper**
- **200 g (7 oz) mushrooms**

Preparation time: 20 minutes
Cooking time: 1 hour
Serves 6

CALVES' LIVER SOUBISE

FOIE DE VEAU SOUBISE

Heat 30 g (1¼ oz) of the butter in a heavy-based pan, add the lardons and cook on a medium heat until they are crisp. Remove them, put in the liver slices and brown on both sides over a high heat. Remove the liver and dry the bottom of the pan. Heat the remaining butter in the pan, add the onions, herbs and garlic and cook, covered, over a gentle heat for 1 hour. Season with salt. When the onions have softened to the consistency of a purée, cover with the slices of liver and simmer for 20 minutes.

- **60 g (2 oz) butter**
- **125 g (4¼ oz) smoked bacon lardons**
- **600 g (1 lb 5 oz) calves' liver, sliced**
- **750 g (1 lb 10 oz) onions, thinly sliced**
- **1 teaspoon chopped thyme leaves**
- **1 bay leaf**
- **1 garlic clove, crushed**
- **Salt**

Preparation time: 30 minutes
Cooking time: 1½ hours
Serves 6

CALVES' LIVER LOAF

GÂTEAU DE FOIE

- 135 g (4½ oz) butter
- 125 g (4¼ oz) flour
- 350 ml (12 fl oz) milk
- 2 eggs, separated
- 500 g (1 lb 2 oz) calves' liver, finely chopped
- Salt and pepper
- 1 quantity tomato sauce (p.57) or mushroom sauce (p.61), to serve

Preparation time: 30 minutes
Cooking time: 1 hour 5 minutes
Serves 6

Preheat the oven to 200°C/400°F/Gas Mark 6. Grease a mould with 10 g (¼ oz) of the butter. Make a béchamel sauce (p.50) using the remaining butter and the flour and milk. Beat the egg whites to stiff peaks. Stir the liver into the sauce, add the egg yolks and the beaten whites. Season with salt and pepper, pour into the prepared mould and bake for 45 minutes. Serve with the chosen sauce.

FRIED KIDNEYS IN WHITE WINE

ROGNONS SAUTÉS AU VIN BLANC

- 6 calves' kidneys, about 500 g (1 lb 2 oz)
- 80 g (2¾ oz) butter
- 60 g (2 oz) onion, finely chopped
- Salt and pepper
- 200 ml (7 fl oz) white wine
- 100 ml (3½ fl oz) any stock
- 1 handful of flat-leaf parsley, chopped

Preparation time: 20 minutes
Cooking time: 25 minutes
Serves 6

Remove the outer membrane and gristle from the kidneys, and cut into diagonal slices. Heat half the butter, add the onion and brown over a very gentle heat. Then turn up the heat, add the kidney slices and fry for 3 minutes on each side. Season with salt and pepper. Remove the kidneys and keep warm, and pour the wine and stock into the pan. Cover and cook for 15 minutes. Cut the remaining butter into small pieces and add to the pan with the parsley, stirring continuously. Pour over the kidneys, and serve hot.

FRIED CALVES' SWEETBREADS

RIS DE VEAU SAUTÉ

Prepare and cook the sweetbreads (p.363) and cut them into slices. Heat the butter in a frying pan, add the sliced sweetbreads and cook on a high heat for 5 minutes on each side, until brown. Sprinkle with the parsley and pour the butter from the pan over the sweetbreads.

- **1 calf's sweetbreads**
- **60 g (2 oz) butter**
- **½ handful of flat-leaf parsley, chopped**

Preparation time: 10 minutes, plus soaking time
Cooking time: 10 minutes
Serves 6

CROQUETTES OF CALVES' SWEETBREADS

CROQUETTES DE RIS DE VEAU

Prepare and cook the sweetbreads (p.363). Meanwhile, blanch the mushrooms in boiling salted water for 10 minutes, then drain and set aside. Make a white sauce (p.50) with the butter, 40 g (1½ oz) of the flour, and water. Stir in the crème fraîche and lemon juice. Add the egg yolks and the egg. Lightly beat the egg whites in a small bowl and set aside. Add the mushrooms to the sauce and season with salt and pepper.

When the sweetbreads are cool, cut them into small dice and stir into the sauce. Allow the mixture to cool. Heat the oil in a deep-fryer to 180°C/350°F, or until a cube of bread browns in 30 seconds. Shape the sweetbreads mixture into croquettes, roll them in the egg whites and then in the flour, and fry in batches until brown. Drain on kitchen paper and serve immediately.

- **1 calf's sweetbreads**
- **200 g (7 oz) mushrooms**
- **40 g (1½ oz) butter**
- **100 g (3½ oz) flour**
- **200 ml (7 fl oz) crème fraîche**
- **Juice of 1 lemon**
- **3 eggs, separated**
- **1 egg**
- **Salt and pepper**
- **Vegetable oil, for deep-frying**

Preparation time: 40 minutes, plus soaking time
Cooking time: 25 minutes
Serves 6

BRAISED CALVES' SWEETBREADS

RIS DE VEAU BRAISÉS

- 1½ calves' sweetbreads
- 60 g (2 oz) bacon lardons
- 50 g (1¾ oz) butter
- 60 g (2 oz) carrot, sliced
- 60 g (2 oz) onion, sliced
- 2 bacon rinds
- 200 ml (7 fl oz) dry white wine
- Salt and pepper

Preparation time: 20 minutes,
plus soaking time
Cooking time: 40 minutes
Serves 6

Prepare and cook the sweetbreads (p.363) and stud with the bacon lardons. Melt the butter in a heavy-based pan and brown the carrot and onion over a medium heat. Add the bacon rinds and sweetbreads and pour in the wine. Season with salt and pepper. Bring to the boil, then reduce the heat and simmer, covered, for 30 minutes. Meanwhile, preheat the oven to 240°C/475°F/Gas Mark 8. Uncover the pan and transfer it to the oven for 5 minutes. Remove the sweetbreads and keep warm. Strain the cooking juices into another pan, and simmer to reduce over a high heat to create a rich brown sauce. Put the sweetbreads on a serving dish, coat with some of the sauce and serve the rest in a sauce boat.

CALVES' SWEETBREADS À L'ANGLAISE

RIS DE VEAU À L'ANGLAISE

- 1 calf's sweetbreads
- 3 eggs
- 30 g (1¾ oz) butter, melted
- Dried breadcrumbs, for coating
- Salt and pepper
- 200 ml (7 fl oz) veal jus
- Cooked peas, to serve

Preparation time: 35 minutes,
plus soaking time
Cooking time: 20 minutes
Serves 6

Prepare and cook the sweetbreads (p.363) and allow to cool. Preheat the oven to 220°C/425°F/Gas Mark 7. Beat together the eggs and butter. Add the sweetbreads to the mixture, then coat in the breadcrumbs. Season with salt and pepper. Place in an ovenproof dish and bake for 20 minutes. Serve with the veal jus, and peas.

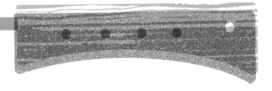

FLAMBÉED KIDNEYS WITH CREAM

ROGNONS FLAMBÉS À LA CRÈME

Remove the outer membrane and gristle from the kidneys and cut them into diagonal slices. Melt the butter in a frying pan and brown the kidney slices over a high heat. Season with salt and pepper. Turn the kidney slices over and add the mushrooms. Pour in the Armagnac and, ensuring the pan is positioned away from anything flammable and standing well back, touch a lighted match to the edge of the pan to set the alcohol alight. Shake the pan to extinguish the flames. Add 3 tablespoons water and stir, scraping to release any sediment on the base of the pan. Add the crème fraîche. Bring to the boil, season with salt and pepper and serve very hot.

- 600 g (1 lb 5 oz) calves' kidneys
- 50 g (1¾ oz) butter
- Salt and pepper
- 150 g (5 oz) mushrooms, sliced
- 2 tablespoons Armagnac
- 2 tablespoons crème fraîche

Preparation time: 20 minutes
Cooking time: 20 minutes
Serves 6

KIDNEYS IN MADEIRA

ROGNONS AU MADÈRE

Remove the outer membrane and gristle from the kidneys and cut them into diagonal slices. Heat the butter in a frying pan, add the kidney slices and fry over a high heat for 3–4 minutes. Remove them from the pan and keep hot. Add the flour to the pan, brown it, stirring constantly, then pour in the stock. Add the mushrooms, herbs and onion. Season with salt and pepper. Cook for 15 minutes over a gentle heat. Return the kidneys to the pan, add the Madeira and lemon juice, and heat for 5 minutes without boiling. Serve in a deep serving dish.

- 600 g (1 lb 5 oz) calves' kidneys
- 100 g (3½ oz) butter
- 30 g (1¼ oz) flour
- 200 ml (7 fl oz) any stock
- 125 g (4¼ oz) mushrooms, quartered
- ½ handful of mixed herbs, chopped
- 1 onion, chopped
- Salt and pepper
- 100 ml (3½ fl oz) Madeira
- Juice of 1 lemon

Preparation time: 25 minutes
Cooking time: 25 minutes
Serves 6

BOILED CALF'S HEAD

TÊTE DE VEAU BOUILLIE

- 1 calf's head, whole or cut into pieces
- 200 ml (7 fl oz) white wine vinegar
- 50 g (1¾ oz) flour
- 1 bouquet garni
- 60 g (2 oz) onion, sliced
- 60 g (2 oz) carrot, sliced
- Salt and pepper
- Vinaigrette (p.66) or ravigote sauce (p.56), to serve (optional)

Preparation time: 10 minutes
Cooking time: 1½–3 hours
Serves 6

Place the calf's head in a large pan with 2 litres (3½ pints) water and the vinegar, and bring to the boil. In a small bowl, mix the flour with 2 tablespoons water and add it to the pan, along with the bouquet garni, onion and carrot. Season with salt and pepper. Boil for 3 hours, covered, if the head is whole. If it is cut into pieces, boil for 1½ hours. Serve hot with the vinaigrette or ravigote sauce (if using).

CALF'S HEAD EN TORTUE

TÊTE DE VEAU EN TORTUE

- 1 calf's head
- 50 g (1¾ oz) butter
- 50 g (1¾ oz) flour
- 500 ml (18 fl oz) any stock
- 100 ml (3½ fl oz) Madeira
- 1 teaspoon tomato purée
- Cayenne pepper, to taste
- Gherkins, chopped, to taste
- Mixed herbs, such as chives, flat-leaf parsley, chervil and tarragon, chopped, to taste

Preparation time: 20 minutes
Cooking time: 3 hours
Serves 6

Boil the calf's head (see above), and cut it into slices. Meanwhile, prepare the sauce. Melt the butter in a pan, add the flour and cook until golden. Pour in the stock, stirring constantly, and simmer for 30 minutes. Add the Madeira and tomato purée, and cayenne pepper, gherkins and herbs to taste. Put the meat in the sauce and simmer for 20 minutes. Arrange the meat on a serving dish and coat with the sauce.

MUTTON & LAMB

Mutton comes from sheep over one year old, reared for their meat, which should be firm and dark red, verging on brown, in colour. The fat should be hard, very white and almost pearly. Mutton is best eaten in winter and spring, as the scent of the lanolin given off by the sheep during the summer shearing season can taint the meat.

Lamb, on the other hand, is a baby sheep, less than 300 days old. Depending on its age, it is termed a milk-fed spring lamb (under two months old), a spring lamb (under four months old) or a hogget (a year-old lamb that has eaten grass). The appearance and the flavour of the meat depend on the animal's age. The colour varies from pale pink to pinkish-red. Many people prefer the more delicate taste of lamb to that of mutton, but mutton is very suitable for stews and dishes that are braised or cooked slowly, in which the meat has time to become tender. For roasts and grilled dishes, it is best to choose a younger animal.

1 • **Scrag end of neck**
2 • **Middle neck**
3 • **Shoulder**
3B • **Fore shank**
4 • **Best end of neck**
5 • **Loin**
6 • **Chump**
7 • **Leg**
7B • **Hind shank**
8 • **Breast**

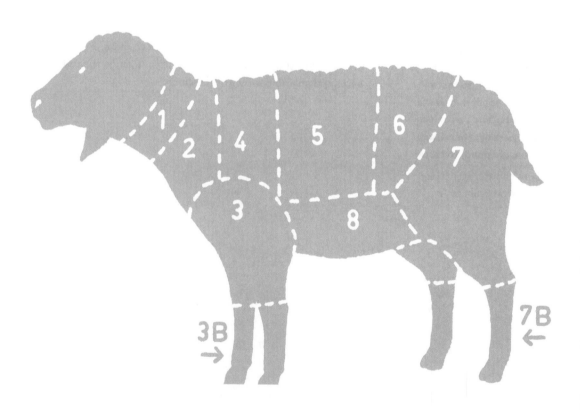

COOKING METHOD	CUTS	COOKING TIMES
POACHING	Breast Neck Leg	15–30 minutes per 500 g (1 lb 2 oz)
PAN FRYING OR GRILLING	Cutlets Loin or chump chops Best end of neck Fillet	10–15 minutes, depending on thickness
ROASTING	Leg Fillet Best end of neck (rack of lamb) Shoulder	15 minutes per 500 g (1 lb 2 oz)
BRAISING	Leg Shoulder	2–3 hours per 1 kg (2¼ lb)
STEWING	Breast Neck	2–3 hours per 1 kg (2¼ lb)

POACHING

LEG OF LAMB À L'ANGLAISE
GIGOT À L'ANGLAISE

In a large pan, bring 3 litres (5¼ pints) water to the boil over a high heat. Add the vegetables, bouquet garni and the lamb, season with salt and pepper, cover and simmer gently until tender, allowing 15 minutes per 500 g (1 lb 2 oz) of lamb. Drain and arrange the vegetables around the lamb. Serve with the caper sauce and haricot beans or mashed potatoes.

* 200 g (7 oz) carrots, chopped
* 100 g (3½ oz) turnips, chopped
* 125 g (4¼ oz) onions, chopped
* 1 bouquet garni
* Salt and pepper
* 1.5 kg (3¼ lb) leg of lamb
* Caper sauce (p.56), to serve
* Haricot beans (p.610) or mashed potatoes (p.566), to serve

Preparation time: 25 minutes
Cooking time: 3 hours
Serves 6

BREAST OF MUTTON MÉNAGÈRE
POITRINE DE MOUTON MÉNAGÈRE

Put the mutton and bacon in a large pan, cover with 2 litres (3½ pints) water, add the vegetables, season with salt, and simmer, covered, for 2½ hours. Remove the mutton and place on a flat work surface. Cover with a board, place a 2-kg (4½-lb) weight on top and allow to cool. Heat the butter in a frying pan over a medium-high heat. Dip each piece of meat in the beaten eggs, and roll in the breadcrumbs. Place carefully in the pan and brown on all sides. Serve the mutton on a dish with the cooked vegetables and bacon arranged around it.

* 1 kg (2¼ lb) breast of mutton, cut into serving pieces
* 500 g (1 lb 2 oz) bacon, chopped
* 1 cabbage, chopped
* 200 g (7 oz) carrots, chopped
* 200 g (7 oz) turnips, chopped
* Salt
* 60 g (2 oz) butter
* 2 eggs, beaten
* Dried breadcrumbs, for rolling

Preparation time: 20 minutes
Cooking time: 2¾ hours
Serves 6

MUTTON SKEWERS
BROCHETTES DE MOUTON

- 150 g (5 oz) bacon, cut into 3.5-cm (1½-inch) squares just under 1 cm (½ inch) thick
- 300 g (11 oz) mutton fillet, cut into 3.5-cm (1½-inch) squares 2 cm (¾ inch) thick
- Bay leaves
- Oil, for brushing
- Salt and pepper

Preparation time: 10 minutes
Cooking time: 20 minutes
Serves 6

Bring a pan of water to the boil, add the bacon and cook for 5–10 minutes. Drain and allow to cool slightly. Thread the mutton, bacon and bay leaves alternately on each of 6 skewers, distributing the meat and bacon equally. Preheat a griddle. Brush the skewers with oil, place on the griddle and cook for 10 minutes, turning regularly. Season with salt and pepper.

ROASTING & FRYING

LAMB CUTLETS
CÔTELETTES D'AGNEAU

 p.419

- 6 lamb cutlets
- Olive oil, for brushing
- Salt
- ½ handful of flat-leaf parsley, chopped
- Juice of ½ lemon
- 1 quantity sauce, such as piquant sauce (p.60), financière sauce (p.57), mushroom sauce (p.61), or tomato sauce (p.57)

Preparation time: 5 minutes
Cooking time: 6 minutes
Serves 6

Preheat a griddle. Brush each cutlet with a little oil, place on the hot griddle and cook for 2–3 minutes on each side. Season with salt. Serve with the parsley and lemon juice, and the chosen sauce.

NOTE
Cutlets can also be cooked in a frying pan. Heat 1 tablespoon olive oil and 15 g (½ oz) butter in a pan, add the cutlets and brown for 2–4 minutes on each side, depending on size and thickness. Serve with macédoine (p.96), braised lettuce (p.556), mashed potatoes (p.568), duchesse potatoes (p.570), tomatoes stuffed with rice (p.580), or onion purée (p.560) or fresh haricot bean purée (p.553).

LAMB CUTLETS IN BREADCRUMBS
CÔTELETTES PANÉES

In a medium bowl, beat the eggs with the oil. Dip the cutlets in the egg mixture, then coat them with the breadcrumbs. Melt the butter in a frying pan, add the chops and fry over a medium-high heat for 5–7 minutes, turning once. Season with salt and pepper.

* **2 eggs**
* **2 teaspoons oil**
* **6 lamb cutlets**
* **Dried breadcrumbs, for coating**
* **40 g (1½ oz) butter**
* **Salt and pepper**

Preparation time: 5 minutes
Cooking time: 6–8 minutes
Serves 6

ROAST LEG OF LAMB
GIGOT RÔTI

Trim the leg of lamb, removing a layer of fat if it is too thick. Insert the garlic clove into the thick end. Preheat the oven to 220°C/425°F/Gas Mark 7. Put the lamb in an ovenproof dish and cook it in the oven: 10 minutes per 500 g (1 lb 2 oz) for very rare meat; 15 minutes per 500 g (1 lb 2 oz) for medium-rare meat.

* **1 x 2-kg (4½-lb) leg of lamb**
* **1 garlic clove**

Preparation time: 10 minutes
Cooking time: 1–1½ hours
Serves 6

NOTE
Shoulder, saddle or loin of lamb can be roasted in the same way. For shoulder, leave the bone in or ask for boneless shoulder, which is easier to carve.

VARIATION

. . . .

LEG OF LAMB FERMIÈRE
GIGOT FERMIÈRE

Proceed as above. Transfer the lamb to a serving plate and keep warm. Strain the cooking juices into a pan, heat very gently and whisk in 50 g (1¾ oz) butter, 3 egg yolks and the juice of 2 lemons. Serve with the lamb, in a sauce boat.

VENISON-STYLE LEG OF LAMB

GIGOT CHEVREUIL

- **400 ml (14 fl oz) red wine**
- **100 g (3½ oz) onions, roughly chopped**
- **1 tablespoon thyme leaves, chopped**
- **1 bay leaf**
- **Salt and pepper**
- **1 x 2-kg (4½-lb) leg of lamb**
- **100 ml (3½ fl oz) crème fraîche**

Preparation time: 15 minutes, plus marinating time
Cooking time: 1–1½ hours
Serves 6

Prepare 3 days before serving. Make a marinade with 400 ml (14 fl oz) water and the wine, onions, thyme, bay leaf, salt and pepper. Put the lamb in a dish, pour over the marinade, and marinate for up to 3 days in the refrigerator, turning the meat occasionally. Preheat the oven to 220°C/425°F/Gas Mark 7. Drain and dry the meat, reserving the marinade, put it in a roasting tin and cook for 10–15 minutes per 500 g (1 lb 2 oz). Make a chasseur sauce (p.65) using the marinade. Just before serving, add the cooking juices from the lamb roast and the crème fraîche to the sauce.

BRAISING

BRAISED LEG OF LAMB

GIGOT BRAISÉ

 p.420

- **50 g (1¾ oz) butter**
- **1 x 1.5-kg (3¼-lb) leg of lamb**
- **125 g (4¼ oz) bacon rashers**
- **Bacon rinds, for barding**
- **150 g (5 oz) carrots, cut into pieces**
- **60 g (2 oz) onion, cut into pieces**
- **200 ml (7 fl oz) white wine**
- **200 ml (7 fl oz) any stock**
- **Salt and pepper**

Preparation time: 15 minutes
Cooking time: 2½ hours
Serves 6

Melt the butter in a heavy-based pan and brown the lamb on all sides. Place the bacon rashers and rinds in the pan. Add the carrots, onion, wine and stock. Season with salt and pepper. Cover with a tightly fitting lid and cook for 50 minutes per 500 g (1 lb 2 oz) meat. Just before serving, strain the cooking juices into a pan and simmer to reduce them to 500 ml (18 fl oz).

BRAISED SHOULDER OF LAMB

ÉPAULE BRAISÉE

- 50 g (1¾ oz) butter
- 1 x 1.2-kg (2½-lb) shoulder of lamb
- 30 g (1¼ oz) flour
- Salt and pepper
- 500 ml (18 fl oz) any stock

Melt the butter in a heavy-based pan, add the lamb and brown it on all sides over a medium heat, then remove it. Add the flour to the cooking juices in the pan, stirring constantly, season with salt and pepper and gradually pour in the stock. Return the lamb to the pan and simmer gently, covered, for 1½ hours, or until tender.

STUFFED SHOULDER OF LAMB

ÉPAULE FARCIE

- 100 g (3½ oz) unsmoked bacon, finely chopped
- 100 g (3½ oz) pork, finely chopped
- 1 handful of flat-leaf parsley, finely chopped
- 1 tablespoon Cognac
- Salt and pepper
- 1 x 1.2-kg (2½-lb) shoulder of lamb, boned
- 50 g (1¾ oz) butter
- 30 g (1¼ oz) flour
- 400 ml (14 fl oz) any stock
- Potatoes or turnips, quartered (optional)

Preparation time: 45 minutes
Cooking time: 2½ hours
Serves 6

To make the stuffing, combine the bacon, pork, parsley and Cognac in a bowl. Season with salt and pepper and mix well. Spread the stuffing over the lamb shoulder, then roll the shoulder up and tie tightly with kitchen string. Melt the butter in a heavy-based pan, add the lamb, brown it on all sides over a medium heat, then remove it. Add the flour to the cooking juices in the pan, stirring constantly, season with salt and pepper and gradually pour in the stock. Return the lamb to the pan, cover and simmer gently for 2½ hours. If desired, add potatoes or turnips when the lamb has been cooking for 1½ hours.

SHOULDER OF LAMB PROVENÇALE

ÉPAULE À LA PROVENÇALE

 p.421

Prepare the stuffing, spread it over the lamb shoulder, then roll the shoulder up and tie tightly with kitchen string. Melt the butter in a heavy-based pan, add the onion and lardons and fry over a medium heat until browned. Add the lamb, carrot and bouquet garni. Season with salt and pepper and pour in the hot stock. Add the tomato purée. Cook, covered, for 2½ hours, turning from time to time.

* 250 g (9 oz) stuffing for red meats (p.80)
* 1 x 1.2-kg (2½-lb) shoulder of lamb, boned
* 50 g (1¾ oz) butter
* 1 onion, chopped
* 125 g (4¼ oz) bacon lardons, chopped
* 1 carrot, sliced
* 1 bouquet garni
* Salt and pepper
* 500 ml (18 fl oz) any stock, hot
* 60 g (2 oz) tomato purée

Preparation time: 35 minutes
Cooking time: 2½ hours
Serves 6

MUTTON NOISETTES

NOISETTES DE MOUTON

Trim most of the fat from around the 'eye' of meat in the chops to create roughly circular noisettes. Stud them with the bacon lardons. Melt the butter in a heavy-based pan, add the noisettes and brown on both sides over a medium-high heat. Pour in the stock, cover and simmer for 1 hour. Serve on the macédoine of vegetables.

* 12 boneless mutton rib or loin chops
* 100 g (3½ oz) streaky bacon lardons
* 40 g (1½ oz) butter
* 100 ml (3½ fl oz) any stock
* 1 quantity macédoine (p.96)

Preparation time: 10 minutes
Cooking time: 1 hour
Serves 6

MUTTON CHOPS À LA CHAMPVALLON
CÔTES DE MOUTON À LA CHAMPVALLON

- 750 g (1 lb 10 oz) potatoes,
  thinly sliced
- 1 onion, finely chopped
- 1 handful of flat-leaf parsley,
  finely chopped
- Salt and pepper
- 50 g (1¾ oz) butter
- 6 mutton chops
- 100 ml (3½ fl oz) white wine
- 100 ml (3½ fl oz) any stock
- 80 g (2¾ oz) tomato purée

Preparation time: 25 minutes
Cooking time: 1 hour
Serves 6

Sprinkle the potato slices with the onion and parsley, and season with salt and pepper. Melt the butter in a frying pan, add the chops and brown for 3 minutes on each side. Transfer the chops and their cooking juices to a large, shallow pan and arrange the potatoes around them. Pour in the wine, stock and tomato purée and bring to the boil. Reduce the heat and simmer, covered, for 1 hour.

MUTTON CURRY
MOUTON AU CURRY

- 60 g (2 oz) butter
- 1.2 kg (2½ lb) mutton,
  cut into pieces
- Salt and pepper
- 10 g (¼ oz) curry powder
- 1 onion, finely chopped
- 30 g (1¼ oz) flour
- 200 ml (7 fl oz) coconut milk
  or water
- 150 g (5 oz) long-grain rice
- 100 ml (3½ fl oz) crème fraîche
- 1 bouquet garni

Preparation time: 25 minutes
Cooking time: 1¾ hours
Serves 6

Melt the butter in a heavy-based pan, add the mutton and cook over a high heat until browned all over. Season with salt and pepper and sprinkle with the curry powder. Add the onion and flour and cook, stirring, until they are pale golden. Pour in the coconut milk or water and add the bouquet garni. Cover and cook over a steady, gentle heat for 1½ hours. Cook the rice as for Indian rice (p.616). Meanwhile, 10 minutes before serving, drain the sauce off the mutton, strain it into a pan and stir in the crème fraîche over a gentle heat. Season to taste with salt and pepper and coat the meat with the sauce. Serve the rice on the side.

NOTE
As a variation, peel and slice 150 g (5 oz) eating apples and fry them in butter until softened, then add to the mutton 5 minutes before the end of the cooking time.

NAVARIN

NAVARIN

Heat the butter in a heavy-based pan over a medium-high heat. Add the mutton, onions, carrots and turnips, and cook until golden brown. Sprinkle with the flour and cook, stirring, until golden. Pour in the hot stock, season with salt and pepper, add the bouquet garni, cover and cook very gently for 2 hours.

VARIATIONS

. . . .

MUTTON STEW WITH POTATOES

RAGOÛT DE MOUTON AUX POMMES DE TERRE

Proceed as above, using only 100 g (3½ oz) turnips, and adding 750 g (1 lb 10 oz) potatoes, quartered, 1 hour before the end of cooking.

. . . .

MUTTON STEW WITH SALSIFY

MOUTON AUX SALSIFIS

Proceed as above, replacing the turnips with salsify.

. . . .

MUTTON WITH CHESTNUTS

MOUTON AUX MARRONS

Prepare 1.25 kg (2½ lb) chestnuts (p.558) and proceed as above, replacing the turnips with chestnuts.

- 60 g (2 oz) butter
- 1 kg (2¼ lb) mutton, cut into pieces
- 125 g (4¼ oz) onions
- 150 g (5 oz) carrots, quartered
- 1.25 kg (2½ lb) turnips, cut into pieces
- 30 g (1¼ oz) flour
- 500 ml (18 fl oz) any stock, hot
- Salt and pepper
- 1 bouquet garni

Preparation time: 25 minutes
Cooking time: 2 hours
Serves 6

SLICED MUTTON

ÉMINCÉ DE MOUTON

Reheat the mutton in a heatproof dish set over a pan of barely simmering water. Make the brown sauce and add the shallot and gherkins. Pour the sauce over the slices of meat.

- 500 g (1 lb 2 oz) leftover mutton, thinly sliced
- 1 quantity brown sauce (p.60)
- 1 shallot, chopped
- 100 g (3½ oz) gherkins, sliced

Preparation time: 10 minutes
Cooking time: 20 minutes
Serves 6

MUTTON & BEANS

HARICOT DE MOUTON

- 1 kg (2¼ lb) dried haricot beans
- 40 g (1½ oz) butter
- 1 kg (2¼ lb) mutton,
  cut into pieces
- 125 g (4¼ oz) onions, chopped
- 20 g (¾ oz) flour
- 500 ml (18 fl oz) any stock, hot
- 1 bouquet garni
- Salt and pepper

Preparation time: 10 minutes,
plus soaking time
Cooking time: 2 hours
Serves 6

Soak the beans in warm water for 6 hours, drain and rinse. Put the beans in a large pan and cover with plenty of water. Bring to the boil and boil gently for 30 minutes, then drain. Meanwhile, heat the butter in a heavy-based pan, add the mutton pieces and onions and cook over a medium-high heat until golden brown. Sprinkle with the flour and cook, stirring, until browned. Pour in the hot stock, add the beans and the bouquet garni, and season with salt and pepper. Cover and cook gently for 1½ hours.

LAMB OFFAL

Offal should be absolutely fresh and it is important to be sure of its origin. The regulations controlling the sale of offal, and its availability, vary from country to country, so it is best to ask your butcher for advice.

PREPARATION

TONGUE
Soak in water for 2 hours, drain, then boil in fresh water for 20 minutes. Remove the rough skin and the bony section.

TROTTER
Soak in water for 12 hours, drain, then boil in fresh water for 10 minutes. Remove any wool growing between the hooves.

KIDNEYS
Split the kidneys in half without completely separating them. Remove the outer membrane and the fat.

BRAISED SHEEP'S TONGUE
LANGUES BRAISÉES

Prepare the tongues (above). Put the bacon, carrots and onions in a heavy-based pan and place the tongues on top of them. Add the stock and season with salt and pepper. Bring to the boil, then reduce the heat, cover and simmer for 2 hours. Allow to cool slightly, then cut the tongues into two, lengthways. Put them on a serving dish, and pour the cooking juices over them. Serve with the chosen sauce in a sauce boat.

NOTE
Braised sheep's tongue can be served with red beans with bacon (p.612), lentils with maître d'hôtel butter (p.612), chestnuts (p.558), sorrel (p.562) or spinach (p.548).

- 4 sheep's tongues
- 125 g (4¼ oz) bacon, diced
- 100 g (3½ oz) carrots, sliced
- 125 g (4¼ oz) onions, sliced
- 500 ml (18 fl oz) any stock
- Salt and pepper
- 1 quantity sauce, such as caper sauce (p.56), piquant sauce (p.60), or tomato sauce (p.57)

Preparation time: 30 minutes, plus soaking time
Cooking time: 2 hours
Serves 6

BOILED SHEEP'S TROTTERS

PIEDS BOUILLIS

- 12 sheep's trotters
- 60 g (2 oz) flour
- 200 ml (7 fl oz) white wine vinegar
- 60 g (2 oz) onion, sliced
- 1 clove • 2 sprigs of thyme
- 1 bay leaf
- Salt and pepper
- 1 quantity sauce, such as poulette sauce (p.52), poivrade sauce (p.63), or tomato sauce (p.57)

Preparation time: 10 minutes, plus soaking time
Cooking time: 3 hours
Serves 6

Prepare the trotters (p.386). In a large heavy-based pan mix the flour with 50 ml (2 fl oz) water. Add the vinegar, 250 ml (8 fl oz) water, onion, clove, thyme and bay leaf. Season with salt and pepper. Bring to the boil and add the trotters, then lower the heat, cover and simmer for 3 hours. Serve with the chosen sauce.

SHEEP'S TROTTER RÉMOULADE

SALADE DE PIEDS DE MOUTON EN RÉMOULADE

- 12 sheep's trotters
- 2 eggs, hard-boiled
- 50 g (1¾ oz) gherkins
- 50 g (1¾ oz) capers
- 50 g (1¾ oz) flat-leaf parsley
- 250 g (9 oz) curly endive
- 1 quantity vinaigrette (p.66)
- 1 quantity mayonnaise (p.70)

Preparation time: 30 minutes, plus soaking time
Cooking time: 10 minutes
Serves 6

Prepare and cook the trotters (p.386). Skin them, remove the bones and slice the meat into small, thin strips. Chop the eggs, gherkins, capers and half the parsley, and mix together. Separate the leaves of the endive, toss them in the vinaigrette and arrange in a ring on a serving dish. Mix the egg mixture with the mayonnaise. Put the slices of sheep's trotter in the centre of the ring and coat with the egg and mayonnaise. Sprinkle with the remaining parsley. Serve cold.

GRILLED KIDNEYS

ROGNONS GRILLÉS

- 750 g (1 lb 10 oz) kidneys
- Oil, for brushing • Salt & pepper
- 1 quantity maître d'hôtel butter (p.48)

Preparation time: 15 minutes
Cooking time: 6 minutes
Serves 6

Preheat the grill. Prepare the kidneys (p.386) and brush them with oil on both sides. Thread them onto 6 skewers, leaving some space between. Grill them on a very high heat for 3 minutes on each side. Season with salt and pepper. Serve with the maître d'hôtel butter.

PORK

Pork is the world's most widely eaten meat. It is tasty and economical, and varies greatly from one cut to another, from lean pork fillet, to the fattier belly and spare ribs. Most of the pigs raised for the table are slaughtered at the age of six months and the meat is pinkish, almost white, firm and close-grained. The fat does not 'marble' the muscle, but forms a thick white layer on the surface, which is rendered down and sold as lard. Pork should always be cooked thoroughly.

1 • Head
2 • Spare rib
3 • Blade
4 • Loin
5 • Chump and leg (fillet end)
6 • Leg (knuckle end)
7 • Hock
8 • Belly (flank)
9 • Hand
10 • Trotter

COOKING METHOD	CUTS	COOKING TIMES
POACHING	Ham, hand, hock Salted belly (*petit salé*) Head Trotters	2 hours per 1 kg (2¼ lb)
GRILLING	Chops Tenderloin Belly or bacon	10–12 minutes
ROASTING	Tenderloin Spare rib or loin Cutlets Brawn Leg/Ham	30 minutes per 500 g (1 lb 2 oz)
BRAISING	Ears Head Trotters Spare ribs Tenderloin	2–3 hours per 1 kg (2¼ lb)

ROASTING & FRYING

PAN-ROASTED PORK CHOPS
CÔTES DE PORC GRILLÉES

Score the fat on the chops with a sharp knife, taking care not to cut into the meat. Heat the oil on a griddle, add the chops and cook over a moderate heat for 7–8 minutes on each side. Season with salt and pepper.

- **6 pork chops**
- **2 tablespoons oil**
- **Salt and pepper**

Preparation time: 10 minutes
Cooking time: 14–16 minutes
Serves 6

PORK CHOPS IN BREADCRUMBS
CÔTES DE PORC PANNÉES

Trim the fat off the chops and preheat a griddle over a moderate heat. Dip each chop in the beaten eggs and sprinkle with some of the breadcrumbs. Place on the griddle and cook for 7–8 minutes on each side. Season with salt and pepper.

- **6 pork chops**
- **3 eggs, beaten**
- **Dried breadcrumbs, for sprinkling**
- **Salt and pepper**

Preparation time: 10 minutes
Cooking time: 14–16 minutes
Serves 6

FRIED PORK CHOPS
CÔTES DE PORC POÊLÉES

Score the fat on the chops with a sharp knife, taking care not to cut into the meat. Melt the butter in a frying pan, then carefully place the chops in. Brown over a medium heat for 7–8 minutes on each side, then season with salt and pepper. Serve with the chosen sauce. If desired, add the sauce after browning, then cover the pan and simmer the chops for 10–12 minutes over a very gentle heat.

- **6 pork chops**
- **10 g (¼ oz) butter**
- **Salt and pepper**
- **1 quantity sauce, such as tomato sauce (p.57), Robert sauce (p.63), piquant sauce (p.60) or mustard sauce (p.68)**

Preparation time: 10 minutes
Cooking time: 24–26 minutes
Serves 6

p.422

ROAST PORK FILLET

CARRÉ DE PORC RÔTI

- **750 g (1 lb 10 oz) pork fillet or boned rack of pork**
- **Salt and pepper**

Preparation time: 15 minutes
Cooking time: 45 minutes
Serves 6

Preheat the oven to 200°C/400°F/Gas Mark 6. Trim any excess fat from the pork and tie it up with kitchen string. Place it on a rack in a roasting tin and roast until it is browned all over. Season with salt and pepper. Reduce the oven temperature to 180°C/350°F/Gas Mark 4, and continue roasting for around 45 minutes or until the juices run clear, basting frequently. This joint can be spit roasted, following the same instructions. Untie and slice the pork to serve.

NOTE
Roast pork is good with mashed potatoes (p.568) or a purée of unsweetened apples (p.669), onions (p.560), chestnuts (p.559), lentils (p.614) or fresh haricot beans (p.553). Put the chosen purée in a serving dish, arrange the meat on top and pour the juices over it.

FILLET OF PORK WITH NEW POTATOES

FILET DE PORC AUX POMMES NOUVELLES

- **750 g (1 lb 10 oz) pork fillet**
- **1.5 kg (3¼ lb) new potatoes**
- **½ bunch of watercress, trimmed**

Preparation time: 25 minutes
Cooking time: 45 minutes
Serves 6

Preheat the oven to 200°C/400°F/Gas Mark 6. Place the fillet on a rack in a roasting tin and roast until it is browned all over, then reduce the oven temperature to 180°C/350°F/Gas Mark 4. Arrange the potatoes in the roasting tin around the meat, 25 minutes before the end of cooking. Turn the meat and baste it with the cooking juices. Cook until the juices run clear, then remove from the oven. Arrange on a long serving dish, in a ring of potatoes and sprigs of the watercress.

PORK LOIN PROVENÇALE

LONGE DE PORC À LA PROVENÇALE

Preheat the oven to 200°C/400°F/Gas Mark 6. Remove the backbone from the pork, trim off the excess fat, leaving a thin layer, and tie the joint with kitchen string. With a sharp knife, make slits in the meat on the side covered by fat and insert the garlic and mushroom slices. Put into an ovenproof dish and cook for around 45 minutes, turning the oven down to 180°C/350°F/Gas Mark 4 as soon as the pork has browned.

Meanwhile, remove the stalks of the mushrooms, reserving the caps. Chop the stalks and put them into a bowl with the sausage meat, any remaining mushroom slices and the herbs. Mix well and season with salt and pepper. Cut out and remove a small circle from the base of each tomato, remove and discard the seeds with a teaspoon and stuff with the sausage meat mixture. Stuff the remaining sausage mixture into the reserved mushroom caps. Heat the oil in a frying pan, add the mushrooms and tomatoes and fry over a high heat for 5 minutes. Reduce the heat and cook, covered, for 20 minutes more. Untie the roast. Arrange on a long serving dish and surround with tomatoes and mushrooms, and pour over the meat juices.

- 800 g (1¾ lb) rack of pork
- 2 garlic cloves, sliced
- 125 g (4¼ oz) mushrooms, sliced
- 6 small ceps or large cultivated mushrooms
- 150 g (5 oz) sausage meat
- 1 handful of chopped mixed herbs, such as flat-leaf parsley, chives, chervil and tarragon
- Salt and pepper
- 6 small round tomatoes
- 120 ml (4 fl oz) oil

Preparation time: 30 minutes
Cooking time: 50 minutes
Serves 6

POACHING

This method is not often used for pork, except for preparing ham, salted pork belly (*petit salé*) and some types of offal.

SALTED PORK BELLY WITH CABBAGE

PETIT SALÉ AUX CHOUX

Prepare the day before. Soak the pork in water for 24 hours, changing the water several times, to get rid of the salt. Put 2 litres (3½ pints) water in a heavy-based pan, add the pork, and bring gently to the boil. Add the bouquet garni, onion and peppercorns, but no salt. Add the cabbage to the rapidly boiling liquid, reduce the heat and simmer on a low heat for 2 hours. Drain, reserving the liquid. Arrange the cabbage in a deep dish, place the pork on top and serve with the boiled potatoes.

NOTE
The cooking liquid can be used to make an excellent soup.

- 800 g (1¾ lb) salted pork belly
- 1 bouquet garni
- 1 onion, quartered
- Peppercorns, to taste
- 1 medium cabbage, cut into large wedges
- 1.5 kg (3¼ lb) potatoes à l'anglaise (p.567)

Preparation time: 24 hours
Cooking time: 2½ hours
Serves 6

BRAISING

BRAISED PORK WITH CABBAGE
PORC BRAISÉ AU CHOU

- 1 kg (2¼ lb) pork roasting joint
- 20 g (¾ oz) lard
- 125 g (4¼ oz) streaky bacon, chopped into lardons
- Salt and pepper
- 1 small cabbage, trimmed and quartered
- 1 handful of flat-leaf parsley
- 500 g (1 lb 2 oz) potatoes

Preparation time: 20 minutes
Cooking time: 2 hours
Serves 6

Bone and trim the joint if necessary, and tie it up with kitchen string. Melt the lard in a heavy-based pan, add the lardons and cook over a high heat until browned. Add the pork and cook, turning regularly, until browned all over. Season with salt and pepper. Reduce the heat and continue to cook, covered, on a gentle heat for about 30 minutes.

Meanwhile, bring a pan of salted water to the boil, add the cabbage and blanch for 15 minutes, then drain. Add the cabbage and parsley to the pork in the pan. Cover and cook for 45 minutes on a gentle heat, then add the potatoes. Cover again and cook on a gentle heat for 45 minutes more. Remove the pork and untie it. Put the cabbage in a deep serving dish and place the pork on top. Arrange the potatoes around it in a ring and pour the juices over it.

RACK OF PORK BORDELAISE
ÉCHINÉE BORDELAISE

- 50 g (1¾ oz) butter
- 800 g (1¾ lb) rack of pork
- 250 ml (8 fl oz) meat consommé or good quality stock
- 500 ml (18 fl oz) white wine
- 1 onion studded with 2 cloves
- 1 bouquet garni
- Salt
- Peppercorns
- 1 quantity chestnut purée (p.559) or lentil purée (p.614)

Preparation time: 10 minutes
Cooking time: 3 hours
Serves 6

Melt the butter in a heavy-based pan, add the pork and cook over a high heat until browned on all sides. Add the consommé and wine. Add the onion and bouquet garni, season with salt and add the peppercorns. Cover and cook for 2½ hours on a low heat, turning the meat several times. Drain and untie the pork, reserving the cooking juices. Place the pork on a serving dish and keep hot. Pour the juices back into the pan and cook over a high heat for 12–15 minutes to reduce, then pour into a sauce boat. Serve the pork with the chestnut or lentil purée, and the sauce.

BURGUNDY HOT-POT

POTÉE BOURGUIGNONNE

Prepare 24 hours in advance. Soak the salt pork in water for 24 hours. Drain and place in a large pan with the sausages, bacon and 2 litres (3½ pints) water. Bring gently to the boil. Remove any tough outer leaves from the cabbage. When the pork comes to the boil, add the turnips, carrots and onions, and the bouquet garni and peppercorns. Simmer, covered, for 1½ hours. Add the potatoes to the pan, and cook for a further 40–45 minutes. Strain the hotpot over a bowl, reserving the stock (this can be used later to make an excellent soup). Cut the cabbage in quarters and place in a serving dish. Arrange the pork on top, surrounded by sausages and the bacon cut into thin slices. Arrange the vegetables in a ring around the meats.

- 600 g (1 lb 5 oz) salt pork
- 6 small sausages
- 1 x 100 g (3½ oz) piece of smoked bacon
- 1 small cabbage
- 250 g (9 oz) small turnips
- 250 g (9 oz) carrots
- 1 onion
- 1 bouquet garni
- ½ teaspoon peppercorns
- 500 g (1 lb 2 oz) small round potatoes

Preparation time: 25 minutes, plus soaking time
Cooking time: 2¼ hours
Serves 6

CASSOULET

CASSOULET

 p.423

Rinse and drain the beans, and place them in a large heavy-based pan or flameproof earthenware dish with the carrot, onion studded with cloves, bacon, bouquet garni and enough water to ensure everything is covered, about 4 litres (7 pints). Bring to the boil and simmer for 1 hour, skimming off any scum. Remove and discard the carrot and onion. In a separate pan, melt the goose fat over a low heat, then increase the heat and fry the pork or mutton in batches until browned. Add the onions, garlic, tomato purée and 500 ml (18 fl oz) of the bean cooking liquor. Simmer for 10 minutes, then transfer to the pan with the beans and bacon and add the sausage and goose or duck confit. Draw off some of the cooking liquor, leaving just enough to cover the meat. Bring to the boil, cover, then simmer over a low heat for 1 hour.

Preheat the oven to 180°C/350°F/Gas Mark 4. Remove the sausage and cut it into pieces. Remove the bacon and cut it into pieces. Arrange alternate layers of beans, cooking liquor, pork or mutton, confit and bacon and sausage pieces in a large ovenproof dish. Season carefully with salt and pepper. Finish with a layer of bacon and sausage. Cover the dish and cook in the oven for 2 hours, then remove the lid and cook for a further 15 minutes before serving.

- 500 g (1 lb 2 oz) dried haricot beans, soaked overnight
- 1 carrot
- 1 onion, studded with cloves
- 1 x 150 g (5 oz) piece of streaky bacon
- 1 bouquet garni
- 60 g (2 oz) goose fat
- 750 g (1 lb 10 oz) pork or mutton, cut into 5-cm (2-inch) pieces
- 200 g (7 oz) onions, chopped
- 25 g (1 oz) garlic, crushed
- 150 g (5 oz) tomato purée
- 150 g (5 oz) raw garlic sausage or Toulouse sausage
- 600 g (1 lb 5 oz) goose or duck confit
- Salt and pepper

Preparation time: 1 hour, plus soaking time
Cooking time: 4½ hours
Serves 6

HOTCHPOTCH
HOCHEPOT

- 250 g (9 oz) beef shoulder
- 200 g (7 oz) salted pork belly
- 40 g (1½ oz) butter
- 250 g (9 oz) breast of mutton
- 250 g (9 oz) neck of veal
- 1 pig's ear
- 1 small cabbage, quartered
- 200 g (7 oz) small turnips, halved
- 200 g (7 oz) carrots, roughly chopped
- 150 g (5 oz) leeks, roughly chopped
- 1 celery stick, roughly chopped
- Salt and pepper
- 6 chipolatas
- 6 slices day-old bread

Preparation time: 40 minutes
Cooking time: 2½–3 hours
Serves 6

Place 3.5 litres (6 pints) water and the beef and pork in a large pan. Rapidly bring to the boil and skim to remove the scum. Meanwhile, melt the butter in a large frying pan and fry the mutton, veal and pig's ear over a high heat until browned. Keep hot. Put the vegetables into the pan with the beef and pork, season with salt and pepper and bring to the boil. Add the mutton, veal and pig's ear, cover and simmer over a low heat for 1½ hours. Add the chipolatas 30 minutes before the end of cooking time. To serve, put the slices of bread in the base of a serving dish, top with the meat, pour the stock over it and surround with the vegetables.

HAM

BOILED HAM
CUISSON DU JAMBON

- 1 x 1.5–2-kg (3¼–4½-lb) raw ham in brine
- 500 ml (18 fl oz) white wine
- 2 carrots, sliced
- 1 onion, sliced
- 1 bouquet garni
- Peppercorns
- Any stock or water, to cover

Preparation time: 15 minutes, plus soaking time
Cooking time: 1½ hours
Serves 6

Prepare the day before. Soak the ham in water to cover overnight to remove the salt, then drain and put it in a large pan. Pour in the wine and add the carrots, onion, bouquet garni and peppercorns. Add stock or water to completely cover the ham. Bring to the boil, then reduce the heat and simmer for 1½ hours. Allow the ham to cool in the pan, then drain. Cut the ham into thin slices with a long, flexible and sharp knife, starting each slice at the fleshy part, and cutting diagonally to finish at the bone.

NOTE
For a ham pot-au-feu, prepare as above and serve with a garnish of cabbage, chicory or braised lettuce.

HAM WITH PARSLEY

JAMBON PERSILLÉ

 p.424

Prepare the day before. Soak the ham in water overnight to remove the salt. Put it in a large pan with water to cover and bring to the boil, then cook over a low heat for 1 hour. Drain, refresh under water and drain again. Put the veal knuckle and calf's foot in a large pan and place the ham on top. Add the dry white wine and enough water to completely cover the meat. Add the shallots and herbs, including 40 g (1½ oz) of the parsley. Bring to the boil, skim, cover and simmer over a low heat for 2 hours. Remove the ham, drain it, remove the rind and mash the flesh with a fork in a terrine. Strain the cooking liquid and season with pepper. Set aside to cool. When the liquid begins to set, pour in the vinegar and the 100 ml (3½ fl oz) wine. Pour the liquid over the meat, sprinkle with the remaining parsley and leave in the refrigerator to set. Serve cold, in slices.

- 1 x 1.5-kg (3¼-lb) raw ham or ham knuckle
- 200 g (7 oz) veal knuckle or shin
- 1 calf's foot, cut into pieces
- 1.5 litres (2½ pints) dry white wine
- 3 shallots
- ½ handful of chervil
- 1 sprig of tarragon
- 1 sprig of thyme
- 1 bay leaf
- 100 g (3½ oz) flat-leaf parsley, chopped
- Pepper
- 1 tablespoon white wine vinegar
- 100 ml (3½ fl oz) good white wine, preferably Burgundy

Preparation time: 30 minutes, plus soaking time
Cooking time: 3 hours
Serves 6

HAM WITH MADEIRA

JAMBON AU MADÈRE

Prepare the day before. Soak the ham in water overnight. Put it in a large pan with water to cover, bring to the boil, and cook over a low heat for 1 hour. Line a heavy-based pan with the bacon and onion, and add the bouquet garni. Put the ham in and pour the mirepoix over it. Cover and simmer for 30 minutes. Add the Madeira, stock and mushrooms and cook for 10 minutes more. Arrange on a dish and serve the sauce separately in a sauce boat.

- 1 x 1.5–2-kg (3¼–4½-lb) raw ham, trimmed
- 100 g (3½ oz) streaky bacon
- 1 onion, sliced
- 1 bouquet garni
- 500 ml (18 fl oz) mirepoix (p.44)
- 50 ml (2 fl oz) Madeira
- 400 ml (14 fl oz) any stock
- 125 g (4¼ oz) mushrooms

Preparation time: 20 minutes, plus soaking time
Cooking time: 1 hour 40 minutes
Serves 6

MARIE-ROSE HAM

JAMBON MARIE-ROSE

- 90 g (3¼ oz) butter
- 1 shallot, chopped
- 40 g (1½ oz) flour
- 200 ml (7 fl oz) white wine
- 200 ml (7 fl oz) any stock
- 100 ml (3½ fl oz) tomato purée
- 1 bouquet garni
- 150 ml (¼ pint) crème fraîche
- 6 slices cooked ham

Preparation time: 5 minutes
Cooking time: 40 minutes
Serves 6

Melt half the butter in a pan, add the shallot and cook gently until softened. Add the flour and cook until golden brown. Gradually add the wine and stock to make a smooth sauce. Add the tomato purée and bouquet garni and simmer for 30 minutes. Add the crème fraîche and cook for 5 minutes. Strain the sauce and add the remaining butter. Meanwhile, reheat the ham in a heatproof dish set over a pan of barely simmering water. Coat the ham slices with the sauce and serve.

HAM SOUFFLÉ

SOUFFLÉ AU JAMBON

Preheat the oven to 200°C/400°F/Gas Mark 6 and brush a soufflé dish or 6 small ramekins with the butter. Make the béchamel sauce and add the cheese, if using. Meanwhile, beat the egg whites to stiff peaks. Stir the egg yolks into the béchamel sauce, then fold in the egg whites and the ham. Season with salt and pepper and pour the mixture into the prepared soufflé dish or ramekins. Cook for 25–30 minutes (10–15 for small soufflés), until risen. Serve immediately.

- 20 g (¾ oz) butter, melted
- 750 ml (1¼ pints) béchamel sauce (p.50)
- Gruyère cheese, grated, to taste (optional)
- 3 eggs, separated
- 150 g (5 oz) cooked ham, chopped
- Salt and pepper

Preparation time: 20 minutes
Cooking time: 15–30 minutes
Serves 6

CANDLEMAS ROLLS

ROULÉS DE LA CHANDELEUR

This recipe is traditionally prepared on Candlemas Day on 2 February, also known as *le jour des crêpes*, or Crêpe Day.

Preheat the oven to 200°C/400°F/Gas Mark 6. Make the crêpes and place a slice of ham on each. Sprinkle with some of the cheese and roll tightly, arranging the rolls in a deep ovenproof dish. Mix the remaining cheese with the tomato sauce and spread over the rolls. Season with a little pepper and bake in the oven for 10 minutes. Serve very hot.

- 6 small crêpes (p.722)
- 6 slices cooked ham
- 125 g (4¼ oz) Gruyère cheese, grated
- 250 ml (8 fl oz) tomato sauce (p.57)
- Pepper

Preparation time: 20 minutes
Cooking time: 30 minutes
Serves 6

HAM KNUCKLE

JAMBONNEAU

Put the knuckle into a large pan with water to cover. Bring to the boil, then reduce the heat and simmer for 1 hour. Allow to cool slowly in the stock. Meanwhile, toast the breadcrumbs in a dry pan over a medium heat until golden. While the ham is still warm, remove it from the pan and drain it. Sprinkle generously with the breadcrumbs.

- 1 pork knuckle
- Dried breadcrumbs, for sprinkling

Preparation time: 10 minutes
Cooking time: 1 hour
Serves 6

NOTE
The knuckle is the part of the pig's leg between the ham and the foot.

HAM CORNETS

- 1 quantity meat jelly or aspic (p.45) made with 1 litre (1¾ pints) court-bouillon with salt (p.82)
- White pepper
- 6 slices of cooked ham
- 900 g (2 lb) macédoine (p.96)
- 225 ml (7½ fl oz) very thick mayonnaise (p.70)
- 3 small tomatoes, sliced
- 2 hard-boiled eggs, sliced

Preparation time: 1 hours, plus setting time
Serves 6

Prepare the meat jelly and season with pepper. Leave to set in the refrigerator for 12 hours. Turn out and chop; set aside. Make the macédoine with the mayonnaise. Roll the slices of ham to form cornets, fill them with the vegetable mixture and arrange on an oval dish. Garnish with the tomatoes, hard-boiled eggs and jelly.

PORK OFFAL

Offal should be absolutely fresh and it is important to be sure of its origin. The regulations controlling the sale of offal, and its availability, vary from country to country, so it is best to ask your butcher for advice.

SAUSAGES WITH WHITE WINE
SAUCISSES AU VIN BLANC

- 6 sausages
- 60 g (2 oz) butter
- 1 onion, thinly sliced
- 100 ml (3½ fl oz) white wine
- Salt and pepper

Preparation time: 10 minutes
Cooking time: 30 minutes
Serves 6

Prick the sausages with a fork. Melt the butter in a frying pan and fry the sausages over a high heat for 8 minutes, turning frequently. Remove from the pan and keep warm. Add the onion to the fat in the pan and cook over a medium heat until browned. Add the wine and season with salt and pepper. Simmer gently for 30 minutes, then pour over the sausages.

LIVER PÂTÉ

PÂTÉ DE FOIE

Preheat the oven to 150°C/300°F/Gas Mark 2. Heat a frying pan, add the bacon and the liver and pork and cook until browned on all sides. Add the onion, shallot and Cognac, and cook until the onion has softened. Remove from the heat and season with salt, pepper and nutmeg. Stir in the eggs and, if using, the breadcrumbs.

Line a terrine, earthenware dish or loaf tin with the bacon rashers, reserving a few. Fill with the meat mixture, cover with the remaining rashers, and arrange the bay leaf and thyme on top. Mix the flour with enough water to make a stiff paste. Cover the terrine with a lid and seal with the paste. Place in a roasting tin half-filled with hot water, and cook in the oven for 1½ hours. Remove the lid and let stand for 20 minutes, then press a board onto the pâté and put a 400-g (14-oz) weight on top. Place the pâté in the refrigerator until it is completely cool. Turn out onto a plate and slice to serve.

- 200 g (7 oz) streaky bacon, roughly chopped
- 350 g (12 oz) pork liver, cut into 2-cm (¾-inch) pieces
- 250 g (9 oz) boneless pork, cut into 2-cm (¾-inch) pieces
- 1 onion, chopped
- 1 shallot, chopped
- 1 tablespoon Cognac
- Salt and pepper
- Freshly grated nutmeg
- 2 eggs, lightly beaten
- 100 g (3½ oz) fresh breadcrumbs soaked in a little milk (optional)
- 6–8 bacon rashers
- 1 bay leaf
- 1 sprig of thyme
- 50 g (2¾ oz) flour

Preparation time: 30 minutes, plus cooling time
Cooking time: 1½ hours
Serves 6

PORK LIVER LOAF

PAIN DE FOIE DE PORC

Preheat the oven to 180°C/350°F/Gas Mark 4. Chop the liver, fat, onion, garlic, shallot and mushrooms together finely. Season with salt and pepper. Grease a charlotte mould with the lard and fill with the chopped mixture. Cover with the bacon bards and arrange the parsley, thyme and bay leaf on top. Cover and cook for 2 hours. Turn out of the mould and serve hot.

- 500 g (1 lb 2 oz) pork liver
- 300 g (11 oz) pork fat (preferably from the kidneys or fillet)
- 1 onion
- 1 garlic clove
- 1 shallot
- 125 g (4¼ oz) mushrooms
- Salt and pepper
- 25 g (1 oz) lard
- 50 g (1¾ oz) bacon, for barding
- 2 sprigs of flat-leaf parsley
- 1 sprig of thyme
- 1 bay leaf

Preparation time: 15 minutes
Cooking time: 2 hours
Serves 6

PIG'S TROTTERS WITH TRUFFLES

PIEDS TRUFFÉS

- 3 pig's trotters, boned and halved lengthways
- 350 g (12 oz) streaky bacon, chopped
- 200 g (7 oz) cooked pork, chopped
- 125 g (4¼ oz) calves' liver, chopped
- Grated truffles, to taste
- Salt
- 1 pinch of ground cloves
- 1 pinch of ground cinnamon
- 1 pinch of freshly grated nutmeg
- 1 egg, lightly beaten
- 6 pieces of caul, 12–15 cm (5–6 inches) square
- 50 g (1¾ oz) butter
- Flat-leaf parsley, to garnish
- 1 lemon, sliced, to garnish

Preparation time: 30 minutes
Cooking time: 15–20 minutes
Serves 6

To bone the trotters, place them flat, palm-side up on a work surface and make 1 long vertical cut from the top of the leg down. Working away from the cut, stretch back the skin on both sides, using a sharp, small knife to sever the connective tissue. Stretch and cut the skin back to the first knuckle, then cut as deeply as possible on all sides just above the joint until the bones are separated from the meat. Alternatively, ask your butcher to do this for you.

Put the bacon in a frying pan and fry over a medium heat for a few minutes, add the pork and liver, and cook until browned on all sides. Sprinkle with truffles to taste, and season with the salt and spices. Stir in the egg and mix thoroughly. Place 1 tablespoon of the mixture on each piece of caul. Place half a trotter on the stuffing. Cover with another spoonful of stuffing and wrap in the caul. Heat the butter in a frying pan, add the trotters and cook for 15–20 minutes, turning once. Serve piping hot, garnished with parsley and slices of lemon.

GRILLED BLACK PUDDING

BOUDIN GRILLÉ

- 500 g (1 lb 2 oz) black pudding
- Mustard, to taste

Preparation time: 5 minutes
Cooking time: 15 minutes
Serves 6

Prick the skin of the pudding with a fork and cut it into as many slices as there are guests. Heat a griddle, and cook on a moderate heat for 12–15 minutes, turning several times. Serve hot with mustard.

VARIATION

. . . .

FRIED BLACK PUDDING
BOUDIN POÊLÉ

Prepare the black pudding as above. Melt 40 g (1½ oz) butter in a frying pan. Cook on a moderate heat for about 12 minutes, turning several times. Serve hot with mustard.

GRILLED CHITTERLING SAUSAGES

ANDOUILLES ET ANDOUILLETTES GRILLÉES

Prick the skin of the sausages with a fork and cut into slices. Heat a griddle and cook the sausages for 12 minutes on a moderate heat, turning several times. Serve with mustard.

NOTE
See p.409 for home-made chitterling sausages.

VARIATION

. . . .

FRIED CHITTERLING SAUSAGES
ANDOUILLES ET ANDOUILLETTES POÊLÉES

Prick the skin of the sausages with a fork and cut into slices. Melt 20 g (¾ oz) butter in a frying pan. Cook over a high heat for 10 minutes, turning several times. Serve with mustard, on a bed of potatoes à l'anglaise (p.567), split pea purée (p.615) or chestnut purée (p.559).

- **500 g (1 lb 2 oz) chitterling sausages**
- **Mustard, to taste**

  Preparation time: 2 minutes
  Cooking time: 12 minutes
  Serves 6

GRILLED SAUSAGES

SAUCISSES GRILLÉES

Prick the sausages with a fork, place them on a griddle and cook for 10 minutes over a moderate heat, turning frequently. If desired, serve on top of rich rice (p.618).

VARIATION

. . . .

FRIED SAUSAGES
SAUCISSES POÊLÉES

Prick the sausages with a fork and place them in a frying pan with a knob of butter. Fry over a high heat for 8 minutes, turning frequently. Serve on a bed of potatoes à l'anglaise (p.567), split pea purée (p.615) chestnut purée (p.559) or rich rice (p.618), or on a plate of braised cabbage with bacon (p.535).

Preparation time: 2 minutes
Cooking time: 10 minutes
Serves 6

BLACK PUDDING FROM ANJOU

GOGUE AU SANG

- 100 g (3½ oz) long-grain rice
- 100 g (3½ oz) crustless white bread
- 200 ml (7 fl oz) milk
- 500 g (1 lb 2 oz) pig's liver, trimmed (p.332)
- 500 g (1 lb 2 oz) pork fat
- 250 g (9 oz) onions
- Small handful mixed herbs, such as flat-leaf parsley, chervil, chives and tarragon
- 3 eggs, beaten
- 1 teaspoon ground coriander
- Salt and pepper
- 1 litre (1¾ pints) pig's blood
- 1 large pig's intestine, washed (p.406)

Preparation time: 1 hour
Cooking time: 20 minutes
Serves 6

Bring a large pan of water to the boil, add the rice and cook for 12–15 minutes, or until just tender, then drain. Cut the bread into cubes and place in a bowl with the milk to soak. Chop the liver, pork fat, onions and herbs, and place in a separate large bowl. Mix in the eggs, cooked rice, coriander, salt and pepper, the bread soaked in the milk, and the pig's blood. Fill the pig's intestine with this mixture. Tie the ends. Prick with a fork. Bring a large pan of salted water to the boil and simmer the black pudding for 20 minutes. Slice, and fry or grill like ordinary black pudding (p.401). Serve accompanied by Swiss chard.

GAYETTES

GAYETTES

- 250 g (9 oz) pig's liver
- 250 g (9 oz) pig's lights (lungs)
- 300 g (11 oz) pig's kidneys
- Salt
- 1 garlic clove, finely chopped
- 300 g (11 oz) sausage meat
- Pig's caul
- 75 g (2½ oz) lard, melted

Preparation time: 45 minutes
Cooking time: 1½ hours
Serves 6

Prepare 6 hours in advance. Cut the liver, lights and kidneys into large pieces. Season well with salt, add the garlic and set aside in the refrigerator, covered, for 6 hours. Preheat the oven to 160°C/325°F/Gas Mark 3. Chop the meat roughly and mix with the sausage meat. Cut the pig's caul into pieces. Divide the meat mixture into balls the size of an apple and wrap in the pieces of pig's caul. Transfer the balls to an ovenproof dish, pour over the lard and cook for 1½ hours. Serve cold.

COOKED PORK

ROAST PORK IN A SAUCE
RÔTI EN SAUCE

Slice the pork and prepare the chosen sauce. Add the pork slices to the sauce and simmer for 10 minutes to reheat. Roast pork can also be sliced and served cold with mayonnaise, garnished with parsley and gherkins.

- Cooked roast pork
- 1 quantity sauce, such as piquant sauce (p.60), mustard sauce (p.68), tomato sauce (p.57) or mayonnaise (p.70)
- 1 sprig of flat-leaf parsley, chopped, to serve (optional)
- 1 tablespoon gherkins, to serve (optional)

Preparation time: 5 minutes
Cooking time: 20 minutes
Serves 6

PÂTÉ FROM GUEUX
PÂTÉ DE GUEUX

Preheat the oven to 200°C/400°F/Gas Mark 6. Grease an ovenproof dish with the butter. Chop the bacon and meat finely and place in a bowl. Add the herbs and onion. Place the potatoes in a pan, add enough milk to cover, and cook until tender. Drain and mash to make a thick purée. Mix the meat and potatoes together, adding the stock a little at a time. Season well with salt and pepper. Transfer to the prepared dish and bake for 25 minutes.

- 15 g (½ oz) butter
- 1 x 125-g (4¼-oz) piece cooked fat bacon
- 350 g (12 oz) mixed cooked meat
- 1 handful of chopped mixed herbs such as flat-leaf parsley, chervil, tarragon and chives
- 1 onion, chopped
- 500 g (1 lb 2 oz) potatoes
- Milk, to cover
- 250 ml (8 fl oz) any stock
- Salt and pepper

Preparation time: 20 minutes
Cooking time: 25 minutes
Serves 6

CHARCUTERIE

Many kinds of charcuterie are now available at good special-ist pork butchers, but cooks with access to farm-fresh pig meat may choose to make their own. Here are a few recipes that require neither complicated equipment nor a professional kitchen, and which have more to do with home cooking than with the craft of charcuterie as we normally think of it.

SAUSAGE MEAT
CHAIR À SAUCISSE

- 1 kg (2¼ lb) lean pork meat, such as neck, minced
- 1 kg (2¼ lb) streaky bacon, minced
- Salt and pepper
- Chopped truffles or truffle peelings (optional)

Preparation time: 10 minutes
Serves 6

In a bowl, mix the pork meat with the bacon. Season with salt and pepper. For very high-quality sausage meat, add chopped truffles or truffle peelings.

CAUL SAUSAGES
CRÉPINETTES

- 6 x 12-cm (5-inch) squares pig's caul
- 1 tablespoon white wine vinegar
- 2 kg (4½ lb) sausage meat (above)
- Oil, for frying

Preparation time: 20 minutes, plus soaking time
Cooking time: 15 minutes
Serves 6

Preheat the oven to 190°C/375°F/Gas Mark 5. Soak the caul squares in water and the vinegar for about 15 minutes, or until the squares are pliable, then rinse, drain and dry them, and lay them out on a work surface. Place a mound of the sausage meat in the middle of each square, wrap it in the caul and flatten slightly so that the sausage is oval in shape. To cook, heat the oil in a frying pan, add the sausages and brown on both sides over a high heat. Transfer to the oven and cook for 8–10 minutes.

NOTE
The uncooked sausages can be brushed with plenty of melted butter, dredged in dried breadcrumbs, then sautéed or cooked on a griddle until golden brown on both sides.

BLACK PUDDING

BOUDIN DE SANG

Prepare the day before. Turn the intestines inside out and wash thoroughly in several changes of warm water, picking them completely clean by hand and scrubbing them with a soft brush, then soak for 12 hours in water and vinegar. Pig's blood should be used while it is still warm. Add the vinegar to prevent it coagulating.

Heat the lard in a frying pan, add the onions and cook over a low heat for 1½ hours stirring occasionally. Add the crème frâiche, pig fat, blood, parsley and garlic, and season with the spices and salt and pepper. Heat, stirring, for 5 minutes. Using a funnel or a sausage-filler, fill the prepared intestines with the mixture, without overstuffing them. Tie both ends with string and tie the ends together.

To cook, bring a large pan of water to the boil, plunge the sausage in and simmer gently for 20 minutes. Prick the skin with a fork; if no blood comes out, the pudding is cooked. Drain, dry and, if desired, rub it with bacon rind to make it shiny. The black pudding is now ready to be grilled or fried (p.401).

- 250 g (9 oz) pig's intestines, cut into 25-cm (10-inch) lengths
- 2 tablespoons white wine vinegar, plus extra for soaking
- 2 litres (3½ pints) pig's blood
- 125 g (4¼ oz) lard
- 125 g (4¼ oz) onions
- 500 ml (18 fl oz) crème fraîche
- 1 kg (2¼ lb) pig fat (preferably fat that surrounds the kidneys or the fillet), finely chopped
- 1 handful of flat-leaf parsley, chopped
- 1 garlic clove, finely chopped
- 1 teaspoon freshly grated nutmeg
- 1 teaspoon ground cloves
- 1 teaspoon ground cinnamon
- Salt and pepper
- Bacon rind, for rubbing (optional)

Preparation time: 2 hours, plus soaking time
Cooking time: 20 minutes
Serves 6

TOULOUSE SAUSAGES

SAUCISSES DE TOULOUSE

 p.427

Prepare the day before. Clean and soak the intestines (above). Remove any sinews from the pork, cut it into pieces and put it through a mincer with the bacon, using the coarsest attachment. (The meat in Toulouse sausages is never very fine.) Alternatively, chop the pork and bacon coarsely in a food processor. Season with the salt, pepper and sugar, cover with a cloth and allow the mixture to rest in the refrigerator until the next day. The next day, work it with a wooden spoon to mix it thoroughly. Using a funnel or a sausage-filler, fill the prepared intestines with the mixture and tie the sausages off with string every 10 cm (4 inches). The sausages can be grilled (p.402), fried (p.402), or served with white wine (p.399).

- 1 pig's small intestines
- 1.5 kg (3¼ lb) lean pork
- 500 g (1 lb 2 oz) streaky bacon
- 40 g (1½ oz) salt
- 8 g (¼ oz) pepper
- 10 g (¼ oz) caster sugar

Preparation time: 1 hour, plus resting time
Serves 6

CHITTERLING SAUSAGES

ANDOUILLES

Prepare at least 3 days before serving. Turn all the intestines inside out, wash thoroughly in several changes of warm water, picking them completely clean by hand and scrubbing with a soft brush, then soak for 12 hours in water and a little vinegar. Put the chopped meats in a bowl, add the onion, shallot and hot peppers, and season with the cloves and salt and pepper. Fill the prepared intestines with this mixture until they are three-quarters full. Tie with string at both ends and hang in a well-ventilated place, then smoke them for at least 48 hours in cool smoke (less than 30°C/86°F).

To cook the sausages, wrap them in a clean kitchen cloth or muslin and put them in a pan of salted water. Poach for 1½ hours over a medium heat at a very slow simmer. Do not allow them to boil. Allow to cool. The chitterlings are now ready to be grilled or fried (p.402).

- 250 g (9 oz) small pig's intestines, cut into 25-cm (10-inch) lengths
- 250 g (9 oz) small calves' intestines, cut into 25-cm (10-inch) lengths
- White wine vinegar, for soaking
- 200 g (7 oz) white tripe, coarsely chopped
- 200 g (7 oz) breast of veal, coarsely chopped
- 200 g (7 oz) breast of pork, coarsely chopped
- 1 onion, chopped
- 1 shallot, chopped
- Hot pepper, chopped, to taste
- 1 pinch of ground cloves
- Salt and pepper

Preparation time: 2 hours, plus soaking and smoking time
Cooking time: 1½ hours
Serves 6

BRAWN

FROMAGE DE TÊTE

 p.425

Prepare the day before serving. Soak the head in cold water with a little vinegar for 24 hours, then drain. Place the head in a large pan, cover with cold water and bring to the boil on a high heat. Cook for 10 minutes, then plunge immediately into cold water. Bone the head, working from the chin to the rest of the head until the meat is free. Cut off the ears and add to the meat. Do not use the tongue. Chop the meat into large pieces and put in a large pan. Add the bacon rind, carrot, onion, bouquet garni, water and wine, and cook on a gentle simmer for 4½ hours. Remove the meat, and continue to simmer the liquid until reduced.

Line the sides of a mould with bacon rashers and arrange the cooked meat in it in layers. Pour in the reduced stock to fill the mould. Cover with a lid or clingfilm and place weights on top. Store in the refrigerator for 24 hours before serving.

- 1 pig's head
- White wine vinegar, for soaking
- 250 g (9 oz) bacon rind, chopped
- 1 carrot
- 1 onion
- 1 bouquet garni
- 1 litre (1¾ pints) water
- 1 litre (1¾ pints) white wine
- 125 g (4¼ oz) bacon rashers

Preparation time: 1 hour, plus soaking and chilling time
Cooking time: 4½ hours
Serves 6

WHITE PUDDING
BOUDIN BLANC

- 250 g (9 oz)
  pig's intestines
- White wine vinegar, for soaking
- 50 g (1¾ oz) lard
- 125 g (4¼ oz) onions,
  finely chopped
- 500 g (1 lb 2 oz) fresh white
  breadcrumbs
- 500 ml (18 fl oz) milk
- 750 g (1 lb 10 oz) pork,
  finely chopped
- 250 g (9 oz) white poultry
  meat, finely chopped
- 150 g (5 oz) pig fat (preferably
  fat that surrounds the kidneys
  or the fillet), finely chopped
- 500 ml (18 fl oz) crème fraîche
- 4 eggs, lightly beaten
- 1 teaspoon freshly grated
  nutmeg
- Salt and pepper

Preparation time: 2 hours,
plus soaking time
Cooking time: 2 hours
Serves 6

Prepare the day before. Turn the intestines inside out, wash thoroughly in several changes of warm water, picking them completely clean by hand and scrubbing them with a soft brush, then soak for 12 hours in water and a little vinegar. Heat the lard in a frying pan, add the onions and cook over a low heat for 1½ hours.

Soak the breadcrumbs in the milk, then put them in another frying pan and simmer gently to evaporate the milk a little and make a thick paste. Add the pork, poultry meat and pig fat to the breadcrumbs, then stir in the onions, crème fraîche and eggs. Season with the nutmeg and salt and pepper. Stuff the prepared intestine with this mixture and tie the ends. Bring a large pan of water to the boil and poach the pudding for 20 minutes. Drain and cool, covered with a thick white cloth so that the pudding stays white. It is now ready to be grilled or fried like black pudding (p.401).

ITALIAN 'CHEESE'
FROMAGE D'ITALIE

- 1 pig's caul
- 1 tablespoon white wine
  vinegar
- 1 kg (2¼ lb) pork liver, chopped
- 1 kg (2¼ lb) bacon, chopped
- 3 eggs, lightly beaten
- Salt and pepper
- Flavourings, such as thyme,
  bay leaf, chopped garlic or
  chopped shallot

Preparation time: 45 minutes,
plus cooling time
Cooking time: 2½ hours
Serves 6

Preheat the oven to 150°C/300°F/Gas Mark 2. Soak the caul in water and the vinegar for about 15 minutes, or until it is pliable, then rinse, drain and dry it. In a bowl, mix the liver and half the bacon. Stir in the eggs and season with salt and pepper and the chosen flavouring. Cover the bottom of a mould with the caul. Put in some of the liver and bacon mixture, then add a layer of some of the remaining bacon. Continue making layers until all the ingredients are used up, finishing with a layer of bacon. Cook for 2½ hours, allow to cool completely, then chill and serve cold.

MEAT PÂTÉ

PÂTÉ DE VIANDES

Preheat the oven to 190°C/375°F/Gas Mark 5. Soak the caul in water and the vinegar for about 15 minutes, or until it is pliable, then rinse, drain and dry it, and lay it out on a work surface. Meanwhile, mix the pork, veal, beef, onion and parsley in a bowl. Soak the breadcrumbs in milk, then add to the meat mixture. Stir in the eggs and season with salt and pepper. Roll the mixture up in the caul, place in an ovenproof dish and pour in the wine. Cook for 1½ hours in the oven, then allow to cool before serving. This pâté keeps in the refrigerator for 48 hours.

- 1 pig's caul
- 1 tablespoon white wine vinegar
- 250 g (9 oz) pork, finely chopped
- 250 g (9 oz) veal, finely chopped
- 250 g (9 oz) beef, finely chopped
- 1 medium onion, finely chopped
- 1 handful of flat-leaf parsley, finely chopped
- 200 g (7 oz) fresh white breadcrumbs
- Milk, for soaking
- 2 eggs, lightly beaten
- Salt and pepper
- 100 ml (3½ fl oz) white wine

Preparation time: 35 minutes, plus cooling time
Cooking time: 1½ hours
Serves 6

PÂTÉ IN ASPIC

PÂTÉ EN GELÉE

Prepare the day before. Preheat the oven to 180°C/350°F/Gas Mark 4. Put a little of the shallots and parsley on the bottom of an ovenproof dish, top with some of the meat slices, add another layer of shallots and parsley and continue making layers until all the ingredients are used up. Place the calf's foot on top, pour in the wine, season with salt and pepper and cook for 3 hours. Remove the calf's foot and place a board or plate the same size as the dish over the meat and place some weights on top while it cools. This pâté keeps in the refrigerator for 48 hours.

- 125 g (4¼ oz) shallots, chopped
- 1 handful of flat-leaf parsley, chopped
- 500 g (1 lb 2 oz) veal, cut into small slices
- 500 g (1 lb 2 oz) pork, cut into small slices
- 1 calf's foot
- 500 ml (18 fl oz) white wine
- Salt and pepper

Preparation time: 30 minutes, plus chilling time
Cooking time: 3 hours
Serves 6

PIG'S TROTTERS
À LA SAINTE-MENEHOULD

PIEDS À LA SAINTE-MENEHOULD

- 6 pig's trotters
- Salt and pepper
- 2 garlic cloves, crushed
- 1 bouquet garni
- Oil, for dipping
- Dried breadcrumbs,
  for coating

Preparation time: 1 hour
Cooking time: 5 hours
Serves 6

 p.426

Prepare the trotters as for sheep's trotters (p.386), then wrap each one tightly in a piece of cloth. Put the trotters in a large pan and place a plate or wedge a wooden spoon on top of them to keep them submerged. Cover with water and season with salt and pepper, and the garlic and bouquet garni. Cook gently for 5 hours. Drain the trotters, and, while they are still warm, untie the cloth. Dip the trotters in oil, then in the breadcrumbs, and fry over a medium-high heat on a griddle or in a frying pan, until browned all over.

PORK RILLETTES

RILLETTES DE PORC

- 200 g (7 oz) lard or
  clarified butter
- 500 g (1 lb 2 oz) pork fillet,
  cut into 3-cm (1¼-inch) pieces
- 500 g (1 lb 2 oz) fat unsmoked
  bacon, cut into 3-cm
  (1¼-inch) pieces
- 1 bouquet garni
- Salt and pepper

Preparation time: 40 minutes
Cooking time: 5 hours
Serves 6

Melt 50 g (1¾ oz) of the lard or butter in a frying pan, add the pork and bacon and cook in batches, turning occasionally, until golden brown. Pour off the fat and set aside, add enough salted water to cover the meat and continue cooking. Add the bouquet garni and simmer for 5 hours over a very low heat. Once the water has evaporated, stir the mixture occasionally so that the meat is lightly browned all over. Process in a mincer or a food processor in batches to make a paste, adding a little water if necessary to make a looser mixture, and stir in the reserved fat. Season with salt and pepper and pack the meat into 6 small pots or ramekins. Cover with a layer of the remaining lard or butter, melted and cooled. Store in the refrigerator and serve cold, with toasts or bread.

LARD

SAINDOUX

- 1.25 kg (2½ lb) pork fat,
  cut into small pieces

Preparation time: 5 minutes,
plus cooling time
Cooking time: 10 minutes

Heat the pork fat gently in a pan over a low heat. When the fat has melted, pass it through a fine-meshed strainer and put it in an earthenware pot. Allow to cool and store in the refrigerator. 1.2 kg (2½ lb) fat yields about 1 kg (2¼ lb) lard.

Entrecôte steak   (p.317)

Beef bourguignon (p.326)

Grilled liver (p.333)

Tripe à la mode   (p.336)

Roast veal (p.348)

Veal chops   (p.343)

Veal paupiettes (p.353)

Lamb cutlets   (p.377)

Braised leg of lamb   (p.379)

Shoulder of lamb provençale   (p.382)

Roast pork fillet   (p.391)

Cassoulet (p.394)

Ham with parsley (p.396)

Brawn (p.408)

Pork rillettes (p.411)

Toulouse sausages   (p.406)

POULTRY

Poultry is the name given to any domesticated bird reared for the table. Poultry is rich in protein, and can be fat or lean, depending on the species. It is usually sold already plucked and cleaned, but any giblets (offal) should be removed before cooking. When buying poultry that has not been plucked and cleaned, a good rule of thumb is to estimate the amount of wastage as about a third of the original weight.

PREPARATION

PLUCKING
Poultry must be plucked immediately after slaughter. Even if it is difficult to remove the feathers, do not soak the bird in hot water; the pores will dilate, which makes the job easier, but the meat will lose its delicate flavour.

CLEANING OUT
Cut off the ring of muscle around the rump, or 'parson's nose'. Make a cut along the neck and pull the upper part of the digestive tract and the crop through this opening. Press down on the breast and push the intestines towards the rump. When cleaning a duck, do not forget to remove the two glands from each side of the rump, which can give it a particularly unpleasant taste. Remove the liver, lungs, heart and gizzard. Remove the gall bladder from the liver. Open the gizzard, clean out its contents, remove the skin covering the inside, wash it and set it aside.

SINGEING
Holding the head in one hand and the feet in the other, pass the bird over a clear flame, until all the down and small feathers have disappeared. After singeing, use the point of a small knife to remove all the small quills that remain in the skin.

TRIMMING
Cut off the head and neck, pinions and feet. Along with the gizzard and the heart, these parts are known as the giblets, and can be used separately.

ADDING TRUFFLES
If desired, make two cuts in the skin of the breast and put slices of truffle underneath it.

STUFFING
Make a stuffing for poultry (p.79). Fill the bird with it through the neck before trussing it.

TRUSSING
Fasten the feet and wings to the body in such a way that the bird retains its shape when being cooked, using a trussing needle and a piece of thin kitchen string. Stick the needle into the right drumstick, under the bone, go through the inside of the body, come out through the other drumstick, and make a knot. Stick the needle into the left wing and go through the inside of the body, coming out through the right wing, then pick up the flap of skin hanging from the neck. Tie a fairly tight knot.

BARDING
Lean or very young birds need to be barded to keep them moist during cooking. To do this, cover the breast and the whole length of the bird with a layer of bacon, wrapping the bird and tying with string a few times.

DUCK

Young, tender ducks are best for roasting, and slightly older ones are good in braised or simmered dishes. A duckling is defined as being less than two months old, a duck four months to one year old. They weigh 1.5 kg (3¼ lb) on average.

JOINTING A DUCK

LEGS
Stick a fork in the leg, press down and lift it, then slide your knife along the carcass, close to the bone, to detach the meat. Cut off the joint.

BREAST FILLETS
Make a long, deep cut down the centre of the breast and on each side of the wishbone to detach the breast fillets, or *magrets*. Score the fat sides with shallow, criss-crossing cuts.

WINGS
Stick a fork under the wing, and find the joint with a knife. Cut through the joint and press down with the fork to lift this part off.

ROAST DUCK

CANARD RÔTI

Preheat the oven to 220°C/425°F/Gas Mark 7. Prepare a duck, clean it out, singe and truss it (p.431). Brush the skin with melted butter and place the duck in an ovenproof dish. Roast, allowing 20 minutes per 500 g (1 lb 2 oz).

Preparation time: 15 minutes
Cooking time: About 1 hour
Serves 6

p.462

DUCK À L'ORANGE

CANARD À L'ORANGE

- **1 duck**
- **2 oranges, 1 peeled and chopped and 1 cut into wedges, to garnish**
- **Zest of 1 orange, finely chopped**
- **100 ml (3½ fl oz) veal stock**
- **50 ml (2 fl oz) Curaçao**
- **Salt and pepper**
- **50 g (1¾ oz) butter**

Preparation time: 15 minutes
Cooking time: 40 minutes
Serves 6

Preheat the oven to 220°C/425°F/Gas Mark 7. Prepare the duck (p.430), setting the liver aside. Put the chopped orange inside the duck, then truss the duck and place it in a roasting tin. Roast for 20 minutes per 500 g (1 lb 2 oz). Meanwhile, bring a small pan of water to the boil, add the orange zest and blanch for 10 minutes. Drain and mash it in a small bowl with the duck liver.

Remove the duck from the roasting tin, then carve it, arrange the pieces on a serving dish and garnish with the orange wedges. Pour off the cooking juices from the roasting tin and strain them. Pour the stock into a pan, bring to the boil, then pour in the strained juices, and the zest and liver mixture and the Curaçao. As soon as it comes back to the boil, remove from the heat. Season with salt and pepper, stir in the butter and pour into a sauce boat to serve.

BRAISED DUCK

CANARD BRAISÉ

- **1 duck**
- **100 g (3½ oz) butter**
- **200 ml (7 fl oz) any stock**
- **Salt and pepper**
- **750 g (1 lb 10 oz) turnips, cut into small balls or barrel shapes**
- **Juice of ½ lemon**

Preparation time: 15 minutes
Cooking time: 2 hours
Serves 6

Prepare the duck and truss it (pp.430–1). Melt 40 g (1½ oz) of the butter in a heavy-based pan, put the duck in and brown it all over. Pour in the stock, season with salt and pepper, cover with a tightly fitting lid and cook over a low heat for 2 hours. Meanwhile, place the turnips in a pan of salted water and bring to the boil over a high heat. Boil for 10 minutes, then drain. Heat the remaining butter in a heavy-based pan, add the turnips and cook over a high heat until browned. Lower the heat, cover and cook for 1½ hours more. Transfer the turnips to the pan containing the duck 10 minutes before serving. Strain the cooking juices and add the lemon juice. Serve the sauce in a sauce boat.

VARIATION

. . . .

DUCK WITH OLIVES
CANARD AUX OLIVES

Proceed as above, omitting the turnips. Shortly before serving, add 200 g (7 oz) stoned olives and a good squeeze of lemon juice to the pan. Season with salt and pepper and simmer for 10 minutes. Serve the duck coated with the strained cooking juices, surrounded by the olives.

DUCK À LA ROUENNAISE

CANARD À LA ROUENNAISE

Preheat the oven to 220°C/425°F/Gas Mark 7. Prepare the duck for roasting (p.430). In a bowl, combine the liver, bacon and parsley, and season with salt and pepper. Fill the duck with this stuffing. Place the duck in a roasting tin and roast for 20 minutes per 500 g (1 lb 2 oz). Remove from the roasting tin and place on a serving dish. Pour the cooking juices from the tin into a pan and add the stock and the wine. Simmer to reduce for 5 minutes over a gentle heat, then stir in the butter. Serve the sauce in a sauce boat.

NOTE
Duck à la rouennaise is a difficult dish to make at home. This recipe is greatly simplified.

- **1 duck**
- **150 g (5 oz) duck liver, chopped**
- **180 g (6¼ oz) bacon, chopped**
- **1 handful of flat-leaf parsley, chopped**
- **Salt and pepper**
- **100 ml (3½ fl oz) any stock**
- **100 ml (3½ fl oz) red wine**
- **30 g (1¼ oz) butter**

Preparation time: 45 minutes
Cooking time: 1 hour
Serves 6

SALMIS OF DUCK

CANARD EN SALMIS

Prepare the duck for roasting (p.430) and set the liver and feet aside. Place the duck in a roasting tin and roast until rare, about 45 minutes. Meanwhile, heat 20 g (¾ oz) of the butter in a frying pan, add the shallot and cook on a gentle heat until softened. Add the brown sauce and continue cooking for about 15 minutes. Season with salt and pepper and set aside. Heat 40 g (1½ oz) of the butter in another frying pan, add the bread and brown on both sides. Remove the duck from the roasting tin and carve it, cutting the breasts into thin strips. Put the feet and breast meat in a frying pan, cover with buttered foil or baking parchment and keep hot, over a gentle heat.

Pound the carcass and wings in a mortar, or put them into a food processor, and reduce them to a fine purée. Strain the purée through a fine-meshed sieve, pour into the sauce and stir to combine. Continue to simmer over a gentle heat. Melt 20 g (¾ oz) of the butter in the roasting tin in which the duck was cooked, add the mushrooms, sauté for a few minutes and stir in the Cognac. Arrange the pieces of duck on a serving dish and pour the mushroom mixture over them. Mash the liver and add it to the simmering sauce. As soon as the sauce comes to the boil, strain it and add the remaining butter. Heat the sauce, without allowing it to boil, and coat the pieces of duck with it. Garnish with the fried bread and serve hot.

- **1 duck**
- **120 g (4 oz) butter**
- **30 g (1¼ oz) shallot, finely chopped**
- **100 ml (3½ fl oz) brown sauce (p.60)**
- **Salt and pepper**
- **6 slices white bread, crusts removed**
- **100 g (3½ oz) mushrooms, roughly chopped**
- **50 ml (2 fl oz) Cognac**

Preparation time: 1 hour
Cooking time: 1 hour
Serves 6

p.463

DUCK TERRINE WITH PRUNES
TERRINE DE CANARD AUX PRUNEAUX

- 300 ml (½ pint) red wine
- 50 g (2 oz) caster sugar
- 200 g (7 oz) prunes
- 1 x 700–800-g (1½–1¾-lb) duck
- 200 g (7 oz) pork belly
- 100 g (3½ oz) breast of veal
- 1 duck liver
- 50 g (2 oz) butter
- 50 g (2 oz) onion, chopped
- 100 ml (3½ fl oz) dry white wine
- 1 pinch of crushed juniper berries
- 2 sprigs of thyme
- 2 bay leaves
- Salt
- 250 g (9 oz) pork fat
- 2 eggs
- 200 g (7 oz) bacon rashers

Preparation time: 45 minutes, plus marinating and chilling time
Cooking time: 1½ hours
Serves 12

Prepare 3 days ahead. In a pan, bring the red wine and sugar to the boil, then reduce the heat and simmer until the sugar has dissolved. Put the prunes in a bowl and pour the marinade over. Allow the prunes to soak for 12 hours. Bone the duck and cut the meat, and the pork and veal, into large pieces. Cut the liver into two and put it in a bowl with the rest of the meat. Melt the butter in a pan and cook the onion until softened. Add the white wine and stir, scraping any sediment from the bottom, then add the juniper, 1 sprig of thyme and 1 bay leaf. Season with salt. Remove from the heat and allow to cool. Pour this liquid over the meat, and marinate in the refrigerator for 24 hours.

Remove the meat and strain the marinade. Put the meat and pork fat through a mincer and add the eggs and half the marinade. Mix thoroughly. Line a terrine with the bacon rashers, letting them hang over the edge. Preheat the oven to 180°C/350°F/Gas Mark 4. Stone the prunes. Arrange alternating layers of the meat mixture and prunes in the terrine, finishing with a layer of meat. Fold the bacon over to cover. Put a sprig of thyme and a bay leaf on top. Cover with foil and cook in a roasting tin half-filled with hot water for 30 minutes, then lower the temperature to 120°C/250°F/Gas Mark 1 for 1 hour. Allow to cool at room temperature, then refrigerate for 48 hours.

DUCKLING

Duckling is prepared in the same way as duck, but because it is more tender, 12 minutes per 500 g (1 lb 2 oz) is sufficient cooking time for roast duckling.

DUCKLING WITH TARRAGON
CANETON À L'ESTRAGON

- 2 ducklings
- 50 g (1¾ oz) butter
- 100 ml (3½ fl oz) any stock
- 1 sprig of tarragon
- Salt and pepper

Preparation time: 25 minutes
Cooking time: 1¼ hours
Serves 6

Prepare the ducklings (p.430). Heat the butter in a heavy-based pan, add the ducklings and fry over a medium heat until browned on all sides. Pour in the stock, add the tarragon and season with salt and pepper. Cover and simmer for 1¼ hours. When ready to serve, strain the juices, removing the sprig of tarragon. Chop the tarragon and stir it into the strained juices. Serve the sauce in a sauce boat.

CAPON

A capon is a young cockerel which has been castrated and fattened, but it is no longer available in many countries. It can be served with the same sauces and treatments as chicken (p.446). Capon is traditionally used in coq au vin, but chicken can be substituted.

COQ AU VIN
COQ AU VIN

 p.464

Prepare the day before serving. Heat the oil and 50 g (1¾ oz) of the butter in a heavy-based pan, add the capon or chicken pieces and the onion and cook over a medium-high heat until browned on all sides. Sprinkle with the flour and continue to cook, stirring. Remove from the heat, pour in the Cognac and simmer vigorously to evaporate the alcohol. Pour in the wine, season with salt and pepper and add the garlic. Cook for 1 hour. Allow to cool and store in the refrigerator until the next day.

The next day, reheat slowly over a low heat. Shortly before serving, divide the remaining butter between 2 frying pans. Add the mushrooms to one and the button onions or shallots and bacon to the other. Cook until the mushrooms are softened and the onions or shallots and bacon are browned. Add the bacon, onions or shallots and mushrooms to the capon or chicken. Serve with potato straws.

- 3 tablespoons oil
- 90 g (3¼ oz) butter
- 1 x 1.5-kg (3¼-lb) capon or chicken, cut into pieces
- 30 g (1¼ oz) onion, chopped
- 40 g (1½ oz) flour
- 50 ml (2 fl oz) Cognac
- 500 ml (18 fl oz) red Burgundy wine
- Salt and pepper
- 2 garlic cloves, crushed or finely chopped
- 185 g (6½ oz) button mushrooms
- 100 g (3½ oz) button onions or shallots
- 100 g (3½ oz) smoked bacon, diced
- Potato straws (p.576), to serve

Preparation time: 25 minutes, plus chilling time
Cooking time: 1 hour
Serves 6

TURKEY

Choose female turkeys because they are smaller and do not have spurs. The flesh should be white. Turkey is carved in the same way as chicken (p.446).

PAN-ROASTED TURKEY BREASTS
RÔTI DE DINDE

Melt the butter in a heavy-based pan, add the breasts and brown on all sides over a high heat. Season with salt and pepper, add half the wine, cover and cook over a moderate heat for 45 minutes–1 hour, until the juices have reduced and the turkey is cooked. Add the remaining wine when the juices have reduced. Cut the turkey into slices to serve.

- **40 g (1½ oz) butter**
- **1 kg (2¼ lb) turkey breasts, rolled and tied**
- **Salt and pepper**
- **200 ml (7 fl oz) dry white wine**

  Preparation time: 10 minutes
  Cooking time: 1 hour
  Serves 6

ROAST TURKEY
DINDE RÔTIE

Preheat the oven to 220°C/425°F/Gas Mark 7. Cover the turkey breast with the bacon rashers and truss the turkey (p.431). Place in a roasting tin and roast, allowing 20 minutes per 450 g (1 lb). If necessary, cover the turkey with a piece of well-buttered foil to prevent it browning too quickly. After 2 hours, untie the turkey and arrange on a serving dish. Garnish with watercress. Add the wine or stock to the roasting tin and simmer, scraping the base of the pan to release any sediment. Serve the juices in a sauce boat.

- **1 x 3-kg (6½-lb) prepared turkey**
- **Bacon rashers, for barding**
- **Watercress, to serve**
- **200 ml (7 fl oz) wine or chicken stock, to deglaze**

  Preparation time: 15 minutes
  Cooking time: 2 hours
  Serves 6

VARIATIONS

. . . .

TURKEY WITH CHESTNUT STUFFING
DINDE FARCIE AUX MARRONS

Mix together 1 turkey liver, finely chopped, and 100 g (3½ oz) each minced veal, pork and bacon. Peel 750 g (1 lb 10 oz) chestnuts (p.558), cook them in 350 ml (12 fl oz) stock or water until softened, then pass through a fine-meshed sieve. Melt 25 g (1 oz) butter in a frying pan, add 10 g (¼ oz) chopped shallots and cook until softened. Mix everything together and, if desired, add a few truffle peelings. Stuff the mixture into the turkey, sew up the opening, truss and roast as above.

. . . .

TURKEY WITH TRUFFLES
DINDE TRUFFÉE

Cut 1 large truffle in half. Cut one of the halves into thin slices and slip them under the skin of the turkey. Finely chop 150 g (5 oz) bacon, 100 g (3½ oz) each pork and veal, 1 turkey liver, the other half of the truffle and the truffle peelings, and mix to make a stuffing. Season with salt and pepper. Stuff the mixture into the turkey, sew up the opening, truss and roast as above.

. . . .

TURKEY WITH APPLES
DINDE AUX POMMES

Peel and cut the apples into wedges, then stuff them into the bird. Sew up the opening, truss and roast as above. The apples absorb the fat and juices from the bird and are delicious.

NOTE
Goose can be substituted for turkey in all these recipes, but do not bard with bacon.

BRAISED TURKEY
DINDE BRAISÉE

Melt the butter in a large heavy-based pan. Prepare and truss the turkey (p.431), put it in the pan and brown it all over on a medium heat. Add the carrots and onions and pour in the stock. Season with salt and pepper. Cover and cook gently for 1 hour. Add the Cognac, boil briefly to evaporate the alcohol, and cook gently for 1½ hours more.

- 100 g (3½ oz) butter
- 1 x 3-kg (6½-lb) turkey
- 100 g (3½ oz) carrots, sliced
- 2 onions, chopped
- 500 ml (18 fl oz) any stock
- Salt and pepper
- 100 ml (3½ fl oz) Cognac

Preparation time: 45 minutes
Cooking time: 2½ hours
Serves 6

GOOSE & FOIE GRAS

Goose is full of flavour, but it is rather fatty. The flesh of a goose should be pinkish and the fat pale yellow. Goose can be bought whole, in which case it will weigh around 5 kg (11 lb), or in pieces, sold as separate joints. Goose can replace turkey in most recipes.

FOIE GRAS WITH PORT
FOIE GRAS AU PORTO

Prepare 2 days before serving. Remove the thin outer membrane, blood vessels and gall bladder from the foie gras. Be careful not to rupture the gall bladder when removing it, as it will taint the flavour of the meat. Place the foie gras in a bowl, add the salt, paprika, Cognac and port, and marinate for 15 hours. After about 14½ hours, soak the caul in cool water with the vinegar for about 15 minutes, or until it is pliable, then rinse, drain and dry it and lay it out on a work surface. Remove the foie gras from the marinade and wrap it in the caul. Prepare and cook a mirepoix in a frying pan, then add the foie gras. Pour in enough port to just cover it. Cook very gently for 15 minutes, without allowing it to boil. Remove from the heat and allow to cool in the liquid. Drain, reserving the liquid, and remove the caul. Make a meat jelly or aspic (p.45) with the reserved liquid. Put the foie gras in a deep dish and glaze with the meat jelly. Place in the refrigerator for 12 hours before serving.

- 1 x 800-g (1¾-lb) fresh goose foie gras
- 12 g (½ oz) salt
- 1 pinch of paprika
- 50 ml (2 fl oz) Cognac
- 50 ml (2 fl oz) port, plus extra for cooking
- 1 piece of pig's caul
- 1 tablespoon white wine vinegar
- Mirepoix (p.44)

Preparation time: 45 minutes, plus marinating and chilling time
Cooking time: 4½ hours
Serves 6

FRESH DUCK FOIE GRAS

FOIE GRAS FRAIS DE CANARD

Prepare 3 days before serving. Use the suggested 500 g (1 lb 2 oz) foie gras before attempting to make a larger quantity. Let the foie gras stand at room temperature for 2 hours. Remove the thin outer membrane, blood vessels and gall bladder from the foie gras. Be careful not to rupture the gall bladder when removing it from the liver, as it will taint the flavour of the meat. Reshape the foie gras and place it on a large piece of clingfilm. Season with salt and pepper and pour the truffle essence and port over it. Wrap the clingfilm around the foie gras and chill in the refrigerator for 12 hours.

The next day, take the foie gras out of its wrapping. Let it stand at room temperature for 1 hour, then preheat the oven to 160°C/325°F/Gas Mark 3. Put the foie gras in an oval terrine, pressing it down carefully with your fingers to get rid of any air. Put the terrine in a roasting tin half-filled with hot water (about 80°C/175°F) and cook for 20 minutes. To check that it is properly cooked, place a skewer inside the terrine next to the foie gras. It should feel warm.

Take the terrine out of the oven, and pour off the fat into a bowl of water, in which it will solidify. Put the terrine aside to cool. Heat the solidified fat in a pan over a low heat, melt it and pour it over the surface of the foie gras. When the fat has set, cover the foie gras with foil and place a wooden board on top, to press it down. Drain to get rid of the blood and chill in the refrigerator for 24 hours before serving.

VARIATION

. . . .

FOIE GRAS IN ASPIC

ASPIC DE FOIE GRAS

Make some aspic (p.45). Rinse a terrine in water, pour in a layer of aspic and allow it to set a little. Then put in the foie gras, prepared as above. Add another layer of aspic and chill overnight in the refrigerator.

- 1 x 500-g (1 lb 2-oz) fresh foie gras
- Salt and pepper
- 1 tablespoon truffle essence
- 50 ml (2 fl oz) port

Preparation time: 30 minutes, plus standing and chilling time
Cooking time: 25 minutes
Serves 6

p.465

FOIE GRAS POACHED IN MADEIRA
FOIE GRAS POCHÉ AU MADÈRE

- 1 x 800-g (1¾-lb) fresh goose foie gras
- Bacon rashers or rinds, for barding
- 1 carrot, sliced
- 4 small mushrooms, sliced
- 120 ml (4 fl oz) any stock
- Madeira

Preparation time: 15 minutes, plus soaking time
Cooking time: 1 hour 20 minutes
Serves 6

Remove the thin outer membrane, blood vessels and gall bladder from the foie gras. Be careful not to rupture the gall bladder when removing it from the liver, as it will taint the flavour of the meat. Soak the foie gras in salted water (10 g/¼ oz salt per 1 litre/1¾ pints) for 6 hours. Preheat the oven to 120°C/250°F/Gas Mark 1. Line a terrine with bacon rinds, carrots and mushrooms, and put the foie gras in it. Pour in the stock and enough Madeira to cover the foie gras. Bring to the boil, then cover and place in the oven for 45 minutes. Remove the foie gras and set aside. Simmer the cooking liquid over a gentle heat and cook for about 20 minutes until reduced, then stir in 2 tablespoons Madeira. Add the foie gras and cook over a gentle heat for 10–12 minutes more. Serve immediately.

FOIE GRAS MOUSSE
MOUSSE DE FOIE GRAS

- 200 g (7 oz) cooked foie gras
- 100 g (3½ oz) butter, softened
- 70 g (2½ oz) truffles
- 200 g (7 oz) double cream
- Salt and pepper

Preparation time: 20 minutes
Serves 6

Mash the liver, butter and truffles together. Add the cream and season with salt and pepper. Use to fill shortcrust pastry tartlets (p.784) baked blind, or serve the mousse on toast.

FOIE GRAS AU TORCHON
FOIE GRAS AU TORCHON

- 800 g (1¾ lb) fresh goose foie gras
- Salt and pepper
- 1 quantity stock (p.176)
- Goose fat, melted, to cover

Preparation time: 30 minutes, plus chilling time
Cooking time: 20 minutes
Serves 6

Prepare 11 days ahead. Remove the thin outer membrane, blood vessels and gall bladder from the foie gras. Be careful not to rupture the gall bladder when removing it from the liver, as it will taint the flavour of the meat. Season with salt and pepper and chill for 24 hours. The next day, prepare the stock, cool it and strain it. To cook the foie gras, wrap the 2 sections together tightly in clean muslin soaked in the cold stock. Twist at each end to secure tightly. Tie it up like a sausage. Put it in a pan, cover with half the stock, bring to the boil, then reduce the heat and simmer for 20 minutes. Remove and plunge into the remaining cold stock. When completely cold, remove and unwrap it. Place in a terrine. Press down, then cover with the melted goose fat. Refrigerate for 10 days before eating.

ALICOT
ALICOT

Melt the goose fat over a medium heat in a heavy-based pan. Fry the giblets in the fat over a high heat until browned, about 5 minutes. Put the salsify and carrots into the pan. Add the stock and bouquet garni, season with salt and pepper and stir in the tomato sauce or purée. Bring to the boil, then reduce the heat to a simmer, cover the pan and cook over a low heat. Meanwhile, make a slit in the chestnut skins, roast or boil the chestnuts until they are half cooked, then peel. Add them to the pan. Continue cooking, covered, for a total of 4 hours.

- 60 g (2 oz) goose fat
- 600 g (1 lb 5 oz) goose giblets
- 250 g (9 oz) salsify, chopped
- 400 g (14 oz) carrots, chopped
- 100 ml (3½ fl oz) any stock
- 1 bouquet garni
- Salt and pepper
- 60 g (2 oz) tomato sauce (p.57) or 1 tablespoon tomato purée
- 250 g (9 oz) uncooked chestnuts

Preparation time: 30 minutes
Cooking time: 4 hours
Serves 6

GUINEA FOWL

Guinea fowl are domestic birds with slightly darker flesh than chicken and a very subtle flavour. If possible, choose a young bird for roasting, and an adult, whose meat is firmer and a little dry, for fricassées. A distinction is made between free-range guinea fowl, reared in the open air, and battery-farmed birds.

GUINEA FOWL WITH CABBAGE
PINTADE AUX CHOUX

 p.466

Prepare the guinea fowl (p.430) and cover the breast with a few slices of the bacon. Put the remaining bacon and the carrot and onion in the bottom of a heavy-based pan. Put the guinea fowl in, put cabbage all around it, season with salt and pepper, and cook over a high heat, covered, for 15 minutes. Pour in the stock and cook over a low heat for 1 hour.

- 1 guinea fowl
- 200 g (7 oz) bacon, sliced
- 1 carrot, sliced
- 1 onion, sliced
- 1.5 kg (3¼ lb) cabbage, cut into wedges
- Salt and pepper
- 100 ml (3½ fl oz) any stock

Preparation time: 25 minutes
Cooking time: 1¼ hours
Serves 6

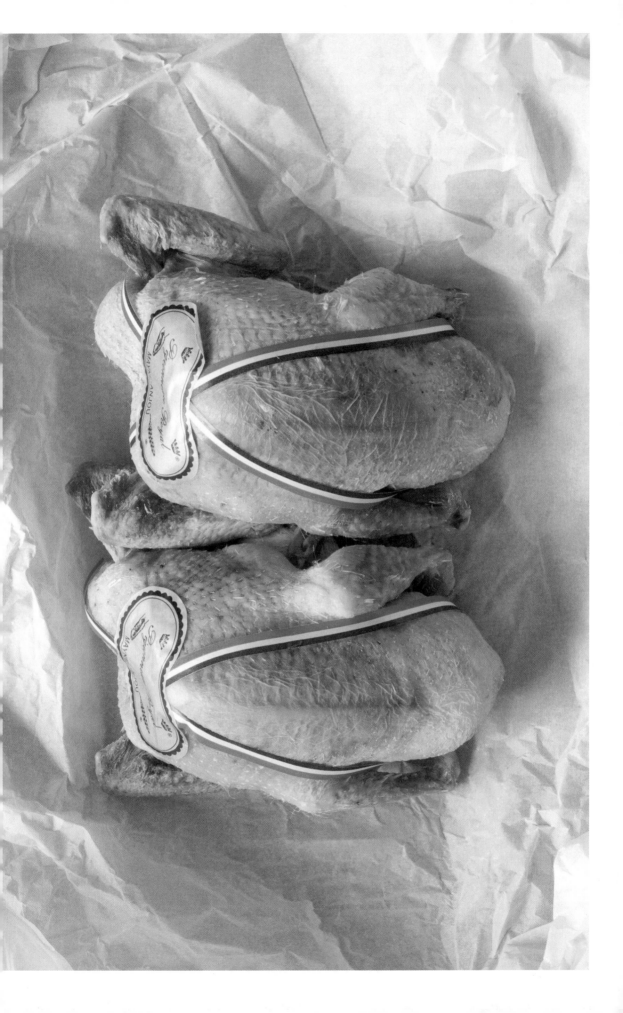

CHICKEN

Chicken has tender meat that may be white or yellow depending on its diet. It is usually slaughtered between the ages of two and four months. Different categories of chicken are defined according to how they are reared, and the age at which they are slaughtered: battery-farmed chickens, which grow fast but have little taste; grain-fed chickens, slaughtered at about 60 days; chickens from a specific locality or source, slaughtered at four months and weighing up to 3 kg (6½ lb), which have firm and tasty flesh. When choosing a chicken, check the information on the packaging, or take your butcher's advice.

To check whether chicken is cooked, pierce the thickest part of the leg with a skewer or sharp knife. If the juices run clear, the chicken is cooked.

CARVING & JOINTING

LEGS
Stick a fork in the leg. Apply pressure to lift it, and slide a knife along the carcass to detach the meat. Cut off at the joint.

WINGS
Stick a fork under the wing. Find the joint with a knife and cut through it. Press down on the fork to remove the wing. Use the knife to hold the chicken steady.

CARCASS
Cut the chicken down the middle, lengthways.

To joint a chicken before cooking, cut up the carcass in the same way as for carving a cooked chicken.

BONING

Starting from the rump and finishing at the neck, make a deep cut along the backbone, going right to the breastbones. Open out this cut, and carefully detach the meat from the carcass on each side. Cut the skin of the neck near the head and stand the bird on its rump. Insert the blade of the knife into the joints attaching the wings to the carcass. Pull the meat away from the body cavity and strip it from the carcass. Break the leg joints. Cut off the feet above the joint and cut off the wing tips.

CHICKEN IN WHITE SAUCE
POULET AU BLANC

- 100 ml (3½ fl oz) white wine
- 1 onion, cut into wedges
- 1 bouquet garni
- 1 x 1.5-kg (3¾-lb) chicken, giblets removed
- Salt
- 60 g (2 oz) butter
- 50 g (1¾ oz) flour
- Juice of 1 lemon
- 2 egg yolks, beaten
- 1 quantity Creole rice (p.617)

Preparation time: 20 minutes
Cooking time: 1¼ hours
Serves 6

Make a court-bouillon with 1.5 litres (2½ pints) water and the wine, onion and bouquet garni (p.82). Allow to cool, then add the chicken. Season with salt, bring to a simmer, cover and cook gently for 1 hour. Strain and reserve the cooking liquid. To make the sauce, melt the butter in a pan, stir in the flour and cook for a few minutes to make a roux. Add the reserved cooking liquid gradually, stirring all the time. When the sauce has thickened slightly, stir in the lemon juice and egg yolks to bind it. Place the chicken on a dish and coat with the sauce. Serve with the Creole rice.

NOTE
A boiling fowl can also be used, but simmer it for 2½ hours instead of 1 hour.

CHICKEN FRICASSÉE

FRICASSÉE DE POULET

Put the chicken pieces in a heavy-based pan with 1.5 litres (2½ pints) water and the bouquet garni, carrot and onion. Bring to the boil, then reduce the heat and simmer for 20 minutes. Drain the chicken pieces, reserving the cooking liquid, and wipe them dry. Melt the butter in the pan, add the chicken pieces, and fry them over a medium heat, taking care not to let them brown. Pour in the wine and 200 ml (7 fl oz) of the reserved cooking liquid. Season with salt and pepper, boil for 2 minutes, then lower the heat and simmer for 35 minutes more.

Meanwhile, prepare the Indian rice. Remove the chicken pieces and keep them warm. Strain the sauce, add the mushrooms and simmer until the liquid has reduced by a third. Stir in the lemon juice and egg yolks and stir until slightly thickened. Serve the chicken pieces coated with the sauce, with a ring of rice and mushrooms around them.

- 1 x 1.5-kg (3¼-lb) chicken, cut into pieces
- 1 bouquet garni
- 1 carrot, sliced
- 1 onion, sliced
- 60 g (2 oz) butter
- 200 ml (7 fl oz) white wine
- Salt and pepper
- 1 quantity Indian rice (p.616)
- 50 g (1¾ oz) mushrooms, roughly chopped
- Juice of 1 lemon
- 2 egg yolks, beaten

Preparation time: 25 minutes
Cooking time: 1 hour
Serves 6

CHICKEN WITH OYSTERS

POULET SAUCE AUX HUÎTRES

Make a court-bouillon with 1.5 litres (2½ pints) water and the wine, onion and bouquet garni. Allow it to cool, then add the chicken. Season with salt and cook gently for 1 hour. Strain and reserve the cooking liquid. To make the sauce, melt the butter in a pan, stir in the flour and cook for a few minutes to make a roux. Add the reserved cooking liquid gradually, stirring all the time. In a separate pan, melt the butter, add the mushrooms and cook over a medium heat for 5 minutes. Add the mushrooms to the sauce. Open the oysters, put them and their liquid in a small pan, and bring to the boil. Season with salt and pepper. Add the oysters and 2–3 tablespoons of their liquid to the sauce, then add the lemon juice. Coat the chicken in the oyster sauce and serve.

- 100 ml (3½ fl oz) white wine
- 1 onion, cut into wedges
- 1 bouquet garni
- 1 x 1.5-kg (3¼-lb) chicken, giblets removed
- 60 g (2 oz) butter
- 50 g (1¾ oz) flour
- Salt and pepper
- 20 g (¾ oz) butter
- 200 g (7 oz) mushrooms, chopped
- 24 oysters
- Juice of 1 lemon

Preparation time: 20 minutes
Cooking time: 1¼ hours
Serves 6

CHICKEN ON A SPIT
POULET À LA BROCHE

* 1 x 1.5-kg (3¼-lb) chicken
* Melted butter, for brushing

Preparation time: 15 minutes
Cooking time: 1 hour 10 minutes
Serves 6

Truss the chicken (p.431). Brush it with melted butter, put it on a spit and roast it over a hot barbecue or in a hot oven. Turn it every 8 minutes and brush it with butter each time.

OVEN-BAKED CHICKEN
POULET AU FOUR

* 1 x 1.5-kg (3¼-lb) chicken
* 60 g (2 oz) butter, cut into small pieces (optional)
* 4 bacon rashers, for barding (optional)
* 2 sprigs of watercress, to garnish
* 200 ml (7 fl oz) chicken stock or white wine

Preparation time: 15 minutes
Cooking time: 1 hour 10 minutes
Serves 6

Preheat the oven to 220°C/425°F/Gas Mark 7. Truss the chicken (p.431), place it in a roasting tin and dot with the butter or cover the breast with the bacon and roast for 1 hour 10 minutes. Turn and baste from time to time. Untruss the chicken, place on a serving dish and garnish with the watercress. Add the stock or wine to the roasting tin and simmer over a low heat, scraping the bottom to release any sediment. Pour into a sauce boat and serve with the chicken.

CHICKEN WITH CHESTNUT STUFFING
POULET FARCI AUX MARRONS

* 375 g (13 oz) chestnuts
* 50 g (1¾ oz) butter
* 200 ml (7 fl oz) milk
* 100 ml (3½ fl oz) meat juices or concentrated meat stock
* Salt and pepper
* 1 x 1-kg (2¼-lb) chicken
* Bacon rashers, for barding

Preparation time: 30 minutes
Cooking time: 1¼ hours
Serves 6

Preheat the oven to 220°C/425°F/Gas Mark 7. Peel the chestnuts and cook them (p.558) in salted water with half the butter. Set aside 12 whole chestnuts and mash the rest, stirring in the milk and meat juices or meat stock. Stir the remaining butter and the whole chestnuts into the mashed chestnuts and season with salt and pepper. Stuff and truss the chicken, cover the breast with the bacon and roast as for oven-baked chicken (above).

CASSEROLED CHICKEN

POULET À LA CASSEROLE

Heat the butter in a heavy-based pan, add the chicken and brown it over a high heat on all sides. Season with salt, cover and cook gently for about 1½ hours. When ready to serve, untie the chicken and place on a serving dish. Add the wine or stock to the pan and simmer, scraping the bottom of the pan to release any sediment. Serve the juices in a sauce boat.

- **40 g (1½ oz) butter**
- **1 x 1-kg (2¼-lb) chicken**
- **Salt**
- **200 ml (7 fl oz) white wine or stock**

Preparation time: 5 minutes
Cooking time: 1½ hours
Serves 6

VARIATIONS

. . . .

CHICKEN CHASSEUR

POULET CHASSEUR

Proceed as above. While the chicken is cooking, heat an additional 50 g (1¾ oz) butter in a frying pan, add 250 g (9 oz) button mushrooms and 100 g (3½ oz) button onions or shallots. Cook over a gentle heat for 25 minutes, then, 15 minutes before serving, add them to the sauce.

. . . .

CHICKEN WITH CREAM

POULET À LA CRÈME

Proceed as above. After 55 minutes, add 125 g (4¼ oz) mushrooms to the pan. Sprinkle with 20 g (¾ oz) flour and cook for 10 minutes, then pour in 500 ml (18 fl oz) crème fraîche and season with salt and pepper. Cut the chicken into pieces, arrange them in a ring on a dish and coat with the sauce.

CHICKEN CASSEROLE
POULET EN COCOTTE

- 40 g (1½ oz) butter
- 125 g (4¼ oz) streaky bacon, diced
- 60 g (2 oz) onion, chopped
- 1 x 1-kg (2¼-lb) chicken
- 100 ml (3½ fl oz) white wine
- Salt and pepper
- 125 g (4¼ oz) mushrooms, chopped

Preparation time: 10 minutes
Cooking time: 1 hour
Serves 6

Preheat the oven to 200°C/400°F/Gas Mark 6. Heat the butter in a heavy-based pan, add the bacon and onions and cook over a high heat until browned. Remove with a slotted spoon and set aside. Add the chicken and brown on all sides. Return the bacon and onion to the pan, and pour in the wine. Season with salt and pepper. Cover with a tight-fitting lid and cook in the oven for 40 minutes. Add the mushrooms to the pan, return to the oven and cook for 20 minutes more.

NOTE
This dish can also be prepared with quails.

 p.467

CHICKEN WITH TARRAGON
POULET À L'ESTRAGON

- 1 x 1-kg (2¼-lb) chicken, prepared, plus its liver, chopped
- 250 g (9 oz) pork, minced
- 125 g (4¼ oz) veal, minced
- 250 g (9 oz) smoked bacon, diced
- 20 ml (¾ fl oz) Cognac
- 40 g (1½ oz) chopped tarragon, plus 1 sprig of tarragon
- Salt and pepper
- 60 g (2 oz) butter
- 60 g (2 oz) onion, chopped

Preparation time: 45 minutes
Cooking time: 40 minutes
Serves 6

Combine the liver, pork, veal and half of the bacon in a bowl to make a stuffing. Stir in the Cognac and 30 g (1¼ oz) of the chopped tarragon. Season with salt and pepper. Fill the inside of the chicken with this mixture, and truss it (p.431). Melt the butter in a heavy-based pan, add the remaining bacon and the onion and cook over a high heat until browned, then remove them with a slotted spoon and set aside. Add the chicken and brown on all sides. Return the bacon and onion to the pan, season with salt and pepper and add the tarragon sprig. Pour in a little water and cook, covered, over a gentle heat for 40 minutes, or until cooked through. When ready to serve, add the remaining chopped tarragon to the cooking juices. Place the chicken on a serving dish and serve the cooking juices in a sauce boat.

PAPRIKA CHICKEN

POULET AU PAPRIKA

Preheat the oven to 180°C/350°F/Gas Mark 4. Joint the chicken (p.446). Heat the butter in a heavy-based ovenproof pan and add the chicken pieces. Cook over a medium-high heat until brown all over. Pour in the stock, cover and cook in the oven for 1 hour. When ready to serve, mix the cooking juices with the crème fraîche and add the paprika. Arrange the chicken pieces in a mound and coat with the sauce.

- 1 x 1-kg (2¼-lb) chicken
- 50 g (1¾ oz) butter
- 200 ml (7 fl oz) any stock
- 300 ml (½ pint) crème fraîche
- 2 pinches of paprika

Preparation time: 10 minutes
Cooking time: 1 hour 10 minutes
Serves 6

FRIED CHICKEN IN SAUCE

POULET SAUTÉ EN SAUCE

Joint the chicken (p.446). Melt half the butter in a heavy-based pan, add the chicken pieces and cook over a medium-high heat until browned. Sprinkle with the flour, stir in the stock and Cognac, and allow to boil for a few minutes to evaporate the alcohol. Season with salt and pepper and add the bouquet garni. In a separate pan, melt the remaining butter and fry the onions until browned, then add them to the pan with the chicken and simmer, covered, for 30 minutes over a low heat. Add the mushrooms and cook for 20 minutes more. Coat the chicken in the sauce and serve.

- 1 x 1.2-kg (2½-lb) chicken
- 50 g (1¾ oz) butter
- 30 g (1¼ oz) flour
- 200 ml (7 fl oz) any stock
- 100 ml (3½ fl oz) Cognac
- Salt and pepper
- 1 bouquet garni
- 100 g (3½ oz) onions, chopped
- 125 g (4¼ oz) mushrooms, chopped

Preparation time: 10 minutes
Cooking time: 1 hour
Serves 6

CHICKEN MARENGO
POULET MARENGO

- 1 x 1.2-kg (2½-lb) chicken
- 2 tablespoons oil
- 30 g (1¼ oz) butter
- 1 handful of flat-leaf parsley, chopped
- 1 shallot, chopped
- 40 g (1½ oz) flour
- 200 ml (7 fl oz) any stock
- 200 ml (7 fl oz) white wine
- Salt and pepper
- 200 g (7 oz) mushrooms, chopped
- 100 g (3½ oz) tomato purée

Preparation time: 20 minutes
Cooking time: 1¾ hours
Serves 6

Joint the chicken (p.446). Heat the oil and butter in a heavy-based pan, add the chicken pieces and begin to brown them over a medium-high heat. When they are half browned, sprinkle with the parsley and shallot. Continue to brown. Add the flour, stock and wine, season with salt and pepper, and cook gently for 1 hour. Add the mushrooms and tomato purée. Cook for at least 30 minutes more.

NOTE
Rabbit can be used in place of chicken.

NAVARRAIS CHICKEN
POULET NAVARRAIS

- 1 x 1-kg (2¼-lb) chicken
- 50 g (1¼ oz) butter
- 200 ml (7 fl oz) Madeira
- Salt and pepper
- 185 g (6½ oz) mushrooms
- 100 g (3½ oz) tomato purée

Preparation time: 15 minutes
Cooking time: 1 hour
Serves 6

Joint the chicken (p.446). Heat the butter in a heavy-based pan, add the chicken pieces and cook over a medium-high heat until browned. Pour in the Madeira and season with salt and pepper. Add the mushrooms and tomato purée, cover with a tight-fitting lid and cook over a low heat for 45 minutes. Put the chicken pieces on a serving dish and coat with the sauce.

CHICKEN CURRY

POULET AU CURRY

Joint the chicken (p. 446). Open the coconut by placing it on a sturdy work surface or clean floor, with a bowl nearby. Carefully strike the middle of the coconut with a hammer. Continue striking very firmly along the equator until the coconut breaks open, taking care to pour the water into the bowl. Break up the large pieces by striking them in the same way, then use a small, flexible knife to remove the white flesh from the shell. Once all the flesh is removed, grate half of it and set aside. Store the other half in the refrigerator for another use.

Melt the butter in a heavy-based pan, add the chicken pieces and the onion, and cook over a high heat for a few minutes. Add the garlic and continue cooking, turning the chicken occasionally until it begins to brown. Sprinkle with the flour and half of the curry powder. Reduce the heat, pour in the coconut water and add the grated coconut flesh. Add as much stock as is needed to give the sauce the desired consistency. Season with salt and pepper and cook, covered, over a gentle heat for about 1 hour. About 5 minutes before serving, add the remaining curry powder. Serve hot with the Creole rice.

- **1 x 1-kg (2¼-lb) chicken**
- **1 coconut**
- **50 g (1¾ oz) butter**
- **1 onion, quartered**
- **2 garlic cloves, crushed**
- **30 g (1¼ oz) flour**
- **30 g (1¼ oz) curry powder**
- **100 ml (3½ fl oz) any stock**
- **Salt and pepper**
- **1 quantity Creole rice (p.617)**

Preparation time: 50 minutes
Cooking time: 1¼ hours
Serves 6

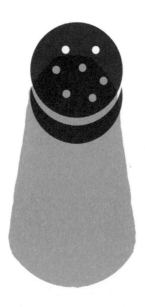

p.468

CHICKEN TERRINE
TERRINE DE POULET

- 1 x 1.2-kg (2½-lb) chicken
- 50 g (1¾ oz) butter
- 100 g (3½ oz) smoked bacon, chopped
- Salt and pepper
- 150 g (5 oz) stuffing for poultry (p.79)
- 200 g (7 oz) ham, cut into strips
- Truffles to taste, cut into strips
- 350 g (12 oz) bacon rashers
- 60 ml (2½ fl oz) Cognac
- 50 g (1¾ oz) flour
- 1 quantity aspic (p.45)

Preparation time: 1¼ hours, plus chilling and setting time
Cooking time: 3 hours
Serves 6

Prepare the day before serving. Joint the chicken (p.446). Heat the butter in a heavy-based pan, add the chicken pieces and bacon, season with salt and pepper, and cook for 30 minutes. Meanwhile, make the stuffing, adding the ham and truffles. Allow the chicken pieces to cool, then bone them.

Preheat the oven to 200°C/400°F/Gas Mark 6. Lay half the bacon rashers in the bottom of a terrine. Put in a layer of stuffing, then a layer of chicken, then another layer of stuffing. Finish with a layer of the bacon cooked with the chicken. Pour in the Cognac and cover the terrine with the remaining bacon rashers. Mix the flour with water, adding enough water to make a stiff paste. Cover the terrine with a lid and seal with the paste. Bake in the oven for 2½ hours. Unseal the lid, make holes in the chicken terrine in several places, and pour in the aspic. Allow to cool and set in the refrigerator. Serve the next day.

VARIATION

RABBIT TERRINE
TERRINE DE LAPIN

Proceed as above, replacing the chicken with 1 rabbit (about 1 kg/2¼ lb). Make the stuffing with 150 g (5 oz) veal, 200 g (7 oz) pork, 250 g (9 oz) ham, 2 lightly beaten eggs, 1 shallot and truffles to taste.

CHICKEN IN ASPIC

POULET EN GELÉE

Prepare the day before serving. Make a stuffing by mashing together the chicken liver, pork and veal. Season with salt and pepper. Bone the chicken (p.447), fill it with the stuffing, truss it, and bard it with the fat bacon. Line a heavy-based pan with the bacon rashers, carrot and onion. Add the chicken and cook, covered, for 15 minutes over a medium heat. Pour in the wine, season with salt and pepper, and braise for 1 hour over a low heat. Remove the fat bacon and put the chicken in an oval terrine. Make the aspic, pour it over the chicken and leave to set in the refrigerator for 12 hours.

- 1 x 1-kg (2¼-lb) chicken, with its liver
- 125 g (4¼ oz) pork, minced
- 125 g (4¼ oz) veal, minced
- Salt and pepper
- 125 g (4¼ oz) fat bacon, sliced, for barding
- 250 g (9 oz) bacon rashers
- 1 carrot, sliced
- 1 onion, sliced
- 100 ml (3½ fl oz) dry white wine
- 1 quantity aspic (p.45)

Preparation time: 1¼ hours, plus setting time
Cooking time: 1¼ hours
Serves 6

BASQUE CHICKEN

POULET BASQUAISE

 p.469

Joint the chicken (p. 446), dividing the legs and wings into two. Heat the oil in a heavy-based pan and fry the chicken pieces for 5–10 minutes over a high heat until golden, cooking in batches if necessary. De-seed and chop the tomatoes. Cut the peppers into quarters and de-seed. Add the tomatoes, peppers and mushrooms to the pan with the chicken. Add the ham and season with salt and pepper. Pour in the wine, cover and cook over a medium heat for 40 minutes. Arrange the chicken pieces on a serving dish. If necessary, simmer the cooking liquid to the desired consistency, then pour it over the chicken. Sprinkle with the parsley and garnish, if liked, with chopped hot Spanish peppers.

- 1 x 1.2-kg (2½-lb) chicken
- 3 tablespoons olive oil
- 250 g (9 oz) tomatoes
- 6 sweet green peppers
- 125 g (4¼ oz) mushrooms, sliced
- 150 g (5 oz) smoked ham, diced
- Salt and pepper
- 150 ml (¼ pint) white wine
- 2 tablespoons flat-leaf parsley, chopped
- Hot Spanish peppers, chopped, to garnish (optional)

Preparation time: 25 minutes
Cooking time: 45 minutes
Serves 6

LIVER PÂTÉ

PÂTÉ DE FOIE

- 300 g (11 oz) calves'
  and chicken livers
- 200 ml (7 fl oz) Madeira
- 300 g (11 oz) fat bacon
- 2 eggs
- 1 shallot, finely chopped
- ½ handful of flat-leaf parsley,
  chopped
- Salt and pepper
- 1 pinch of freshly grated
  nutmeg
- Butter, for greasing

Preparation time: 25 minutes,
plus marinating time
Cooking time: 2–3 hours
Serves 6

Prepare the day before serving. Marinate the livers in the Madeira for 24 hours, then finely chop the livers and bacon. Stir in the eggs, shallot and parsley. Season with salt, pepper and nutmeg. Preheat the oven to 150°C/300°F/Gas Mark 2. Grease a pâté mould with butter, press the mixture into it and place in a roasting tin half-filled with hot water. Cover with foil, or the lid of the terrine, and bake for 2–3 hours. When the blade of a knife comes out clean, the pâté is cooked. Allow to cool.

CHICKEN LIVER LOAF

PAIN DE FOIES DE VOLAILLE

- 4 large chicken livers
- 200 g (7 oz) beef marrow
- 4 eggs, separated
- 500 ml (18 fl oz) béchamel
  sauce (p.50)
- Salt and pepper
- Butter, for greasing
- Dried breadcrumbs,
  for sprinkling
- Tomato sauce (p.57)
  or financière sauce (p.57),
  to serve

Preparation time: 35 minutes
Cooking time: 1 hour
Serves 6

Preheat the oven to 150°C/300°F/Gas Mark 2. Clean the livers and chop them finely with the beef marrow. Add the egg yolks and béchamel sauce, whisk the egg whites to stiff peaks and fold them in. Season with salt and pepper. Grease a terrine with butter, sprinkle it with the breadcrumbs, and press the mixture into it. Place in a roasting tin half-filled with hot water, cover with foil or the lid of the terrine, and bake for 1 hour. Serve with the chosen sauce.

BOILING FOWL

Since boiling fowls are older than chickens, they require longer cooking to make them tender. Boiling fowls can be cooked in a pot-au-feu (p.316) or in a white sauce (p.447).

JELLIED BOILING FOWL

POULE EN GELÉE

Prepare the fowl and truss it (p.431), reserving the giblets. Put the veal leg and hock and the calf's foot in a large pan, pour in 2.5 litres (4½ pints) water and add the salt, carrot, onion, bouquet garni and reserved giblets. Add the fowl and bring to the boil, then reduce the heat and simmer over a low heat for 1½ hours. Remove the fowl and cook for 2½ hours more. Strain the cooking juices and add the Madeira. Put the fowl in an oval serving dish, pour the cooking juices over it and chill in the refrigerator until the juices set.

- 1 x 1.3-kg (2¾-lb) boiling fowl
- 250 g (9 oz) leg of veal
- 500 g (1 lb 2 oz) veal hock
- 1 calf's foot
- 25 g (1 oz) salt
- 1 carrot, sliced
- 1 onion, sliced
- 1 bouquet garni
- 100 ml (3½ fl oz) Madeira

Preparation time: 20 minutes, plus chilling and setting time
Cooking time: 4 hours
Serves 6

BOILING FOWL WITH RICE

POULE AU RIZ

Prepare the fowl and truss it (p.431) and put it in a large pan. Pour in 2.5 litres (4½ pints) water and add the carrot, onion and bouquet garni. Season with salt and pepper, cover and simmer over a low heat for 2½ hours. Skim the stock to remove the fat. Wash the rice, add it to the pan and cook for 30 minutes more over a low heat. Untruss the fowl, serve surrounded with rice.

- 1 x 1.3-kg (2¾-lb) boiling fowl
- 1 carrot, sliced
- 1 onion, sliced
- 1 bouquet garni
- Salt and pepper
- 375 g (13 oz) rice

Preparation time: 5 minutes
Cooking time: 3 hours
Serves 6

BOILING FOWL À LA COMTOISE

POULE À LA COMTOISE

- 1 x 1.5–2-kg (3¼–4½-lb)
  boiling fowl
- 60 g (2 oz) butter
- 50 ml (2 fl oz) Armagnac
- 100 ml (3½ fl oz) Cognac
- 1 onion, chopped
- 1 shallot, chopped
- 1 garlic clove, crushed
- 1 bouquet garni
- Salt and pepper
- 300 ml (½ pint) Arbois
  or Jura white wine
- 300 ml (½ pint) light stock
- 200 g (7 oz) mushrooms,
  chopped

Preparation time: 10 minutes
Cooking time: 1 hour 40 minutes
Serves 6

Joint the fowl (p.446). Melt the butter in a heavy-based pan and fry the pieces of fowl over a high heat until golden all over, in batches if necessary. Pour in the Armagnac and Cognac and simmer for a few minutes to evaporate the alcohol. Add the onion, shallot, garlic and bouquet garni, and season with salt and pepper. Pour in the wine and stock. Simmer, covered, over a low heat for 1 hour. Add the mushrooms and cook for a further 40 minutes.

COOKED POULTRY

COLD LEFTOVERS

Arrange pieces of leftover meat on a dish and garnish to taste with hard-boiled eggs and parsley. Serve with mayonnaise (p.70) in a sauce boat. Alternatively, slice the leftover poultry thinly and put it in a salad bowl with trimmed lettuce and hard-boiled eggs (p.134) cut in quarters. Season with a vinaigrette dressing (p.66), and serve with a little mayonnaise.

HOT LEFTOVERS

Make a sauce, such as velouté (p.59), tomato (p.57), finan-cière (p.57) or Bordelaise (p.58). Add the pieces of meat and simmer for no more than 10 minutes.

OMELETTE
EN OMELETTE

Put the poultry meat in a bowl, break the eggs over it and season with salt and pepper. Heat the butter in a frying pan, beat the egg mixture and pour it into the hot pan. Cook until small bubbles form around the edge of the omelette and the eggs are almost set. Tip and gently shake the pan to allow any runny egg to reach the hot surface of the pan. Using a fork, fold the edges of the omelette towards the centre, slide onto a hot dish and serve with the tomato sauce.

- **150 g (5 oz) boneless and skinless poultry meat, finely chopped**
- **6 eggs**
- **Salt and pepper**
- **40 g (1½ oz) butter**
- **1 quantity tomato sauce (p.57), to serve**

Preparation time: 5 minutes
Cooking time: 5 minutes
Serves 6

FRITTERS

EN BEIGNETS

- 1 quantity batter (p.725)
- 1 tablespoon white wine vinegar
- 2 tablespoons oil, plus extra for deep-frying
- Salt and pepper
- 150 g (5 oz) boneless and skinless poultry meat, cut into evenly sized pieces
- Lemon wedges, to garnish

Preparation time: 30 minutes, plus marinating time
Cooking time: 15 minutes
Serves 6

Prepare the batter and while it is resting combine the vinegar, oil, salt and pepper in a dish. Add the poultry and marinate for 1 hour. When the batter has rested, heat the oil in a deep-fryer to 180°C/350°F, or until a cube of bread browns in 30 seconds. Plunge the marinated meat into the batter, then cook in batches in the oil until browned. Drain on kitchen paper. Serve with lemon wedges.

CROQUETTES

EN CROQUETTES

- 50 g (1¾ oz) butter
- 50 g (1¾ oz) flour
- 200 ml (7 fl oz) milk
- 125 g (4¼ oz) mushrooms, finely chopped
- 200 g (7 oz) boneless and skinless poultry meat, finely chopped
- 60 g (2 oz) ham, finely chopped
- Salt and pepper
- Oil, for deep-frying
- 1 egg, beaten with 1 tablespoon water and oil
- Dried breadcrumbs, for rolling

Preparation time: 25 minutes
Cooking time: 35 minutes
Serves 6

Make a béchamel sauce (p.50) with the butter, flour and milk, add the mushrooms and cook for 5 minutes. Allow the sauce to cool, then stir in the poultry and ham. Season with salt and pepper, and shape the mixture into little balls. Heat the oil in a deep-fryer to 180°C/350°F, or until a cube of bread browns in 30 seconds. Dip the balls in the beaten egg, then roll them in the breadcrumbs. Carefully place them into the hot oil and deep-fry in batches until golden brown. Drain on kitchen paper and serve hot.

Duck à l'orange   (p.433)

Duck terrine with prunes   (p.435)

Coq au vin (p.436)

Foie gras poached in Madeira   (p.443)

Guinea fowl with cabbage   (p.444)

Chicken with tarragon   (p.451)

Chicken terrine (p.455)

Basque chicken   (p.456)

- 8 -
GAME

GAME

The term 'game' can be applied to all edible wild animals that are hunted. The texture and taste of their meat depends on their age, way of life and diet. Their meat is dark and often very strongly flavoured, and much leaner than other types of meat. Game is hung in order to tenderize it, but it must not be hung for more than four or five days.

Wild game, as opposed to game specially reared for the table, is available in France and in the UK during the different hunting seasons. However, the availability of game varies widely from country to country. Wild game is divided into two categories: game animals, or furred game (wild boar, roe deer, red deer, fallow deer, wild rabbit and hare) and game birds, or feathered game, (young partridge, partridge, woodcock, snipe, quail, pheasant, black grouse, golden plover and teal). Some former game birds, such as thrush, lapwing, lark, warblers, blackbird and hazel grouse or hazel hen, are now protected. Good sauces to serve with game include 'poor man's' (p.47), Périgueux (p.61), poivrade (p.63), chasseur (p.65) and blood sauce (p.65).

WILD BOAR

The fillet, cutlets, haunch and head are the best cuts of wild boar. Use only fresh meat that smells good and has bright red flesh and light iron-grey hairs. Wild boar is always marinated, especially if it has not been hung. Roast boar is cooked in a moderate oven for 30–35 minutes per 450 g (1 lb). Most recipes for pork can be used for wild boar.

ROAST FILLET OF WILD BOAR

FILET DE SANGLIER RÔTI

- 750 g (1 lb 10 oz) fillet of wild boar, trimmed
- Bacon rashers, for barding
- 1 quantity uncooked marinade (p.78)
- 250 ml (8 fl oz) chasseur sauce (p.65)

Preparation time: 10 minutes, plus marinating time
Cooking time: 45 minutes
Serves 6

Prepare 2–3 days before serving. Cover the fillet with the bacon, truss it with kitchen string and put it in a bowl. Pour the marinade over the meat to cover it completely, refrigerate and marinate for 2–3 days. Preheat the oven to 240°C/475°F/Gas Mark 8. Remove the meat from the marinade, drain and dry it, then place it on a rack or grid in a roasting tin. Cook as for roast beef (p.322). Serve the chasseur sauce separately.

HAUNCH OF WILD BOAR

CUISSOT DE SANGLIER

- 1 haunch of wild boar, trimmed
- 1 quantity cooked marinade with white wine (p.77)
- 1–2 thin bacon rashers for lardons
- Scraps of ham and bacon, to taste
- 60 g (2 oz) onion, sliced
- 1 kg (2¼ lb) carrots, sliced
- 200 ml (7 fl oz) white wine
- 1 bouquet garni
- Salt and pepper
- 50 ml (2 fl oz) Cognac

Preparation time: 10 minutes, plus marinating time
Cooking time: 5 hours

Prepare 3–4 days before serving. Pour the marinade over the meat to cover it completely, refrigerate and marinate for 3–4 days. Remove the meat, reserving the marinade. Using a larding needle, lard the meat with the bacon (p.312). Put the ham and bacon scraps in the bottom of a heavy-based pan, add the boar, onion and carrots, and pour in the reserved marinade and the wine. Add the bouquet garni and season with salt and pepper. Bring to the boil, then reduce the heat and simmer, covered, for 4½–5 hours. Add the Cognac 1 hour before serving.

WILD BOAR FILLET

FILETS MIGNONS DE SANGLIER

Prepare 1–2 days before serving. Trim the fillet and cut it into even slices about 4 cm (1½ inches) thick. Pour the marinade over the meat to cover it completely, refrigerate and marinate for 1–2 days. Remove the meat, reserving the marinade, and dry. Put the bacon, garlic, shallots and bouquet garni in the bottom of a high-sided frying pan. Melt the butter in another frying pan and brown each slice of fillet over a medium-high heat on both sides. Place the slices on top of the vegetables in the first pan, and add the oil, salt, pepper, Cognac and 2 tablespoons of the reserved marinade. Cover and simmer for 1½ hours on a gentle heat.

- 650 g (1 lb 7 oz) fillet of wild boar
- 1 quantity uncooked marinade (p.78)
- 125 g (4¼ oz) bacon, chopped
- 1 garlic clove, chopped
- 5 shallots, chopped
- 1 large bouquet garni
- 75 g (2½ oz) butter
- 1 tablespoon olive oil
- Salt and pepper
- 100 ml (3½ fl oz) Cognac

Preparation time: 15 minutes, plus marinating time
Cooking time: 1 hour 40 minutes
Serves 6

WILD BOAR & TURNIP STEW

SANGLIER EN HARICOT

Put the wild boar in a pan with the stock, vinegar, wine and bouquet garni. Season with salt and pepper and simmer, covered, over a gentle heat for 2 hours. Add the turnips to the stew and cook, uncovered, for about 1 hour, to reduce the sauce. Add the stock and simmer for 10 minutes more. Arrange the meat on a serving dish with the turnips around it and coat with the sauce.

- 600 g (1 lb 5 oz) breast of wild boar, cut into pieces
- 500 ml (18 fl oz) any stock
- 2 tablespoons white wine vinegar
- 500 ml (18 fl oz) white wine
- 1 bouquet garni
- Salt and pepper
- 300 g (11 oz) turnips, trimmed and halved
- 100 ml (3½ fl oz) veal stock

Preparation time: 20 minutes
Cooking time: 3 hours 10 minutes
Serves 6

ROAST WILD PIGLET

MARCASSIN RÔTI

* 700 g (1 lb 8½ oz) saddle of wild piglet
* 500 ml (18 fl oz) uncooked marinade with red or white wine (p.78)
* 125 g (4¼ oz) bacon rashers, for barding
* 20 g (¾ oz) juniper berries
* 250 ml (8 fl oz) sherry
* 250 ml (8 fl oz) poivrade sauce (p.63)
* Salt and pepper

Preparation time: 20 minutes, plus marinating time
Cooking time: 30 minutes per 1 kg (2¼ lb)
Serves 6

Prepare 2–3 days before serving. Rinse the saddle, pour the marinade over it to cover it completely, refrigerate and marinate for 2–3 days. Preheat the oven to 240°C/475°F/Gas Mark 8. Remove the saddle, reserving the marinade, pat dry and cover it with the bacon rashers. Place in an ovenproof dish, add a little water and roast until browned, then lower the oven temperature to 200°C/400°F/Gas Mark 6 and roast for 20–25 minutes more. Strain the reserved marinade into a pan and add the juniper berries, sherry, poivrade sauce and any juices from the roast. Cook over a high heat for 15 minutes to reduce, then strain the reduction. Season carefully with salt and pepper. Serve separately in a sauce boat to accompany the roast piglet.

VENISON

Roe deer are particularly abundant in French and British forests, and are prized for their excellent meat. The meat of animals younger than 18 months is tender and does not have to be marinated. Older animals are cooked in stews. A young animal can be identified by the fact that its antlers are not fully developed and have no branches. The female has no antlers, only some very small lumps on the front of the head. The meat of the roe deer takes 3–4 days to become tender and is almost always marinated. The best cuts are the haunch, ribs and fillet. The meat of red deer and fallow deer is tougher and firmer, but it can be used in the recipes that follow.

VENISON CHASSEUR

FILET CHASSEUR

Prepare 2–3 days before serving. Pour the marinade over the meat to cover it completely, refrigerate and marinate for 2–3 days. Remove, drain and dry the meat. Reserve the marinade. Put the bacon in a high-sided frying pan and cook over a moderate heat until browned. Add the meat and brown it, turning occasionally. Pour in the wine, stock and 250 ml (8 fl oz) of the reserved marinade. Season with salt and pepper and simmer, covered, for 1 hour. Transfer to a serving dish. Strain the sauce and serve separately in a sauce boat.

- 1 kg (2¼ lb) fillet of venison
- 1 quantity uncooked marinade (p.78)
- 75 g (2½ oz) streaky bacon, diced
- 250 ml (8 fl oz) white wine
- 250 ml (8 fl oz) any stock
- Salt and pepper

Preparation time: 15 minutes, plus marinating time
Cooking time: 1 hour 10 minutes
Serves 6

HAUNCH OF VENISON WITH BERRIES

GIGUE DE CHEVREUIL AUX AIRELLES

- 50 ml (2 fl oz) olive oil
- 1 carrot, chopped
- 1 onion, chopped
- ½ celery stick, chopped
- 1 litre (1¾ pints) red wine
- Sprig of thyme
- 1 bay leaf
- 20 g (¾ oz) juniper berries, crushed
- 1 tablespoon tomato purée
- Salt and pepper
- 1.5 kg (3¼ lb) haunch of venison, trimmed
- 60 g (2 oz) butter
- 500 ml (18 fl oz) poivrade sauce (p.63)
- 1 tablespoon cranberry or redcurrant jelly
- 50 g (2 oz) crème fraîche
- 1 tablespoon fresh cranberries or redcurrants

Preparation time: 40 minutes, plus marinating time
Cooking time: 40 minutes
Serves 6

Prepare 3 days before serving. To make the marinade, heat the oil in a pan, add the carrot, onion and celery and cook gently until softened. Add the wine and simmer until reduced by half. Add the thyme, bay leaf, juniper berries and tomato paste. Season with salt and pepper and allow to cool. Add the haunch and marinate it for up to 3 days in the refrigerator, turning it from time to time.

To make the dish, take the haunch out of the marinade, drain it and wipe it dry. Reserve the marinade. Melt half the butter in a high-sided frying pan, add the venison and brown all over, basting regularly. When the haunch is cooked (about 40 minutes) put it on a serving dish, cover with foil and keep warm. Add the reserved marinade to the pan and simmer, scraping the bottom of the pan. Reduce slightly, add the poivrade sauce and the jelly. Process the sauce in the blender and thicken it by whisking in the remaining butter and the crème fraîche. Beating constantly, add the cranberries. Serve in a sauce boat with the venison.

RABBIT

Most of the rabbits for sale are slaughtered at under three months and weigh about 1.5 kg (3¼ lb) without the legs. Choose one that is rather solid, with a good amount of meat on the back (or saddle), pearly pink flesh and solid white fat around the kidneys. Farmed rabbit is larger, and its diet of grain and grass makes it an excellent dish.

Wild rabbit is smaller than farmed rabbit, its flesh is darker and has a stronger flavour, although young wild rabbits have a delicate flavour.

CLEANING

Place the rabbit on its back and make a cut from top to bottom; separate the back legs by inserting the knife at the bottom of the saddle. Remove the intestines.

JOINTING

A rabbit can be roasted and served whole. You can use the whole saddle and cut off only the forequarters, or you can joint the rabbit into smaller pieces. Cut each shoulder into two pieces and each leg into three. Separate the thorax from the saddle. Cut the thorax into two lengthways, then into two widthways. Cut the saddle into pieces 2–3 cm (¾–1¼ inch) wide, at right angles to the spine.

ROAST RABBIT
LAPIN RÔTI

 p.502

Preheat the oven to 240°C/475°F/Gas Mark 8. Lard the fleshy parts of the rabbit with the bacon using a larding needle, or wrap the joint in the bacon rashers. Tie with string and place in a roasting tin. Roast, allowing 20 minutes per 500 g (1 lb 2 oz). Untie and serve with the poivrade sauce or strong mustard, or simply with the cooking juices, along with the bacon.

VARIATION

• •

ROAST RABBIT WITH MUSTARD
LAPIN RÔTI À LA MOUTARDE

Proceed as above, but spread the rabbit with 50 g (1¾ oz) strong mustard before wrapping it in bacon.

- **1 small rabbit, cleaned, or the saddle of a large rabbit, rolled and tied**
- **Streaky bacon, for larding or barding**
- **1 quantity poivrade sauce (p.63), optional**
- **60 g (2 oz) strong mustard (optional)**

Preparation time: 10 minutes
Cooking time: About 45 minutes
Serves 6

SAUTÉED RABBIT

LAPIN SAUTÉ

50 g (1¾ oz) butter

1 x 900-g (2-lb) very young rabbit, jointed

1 onion, chopped

1 shallot, chopped

1 handful of flat-leaf parsley, chopped

100 g (3½ oz) mushrooms, chopped

Salt and pepper

200 ml (7 fl oz) white wine

100 ml (3½ fl oz) hot water

Preparation time: 10 minutes
Cooking time: 25 minutes
Serves 6

Melt the butter in a frying pan, add the rabbit and brown over a high heat for 10 minutes. Sprinkle with the onion, shallot, parsley and mushrooms. Season with salt and pepper. Pour in the wine and cook for 15 minutes. When ready to serve, arrange the rabbit pieces on a dish. Add the hot water to the pan, stirring and scraping the bottom to release any sediment. Bring to the boil and cook to reduce to the desired consistency. Coat the rabbit with the juices or serve them in a sauce boat.

SEMI-CURED SADDLE OF YOUNG RABBIT

RÂBLE DE LAPEREAU AU DEMI-SEL

30 g (1¼ oz) salt

1 x 1.5-kg (3¼-lb) saddle of rabbit

50 ml (2 fl oz) olive oil

300 g (11 oz) tomatoes, cut into strips

250 g (9 oz) courgettes, cut into strips

Salt and pepper

1 tablespoon dried Provençal herbs

1 tablespoon thyme, chopped

100 ml (3½ fl oz) jellied veal stock

30 g (1¼ oz) butter

150 g (5 oz) onions, sliced

50 ml (2 fl oz) sherry vinegar

Preparation time: 3 hours, plus brining time
Cooking time: 40–45 minutes
Serves 6

Prepare 2 hours before serving. Dissolve the salt in 1 litre (1¾ pints) water to make the brine. Bone the saddle, starting with the spine. Roll the meat to form a small joint and tie it with string. Put in the brine for 2 hours. After 1½ hours of brining, preheat the oven to 180°C/350°F/Gas Mark 4. Brush a gratin dish with some of the oil, and arrange the tomatoes and courgettes in it, in alternating layers. Brush with the remaining oil, season with salt and pepper, and sprinkle with the herbs and half the thyme. Cook in the oven for 20–25 minutes.

Drain the rabbit. Take a sheet of heat-safe clingfilm and place half the jellied stock in the centre. Place the rabbit on it and sprinkle with the remaining thyme. Put the remaining jelly on top and wrap it all up in the clingfilm. Put in a steamer and steam for 15 minutes. Meanwhile, melt the butter in a small pan, add the onions and cook over a low heat until golden. Add the vinegar and simmer, scraping the bottom of the pan. Season with salt and pepper. Place the baked tomatoes and courgettes in a serving dish. Open and untie the rabbit, reserving the juices. Cut it into thin slices and arrange them on the tomatoes and courgettes. Place the softened onions in the centre and coat everything with the rabbit cooking juices. Sprinkle with a little freshly ground pepper.

RABBIT IN WHITE WINE

LAPIN EN GIBELOTTE

Melt the butter in a heavy-based pan, add the onions or shallots and the bacon and cook over a medium heat until browned. Remove and set aside, and put rabbit into the pan. Cook until golden brown, then sprinkle with flour and pour in the hot stock and the wine. Season with salt and pepper. Add the bouquet garni and the reserved bacon and onions or shallots. Cook gently for 45 minutes. Add the potatoes, season with salt and pepper and cook for 30 minutes more. About 15 minutes before serving, add the mushrooms. Transfer to a serving dish and serve hot.

- 50 g (1¾ oz) butter
- 100 g (3½ oz) button onions or shallots
- 150 g (5 oz) bacon, diced
- 1 x 1.5-kg (3¼-lb) rabbit, cut into pieces
- 40 g (1½ oz) flour
- 200 ml (7 fl oz) any stock, hot
- 400 ml (14 fl oz) white wine
- Salt and pepper
- 1 bouquet garni
- 800 g (1¾ lb) small potatoes
- 125 g (4¼ oz) mushrooms

Preparation time: 20 minutes
Cooking time: 1¼ hours
Serves 6

RABBIT IN CREAM

LAPIN À LA CRÈME

Preheat the oven to 220°C/425°F/Gas Mark 7. Soak the caul in the vinegar and enough water to cover for about 15 minutes, or until it is pliable, then rinse, drain and dry it, and lay it out on a work surface. Meanwhile, coat each rabbit piece with some of the mustard and season with salt and pepper. Put all the rabbit in the prepared caul, wrap the caul into a parcel and put it in a baking dish. Bake for 1½ hours. Remove the rabbit from the caul, put the pieces in a serving dish and pour the crème fraîche into the hot baking dish, stirring carefully. Cover the rabbit with this sauce and serve.

- 1 pig's caul
- 1 tablespoon white wine vinegar
- 1 large saddle of rabbit, cut into pieces
- Dijon mustard, for coating
- Salt and pepper
- 185 g (6½ oz) crème fraîche

Preparation time: 30 minutes
Cooking time: 1½ hours
Serves 6

RABBIT STEW

CIVET DE LAPIN

Heat the butter in a heavy-based pan, add the onions and bacon and fry over a medium heat until browned. Remove them, add the rabbit and cook until golden brown, then remove. Make a brown roux (p.60) with the flour, hot stock and wine. Return the rabbit, bacon and onions to the pan, season with salt and pepper, and add the bouquet garni. Simmer gently for 1 hour. Mash the liver 10 minutes before serving and add it, along with the blood, to the sauce, stirring well.

- 30 g (1¼ oz) butter
- 125 g (4¼ oz) onions
- 125 g (4¼ oz) diced bacon
- 1 x 1.5-kg (3¼-lb) rabbit, cut into pieces, with its liver and blood
- 30 g (1¼ oz) flour
- 200 ml (7 fl oz) any stock, hot
- 400 ml (14 fl oz) red wine
- Salt and pepper
- 1 bouquet garni

Preparation time: 25 minutes
Cooking time: 1 hour 10 minutes
Serves 6

RABBIT WITH PRUNES

LAPIN AUX PRUNEAUX

Prepare the day before serving. Rinse the prunes and soak in water for 24 hours, then drain. Put the rabbit in a bowl. Make a marinade made by combining the wine, carrot, thyme and bay leaf in a pan. Bring to the boil and cook for a few minutes, then pour the warm marinade over the rabbit to completely cover it. Leave to marinate in the refrigerator for 12 hours. The next day, heat the butter in a heavy-based pan, add the onion and bacon and fry over a medium heat until browned, then remove and set aside. Remove the rabbit from the marinade, wipe the pieces, add to the pan and fry until golden brown. Strain the marinade.

Return the bacon and onion to the pan. Pour in a little of the strained marinade, season with salt and pepper and add the drained prunes. Cover and simmer for 45 minutes to 1 hour. Serve in a deep serving dish, coated with the cooking juices, which you can thicken with the redcurrant jelly, if desired.

- 500 g (1 lb 2 oz) prunes
- 1 x 1.5-kg (3¼-lb) rabbit, cut into pieces
- 1 litre (1¾ pints) red wine
- 1 carrot, sliced
- 1 pinch of thyme
- 1 bay leaf
- 50 g (1¾ oz) butter
- 1 onion, sliced
- 125 g (4¼ oz) salted bacon, diced
- Salt and pepper
- 1 tablespoon redcurrant jelly (optional)

Preparation time: 20 minutes, plus soaking and marinating time
Cooking time: 1 hour
Serves 6

RABBIT LOAF

PAIN DE LAPIN

- 1 x 1-kg (2¼-lb) rabbit, cut into pieces
- 1 quantity uncooked marinade (p.78)
- 350 g (12 oz) bacon
- 2 eggs, separated
- 100 g (3½ oz) fresh breadcrumbs
- 100 ml (3½ fl oz) Cognac
- ½ handful of flat-leaf parsley, chopped
- Salt and pepper
- Butter, for greasing
- 1 quantity tomato sauce (p.57)

Preparation time: 30 minutes, plus marinating time
Cooking time: 2 hours
Serves 6

Prepare the day before serving. Pour the marinade over the rabbit to cover it completely, refrigerate and marinate for 24 hours. Remove the meat from the bones and chop finely with the bacon. Beat the egg yolks, mash the breadcrumbs into them with a fork and add to the meat mixture, along with the Cognac. Whisk the egg whites to stiff peaks and fold into the mixture along with the parsley. Season with salt and pepper. Preheat the oven to 150°C/300°F/Gas Mark 2. Grease a rectangular mould with butter and press the meat mixture into it. Place in a roasting tin half-filled with hot water and bake for 2 hours. Turn out and serve with the tomato sauce.

YOUNG RABBIT NIÇOISE

LAPEREAU À LA NIÇOISE

- 1 young rabbit
- 50 g (1¾ oz) flour
- 1 tablespoon olive oil
- Salt and pepper
- 100 ml (3½ fl oz) white wine
- 18 black olives, stoned
- 1 quantity tomato sauce (p.57)
- 1 bouquet garni
- 50 g (1¾ oz) butter

Preparation time: 15 minutes
Cooking time: 35 minutes
Serves 6

Skin, clean and joint the rabbit (p.478). Dip each piece in the flour. Heat the oil in a frying pan, add the meat and fry over a high heat until golden brown. Season with salt and pepper and pour in the wine. Add the olives, tomato sauce and bouquet garni. Simmer over a gentle heat for 25 minutes. Arrange the rabbit in a deep serving dish, thicken the sauce with the butter and pour it over the meat.

SLICED RABBIT
ÉMINCÉ DE LAPIN

Slice the rabbit meat. Put the meat slices and bacon in a frying pan and fry over a medium-high heat until browned on both sides. Prepare the piquant sauce, add the rabbit slices and simmer for 20 minutes, taking care not to let it boil.

- 1 cooked rabbit
- 75 g (2½ oz) streaky bacon, chopped
- 500 ml (18 fl oz) piquant sauce (p.60)

Preparation time: 30 minutes
Cooking time: 40 minutes
Serves 6

HARE

Unlike rabbits, which have pale meat, hare meat is darker. A young hare (less than one year old) can be prepared in the same way as rabbit. Older animals should be marinated before being cooked in a stew or made into a terrine.

ROAST SADDLE OF HARE
RÂBLE DE LIÈVRE RÔTI

Preheat the oven to 220°C/425°F/Gas Mark 7. Using a larding needle, lard the saddles with the bacon strips. Season with salt and pepper, put them on a rack and roast for 8 minutes, basting regularly with the butter. Reduce the oven temperature to 160°C/325°F/Gas Mark 3 and continue roasting and basting for another 7–8 minutes. Place the saddles on a long serving dish and serve the chestnuts or mushrooms separately. Add the stock to the pan in which the hare was cooked and simmer for a few minutes, scraping the bottom of the pan. Serve separately in a sauce boat.

- 3 saddles of hare
- 120 g (4 oz) streaky bacon, cut into small strips
- Salt and pepper
- 120 g (4 oz) butter, melted
- Whole chestnuts (p.558) or chanterelles with cream (p.530), to serve
- 50 ml (2 fl oz) concentrated veal stock

Preparation time: 10 minutes
Cooking time: 20 minutes
Serves 6

HARE TERRINE

TERRINE DE LIÈVRE

- 2 good-sized hare's legs
- 250 g (9 oz) pork fat or fat pork belly, chopped
- 375 g (13 oz) streaky bacon, chopped
- 40 g (1½ oz) butter
- 1 onion, sliced
- 200 ml (7 fl oz) white wine
- 2 sprigs of thyme
- 2 bay leaves
- 50 ml (2 fl oz) Cognac
- 10 g (¼ oz) juniper berries, crushed
- 3 shallots, chopped
- 2 garlic cloves, chopped
- 2 eggs, lightly beaten
- Salt and pepper
- 300 g (11 oz) bacon rashers

Preparation time: 40 minutes, plus marinating time
Cooking time: 1 hour
Serves 6

Prepare 1 week before serving. Bone the hare's legs and cut the meat into pieces. Put the hare meat, pork fat or belly and streaky bacon in a bowl. Melt half the butter in a frying pan over a medium heat. Add the onion and cook slowly until softened, taking care not to let it brown. Add half the white wine, simmer for a few minutes, and pour this sauce over the meats in the bowl. Add 1 thyme sprig, 1 bay leaf, the Cognac and the juniper. Cover and marinate in the refrigerator for 24 hours.

The next day, heat the remaining butter in a frying pan over a medium heat. Add the shallots and garlic and cook slowly until softened, taking care not to let them brown. Remove the meats from the marinade, discard the flavourings and put the meats through a food processor with the shallots and garlic. Pour it all into a bowl and add the eggs. Season with salt and pepper and mix thoroughly.

Preheat the oven to 240°C/475°F/Gas Mark 8. Line a pâté terrine with the bacon rashers, letting them hang over the edge. Fill with the meat mixture and pour in the remaining wine. Press it down hard and fold the bacon rashers over it. Put the remaining thyme and bay leaf on the top and put in a roasting tin half-filled with hot water, then place in the oven. Cook for 20 minutes, then lower the oven temperature to 200°C/400°F/Gas Mark 6. Cook for 30 minutes more, allow to cool, and store in the refrigerator for 48 hours.

PARTRIDGE

The partridge is a delicate game bird. When the birds are younger than eight months they are known as *perdreaux*, and can be identified by their flexible beaks and the white spot on their first wing feather. Young birds should be cooked rapidly; when they are older they are braised, often with cabbage.

PARTRIDGE STEW

PERDRIX À L'ÉTOUFFADE

Prepare the partridges for cooking (pp.430–1). Put the bacon, ham, onions and carrots in a heavy-based pan. Place the partridges on top and add the stock and wine. Season with salt and pepper and add the bouquet garni. Cover with a tight-fitting lid and cook for 1 hour on a very low heat. Add the meat glaze to the sauce, if you wish. Arrange the partridges on a serving dish and serve the sauce separately in a sauce boat.

- **2 partridges**
- **150 g (5 oz) bacon, sliced**
- **100 g (3½ oz) ham, diced**
- **2 onions, chopped**
- **2 carrots, chopped**
- **250 ml (8 fl oz) any stock**
- **175 ml (6 fl oz) white wine**
- **Salt and pepper**
- **1 bouquet garni**
- **1 quantity meat glaze (p.45), optional**

Preparation time: 20 minutes
Cooking time: 1 hour
Serves 6

PARTRIDGES WITH CABBAGE

PERDRIX AU CHOU

Prepare the partridges for cooking (pp.430–1). Put them in a heavy-based pan with the bacon, ham, onions, carrot, saveloy and chipolatas. Cook over a medium heat, stirring, until everything is well browned. Bring a pan of salted water to the boil and blanch the cabbage for 15 minutes. Drain and press it to squeeze out any excess water. Add the cabbage to the partridges and season with salt and pepper. Pour in the stock and add the bouquet garni. Cover the pan and simmer for 2–3 hours, depending on the age and tenderness of the partridges.

When the partridges are tender, remove and slice the saveloy. Arrange the birds on a dish, surround them with the vegetables and flavourings, and garnish with the sausage. Continue simmering the sauce over a high heat to reduce it to about 150 ml (¼ pint), then coat the birds with the sauce.

- **2 partridges**
- **150 g (5 oz) streaky bacon, diced**
- **150 g (5 oz) ham, thinly sliced**
- **2 onions, cut into wedges**
- **1 carrot, cut into large pieces**
- **1 saveloy or other large, lightly seasoned sausage**
- **3 chipolata sausages, sliced**
- **1 Savoy cabbage, thickly sliced**
- **Salt and pepper**
- **500 ml (18 fl oz) any stock**
- **1 bouquet garni**

Preparation time: 30 minutes
Cooking time: 2–3 hours
Serves 6

ROAST YOUNG PARTRIDGES

PERDREAUX RÔTIS

- **6 young partridges**
- **200 g (7 oz) streaky bacon**
- **Salt and pepper**
- **1 quantity crouton garnish (see below)**
- **25 g (1 oz) butter**
- **6 slices bread**

Preparation time: 30 minutes
Cooking time: 30 minutes
Serves 6

Preheat the oven to 220°C/425°F/Gas Mark 7. Prepare the partridges for cooking (pp.430–1), reserving the livers. Roast them on a spit or in the oven for 15 minutes, season with salt and pepper, then continue roasting for 10–15 minutes more. Remove the birds and add a little water to the roasting tin, stirring to dislodge any sediment. Meanwhile, make the crouton garnish with the reserved livers. Heat the butter in a frying pan, add the slices of bread and brown on both sides. Spread some of the crouton garnish on each slice of fried bread and arrange a partridge on top of each one. Place in the oven for 2 minutes, then serve with the cooking juices in a sauce boat.

NOTE
For a more delicate dish, slip slices of truffle under the skin of the partridges before trussing them.

CROUTON GARNISH (FOR YOUNG PARTRIDGES)

GARNITURE DES CROÛTONS

- **150 g (5 oz) partridge livers, each cut into 3 pieces**
- **150 g (5 oz) fat unsmoked bacon, finely chopped**
- **Salt and pepper**
- **1 pinch of freshly grated nutmeg**
- **1 tablespoon Cognac**

Preparation time: 5 minutes
Cooking time: 5 minutes
Serves 6

Put the liver and bacon in a small pan and fry over a medium-high heat until the bacon is browned. Season with salt, pepper and nutmeg and pour in the Cognac. Crush with a pestle to reach the consistency of a paste. To serve, spread on slices of bread fried in butter.

YOUNG PARTRIDGES WITH GRAPES

PERDREAUX AU RAISIN

Prepare the partridges for cooking (pp.430–1). Line a heavy-based pan with the bacon and the ham, if using, and put the partridges on top. Add the grapes and the bouquet garni, and season with salt and pepper. Cook, covered, for 1 hour. Serve the birds with the grapes around them, topped with the cooking juices.

- 6 young partridges
- 125 g (4¼ oz) streaky bacon
- 200 g (7 oz) ham, thinly sliced (optional)
- 800 g (1¾ lb) white grapes, de-seeded
- 1 bouquet garni
- Salt and pepper

Preparation time: 15 minutes
Cooking time: 1 hour
Serves 6

YOUNG PARTRIDGE MANSELLE

MANSELLE DE PERDREAUX

Preheat the oven to 220°C/425°F/Gas Mark 7. Prepare the partridges for cooking (pp.430–1) and cover them with the streaky bacon. Roast them for 20–25 minutes. Remove the legs and wings and keep warm. Bone the partridges and keep the meat warm. In a mortar, pound the carcass, bones, head and neck with the shallot, pepper and bouquet garni. Put this mixture in a heavy-based pan with the Portuguese sauce, wine and stock. Season with salt, pepper and nutmeg. Simmer for 1 hour over a gentle heat. Strain the sauce through muslin or a fine-meshed strainer and pour over the hot partridge meat, legs and wings.

- 6 young partridges
- 200 g (7 oz) streaky bacon
- 1 shallot
- Salt and pepper
- 1 bouquet garni
- 400 ml (14 fl oz) Portuguese sauce (p.62)
- 100 ml (3½ fl oz) white wine
- 500 ml (18 fl oz) any stock
- 1 teaspoon freshly grated nutmeg

Preparation time: 30 minutes
Cooking time: 1½ hours
Serves 6

SUPREME OF YOUNG PARTRIDGES

SUPRÊME DE PERDREAUX

- 6 young partridges
- 2 truffles, peeled and sliced
- 250 g (9 oz) streaky bacon, finely chopped
- 1 handful of chopped herbs, such as flat-leaf parsley, chervil, chives and tarragon
- Salt
- 1 pinch of cayenne pepper
- 150 g (5 oz) butter
- 400 ml (14 fl oz) white wine
- 150 ml (¼ pint) any stock
- 3 shallots
- 200 ml (7 fl oz) crème fraîche
- Foie gras, to taste

Preparation time: 20 minutes
Cooking time: 1¼ hours
Serves 6

Prepare the partridges for cooking (pp.430–1). Finely chop the truffle peelings. Combine the bacon, herbs, salt, cayenne pepper, any partridge trimmings and the truffle peelings to make a stuffing. Fill the insides of the birds with this stuffing and sew up with fine string. Melt the butter in a frying pan, carefully add the birds and cook over a high heat until well browned. Lower the heat and cook, covered, for 30 minutes more.

Cut up the partridges, put the legs, wings and white meat aside and keep them hot. In a mortar, pound the partridge carcass and return it to the pan. Pour in the wine and stock, and add the shallots. Simmer over a gentle heat for 30–35 minutes. Strain the mixture through muslin or a fine strainer and put it back in the pan with the legs and wings. Add the crème fraîche, foie gras and sliced truffles, stirring constantly. Simmer for 5 minutes, arrange on a serving dish and serve very hot.

WOODCOCK & SNIPE

Woodcock is a highly prized game bird, but it is rare and difficult to hunt. It used to be the practice to hang it for four to five days, but many people now prefer to eat it fresh, without cleaning it out. Snipe is a small bird belonging to the same family, which lives in marshes and wetlands. Its meat has the best flavour in autumn, so try to buy it fresh during its open season, from August to January.

ROAST WOODCOCK IN CREAM SAUCE
BÉCASSE RÔTIE SAUCE CRÈME

Preheat the oven to 200°C / 400°F / Gas Mark 6. Pluck and singe the woodcock (p.430). Do not clean them out, but remove the gizzard and eyes; cover them with the bacon and truss. Roast in the oven or on a spit, for 20 minutes. Cut up, separate the legs and wings and white meat, and keep them warm. In a mortar, pound together the carcass, intestines, heart, liver and lungs. Strain through a piece of muslin. Put the resulting juices in a pan with 100 g (3½ oz) of the butter, and the stock, salt, cayenne pepper and a little of the foie gras. Boil for 5 minutes. Add the Cognac and simmer briefly to evaporate the alcohol.

Take the sauce off the heat and gently pour in the crème fraîche, stirring as you pour, to thicken it. Put the pieces of woodcock back into the sauce and heat gently, stirring frequently, without allowing it to boil, for about 10 minutes. Heat the remaining butter in a frying pan, add the bread slices and brown on both sides. Spread them with the remaining foie gras. Arrange the woodcock on the fried bread, coat with the sauce and serve piping hot.

- 2 woodcock
- 125 g (4¼ oz) streaky bacon
- 125 g (4¼ oz) butter
- 50 ml (2 fl oz) any stock
- Salt
- 1 pinch of cayenne pepper
- Foie gras, to taste
- 50 ml (2 fl oz) Cognac
- 125 ml (4¼ fl oz) crème fraîche
- 6 slices bread, crusts removed

Preparation time: 25 minutes
Cooking time: 35 minutes
Serves 6

SNIPE À LA GRASSOISE

BÉCASSINES À LA GRASSOISE

- 6 snipe
- 2 tablespoons oil
- 2 shallots, chopped
- 1 garlic clove, chopped
- 1 bouquet garni
- Salt and pepper
- 250 ml (8 fl oz) white wine
- 250 ml (8 fl oz) any stock
- 135 g (4½ oz) butter
- 6 slices of white bread, crusts removed
- 1 lemon, sliced, to serve

Preparation time: 30 minutes
Cooking time: 1¾ hours
Serves 6

Bone the snipe and set the fillets aside. Crush the bones. Put the trimmings, crushed bones and offal in a frying pan with the oil and fry over a medium heat for 5–6 minutes. Add the shallots, garlic and bouquet garni, season with salt and pepper, and pour in the wine and stock. Simmer for 1½ hours, then strain and reserve the sauce. Melt 75 g (2½ oz) of the butter in a frying pan, add the snipe fillets and cook for 7–8 minutes, or until they are golden brown on all sides. Heat the remaining butter in a frying pan, add the bread slices and fry on both sides until golden brown. Reheat the sauce. Arrange the fillets on the fried bread, coat with the sauce and serve with slices of lemon.

QUAIL

Quails living in the wild are becoming increasingly rare, but autumn is the season when they are fattest and therefore have the most flavour. Farmed quails, which have less flavour, can be cooked in the same way as wild quails. Both kinds must be cleaned out and barded with bacon before being roasted. Quails are usually sold fully prepared and trussed for the oven.

ROAST QUAILS

CAILLES RÔTIES

- 6 quails
- Salt and pepper
- 100 g (3½ oz) streaky bacon

Preparation time: 15 minutes
Cooking time: 10 minutes
Serves 6

Preheat the oven to 220°C/425°F/Gas Mark 7. Prepare the quails for cooking (p.430) and season the insides with salt and pepper. Cover them with the bacon, tie with string and roast for no more than 10 minutes.

QUAILS WITH ASTI SPUMANTE

CAILLES À L'ASTI

Prepare the quails for cooking (p.430) and cover with the bacon, then truss with kitchen string. Melt the butter in a frying pan and brown the quails over a medium heat for 10 minutes. Pour in the wine and stock and arrange the truffle slices around the quails. Season with salt and pepper and simmer, covered, for 10 minutes. Arrange in a deep serving dish and serve hot.

- ◆ 6 quails
- ◆ 100 g (3½ oz) streaky bacon
- ◆ 75 g (2½ oz) butter
- ◆ 175 ml (6 fl oz) Asti Spumante or other sweet sparkling white wine
- ◆ 50 ml (2 fl oz) any stock
- ◆ White truffles, peeled and sliced, to taste
- ◆ Salt and pepper

Preparation time: 15 minutes
Cooking time: 20 minutes
Serves 6

QUAIL CASSEROLE

CAILLES EN COCOTTE

 p.504

Preheat the oven to 200°C/400°F/Gas Mark 6. Prepare the quails for cooking (p.430). Melt the butter in a heavy-based pan, add the bacon and onion and cook over a medium-high heat until browned. Remove with a slotted spoon and set aside. Put the quails in the pan and brown on all sides. Return the bacon and onion to the pan, and pour in the wine. Season with salt and pepper. Cover with a tight-fitting lid and cook in the oven for 15 minutes. Add the mushrooms to the pan, return to the oven and cook for 15 minutes more.

- ◆ 6 quails
- ◆ 40 g (1½ oz) butter
- ◆ 125 g (4¼ oz) streaky bacon, diced
- ◆ 60 g (2 oz) onion, chopped
- ◆ 100 ml (3½ fl oz) white wine
- ◆ Salt and pepper
- ◆ 125 g (4¼ oz) mushrooms, chopped

Preparation time: 10 minutes
Cooking time: 30 minutes
Serves 6

QUAILS WITH GRAPES

CAILLES AUX RAISINS

- **6 quails**
- **40 g (1½ oz) butter**
- **Salt and pepper**
- **50 g (1¾ oz) white grapes**
- **100 ml (3½ fl oz) Pineau des Charentes or other sweet white wine**
- **1 tablespoon veal stock**

Preparation time: 15 minutes
Cooking time: 20 minutes
Serves 6

Prepare the quails for cooking (p.430). Melt the butter in a frying pan, add the quails and cook over medium-high heat until golden brown. Season with salt and pepper, then continue cooking for 12 minutes more. Add the grapes and pour in the wine and stock. Bring to the boil and serve immediately, preferably in the frying pan.

QUAILS IN PAPER
CAILLES EN CAISSETTES

Preheat the oven to 200°C/400°F/Gas Mark 6. Prepare the quails for cooking (p.430), and wipe them dry. Soak the breadcrumbs in the milk. In a bowl, mix together the butter, livers, mushrooms, breadcrumbs soaked in milk, and the herbs. Use half the mixture to stuff the birds, then cover the quails with the bacon rashers, putting a few peppercorns and juniper berries between the bard and the skin. Tie up the birds with string. Make small packages out of 4 layers of greaseproof paper and brush them lightly with oil. Fill them with the remaining stuffing, then put a bird in each package. Arrange the packages on a baking tray and cover each one with a piece of oiled greaseproof paper. Place in the oven and cook for 1 hour. Open the packages, untruss the birds and serve them in the paper.

- 6 quails
- 125 g (4¼ oz) fresh breadcrumbs
- 100 ml (3½ fl oz) milk
- 75 g (2½ oz) butter
- 6 chicken livers, chopped
- 125 g (4¼ oz) mushrooms, finely chopped
- 1 handful of chopped herbs, such as flat-leaf parsley, chives, chervil or tarragon
- 75 g (2½ oz) bacon rashers
- Whole peppercorns
- Juniper berries
- Oil, for brushing

Preparation time: 45 minutes
Cooking time: 1 hour
Serves 6

PHEASANT & BLACK GROUSE

Pheasants have magnificent tails of golden-brown feathers. The wild pheasant has become rare, and its natural habitat has been restocked with farmed birds, which can be less flavoursome. The male is bigger, but the meat of the female is more delicate. The best pheasants are shot in autumn, when they are young and tender, and are best eaten roasted. Older birds can be hung for three days, without being plucked, and then cooked in a stew or in the form of a terrine. Black grouse is rare and its hunting strictly regulated. Its strongly flavoured meat is treated in the same way as pheasant.

ROAST PHEASANT

FAISAN RÔTI

If the pheasant is old, hang it in the refrigerator for 2–3 days, then pluck it, clean it, cover it with the bacon rashers and truss it (pp.430–1). Preheat the oven to 220°C/425°F/Gas Mark 7. Place the pheasant in a roasting tin and roast for 35–40 minutes, turning and basting from time to time. Untie the pheasant and place on a serving dish. Add a little water to the roasting tin and stir to dislodge any sediment, then simmer for a few minutes. Serve the juices in a sauce boat.

- **1 pheasant**
- **4 bacon rashers**

Preparation time: 15 minutes
Cooking time: 35–40 minutes
Serves 6

PAN-ROASTED STUFFED PHEASANT

FAISAN FARCI À CASSEROLE

Pluck and clean the pheasant, bard it with the bacon rashers and truss it (pp.430–1). Cook and peel the chestnuts. Make a stuffing by pounding together the chestnuts, streaky bacon, truffles and foie gras. Stuff the pheasant with this mixture and sew it up with a trussing needle. Heat the butter in a heavy-based pan, add the bird and cook over a medium-high heat until browned all over. Pour in the Madeira, add the bouquet garni, season with salt and pepper and cook, covered, on a very low heat for 1¼ hours. Serve with the chestnut purée and with the cooking juices in a sauce boat.

- **1 pheasant**
- **4 bacon rashers**
- **250 g (9 oz) chestnuts (p.558)**
- **125 g (4¼ oz) streaky bacon, finely chopped**
- **Truffles, to taste**
- **Foie gras, to taste**
- **75 g (2½ oz) butter**
- **300 ml (½ pint) Madeira**
- **1 bouquet garni**
- **Salt and pepper**
- **1 quantity chestnut purée (p.559), to serve**

Preparation time: 1 hour
Cooking time: 1¼ hours
Serves 6

p.505

WARM PHEASANT SALAD
SALADE TIÈDE DE FAISAN

- 800 g (1¾ lb) cooked pheasant, and its cooking juices
- 2 tablespoons stock (optional)
- 200 g (7 oz) curly endive
- 200 g (7 oz) oak-leaf lettuce
- 50 g (2 oz) lamb's lettuce
- 1 quantity vinaigrette (p.66)
- 30 g (1¼ oz) butter
- 200 g (7 oz) mushrooms, sliced
- Salt and pepper

Preparation time: 40 minutes
Cooking time: 10 minutes
Serves 6

Cut the pheasant into strips, and reheat it gently in a pan in its cooking juices or a little stock. Remove the meat and reserve the liquid. Clean, wash and drain the salad leaves, place the strips of meat on them, and dress with the vinaigrette. Melt the butter in a pan and cook the mushrooms over a medium heat until softened, season with salt and pepper, then add them to the salad. Pour over the reserved liquid. If you have only a little pheasant, you can enhance the dish with strips of foie gras.

PIGEON

A young pigeon has a white rump, light-coloured feet, a rather soft wishbone, and a thick neck and feet. The skin is pinkish and the flesh is red. Most pigeons are sold ready prepared for cooking.

CARVING & JOINTING

Cut a cooked pigeon into two or four pieces: if in two, cut lengthways, if in four, lengthways and widthways. Pigeons can also be jointed in this way before cooking.

ROAST PIGEON

PIGEONS RÔTIS

 p.503

Preheat the oven to 220°C/425°F/Gas Mark 7. Prepare the pigeons for cooking (pp.430–1) and season the insides with salt. Cover them with the bacon rashers, tie with string, place in a roasting tin and roast for 25–30 minutes.

VARIATION

. . . .

STUFFED PIGEON

PIGEON FARCIS

Combine 100 g (3½ oz) sausage meat, 100 g (3½ oz) chopped bacon, white bread soaked in milk and 100 g (3½ oz) finely chopped onions to make a stuffing. Spoon the stuffing into the pigeons, bard with bacon, tie with string and roast as above. The pigeons' livers and gizzards, chopped and mixed with the bread soaked in milk, can also be added. Bind with 1 egg and stuff as above.

- **3 pigeons**
- **Salt**
- **Bacon rashers, for barding**

  Preparation time: 15 minutes
  Cooking time: 30 minutes
  Serves 6

PIGEON À LA CRAPAUDINE

PIGEONS À LA CRAPAUDINE

First, spatchcock the pigeons. Split them down the back, leaving them attached on the stomach side. Leave the liver and lungs in place, and flatten the birds slightly. Melt half the butter in a heavy-based pan, add the birds and cook them gently for 10 minutes on each side, taking care not to let them brown. Remove the birds from the pan and set aside to cool. Meanwhile, add the vinegar, shallots, garlic, tarragon, meat glaze and lemon juice to the butter used to cook the birds and simmer until reduced by half. Sieve the sauce and serve in a sauce boat. When the pigeons have cooled, dip them in the remaining butter, roll them in the breadcrumbs and cook for 20 minutes on a griddle over a moderate heat, until browned.

- **3 pigeons**
- **60 g (2 oz) butter, melted**
- **100 ml (3½ fl oz) white wine vinegar**
- **2 shallots, finely chopped**
- **½ garlic clove, finely chopped**
- **1 sprig of tarragon, finely chopped**
- **150 g (5 oz) meat glaze (p.45)**
- **1 tablespoon lemon juice**
- **Dried breadcrumbs, for rolling**
- **Salt and pepper**

  Preparation time: 20 minutes
  Cooking time: 1 hour
  Serves 6

TEAL

Teals are small wild ducks. Their meat is slightly bitter but it is considered a delicacy. It can be cooked like other wild duck.

TEAL WITH BITTER ORANGE SAUCE

SARCELLE À LA BIGARADE

- 2 small teals, with livers and hearts
- 30 g (1¼ oz) bacon, finely chopped
- 75 g (2½ oz) butter, cut into very small pieces
- Grated zest of ½ lemon
- Salt and pepper
- Juice of 1 lemon
- 70 g (2½ oz) streaky bacon
- 125 g (4¼ oz) mirepoix (p.44)
- 250 ml (8 fl oz) blond roux (p.57)
- Juice of 3 bitter (Seville) oranges

Preparation time: 30 minutes
Cooking time: 40 minutes
Serves 6

Pluck, singe and clean out the teal (p.430). Preheat the oven to 220°C/425°F/Gas Mark 7. Chop the livers and hearts, and mix with the chopped bacon, butter, lemon zest, and salt and pepper to make a stuffing. Stuff each bird with this mixture. Pour the lemon juice over the birds, cover them with the streaky bacon, truss and season with salt and pepper. Wrap each bird in foil, closing it firmly so that the juices do not run out. Roast in the oven for 40 minutes. Meanwhile, prepare the mirepoix and add it to the blond roux, along with the orange juice. Unwrap and untie the teals and serve with the sauce in a sauce boat.

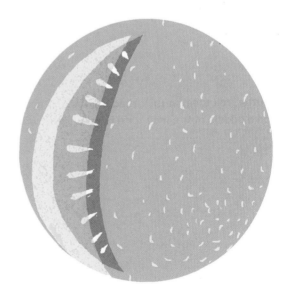

ROAST TEAL

SARCELLE RÔTIE

Preheat the oven to 220°C/425°F/Gas Mark 7. Pluck, singe and clean out the teal, cover with the bacon and truss it (pp.430–1). Roast it in the oven or on a spit for about 8 minutes. Season with salt and pepper, then continue roasting for about 7 minutes more. Arrange the teal on a long serving dish, with bunches of watercress around it. Add a little hot water to the pan, stirring to release any sediment, and serve the juices separately in a sauce boat.

- **1 teal**
- **75 g (2½ oz) streaky bacon**
- **Salt and pepper**
- **Bunches of watercress, to garnish**

Preparation time: 25 minutes
Cooking time: 15 minutes
Serves 6

TEAL WITH OLIVES

SARCELLES AUX OLIVES

Pluck, singe and clean out the teal, cover with the bacon and truss it (pp.430–1). Preheat the oven to 200°C/400°F/Gas Mark 6. Heat the butter in a heavy-based pan, add the teal and brown it on all sides. Season with salt and pepper, add the bouquet garni and cook for 20 minutes. Add the olives and cook for 20–25 minutes more. Arrange the bird on a dish with the cooking juices and olives around it.

- **1 teal**
- **100 g (3½ oz) streaky bacon**
- **40 g (1½ oz) butter**
- **Salt and pepper**
- **1 bouquet garni**
- **250 g (9 oz) green olives, stoned and rinsed in cold water**

Preparation time: 10 minutes
Cooking time: 45 minutes
Serves 6

Haunch of venison with berries   (p.477)

Roast rabbit   (p.478)

Roast pigeon   (p.498)

Quail casserole   (p.492)

Warm pheasant salad   (p.497)

- 9 -
VEGETABLES
&
SALADS

FRESH VEGETABLES

Fresh vegetables play a vital role in our diet, because they contain easily absorbed minerals, vitamins and fibre. The great variety of vegetables available means that menus can be varied almost infinitely. Most vegetables can be eaten raw or cooked. Even though they keep relatively well for several days, it is better to use them quickly to preserve their nutritional value.

COOKING

Fresh vegetables lose their nutritional value and flavour if they are cooked for too long. They should be boiled rapidly in salted water, steamed or grilled, depending on the vegetable.

The water should be salted with 1 teaspoon salt per 1 litre (1¾ pints). Some vegetables that take longer to cook may be cooked more quickly in a pressure cooker, which can considerably reduce the cooking times for artichokes, cabbage, salsify and so on. Green vegetables, such as beans and spinach, should be blanched briefly and vigorously.

SAUCES FOR VEGETABLES

- Maître d'hôtel butter (p.48)
- Black butter (p.48)
- Béchamel sauce (p.50)
- Cheese sauce (p.51)
- Printanière or Chivry sauce (p.54)
- Tomato sauce (p.57)
- Madeira sauce (p.61)
- Mushroom sauce (p.61)
- Portuguese sauce (p.62)
- Rémoulade sauce (p.68)
- Mousseline mayonnaise (p.71)

ARTICHOKES

To prepare whole globe artichokes, break off the stalk and, using a very sharp knife, remove the tough outer leaves and trim the base. Neatly cut the tips off the remaining inner leaves. Wash thoroughly in water and keep in water with 1 tablespoon lemon juice to prevent discolouring.

To prepare artichoke hearts, peel the tough leaves off before cooking, so that the softer, edible part of each leaf remains attached to the heart. Cut off all the stringy parts, remove the hairy choke from the centre of the artichoke and rub each heart with lemon. Boil in salted water for 15–25 minutes, depending on the size of the artichokes.

BOILED ARTICHOKES
ARTICHAUTS BOUILLIS

First, prepare the artichokes (see above). Boil the artichokes in plenty of salted water or steam them. Cooking time will depend on the size of the artichoke, so check that the base of the artichoke is tender with the point of a sharp knife.

Once cooked, drain by turning the artichokes with the tips of the leaves pointing downwards. If desired, the whole cap of leaves can now be lifted off. Cut away the hairy choke and discard, then replace the leaves on the tender base of the artichoke. Serve with the vinaigrette or your chosen sauce in a sauce boat.

- **6 globe artichokes**
- **1 quantity vinaigrette (p.66), white sauce (p.50), or cream sauce (p.51), to serve**

Preparation time: 20 minutes
Cooking time: 30 minutes
Serves 6

p.589

ARTICHOKES À LA BARIGOULE
ARTICHAUTS À LA BARIGOULE

- 6 globe artichokes
- 200 g (7 oz) mushrooms
- 125 g (4¼ oz) bacon
- 1 handful of flat-leaf parsley
- Salt and pepper
- 12 bacon rashers
- 30 g (1¼ oz) butter
- 2 tablespoons oil
- 125 g (4¼ oz) carrots, roughly chopped
- 100 g (3½ oz) onions, roughly chopped
- Bacon rinds
- 300 ml (½ pint) white wine
- 500 ml (18 fl oz) stock

Preparation time: 1 hour
Cooking time: 30 minutes
Serves 6

Prepare the artichokes (p.510). Boil them in plenty of salted water for 5 minutes. Meanwhile, make the stuffing by finely chopping the mushrooms, bacon and parsley and seasoning with salt and pepper. Drain the artichokes, then lift off the cap of leaves and remove the hairy choke. Top the artichokes with the stuffing. Wrap each artichoke in 2 bacon rashers, arranged in a cross, tie with string and fry them in the butter and oil until golden, about 5 minutes.

Preheat the oven to 190°C/375°F/Gas Mark 5. Put the carrots, onions and bacon rinds in a heavy-based ovenproof pan and put the artichokes on top. Pour on the wine, bring to the boil and reduce over a high heat for 10 minutes, then add the stock and cook, covered, in the oven for 30 minutes. Remove the string from the artichokes and place in a warmed serving dish. Strain the cooking juices over and serve.

STUFFED ARTICHOKE HEARTS
FONDS D'ARTICHAUTS FARCIS

- 6 globe artichokes
- 30 g (1¼ oz) butter
- 1 carrot, chopped
- 1 onion, chopped
- 500 ml (18 fl oz) any stock
- Salt and pepper
- 1 quantity stuffing for red meats (p.80)

Preparation time: 30 minutes
Cooking time: 1 hour
Serves 6

Prepare the artichoke hearts (p.510). Melt the butter in a frying pan and cook them over a high heat for 5 minutes. Add the carrot, onion and stock to the pan and season with salt and pepper. Lower the heat and cook gently for 45 minutes. Preheat the oven to 200°C/400°F/Gas Mark 6. Fill the hearts with your chosen stuffing. Put them in an ovenproof serving dish, strain over the cooking juices, and bake in the oven for 10 minutes.

ARTICHOKE HEARTS PRINTANIÈRE

FONDS D'ARTICHAUTS PRINTANIÈRE

Preheat the oven to 180°C / 350°F / Gas Mark 4. Prepare the artichokes (p.510). Boil the artichokes in plenty of salted water for 15–20 minutes; do not overcook. Meanwhile, make a blond roux (p.57) using 30 g (1¼ oz) of the butter and the flour and stock. Season well with salt and pepper. In another pan, gently fry the mushrooms and shallot in 20 g (¾ oz) of the butter until softened, about 5 minutes. Mix with the roux and set aside. Drain the artichokes and peel off the leaves.

Remove the hairy choke from the centre of each artichoke and discard. Cut off the lower, edible part from each leaf and mix with the hard-boiled egg and ham. Stir into the mushroom sauce with the tarragon and parsley. Fill the hearts with this mixture and place in an ovenproof dish. Sprinkle the artichokes with the breadcrumbs, divide the remaining butter between each one and brown in the oven for 20 minutes.

* 6 globe artichokes
* 70 g (2½ oz) butter
* 30 g (1¼ oz) flour
* 200 ml (7 fl oz) any stock
* Salt and pepper
* 100 g (3½ oz) mushrooms, finely chopped
* 1 shallot, finely chopped
* 1 hard-boiled egg, finely chopped
* 100 g (3½ oz) ham, chopped
* 1 tablespoon finely chopped tarragon
* 1 tablespoon finely chopped flat-leaf parsley
* Dried breadcrumbs, for sprinkling

Preparation time: 45 minutes
Cooking time: 45 minutes
Serves 6

ARTICHOKE HEARTS IN CHEESE SAUCE

FONDS D'ARTICHAUTS À LA MORNAY

Preheat the oven to 220°C/425°F/Gas Mark 7. Prepare and cook the artichoke hearts (p.510). Meanwhile, heat the butter in a frying pan and fry the mushrooms over a gentle heat until softened, about 5 minutes. Once the artichokes are cooked, drain and peel off the leaves. Remove the hairy choke from the centre of each artichoke and discard. Cut off the lower, fleshy part of each leaf and mix it with the mushrooms. Season with salt and pepper. Place the mushroom stuffing on each artichoke heart and arrange in a buttered ovenproof dish. Coat the hearts with the cheese sauce and brown in the oven for 20 minutes.

* 6 globe artichokes
* 20 g (¾ oz) butter
* 200 g (7 oz) mushrooms, chopped
* Salt and pepper
* 1 quantity cheese sauce (p.51)

Preparation time: 1 hour
Cooking time: 1 hour
Serves 6

ASPARAGUS

To prepare white or green asparagus, cut off the earthy end and peel the outer part of the stem (this may not be necessary with fine asparagus spears, of which more spears are required per person). Wash thoroughly in water. Lower into a large pan of boiling salted water and cook at a rolling boil until just tender, about 4–8 minutes, depending on the thickness of the spears. Drain and serve on a napkin or in a special basket known as a *berceau*, with a mayonnaise (p.70), mousseline mayonnaise (p.71), vinaigrette (p.66), white sauce (p.50) or cheese sauce (p.51). Allow 8–10 thick asparagus spears per person, or 2.5 kg (5½ lb) for six people.

ASPARAGUS TIPS IN PUFF PASTRY
FEUILLETÉ AUX POINTES D'ASPERGES

Preheat the oven to 220°C/425°F/Gas Mark 7 and grease a baking tray with butter. Roll the puff pastry out to a thickness of 2.5 cm (1 inch) and cut it into 6 squares or diamonds. Using a sharp knife, mark a 1.5-cm (½-inch) deep lid in the centre of each square, without cutting all the way through. Mix the egg yolk with a little cold water and brush onto the top of the pastry. Score diagonal lines across with a knife. Place the pastry cases on the prepared baking tray and bake for 20–25 minutes, until deep golden brown.

Meanwhile, prepare and cook the asparagus (see above). Drain and refresh under cold running water. Cut the tips of about 4 cm (1¾ inches) off the asparagus, and cut the stems into small dice. Melt the butter in a frying pan and gently heat the diced asparagus with the nutmeg, chervil and half the beurre blanc for 2–3 minutes. Carefully detach the lids from the pastry cases. Fill the cases with the diced asparagus and replace the lids. Place on a serving plate. Thinly coat the asparagus tips with the remaining beurre blanc and arrange round the pastry cases. Serve immediately.

- 400 g (14 oz) ready-made or home-made puff pastry (p.776)
- 30 g (1¼ oz) butter, plus extra for greasing
- 1 egg yolk
- 1.5 kg (3¼ lb) asparagus
- Freshly grated nutmeg
- 20 g (¾ oz) chervil, chopped
- 100 ml (3½ fl oz) beurre blanc (p.49)

Preparation time: 30 minutes
Cooking time: 40 minutes
Serves 6

ASPARAGUS SERVED LIKE PEAS

ASPERGES EN PETITS POIS

- **50 asparagus spears**
- **50 g (1¾ oz) butter**
- **60 g (2 oz) button or pearl onions**
- **50 g (1¾ oz) flour**
- **500 ml (18 fl oz) chicken or vegetable stock**
- **1 bouquet garni**
- **Salt and pepper**
- **1 egg, beaten**

Preparation time: 45 minutes
Cooking time: 15–20 minutes
Serves 6

Prepare the asparagus (p.514) and cut into dice. In a large pan, melt the butter and cook the onions over a low heat until soft, then stir in the flour. Cook for a minute, then add the stock and stir to make a white sauce (p.50). Add the bouquet garni, salt, pepper and asparagus. Cook gently for 15–20 minutes. When ready to serve, add the egg and stir until thickened.

AUBERGINES

Choose firm aubergines with very smooth skin. If they are to be braised, shallow-fried or baked *au gratin*, they should be peeled and sliced or cut into quarters, and then sprinkled with salt and left to release their liquid for 30 minutes in a colander. Rinse and wipe them dry before preparing them. If the aubergines are to be stuffed, they should be cut in half, scored in a few places with a knife and carefully lowered into a high-sided pan half-filled with very hot oil for 6–7 minutes, white flesh downwards. Drain and, using a spoon, remove some of the pulp to use for the stuffing. Fill the aubergine halves with the mixture of your choice. Allow one small aubergine or half a large one per person.

STUFFED AUBERGINES WITHOUT MEAT
AUBERGINES FARCIES AU MAIGRE

Preheat the oven to 200°C/400°F/Gas Mark 6. Cut the aubergines in half lengthways and prepare them for stuffing (above), frying them in the oil. Remove some of the pulp from the aubergines and mix it with the duxelles. Season with salt and pepper and fill the aubergine halves with the mixture. Sprinkle with the breadcrumbs, dot with the butter and bake in the oven for 45 minutes.

- 3 aubergines
- Oil, for frying
- 1 quantity duxelles (p.81)
- Salt and pepper
- Dried breadcrumbs, for sprinkling
- 40 g (1½ oz) butter

Preparation time: 30 minutes
Cooking time: 45 minutes
Serves 6

FRIED AUBERGINES
AUBERGINES FRITES

Prepare the aubergines for frying (see above), cutting them into 1-cm (½-inch) slices. Drain, wipe dry and dip the slices into the batter. Heat the oil in a deep-fryer to 180°C/350°F, or until a cube of bread browns in 30 seconds. Using a slotted spoon, lift out each slice with its coating of batter and deep-fry the slices in batches in the hot oil, until golden brown. Drain on kitchen paper and serve hot.

- 3 aubergines
- 1 quantity batter (p.725)
- Vegetable oil, for deep-frying

Preparation time: 25 minutes
Cooking time: 10 minutes
Serves 6

p.590

AUBERGINES WITH TOMATOES

AUBERGINES AUX TOMATES

- 750 g (1 lb 10 oz) tomatoes, chopped
- 3 aubergines
- Oil, for frying
- Salt and pepper
- 1 handful of flat-leaf parsley, chopped
- 1 garlic clove, chopped
- 40 g (1½ oz) butter

Preparation time: 45 minutes
Cooking time: 45 minutes
Serves 6

Make a tomato purée by cooking the tomatoes in a dry pan for 10 minutes, stirring constantly. Press through a sieve and set aside. Cut the aubergines into 1-cm (½-inch) slices. Heat oil to a depth of 2 cm (¾ inch) in a high-sided frying pan. Fry the aubergines in batches in the hot oil until golden, about 5 minutes per batch. Meanwhile, preheat the oven to 180°C/350°F/Gas Mark 4. Arrange a layer of tomato purée and a layer of aubergines in an ovenproof dish, season with salt and pepper, and sprinkle each layer with the parsley and garlic. Dot with the butter and bake for 45 minutes.

AUBERGINE GRATIN

GRATIN D'AUBERGINES

- 3 aubergines
- 100 ml (3½ fl oz) oil
- 40 g (1½ oz) butter
- 1 onion, finely chopped
- 1 garlic clove, finely chopped
- 150 g (5 oz) cooked meat, chopped
- 2 tablespoons tomato purée
- 1 handful of flat-leaf parsley, chopped
- Salt and pepper
- Dried breadcrumbs, for sprinkling

Preparation time: 25 minutes
Cooking time: 45 minutes
Serves 6

Preheat the oven to 200°C/400°F/Gas Mark 6. Prepare the aubergines for frying (p.516), cutting them into 1-cm (½-inch) slices. Heat the oil in a high-sided frying pan and fry until golden, in batches. Meanwhile, melt half the butter in a pan and gently cook the onion and garlic for 10 minutes. Add the meat, tomato purée and parsley. Season with salt and pepper and cook for 5 minutes. Arrange alternating layers of the aubergines and the meat mixture in an ovenproof dish, sprinkle with the breadcrumbs and dot with the remaining butter. Bake for 45 minutes.

SWISS CHARD

To prepare, cut off the earthy ends. Strip the leaves from the stalks. Using a knife, remove the thin outer skin from the stalks. If this is particularly tough, cut them into 2.5–4-cm (1–1½-inch) slices, and rinse and drain. Cook for 3–5 minutes in boiling water with very little salt, as chard absorbs salt. The leaves can be shredded and added to the cooking water a few minutes after the stalks, or they can be used in a separate recipe. Drain the chard and serve with a white sauce (p.50), cream sauce (p.51), cheese sauce (p.51), or poulette sauce (p.52).

PROVENÇALE SWISS CHARD
BETTES À LA PROVENÇALE

Prepare the chard stalks (see above). Boil in lightly salted water for 3–5 minutes, then drain thoroughly. Melt the butter in a frying pan, add the pieces of chard and garlic and fry over a high heat for 3–4 minutes. Sprinkle with the parsley and serve.

- 1 kg (2¼ lb) Swiss chard
- 50 g (1¾ oz) butter
- 1 garlic clove, finely chopped
- 1 tablespoon flat-leaf parsley, chopped

Preparation time: 10 minutes
Cooking time: 10 minutes
Serves 6

BROCCOLI

Broccoli should be dark green in colour. To trim it, remove only the leaves and separate the florets. Wash thoroughly.

STEAMED BROCCOLI
BROCOLIS À LA VAPEUR

Trim the broccoli and steam it for 4–5 minutes. Serve it hot with the butter or single cream, or serve it warm, as a salad, with a dash of olive oil or Parmesan shavings.

- 1 kg (2¼ lb) broccoli
- 40 g (1½ oz) butter, melted, or warm single cream (optional)
- Olive oil or Parmesan cheese, to serve (optional)

Preparation time: 10 minutes
Cooking time: 5 minutes
Serves 6

BROCCOLI IN CHEESE SAUCE
BROCOLIS SAUCE MORNAY

- **1 kg (2¼ lb) broccoli**
- **1 quantity cheese sauce (p.51)**

Preparation time: 20 minutes
Cooking time: 5 minutes
Serves 6

Preheat the oven to 220°C/425°F/Gas Mark 7. Steam the broccoli for 4–5 minutes or boil it in salted water for 6 minutes. Drain and put in an ovenproof serving dish. Coat the broccoli with the cheese sauce. Brown in the oven for 5 minutes before serving.

CARDOONS

Cardoons are similar to globe artichokes, but are taller and more prickly. The flower head and the most tender part of the stem, close to the head, are edible if the plants are young but have to be trimmed very carefully. Remove any tough, withered or hollow, spongy stems; expect two-thirds wastage from freshly picked cardoons, less if purchased pre-trimmed.

Retaining only the tender white parts, cut the cardoons into 10-cm (4-inch) pieces, removing any stringy filaments. Rub them immediately with lemon and place in water acidulated with a few drops of vinegar or lemon juice. Cook them in boiling water for 30–45 minutes, until tender. To further prevent them discolouring, add 100 g (3½ oz) small pieces of veal fat per 1 litre (1¾ pints) to the boiling water if desired. When they are cooked, leave the pieces of cardoon in acidulated water. They will keep very well for 24 hours. Serve with a white sauce (p.50), cheese sauce (p.51) or hollandaise sauce (p.74).

BRAISED CARDOONS
CARDONS AU JUS

- **1 kg (2¼ lb) cardoons**
- **40 g (1½ oz) butter**
- **100 ml (3½ fl oz) rich veal stock**

Preparation time: 5 minutes
Cooking time: 20 minutes
Serves 6

Prepare and cook the cardoons (see above). Put the butter in a frying pan, add the cardoons and reheat them over a gentle heat for 10 minutes. Pour in the veal stock and simmer for a further 10 minutes. Put the cardoons on a serving dish and serve immediately.

CARDOON GRATIN

CARDONS EN GRATIN

Prepare and cook the cardoons (p.519). Preheat the oven to 240°C/475°F/Gas Mark 8. Chop 250 g (9 oz) of the cardoons, and the mushrooms, and mix together. Arrange the remaining cardoons in an ovenproof dish, cover with the chopped cardoons and mushrooms and season with salt and pepper. Pour in the lemon juice, sprinkle with the breadcrumbs and bake for 20 minutes. Heat the stock and pour it over the gratin just before serving.

- **3 kg (6½ lb) cardoons, trimmed but not cut**
- **150 g (5 oz) mushrooms**
- **Salt and pepper**
- **150 ml (¼ pint) rich meat stock**
- **Juice of 1 lemon**
- **6 tablespoons dried breadcrumbs**

Preparation time: 1½ hours
Cooking time: 20 minutes
Serves 6

CARROTS

Carrots should be trimmed, thinly peeled and rinsed. Young, tender carrots can simply be scraped rather than peeled. Old carrots can develop a woody core that should be removed. Boil carrots in salted water for 5–15 minutes, depending on whether they are to be cooked whole or sliced. Carrots can be diced, sliced, cut into strips or trimmed into barrel shapes.

CARROTS IN BUTTER

CAROTTES AU BEURRE

Scrape and wash the carrots. Put them in a pan with just enough water to cover them. Add the salt and bring to the boil, then reduce the heat and simmer gently, shaking the pan from time to time. When the carrots are cooked (the cooking time will depend on their size), drain and return them to the pan with the butter, shaking until the butter has melted and coated the carrots. Sprinkle with the parsley and serve.

- **600 g (1 lb 5 oz) new carrots**
- **1 pinch of salt**
- **50 g (1¾ oz) butter**
- **1 tablespoon flat-leaf parsley, chopped**

Preparation time: 10 minutes
Cooking time: 20 minutes
Serves 6

p.591

CARROTS IN BÉCHAMEL SAUCE
CAROTTES À LA BÉCHAMEL

- **600 g (1 lb 5 oz) carrots**
- **1 quantity béchamel sauce (p.50)**
- **1 egg yolk**

Preparation time: 15 minutes
Cooking time: 30 minutes
Serves 6

Prepare and cook the carrots (p.520). Prepare the béchamel sauce and whisk in the egg yolk. When ready to serve, coat the carrots with the sauce.

VARIATION

. . . .

CARROTS IN CREAM
CAROTTES À LA CRÈME

Proceed as above, replacing the egg yolk with 100 ml (3½ fl oz) crème fraîche.

CARROTS WITH BACON
CAROTTES AU LARD

- **1 x 100-g (3½-oz) piece of salt bacon**
- **20 g (¾ oz) butter**
- **700 g (1 lb 8½ oz) carrots, peeled or scraped and sliced**
- **500 ml (18 fl oz) any stock**
- **1 bouquet garni**
- **Salt and pepper**

Preparation time: 15 minutes
Cooking time: 20–30 minutes
Serves 6

Dice the bacon and fry in the butter over a medium heat for 5 minutes until starting to brown. Add the carrots, stock and bouquet garni. Season with salt and pepper. Cook gently until the carrots are very tender, about 20–30 minutes depending on their size.

VICHY CARROTS
CAROTTES À LA VICHY

- **600 g (1 lb 5 oz) carrots**
- **40 g (1½ oz) butter**
- **1 teaspoon salt**
- **1 tablespoon caster sugar**
- **1 pinch of bicarbonate of soda**
- **1 handful of flat-leaf parsley, chopped**

Preparation time: 10 minutes
Cooking time: 20 minutes
Serves 6

Peel and trim the carrots, slice them evenly and put them in a fairly large pan. Add the butter, salt, sugar, bicarbonate of soda and 400 ml (14 fl oz) water. Bring to the boil, then reduce the heat and cook gently until tender, about 15 minutes. Continue cooking, shaking the pan every few minutes, until the cooking liquid is completely reduced and the carrots are coated in a shiny glaze. Sprinkle with the parsley and serve.

CELERY

To prepare, remove any tough green stalks and leaves. Reserve the part nearest to the root and peel and trim it if necessary. A head of celery approximately 18–20 cm (7–8 inches) long is usually enough for two people. Wash thoroughly in water. Tie the heads with string and plunge into boiling salted water for 15 minutes, or until tender. Drain.

CELERY IN SAUCE
CÉLERI-BRANCHE EN SAUCE

Cook the celery heads as described above. Drain and untie them and serve with a white or cream sauce served separately or poured over the celery, or maître d'hôtel butter. Celery can also be served cold, with a vinaigrette or mayonnaise.

- 3 heads of celery
- 1 quantity white sauce (p.50), cream sauce (p.51), maître d'hôtel butter (p.48), vinaigrette (p.66) or mayonnaise (p.70)

Preparation time: 15 minutes
Cooking time: 15 minutes
Serves 6

CELERY WITH BEEF MARROW
CÉLERI-BRANCHE À LA MOELLE

Prepare the celery (see above). Heat the butter in a heavy-based pan or frying pan and cook the celery over a low heat for 5–10 minutes. Add the stock and simmer for 20 minutes. Season with salt and pepper. Meanwhile, cut the marrow into 5-mm (¼-inch) thick slices, with a knife dipped in hot water. Bring a small pan of water to a simmer and add the marrow slices. Simmer gently for 2 minutes, without allowing the water to boil, then remove the marrow carefully with a slotted spoon. Untie the celery heads, cut them in half lengthways and return to the pan. Cover with the marrow and cook over a gentle heat for a further 5 minutes.

- 3 heads of celery
- 40 g (1½ oz) butter
- 150 ml (¼ pint) beef stock
- Salt and pepper
- 120 g (4 oz) beef marrow

Preparation time: 20 minutes
Cooking time: 40 minutes
Serves 6

BRAISED CELERY

CÉLERI AU JUS

- **30 g (1¼ oz) butter**
- **1 carrot, sliced**
- **1 onion, sliced**
- **3 heads of celery**
- **Salt and pepper**
- **250 ml (8 fl oz) any stock**
- **250 ml (8 fl oz) concentrated meat stock or juices from a roast**

Preparation time: 10 minutes
Cooking time: 1 hour
Serves 6

Prepare the celery (p.522). Melt the butter in a frying pan and fry the carrot and onion over a medium heat until softened, about 5 minutes. Place the celery in the pan, season with salt and pepper and pour in the stock. Cover and cook gently for 45 minutes. Add the concentrated stock or meat juices and cook for a further 10 minutes.

CELERIAC

To prepare, peel and cut into wedges or thin slices, tossing with lemon juice to prevent discolouration. Place the celeriac in salted water, then bring to the boil and cook for 10–20 minutes or until tender, depending on the size of the pieces.

CELERIAC WITH CREAM

CÉLERI-RAVE À LA CRÈME

- **750 g (1 lb 10 oz) celeriac**
- **1 quantity white sauce (p.50)**
- **100 ml (3½ fl oz) crème fraîche**

Preparation time: 15 minutes
Cooking time: 20 minutes
Serves 6

Prepare and cook the celeriac (see above). Prepare the white sauce, add the crème fraîche and coat the cooked celeriac with it.

CELERIAC PURÉE

CÉLERI-RAVE EN PURÉE

Cut the celeriac into wedges, bring a pan of salted water to the boil and cook the celeriac for 5 minutes. Cut the potatoes into wedges, add to the pan and cook for a further 15 minutes. Drain thoroughly and push through a sieve or process in a blender to make a purée. Stir in the crème fraîche and the butter, beating the purée vigorously. Season with salt and pepper. Less celeriac and more potatoes can be used for a mildly flavoured purée.

- 800 g (1¾ lb) celeriac
- 250 g (9 oz) potatoes
- 175 ml (6 fl oz) crème fraîche
- 40 g (1½ oz) butter
- Salt and pepper

Preparation time: 10 minutes
Cooking time: 20 minutes
Serves 6

CELERIAC SALAD

CÉLERI-RAVE EN SALADE

Prepare 6–8 hours in advance. Peel the celeriac, cut it into wedges and blanch it in salted boiling water for 4–5 minutes. Cut the celeriac into fine strips or grate it coarsely. Cover with the rémoulade sauce and chill in the refrigerator for 6–8 hours before serving.

- 1 celeriac
- 1 quantity rémoulade sauce (p.68)

Preparation time: 20 minutes, plus chilling time
Cooking time: 10 minutes
Serves 6

CELERIAC LOAF

PAIN DE CÉLERI

Preheat the oven to 160°C/325°F/Gas Mark 3. Grease a deep ovenproof dish, terrine or loaf tin with the butter. Prepare and cook the celeriac (p.523). Mash it, stir in the egg yolks, egg and crème fraîche and season with salt and pepper. Put the mixture in the prepared dish, cover tightly with foil or a lid and set in a roasting tin half-filled with hot water. Cook in the oven for 1½ hours.

- 10 g (¼ oz) butter
- 1 kg (2¼ lb) celeriac
- 5 egg yolks
- 1 egg
- 250 ml (8 fl oz) crème fraîche
- Salt and pepper

Preparation time: 20 minutes
Cooking time: 1½ hours
Serves 6

MUSHROOMS

Mushrooms are highly regarded for their nutritional content as well as for their gastronomic properties. Their flavour, whether they are cultivated or wild, can considerably enhance the taste of a dish. When picking wild mushrooms, it is essential to know them very well, because it is very difficult to distinguish the poisonous ones from those that are edible. To preserve their flavour, it is best to cook mushrooms soon after they have been picked, and to clean them with a damp cloth rather than in water, since this causes them to become watery. Alternatively, brush off any loose dirt with a clean brush. Mushrooms can be added to sauces or slowly cooked dishes, or they can be served as a side dish or starter.

GRIDDLED MUSHROOMS WITH HERB BUTTER
CHAMPIGNONS SUR LE GRIL

 p.592

- 6–12 large ceps, white or field mushrooms, depending on size
- 75 g (2½ oz) butter, melted
- 1 handful of mixed herbs, such as flat-leaf parsley, chervil and tarragon, chopped
- Salt and pepper

Preparation time: 10 minutes
Cooking time: 12 minutes
Serves 6

Wipe the mushrooms clean with a damp cloth. Cut off the stalks and put the caps on a griddle pan, rounded sides downwards. Pour 40 g (1½ oz) of the butter over them and cook for 10–12 minutes over a gentle heat. Mix the remaining butter with the herbs and season with salt and pepper. Arrange the mushrooms on a serving dish and fill with the herb butter. Serve as a starter or to accompany roast red meat or game.

MUSHROOM PURÉE
PURÉE DE CHAMPIGNONS

- 600 g (1 lb 5 oz) mushrooms
- 80 g (2¾ oz) butter
- Juice of 1 lemon
- 1 quantity blond roux (p.57)
- 100 ml (3½ fl oz) crème fraîche
- Salt and pepper
- 6 slices bread

Preparation time: 10 minutes
Cooking time: 15 minutes
Serves 6

Clean and very finely chop the mushrooms. Place in a pan with 50 g (1¾ oz) of butter and the lemon juice. Cook for 5–6 minutes over a medium heat. Add the blond roux and crème fraîche, stir and simmer to reduce for 5 minutes. Season with salt and pepper. Fry the bread in the remaining butter and serve the mushroom purée on the fried bread.

STUFFED MUSHROOMS

CHAMPIGNONS FARCIS

Preheat the oven to 200°C/400°F/Gas Mark 6. Clean the mushrooms, cut the stalks off and set aside. Sprinkle the caps with a little of the melted butter or oil. Put the mushrooms on a baking tray, gills upward, and bake for 7–8 minutes. Remove from the oven, turn them over and allow to cool. Use the stalks to make a duxelles (p.81) with the onion, shallot, nutmeg and 30 g (1¼ oz) butter or oil. Heap the duxelles into the mushrooms and sprinkle with breadcrumbs. Arrange on a baking tray, drizzle with the remaining butter or oil and bake for 12–15 minutes.

- 12 large cultivated mushrooms
- 90 g (3¼ oz) butter, melted, or 3 tablespoons olive oil
- 60 g (2 oz) onion, finely chopped
- 1 shallot, finely chopped
- Freshly grated nutmeg
- 6 tablespoons dried breadcrumbs

Preparation time: 30 minutes
Cooking time: 25 minutes
Serves 6

MUSHROOM STEW

RAGOÛT DE CHAMPIGNONS

- 600 g (1 lb 5 oz) mushrooms, sliced if large
- 50 g (1¾ oz) butter
- ½ tablespoon white wine vinegar or lemon juice
- 1 handful of mixed herbs, such as flat-leaf parsley, chives, chervil or tarragon, chopped
- Freshly grated nutmeg
- Salt and pepper
- 2 egg yolks

Preparation time: 10 minutes
Cooking time: 15 minutes
Serves 6

Clean the mushrooms with a damp cloth. Put them in a pan with the butter, vinegar or lemon juice and herbs. Season with nutmeg, salt and pepper. Cover and simmer for 12–15 minutes. When ready to serve, remove from the heat and stir in the egg yolks to thicken the juices.

COOKED MUSHROOM SALAD

SALADE DE CHAMPIGNONS CUITS

- 250 g (9 oz) cultivated mushrooms
- Juice of 1 lemon
- 1 egg yolk
- 120 ml (4 fl oz) oil
- 1 pinch of salt

Preparation time: 25 minutes
Cooking time: 3 minutes
Serves 6

Wipe the mushrooms clean with a damp cloth. Bring a pan of salted water to the boil and add half the lemon juice. Add the mushrooms and simmer for 3 minutes. Meanwhile, make a mayonnaise (p.70) with the remaining lemon juice and the egg yolk, oil and salt. Drain the mushrooms and allow to cool completely, then cut them into small pieces and mix with the mayonnaise. This mixture can be used to fill sandwiches.

RAW MUSHROOM SALAD

SALADE DE CHAMPIGNONS CRUS

- 250 g (9 oz) cultivated mushrooms
- Juice of 1 lemon
- 2 tablespoons oil
- Salt and pepper
- 1 handful of flat-leaf parsley, chopped, to garnish

Preparation time: 10 minutes
Serves 6

Make just before serving. Clean some very fresh mushrooms with a damp cloth, cut into thin strips and place in a bowl. Whisk together the lemon juice, oil, salt and pepper to make a dressing, and toss this with the mushrooms. Garnish with the parsley.

CEPS WITH HERBS
CÈPES AUX FINES HERBES

Make 3 hours in advance. Clean the ceps with a damp cloth and cut off and reserve their stalks. Place the caps in a bowl and toss with the oil, then season with salt and pepper. Set aside to marinate for 3 hours. Finely chop the shallots and the stalks from the ceps. Melt the butter in a frying pan and cook the shallots, stalks and herbs over a gentle heat for 15 minutes. In a separate pan, brown the mushroom caps in their oil over a high heat for 5 minutes. Add the chopped mushroom mixture to the pan and cook for a further 5 minutes. Season with more salt and pepper if necessary and serve very hot.

- 6 large, firm ceps
- 100 ml (3½ fl oz) oil
- Salt and pepper
- 2 shallots
- 25 g (1 oz) butter
- 1 tablespoon chopped mixed herbs, such as flat-leaf parsley, chives, chervil and tarragon

Preparation time: 15 minutes, plus marinating time
Cooking time: 20 minutes
Serves 6

CEPS À LA BORDELAISE
CÈPES À LA BORDELAISE

Clean the ceps with a damp cloth and remove the stalks. Finely chop the stalks and mix with the shallot and breadcrumbs. Season with salt and pepper. Fry the caps on a griddle or in a frying pan for 5 minutes, without any fat. Remove from the heat and cut into diagonal 1-cm (½-inch) slices. Heat half the oil in a frying pan, add the slices and fry over a high heat until browned, then drain. In another pan, heat the remaining oil and fry the chopped stalks and breadcrumb mixture for 2–3 minutes. Put the caps on a dish, season with salt and pepper and cover with the breadcrumb mixture. Sprinkle with the parsley.

- 750 g (1 lb 10 oz) very fresh ceps
- 1 shallot, finely chopped
- 40 g (1½ oz) dried breadcrumbs
- Salt and pepper
- 3 tablespoons olive oil
- ½ handful of flat-leaf parsley, chopped

Preparation time: 20 minutes
Cooking time: 15 minutes
Serves 6

STUFFED CEPS
CÈPES FARCIS

Clean the ceps with a damp cloth and remove the stalks. Make a stuffing by chopping and mixing together the stalks, bread, eggs and herbs. Season the caps with salt and pepper. Melt 40 g (1½ oz) of the butter in a frying pan, add the caps, cover and cook over a low heat for 20 minutes. Stuff each cap with the stuffing. Heat the remaining butter in the frying pan, return the stuffed ceps to the pan and cook gently for 10 minutes, without turning.

- 6 large ceps
- 100 g (3½ oz) crustless white bread, torn into pieces
- 2 eggs, hard-boiled (p.134)
- ½ handful of mixed herbs, such as flat-leaf parsley, chives, chervil and tarragon
- Salt and pepper
- 60 g (2 oz) butter

Preparation time: 20 minutes
Cooking time: 30 minutes
Serves 6

CEP CASSOLETTES
CASSOLETTES DE CÈPES

- 1 kg (2¼ lb) ceps
- 100 g (3½ oz) butter or
  goose fat
- ½ handful of flat-leaf parsley,
  chopped
- 1 garlic clove, crushed
- 50 g (1¾ oz) shallot,
  very finely chopped
- 100 ml (3½ fl oz) truffle juice
  or 1 tablespoon truffle essence
- Salt and pepper
- Veal stock (optional)
- 1 quantity Périgueux sauce
  (p.61), to serve (optional)

Preparation time: 15 minutes
Cooking time: 10 minutes
Serves 6

Clean the ceps with a damp cloth and separate the caps from the stalks. Slice both. Heat 60g (2 oz) of the butter or goose fat in a frying pan and gently cook the slices for 5 minutes. Remove from the pan and drain. Melt the remaining butter or goose fat in the frying pan and, when it is hot, add the parsley, garlic and ceps slices, and fry over a high heat until brown, about 5 minutes. Off the heat, add the shallot and truffle juice or essence and season with salt and a pinch of pepper. If the mixture seems dry, add a little veal stock. Serve very hot. Serve the ceps with the Périgueux sauce, if desired.

CEPS À LA BRETONNE
CÈPES À LA BRETONNE

- 30 g (1¼ oz) butter, plus extra
  for greasing
- 6–8 large ceps
- 5 shallots
- ½ handful of mixed herbs,
  such as flat-leaf parsley, chives,
  chervil and tarragon
- Salt and pepper
- 50 ml (2 fl oz) white wine
- 100 ml (3½ fl oz) any stock
- 4 tablespoons dried
  breadcrumbs

Preparation time: 10 minutes
Cooking time: 15 minutes
Serves 6

Preheat the oven to 220°C/425°F/Gas Mark 7 and grease an ovenproof dish with butter. Clean the ceps with a damp cloth. Cut off the stalks. Melt the butter in a frying pan and fry the stalks and caps over a medium heat for 5 minutes. Finely chop and mix together the stalks, shallots and herbs and season with salt and pepper. Fill each cap with the mixture. Arrange in the prepared dish. Add the wine and stock, sprinkle with the breadcrumbs and bake until browned, about 10 minutes.

CHANTERELLES IN BUTTER

CHANTERELLES AU BEURRE

Clean the chanterelles with a soft brush, put them in a frying pan with the butter and fry over a high heat for 10 minutes until brown. Add the shallot, garlic and parsley, and season with salt and pepper. Cover the pan with a tightly fitting lid and cook over a gentle heat for 15 minutes. Good served with roast veal and other meats.

VARIATION

. . . .

CHANTERELLES WITH CREAM

CHANTERELLES À LA CRÈME

Proceed as above, omitting the shallot and stirring in 120 ml (4 fl oz) double cream just before serving.

- 350 g (12 oz) chanterelles
- 30 g (1¼ oz) butter
- 1 shallot, chopped
- 1 garlic clove, crushed
- 2 tablespoons flat-leaf parsley, chopped
- Salt and pepper

Preparation time: 10 minutes
Cooking time: 25 minutes
Serves 6

CHANTERELLES BONNE FEMME

CHANTERELLES BONNE FEMME

 p.593

Clean the chanterelles with a soft brush. Melt the butter in a frying pan and fry the bacon over a high heat for 5 minutes. Add the onion, parsley, and chanterelles and season with salt and pepper. When everything has browned, sprinkle with the flour. Moisten with a little hot water and the wine, and simmer over a low heat for 40 minutes. When ready to serve, stir in the crème fraîche.

NOTE
Morels can be used instead of chanterelles.

- 750 g (1 lb 10 oz) chanterelles
- 40 g (1½ oz) butter
- 125 g (4¼ oz) smoked bacon, diced
- 1 onion, chopped
- 2 tablespoons flat-leaf parsley, chopped
- Salt and pepper
- 30 g (1¼ oz) flour
- 75 ml (2½ fl oz) white wine
- 60 ml (2 fl oz) crème fraîche

Preparation time: 20 minutes
Cooking time: 50 minutes
Serves 6

PLAINLY COOKED TRUFFLES

TRUFFES AU NATUREL

Preparation time: 20 minutes
Cooking time: 35 minutes

Preheat the oven to 190°C/375°F/Gas Mark 5. Gently clean some good-sized truffles with a soft brush. Wrap them in 2 layers of foil and dip the parcel briefly in water. Place on a baking tray and bake in the oven for 35 minutes, or cook under very hot ashes. Remove the foil and serve the truffles in a warm napkin.

VARIATION

. . . .

TRUFFLE PARCELS
TRUFFES EN PAPILLOTES

Preparation time: 30 minutes
Cooking time: 45 minutes

Proceed as above, but first season the truffles with salt and pepper, soak them in Cognac and wrap them in a very thin layer of bacon before placing them in the double-layer foil parcel. The truffles are served in their parcels, with the outer layer of foil removed.

TRUFFLES IN CHAMPAGNE

TRUFFES AU CHAMPAGNE

- ½ bottle of Champagne or other sparkling white wine
- 500 ml (18 fl oz) cooked marinade (p.77)
- 125 g (4¼ oz) cured ham, chopped
- 1 garlic clove, crushed
- 2 tablespoons flat-leaf parsley, chopped
- Truffles, cleaned
- Salt and pepper

Preparation time: 20 minutes
Cooking time: 30 minutes
Serves 6

Use the Champagne or sparkling wine to prepare the marinade. Stir the ham, garlic and parsley into the pan containing the marinade. Season the truffles lightly with salt and pepper, add them to the pan and cook gently over a low heat for 30 minutes. Cool. Drain the truffles, sponge them dry on a clean cloth and serve in a napkin.

TRUFFLE 'ROCK'

TRUFFES EN ROCHE

Preheat the oven to 200°C/400°F/Gas Mark 6. Clean the truffles with a soft brush and set aside. Make a stuffing by mixing together the bacon, Cognac and herbs and seasoning well with salt and pepper. Roll out the puff pastry to a thickness of 1 cm (½ inch), then spread with one-third of the stuffing. Arrange the truffles on top in a pyramid, with another third of the stuffing in between them. Cover the pyramid with the remaining stuffing, then with another very thin layer of puff pastry, sealed closely round the truffles to give the effect of a boulder. Make a small hole in the top, brush with the egg yolk and bake for 1 hour. Serve hot.

- 250 g (9 oz) truffles
- 200 g (7 oz) streaky bacon, finely chopped
- 100 ml (3½ fl oz) Cognac
- ½ handful of mixed herbs, such as flat-leaf parsley, chives, chervil and tarragon, chopped
- Salt and pepper
- 250 g (9 oz) puff pastry (p.776)
- 1 egg yolk, beaten

Preparation time: 30 minutes
Cooking time: 1 hour
Serves 6

TRUFFLES IN A NAPKIN

TRUFFES À LA SERVIETTE

Thoroughly clean the truffles with a soft brush. Pour about 1 cm (½ inch) water into a flameproof earthenware dish. Put in the truffles and season very lightly with salt. Cover tightly. Simmer for 30–35 minutes. Remove and arrange the truffles inside a folded napkin. Add the Cognac to the cooking liquid, and, ensuring the pan is well away from anything flammable, touch a lighted match to the edge of the pan to ignite it, standing well back. When the flames have died down, serve the liquid separately in small bowls or heatproof glasses.

- Truffles, to taste
- Salt
- Cognac, to taste

Preparation time: 20 minutes
Cooking time: 35 minutes

ENDIVE

Endive, curly endive and batavia are the names given to several kinds of salad leaves that have tall, thin stems, sometimes curly, and which are usually loosely joined together. To prepare them, remove any coarse or wilted outer leaves and cut them into four lengthways. Wash carefully and blanch in boiling salted water for 5 minutes.

ENDIVE PURÉE
CHICORÉE EN PURÉE

- 3 kg (6½ lb) endive
- 1 quantity béchamel sauce (p.50)
- Salt and pepper
- Freshly grated nutmeg
- 50 g (1¾ oz) butter
- 6 slices bread, cut into triangles

Preparation time: 30 minutes
Cooking time: 25 minutes
Serves 6

Prepare the endive as described above, and cook for 15 minutes. Drain the endive carefully, pressing between your hands to squeeze out all the cooking liquid. Process through a food mill or food processor to make a purée. Make the béchamel sauce, add it to the purée and season with salt, pepper and nutmeg. Melt the butter in a frying pan, add the bread triangles and fry for 1 minute on each side until browned. Garnish the purée with the triangles.

ENDIVE BRAISED IN MEAT STOCK
CHICORÉE AU GRAS

- 3 kg (6½ lb) endive
- 60 g (2 oz) butter
- Salt and pepper
- 200 ml (7 fl oz) stock or meat juices

Preparation time: 25 minutes
Cooking time: 1 hour
Serves 6

Prepare the endive as described above. Drain the endive carefully, pressing between your hands to squeeze out all the cooking liquid. Melt half the butter in a heavy-based pan, add the drained endive, cover and cook over a low heat for 10 minutes. Season with salt and pepper and add the stock or meat juices. Cover and simmer for 45 minutes. Stir in the rest of the butter before serving.

ENDIVE BRAISED WITHOUT MEAT
CHICORÉE AU MAIGRE

Prepare and cook the endive (p.533). Drain the endive carefully, pressing between your hands to squeeze out all the cooking liquid. Place the drained endive in a heavy-based pan with the butter and crème fraîche. Season with salt and pepper and cook over a gentle heat for 1 hour. Carefully remove the endive from the pan with a slotted spoon and place on a warm serving dish. Cut the hard-boiled eggs into quarters and arrange on the endive. Thicken the cooking liquid in the pan by whisking in the egg yolks over a gentle heat, and pour it over the endive to serve.

- 3 kg (6½ lb) endive
- 50 g (1¾ oz) butter
- 200 ml (7 fl oz) crème fraîche
- Salt and pepper
- 3 eggs, hard-boiled
- 2 egg yolks

Preparation time: 25 minutes
Cooking time: 1 hour
Serves 6

OLD-FASHIONED ENDIVE LOAF
PAIN DE CHICORÉE À L'ANCIENNE

Prepare an endive purée (p.533) with the béchamel sauce, salt, pepper and nutmeg. Preheat the oven to 190°C/375°F/Gas Mark 5 and grease a ring mould with butter. Beat the eggs and add them to the purée with the butter. Pour into the prepared mould. Place in a roasting tin half-filled with hot water and bake for 45 minutes. Turn out and serve with the cream sauce.

- 3 kg (6½ lb) endive
- 1 quantity béchamel sauce (p.50)
- Salt and pepper
- Freshly grated nutmeg
- 3 eggs
- 50 g (1¾ oz) butter, plus extra for greasing
- 1 quantity cream sauce (p.51), to serve

Preparation time: 30 minutes
Cooking time: 45 minutes
Serves 6

CABBAGE

To prepare cabbage for cooking, cut off the base and remove any wilted outer leaves. Wash thoroughly, cut into pieces and blanch in boiling salted water for 5–10 minutes.

PLAIN BRAISED CABBAGE

CHOU À L'ÉTOUFFÉE

- 100 g (3½ oz) lard
- 1 x 1.5-kg (3¼-lb) cabbage
- Salt and pepper
- 200 ml (7 fl oz) any stock, hot

Preparation time: 5 minutes
Cooking time: 1 hour
Serves 6

Melt the lard over a medium heat in a high-sided frying pan. Trim the cabbage, cut it into pieces and add to the pan. Season with salt and pepper, pour on the hot stock and simmer over a low heat for 1 hour.

BRAISED CABBAGE WITH BACON

CHOU BRAISÉ

- 1 x 1.5-kg (3¼-lb) cabbage
- 200 g (7 oz) bacon rashers
- 100 g (3½ oz) carrots, sliced
- 1 onion, sliced
- 1 sprig of thyme
- 1 bay leaf
- Salt and pepper
- 200 ml (7 fl oz) any stock, hot

Preparation time: 15 minutes
Cooking time: 1–1½ hours
Serves 6

Trim the cabbage and cut it into quarters. Line a heavy-based pan with the bacon rashers, reserving 3 rashers. Place the cabbage on top of the bacon, along with the carrots, onion, thyme and bay leaf, and season with salt and pepper. Cover with the reserved bacon rashers, pour on the hot stock and simmer over a low heat for 1–1½ hours.

STUFFED CABBAGE

CHOU FARCI

 p.594

Trim the cabbage, removing any wilted or damaged leaves. Cut a deep cross in the base. Bring a large pan of salted water to the boil and blanch the cabbage in boiling water for 10 minutes. Drain the cabbage, remove some of the core to expose the ends of the leaves and drain again with the base facing downwards. Beginning in the centre of the cabbage, slip a little stuffing into the base of each leaf without pulling the cabbage completely apart. Wrap the bacon rashers around the cabbage and tie with kitchen string. Put it in a heavy-based pan with the onion and carrot, and pour on the stock and wine. Season with salt and pepper, cover with a lid and simmer gently for 2 hours.

- 1 x 1.5-kg (3¼-lb) cabbage
- 250 g (9 oz) stuffing for red meats (153)
- 125 g (4¼ oz) bacon rashers
- 1 onion, sliced
- 1 carrot, sliced
- 200 ml (7 fl oz) any stock
- 100 ml (3½ fl oz) white wine
- Salt and pepper

Preparation time: 45 minutes
Cooking time: 2 hours
Serves 6

STUFFED CABBAGE À LA CHÂTELAINE

CHOU FARCI À LA CHÂTELAINE

Trim and blanch the cabbage (p.535) and make the stuffing. Preheat the oven to 160°C/325°F/Gas Mark 3. Arrange alternating layers of cabbage, stuffing and bacon rashers in an ovenproof dish, finishing with the bacon. Sprinkle with the breadcrumbs, dot with the butter and bake for 2 hours. Serve with the tomato sauce.

- 1 x 1.5-kg (3¼-lb) cabbage
- 250 g (9 oz) stuffing for red meats (p.80)
- 150 g (5 oz) bacon rashers
- 4 tablespoons dried breadcrumbs
- 30 g (1¼ oz) butter
- 1 quantity tomato sauce (p.57), to serve

Preparation time: 45 minutes
Cooking time: 2 hours
Serves 6

CABBAGE PURÉE

CHOUÉE VENDÉENNE

This recipe comes from the Vendée region on the west coast of France.

Choose very young green cabbages, trim and wash them, and cook for 1 hour in boiling salted water. Drain. Press out the water and press the cabbages through a sieve, or process them to a purée in a blender. Melt the butter in a frying pan and fry the cabbage purée over a medium heat. Season with salt and pepper, and stir in the vinegar.

- 1 kg (2¼ lb) young green cabbages
- 125 g (4¼ oz) butter
- Salt and pepper
- 1 tablespoon white wine vinegar

Preparation time: 10 minutes
Cooking time: 1¼ hours
Serves 6

BRUSSELS SPROUTS

To prepare, trim each sprout individually and remove any wilted leaves. Boil without a lid in salted water for 5–10 minutes, depending on size, until just tender.

SAUTÉED BRUSSELS SPROUTS
CHOUX DE BRUXELLES SAUTÉS

- **1 kg (2¼ lb) Brussels sprouts**
- **80 g (2¾ oz) butter**
- **Salt and pepper**

Preparation time: 30 minutes
Cooking time: 20 minutes
Serves 6

Trim and cook the sprouts (see above). Melt 60 g (2 oz) of the butter in a frying pan and fry the sprouts over a high heat. When they begin to brown, season with salt and pepper and add the remaining butter.

BRUSSELS SPROUTS WITH CHESTNUTS
CHOUX DE BRUXELLES AUX MARRONS

- **500 g (1 lb 2 oz) chestnuts**
- **700 g (1 lb 8½ oz) Brussels sprouts**
- **50 g (1¾ oz) butter, melted**

Preparation time: 1 hour
Cooking time: 25 minutes
Serves 6

Prepare and cook the chestnuts (p.558), and the sprouts (see above). When both are cooked, mix them together and place in a serving bowl. Just before serving, pour the butter over them.

CAULIFLOWER

To prepare, cut the cauliflower into florets. Place in boiling salted water and boil for 5–10 minutes, depending on the size of the florets.

CAULIFLOWER IN WHITE SAUCE
CHOU-FLEUR À LA SAUCE BLANCHE

Prepare and cook the cauliflower (see above), and place the florets in a large round bowl, with the stalks facing upwards. Turn out carefully onto a serving dish so that they resemble a whole cauliflower, and coat with your chosen sauce.

- 1 x 1-kg (2¼-lb) cauliflower
- 1 quantity white sauce (p.50) or tomato sauce (p.57), hot

Preparation time: 20 minutes
Cooking time: 20 minutes
Serves 6

CAULIFLOWER GRATIN
CHOU-FLEUR EN GRATIN

Prepare and cook the cauliflower (see above). Preheat the oven to 220°C/425°F/Gas Mark 7. Place the florets in a buttered ovenproof dish. Coat with the cheese sauce, sprinkle with the cheese and bake for 10–15 minutes, until golden.

- 1 kg (2¼ lb) cauliflower
- 1 quantity cheese sauce (p.51)
- 60 g (2 oz) Gruyère cheese, grated

Preparation time: 20 minutes
Cooking time: 10–15 minutes
Serves 6

CAULIFLOWER TIMBALE
TIMBALE DE CHOU-FLEUR

Preheat the oven to 180°C/350°F/Gas Mark 4. Prepare and cook the cauliflower (see above). Make the stuffing and arrange alternating layers of the florets and stuffing in an ovenproof dish, finishing with florets. Place in a roasting tin half-filled with hot water and bake for 40 minutes. Serve with the mushroom sauce.

- 1 kg (2¼ lb) cauliflower
- 250 g (9 oz) stuffing for red meats (p.80)
- 1 quantity mushroom sauce (p.61)

Preparation time: 45 minutes
Cooking time: 40 minutes
Serves 6

CAULIFLOWER CROQUETTES

CHOU-FLEUR EN CROQUETTES

- 750 g (1 lb 10 oz) cauliflower
- 30 g (1¼ oz) butter
- 50 g (1¾ oz) flour
- 500 ml (18 fl oz) milk
- 60 g (2 oz) Gruyère cheese, grated
- 1 egg
- 1 egg, separated
- Salt and pepper
- Dried breadcrumbs, for rolling
- Vegetable oil, for deep-frying

Preparation time: 35 minutes
Cooking time: 25 minutes
Serves 6

Cook the cauliflower (p.538), then drain and cut the florets into small pieces. Make a béchamel sauce (p.50), with the butter, flour and milk, and add the cheese. Stir the egg and egg yolk into the sauce to thicken it, and mix the cauliflower into the sauce. Season with salt and pepper and set aside to cool. Whisk the remaining egg white to stiff peaks. Shape the cauliflower mixture into croquettes and roll them in the egg white, then in the breadcrumbs. Heat the oil in a deep-fryer to 180°C/350°F, or until a cube of bread browns in 30 seconds. Add the croquettes and deep-fry in batches until golden. Drain well before serving.

CAULIFLOWER FRITTERS

CHOU-FLEUR EN BEIGNETS

- 1 quantity sweet marinade (p.78)
- 1 cauliflower
- 1 quantity batter for frying (p.725)
- Vegetable oil, for deep-frying

Preparation time: 20 minutes
Cooking time: 10 minutes
Serves 6

Prepare and cook the cauliflower (p.538) and mix the florets into the marinade. Cover and set aside for 2 hours. Make the batter. Heat the oil in a deep-fryer to 180°C/350°F, or until a cube of bread browns in 30 seconds. Dip the florets in the batter and deep-fry in batches for 2–3 minutes until golden. Drain well before serving.

CAULIFLOWER SOUFFLÉ

PAIN DE CHOU-FLEUR

- Butter, for greasing
- 300 g (11 oz) cauliflower
- ½ quantity béchamel sauce (p.50)
- 100 ml (3½ fl oz) crème fraîche
- 60 g (2 oz) Gruyère cheese, grated
- 3 eggs, separated
- Pepper
- 1 quantity tomato sauce (p.57)

Preparation time: 5 minutes
Cooking time: 1 hour
Serves 6

Preheat the oven to 180°C/350°F/Gas Mark 4. Grease a loaf tin with butter. Prepare and cook the cauliflower (p.538). Drain the florets well and pass through a food mill or process in a food processor to make a purée. Mix the purée with the béchamel sauce and stir in the crème fraîche, cheese and egg yolks. Whisk the egg whites to medium peaks and fold them into the sauce. Season with pepper. Put the mixture in the prepared loaf tin and place in a roasting tin half-filled with hot water. Cover and cook for 30 minutes. Remove from the roasting tin and return to the oven for another 10 minutes. Turn out and serve with tomato sauce.

RED CABBAGE

To prepare, cut off the base and remove any wilted leaves. Wash thoroughly, cut into thin strips and blanch in boiling salted water for 5–10 minutes.

RED CABBAGE WITH BACON
CHOU ROUGE AU LARD

Wash the cabbage and cut it into strips. In a heavy-based pan, melt the lard or butter over a high heat, add the onion, and cook for 5 minutes, stirring, until browned. Add the cabbage and 250 ml (8 fl oz) water. Season with salt and pepper. Cook gently for 15 minutes. Add the bacon to the pan, cover and cook for a further 45 minutes.

VARIATION

. . . .

RED CABBAGE WITH CHESTNUTS
CHOU ROUGE AUX MARRONS

Proceed as above, replacing the bacon with 500 g (1 lb 2 oz) chestnuts, peeled and roughly chopped.

* 750 g (1 lb 10 oz) red cabbage
* 60 g (2 oz) lard or butter
* 1 onion, sliced
* Salt and pepper
* 300 g (11 oz) smoked bacon, diced

Preparation time: 10 minutes
Cooking time: 1 hour
Serves 6

RED CABBAGE IN RED WINE
CHOU ROUGE AU VIN ROUGE

Wash the cabbage and cut it into strips. Melt the butter in a heavy-based pan. Add the cabbage and cook very gently for 15 minutes. Season with salt and pepper and pour in the wine. Cover and simmer over a very low heat for 2 hours.

* 1 kg (2¼ lb) red cabbage
* 60 g (2 oz) butter
* Salt and pepper
* 200 ml (7 fl oz) red wine

Preparation time: 10 minutes
Cooking time: 2¼ hours
Serves 6

p.595

ALSACE CHOUCROUTE
CHOUCROUTE À L'ALSACIENNE

- 1 kg (2¼ lb) sauerkraut
- 50 g (1¾ oz) lard or oil
- 100 g (3½ oz) onion, chopped
- 250 ml (8 fl oz) white wine
- Salt and pepper
- 1 x 300-g (11-oz) piece of smoked bacon
- 1 x 250-g (9-oz) piece of cured sausage
- 500 g (1 lb 2 oz) potatoes, quartered
- 6 slices ham

Preparation time: 10 minutes
Cooking time: 3½ hours
Serves 6

Rinse the sauerkraut. Melt the lard or oil over a low heat in a large pan. Add the onion and sauerkraut. Pour in the wine, season with salt and pepper, cover and cook for 2½ hours over a low heat. Add the bacon and cook, covered, for a further 30 minutes. Add the sausage, potatoes and ham and cook, covered, for a final 30 minutes. Slice the bacon and sausage and serve on a warmed serving dish.

CUCUMBER

To prepare, peel the cucumbers, cut them in half lengthways and remove the seeds with the tip of a teaspoon. Cut into thin slices and cook for 5 minutes in boiling salted water. For cucumber in a sauce, prepare the cucumbers as above and add a poulette sauce (p.52) or a béchamel sauce (p.50). Allow 1.25–1.5 kg (2¾–3¼ lb) cucumber for six people as a vegetable accompaniment.

CUCUMBER À L'ANTIBOISE
CONCOMBRE À L'ANTIBOISE

- 700 g (1 lb 8½ oz) cucumber
- 200 g (7 oz) tuna in brine
- 250 ml (8 fl oz) mayonnaise (p.70)
- 1 quantity yoghurt sauce (p.66)
- 1 tablespoon tomato purée
- 1 tablespoon flat-leaf parsley, chopped

Preparation time: 40 minutes
Cooking time: 5 minutes
Serves 6

Prepare and cook the cucumber (see above), cutting it into thin slices. Drain the tuna and mix with half the mayonnaise. Arrange the slices of cucumber on a dish and arrange spoonfuls of the tuna and mayonnaise mixture on top. Mix the yoghurt sauce with the tomato purée and remaining mayonnaise. Coat the tuna and cucumber with this sauce and sprinkle with the parsley. Serve well chilled.

STUFFED CUCUMBERS
CONCOMBRES FARCIS

Prepare the stuffing. Cut off the stalk end of each of the cucumbers and set aside. Hollow out the inside with a long-handled spoon and replace the seeds with the stuffing. Replace the stalk end and tie it on with kitchen string. Melt the butter in a large sauté pan, add the cucumbers and pour in the stock. Season with salt and pepper and cook over a very low heat, covered, for 1 hour. When ready to serve, pour the lemon juice over the cucumbers and serve with their sauce.

- 200 g (7 oz) stuffing for red meats (p.80) or duxelles (p.81)
- 6 small cucumbers
- 50 g (1¾ oz) butter
- 200 ml (7 fl oz) light chicken or vegetable stock
- Salt and pepper
- Juice of 1 lemon

Preparation time: 30 minutes
Cooking time: 1 hour
Serves 6

COURGETTES

To prepare, wash the courgettes and peel thinly if the skins are tough. Small courgettes are normally used whole. Freshly picked courgette flowers can be stuffed and lightly braised, or coated with batter and deep-fried.

COURGETTES SAUTÉED WITH HERBS
COURGETTES SAUTÉES AUX FINES HERBES

Season the flour with salt and pepper. Cut the courgettes into 1-cm (½-inch) dice and toss in the flour. Melt the butter in a frying pan and brown the courgettes over a high heat for 5 minutes. Sprinkle with the chopped herbs and serve.

- 3 tablespoons flour
- Salt and pepper
- 4 large courgettes
- 50 g (1¾ oz) butter
- 2 tablespoons chervil, chopped
- 2 tablespoons flat-leaf parsley, chopped
- 1 tablespoon tarragon, chopped

Preparation time: 5 minutes
Cooking time: 5 minutes
Serves 6

COURGETTE GRATIN

COURGETTES EN GRATIN

- 40 g (1½ oz) butter or oil
- 4 large courgettes
- Salt and pepper
- 1 quantity béchamel sauce (p.50)
- 40 g (1½ oz) Gruyère cheese, grated

Preparation time: 15 minutes
Cooking time: 5–10 minutes
Serves 6

Preheat the oven to 240°C / 475°F / Gas Mark 8 and grease an ovenproof dish with a little of the butter or oil. Cut the courgettes into 1.5-cm (¾-inch) slices. Heat the remaining butter or oil in a pan, add the courgettes and cook gently for 10 minutes. Season with salt and pepper. Make the béchamel sauce. Arrange the courgette slices in the prepared dish. Coat with the sauce, sprinkle with cheese and bake for 5–10 minutes, until golden brown.

COURGETTE & TOMATO GÂTEAU
GÂTEAU DE COURGETTES ET DE TOMATES

Preheat the oven to 190°C/375°F/Gas Mark 5. Slice the tomatoes and courgettes. The slices of tomato should be a little larger than the courgette slices. Brush an ovenproof dish with a little of the oil. Arrange alternating slices of tomato and courgette in the dish. Sprinkle with salt and pepper and brush with oil. Sprinkle with the thyme flowers or leaves and bake for 20 minutes.

NOTE
The dish may be sprinkled with dried breadcrumbs and, once cooked, dotted with butter and browned under a hot grill.

- 600 g (1 lb 5 oz) tomatoes
- 400 g (14 oz) courgettes
- 3 tablespoons olive oil
- Salt and pepper
- Thyme flowers or young thyme leaves, to taste

Preparation time: 20 minutes
Cooking time: 20 minutes
Serves 6

WATERCRESS

WATERCRESS PURÉE
CRESSON EN PURÉE

Trim the watercress, removing any thick stems and wilted leaves. Blanch in boiling salted water for 1 minute. Drain and refresh under cold running water. Drain the watercress carefully, pressing to squeeze out all the cooking liquid. Process through a food mill or food processor to make a purée. Make the white sauce, add it to the purée and season with nutmeg.

- 6 bunches of watercress
- 1 quantity white sauce (p.50)
- Freshly grated nutmeg

Preparation time: 5 minutes
Cooking time: 15 minutes
Serves 6

CHICORY

Chicory (confusingly, also sometimes known as Belgian endive) is a bitter-tasting leaf that grows in tightly packed bunches, which are very pale yellow and pointed at one end. To prepare, cut the root end off each head of chicory. Remove any withered leaves and rinse quickly but carefully under cold running water to remove earth or sand. Drain and wipe dry.

BRAISED CHICORY

ENDIVES À L'ÉTUVÉE

- 1 kg (2¼ lb) chicory
- 60 g (2 oz) butter
- Salt and pepper
- Juice of 1 lemon

Preparation time: 10 minutes
Cooking time: 30 minutes
Serves 6

Prepare the chicory (p.544). Melt the butter in a high-sided frying pan, add the chicory, season with salt and pepper and pour over the lemon juice. Cover tightly and cook over a very low heat for 30 minutes, until soft.

CHICORY WITH CHEESE

ENDIVES AU FROMAGE

- Butter, for greasing
- 1 kg (2¼ lb) chicory, braised (see above)
- 1 quantity béchamel sauce (p.50)
- 40 g (1½ oz) Gruyère cheese, grated

Preparation time: 20 minutes
Cooking time: 40 minutes
Serves 6

Preheat the oven to 220°C/425°F/Gas Mark 7 and grease an ovenproof dish with butter. Place the chicory in the prepared dish, coat with the béchamel sauce and sprinkle with the cheese. Bake for 10 minutes, until golden brown.

STUFFED CHICORY

ENDIVES FARCIES

- Butter, for greasing
- 1 kg (2¼ lb) chicory
- 250 g (9 oz) stuffing for red meat (p.80)
- Salt and pepper
- 1 quantity white sauce (p.50)

Preparation time: 45 minutes
Cooking time: 1 hour
Serves 6

Preheat the oven to 190°C/375°F/Gas Mark 5 and grease an ovenproof dish with butter. Prepare the chicory (p.544). Bring a large pan of salted water to the boil, add the chicory, reduce the heat and simmer for 5 minutes. Drain well. Arrange alternating layers of chicory and stuffing in the prepared dish. Season with salt and pepper, coat with the white sauce and bake for 1 hour, covering with foil if the chicory browns too quickly.

CHICORY LOAF

PAIN D'ENDIVES

Preheat the oven to 190°C/375°F/Gas Mark 5, and grease an ovenproof terrine or loaf tin with butter. Cut the chicory into 2-cm (¾-inch) slices. Thoroughly combine with the meat and eggs. Season with salt and pepper. Put in the terrine or loaf tin, place in a roasting tin half-filled with hot water and bake for 2 hours. Meanwhile, prepare the white sauce and add the Madeira, mushroom stock and tomato purée. Turn out the chicory loaf and coat with the sauce.

- Butter, for greasing
- 1 kg (2¼ lb) chicory
- 500 g (1 lb 2 oz) minced meat
- 2 eggs, beaten
- Salt and pepper
- 20 g (¾ oz) butter
- 1 quantity white sauce (p.50)
- 1 tablespoon Madeira
- 50 ml (2 fl oz) mushroom stock (p.46)
- 1 teaspoon tomato purée

Preparation time: 10 minutes
Cooking time: 2 hours
Serves 6

CROSNES

Crosnes resemble, and taste similar to, small Jerusalem artichokes. They are sometimes known as Chinese artichokes, although they are not related. To prepare, wash them, trim the ends and, if desired, remove the skin by rubbing them gently in a clean cloth with coarse salt. Wash well. Cook in boiling salted water for 10–15 minutes. Serve as they are or dress with vinaigrette (p.66) or mayonnaise (p.70).

SAUTÉED CROSNES

CROSNES SAUTÉS

Prepare the crosnes as above, and cut them into slices. Heat the butter in a medium pan and fry the crosnes for 5–10 minutes over a medium heat, until golden. Sprinkle with salt and the parsley, and serve. Crosnes can also be served with maître d'hôtel butter (p.48).

- 600 g (1 lb 5 oz) crosnes
- 60 g (2 oz) butter
- Salt
- 1 tablespoon flat-leaf parsley, chopped

Preparation time: 20 minutes
Cooking time: 25 minutes
Serves 6

SPINACH

To prepare, remove any large or tough stalks from the leaves. Wash the spinach in several changes of water, then cook uncovered in plenty of boiling salted water for 5 minutes, using about 3 litres (5¼ pints) water per 1 kg (2¼ lb) spinach. Drain and press out the water. The cooked weight will be approximately two-thirds less than the raw weight.

SPINACH & RICE LOAF

PAIN D'ÉPINARDS ET DE RIZ FLORENTIN

Wash and cook the spinach (as above). Chop the cooked and drained spinach. Prepare the Indian rice and make the béchamel sauce. Preheat the oven to 220°C/425°F/Gas Mark 7 and grease an ovenproof dish with butter. Mix the béchamel sauce with the spinach. Mix the eggs with the Indian rice, then put alternate layers of rice and spinach in the prepared dish. Dot with the butter and bake for 20 minutes.

NOTE

The spinach and rice loaf may be coated with tomato sauce (p.57) or Madeira sauce (p.61) and served with slices of ham or roast meat.

- **3 kg (6½ lb) spinach**
- **200 g (7 oz) Indian rice (p.616)**
- **500 ml (18 fl oz) béchamel sauce (p.50)**
- **60 g (2 oz) butter, plus extra for greasing**
- **2 eggs, beaten**

Preparation time: 45 minutes
Cooking time: 20 minutes
Serves 6

SPINACH CROQUETTES

SUBRICS D'ÉPINARDS

 p.596

Make the béchamel sauce. Process the spinach in a food processor or pass through a food mill until smooth, and mix with the sauce. Add the eggs and cheese. Heat the butter in a frying pan. When it is hot, drop spoonfuls of the spinach mixture gently into the pan and cook for 2–3 minutes on each side, until browned.

- **250 ml (8 fl oz) béchamel sauce (p.50)**
- **800 g (1¾ lb) cooked spinach (see above)**
- **2 eggs, beaten**
- **100 g (3½ oz) Gruyère cheese, grated**
- **100 g (3½ oz) butter**

Preparation time: 20 minutes
Cooking time: 5 minutes
Serves 6

FENNEL

To prepare, remove any damaged stems and leaves. Trim the base to make it even and remove any blemishes, and wash carefully. Place in boiling salted water for 15 minutes, or until tender, depending on the size of the bulbs. Drain well. Fennel can be served coated in béchamel sauce (p.50), Madeira sauce (p.61) or cream sauce (p.51).

BRAISED FENNEL
FENOUIL À L'ÉTUVÉE

- **1 kg (2¼ lb) fennel**
- **50 g (1¾ oz) butter**
- **Salt and pepper**
- **Juice of 1 lemon**

Preparation time: 10 minutes
Cooking time: 35–45 minutes
Serves 6

Prepare and cook the fennel (see above), but boil for 5 minutes only. Drain well. Melt the butter in a high-sided frying pan, add the fennel and season with salt and pepper. Pour over the lemon juice. Cover tightly and cook over a very low heat for 30–40 minutes, until tender.

STEWED FENNEL WITH THYME
TOMBÉE DE FENOUIL AU THYM

- **1 kg (2¼ lb) fennel**
- **Salt and pepper**
- **Juice of 2 lemons**
- **4 tablespoons olive oil**
- **1 bay leaf**
- **2–3 sprigs of thyme**

Preparation time: 10 minutes
Cooking time: 30 minutes
Serves 6

Prepare the fennel (see above), removing any long tough stems, and cut lengthways into quarters. Cut out the hard base and lower part of the central core, keeping the quarters intact. Arrange the fennel in a frying pan and season with salt and pepper. Pour on the lemon juice and oil, and add the bay leaf and thyme and enough water to half cover the fennel. Cover and simmer over a steady heat for 20–30 minutes, or until tender. Remove the bay leaf and thyme. The fennel can be served drained or, preferably, in the cooking liquid.

NOTE
This fennel stew goes very well with grilled fish.

BROAD BEANS

To prepare, first shell the broad beans. Pop them out of their whitish skins and separate the beans into halves. Cook for 5 minutes in boiling salted water, adding a few sprigs of savory to the water, if available. Alternatively, it is easier to remove the skins before cooking, after blanching the beans for 1 minute, then continue cooking the beans. Drain and remove the savory before serving. Serve with maître d'hôtel butter (p.48), if desired.

BROAD BEANS WITH BACON
FÈVES AU LARD

Cook the broad beans (see above). Melt the butter in a pan and fry the bacon over a high heat until golden brown. Add the beans, salt, pepper and savory. Cook over a very low heat for 20 minutes. French beans can be used instead of broad beans.

- **1 kg (2¼ lb) shelled broad beans**
- **20 g (¾ oz) butter**
- **150 g (5 oz) bacon, diced**
- **Salt and pepper**
- **2–3 sprigs of savory**

Preparation time: 15 minutes
Cooking time: 20 minutes
Serves 6

BROAD BEANS WITH CREAM
FÈVES À LA CRÈME

Cook the broad beans (see above). Heat the butter in a pan, add the broad beans and cook gently for 30 minutes. Season with salt and pepper. Add the crème fraîche or poulette sauce 5 minutes before serving.

- **1 kg (2¼ lb) shelled broad beans**
- **50 g (1¾ oz) butter**
- **Salt and pepper**
- **100 ml (3½ fl oz) crème fraîche or 1 quantity poulette sauce (p.52)**

Preparation time: 10 minutes
Cooking time: 35 minutes
Serves 6

FRENCH BEANS

To prepare, top and tail each bean. If the beans are large, split them in two lengthways. Wash in warm water and cook immediately in boiling salted water. To keep the beans green, put them in one handful at a time, and wait for the water to come back to the boil before adding the next handful. Allow 8–12 minutes for cooking. The beans should remain slightly firm.

FRENCH BEANS À L'ANGLAISE
HARICOTS VERTS À L'ANGLAISE

* 1 kg (2¼ lb) French beans
* Salt and pepper
* 50 g (1¾ oz) butter
* 2 tablespoons flat-leaf parsley, chopped

Preparation time: 30 minutes
Cooking time: 20 minutes
Serves 6

Prepare and cook the beans (see above). Drain, season with salt and pepper and toss in the butter and parsley. Maître d'hôtel butter (p.48) can be used instead of the butter and parsley.

FRENCH BEANS À LA NIÇOISE
HARICOTS VERTS À LA NIÇOISE

📷 p.597

* 1 kg (2¼ lb) French beans
* 500 ml (18 fl oz) tomato sauce (p.57)
* 1 handful of flat-leaf parsley, chopped

Preparation time: 30 minutes
Cooking time: 40 minutes
Serves 6

Prepare and cook the beans (see above). Drain and place in a pan with the tomato sauce. Simmer over a low heat for 20 minutes. Add the parsley and serve.

FRESH HARICOT BEANS

To prepare, shell the beans and cook in boiling salted water along with 1 garlic clove, 1 bouquet garni and a few slices of carrot. Cook gently for 30–40 minutes until tender. 1 kg (2¼ lb) beans in their pods will yield about 350 g (12 oz) shelled beans. Allow 150 g (5 oz) shelled beans per person.

FRESH HARICOT BEANS WITH MAÎTRE D'HÔTEL BUTTER
HARICOTS BLANCS À LA MAÎTRE D'HÔTEL

Shell the beans and cook them as described above. Prepare a maître d'hôtel butter (p.48) with the remaining ingredients. Drain the cooked beans and add the butter immediately before serving.

- 2 kg (4½ lb) fresh haricot beans
- 120 g (4 oz) butter, softened
- 1 handful of flat-leaf parsley, chopped
- Juice of 1 lemon
- Salt and pepper

Preparation time: 40 minutes
Cooking time: 1 hour 10 minutes
Serves 6

FRESH HARICOT BEANS WITH TOMATOES
HARICOTS BLANCS FRAIS AUX TOMATES

Shell the beans and cook them as described above. Heat the butter in a high-sided frying pan and fry the onions until golden. Stir in the tomatoes, then the beans, and season with salt and pepper. Simmer over a low heat, uncovered, for 20 minutes. Serve with the tomato sauce in a sauce boat, if desired.

- 2 kg (4½ lb) fresh haricot beans
- 60 g (2 oz) butter
- 100 g (3½ oz) onions, chopped
- 500 g (1 lb 2 oz) tomatoes, skinned, de-seeded and diced
- Salt and pepper
- 1 quantity tomato sauce (p.57), optional

Preparation time: 40 minutes
Cooking time: 1 hour 10 minutes
Serves 6

FRESH HARICOT BEANS
À LA PROVENÇALE

HARICOTS BLANCS À LA PROVENÇALE

- 2 kg (4½ lb) fresh haricot beans
- 60 g (2 oz) butter
- 125 g (4¼ oz) onions, chopped
- 800 ml (1½ pints) any stock
- 1 garlic clove
- 1 shallot
- 1 tomato
- 1 bay leaf
- 3 cloves
- Salt and pepper

Preparation time: 40 minutes
Cooking time: 3½ hours
Serves 6

Shell the beans (p.552) but do not cook them. Heat the butter in a high-sided frying pan and fry the onions until golden. Add 500 ml (18 fl oz) of the stock. When it comes to the boil, add the beans. Add the garlic, shallot, tomato, bay leaf and cloves. Reduce the heat and simmer gently for 1 hour, adding more hot stock as necessary. Season with salt and pepper after 2 hours, and continue to simmer for about 1 hour more, until the beans are very tender.

FRESH HARICOT BEAN PURÉE

HARICOTS BLANCS EN PURÉE

- 2 kg (4½ lb) fresh haricot beans
- 500 ml (18 fl oz) hot milk
- 100 g (3½ oz) butter
- Salt and pepper
- 12 small slices bread

Preparation time: 40 minutes
Cooking time: 40 minutes
Serves 6

Shell the beans and cook them as described on p.552. Drain and process in a food mill or food processor to make a smooth purée. Beat in the hot milk and half the butter. Season with salt and pepper. Heat the remaining butter in a frying pan, add the bread and fry on both sides until golden. Serve with the purée.

BRAISED FRESH HARICOT BEANS

HARICOTS BLANCS AU JUS

- 2 kg (4½ lb) fresh haricot beans
- 500 ml (18 fl oz) chicken stock
- 1 onion, sliced
- 1 handful of flat-leaf parsley, chopped
- Salt and pepper

Preparation time: 40 minutes
Cooking time: 45 minutes
Serves 6

Shell the beans and cook them as described on p.552. Bring the stock to the boil and add the onion. Reduce the heat and simmer for 15 minutes. Drain the beans and add them to the stock with the parsley. Simmer for 20 minutes. Season with salt and pepper before serving.

MOGETTE BEANS WITH CREAM

MOUGETTES À LA CRÈME

Put the beans in a large pan. Put in enough water to cover them by at least 5 cm (2 inches). Add the onion, carrot, celeriac, garlic and thyme, and season with pepper. Cook over a very low heat for 2½–3 hours, topping up with boiling water if necessary. Drain the beans and remove the vegetables and thyme. Stir in the salt, butter and crème fraîche and serve.

- 1 kg (2¼ lb) mogette, haricot or white kidney beans, soaked according to the instructions on the packet
- 1 onion, studded with cloves
- 1 carrot
- 60 g (2 oz) celeriac
- 1 garlic clove
- 1 sprig of thyme
- Pepper
- 1 teaspoon salt
- 80 g (2¾ oz) butter
- 80 ml (3 fl oz) crème fraîche

Preparation time: 15 minutes
Cooking time: 3 hours
Serves 6

MIXED BEANS

HARICOTS PANACHÉS

In separate pans, cook the French beans (p.551) and the haricot beans (p.552). Combine in a serving dish, season with salt and pepper and add butter if desired.

- 500 g (1 lb 2 oz) French beans
- 500 g (1 lb 2 oz) fresh haricot beans
- Salt and pepper
- Butter, to taste (optional)

Preparation time: 15 minutes
Cooking time: 30–40 minutes
Serves 6

JARDINIÈRE OF VEGETABLES

JARDINIÈRE DE LÉGUMES

- 150 g (5 oz) carrots
- 150 g (5 oz) turnips
- 1 small cauliflower
- 200 g (7 oz) French beans
- 200 g (7 oz) shelled peas
- 150 g (5 oz) flageolet beans
- 60 g (2 oz) butter

Preparation time: 30 minutes
Cooking time: 45 minutes
Serves 6

Cut the carrots and turnips into small batons. Separate the cauliflower into small florets. Cook all the vegetables separately in boiling salted water until tender. Cut the French beans into dice after cooking. Serve the vegetables topped with the butter, either separately or mixed together.

 p.598

VEGETABLE TART

TARTE AUX LÉGUMES

- 1 quantity shortcrust pastry (p.784)
- 120 g (4 oz) French beans, diced
- 120 g (4 oz) shelled peas
- 120 g (4 oz) carrots, diced
- 120 g (4 oz) potatoes, diced
- ½ quantity béchamel sauce (p.50)
- 60 g (2 oz) Gruyère cheese, grated
- 3 tablespoons dried breadcrumbs

Preparation time: 45 minutes
Cooking time: 45 minutes
Serves 6

Preheat the oven to 200°C/400°F/Gas Mark 6. Line a 23-cm (9-inch) tart tin with the pastry and bake the pastry blind. Cook the vegetables in salted water for 3–4 minutes, until just tender. Drain thoroughly. Gently spread half the béchamel sauce over the base of the cooked pastry case, then add the vegetables. Cover with the remaining sauce. Sprinkle with the cheese and breadcrumbs. Bake for 10–15 minutes, or until golden brown.

LETTUCE

To prepare, cut off any wilted leaves. Cut out the core. Wash carefully by plunging the leaves head first into cold water. Wash in several changes of water and drain. If the lettuce is to be cooked, blanch it in boiling salted water for 1–2 minutes. Refresh in a bowl of chilled water and drain well.

BRAISED LETTUCE
LAITUES À L'ÉTUVÉE

Melt 60 g (2 oz) of the butter in a large pan. Prepare the lettuces (see above), add to the pan and braise over a gentle heat for 10 minutes. Add the onion and stock and season with salt and pepper. Cover tightly and cook for 1 hour. Prepare the printanière or Chivry sauce. Melt the remaining butter in a frying pan and fry the bread slices over a medium heat until golden brown on both sides. Arrange a lettuce (or half a lettuce, if using large ones) on each slice. Serve with the sauce in a sauce boat.

- 80 g (2¾ oz) butter
- 3 large or 6 small lettuces
- 1 onion, finely chopped
- 100 ml (3½ fl oz) light stock
- Salt and pepper
- 1 quantity printanière or Chivry sauce (p.54)
- 6 slices bread

Preparation time: 25 minutes
Cooking time: 1 hour 20 minutes
Serves 6

BOUQUETIÈRE OF VEGETABLES
BOUQUETIÈRE DE LÉGUMES

Cut the carrots, turnips and potatoes into small olive-shaped pieces. Separate the cauliflower into small florets. Cook all the vegetables separately in boiling salted water until tender, and cut the French beans into dice after cooking. Place the vegetables separately on a serving dish and top with the parsley and butter. If desired, the potatoes may be fried in butter after cooking.

- 150 g (5 oz) carrots
- 150 g (5 oz) turnips
- 200 g (7 oz) potatoes
- 1 small cauliflower
- 200 g (7 oz) French beans
- 200 g (7 oz) shelled peas
- 150 g (5 oz) flageolet beans
- 1 handful of flat-leaf parsley, chopped
- 50 g (1¾ oz) butter

Preparation time: 30 minutes
Cooking time: 45 minutes
Serves 6

CORN ON THE COB

To prepare, remove the leaves and any long fibres. Cut the stalk so that it is level with the bottom of the cob. Wash in cold water. Place in boiling water with a little milk, allowing 100 ml (3½ fl oz) of milk per 2 litres (3½ pints) water. Do not add salt, as this toughens the corn. Simmer for 15–20 minutes until tender. The kernels should come away easily from the cobs. Drain and serve hot.

CORN ON THE COB WITH BUTTER
MAÏS AU BEURRE

Prepare and cook the corn on the cobs (see above). Serve hot on a dish covered with a napkin, with butter and salt.

- **6 corn on the cobs**
- **Butter, to taste**
- **Salt**

  Preparation time: 5 minutes
  Cooking time: 20 minutes
  Serves 6

CHESTNUTS

To prepare, carefully cut a cross in the rounded part of the shell of each chestnut with a sharp knife. Bring a large pan of water to the boil and blanch the chestnuts in the water for 2 minutes. Drain, allow to cool slightly and remove the shells. Cook the chestnuts for another 10 minutes in fresh boiling water. Remove them from the water in batches and remove the inner skins while they are still hot (the skin sticks to the nuts as they cool). Cook for a further 10–15 minutes in simmering water or milk. Drain and serve with salt and butter.

CHESTNUTS WITH ONIONS

MARRONS AUX OIGNONS

- 1 kg (2¼ lb) small chestnuts
- 40 g (1½ oz) butter
- 250 g (9 oz) onions, chopped
- Salt and pepper
- 1 litre (1¾ pints) stock

Preparation time: 45 minutes
Cooking time: 40 minutes
Serves 6

Prepare the chestnuts (p.558). Melt the butter in a pan and cook the onions over a medium heat for 5 minutes, until golden. Add the chestnuts and season with salt and pepper. Pour in the stock and simmer for 15–20 minutes.

CHESTNUT PURÉE

MARRONS EN PURÉE

- 1 kg (2¼ lb) chestnuts
- 750 ml (1¼ pints) milk
- 1 teaspoon caster sugar
- 1 teaspoon salt
- 40 g (1½ oz) butter

Preparation time: 1 hour
Cooking time: 30 minutes
Serves 6

Prepare the chestnuts (p.558). Place them in a pan with the milk, sugar and salt and bring to the boil. Reduce the heat and simmer for 30 minutes. Remove the chestnuts and process to a purée in a food processor. Moisten with a little of the cooking liquid, and beat in the butter. Season with salt and pepper for a savoury purée, or add sugar to make a sweet purée.

TURNIPS

To prepare, peel the turnips. Cut in slices, dice or quarters, as required, and cook in boiling salted water until tender, about 10–20 minutes depending on the size of the pieces.

TURNIP & POTATO PURÉE

NAVETS EN PURÉE

- 500 g (1 lb 2 oz) turnips
- 500 g (1 lb 2 oz) potatoes
- 40 g (1½ oz) butter
- Milk, to taste (optional)
- Pepper

Preparation time: 30 minutes
Cooking time: 15 minutes
Serves 6

Bring a large pan of salted water to the boil. Cut the turnips and potatoes into pieces and cook together for 15 minutes, or until tender. Drain thoroughly and pass through a food mill or potato ricer. Beat the butter and, if desired, a little milk into the mashed vegetables. Season with pepper.

ONIONS

To cook, peel the onions and place, whole, in boiling salted water. Simmer for 10–15 minutes, depending on size.

GLAZED ONIONS
OIGNONS GLACÉS

Put the onions in a frying pan and add enough veal stock, if using, or water to just cover them. Season with salt and pepper and add the butter. Cover with a disc of greaseproof paper or half cover with a lid and cook over a gentle heat until the onions are tender and most of the liquid has evaporated. Gently roll the onions in the bottom of the frying pan so that they become glazed with the remaining liquid. They can be used as a garnish for many dishes.

- 500 g (1 lb 2 oz) pearl or button onions, peeled
- Veal stock, to cover (optional)
- Salt and pepper
- 100 g (3½ oz) butter

Preparation time: 10 minutes
Cooking time: 30 minutes
Serves 6

ONION PURÉE
OIGNONS EN PURÉE

Cook the onions (see above) and make the béchamel sauce. Process the onions in a blender or food processor until smooth, then stir them into the sauce. Season with salt and pepper.

- 750 g (1 lb 10 oz) medium onions
- 1 quantity béchamel sauce (p.50)
- Salt and pepper

Preparation time: 20 minutes
Cooking time: 30 minutes
Serves 6

STUFFED ONIONS
OIGNONS FARCIS

 p.599

Bring a large pan of water to the boil and add the onions, then reduce the heat and simmer for 15 minutes. Preheat the oven to 200°C/400°F/Gas Mark 6 and grease an ovenproof dish with butter. Prepare the stuffing. Drain the cooked onions and hollow each one out with a spoon, without cutting through the base. Mix the stuffing and white sauce together and fill the hollowed-out onions with this mixture. Place in the prepared dish. Sprinkle with the breadcrumbs, dot with the butter and bake for 25 minutes.

- 40 g (1½ oz) butter, plus extra for greasing
- 6 large Spanish onions
- 200 g (7 oz) stuffing for red meats (p.80) or duxelles (p.81)
- ½ quantity white sauce (p.50)
- 3 tablespoons dried breadcrumbs

Preparation time: 45 minutes
Cooking time: 45 minutes
Serves 6

ONION TART

TARTE À L'OIGNON

This recipe comes from the Alsace region in eastern France.

Preheat the oven to 200°C/400°F/Gas Mark 6. Make the shortcrust pastry and allow it to rest while making the filling. In a pan, melt 60 g (2 oz) of the butter and fry the onions over a medium heat until all the liquid has evaporated and they are starting to brown. Stir in the flour and eggs. Season with salt and pepper, and add a little milk to loosen the mixture if necessary. Roll out the pastry and use it to line a tart tin. Cover the pastry with the onion filling and bake for 30 minutes.

- 1 quantity shortcrust pastry (p.784)

For the filling:
- 75 g (2½ oz) butter
- 500 g (1 lb 2 oz) onions, sliced
- 30 g (1¼ oz) flour
- 2 eggs, beaten
- Salt and pepper
- Milk (optional)

Preparation time: 30 minutes
Cooking time: 30 minutes
Serves 6

SORREL

To prepare, remove the stalks from any large leaves. Wash the leaves in plenty of cold water. Blanch in boiling water for 1–2 minutes. Drain immediately and use in a dish, or add a little butter and allow to wilt. Since sorrel's volume reduces greatly in cooking, at least 200 g (7 oz) per person should be allowed.

BRAISED SORREL

OSEILLE AU JUS

Heat the butter in a large pan and add the sorrel a handful at a time. Sprinkle with the flour. Add the sugar, season with salt and pepper and simmer for 5 minutes. Add the stock and simmer gently for 30 minutes. Process in a blender to a smooth purée, thinning if necessary with a little more stock.

- 40 g (1½ oz) butter
- 1.2 kg (2½ lb) sorrel
- 20 g (¾ oz) flour
- 1 pinch of caster sugar
- Salt and pepper
- 400 ml (14 fl oz) veal stock, plus extra for thinning

Preparation time: 5 minutes
Cooking time: 35 minutes
Serves 6

PEAS

To prepare, shell the peas shortly before cooking. Keep them wrapped in a cloth until ready to cook. 1 kg (2¼ lb) unshelled peas yields 350–400 g (12–14 oz) shelled peas. Mangetout peas can be cooked in the same way as peas, but the pod is also eaten. Each pod should have the string removed like a runner bean, by breaking each end and pulling away the string, although this is often not necessary for very young mangetout.

PEAS À L'ANGLAISE
PETITS POIS À L'ANGLAISE

- 3 teaspoons salt, plus extra to taste
- 1 kg (2¼ lb) shelled peas
- 40 g (1½ oz) butter
- Chopped herbs, such as mint, savory and fennel, to serve

Preparation time: 10 minutes
Cooking time: 10 minutes
Serves 6

Place 3 litres (5¼ pints) water and the salt in a pan and bring to the boil. Once boiling, add the peas and cook for 6–8 minutes. They should be tender but firm. Drain and season with extra salt, if desired. Serve the peas in a warm dish and offer the butter and selection of herbs separately.

VARIATION

PEAS WITH CREAM
PETITS POIS À LA CRÈME

Proceed as above and stir in 250 ml (8 fl oz) cream sauce (p.51). Serve with the selection of herbs, but omit the butter.

PEAS À LA PAYSANNE
PETITS POIS À LA PAYSANNE

- 1 kg (2¼ lb) shelled peas
- 60 g (2 oz) butter, chilled
- 1 lettuce, shredded
- 1 onion, finely chopped
- Salt
- 1 teaspoon caster sugar

Preparation time: 15 minutes
Cooking time: 20 minutes
Serves 6

Put the peas in a pan with 750 ml (1¼ pints) water, half the butter, and the lettuce and onion. Season with salt. Bring rapidly to the boil, then reduce the heat and simmer for 15 minutes. Add the sugar and remaining butter just before serving.

PEAS À LA FRANÇAISE
PETITS POIS À LA FRANÇAISE

Heat the butter in a large pan or high-sided frying pan. Add the onions, cover and braise over a very low heat for 10 minutes. Add the peas, lettuces and sugar and season with salt. Cover and simmer over a very low heat for 30 minutes.

NOTE
If using frozen peas, add them to the pan 10 minutes before the end of cooking time.

- **40 g (1½ oz) butter**
- **50 g (1¾ oz) pearl onions**
- **1 kg (2¼ lb) shelled peas**
- **2 lettuces, shredded**
- **1 teaspoon caster sugar**
- **Salt**

Preparation time: 15 minutes
Cooking time: 45 minutes
Serves 6

PEAS À LA FLAMANDE
PETITS POIS À LA FLAMANDE

Put the butter and carrots in a pan with 500 ml (18 fl oz) water. Bring to the boil and cook for 15 minutes. Add the peas and salt and cook gently for 30 minutes. To add more flavour, the pea pods can be cooked with the carrots. They should be removed before serving.

- **750 g (1 lb 10 oz) shelled peas**
- **40 g (1½ oz) butter**
- **250 g (9 oz) young carrots, diced**
- **Salt**

Preparation time: 40 minutes
Cooking time: 45 minutes
Serves 6

LEEKS

The white part of the leek is the best part to use, although the tougher green upper part is good for soups and stews. Remove the roots, cut out any damaged leaves and wash very carefully to remove any soil trapped between the layers. Place in boiling salted water and boil, uncovered, for around 20 minutes if cooking whole small leeks, or around 8 minutes if sliced.

LEEKS SERVED LIKE ASPARAGUS
POIREAUX EN ASPERGES

- ◆ 24 medium leeks
- ◆ 1 quantity mousseline sauce
  (p.75), white sauce (p.50),
  poulette sauce (p.52),
  vinaigrette (p.66)
  or mayonnaise (p.70)

Preparation time: 10 minutes
Cooking time: 20 minutes
Serves 6

Prepare and cook the leeks (p.564). Drain well and serve with mousseline, white or poulette sauce, or with vinaigrette or mayonaise, in a sauce boat.

 p.600

LEEK GRATIN
POIREAUX EN GRATIN

- ◆ 24 medium leeks
- ◆ 1 quantity white sauce (p.50)
- ◆ Grated Gruyère cheese,
  for sprinkling

Preparation time: 20 minutes
Cooking time: 40 minutes
Serves 6

Preheat the oven to 200°C/400°F/Gas Mark 6. Prepare and cook the leeks whole (p.564) and prepare the white sauce. Drain the leeks well and put in a large ovenproof dish, or several individual ovenproof dishes. Coat with the sauce, sprinkle with the cheese and bake for 20 minutes, or until golden brown.

LEEK PURÉE
PURÉE DE POIREAUX

- ◆ 12 leeks, sliced
- ◆ 500 g (1 lb 2 oz) potatoes,
  chopped
- ◆ Salt
- ◆ 200 ml (7 fl oz) crème fraîche

Preparation time: 20 minutes
Cooking time: 40 minutes
Serves 6

Prepare the leeks (p.564). Bring a pan of salted water to the boil, add the leeks and cook for 8 minutes, or until tender. Add the potatoes, reduce the heat and simmer for a further 15–20 minutes. When the potatoes are tender, drain thoroughly and process the leeks and potatoes in a blender or food processor to make a smooth purée. Season with salt, stir in the crème fraîche and serve.

LEEK PIE

FLAMICHE PICARDE

Wash and thinly slice the leeks, put them in a pan with 40 g (1½ oz) of the butter, and season with salt and pepper. Cook over a very low heat for 30 minutes, stirring frequently. Preheat the oven to 220°C/425°F/Gas Mark 7 and grease a pie dish with 15 g (½ oz) of the butter. In a bowl, combine the flour, the remaining butter, the eggs and egg whites, and a pinch of salt. Knead to make a dough and divide into 2 balls.

Roll the dough balls out thinly on a well-floured work surface. Line the prepared dish with one of the pieces of dough. Remove the leeks from the heat, and stir in the egg yolks and crème fraîche. Taste and season again if necessary. Fill the pastry-lined dish with the leek and crème fraîche mixture. Cover with the remaining dough and decorate by scoring patterns with a knife. Seal the edges of the pastry with a little water. Bake for 30 minutes, or until brown. Serve hot.

- 10 large leeks, white parts only
- 140 g (4½ oz) butter, softened
- Salt and pepper
- 250 g (9 oz) flour, plus extra for dusting
- 3 eggs
- 2 eggs, separated
- 125 ml (4½ fl oz) crème fraîche

Preparation time: 30 minutes
Cooking time: 30 minutes
Serves 6

POTATOES

There are many varieties of potato which, for culinary purposes, can be divided into two groups: floury potatoes used for soups, mashed potatoes and toppings, such as King Edward, Desirée and Maris Piper, and waxy potatoes used for chips, fried potatoes, garnishes, and salads, such as Charlotte, Nicola, Ratte or Roseval. Both kinds can be used in a huge variety of dishes.

POTATOES BOILED IN THEIR SKINS

POMMES DE TERRE EN ROBE DES CHAMPS

Wash the potatoes thoroughly. Put them in a pan, cover with cold salted water and bring to the boil. Reduce the heat and simmer gently for 20 minutes or until tender. Drain and, if possible, dry out for 10 minutes over a very low heat, stirring constantly, before serving with the butter.

- 1.5 kg (3¼ lb) small potatoes, unpeeled
- Salt
- Cold butter, to serve

Preparation time: 5 minutes
Cooking time: 20 minutes
Serves 6

POTATOES À L'ANGLAISE

POMMES DE TERRE À L'ANGLAISE

- 1.5 kg (3¼ lb) small potatoes
- 50 g (1¾ oz) butter, melted
- Salt
- 1 handful of flat-leaf parsley, chopped

Preparation time: 20 minutes
Cooking time: 25 minutes
Serves 6

Bring a pan of salted water to the boil and add the potatoes, then reduce the heat and simmer for 15 minutes, or until tender. Drain. Pour the butter over the potatoes, season with salt and sprinkle with the parsley.

STEAMED POTATOES

POMMES DE TERRE VAPEUR

- 1.5 kg (3¼ lb) small potatoes
- 50 g (1¾ oz) butter, melted
- Salt
- 1 handful of flat-leaf parsley, chopped

Preparation time: 20 minutes
Cooking time: 25 minutes
Serves 6

Rinse the potatoes and put them in a steaming basket set over a covered pan of water. Bring to the boil, then reduce the heat and simmer for 15–20 minutes. Pour the butter over the potatoes, season with salt and sprinkle with the parsley.

POTATO SALAD

POMMES DE TERRE EN SALADE

- 1 kg (2¼ lb) waxy potatoes, unpeeled
- 1 quantity vinaigrette (p.66)
- 1 onion, finely chopped
- 1 tablespoon finely chopped flat-leaf parsley
- 2 eggs, hard boiled and sliced (optional)
- 1 beetroot, cooked and sliced (optional)

Preparation time: 20 minutes
Cooking time: 20 minutes
Serves 6

Bring a pan of salted water to the boil, and add the potatoes, then reduce the heat and simmer for 20 minutes, or until tender. Allow to cool slightly, then peel and slice thinly into a salad bowl. Dress with the vinaigrette, then gently stir in the onion and parsley, and hard-boiled eggs and beetroot, if using.

NOTE
To prevent the salad being too dry, a little stock or milk can be placed in the bottom of the salad bowl, before the salad ingredients are combined.

STUFFED POTATOES

POMMES DE TERRE FARCIES

Cut the potatoes in half. Hollow them out with a teaspoon and cook in boiling salted water for 10 minutes, or until tender. Drain well. Preheat the oven to 220°C/425°F/Gas Mark 7, and grease an ovenproof dish with the butter. Fill the potato halves with the stuffing. Place them in the prepared dish and pour over the meat juices or stock and the hot water. Bake for 25 minutes.

- 1 kg (2¼ lb) evenly sized potatoes
- 10 g (¼ oz) butter
- 200 g (7 oz) stuffing for red meat (p.80) or duxelles (p.81)
- 100 ml (3½ fl oz) meat juices or concentrated meat stock
- 100 ml (3½ fl oz) hot water

Preparation time: 15 minutes
Cooking time: 35 minutes
Serves 6

POTATOES À LA POULETTE

POMMES DE TERRE À LA POULETTE

Cook the potatoes in their skins (p.566). Preheat the oven to 220°C/425°F/Gas Mark 7 and grease an ovenproof dish with butter. Drain the potatoes, peel them and cut into slices. Put a layer of half the potatoes in the prepared dish. Cover with half the white sauce and half the cheese. Put in a layer of the remaining potatoes and cover with the remaining sauce and cheese. Bake for 20 minutes, or until golden brown.

- 750 g (1 lb 10 oz) potatoes, unpeeled
- Butter, for greasing
- 1 quantity white sauce (p.50)
- 125 g (4¼ oz) Gruyère cheese, grated

Preparation time: 20 minutes
Cooking time: 50 minutes
Serves 6

MASHED POTATOES

PURÉE DE POMMES DE TERRE

Put the potatoes in a pan and cover with cold salted water. Bring to the boil, then reduce the heat and simmer for 20 minutes, or until tender. Drain thoroughly and pass through a food mill or potato ricer while the potatoes are still hot. Beat in the butter and milk with a wooden spoon. Season with salt. Do not cook or beat the purée after adding the butter and milk.

- 1 kg (2¼ lb) potatoes
- 60 g (2 oz) butter
- 500 ml (18 fl oz) hot milk
- Salt

Preparation time: 15 minutes
Cooking time: 20 minutes
Serves 6

POTATO GRATIN

POMMES DE TERRE EN GRATIN

- 60 g (2 oz) butter
- 1 quantity mashed potatoes (p.568)
- 125 g (4¼ oz) Gruyère cheese, grated (optional)
- 2 egg yolks (optional)
- 100 ml (3½ fl oz) crème fraîche

Preparation time: 10 minutes
Cooking time: 20–25 minutes
Serves 6

Preheat the oven to 220°C/425°F/Gas Mark 7 and grease a gratin dish with some of the butter. Spread the potatoes in the prepared dish and dot with the remaining butter. The potatoes can be enriched by adding the cheese, egg yolks or crème fraîche. Bake for 20–25 minutes, or until golden brown.

POTATO CROQUETTES

POMMES DE TERRE EN CROQUETTES

- 1 quantity mashed potatoes (p.568)
- Salt and pepper
- Flour, for rolling
- 2 eggs, beaten
- Dried breadcrumbs, for rolling
- Vegetable oil, for deep-frying

Preparation time: 30 minutes
Cooking time: 20 minutes
Serves 6

Season the potatoes with salt and pepper and allow to cool. Shape into croquettes, and roll them in the flour. Dip the croquettes in the beaten egg, then in the breadcrumbs. Heat the oil in a deep-fryer to 180°C/350°F, or until a cube of bread browns in 30 seconds. Fry the croquettes in batches until golden brown, then drain well.

COTTAGE PIE

HACHIS PARMENTIER

- Butter, for greasing and dotting
- 1 quantity mashed potatoes (p.568)
- Salt and pepper
- 1 quantity stuffing for red meats (p.80)
- Gruyère cheese, grated, for sprinkling

Preparation time: 35 minutes
Cooking time: 20–25 minutes
Serves 6

Preheat the oven to 200°C/400°F/Gas Mark 6 and grease an ovenproof dish with butter. Season the potatoes with salt and pepper. Put a layer of potatoes in the prepared dish, cover with the stuffing and top with another layer of potatoes. Dot with butter and sprinkle with the cheese. Bake for 20–25 minutes, until golden brown.

EGGS IN POTATO NESTS

ŒUFS PARMENTIER

Make fairly thick mashed potatoes (p.568) with the potatoes, milk and butter. Season with salt and pepper. Preheat the oven to 220°C/425°F/Gas Mark 7 and grease a shallow ovenproof dish with butter. Spread the potatoes in the prepared dish. Hollow out 6 holes with the back of a spoon and break 1 egg into each hole. Cover with the crème fraîche, season again lightly with salt and pepper and bake for 15 minutes, or until browned.

- 750 g (1 lb 10 oz) potatoes
- 500 ml (18 fl oz) milk
- 50 g (1¾ oz) butter
- Salt and pepper
- 6 eggs
- 200 ml (7 fl oz) crème fraîche

Preparation time: 45 minutes
Cooking time: 15 minutes
Serves 6

DUCHESSE POTATOES

POMMES DE TERRE DUCHESSE

Cook and mash the potatoes (p.568). Beat in the butter, 2 of the eggs and the egg yolks, and season with salt, pepper and nutmeg. Preheat the oven to 220°C/425°F/Gas Mark 7 and grease a baking tray with butter. Spread out the potatoes to a thickness of 1 cm (½ inch) on another tray, allow to cool, then chill in the refrigerator until firm. Cut the potatoes into squares, diamonds, rectangles or bun shapes as desired. Dip in the flour, brush with the remaining egg and place on the prepared tray. Bake for 15 minutes, until well browned. Serve as a garnish.

- 1 kg (2¼ lb) potatoes
- 70 g (2½ oz) butter, plus extra for greasing
- 3 eggs, lightly beaten
- 3 egg yolks
- Freshly grated nutmeg
- Flour, for dipping
- Salt and pepper

Preparation time: 30 minutes
Cooking time: 35 minutes
Serves 6

DAUPHINE POTATOES

POMMES DE TERRE DAUPHINE

Cook and mash the potatoes (p.568) with the egg yolks, 1 of the eggs and the butter. Make the choux pastry and mix it with the potatoes in the proportion of one-third pastry to two-thirds mashed potatoes. Season well with salt, pepper and nutmeg. Form the mixture into small egg shapes. Dip in the remaining eggs, then roll in the breadcrumbs. Heat the oil in a deep-fryer to 180°C/350°F, or until a cube of bread browns in 30 seconds. Fry in batches until golden brown. Serve as a garnish.

- 500 g (1 lb 2 oz) potatoes
- 3 egg yolks
- 3 eggs, lightly beaten
- 40 g (1½ oz) butter
- ½ quantity choux pastry (p.774)
- Salt and pepper
- Freshly grated nutmeg
- 100 g (3½ oz) dried breadcrumbs
- Vegetable oil, for deep-frying

Preparation time: 40 minutes
Cooking time: 45 minutes
Serves 6

p.601

DAUPHINOIS POTATOES
GRATIN DAUPHINOIS

- **50 g (1¾ oz) butter, plus extra for greasing**
- **1 kg (2¼ lb) potatoes**
- **Salt and pepper**
- **1 garlic clove (optional)**
- **250 ml (8 fl oz) crème fraîche**

Preparation time: 20 minutes
Cooking time: 1½ hours
Serves 6

Preheat the oven to 180°C/350°F/Gas Mark 4 and grease an ovenproof dish with butter. Cut the potatoes into thin slices. Wash and pat dry in a cloth and season with salt and pepper. Rub the prepared dish with a garlic clove, if desired. Layer the potatoes in the dish to within 1 cm (½ inch) of the rim. Cover with the crème fraîche. Dot with the butter and bake for 1½ hours, or until the potatoes are tender.

POTATO GNOCCHI
GNOCCHIS AUX POMMES DE TERRE

- **1 kg (2¼ lb) potatoes, quartered**
- **2 eggs**
- **2 egg yolks**
- **70 g (2½ oz) butter, plus extra for greasing**
- **100 g (3½ oz) flour**
- **Salt**
- **Freshly grated nutmeg**
- **60 g (2 oz) Gruyère cheese, grated**

Preparation time: 40 minutes
Cooking time: 45 minutes
Serves 6

Preheat the oven to 220°C/425°F/Gas Mark 7 and grease an ovenproof dish with butter. Cook the potatoes in boiling salted water until tender. Drain well, mash and beat in the eggs, egg yolks, 30 g (1¼ oz) of the butter and the flour. Season with salt and nutmeg. Bring a large pan of water to the boil over a high heat. Form the potato mixture into small egg shapes. Flatten them slightly, then poach them, in batches, in the boiling water for 3–4 minutes. Lift out with a slotted spoon and drain on kitchen paper. Arrange the gnocchi in the prepared dish. Sprinkle with the cheese, dot with the remaining butter and bake for 15 minutes, until golden.

POTATO FRITTERS
BEIGNETS DE POMMES DE TERRE

- **1 kg (2¼ lb) potatoes**
- **5 eggs**
- **Mixed herbs, such as flat-leaf parsley, chives, chervil and tarragon, chopped**
- **Salt and pepper**
- **Vegetable oil, for deep-frying**

Preparation time: 15 minutes
Cooking time: 10 minutes
Makes 10 fritters

Grate the potatoes. Place in a colander and press down firmly to drain off the liquid. Beat the eggs in a large bowl and stir in the potatoes. Stir in the herbs and season with salt and pepper. Heat the oil in a deep-fryer to 180°C/350°F, or until a cube of bread browns in 30 seconds. Carefully lower spoonfuls of the potatoes, in batches, into the hot oil. Cook for 3 minutes on each side and drain well before serving.

AUVERGNE-STYLE POTATOES
POMMES DE TERRE À L'AUVERGNATE

Preheat the oven to 240°C/475°F/Gas Mark 8 and grease a flameproof dish with butter. Rinse the potatoes under cold running water and cut into thin slices. Layer some of the slices in the prepared dish. Sprinkle with a little of the garlic, season with salt and pepper, and add a few small knobs of butter and a little oil. Continue layering until all the ingredients are used up. Cover with the bacon. Pour the stock over the potatoes. Bring to the boil on top of the stove, then transfer to the oven and bake for 50 minutes, or until the potatoes are tender.

- 40 g (1½ oz) butter, plus extra for greasing
- 1 kg (2¼ lb) potatoes
- 1 garlic clove, finely chopped
- Salt and pepper
- 40 g (1½ oz) oil
- 60 g (2 oz) thin smoked bacon rashers
- 100 ml (3½ fl oz) any stock

Preparation time: 20 minutes
Cooking time: 1 hour
Serves 6

POTATO CAKE
GÂTEAU DE POMMES DE TERRE

Preheat the oven to 220°C/425°F/Gas Mark 7 and grease a baking tray with butter. Cook the potatoes in simmering salted water until tender, then drain and cool. Peel the potatoes, mash them, and add the flour, milk and 1 of the eggs. Season with salt and pepper. Place the potatoes on the prepared baking tray and shape into a flat cake. Score the top in a diamond pattern, brush with the remaining egg and dot with the butter. Bake until browned, about 15 minutes.

- 60 g (2 oz) butter, plus extra for greasing
- 1 kg (2¼ lb) potatoes, unpeeled
- 80 g (2¾ oz) flour
- 200 ml (7 fl oz) milk
- 2 eggs
- Salt and pepper

Preparation time: 15 minutes
Cooking time: 45 minutes
Serves 6

RENAISSANCE TIMBALE
TIMBALE RENAISSANCE

Cook the potatoes in boiling salted water for 20 minutes, or until tender. Drain and allow to cool. Preheat the oven to 200°C/400°F/Gas Mark 6 and grease a charlotte mould with butter. Peel and mash the potatoes, then stir in the ham and eggs. Stir in the crème fraîche and butter. Season with salt and pepper. When the mixture is very smooth, place it in the prepared mould. Bake for 45 minutes. Turn out and serve very hot.

- 1 kg (2¼ lb) evenly sized potatoes, unpeeled
- 60 g (2 oz) butter, softened, plus extra for greasing
- 125 g (4¼ oz) ham, diced
- 3 eggs, beaten
- 100 ml (3½ fl oz) crème fraîche
- Salt and pepper

Preparation time: 20 minutes
Cooking time: 45 minutes
Serves 6

SAVOY POTATO LOAF

FARÇON SAVOYARD

- 40 g (1½ oz) butter, plus extra for greasing
- 1 kg (2¼ lb) potatoes
- 500 ml (18 fl oz) hot milk
- 100 g (3½ oz) chervil, finely chopped
- 6 eggs
- Salt and pepper

Preparation time: 30 minutes
Cooking time: 45 minutes
Serves 6

Preheat the oven to 200°C/400°F/Gas Mark 6 and grease an ovenproof dish with butter. Cook the potatoes in boiling salted water until tender, then mash them with the hot milk, chervil and butter. Beat in the eggs and season with salt and pepper. Put in the prepared dish and brown in the oven for 25 minutes.

POTATO CAKES

POMMES MACAIRE

- 1 kg (2¼ lb) large potatoes, unpeeled
- 120 g (4 oz) butter
- Salt and pepper
- Freshly grated nutmeg

Preparation time: 20 minutes
Cooking time: 1 hour 20 minutes
Serves 6

Preheat the oven to 200°C/400°F/Gas Mark 6. Wash the potatoes, dry them and bake them in their skins until tender (about 45–60 minutes depending on their size). Scoop the flesh out of the skins and place in a bowl. Mash with a fork, mixing in 100 g (3½ oz) of the butter. Season with salt, pepper and nutmeg. Melt a knob of the remaining butter in a frying pan. Cover the pan with 3 cm (1¼ inches) of potato and cook over a medium heat until the base is browned, about 5–10 minutes. Gently slide the potato cake out onto a plate, cover with another plate and turn over. Heat another knob of butter in the pan, return the potato cake to the pan (uncooked side down), and cook until browned. Depending on the size of the frying pan, 2, 3 or 4 cakes may be made. Serve as a side dish.

SURPRISE POTATOES

POMMES DE TERRE SURPRISE

- 500 g (1 lb 2 oz) potatoes
- 50 g (1¾ oz) butter
- Salt and pepper
- 1 quantity choux pastry (p.774)
- Vegetable oil, for deep-frying

Preparation time: 30 minutes
Cooking time: 30 minutes
Serves 6

Cook the potatoes in boiling salted water for 20 minutes, or until tender. Mash through a ricer or food mill, beat in the butter and season with salt and pepper. Make the choux pastry dough and mix it with the mashed potatoes. Butter a shallow dish and spread the mixture 1 cm (½ inch) deep on the dish. Cool, then chill in the refrigerator until firm. Cut into small rounds using a plain pastry cutter. Heat the oil in a deep-fryer to 180°C/350°F or until a cube of bread browns in 30 seconds. Fry in batches in the hot oil until golden brown.

POTATOES COOKED IN BUTTER

POMMES DE TERRE AU BEURRE

If using large potatoes, make small balls with a melon baller and dry them on kitchen paper. Heat the butter in a heavy-based pan, add the potatoes and cook over a gentle heat for 15–20 minutes, shaking the pan frequently so that the potatoes brown evenly. Sprinkle with salt and the parsley and serve.

- 1 kg (2¼ lb) small new potatoes or large potatoes
- 60 g (2 oz) butter
- ½ teaspoon salt
- 1 tablespoon flat-leaf parsley, finely chopped

Preparation time: 25 minutes
Cooking time: 15–20 minutes
Serves 6

SAUTÉ POTATOES

POMMES DE TERRE SAUTÉES

Bring a pan of water to the boil, add the potatoes, then reduce the heat and simmer for 15 minutes, or until almost cooked. Drain. Allow to cool, then slice. Heat the butter in a frying pan and fry the potatoes over a medium heat until golden, shaking the pan frequently so that they brown evenly. Sprinkle with salt and the parsley and serve.

- 750 g (1 lb 10 oz) potatoes
- 60 g (2 oz) butter
- ½ teaspoon salt
- 1 tablespoon flat-leaf parsley, finely chopped

Preparation time: 10 minutes
Cooking time: 25 minutes
Serves 6

POTATO STEW

POMMES DE TERRE EN RAGOUT

Heat the butter in a large pan and fry the bacon and onions for 5–10 minutes over a medium heat, until golden. Add the flour and make a blond roux (p.57) with the stock. Season with salt and pepper and add the bouquet garni. Add the potatoes and cook over a very low heat for 1¼ hours, or until the potatoes are tender. Remove the bouquet garni before serving.

- 20 g (¾ oz) butter
- 125 g (4¼ oz) bacon, diced
- 100 g (3½ oz) onions, chopped
- 30 g (1¼ oz) flour
- 500 ml (18 fl oz) any stock
- Salt and pepper
- 1 bouquet garni
- 750 g (1 lb 10 oz) medium potatoes, quartered

Preparation time: 30 minutes
Cooking time: 1¼ hours
Serves 6

p.602

ANNA POTATOES
POMMES DE TERRE ANNA

- **1 kg (2¼ lb) new potatoes**
- **1 tablespoon goose fat or oil**
- **100 g (3½ oz) butter, melted**
- **Salt and pepper**

Preparation time: 30 minutes
Cooking time: 1¼ hours
Serves 6

Peel or scrub the potatoes. Cut one-third of them into 2-mm (⅛-inch) slices and place in a bowl of salted water for 10 minutes. Meanwhile, heat the goose fat or oil in a solid-based round cake tin or shallow ovenproof pan until very hot. Drain the potato slices and dry with kitchen paper. Protecting your hands with oven gloves, carefully tilt the hot fat in the tin to coat the sides and base, then pour any surplus out. Arrange the potato slices neatly around the base and sides of the tin, overlapping them. Preheat the oven to 200°C/400°F/Gas Mark 6.

Cut the remaining potatoes into 1-cm (½-inch) slices. Heat some of the butter in a frying pan, add the potatoes and fry them over a high heat until they start to brown. Arrange in the prepared cake tin in layers, pressing each layer down, seasoning them with salt and pepper and brushing with the remaining butter. Continue until the tin is full. Cover and cook for about 1 hour. Turn out and serve hot. The potatoes should form a golden-brown cake.

CHIPS
POMMES DE TERRE FRITES OU PONT-NEUF

- **1.2 kg (2½ lb) potatoes**
- **Vegetable oil, for deep-frying**
- **Salt**

Preparation time: 20 minutes
Cooking time: 15 minutes
Serves 6

Cut the potatoes into fingers 1 cm (½ inch) thick. Dry on kitchen paper. Heat the oil in a deep-fryer to 180°C/350°F or until a cube of bread browns in 30 seconds. Carefully lower the potatoes into the hot oil and cook until softened but not coloured. Remove the chips from the oil and heat it to 190°C/375°F. Put the chips back in the oil and cook until brown. Serve hot, sprinkled with salt.

CRISPS
POMMES DE TERRE CHIPS

- **800 g (1¾ lb) potatoes**
- **Vegetable oil, for deep-frying**
- **Salt**

Preparation time: 20 minutes
Cooking time: 5 minutes
Serves 6

Cut the potatoes into very thin slices, preferably with a mandolin. Heat the oil in a deep-fryer to 180°C/350°F, or until a cube of bread browns in 30 seconds. Carefully lower the potatoes into the hot oil and fry until the crisps rise to the surface. As they cook, they may need to be gently separated with a long-handled spoon. Drain and serve immediately, sprinkled with salt.

POTATO STRAWS
POMMES DE TERRE PAILLE

Cut the potatoes into 3-mm (⅛-inch) thick straws. Heat the oil in a deep-fryer to 180°C/350°F, or until a cube of bread browns in 30 seconds. Carefully lower the straws into the hot oil and cook until tender but not coloured. Remove the straws. Increase the heat to 190°C/375°F and cook again for about 10 seconds, until browned. Drain well and sprinkle with salt to serve.

- **1 kg (2¼ lb) potatoes**
- **Vegetable oil, for deep-frying**
- **Salt**

Preparation time: 20 minutes
Cooking time: 2 minutes
Serves 6

POTATO PUFFS
POMMES DE TERRE SOUFFLÉS

Cut the potatoes into 3-mm (⅛-inch) slices. Dry the slices. Heat the oil in 2 deep-fryers to 180°C/350°F, or until a cube of bread browns in 30 seconds. Increase the heat in the second fryer to 190°C/375°F. This will be used to puff the potatoes. Lower the slices into the hot oil in the first fryer and cook for 7 minutes. Remove from the oil and drain. The oil in the second fryer should be very hot. Immediately add the slices to this fryer and stir carefully. The potato slices will puff up. When they are golden brown and firm, remove with a slotted spoon, drain well and sprinkle with salt to serve.

- **800 g (1¾ lb) waxy potatoes**
- **Vegetable oil, for deep-frying**
- **Salt**

Preparation time: 15 minutes
Cooking time: 8 minutes
Serves 6

PUMPKIN

To prepare, carefully cut off the thick skin of the pumpkin with a heavy, sharp knife. Remove the seeds with a spoon. Cut the flesh into dice and boil in salted water for 15–20 minutes, or until tender.

PUMPKIN GRATIN
POTIRON EN GRATIN

- 750 g (1 lb 10 oz) peeled pumpkin
- 250 g (9 oz) potatoes
- 2 eggs, beaten
- 50 g (1¾ oz) butter
- Salt and pepper
- 100 g (3½ oz) Gruyère cheese, grated

Preparation time: 35 minutes
Cooking time: 20 minutes
Serves 6

Cook the pumpkin (p.576). Meanwhile, cook the potatoes separately in boiling salted water until tender. Preheat the oven to 220°C/425°F/Gas Mark 7. Drain the pumpkin and potatoes, mash them with the eggs and butter, and season with salt and pepper. Put in an ovenproof dish, sprinkle with the cheese and bake for 20 minutes, until browned.

SALSIFY

To prepare, cut the end off each piece of salsify, scrape and rinse in water with vinegar added to it. Cook in boiling salted water for 30–45 minutes, or until tender, depending on size.

SALSIFY IN WHITE SAUCE
SALSIFIS EN SAUCE BLANCHE

- 30 stems of salsify
- 1 quantity white sauce (p.50) or poulette sauce (p.52)

Preparation time: 30 minutes
Cooking time: 30–40 minutes
Serves 6

Prepare the salsify and slice it into 5-cm (2-inch) pieces. Cook until tender (see above), then drain. Make your chosen sauce and add it to the salsify.

FRIED SALSIFY

SALSIFIS FRITS

Prepare and cook the salsify (p.577). Meanwhile, prepare the marinade and batter. Drain the salsify and leave to cool in the marinade. Remove from the marinade, cut into slices, and dry with kitchen paper. Heat the oil in a deep-fryer to 180°C/350°F, or until a cube of bread browns in 30 seconds. Dip the salsify into the batter and fry in batches, until brown. Drain well and serve hot.

- **30 stems of salsify**
- **1 quantity sweet marinade (p.78)**
- **1 quantity batter (p.725)**
- **Vegetable oil, for deep-frying**

Preparation time: 30 minutes
Cooking time: 15 minutes
Serves 6

TOMATOES

Raw tomatoes, with a good colour and even size, are an important decorative element in many dishes as well as adding great flavour. Always wash or wipe them carefully before use.

TOMATOES STUFFED WITH PRAWNS

TOMATES FARCIES AUX CREVETTES

Slice the top off each tomato to make a lid. Scoop out the seeds with a small spoon, lightly salt the insides and turn the tomatoes upside down for 30 minutes to release their liquid. Stir the peeled prawns into the mayonaise. Fill the tomatoes with this mixture, cover with the lids and serve on lettuce leaves.

- **12 small tomatoes**
- **Salt**
- **125 g (4¼ oz) cooked peeled prawns**
- **½ quantity mayonnaise (p.70)**
- **Lettuce leaves, to serve**

Preparation time: 45 minutes
Serves 6

VARIATION

· ·

TOMATOES STUFFED WITH CRAB

TOMATES FARCIES AU CRABE

Proceed as above, replacing the prawns with 300 g (11 oz) crab meat (preferably fresh). Garnish with slices of hard-boiled egg (p.134). The same method can be used to stuff tomatoes with tuna and mayonnaise (p.70), hard-boiled eggs and herbs, a macédoine of vegetables (p.96) dressed with mayonnaise, or with 8 anchovy fillets pounded with 2 hard-boiled eggs and mayonnaise.

TOMATOES À L'ANTIBOISE
TOMATES À L'ANTIBOISE

- 6 medium tomatoes
- 200 g (7 oz) tuna in brine, drained
- 250 ml (8 fl oz) mayonnaise (p.70)
- Salt and pepper
- ½ quantity yoghurt sauce (p.66)
- 1 tablespoon tomato purée
- 2 tablespoons flat-leaf parsley, chopped

Preparation time: 30 minutes
Serves 6

Cut the tomatoes into even slices 1.5 cm (½ inch) thick. Mix the tuna with half the mayonnaise. Season lightly with salt and pepper. Arrange the slices of tomatoes in a circle. Place 1 tablespoon of the tuna mixture between each tomato slice. Mix the yoghurt sauce with the tomato purée and the remaining mayonnaise. Coat the dish with this sauce and sprinkle with the parsley. Serve chilled.

BRAISED TOMATOES
TOMATES À L'ÉTUVÉE

- 1 kg (2¼ lb) tomatoes
- 40 g (1½ oz) butter
- 4 garlic cloves, crushed
- Salt and pepper

Preparation time: 10 minutes
Cooking time: 40 minutes
Serves 6

Fill a heatproof bowl with boiling water and put the tomatoes in for 2 minutes. Drain and allow to cool slightly. Cut the tomatoes into quarters and remove the skin and seeds. Place the flesh in a pan with the butter and garlic. Season with salt and pepper. Simmer gently for 40 minutes.

FRIED TOMATOES
TOMATES FRITES

- 600 g (1 lb 5 oz) tomatoes
- 3 tablespoons olive oil
- Salt and pepper

Preparation time: 5 minutes
Cooking time: 8 minutes
Serves 6

 p.603

Slice the tomatoes. Heat the oil in a frying pan. Add the tomatoes and fry for 3–4 minutes on each side. Season with salt and pepper.

VARIATION

. . . .

FRIED TOMATOES WITH EGGS
TOMATES FRITS AUX OEUFS

Proceed as above, and crack 6 eggs on top of the tomatoes, then continue to cook for 4 minutes, until the eggs have set. Serve immediately.

TOMATOES STUFFED WITH MUSHROOMS

TOMATES FARCIES AU MAIGRE

Slice the top off each tomato to make a lid. Scoop out the seeds with a small spoon, lightly salt the insides and turn the tomatoes upside down for 30 minutes to release their liquid. Meanwhile, make the duxelles. Preheat the oven to 190°C/375°F/Gas Mark 5. Stuff the tomatoes with the duxelles. Add a knob of butter to each, sprinkle with the breadcrumbs and cover with the lids. Bake for 40 minutes.

- 6 large tomatoes
- Salt and pepper
- 250 g (9 oz) duxelles (p.81)
- 40 g (1½ oz) butter
- Dried breadcrumbs, for sprinkling

Preparation time: 35 minutes
Cooking time: 40 minutes
Serves 6

TOMATOES STUFFED WITH RICE

TOMATES FARCIES AU RIZ

Prepare the Indian rice. Preheat the oven to 190°C/375°F/Gas Mark 5. Chop the eggs and place in a bowl with the rice, parsley, onion and chervil. Season with salt and pepper. Slice the top off each tomato to make a lid. Scoop out the seeds with a small spoon, lightly salt the insides and turn the tomatoes upside down for 30 minutes to release their liquid. Stuff each tomato with the rice mixture. Sprinkle with the breadcrumbs or cheese and bake for 25 minutes, until golden.

- 180 g (6¼ oz) Indian rice (p.616)
- 2 hard-boiled eggs (p.134)
- 2 tablespoons flat-leaf parsley, chopped
- 1 onion, chopped
- 1 tablespoon chervil, chopped
- Salt and pepper
- 6 large tomatoes
- 3 tablespoons dried breadcrumbs or 150 g (5 oz) Gruyère cheese, grated

Preparation time: 35 minutes
Cooking time: 1 hour
Serves 6

VARIATION

. . . .

TOMATOES STUFFED WITH MEAT
TOMATES FARCIES AU GRAS

Proceed as above, replacing the rice stuffing with stuffing for red meats (p.80) or sausage meat. Bake for 30 minutes.

TOMATOES WITH EGGS
TOMATES AUX ŒUFS

- **40 g (1½ oz) butter**
- **6 large tomatoes, sliced**
- **Salt and pepper**
- **6 eggs**

Preparation time: 10 minutes
Cooking time: 10 minutes
Serves 6

Heat the butter in a frying pan, add the tomatoes and cook, covered, until softened. Season lightly with salt. Break the eggs into the pan one by one, keeping the yolks whole. Cook for 5 minutes, as for fried eggs. Season lightly with salt and pepper and serve immediately.

RATATOUILLE
RATATOUILLE PROVENÇALE

- **750 g (1 lb 10 oz) aubergines**
- **1 kg (2¼ lb) courgettes**
- **120 g (4 oz) onions**
- **1 garlic clove**
- **750 g (1 lb 10 oz) sweet peppers**
- **600 g (1 lb 5 oz) tomatoes**
- **5 tablespoons olive oil**
- **Salt and pepper**

Preparation time: 25 minutes
Cooking time: 2 hours
Serves 6

Cut all the vegetables into slices about 1 cm (½ inch) thick. Put them in a heavy-based pan, pour over the oil, season with salt and pepper and add 500 ml (¼ pint) water. Cover and simmer for 2 hours. If desired, pound with a pestle and mortar. Serve hot or cold.

JERUSALEM ARTICHOKES

To prepare, peel and wash the artichokes, and cut them into slices about 2 cm (¾ inch) thick. Pour equal quantities of water and milk into a pan. Bring to the boil and add the artichokes, then reduce the heat and simmer for 15–20 minutes, or braise the artichokes in the same liquid in a low oven for 20 minutes, until tender. They may be cooked for longer if they are to be served in a sauce.

JERUSALEM ARTICHOKES IN WHITE SAUCE

TOPINAMBOURS EN SAUCE BLANCHE

Prepare the artichokes and braise them (see above). Add your chosen sauce and cook over a gentle heat for a further 10 minutes.

- 1 kg (2¼ lb) Jerusalem artichokes
- 1 quantity white sauce (p.50), cream sauce (p.51) or tomato sauce (p.57)

Preparation time: 15 minutes
Cooking time: 30 minutes
Serves 6

JERUSALEM ARTICHOKE PURÉE

TOPINAMBOURS EN PURÉE

Cook the Jerusalem artichokes (see above). Cook the potatoes in boiling water for 15 minutes, or until tender. Drain both vegetables thoroughly and pass through a food mill or potato ricer. Beat the butter and, if desired, a little milk into the puréed vegetables. Season with salt and pepper.

- 500 g (1 lb 2 oz) Jerusalem artichokes
- 500 g (1 lb 2 oz) potatoes
- 60 g (2 oz) butter
- Milk, for mashing (optional)
- Salt and pepper

Preparation time: 20 minutes
Cooking time: 15 minutes
Serves 6

FRIED JERUSALEM ARTICHOKES
TOPINAMBOURS FRITS

- 700 g (1 lb 8½ oz) Jerusalem artichokes
- 1 quantity sweet marinade (p.78)
- 1 quantity batter (p.725)
- Vegetable oil, for deep-frying

Preparation time: 20 minutes
Cooking time: 15 minutes
Serves 6

Braise the Jerusalem artichokes (p.582). Meanwhile, prepare the marinade and batter. Drain the artichokes, cut into slices, add to the marinade and leave to cool. Remove from the marinade and dry with kitchen paper. Heat the oil in a deep-fryer to 180°C/350°F, or until a cube of bread browns in 30 seconds. Dip the artichoke slices into the batter and cook in the hot oil in batches, until golden brown.

SALADS

Strictly speaking, salads are green leafy vegetables that are eaten raw, lightly dressed, and served as a starter or palate cleanser before, or alongside, the cheese course. By extension, the term is used for all kinds of cold vegetable-based recipes, and also those incorporating meat, eggs, rice, pasta or dried pulses. These more substantial salads are sometimes served as a main course in themselves. All raw salad ingredients should be washed carefully and drained thoroughly before use.

LETTUCE SALAD
LAITUE

- 2 medium lettuces
- 4 tablespoons olive oil, or a mixture of olive and mild-flavoured oils such as sunflower
- 2 tablespoons white wine vinegar
- Salt and pepper
- Finely chopped chervil, tarragon or chives (optional)
- 3 tablespoons crème fraîche (optional)
- 1 tablespoon lemon juice (optional)

Preparation time: 10 minutes
Serves 6

The oil and vinegar in the vinaigrette can be varied according to the ingredients it is to dress. For example, a milder-tasting sunflower oil would complement stronger flavoured leaves. Romaine (Cos), curly endive, oak leaf or little gem lettuces can be used.

Carefully wash the lettuces, separating the leaves. Drain or spin in a salad spinner to remove as much excess water as possible without damaging the delicate leaves. Whisk the oil, vinegar and salt and pepper together to make the dressing. This can be prepared in advance, but do not dress the leaves until the last minute. Herbs can be added, or a cream dressing can be made by whisking the crème fraîche with the lemon juice and salt and pepper.

CHICORY & WILD CHICORY
ENDIVES, BARBE-DE-CAPUCIN

Young wild salad leaves such as salsify, wild chicory and dandelion can be rather tough when older, so choose small young leaves where possible. Their distinctive bitterness can add character to a bowl of milder leaves. Wash well, drain, and slice into very long pieces. Dress 5–10 minutes in advance with the vinaigrette for lettuce salad (p.583).

Preparation time: 10 minutes
Serves 6

SALAD WITH BACON
SALADE AU LARD

 p.604

Heat a frying pan, add the bacon and cook over a medium heat until the fat runs out. Tip into a small bowl with the remaining ingredients and whisk together. Use to dress any salad leaves, such as Romaine (Cos), curly endive, oak leaf or little gem lettuces.

- 200 g (7 oz) bacon, diced
- 1 tablespoon white wine vinegar
- 1 tablespoon chopped mixed herbs, such as flat-leaf parsley, chives, chervil and tarragon
- Salt and pepper

Preparation time: 15 minutes
Serves 6

NINON SALAD
SALADE NINON

p.605

Hard boil the eggs in a pan of boiling water for 10 minutes and allow to cool completely. Trim and wash the chicory and endive. Dress with the rémoulade sauce. Slice the egg whites into fine strips, and chop or sieve the yolks. Use to decorate the salad.

- 3 eggs
- 1 head of chicory
- 3 heads of endive
- 6 tablespoons rémoulade sauce (p.68)

Preparation time: 10 minutes, plus cooling time
Cooking time: 10 minutes
Serves 6

PASTOURELLE SALAD

SALADE PASTOURELLE

Put the onions into a small pan of salted boiling water and cook for 10 minutes, or until tender. Drain. Hard boil the eggs (p.134) and once cool remove and reserve the yolks. Cut the anchovy fillets into very thin strips and the tuna into chunks. Gently mix the onions, anchovies, tuna, capers, gherkins and olives together. Halve the egg yolks. Dress with the vinaigrette. Decorate with the halved egg yolks and the herbs. Serve as an hors-d'oeuvre.

- 10 small round onions
- 6 eggs
- 6 anchovy fillets
- 80 g (2¾ oz) tuna in oil, drained
- 1 tablespoon capers, rinsed
- 2 gherkins, sliced
- 10–15 olives, stoned
- 50 ml (2 fl oz) vinaigrette (p.66)
- Mixed herbs, such as flat-leaf parsley, chives, chervil or tarrago finely chopped, to decorate

Preparation time: 20 minutes
Cooking time: 20 minutes
Serves 6

ANDRÉA SALAD

SALADE ANDRÉA

Hard boil the eggs (p.134). Cook the potatoes and beans in separate pans of salted boiling water until tender. Drain. Peel the potatoes and cut into thin slices. Blanch the celery for 2 minutes in boiling water. Trim, remove the strings and cut into thin slices. Halve the hard-boiled eggs and tomatoes. Gently combine the potato and celery slices with the beans. Dress with the vinaigrette. Decorate with the halved hard-boiled eggs and tomatoes and serve with the mayonnaise.

- 4 eggs
- 250 g (9 oz) potatoes, unpeeled
- 250 g (9 oz) French beans, trimm
- 1 head of celery
- 50 ml (2 fl oz) vinaigrette (p.66)
- 4 tomatoes
- 4 tablespoons mayonnaise (p.70)

Preparation time: 20 minutes
Cooking time: 30 minutes
Serves 6

RACHEL SALAD

SALADE RACHEL

 p.606

Prepare the vinaigrette. Cut the celery into thin strips and leave to marinate for 2 hours in the vinaigrette in a non-metallic bowl. Cut each walnut into quarters and add to the celery with the apples. Toss gently. Carefully wash the endive, separating the leaves. Drain or spin in a salad spinner. Garnish the top of the salad with the endive leaves and beetroot slices.

- 50 ml (2 fl oz) vinaigrette (p.66)
- 85 g (3 oz) celery
- 12 large fresh walnuts
- 2 eating apples, thinly sliced
- 2 heads of chicory
- 125 g (4¼ oz) beetroot, sliced

Preparation time: 20 minutes, plus marinating time
Serves 6

YVETTE SALAD
SALADE YVETTE

- 500 g (1 lb 2 oz) potatoes, unpeeled
- 2 small heads of celery
- 4 eggs
- 50 ml (2 fl oz) vinaigrette (p.66)
- 4 tablespoons mayonnaise (p.70)

Preparation time: 25 minutes
Cooking time: 20 minutes
Serves 6

Boil or steam the potatoes until tender. Blanch the celery for 2–3 minutes in boiling water. Hard boil the eggs (p.134). Peel the potatoes and slice thinly. Trim the celery and slice thinly. Cut the eggs into quarters. Combine the potatoes, celery and eggs in a bowl. Dress with the vinaigrette and gently stir in the mayonnaise.

 p.607

TOURANGELLE SALAD
SALADE TOURANGELLE

- 250 g (9 oz) French beans
- 250 g (9 oz) new potatoes
- 1 Romaine lettuce
- 150 ml (¼ pint) crème fraîche
- Juice of 1 lemon
- Salt and pepper
- 2 tomatoes, sliced

Preparation time: 10 minutes
Cooking time: 20 minutes
Serves 6

Cook the beans and potatoes in separate pans of salted boiling water until tender. Drain and cool. Cut into very small pieces. Separate the lettuce leaves, wash them and drain well. Shred finely. Add the lettuce to the beans and potatoes and stir in the crème fraîche and lemon juice. Season with salt and pepper and decorate with the tomato slices.

AMERICAN SALAD
SALADE AMÉRICAINE

- 3 oranges
- 1 Romaine lettuce
- 20 large walnuts, chopped
- 100 ml (3½ fl oz) crème fraîche
- Juice of 1 lemon
- Salt and pepper

Preparation time: 20 minutes
Serves 6

Wash the oranges and slice them thinly, without removing the skin. Discard the end slices. Separate the lettuce leaves, and wash and drain them well. Select only the pale, inside leaves and cut them in half. Put the orange slices, walnuts and lettuce in a salad bowl. Add the crème fraîche, lemon juice and salt and pepper. Stir to combine.

RUSSIAN SALAD

SALADE RUSSE

Cook each vegetable separately in boiling water until tender. Drain and cool. Cut into small dice, and mix with the mayonnaise. Hard boil the eggs (p.134) and cut into slices once cool. Separate the lettuce leaves and wash and drain them well. Arrange the lettuce in a salad bowl and add the vegetables. Decorate with the tomatoes, egg slices and olives.

- Artichoke hearts, French beans, fresh haricot beans, young turnips, carrots, peas, cauliflower, to taste
- 1 quantity mayonnaise (p.70)

To decorate:
- 2 eggs
- 1 lettuce
- 2 tomatoes, sliced
- 7–8 olives, stoned

Preparation time: 45 minutes
Cooking time: 30 minutes
Serves 6

NORWEGIAN SALAD

MACÉDOINE NORVÉGIENNE

Cook each vegetable separately in boiling water until tender. Drain and cool. Cut into small dice. Hard boil the eggs (p.134). Cool, and separate the whites from the yolks. Slice the egg whites and gherkins and put in a large salad bowl with the cooked vegetables. Pound the egg yolks in a smaller bowl. Add the oil to the yolks, drop by drop, to make a smooth creamy sauce, stirring constantly. Add the herbs and season with the vinegar, and salt and pepper. Pour over the salad and mix well. Decorate with the anchovies. The salad can be coated with mayonnaise.

- 125 g (4¼ oz) each of the following vegetables: artichoke hearts, potatoes, French beans, fresh haricot beans, turnips, carrots, peas
- 4 eggs
- 4 gherkins
- 200 ml (7 fl oz) sunflower oil
- Mixed herbs, such as flat-leaf parsley, chervil, chives and tarragon, finely chopped, to taste
- 1 tablespoon white wine vinegar
- Salt and pepper
- 12 anchovy fillets
- 1 quantity mayonaise (p.70), optional

Preparation time: 45 minutes
Cooking time: 30 minutes
Serves 6

Artichokes à la barigoule   (p.511)

Aubergines with tomatoes (p.517)

Carrots in béchamel sauce (p.521)

Griddled mushrooms with herb butter (p.525)

Chanterelles bonne femme   (p.530)

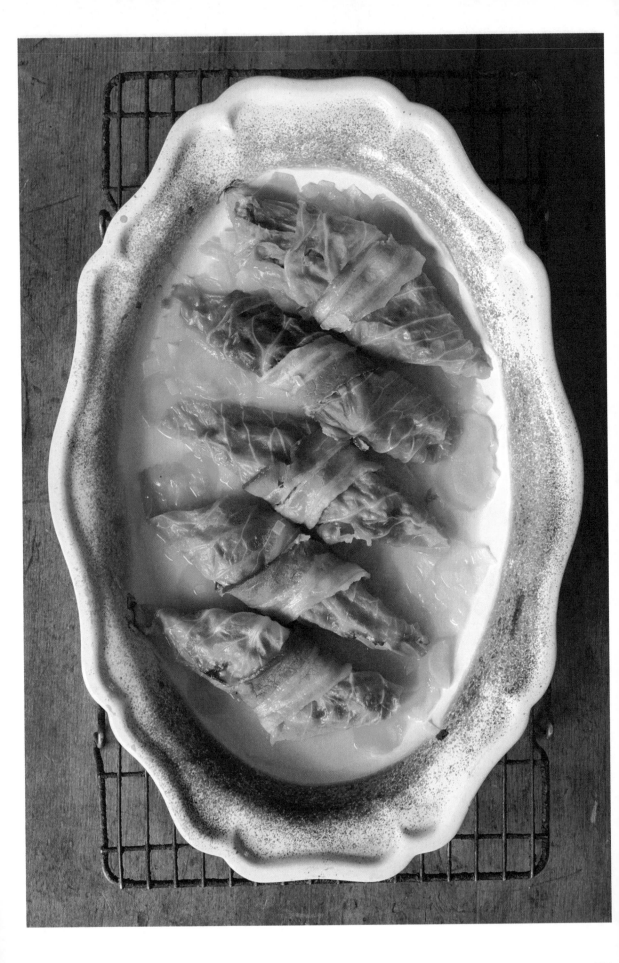

Stuffed cabbage (p.536)

Alsace choucroute (p.541)

Spinach croquettes (p.548)

French beans à la niçoise   (p.551)

Vegetable tart   (p.555)

Stuffed onions (p.560)

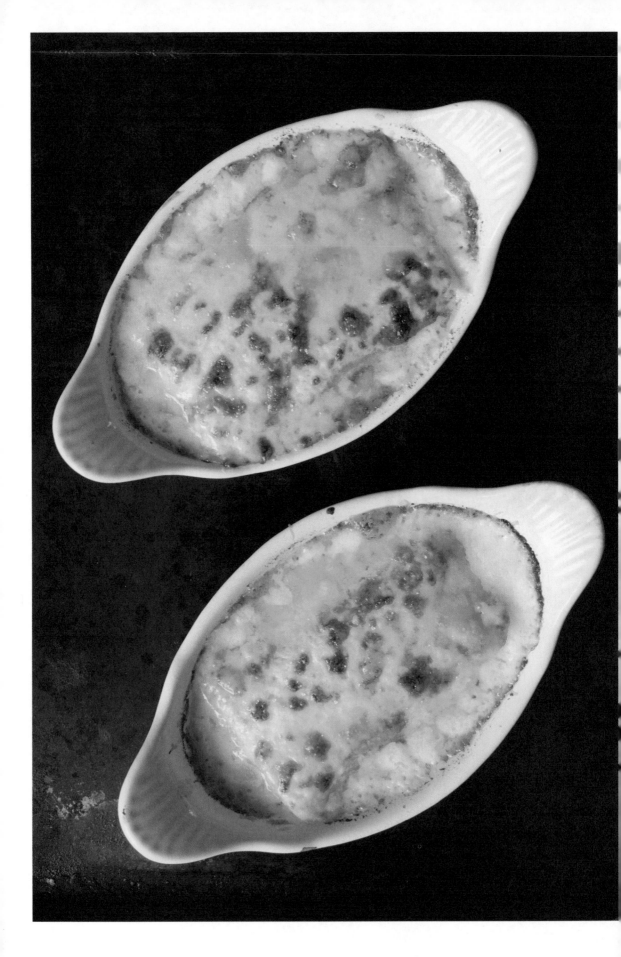

Leek gratin (p.565)

Dauphinois potatoes (p.571)

Anna potatoes   (p.575)

Fried tomatoes with eggs   (p.579)

Salad with bacon (p.584)

Ninon salad   (p.584)

Rachel salad   (p.586)

Tourangelle salad (p.587)

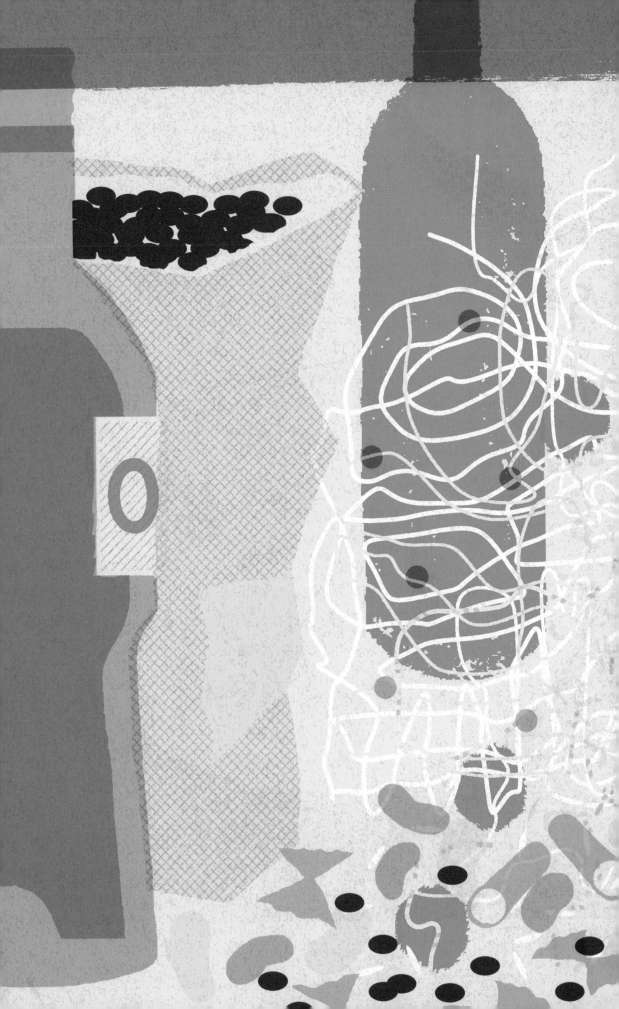

PULSES, RICE, RICE & PASTA

SALT

PULSES

Dried pulses (such as beans, lentils and split peas) are seeds of the bean family. Low in fat, rich in complex carbohydrates, protein, fibre and vitamins, pulses are nutritious, inexpensive and versatile. They should be rehydrated by soaking in cold water before cooking according to the packet instructions. A number of factors, such as how long the beans have been stored and the hardness of the local water, will affect the final cooking time. Try to buy pulses from a shop with a rapid turnover to ensure that they are fresh. Acidic ingredients, such as tomatoes, lemon juice and vinegar, will lengthen the cooking time significantly if added early on.

To prepare pulses, rinse and check the beans over for any grit before putting them in a large pan of water. If the liquid runs dry while the pulses are simmering, extra hot water should be added. In hard-water areas, add one teaspoon of bicarbonate of soda to the pan.

BRETON HARICOT BEANS

HARICOTS SECS À LA BRETONNE

 p.636

Put the beans in a large pan, cover generously with water and bring to the boil. Reduce the heat, add the bouquet garni and simmer gently for up to 3 hours, or until tender. While the beans are cooking, prepare the sauce. Melt the butter in a medium pan and add the onions. Fry until golden, then sprinkle over the flour and cook for a few minutes to make a blond roux (p.57). Gradually add the stock and tomato coulis or passata. Add the garlic and season with salt and pepper. Simmer gently for 10 minutes, or until the sauce is reduced by half. When the beans are cooked, discard the bouquet garni, drain and force through a coarse sieve. Mix the sauce into the purée. Simmer for a further 10 minutes.

- 500 g (1 lb 2 oz) dried haricot or cannellini beans, soaked
- 1 bouquet garni
- 30 g (1¼ oz) butter
- 200 g (7 oz) onions, chopped
- 30 g (1¼ oz) flour
- 300 ml (½ pint) hot stock
- 60 g (2 oz) tomato coulis or passata
- ½ garlic clove, crushed
- Salt and pepper

Preparation time: 20 minutes, plus soaking time
Cooking time: 3 hours
Serves 6

RED BEANS WITH BACON

HARICOTS ROUGES AU LARD

Put the beans in a large pan, cover with water, bring to the boil and cook vigorously for 15 minutes. Drain, rinse well and return to the pan. Cover with fresh water and add the bacon and wine. Bring to the boil, reduce the heat and simmer gently for 1½ hours, or until tender. Remove the bacon, allow to cool, then dice it. Fry the bacon and onion in half the butter, until golden brown. Drain the beans, reserving a few spoonfuls of the cooking liquid. Place them in a serving dish and add the bacon and onion. Season with salt and pepper. Dot with the remaining butter and coat with a few spoons of the liquid.

- 350 g (12 oz) dried red haricot or kidney beans, soaked overnight
- 1 x 125-g (4¼-oz) piece bacon
- 200 ml (7 fl oz) red wine
- 30 g (1¼ oz) butter
- 1 onion, chopped
- Salt and pepper

Preparation time: 10 minutes, plus soaking time
Cooking time: 2 hours
Serves 6

LENTILS WITH MAÎTRE D'HÔTEL BUTTER

LENTILLES À LA MAÎTRE D'HÔTEL

Put the lentils in a large pan and cover with water. Bring to the boil, reduce the heat and simmer very gently until tender, about 25–45 minutes. The exact timing will depend on the size and type of lentil chosen (consult the instructions on the packet). Drain, and when ready to serve, stir in the butter, parsley, lemon juice or vinegar and season with salt and pepper.

- 500 g (1 lb 2 oz) lentils
- 60 g (2 oz) butter
- 1 handful of flat-leaf parsley, finely chopped
- Dash of lemon juice or balsamic vinegar
- Salt and pepper

Preparation time: 10 minutes
Cooking time: 45 minutes
Serves 6

BRAISED LENTILS

LENTILLES AU JUS

Put the lentils in a large pan and cover with water. Bring to the boil, reduce the heat and simmer very gently until tender, about 25–45 minutes. The exact timing will depend on the size and type of lentil chosen (consult the instructions on the packet). Meanwhile, heat the stock in a pan, add the onion and simmer for 15 minutes. Drain the lentils and add them to the stock with the parsley. Simmer for 20 minutes more.

- 500 g (1 lb 2 oz) lentils
- 500 ml (18 fl oz) chicken stock
- 1 onion, sliced
- 1 handful of flat-leaf parsley, chopped
- Salt and pepper

Preparation time: 10 minutes
Cooking time: 45 minutes
Serves 6

LENTILS WITH TOMATOES

LENTILLES AUX TOMATES

Put the lentils in a large pan and cover with water. Bring to the boil, reduce the heat and simmer very gently until tender, about 25–45 minutes, then drain. The exact timing will depend on the size and type of lentil chosen (consult the instructions on the packet). Meanwhile, melt the butter in a pan, add the onions and fry until golden. Add the tomatoes, then the drained lentils, season with salt and pepper and simmer for 30 minutes. If desired, tomato sauce, served in sauce boat, can be offered separately.

- 500 g (1 lb 2 oz) lentils
- 30 g (1¼ oz) butter
- 100 g (3½ oz) onions, chopped
- 500 g (1 lb 2 oz) tomatoes, skinned, de-seeded and diced
- Salt and pepper
- 1 quantity tomato sauce (p.57), to serve (optional)

Preparation time: 10 minutes
Cooking time: 45 minutes
Serves 6

LENTILS WITH MUSTARD

LENTILLES À LA DIJONNAISE

Put the lentils in a large pan and cover with water. Bring to the boil, reduce the heat and simmer very gently until tender, about 25–45 minutes, then drain. The exact timing will depend on the size and type of lentil chosen (consult the instructions on the packet). Meanwhile, melt the butter in a pan and fry the onion and ham until golden brown. Add the stock. Season with salt and pepper and the mustard. Stir this sauce into the drained lentils.

- 500 g (1 lb 2 oz) lentils
- 30 g (1¼ oz) butter
- 1 onion, chopped
- 150 g (5 oz) raw ham, chopped
- 100 ml (3½ fl oz) hot stock
- Salt and pepper
- 30 g (1¼ oz) Dijon mustard

Preparation time: 10 minutes
Cooking time: 1 hour
Serves 6

LENTIL PURÉE

LENTILLES EN PURÉE

Put the lentils in a large pan, cover with water, add the carrots, onion and bouquet garni, and bring to a slow simmer. Cook until tender, about 25–45 minutes, then drain. The exact timing will depend on the size and type of lentil chosen (consult the instructions on the packet). Discard the bouquet garni. Process the lentils until smooth in a blender and beat the butter into the purée. Season with salt and pepper.

- 500 g (1 lb 2 oz) lentils
- 100 g (3½ oz) carrots, chopped
- 1 onion, chopped
- 1 bouquet garni
- 40 g (1½ oz) butter
- Salt and pepper

Preparation time: 10 minutes
Cooking time: 1½ hours
Serves 6

LENTIL SALAD

LENTILLES EN SALADE

- **500 g (1 lb 2 oz) lentils**
- **1 quantity vinaigrette (p.66)**

  Preparation time: 5 minutes
  Cooking time: 45 minutes
  Serves 6

Put the lentils in a large pan and cover with water. Bring to the boil, reduce the heat and simmer very gently until tender, about 25–45 minutes. Exact timing will depend on the size and type of lentil chosen (consult the instructions on the packet). Drain the lentils and, when cool, dress with the vinaigrette.

SPLIT PEA PURÉE

PURÉE DE POIS CASSÉS

- **500 g (1 lb 2 oz) dried split peas, soaked overnight**
- **250 ml (8 fl oz) hot milk**
- **60 g (2 oz) butter**
- **Salt and pepper**
- **Small cubes of bread, for croutons**

  Preparation time: 20 minutes, plus soaking time
  Cooking time: 2½ hours
  Serves 6

Put the split peas into a large pan and cover with water. Bring to the boil, reduce the heat and simmer until tender, about 2 hours. Drain and mash the split peas, then return the purée to the pan and stir continuously over a low heat until dry. Add the milk and half the butter. Season with salt and pepper. Heat the remaining butter in a frying pan until bubbling and fry the bread until golden to make croutons. Make a mound of the purée on a serving dish and arrange the croutons on top.

RICE

Rice is a high-energy grain that is easy to prepare and can be eaten hot, or cold in a salad. There are many varieties of rice, all with slightly different flavours and uses. Brown rice is a naturally healthier option, since milling rice to remove the seed husk removes much of the vitamin content. For precise cooking times, refer to the instructions on the packet.

VARIETIES OF RICE

WHITE SHORT-GRAIN RICE
Cooks quickly and is high in starch. It is particularly suitable for soups, risottos and rice puddings.

WHITE LONG-GRAIN RICE

Harder than short-grain rice, and does not become sticky when cooked. Its flavour varies according to the area in which it is grown: Indian basmati rice has a delicately perfumed flavour. American long-grain rice is often parboiled, which ensures that it holds its shape when cooked.

BROWN RICE

Sold with its bran layer intact. It is higher in vitamins and minerals and takes longer to cook than white rice. It is excellent in salads.

WILD RICE

Comes from a North American water grass. It has very long dark brown grains and tastes similar to hazelnuts. It is more expensive than other varieties of rice and is often sold mixed with American parboiled rice or brown rice.

RED, GREEN AND BLACK RICE

Less widely available and more expensive than white or brown rice. The colour is natural and, although once considered a nuisance in a field of otherwise 'normal' rice, these varieties are now cultivated for their colour. Like brown rice, coloured rice is flavoursome and excellent in salads.

INDIAN RICE

RIZ À L'INDIENNE

Preheat the oven to 150°C/300°F/Gas Mark 2. Add the salt to a large pan of water and bring to the boil. Add the rice and boil for 10 minutes. Drain, then put the rice into an ovenproof dish with a lid. Gently mix in the butter. Cover the dish tightly and place in the oven for 20 minutes. The rice grains remain whole, but become soft. The rice may be served alone, or alongside numerous dishes.

- **15 g (½ oz) salt**
- **350 g (12 oz) long-grain rice**
- **25 g (1 oz) butter**

Preparation time: 3 minutes
Cooking time: 25 minutes
Serves 6

VARIATIONS

. . . .

ITALIAN RICE

RIZ À L'ITALIENNE

Proceed as above, then stir in 60 g (2 oz) grated Parmesan, pepper and a little grated nutmeg. Dot with 20 g (¾ oz) butter and serve.

. . . .

RICE WITH TOMATO
RIZ À LA TOMATE

Cook the rice as above, then stir in 30 g (1¼ oz) grated cheese, 40 g (1½ oz) grated Parmesan and 200 g (7 oz) tomato coulis or passata. Dot with 20 g (¾ oz) butter and serve.

. . . .

RICE WITH FINANCIÈRE SAUCE
RIZ À LA FINANCIÈRE

Cook the rice as above and stir in 500 ml (18 fl oz) financière sauce (p.57) before serving.

CREOLE RICE
RIZ À LA CRÉOLE

- **15 g (½ oz) salt**
- **350 g (12 oz) long-grain rice**
- **30 g (1¼ oz) butter**

Preparation time: 3 minutes
Cooking time: 10 minutes
Serves 6

Add the salt to 3 litres (5¼ pints) water in a large pan and bring to the boil. Add the rice and boil for 10 minutes. Taste the rice to check that it is tender. When cooked, tip the rice into a fine sieve and rinse quickly under running cold water. Drain. Melt the butter in a large pan, add the rice and reheat, gently stirring to ensure the rice does not stick to the base of the pan. Check the seasoning and add a little more salt if necessary.

FRIED RICE
RIZ REVENU

- **350 g (12 oz) long-grain rice**
- **50 g (1¼ oz) butter
  or chicken fat**
- **1 litre (1¾ pints) hot water
  or stock**
- **Salt and pepper**

Preparation time: 5 minutes
Cooking time: 20 minutes
Serves 6

Rinse the rice under running cold water and dry it. In a large pan, melt the butter or fat and fry the rice, stirring constantly, for 4–5 minutes. When the rice is golden brown, pour in the hot water or stock (use stock for preference) and season with salt and pepper. Simmer the rice for a further 15 minutes. Taste the rice to check that it is cooked and tender, then drain through a fine sieve before serving.

RICH RICE

RIZ AU GRAS

Bring the stock to the boil in a large pan. Add the rice and the onion, butter or fat and bouquet garni. Season with salt and pepper. Simmer gently, for 15 minutes. Taste the rice to check that it is tender, then discard the bouquet garni, drain and serve. This rice may be served alone or with white meat, for example poultry or veal in white sauce.

- 1 litre (1¾ pints) stock
- 350 g (12 oz) long-grain rice
- 1 onion, chopped
- 50 g (1¾ oz) butter
  or poultry fat
- 1 bouquet garni
- Salt and pepper

Preparation time: 5 minutes
Cooking time: 25 minutes
Serves 6

COUNTRY-STYLE RICE

RIZ À LA PAYSANNE

 p.637

This rustic, satisfying rice relies on tasty ingredients, so choose full-flavoured bacon and a well-reduced, rich stock such as veal or beef.

Melt the butter in a large pan. Fry the bacon and onion for 5 minutes, until softened. Add the rice. Fry, stirring, for 2–3 minutes to coat the rice in fat, then add the stock. Tie the herbs in a bunch with string (these are known as *fines herbes*; other soft herbs can be substituted) and add to the pan with salt and pepper. Cook for 15 minutes, or until the rice is tender (which will take longer if using brown rice), discard the herbs, stir in the cheese and serve.

- 20 g (¾ oz) butter
- 75 g (2½ oz) lean bacon, diced
- 75 g (2½ oz) fatty bacon, diced
- 1 onion, sliced
- 300 g (11 oz) long-grain white
  or brown rice
- 2 litres (3½ pints) hot stock
- 1 sprig of parsley
- 1 sprig of thyme
- 1 sprig of chervil
- 1 small bunch of chives
- Salt and pepper
- 80 g (2¾ oz) Gruyère
  cheese, finely grated

Preparation time: 10 minutes
Cooking time: 20 minutes
Serves 6

RICE MOUND À L'AURORE
MONT DE RIZ À L'AURORE

- 350 g (12 oz) long-grain rice
- 65 g (2¼ oz) butter
- 40 g (1½ oz) flour
- 250 ml (8 fl oz) hot milk
- 25 g (1 oz) mild paprika
- 125 g (4¼ oz) mushrooms, sliced
- 100 ml (3½ fl oz) double cream
- Salt and pepper

Preparation time: 15 minutes
Cooking time: 45 minutes
Serves 6

Prepare Indian rice (p.616) with the rice and 25 g (1 oz) of the butter. Prepare the sauce while the rice is cooking. Melt the remaining butter in a frying pan over a low heat. Add the flour and stir briskly until blended. Pour in the milk and whisk for 1–2 minutes until perfectly smooth. Add the paprika, mushrooms, cream, and salt and pepper, and cook over a gentle heat for 15 minutes until the sauce is thick. Arrange the cooked rice in a pyramid or mound on a large serving dish. Coat the rice with the sauce and serve hot.

RICE À LA REINE
RIZ À LA REINE

- 3 litres (5¼ pints) chicken stock
- 65 g (2¼ oz) butter
- 300 g (11 oz) long-grain rice
- 500 ml (18 fl oz) velouté sauce (p.59)
- Leftover cooked poultry, sliced
- 200 g (7 oz) mushrooms, chopped
- 6 tablespoons crème fraîche
- 200 g (7 oz) veal quenelles (p.104)
- Salt and pepper

Preparation time: 15 minutes
Cooking time: 50 minutes
Serves 6

Bring the stock to the boil in a large pan and add half the butter. Cook the rice for 10 minutes, or until tender. Drain, reserving the stock, and prepare the velouté sauce using the remaining butter and the reserved stock. Stir the poultry into the sauce and add the mushrooms. Simmer for 20 minutes, then add the crème fraîche and the quenelles. Simmer for a few more minutes to heat through, then mix the sauce with the drained rice. Season with salt and pepper.

PORK JAMBALAYA

RIZ JAMBALAYA AU PORC

Jambalaya, the characteristic dish of French-speaking New Orleans, can be made with any kind of meat, crustacean or fish, but rice is always the main ingredient and a jambalaya should be spicy.

In a large pan, slowly fry the bacon over a gentle heat for about 5 minutes, or until the fat runs, and then add the onions. Raise the heat to medium and continue to fry for 5 minutes, until softened. Remove the bacon and onions from the pan and brown the pork in the fat. Return the bacon and onions to the pan with the ham. Pour in the hot water or stock, bring to the boil, then reduce the heat and simmer for 15 minutes. Stir in the rice and herbs, and season with salt and cayenne pepper. Cook for a further 10 minutes, or until the rice has absorbed the liquid and is tender.

- 100 g (3½ oz) fatty bacon, diced
- 2 onions, sliced
- 400 g (14 oz) roast pork
- 100 g (3½ oz) ham, diced
- 1 litre (1¾ pints) hot water or stock
- 300 g (11 oz) long-grain rice
- 1 tablespoon parsley, chopped
- 1 tablespoon thyme
- 1 tablespoon chervil, chopped
- 1 small bunch of chives, chopped
- Salt and cayenne pepper

Preparation time: 15 minutes
Cooking time: 30 minutes
Serves 6

OYSTER JAMBALAYA

RIZ JAMBALAYA AUX HUÎTRES

Melt the butter in a large pan and fry the onions for 5 minutes, until softened. Add the rice and stir well, then add the hot water or stock and bouquet garni. Season well with salt and cayenne pepper, then simmer for 12 minutes or until the rice is almost cooked. Shuck the oysters and add them, with their juices, to the rice. Place a lid on the pan to gently steam them for 3 minutes. Discard the bouquet garni and serve immediately.

- 30 g (1¼ oz) butter
- 2 onions, sliced
- 350 g (12 oz) long-grain rice
- 1 litre (1¾ pints) hot water or fish stock
- 1 bouquet garni
- Salt and cayenne pepper
- 24 oysters

Preparation time: 15 minutes
Cooking time: 15 minutes
Serves 6

CRAB JAMBALAYA

RIZ JAMBALAYA AU CRABE

- **1 litre (1¾ pints) court-bouillon with salt (p.82)**
- **1 large crab**
- **100 g (3½ oz) bacon, diced**
- **2 onions, sliced**
- **350 g (12 oz) long-grain rice**
- **Salt and pepper**

Preparation time: 30 minutes
Cooking time: 30 minutes
Serves 6

Pour the court-bouillon into a large pan and bring to a vigorous boil. Place the crab in the liquid, cover and boil for 15 minutes. Turn off the heat and let the crab cool in the liquid. Remove the meat from the shell, chop finely and set aside. Fry the bacon and onions over a medium heat for 5–10 minutes until golden brown. Meanwhile, reheat the court-bouillon. Add the rice to the pan and carefully strain in the court-bouillon. Simmer for 10 minutes, adding the reserved crab meat for the final 2 minutes. Season with salt and pepper and serve immediately.

RICE WITH ASPARAGUS CREAM

RIZ À LA CRÈME D'ASPERGES

- **300 g (11 oz) long-grain rice**
- **65 g (2¼ oz) butter**
- **1 small bunch of asparagus**
- **20 g (¾ oz) rice flour**
- **100 ml (3½ fl oz) hot water**
- **200 ml (7 fl oz) double cream**
- **Salt and pepper**
- **250 g (9 oz) crustless white bread**

Preparation time: 30 minutes
Cooking time: 30 minutes
Serves 6

Prepare Indian rice (p.616) with the rice and 25 g (1 oz) of the butter. Meanwhile, prepare the asparagus cream. Trim the asparagus and place them in salted, boiling water. Cook for 5–10 minutes, or until the spears are tender, then process to a purée in a blender. Set aside. Melt 20 g (¾ oz) of the butter in a pan over a medium heat. When it is bubbling, add the flour and gradually stir in the hot water. Stir in the cream and the asparagus purée. Season with salt and pepper. Add the rice to the asparagus cream. Cut the bread into small cubes and fry in the remaining butter for 2–3 minutes until golden brown. Arrange the croutons in a ring shape on a serving dish and garnish with some of the rice and asparagus mixture. Pour the remaining mixture into the centre of the ring.

RICE WITH ARTICHOKES

RIZ AUX ARTICHAUTS

Prepare Indian rice (p.616) with the rice and half the butter. Melt the remaining butter in a large pan and fry the artichokes, tomatoes and onion for 20 minutes, stirring occasionally. Add the rice, cheese, salt and pepper. Serve very hot.

- 300 g (11 oz) long-grain rice
- 50 g (1¾ oz) butter
- 4 artichoke hearts, diced
- 500 g (1 lb 2 oz) tomatoes, quartered
- 1 onion, chopped
- 60 g (2 oz) Parmesan cheese, grated
- Salt and pepper

Preparation time: 25 minutes
Cooking time: 45 minutes
Serves 6

CURRIED RICE

RIZ AU CURRY

Melt half the butter in a large pan over a medium heat. Fry the onions for 5–10 minutes, or until golden brown. Stir in the rice and curry powder. Stir carefully. Add the stock and cook over a low heat for 15 minutes until all the liquid is absorbed and the rice is tender. Stir in the remaining butter, and season with salt and pepper just before serving.

- 40 g (1½ oz) butter
- 2 onions, sliced
- 350 g (12 oz) long-grain rice
- Curry powder, to taste
- Salt and pepper
- 1 litre (1¾ pints) hot stock

Preparation time: 5 minutes
Cooking time: 20 minutes
Serves 6

VARIATIONS

. . . .

PAPRIKA RICE

RIZ AU PAPRIKA

Proceed as above, replacing the curry powder with paprika.

. . . .

SAFFRON RICE

RIZ AU SAFRAN

Proceed as above, replacing the curry powder with a pinch of saffron threads, and stir in 100 ml (3½ fl oz) tomato coulis or passata a few minutes before the rice is cooked.

PILAF

RIZ PILAF

Pour water or stock, equal to 1½ times the volume of the rice, into a large pan and bring to the boil. Melt 30 g (1¼ oz) of the butter in a large pan. Add the rice and onion to the butter and stir over a medium heat for 2–3 minutes, without browning. Pour the boiling water or stock carefully over the rice. Season with salt and pepper. Cover the pan and simmer gently over a low heat for 15 minutes, or until the liquid has been absorbed. When ready to serve, dot the rice with the remaining butter and stir it in with a fork.

- Water or stock (see method)
- 50 g (1¼ oz) butter
- 350 g (12 oz) long-grain rice
- 1 onion, chopped
- Salt and pepper

Preparation time: 5 minutes
Cooking time: 30 minutes
Serves 6

LETTUCE PARCELS

LAITUES DE LA MÈRE MARIE

 p.638

Preheat the oven to 180°C/350°F/Gas Mark 4. Bring a large pan of water to the boil and blanch the lettuce leaves for 30 seconds–1 minute, so that they can be easily rolled up. Drain well. Mix together the rice, meat and egg. Season with salt and pepper. Roll the meat mixture into small balls and wrap each one in a lettuce leaf. Fit the parcels snugly in an ovenproof dish, whisk the crème fraîche with 100 ml (3½ fl oz) water, pour it over the parcels and bake for 45 minutes.

- 1 large-leafed lettuce, leaves separated
- 150 g (5 oz) cooked long-grain rice
- 200 g (7 oz) leftover veal or chicken, finely chopped
- 1 egg, lightly beaten
- Salt and pepper
- 100 ml (3½ fl oz) crème fraîche

Preparation time: 30 minutes
Cooking time: 45 minutes
Serves 6

PASTA

Pasta is a very useful food, from both a nutritional and an economical point of view. In Italy, the home of pasta, it is considered to be not just the country's most important staple, but almost an art form. There are countless names for all the different shapes and sizes available.

The best pasta is made from fresh eggs and strong white durum wheat flour, specifically produced for pasta making and often labelled '00'. Handmade pasta dough is pleasingly yellow, taking its colour from egg yolks, and slightly rough in texture, which helps the sauce cling to it. Commercially produced pasta tends to be smoother in texture. Any type of pasta dough can be flavoured or coloured by adding spinach, tomato or saffron, among other things. Pasta can be prepared in many different ways and served as a side dish, in a salad or as a main dish. Some simple serving suggestions are given below.

WITH ROASTS
Long fresh pasta, such as tagliatelle, is usually served with roasts. It is cooked in water and dressed with the meat juices and a little cheese, if desired.

WITH GRILLED MEAT
Make a bed of plainly cooked pasta, top with the grilled meat and dress with the meat juices.

WITH BRAISED MEAT AND STEWS
Conchiglie pasta is mainly used in stews. It should be cooked separately and plainly, and is excellent with hot meat in a sauce.

IN SOUPS
Pasta can be used in place of croutons in soups. Small pasta shapes or vermicelli are generally used.

AS A MAIN DISH
Pasta with butter, cheese, sauce or *au gratin* can be served as a main course. Allow 100 g (3½ oz) per person.

WITH SAUCES
Suitable sauces include white sauce (p.50), béchamel sauce (p.50), cheese sauce (p.51), poulette sauce (p.52), maître d'hôtel butter (p.48), and financière sauce (p.57).

MAKING FRESH PASTA

PREPARATION DE LA PÂTE À NOUILLES

Make a mound of flour on a large, clean work surface and make a well in the centre. Break the eggs into the well. Gradually stir the flour into the eggs using a knife or your fingertips. Once a single piece of dough has formed, knead it rhythmically, giving a quarter turn between each kneading action. Frequent turning helps prevent the dough from sticking and forms a consistently smooth, elastic dough. Dust the work surface with as little flour as possible during the kneading and rolling process. Cover the dough with a bowl or clingfilm and leave to rest for at least 30 minutes.

Uncover the dough and knead briefly. Dust the work surface with a little flour. Using a large rolling pin and firm movements, roll out the dough to 3 mm (⅛ inch) thick, turning it frequently to prevent sticking and maintaining a reasonably circular shape. Rest for 3 hours. Loosely roll the dough up into a cylinder shape and, using the heel of a sharp knife, cut it into strips 5 mm–2.5 cm (¼–1 inch) wide, depending upon the desired width of the pasta. Gently shake the strands apart and leave to dry for at least 30 minutes on a clean, lightly floured cloth. The pasta may then be cooked, or can be kept in a cool, dry place for 2–3 days before cooking.

- **300 g (11 oz) pasta flour, plus extra for dusting**
- **3 eggs**

  Preparation time: 30 minutes, plus resting and drying time
  Makes 800 g (1¾ lb)

BASIC METHOD FOR COOKING PASTA

CUISSON ÉLÉMENTAIRE DES PÂTES

Pasta should be cooked in a large quantity of boiling salted water. For 250 g (9 oz) dried pasta, boil at least 3 litres (5¼ pints) water, 30 g (1¼ oz) salt and 1 teaspoon oil in a capacious pan. Quickly but carefully place the pasta in the boiling water and bring back to the boil quickly to ensure the pasta does not sink and stick to the bottom of the pan. Do not cover. Stir once or twice during cooking to separate the pasta. Drain in a large colander. Cooking time is calculated from the time the water comes back to the boil and varies according to the type of pasta. Freshly made pasta will require only 2–3 minutes. Otherwise, refer to the packet instructions.

Preparation time: 5 minutes
Cooking time: 5–12 minutes

RÉGENCE NOODLES

NOUILLES RÉGENCE

- 350 g (12 oz) tagliatelle
  or spaghetti
- 30 g (1¼ oz) butter
- 100 g (3½ oz) Gruyère
  cheese, grated
- 50 g (1¼ oz) dried breadcrumbs

Preparation time: 5 minutes
Cooking time: 30 minutes
Serves 6

Bring a large pan of salted water to the boil, add the tagliatelle and boil for for 12 minutes, or until al dente. Preheat the oven to 190°C/375°F/Gas Mark 5. Grease an ovenproof dish with some of the butter. Put in a layer of cooked pasta, a layer of cheese and dot with butter. Repeat until the dish is full, finishing with a layer of cheese and breadcrumbs. Bake for 15 minutes, or until golden.

NOODLE SOUFFLÉ

SOUFFLÉ AUX NOUILLES

- 1 quantity béchamel sauce
  (p.50)
- 500 ml (18 fl oz) milk
- 250 g (9 oz) tagliatelle or
  spaghetti, broken into 5-cm
  (2½-inch) lengths
- 4 eggs, separated
- Salt and pepper
- 1 quantity tomato sauce (p.57)

Preparation time: 30 minutes
Cooking time: 25 minutes
Serves 6

Make the béchamel sauce. Bring the milk and 2 litres (3½ pints) water to the boil in a large pan. Add the tagliatelle and boil for 12 minutes, or until al dente. Preheat the oven to 180°C/350°F/ Gas Mark 4. In a large bowl, whisk together the béchamel sauce and egg yolks and gently stir in the noodles. Season with salt and pepper. Beat the egg whites to stiff peaks and fold into the noodle mixture. Place in a gratin dish and bake for 25 minutes. Serve immediately.

MACARONI À LA NAPOLITAINE

MACARONIS À LA NAPOLITAINE

- 350 g (12 oz) macaroni
- 200 ml (7 fl oz) tomato sauce
  (p.57)
- 30 g (1¼ oz) butter
- 100 g (3½ oz) Gruyère
  cheese, grated
- Freshly grated nutmeg
- Salt and pepper

Preparation time: 15 minutes
Cooking time: 25 minutes
Serves 6

Bring a large pan of salted water to the boil, add the macaroni and boil for 8–10 minutes, or until al dente. Meanwhile, heat the tomato sauce. Drain the macaroni well, put in a serving dish and stir in the butter, cheese, freshly grated nutmeg and season with salt and pepper. Just before serving, pour over the hot tomato sauce.

MACARONI NIÇOIS

MACARONIS NIÇOIS

 p.639

Bring a large pan of salted water to the boil, add the macaroni and boil for 8–10 minutes, or until al dente. Drain and set aside. Sprinkle the slices of aubergine with salt and drain in a colander for 30 minutes. Rinse under cold running water and dry the slices. Heat the oil in a deep-fryer to 180°C/350°F, or until a cube of bread browns in 30 seconds, and fry the aubergines, in batches, for 5 minutes, or until crisp and golden. Drain on kitchen paper. Melt the butter in a pan and fry the tomatoes, mushrooms, ham and garlic for 5 minutes. Add the meat jus and the cheese. Season with salt and pepper. Mix the sauce with the macaroni and garnish with the fried aubergines.

- 200 g (7 oz) macaroni
- 3 large aubergines, thinly sliced
- Salt, for sprinkling
- Vegetable oil, for deep-frying
- 30 g (1¼ oz) butter
- 3 tomatoes, thinly sliced
- 100 g (3½ oz) mushrooms, thinly sliced
- 180 g (6¼ oz) ham, diced
- 1 garlic clove, crushed
- 100 ml (3½ fl oz) meat jus
- 60 g (2 oz) Parmesan cheese, grated
- Salt and pepper

Preparation time: 30 minutes
Cooking time: 25 minutes
Serves 6

MACARONI TIMBALE

TIMBALE MILANAISE

Bring a large pan of salted water to the boil, add the macaroni and boil for 8–10 minutes, or until al dente. Drain, return to the pan, stir in the butter and cheeses, and season with salt and pepper. In a large pan, bring the blond roux to a simmer, add the chosen diced meat or mushrooms and the bouquet garni and cook for 15 minutes. Season with salt and pepper, add the crème fraîche and simmer for a further 5 minutes. Discard the bouquet garni. Arrange alternate layers of the meat mixture and the macaroni in a serving dish, or a puff pastry case, if using. Finish with a layer of the meat mixture and sprinkle with grated truffle.

- 250 g (9 oz) macaroni
- 75 g (2½ oz) butter
- 75 g (2½ oz) Gruyère cheese
- 50 g (1¾ oz) Parmesan cheese
- Salt and pepper
- 300 ml (½ pint) blond roux (p.57)
- Your choice of: calves' sweetbreads, cooked and diced; ham, diced; poultry quenelles (p.104), diced; mushrooms, diced; or chipolata sausages, cooked and diced
- 1 bouquet garni
- 100 ml (3½ fl oz) crème fraîche
- Puff pastry case, cooked (optional)
- Truffle, grated, for sprinkling

Preparation time: 30 minutes
Cooking time: 45 minutes
Serves 6

MACARONI À LA CUSSY

MACARONIS À LA CUSSY

- 360 g (12½ oz) macaroni
- 100 g (3½ oz) butter
- 50 g (1¾ oz) truffles, peeled and sliced
- 100 ml (3½ fl oz) Madeira
- 1 prepared calves' sweetbread (p.370), diced
- Salt and pepper
- 50 ml (2 fl oz) veal stock
- 125 g (4¼ oz) Parmesan cheese, grated

Preparation time: 20 minutes
Cooking time: 20 minutes
Serves 6

Bring a large pan of salted water to the boil, add the macaroni and boil for 8–10 minutes, or until al dente. Drain and set aside. Meanwhile, melt a quarter of the butter in a pan and fry the truffles for a few minutes. Add the Madeira and the sweetbread and continue to cook for 10–15 minutes. Season with salt and pepper and add the stock. Put the macaroni in a serving dish and stir in the cheese and the remaining butter. Pour the sweetbread mixture over the macaroni and serve immediately.

MACARONI LOAF

PAIN DE MACARONIS

Preheat the oven to 150°C/300°F/Gas Mark 2 and grease a charlotte or other domed mould with butter. Bring a large pan of salted water to the boil, add the macaroni and boil for 8–10 minutes, or until al dente. Drain and stir in the egg yolks, cheese, ham and half the mushrooms. Season with salt and pepper. In a large bowl, beat the egg whites to stiff peaks, and fold them into the macaroni mixture. Pour the macaroni mixture into the prepared mould and place in a roasting tin half-filled with hot water. Bake for 1½ hours. Meanwhile, prepare the sauce. Melt the butter in a medium pan and fry the remaining mushrooms for 10 minutes. Season with salt, pepper and nutmeg, then stir in the crème fraîche. Turn out the macaroni loaf and pour the sauce over it to serve.

- 20 g (¾ oz) butter, plus extra for greasing
- 300 g (11 oz) macaroni
- 6 eggs, separated
- 100 g (3½ oz) mixed Gruyère and Parmesan cheese, grated
- 150 g (5 oz) ham, chopped
- 250 g (9 oz) mushrooms, sliced
- Salt and pepper
- Freshly grated nutmeg
- 125 ml (4½ oz) crème fraîche

Preparation time: 20 minutes
Cooking time: 1¾ hours
Serves 6

FRIED MACARONI

MACARONIS FRITS

Bring a large pan of salted water to the boil, add the macaroni and boil for 8–10 minutes, or until al dente. Drain well. Heat the oil in a deep-fryer to 180°C/350°F, or until a cube of bread browns in 30 seconds, and carefully place batches of macaroni in the hot oil and cook for 5 minutes, or until golden brown. Remove, drain and season with salt and pepper. Deep-fry the parsley (p.81). Use to garnish the fried macaroni.

- 250 g (9 oz) macaroni
- Vegetable oil, for deep-frying
- Salt and pepper
- 6 sprigs of flat-leaf parsley

Preparation time: 5 minutes
Cooking time: 25 minutes
Serves 6

MACARONI SALAD

SALADE DE MACARONIS

Bring a large pan of salted water to the boil, add the macaroni and boil for 8–10 minutes, or until al dente. Drain and season with salt and pepper. Dice the artichoke hearts and hard-boiled egg. Add to the macaroni along with the parsley. Make a well-seasoned mayonnaise and stir in the tomato purée. Fold gently into the macaroni mixture. Serve warm or cold.

- 200 g (7 oz) macaroni
- Salt and pepper
- 4 cooked artichoke hearts (p.510)
- 1 hard-boiled egg (p.134)
- Flat-leaf parsley, chopped
- 4 tablespoons mayonnaise (p.70)
- 60 g (2 oz) tomato purée

Preparation time: 1 hour
Cooking time: 25 minutes
Serves 6

NEAPOLITAN CROQUETTES

CROQUETTES NAPOLITAINES

- 250 g (9 oz) macaroni
- 200 g (7 oz) Gruyère cheese, grated
- 200 g (7 oz) ham, chopped
- 1 egg
- 2 eggs, separated
- Salt and pepper
- Dried breadcrumbs, for rolling
- Vegetable oil, for deep-frying

Preparation time: 20 minutes
Cooking time: 25 minutes
Serves 6

Bring a large pan of salted water to the boil, add the macaroni and boil for 8–10 minutes, or until al dente. Drain. In a bowl, mix the macaroni with the cheese, ham, whole egg and the egg yolks. Season with salt and pepper and shape the mixture into croquettes. Whisk the egg whites to soft peaks and dip the croquettes into the whites and then in the breadcrumbs. Heat the oil in a deep-fryer to 180°C/350°F, or until a cube of bread browns in 30 seconds, and fry the croquettes, in batches, for 5 minutes, or until golden.

MACARONI À LA CÉVENOLE

MACARONI À LA CÉVENOLE

- 250 g (9 oz) macaroni
- 60 g (2 oz) butter
- 500 g (1 lb 2 oz) chestnuts
- Salt and pepper
- 125 g (4¼ oz) Gruyère cheese, grated
- 60 ml (2 fl oz) crème fraîche

Preparation time: 20 minutes
Cooking time: 30 minutes
Serves 6

Bring a large pan of salted water to the boil, add the macaroni and boil for 8–10 minutes, or until al dente. Drain. Preheat the oven to 180°C/350°F/Gas Mark 4 and grease an ovenproof dish with some of the butter. Make a slit in the skins of the chestnuts and roast them for 20 minutes. Allow to cool, then peel and halve them. Mix the macaroni and chestnuts together and transfer to the prepared dish. Season with salt and pepper. Sprinkle with the cheese, dot with the remaining butter and pour on the crème fraîche. Bake for 15 minutes.

MACARONI GRATIN

MACARONIS GRATINS

Bring a large pan of salted water to the boil, add the macaroni and boil for 8–10 minutes, or until al dente, and then drain it. Finely mince or chop together the ham, meat and parsley and place in a bowl. Preheat the oven to 240°C/475°F/Gas Mark 8 and grease an ovenproof dish with butter. Melt 20 g (¾ oz) of the butter in a small pan and fry the mushrooms and onion for 5 minutes, until softened. Add to the meat with the stock and tomato sauce. Season with salt and pepper. Spread half the macaroni in the prepared dish, then add the meat and finally the remaining macaroni. Sprinkle with the cheese and dot with butter. Bake for 7–8 minutes.

- 250 g (9 oz) macaroni or elbow macaroni
- 120 g (4 oz) ham
- 120 g (4 oz) leftover meat (chicken, veal, beef)
- 1 handful of flat-leaf parsley
- 40 g (1½ oz) butter, plus extra for greasing and dotting
- 120 g (4 oz) mushrooms, sliced
- 1 onion, sliced
- 3 tablespoons rich stock or meat juices
- 100 ml (3½ fl oz) tomato sauce (p.57)
- Salt and pepper
- 85 g (3 oz) Gruyère cheese, grated

Preparation time: 20 minutes
Cooking time: 30 minutes
Serves 6

MACARONI À LA REINE

COQUILLETTES À LA REINE

Bring a large pan of salted water to the boil, add the macaroni and boil for 8–10 minutes, or until al dente. Drain. Stir in the cheese. Meanwhile, prepare the béchamel sauce, then stir the poultry into the sauce and add the meat juices. Reheat, if necessary, then stir in the pasta. Season with salt and pepper.

- 250 g (9 oz) small macaroni or elbow macaroni
- 150 g (5 oz) Gruyère cheese, grated
- 250 ml (8 fl oz) béchamel sauce (p.50)
- 150 g (5 oz) leftover roast poultry, sliced
- 100 ml (3½ fl oz) rich stock or meat juices
- Salt and pepper

Preparation time: 15 minutes
Cooking time: 15 minutes
Serves 6

CANNELLONI

CANNELLONIS

- 250 g (9 oz) pasta dough (p.626)
- 150 g (5 oz) cooked meat (beef, veal, chicken), finely chopped
- 100 g (3½ oz) sausage meat
- 200 g (7 oz) spinach purée
- 30 g (1¼ oz) Gruyère cheese, grated, plus extra for sprinkling (optional)
- 1 whole egg
- 1 egg yolk
- Freshly grated nutmeg
- 300 ml (½ pint) tomato sauce (p.57)
- Salt and pepper

Preparation time: 30 minutes
Cooking time: 30 minutes
Serves 6

Make the pasta dough and roll out to a thickness of 3 mm (⅛ inch). Cut into 12 x 12-cm (5-inch) squares. Bring a large pan of salted water to the boil, add the squares of pasta and simmer for 8 minutes, or until al dente. Drain. Make the stuffing. Mix together the cooked meat, sausage meat, spinach purée, Gruyère cheese, whole egg and egg yolk. Season with nutmeg, salt and pepper. Preheat the oven to 200°C/400°F/Gas Mark 6. Put a small portion of the stuffing mixture onto each square of pasta. Roll up each square so that it looks like very large macaroni, sealing the edge with a little water. Arrange the cannelloni in an ovenproof dish. Coat with the tomato sauce. Sprinkle with a little extra grated cheese, if desired. Bake for 10 minutes.

RAVIOLI

RAVIOLIS

- 250 g (9 oz) pasta dough (p.626)
- 125 g (4¼ oz) cooked meat, minced
- 2 tablespoons flat-leaf parsley, chopped
- Salt and pepper
- 1.5 litres (2½ pints) stock or water

Preparation time: 50 minutes
Cooking time: 10 minutes
Serves 6

Make the pasta dough. Roll out to a thickness of 3 mm (⅛ inch). Cut into circles approximately 15 cm (6 inches) in diameter. Mix the meat with the parsley and season with salt and pepper. Put a small quantity of this mixture on each circle. Moisten the edge of each circle with water, fold over and seal carefully like a small turnover. Bring the stock or water to the boil in a large pan, add the ravioli and simmer for 10 minutes. Serve as a garnish for soup, meat or vegetables, or alone with butter and grated Parmesan cheese.

SPAGHETTI WITH WALNUT SAUCE

SPAGHETTIS SAUCE AUX NOIX

Crush the garlic, walnuts and parsley in a mortar, then add the oil, drop by drop, to create an emulsified sauce. Season with salt and pepper. Bring a large pan of salted water to the boil, add the spaghetti and boil for 8–10 minutes, or until al dente. Drain. Coat the drained pasta in the sauce and sprinkle with the cheese.

+ **1 garlic clove**
+ **60 g (2 oz) walnut pieces**
+ **2 tablespoons flat-leaf parsley, chopped**
+ **2 tablespoons olive oil**
+ **Salt and pepper**
+ **250 g (9 oz) spaghetti**
+ **120 g (4 oz) Parmesan cheese, grated**

Preparation time: 30 minutes
Cooking time: 12 minutes
Serves 6

PROVENÇALE SPAGHETTI

TIMBALE PROVENÇALE

Bring a large pan of salted water to the boil, add the spaghetti and boil for 8–10 minutes, or until al dente. Drain. Melt the butter in a large pan and fry the onions and mushrooms for 2–3 minutes over a high heat, then reduce the heat to low, add the thyme and the bay leaf, and cook for 10 minutes, or until softened. Add the tomato sauce and spaghetti to the onions and mushrooms. Stir in the olives and cheese. Simmer for 2–3 minutes and serve very hot.

+ **250 g (9 oz) spaghetti**
+ **30 g (1¼ oz) butter**
+ **100 g (3½ oz) button onions**
+ **250 g (9 oz) button mushrooms**
+ **2 teaspoons thyme leaves**
+ **1 bay leaf**
+ **¼ quantity tomato sauce (p.57)**
+ **120 g (4 oz) olives, stoned**
+ **100 g (3½ oz) Parmesan cheese, grated**

Preparation time: 30 minutes
Cooking time: 40 minutes
Serves 6

GAUDES

GAUDES

This recipe comes from the Burgundy region in eastern France.

Bring 1 litre (1¾ pints) water and the salt to the boil in a large pan. Add the cornmeal, reduce the heat, and simmer for 25 minutes, stirring frequently. Add the butter. In a separate pan, heat the milk. Serve the cornmeal with the hot milk poured over it. Alternatively, the cornmeal mixture can be poured into a loaf tin, left to cool and set, then cut into slices and fried in butter.

+ **2 teaspoons salt**
+ **200 g (7 oz) cornmeal**
+ **125 g (4½ oz) butter**
+ **1 litre (1¾ pints) milk**
+ **Butter, for frying (optional)**

Preparation time: 5 minutes
Cooking time: 25 minutes
Serves 6

GNOCCHI

GNOCCHIS

- 300 g (11 oz) choux pastry dough (p.774)
- 25 g (1 oz) butter
- 500 ml (18 fl oz) cheese sauce (p.51)

Preparation time: 20 minutes, plus resting time
Cooking time: 30 minutes
Serves 6

Make the choux pastry dough and leave it to rest for 2 hours. Preheat the oven to 240°C/475°F/Gas Mark 8 and grease a dish with some of the butter. Bring a large pan of salted water to the boil and drop walnut-sized balls of the dough into the water. Poach the gnocchi for 15 minutes, then drain well. Arrange in the prepared dish. Pour over the cheese sauce. Dot with the remaining butter and bake for 10 minutes until golden brown.

CROSETS SAVOYARDS

CROSETS SAVOYARDS

- 500 g (1 lb 2 oz) flour
- 4 eggs
- 250 ml (8 fl oz) milk
- 1 teaspoon salt
- 100 g (3½ oz) Gruyère cheese, grated
- 100 ml (3½ fl oz) butter or meat juices, to serve

Preparation time: 30 minutes
Cooking time: 25 minutes
Serves 6

Traditionally, crosets are made from a combination of wheat and buckwheat flour. They come from the Savoie region near the French Alps.

Put the flour in a bowl, add the eggs, milk and salt and mix to make a firm dough. Roll the dough out to a thickness of about 3 mm (⅛ inch) and cut into small dice. Bring a large pan of salted water to the boil, add the diced pasta and cook for about 5 minutes, or until al dente. Drain. Sprinkle with the cheese and serve with the butter or meat juices.

KNEPFLES

KNEPFLES

- 300 g (11 oz) flour
- 2 eggs
- Salt and pepper
- 100 ml (3½ fl oz) milk
- 50 g (1¾ oz) butter, melted

Preparation time 25 minutes, plus resting time
Cooking time: 2 minutes
Serves 6

Prepare 2 hours in advance. Put the flour in a bowl, and add the eggs, salt, pepper and milk. Mix to make a dough and knead until smooth. Cover and set aside for 2 hours. Bring 3 litres (5¼ pints) salted water to the boil in a large pan. Shape the dough into cylinders 4 cm (1½ inches) long, then cut them into discs 2 cm (¾ inch) in diameter. Cook in the boiling water until they float to the surface, then continue to cook for 5 minutes more, until cooked through. Transfer to a serving dish and pour the butter over them. Serve immediately.

NOTE
Herbs such as chives, parsley or chervil can be added to the dough for these dumplings from Alsace.

Breton haricot beans (p.610)

Country-style rice   (p.618)

Lettuce parcels   (p.624)

Macaroni Niçois   (p.628)

FRUIT

Fruit is a high-quality food, not only from a nutritional point of view (it contains vitamins, minerals and fibre), but also because it offers a wide range of appealing flavours, textures, colours and aromas: a wealth of ideas for the creative cook. For the most nutritional benefit and best flavour, fruit should be eaten in season when it is fully ripe and free from disease. In the winter months, when fresh fruit is not so readily available, there is always the option of enjoying fruit that has been preserved by one of many methods such as bottling in alcohol or syrup, candying, drying or freezing.

SUGAR

Sugar is used in making desserts, cakes and pastries, and it also plays an essential role in preserving fruit in jams and syrup, or as candied fruit. In many recipes, sugar is cooked to a syrup. As the temperature of the syrup increases it takes on different characteristics and can be used in different ways. The syrup can be assessed by measuring the temperature it has reached, or by observing its physical characteristics, as described in the sugar syrup recipe and listed opposite. If using a sugar thermometer, ensure that the tip is suspended in the syrup, rather than resting against the side of the pan. Great care should be taken when making all types of sugar syrup, as very high temperatures are involved.

SUGAR SYRUP
SIROP DE SUCRE

Pour 250 ml (8 fl oz) water into a large, clean pan. Add the sugar and place over a low heat, stirring, until the sugar dissolves. Increase the heat and boil without stirring, observing closely until the syrup reaches the desired temperature or stage required for the recipe. To check the consistency using your fingers, remove a small quantity of syrup with a teaspoon, dip your fingers in cold water and immediately into the syrup on the spoon to check the consistency. When the correct temperature has been reached, remove the pan carefully from the heat and stop the cooking by adding one or two drops of iced water to the pan.

- **1 kg (2¼ lb) white sugar, caster or granulated**

  Preparation time: 2 minutes
  Cooking time: 5–25 minutes
  Makes 1.2 litres (2 pints)

VARIATION

. . . .

LIGHT SUGAR SYRUP
Dissolve 500 g (1 lb 2 oz) sugar in 1 litre (1¾ pints) water over a gentle heat, then boil for 1 minute. Makes 1.5 litres (2½ pints).

GLAZING SYRUP OR PEARL
105°C (221°F)
The syrup forms a fairly thin layer on the spoon.

SHORT THREAD
107°C (225°F)
When taken between the fingers (previously dipped in cold water), the syrup forms a small thread about 1 cm (½ inch) long that breaks immediately.

LONG THREAD
109–110°C (228–230°F)
A thread 2–3 cm (¾–1 inch) long is formed between the fingers.

FEATHER
111°C (232°F)
As it boils, the sugar forms small round beads on the surface. When taken between the fingers, it forms a thread 4–5 cm (1¾–2 inches) long.

SOUFFLÉ
114°C (237°F)
Small beads appear on the surface of the syrup. If you blow carefully on a spoon covered with the syrup, bubbles form.

SOFT BALL
115–117°C (239–242°F)
If you blow carefully on the spoon, the bubbles separate.

FIRM BALL
120°C (248°F)
When rolled between the fingers, the syrup forms a small soft ball, the size of a pea.

HARD BALL
125–130°C (257–266°F)
When rolled between the fingers, the syrup forms a fairly hard ball the size of a hazelnut.

SOFT CRACK
135–140°C (275–284°F)
The small ball of sugar is hard and brittle. It sticks to the teeth.

HARD CRACK
145–150°C (293–302°F)
The ball can be cracked between the fingers or the teeth.

LIGHT CARAMEL
DARK CARAMEL
155–165°C (311–329°F)
166–175°C (330–347°F)
All the water has evaporated and the sugar is starting to caramelize, moving from light gold to deeper brown.

POACHED APRICOTS

ABRICOTS À L'ANGLAISE

Bring 2 litres (3½ pints) water to the boil in a large pan. Wash, halve and stone the apricots. Place the halved fruits carefully in boiling water. Remove them with a slotted spoon as soon as they rise to the surface. Arrange in a dish and sprinkle with caster sugar. Serve cold.

- **1 kg (2¼ lb) apricots**
- **Caster sugar, to taste**

Preparation time: 10 minutes
Cooking time: 10 minutes
Serves 6

APRICOT COMPOTE

COMPOTE D'ABRICOTS

Prepare a syrup to the long-thread stage (p.643) with the sugar and 250 ml (8 fl oz) water. Wash the apricots, cut them in half and remove the stones. Simmer in the syrup for 10–12 minutes. Arrange on a dish and pour the juices over them.

- **125 g (4¼ oz) caster sugar**
- **1 kg (2¼ lb) apricots**

Preparation time: 10 minutes
Cooking time: 20 minutes
Serves 6

DRIED APRICOT COMPOTE

ABRICOTS SECS EN COMPOTE

The day before serving them, wash and soak the apricots in enough water to cover generously. The next day, drain the apricots and bring 500 ml (18 fl oz) of the soaking water and the sugar to the boil in a medium pan. Carefully place the apricots in the boiling syrup. Reduce the heat and simmer gently for 1 hour. Serve warm or cold with the cooking liquid.

- **300 g (11 oz) dried apricots**
- **90 g (3¼ oz) caster sugar**

Preparation time: 5 minutes,
plus soaking time
Cooking time: 1 hour
Serves 6

SURPRISE EGGS

ŒUFS SURPRISE

Cut the apricots in half, remove the kernels and reserve. Bring 100 ml (3½ fl oz) water and sugar to the boil in a medium pan. Add the kernels and boil for 10–12 minutes. Remove the kernels with a slotted spoon. Carefully lower the apricot halves into the syrup, reduce the heat and poach for 5–6 minutes in the simmering syrup. Remove the apricots with a slotted spoon and drain. Cool. Spread the cold rice pudding on a round dish, cover with the crème fraîche and arrange the apricot halves on top to resemble egg yolks. Serve cold.

- **12 very large apricots**
- **100 g (3½ oz) caster sugar**
- **200 g (7 oz) rice pudding (p.711)**
- **125 ml (4½ fl oz) crème fraîche**

Preparation time: 10 minutes
Cooking time: 20 minutes
Serves 6

DIPLOMAT PUDDING
DIPLOMATE

Prepare the day before. Combine the rum and light sugar syrup in a shallow bowl. Dip the flat side of the sponge fingers in this mixture and arrange them around the base and sides of a charlotte mould. Spread the sponge fingers with a third of the apricot marmalade. Sprinkle with the raisins and candied fruit. Fill the mould with alternating layers of soaked sponge fingers, compote, and raisins and candied fruit. Finish with a layer of sponge fingers. Cover with a plate and put a 200-g (7-oz) weight on top. Leave in the refrigerator for 24 hours. Turn out on a dish and serve with the crème anglaise.

- 5 tablespoons rum
- 5 tablespoons light sugar syrup (p.643)
- 300 g (11 oz) sponge fingers
- 350 g (12 oz) apricot marmalade (p.855)
- 85 g (3 oz) raisins
- 3 tablespoons candied fruit, chopped
- 500 ml (18 fl oz) crème anglaise (p.694)

Preparation time: 20 minutes, plus standing time
Cooking time: 20 minutes
Serves 6

APRICOT OMELETTE
OMELETTE AUX ABRICOTS

 p.680

Preheat the grill. Make an omelette (p.157) with the eggs and butter, adding a pinch of salt to the beaten eggs. Before folding, fill with the apricot marmalade. Fold. Slide onto an ovenproof dish. Sprinkle with the sugar and brown under a hot grill for 3–5 minutes.

- 6 eggs
- 50 g (1¾ oz) butter
- Salt
- 120 g (4 oz) apricot marmalade (p.855)
- 2–3 tablespoons icing sugar

Preparation time: 10 minutes
Cooking time: 10 minutes
Serves 6

ALMOND PASTE
PÂTE D'AMANDES

Blanch the almonds for 2 minutes in boiling water. Drain and rub off the skins with a clean dry tea towel. Pound the almonds with the sugar and egg white in a mortar to form a smooth paste; this can also be done in a food processor. Shop-bought blanched or ground almonds may be used for speed and convenience.

- 200 g (7 oz) sweet almonds
- 5–6 bitter almonds
- 200 g (7 oz) caster sugar
- 1 egg white

Preparation time: 35 minutes
Cooking time: 2 minutes
Serves 6

ALMOND MILK JELLY

BLANC-MANGER

- 500 g (1 lb 2 oz) sweet almonds
- 30 g (1¼ oz) bitter almonds
- 15 g (½ oz) powdered gelatine, or 4 gelatine leaves
- 350 g (12 oz) caster sugar
- 1 tablespoon orange-flower water

Preparation time: 1 hour, plus setting time
Cooking time: 5 minutes
Serves 6

Prepare 3 or 4 hours in advance. Blanch the almonds for 2 minutes in boiling water. Drain and rub off the skins with a clean dry tea towel, and then pound them in a mortar adding 450 ml (16 fl oz) water, a little at a time. A food processor may be used for speed and convenience. Put the mixture in a strong, clean cloth and twist over a bowl to collect the almond milk.

Combine the gelatine and 50 ml (2 fl oz) water in a small pan and soak for 5 minutes until softened. Set the pan over very gentle heat and allow the gelatine to dissolve, without letting the liquid boil. Add this and the sugar to the almond milk, and stir to combine. Stir in the orange-flower water. Pour into a mould or individual ramekins and put in a refrigerator or on ice to set. To turn out, soak the mould for 30 seconds in warm water and turn out onto a serving dish.

SALTED ALMONDS

AMANDES SALÉES

- 250 g (9 oz) almonds
- 25 g (1 oz) salt

Preparation time: 5 minutes
Cooking time: 15 minutes
Serves 6

Preheat the oven to 200°C/400°F/Gas Mark 6. Blanch the almonds for 2 minutes in boiling water. Drain and rub off the skins with a clean dry tea towel. While the almonds are still damp, roll them in the salt. Spread the almonds in a single layer on a baking sheet and bake for 10 minutes, until golden. Cool, and shake off any excess salt before serving.

PINEAPPLE WITH KIRSCH

ANANAS AU KIRSCH

- 1 pineapple, about 1.2 kg (2½ lb)
- 200 ml (7 fl oz) light sugar syrup (p.643)
- 50 ml (2 fl oz) Kirsch

Preparation time: 5 minutes
Serves 6

Remove the skin and eyes from the pineapple. Cut into slices and pour the sugar syrup and Kirsch over them. Macerate for 1 hour. Serve very cold. Other kinds of alcohol can be substituted for the Kirsch, such as Champagne or rum.

PINEAPPLE COMPOTE

COMPOTE D'ANANAS

Put the sugar and 250 ml (8 fl oz) water into a medium pan. Bring to the boil, stirring to dissolve the sugar. Remove the skin and eyes from the pineapple and cut it into chunks, discarding the tough core. Peel the oranges, divide into segments and remove any pips. Carefully lower the pineapple chunks and orange segments into the boiling syrup and reduce the heat to a simmer. Cook for 12 minutes. Remove from the heat and arrange on a serving dish. Pour the maraschino liqueur over the fruit.

- 150 g (5 oz) sugar
- 1 pineapple, about 1.2 kg (2½ lb)
- 2 oranges
- 50 ml (2 fl oz) maraschino liqueur

Preparation time: 10 minutes
Cooking time: 35 minutes
Serves 6

PINEAPPLE RING

COURONNE D'ANANAS

Make a rice pudding (p.711) with the rice, milk, 85 g (3 oz) of the sugar, and the vanilla and salt. Lightly oil a ring mould. Pour the rice pudding into the ring mould and level the surface. Allow to cool and set in the refrigerator. Turn out onto a serving dish. Remove the skin and eyes from the pineapple. Slice thinly, cut the slices in half and arrange them around the rice ring. Put the strawberries in a blender with the remaining sugar, process to a purée and pour this sauce into the centre of the ring. Serve very cold.

- 250 g (9 oz) pudding rice
- 750 ml (1¼ pints) milk
- 120 g (4 oz) caster sugar
- 1 teaspoon vanilla extract
- 1 teaspoon salt
- Flavourless oil, for greasing
- 1 pineapple, about 1.2 kg (2½ lb)
- 125 g (4¼ oz) strawberries

Preparation time: 15 minutes, plus setting time
Cooking time: 45 minutes
Serves 6

BANANA COMPOTE

COMPOTE DE BANANES

In a medium pan, bring the sugar and 250 ml (8 fl oz) water to the boil. Peel the bananas and remove any fibres. Cut into slices and carefully place them in the syrup. Reduce the heat and simmer gently for 10 minutes, stirring occasionally. Serve cold.

- 100 g (3½ oz) sugar
- 6 bananas

Preparation time: 3 minutes
Cooking time: 10 minutes
Serves 6

p.681

FLAMBÉED BANANAS
BANANES FLAMBANTES

- **85 g (3 oz) sugar**
- **1 teaspoon vanilla extract**
- **6 bananas**
- **1½ tablespoons rum**

Preparation time: 5 minutes
Cooking time: 15 minutes
Serves 6

In a wide, shallow pan, bring the sugar, 250 ml (8 fl oz) water and the vanilla to the boil. Peel the bananas, removing any fibres, and poach for 3–4 minutes in the syrup. Lift out the bananas carefully, using a slotted spoon to keep them whole. Reserve the syrup. Arrange the bananas on a serving dish. Just before serving, add the rum to the syrup and reheat over a medium heat, without letting it boil. Pour over the bananas and, keeping the serving dish well away from anything flammable and standing well back, very carefully touch a lighted match to the edge of the dish to ignite the rum. Serve while still flaming.

FRIED BANANAS
BANANES FRITES

- **6 bananas**
- **50 g (1¾ oz) butter**
- **30 g (1¼ oz) caster sugar**

Preparation time: 3 minutes
Cooking time: 3 minutes
Serves 6

Peel the bananas, removing any fibres, and cut them in half lengthways. Melt the butter in a frying pan and fry the bananas over a high heat for 2–3 minutes on each side. Arrange on a dish, sprinkle with the sugar and serve immediately. The bananas can also be served on a bed of hot rice pudding.

BANANA CRÊPES
CRÊPES AUX BANANES

- **½ quantity crêpe batter (p.721)**
- **1 quantity crème pâtissière (p.706)**
- **2 tablespoons rum**
- **30 g (1¼ oz) butter**
- **6 bananas**

Preparation time: 20 minutes
Cooking time: 30 minutes
Makes 12 crêpes

Make the crêpe batter and set it aside to rest. Meanwhile, make the crème pâtissière and stir in the rum. Cook 12 crêpes, using 20 g (¾ oz) of the butter to grease the pan. Preheat the oven to 200°C/400°F/Gas Mark 6. Peel the bananas and cut them in half lengthways. Put 1 tablespoon crème pâtissière and half a banana on each crêpe and roll up. Use the remaining butter to grease a gratin dish and arrange the stuffed crêpes in it. Bake for 7–8 minutes, until golden, and serve immediately.

BANANA BOATS

BATEAUX DE BANANES

Prepare the day before. Choose unblemished bananas that are not too ripe. Keeping the peel on, cut them in half lengthways. Remove the flesh from the skins without damaging them and put the skins aside, covered. Combine the rum, caster sugar and lemon juice in a shallow dish. Dice the banana flesh and add to the dish. Hull, wash, and slice the large strawberries and add them to the dish. Stir gently to coat, cover, and macerate for 12 hours, stirring gently from time to time. Press the wild strawberries and the raspberries through a sieve and place the purée and sugar in a small pan. Boil for 10 minutes to make a syrup, then leave to cool. Before serving, drain the banana and strawberry mixture. Fill the reserved banana skin boats with it, coat with the strawberry syrup and serve very cold.

* 6 bananas
* 1 teaspoon rum
* 50 g (1¾ oz) caster sugar
* Juice of 1 lemon
* 250 g (9 oz) large strawberries
* 120 g (4 oz) wild strawberries
* 120 g (4 oz) raspberries
* 100 g (3½ oz) icing sugar

Preparation time: 20 minutes, plus macerating time
Cooking time: 10 minutes
Serves 6

BANANA CONDÉ

CONDÉ DE BANANES

Make a thick rice pudding, and use it to fill a lightly oiled ring mould. Leave to cool and set in the refrigerator. Peel the bananas, cut them in half, and then in half again lengthways. Cut the oranges, mandarins and apples into small dice. Place 100 ml (3½ fl oz) water and the sugar in a pan, bring to the boil and poach the bananas for 3–4 minutes. Remove with a slotted spoon and drain. Poach the diced fruit for 3–4 minutes. Remove with a slotted spoon and drain. Turn the rice ring out onto a serving dish and arrange the bananas round it. Put the diced fruit in the middle. Decorate with glacé or tinned cherries. Stir the apricot marmalade into the poaching syrup, if using, and pour the syrup over the entire dessert.

* 500 ml (18 fl oz) rice pudding (p.711)
* Flavourless oil, for greasing
* 6 bananas
* 2 oranges
* 2 mandarins
* 2 apples
* 80 g (2¾ oz) sugar
* A few glacé cherries or tinned cherries, to serve
* 1–2 tablespoons apricot marmalade (p.855), optional

Preparation time: 15 minutes, plus cooling time
Cooking time: 30 minutes
Serves 6

VARIATIONS

· ·

PEACH CONDÉ

CONDÉ DE PÊCHES

Halve, stone and peel 6 large, ripe peaches. Continue as for banana condé. The fruit filling in the centre should consist of 125 g (4¼ oz) each diced and poached apricots, plums and mirabelle plums.

APRICOT CONDÉ
CONDÉ D'ABRICOTS

Halve and stone 12 ripe apricots. Proceed as for banana condé. The fruit filling in the centre should consist of 125 g (4¼ oz) each diced and poached peaches, plums and mirabelle plums.

PEAR CONDÉ
CONDÉ DE POIRES

Peel 6 ripe pears, cut in half and remove the stalks and cores. Proceed as for banana condé, poaching the pears for 10 minutes in the syrup, made with 250 ml (8 fl oz) water. The fruit filling in the centre should consist of 125 g (4¼ oz) each redcurrants, raspberries and strawberries.

APPLE CONDÉ
CONDÉ DE POMMES

Peel 6 eating apples, cut in half and remove the stalks and cores. Proceed as for banana condé, poaching the apples for 10–15 minutes in the syrup, made with 250 ml (8 fl oz) water. The central filling is replaced by ½ jar redcurrant jelly mixed into a little hot water.

BANANA SOUFFLÉ
SOUFFLÉ DE BANANES

- 20 g (¾ oz) butter, plus extra for greasing
- 25 g (1 oz) flour
- 100 ml (3½ fl oz) hot milk
- 6 bananas
- 3 eggs, separated
- 50 g (1¾ oz) caster sugar
- 1 teaspoon vanilla extract
- 1 pinch of salt

Preparation time: 20 minutes
Cooking time: 50 minutes
Serves 6

Make a béchamel sauce (p.50) with the butter, flour and milk. Purée the bananas in a blender or food processor and mix them into the sauce. Beat in the egg yolks and sugar and add the vanilla. Preheat the oven to 220°C/425°F/Gas Mark 7 and butter a soufflé dish. Whisk the egg whites to stiff peaks with the salt and fold into the banana purée. Pour this mixture into the prepared soufflé dish, gently level the surface, and bake for 30 minutes, until well risen and golden brown.

POACHED CHERRIES

CERISES À L'ANGLAISE

Wash the fruit. Cut the stalks with scissors, leaving only 1 cm (½ inch) still attached. Bring a large pan of water to the boil. Add a few cherries at a time to the water, where they will fall to the bottom. As soon as they rise to the surface, remove the cherries with a slotted spoon and put them in a dish. Sprinkle with sugar and leave to cool.

- **1 kg (2¼ lb) cherries**
- **Caster sugar, to taste**

Preparation time: 10 minutes
Cooking time: 5 minutes
Serves 6

CHERRY COMPOTE

COMPOTE DE CERISES

Remove the stalks and stone the cherries. Put 120 ml (4 fl oz) water and the sugar (exactly how much will depend upon the natural sweetness of the cherries) in a pan and bring to the boil. Add the cherries and simmer for 10 minutes. Serve cold, in the syrup.

- **1 kg (2¼ lb) cherries**
- **100 –120 g (3½–4 oz) caster sugar**

Preparation time: 15 minutes
Cooking time: 10 minutes
Serves 6

CHERRIES WITH KIRSCH

CERISES AU KIRSCH

Remove the stalks and stone the cherries. Put the sugar and 100 ml (3½ fl oz) water in a pan and bring to the boil. Add the cherries and simmer for 10 minutes. Mix the flour with a few teaspoons of cold water in a bowl. Pour into the cherry compote and stir until thickened. Boil for a further 2 minutes. Remove from the heat. Pour the compote into a bowl. Warm the Kirsch and pour it over the compote. Ensure the dish is well away from anything flammable and, standing well back, very carefully touch a lighted match to its edge to ignite the Kirsch. Serve while flaming.

- **1 kg (2¼ lb) cherries**
- **200 g (7 oz) sugar**
- **15 g (½ oz) potato or rice flour**
- **1 tablespoon Kirsch**

Preparation time: 20 minutes
Cooking time: 20 minutes
Serves 6

DUCHESSE CHERRIES

CERISES DUCHESSE

- 600 g (1 lb 5 oz) large Morello or other tart cherries
- 2 egg whites
- 125 g (4¼ oz) caster sugar

Preparation time: 20 minutes
Cooking time: 15 minutes
Serves 6

Preheat the oven to 180°C / 350°F / Gas Mark 4. Trim the cherry stalks, leaving about 2 cm (¾ inch) still attached. Wash and dry lightly. Beat the egg whites for 5 minutes with a fork. Dip the cherries in the egg whites, then in the sugar. Sprinkle a baking sheet with some of the remaining sugar. Arrange the cherries on the sheet and bake for 15 minutes. Serve hot, warm or cold.

CLAFOUTIS

CLAFOUTIS

- Butter, for greasing
- 100 g (3½ oz) flour
- 6 eggs
- 1 pinch of salt
- 250 ml (8 fl oz) milk
- 750 g (1 lb 10 oz) black cherries, stoned
- 1 tablespoon Kirsch
- 90 g (3¼ oz) caster sugar

Preparation time: 30 minutes
Cooking time: 35 minutes
Serves 6

This recipe comes from the Limousin region in central France. Black cherries are the classic ingredient, but clafoutis is often made with other stone fruit, such as apricots or plums.

Preheat the oven to 200°C/400°F/Gas Mark 6 and butter an ovenproof dish. Mix the flour with the eggs and salt. Add a little of the milk. Beat the batter to make it light and smooth. Beat in the remaining milk a little at a time. The batter should have the consistency of crêpe batter. Add the cherries and Kirsch to the batter. Pour into the prepared dish and bake for 35 minutes. Sprinkle with the sugar. Serve warm or cold.

STRAWBERRIES & CREAM

FRAISES À LA CRÈME

- 500 g (1 lb 2 oz) strawberries
- 250 ml (8 fl oz) sweetened whipped cream (p.121)
- Caster sugar, to serve

Preparation time: 10 minutes
Serves 6

Wash, drain and trim the strawberries. Arrange on a dish in the shape of a pyramid and coat the pyramid with the cream. Serve with caster sugar. If preferred, strawberries may be served with crème fraîche, handed separately.

STRAWBERRIES MARINATED IN WINE

FRAISES AU JUS

 p.682

Prepare several hours in advance. Wash, drain and trim the strawberries and place in a bowl. Add sugar to taste and just cover the fruit with wine, maraschino or Champagne. Macerate in the refrigerator for several hours before serving.

- **500 g (1 lb 2 oz) strawberries**
- **Caster sugar, to taste**
- **½ bottle red wine, maraschino or Champagne, chilled**

Preparation time: 10 minutes, plus macerating time
Serves 6

ITALIAN-STYLE STRAWBERRIES

FRAISES À L'ITALIENNE

Prepare 2 hours in advance. Wash, drain and trim the strawberries and place in a bowl. Add the sugar, lemon juice and Kirsch. Macerate in the refrigerator for 2 hours before serving.

- **500 g (1 lb 2 oz) strawberries**
- **85 g (3 oz) caster sugar**
- **Juice of 2 lemons**
- **2 tablespoons Kirsch**

Preparation time: 10 minutes, plus macerating time
Serves 6

p.683

RASPBERRY LOAF

PAIN DE FRAMBOISES

- Butter, for greasing
- 250 ml (8 fl oz) white wine
- 130 g (4½ oz) caster sugar
- Juice of 1 lemon
- 1 teaspoon vanilla extract
- 125 g (4¼ oz) semolina

For the coulis:
- 250 g (9 oz) raspberries
- 100 g (3½ oz) icing sugar
- Juice of ½ lemon

Preparation time: 20 minutes,
plus cooling time
Cooking time: 1 hour
Serves 6

Preheat the oven to 150°C/300°F/Gas Mark 2, and butter 1 large or several small charlotte moulds. Put 250 ml (8 fl oz) water and the wine, sugar, lemon juice and vanilla in a large pan. Boil for 5 minutes and then add the semolina all at once. Simmer for 15 minutes, stirring. Pour the semolina mixture into the prepared moulds. Place in a roasting tin half-filled with hot water and bake for 30 minutes. Allow to cool, then turn out onto a serving dish. Meanwhile, prepare the raspberry coulis (see below), and use it to coat the semolina before serving.

RASPBERRY COULIS

COULIS DE FRAMBOISE

- 500 g (1 lb 2 oz) raspberries
- 200 g (7 oz) icing sugar
- Juice of ½ lemon

Preparation time: 5 minutes
Serves 6

Purée the raspberries in a blender, and add the sugar and lemon juice. Blend again for 2 minutes. Pass through a fine-meshed sieve to remove the pips and refrigerate in a sealed container until ready to serve.

COOKED RASPBERRY COULIS

COULIS DE FRAMBOISE (CHAUD)

- 500 g (1 lb 2 oz) raspberries
- 200 g (7 oz) sugar
- Juice of ½ lemon

Preparation time: 12 minutes
Cooking time: 5 minutes
Serves 6

Purée the raspberries in a blender for 1 minute. Add the sugar and lemon juice and blend again briefly. Pour into a pan and bring to the boil while stirring with a wooden spoon. Remove immediately from the heat. Pass through a fine-meshed sieve and refrigerate in a sealed container until ready to serve.

NOTE
For a simple fruit dessert, the coulis may be mixed with 250 g (9 oz) sweetened whipped cream (p.121) or 200 ml (7 fl oz) crème anglaise (p.694) flavoured with vanilla.

REDCURRANTS IN THEIR JUICE

GROSEILLES AU JUS

Prepare 2 hours in advance. Wash and drain the redcurrants and strip them from their stalks. Put them in a glass bowl, add the sugar and lemon juice and stir gently to coat. Macerate for 2 hours.

- 500 g (1 lb 2 oz) redcurrants
- 200 g (7 oz) caster sugar
- Juice of 1 lemon

Preparation time: 15 minutes, plus macerating time
Serves 6

CARDINAL CURRANTS

GROSEILLES CARDINAL

Prepare 3 hours in advance. Wash and drain the currants and strip them from their stalks. Put them in a glass bowl. Wash the raspberries. Put them in a sieve lined with muslin cloth and press out all the juice. Pour the raspberry juice over the currants and add the vanilla sugar and lemon juice. Surround the bowl with ice or place in the refrigerator. Cool for 3 hours.

- 250 g (9 oz) redcurrants
- 250 g (9 oz) whitecurrants
- 150 g (5 oz) raspberries
- 150 g (5 oz) vanilla sugar
- Juice of 1 lemon

Preparation time: 20 minutes, plus cooling time
Serves 6

MANDARIN COMPOTE

MARMELADE DE MANDARINS

Bring a large pan of water to the boil. Wash and dry the mandarins. Remove the skin and remove any fibres and pith. Divide the segments, discarding any pips, and reserve. Place the cleaned peel in the boiling water and cook for about 30 minutes, until tender. Drain. Process to a smooth, thick purée in a blender or food processor. Place the sugar and 250 ml (8 fl oz) water in a pan and bring to the boil. Boil for 10 minutes over a high heat. Reduce the heat, add the mandarin purée and the mandarin segments and simmer very gently for 12–15 minutes. Remove, cool and serve cold.

- 500 g (1 lb 2 oz) large unblemished mandarins
- 200 g (7 oz) sugar

Preparation time: 20 minutes
Cooking time: 1 hour
Serves 6

CHESTNUT VERMICELLI
VERMICELLERIE DE MARRONS

- 500 g (1 lb 2 oz) chestnuts
- 120 g (4 oz) caster sugar
- 250 ml (8 fl oz) sweetened whipped cream (p.121)

Preparation time: 45 minutes
Cooking time: 35 minutes
Serves 6

📷 p.684

Peel and cook the chestnuts (p.558). Mash them, then force them through a sieve or colander with large holes, straight onto a serving dish so that they look like vermicelli. Sprinkle with the sugar. Arrange a pyramid of the cream over the chestnuts.

MONT BLANC
MONT-BLANC

- 500 g (1 lb 2 oz) peeled chestnuts
- 175 g (6 oz) vanilla sugar
- 250 ml (8 fl oz) double cream

Preparation time: 30 minutes
Cooking time: 30 minutes
Serves 6

Prepare a chestnut purée (p.559) and stir in the sugar. Pile or pipe into a pyramid shape on a serving dish. Whip the cream to stiff peaks and spread or pipe it onto the chestnut purée. Serve very cold.

CHESTNUTS IN SYRUP
MARRONS AU SIROP

- 500 g (1 lb 2 oz) chestnuts
- 300 g (11 oz) sugar
- 1 teaspoon vanilla extract

Preparation time: 30 minutes
Cooking time: 50 minutes
Serves 6

Cook the chestnuts in water (p.558) for 20 minutes. Drain and allow to cool slightly, then peel off the skins while still warm, without damaging the flesh. Place the sugar and 100 ml (3½ fl oz) water in a medium pan and heat gently to simmering point to dissolve the sugar. Add the vanilla. Lower the chestnuts carefully into the syrup. Cook on a very low heat for 30 minutes. Arrange the chestnuts on a dish and spoon over the syrup. Allow to cool before serving.

CHRISTMAS LOG

BÛCHE DE NOËL

Make a chestnut purée (p.559) and mix the butter into it. Put the chocolate in the milk or water and melt over a gentle heat, stirring occasionally. Mix the chocolate into the chestnut purée very thoroughly. Allow to cool for several hours. Shape into a log, decorate with the crystallized flowers and surround with the cream.

- 1 kg (2¼ lb) chestnuts
- 100 g (3½ oz) butter
- 250 g (9 oz) dark chocolate
- 50 ml (2 fl oz) milk or water
- 60 g (2 oz) crystallized flowers, such as violets
- 250 ml (8 fl oz) sweetened whipped cream (p.121)

Preparation time: 40 minutes, plus cooling time
Cooking time: 30 minutes
Serves 6

CHESTNUT CAKE

GÂTEAU DE MARRONS

Make a slit in the skin of each chestnut and cook in boiling water for 30 minutes. Drain and allow to cool slightly, then peel off the skins while still warm. Preheat the oven to 160°C/325°F/Gas Mark 3. Put the chestnuts, milk, sugar and vanilla in a pan and simmer for 15 minutes. Remove from the heat, cool a little and then process the chestnut mixture in a blender until smooth. Whisk the egg whites to stiff peaks and fold into the purée. Coat a charlotte mould with the light caramel. Pour in the chestnut mixture. Bake for 1½–1¾ hours. Serve with the crème anglaise.

- 1 kg (2¼ lb) chestnuts
- 250 ml (8 fl oz) milk
- 100 g (3½ oz) sugar
- 1 teaspoon vanilla extract
- 4 egg whites
- 1 quantity light caramel (p.643)
- 500 ml (18 fl oz) crème anglaise (p.694), to serve

Preparation time: 45 minutes
Cooking time: 2½ hours
Serves 6

p.685

CHESTNUT & CHOCOLATE TERRINE

PAVÉ DE MARRONS AU CHOCOLAT

- 2 fresh egg yolks
- 50 g (1¾ oz) caster sugar
- 150 g (5 oz) dark chocolate
- 125 g (4¼ oz) butter at room temperature
- 400 g (14 oz) chestnut purée (p.559)
- 40 ml (1½ fl oz) crème fraîche
- 50 ml (2 fl oz) Kirsch
- 24 sponge fingers
- 1 quantity light caramel (p.643), crème anglaise (p.694) or rum sauce (p.729), to serve

Preparation time: 30 minutes, plus chilling time
Serves 6

Prepare the day before. Whisk the egg yolks with the sugar until the mixture becomes thick, white and creamy. Melt the chocolate with very little water in a heatproof bowl set over a pan of barely simmering water, and stir into the eggs. Beat the butter to soften it and add to the egg and chocolate mixture. Mix the chestnut purée a little at a time into the mixture. Finally, stir in the crème fraîche and Kirsch.

Arrange the sponge fingers in a loaf tin, covering the base and sides. Spoon in a layer of the chestnut mixture. Add a layer of sponge fingers and another layer of chestnut mixture. Finish with a layer of sponge fingers. Cover the sponge fingers with foil and press down with a few weights. Refrigerate for 12 hours. Turn out. Serve the terrine as it is, or coated with very light caramel, crème anglaise or rum sauce.

CHESTNUT SOUFFLÉ

SOUFFLÉ AUX MARRONS

- 500 g (1 lb 2 oz) chestnuts
- 30 g (1¼ oz) butter, plus extra for greasing
- 500 ml (18 fl oz) milk
- 1 teaspoon vanilla extract
- 125 g (4¼ oz) caster sugar
- 4 eggs, separated

Preparation time: 30 minutes
Cooking time: 1¼ hour
Serves 6

Make a slit in the skin of each chestnut and cook in boiling water for 30 minutes. Drain and allow to cool slightly, then peel off the skins while still warm. Preheat the oven to 180°C/350°F/Gas Mark 4 and butter an ovenproof dish. Put the chestnuts and milk in a pan, and bring to the boil, then reduce the heat and simmer for 15 minutes. Stir in the vanilla and sugar. Allow to cool a little and then process the chestnut mixture in a blender until smooth. Return to the pan and add the egg yolks, stirring constantly. Whisk the egg whites until stiff and fold into the mixture. Pour into the prepared dish and bake for 25 minutes, or until golden and risen.

GREEN MELON COMPOTE

COMPOTE DE MELON VERT

Peel the melons, removing a thick layer of rind, and scoop out the seeds. Cut in thin slices. Place the sugar and vinegar in a non-reactive pan. Heat gently to dissolve the sugar and then add the melon slices. Simmer for 30–35 minutes, or until tender. Serve cold.

- **3 small unripe melons**
- **250 g (9 oz) caster sugar**
- **50 ml (2 fl oz) white wine vinegar**

Preparation time: 10 minutes
Cooking time: 35 minutes
Serves 6

MELON SURPRISE

MELON SURPRISE

Prepare the day before. Cut the melon in half and remove the seeds. Carefully cut out the flesh without damaging the peel, and dice it. Mix the diced flesh with the strawberries, sugar and Kirsch. Fill the melon halves with this mixture, then bring the halves together and tie tightly with string. Chill in the refrigerator for 24 hours and serve very cold.

- **1 large ripe melon**
- **250 g (9 oz) strawberries, cut into pieces if large**
- **80 g (2¾ oz) caster sugar**
- **50 ml (2 fl oz) Kirsch**

Preparation time: 15 minutes, plus chilling time
Serves 6

WALNUT TERRINE

GRENOBLOIS (AUX NOIX)

Prepare the day before. Whisk the egg yolks with the sugar until thick, white and creamy. Crush the walnuts to a paste. Crush 3 sponge fingers to a powder. Fold the walnut paste, powdered sponge fingers and the softened butter into the egg yolk mixture. Whisk the egg whites to stiff peaks and fold them into the mixture. Line a loaf tin with greaseproof paper. Soak the remaining sponge fingers in the coffee extract and Cognac and use to line the sides and base of the tin. Place the walnut mixture and sponge fingers in the tin in alternate layers, finishing with a layer of sponge fingers. Cover with greaseproof paper, put a few weights on top and refrigerate until the next day. Turn out and serve as it is, or accompanied by coffee crème anglaise.

- **4 egg yolks**
- **25 g (1 oz) caster sugar**
- **100 g (3½ oz) shelled walnuts**
- **28 sponge fingers**
- **90 g (3¼ oz) butter, softened**
- **2 egg whites**
- **100 ml (3½ fl oz) coffee extract**
- **50 ml (2 fl oz) Cognac**
- **Coffee crème anglaise (p.694), to serve (optional)**

Preparation time: 30 minutes, plus chilling time
Serves 6

ORANGE SURPRISE

ORANGES SURPRISE

- 6 oranges
- 1 apple, peeled and diced
- 1 pear, peeled and diced
- 2 bananas, peeled and diced
- 2 tablespoons raisins
- 2 tablespoons glacé cherries, halved
- 60 g (2 oz) caster sugar
- Rum, to taste

Preparation time: 30 minutes
Serves 6

Make small 'lids' by slicing the top off each orange. Reserve the lids and scoop out the flesh. Reserve the hollowed-out orange skins. Cut the flesh into small pieces and put in a dish. Add all the other fruit, and the raisins and cherries. Stir in the sugar, and rum to taste. Fill the hollowed-out skins with the fruit salad and cover with the orange lids. Refrigerate until ready to serve.

ORANGE SALAD

SALADE D'ORANGES

- 5 oranges
- 100 g (3½ oz) caster sugar
- 50 ml (2 fl oz) rum

Preparation time: 10 minutes, plus chilling time
Serves 6

Prepare 1–2 hours in advance. Peel the oranges, remove the pith and cut the flesh into thin slices. Arrange in a bowl and sprinkle with the sugar. Mix the rum with 50 ml (2 fl oz) water and pour over the oranges. Refrigerate until ready to serve.

TAHITIAN ORANGES

ORANGES TAHITIENNES

- 6 slices pineapple, peeled
- 6 oranges, peeled
- Redcurrant jelly, for coating
- 125 g (4¼ oz) candied fruit, chopped

Preparation time: 20 minutes
Serves 6

Put the pineapple slices on a dish. Put an orange on top of each slice. Coat with redcurrant jelly and surround with the candied fruit. Refrigerate until ready to serve.

ORANGE JELLY

ASPIC D'ORANGES

Prepare 5–6 hours in advance. Dissolve the sugar and gelatine in the water. Grate the zest of 2 oranges and add it to the gelatine syrup. Squeeze the juice from all the oranges and lemons and mix into the syrup. Strain through fine muslin or a fine-meshed sieve. Pour into a charlotte mould or individual ramekins. Leave to set for 5–6 hours in a refrigerator. To turn out, dip the mould or ramekins in hot water for 30 seconds and invert onto a serving dish.

- 60 g (2 oz) caster sugar
- 30 g (1¼ oz) powdered gelatine or 8 leaves
- 250 ml (8 fl oz) hot water
- 12 oranges
- 3 lemons

Preparation time: 20 minutes, plus setting time
Serves 6

ORANGE SOUFFLÉ

SOUFFLÉ À L'ORANGE

Preheat the oven to 190°C/375°F/Gas Mark 5 and grease a charlotte mould or soufflé dish with butter. In a medium bowl, mix the flour with 50 ml (2 fl oz) of the milk, stirring until smooth. Pour the remaining milk into a pan and bring to just below boiling point. Pour the hot milk over the flour mixture, mix and return to the pan. Cook over a low heat for 5–10 minutes, stirring until thickened. Remove from the heat. Mix in the butter with the sugar, egg yolks, orange zest and candied peel. Whisk the egg whites until stiff and fold gently into the soufflé mixture. Pour the soufflé mixture into the prepared dish and bake for 20 minutes, until well risen and golden brown.

- 25 g (1 oz) butter, plus extra for greasing
- 30 g (1¼ oz) flour
- 200 ml (7 fl oz) milk
- 50 g (1¼ oz) caster sugar
- 4 egg yolks
- Zest of 2 oranges
- 30 g (1¼ oz) candied orange peel, chopped
- 5 egg whites

Preparation time: 15 minutes
Cooking time: 25 minutes
Serves 6

ORANGE COMPOTE

MARMELADE D'ORANGES

Peel the oranges, slice them and put them and their juices in a pan with the sugar, but without water. Bring slowly to the boil to dissolve the sugar, then reduce the heat and simmer for 10 minutes. Serve hot or cold.

- 1 kg (2¼ lb) oranges
- About 400 g (14 oz) caster sugar, depending on the sweetness of the fruit

Preparation time: 10 minutes
Cooking time: 15 minutes
Serves 6

POACHED PEACHES

PÊCHES POCHÉES

- **6 large peaches**
- **Caster sugar, for sprinkling**

Preparation time: 4 minutes
Cooking time: 10 minutes
Serves 6

Wipe the peaches. Bring a large pan of water to the boil. Add the peaches carefully to the boiling water and cook for 3–4 minutes. Remove, drain and peel the peaches. Arrange, either whole or cut in half and stoned, on a serving dish. Sprinkle with caster sugar.

PEACHES IN WINE

PÊCHES AU VIN

- **6 peaches**
- **250 ml (8 fl oz) sparkling white wine or Champagne**
- **30 g (1¼ oz) caster sugar**

Preparation time: 10 minutes,
plus macerating time
Serves 6

Prepare 2 hours in advance. Peel the peaches and cut them into quarters, removing the stones. Put in a bowl, pour over the wine or Champagne and sprinkle with the sugar. Macerate for 1–2 hours. Serve cold, on a bed of ice if desired.

PEACHES COLOMBINE

PÊCHES COLOMBINE

- **250 g (9 oz) rice pudding (p.711)**
- **100 g (3½ oz) sugar**
- **6 peaches**
- **Glacé cherries, halved and angelica, cut into strips, to decorate**
- **250 ml (8 fl oz) sabayon (p.727)**

Preparation time: 20 minutes
Cooking time: 30 minutes
Serves 6

Make the rice pudding. Using a large spoon, use most of it to put 6 egg-shaped, evenly sized mounds in the centre of a round dish. Add the sugar to a large pan of water and bring slowly to the boil. Reduce the heat and poach the peaches for 5 minutes in simmering water. Drain, peel, cut in half and remove the stones. Stuff each half with a little of the remaining rice pudding and put the halves back together. Arrange the peaches in a ring around the rice mounds and decorate with glacé cherries and angelica. Coat the rice pudding mounds with the sabayon.

PEACHES MELBA-STYLE

PÊCHES FAÇON MELBA

 p.686

Prepare several hours in advance. Make a light syrup by dissolving 100 g (3½ oz) of the sugar in 500 ml (18 fl oz) water in a small pan, then boiling for 1 minute. Peel the peaches and poach them for 5 minutes in the syrup. Put the peaches in a bowl, coat with the redcurrant jelly and sprinkle with the almonds. Make a crème anglaise (p.694) with the milk, egg yolks and remaining sugar. Allow to cool. Pour the crème anglaise round the peaches. Alternatively, layer the redcurrant jelly, peaches and crème anglaise in individual dessert glasses. Chill in the refrigerator for a few hours before serving.

- 150 g (5 oz) caster sugar
- 6 peaches
- Redcurrant jelly, for coating
- 50 g (1¾ oz) toasted almonds, chopped
- 500 ml (18 fl oz) milk
- 5 egg yolks

Preparation time: 30 minutes, plus chilling time
Cooking time: 25 minutes
Serves 6

PEACH MOUSSE
MOUSSE DE PÊCHES

- 3 peaches, peeled and stoned
- 100 g (3½ oz) caster sugar
- 250 ml (8 fl oz) double cream, whipped
- 125 g (4¼ oz) sponge fingers
- 15 g (½ oz) powdered gelatine, or 4 gelatine leaves (optional)

Preparation time: 10 minutes, plus setting time

Serves 6

Put the peaches in a blender and process until smooth. Put the purée into a bowl and add the sugar, then fold in the cream. Arrange on a dish and surround with sponge fingers. If the dessert is made in advance, gelatine dissolved in a small amount of hot water should be stirred into the peach purée. Chill in the refrigerator for a few hours to set.

VARIATIONS

. . . .

BANANA MOUSSE
MOUSSE DE BANANES

Proceed as above, replacing the peaches with 6 peeled bananas and using 50 g (1¾ oz) sugar.

. . . .

APRICOT MOUSSE
MOUSSE D'ABRICOTS

Proceed as above, replacing the peaches with 250 g (9 oz) stoned apricots and using 100 g (3½ oz) sugar.

. . . .

PINEAPPLE MOUSSE
MOUSSE D'ANANAS

Proceed as above, replacing the peaches with 4 slices pineapple and using 75 g (2½ oz) sugar.

PEACHES BONNE FEMME
PÊCHES BONNE FEMME

- 100 g (3½ oz) butter, plus extra for greasing
- 6 slices white bread
- 6 large peaches
- 40 g (1½ oz) sugar

Preparation time: 10 minutes

Cooking time: 40 minutes

Serves 6

Preheat the oven to 160°C/325°F/Gas Mark 3 and butter an ovenproof dish. Spread about half the butter over the bread slices. Peel the peaches and cut them in half, removing the stones. Fill the hollows with the sugar and remaining butter. Place them on the bread in the prepared dish. Pour a little water over them and bake for 40 minutes.

PEAR COMPOTE

COMPOTE DE POIRES

Peel, quarter and core the pears, placing them in a bowl of cold water to prevent them discolouring. Place the pear quarters in a non-reactive pan with 250 ml (8 fl oz) water and the sugar and lemon zest or vanilla. Bring to a simmer and cook for 10–20 minutes, or until the pears are tender. Arrange on a serving dish and serve cold.

- **500 g (1 lb 2 oz) pears**
- **80 g (2¾ oz) sugar**
- **Zest of 1 lemon or 1 teaspoon vanilla extract**

Preparation time: 15 minutes
Cooking time: 30 minutes
Serves 6

PEARS IN WINE

POIRES AU VIN

 p.687

Peel the pears, leaving the stalks attached. Put them in a non-reactive pan with the wine, sugar, cinnamon, clove and nutmeg. Bring to a simmer and cook for 30 minutes, or until the pears are tender. Arrange the pears in a dish with their stalks uppermost and pour the cooking liquid over them.

- **500 g (1 lb 2 oz) small, firm pears**
- **100 ml (3½ fl oz) red wine**
- **200 g (7 oz) caster sugar**
- **1 pinch of ground cinnamon**
- **1 clove**
- **1 scrape of nutmeg**

Preparation time: 15 minutes
Cooking time: 30 minutes
Serves 6

PEARS WITH CREAM

POIRES À LA CRÈME

Peel the pears, leaving the stalks attached. Place the sugar, vanilla and 250 ml (8 fl oz) water in a large pan and slowly bring to a simmer. Gently simmer the pears in the syrup for 30 minutes, or until the pears are tender. Remove and drain. Increase the heat to medium-high and boil to reduce the syrup to half its volume. Pour over the pears. Make a thick crème anglaise (p.694) with the milk, sugar and egg yolks. Coat the pears with the sauce.

- **12 small, firm pears**
- **100 g (3½ oz) caster sugar**
- **1 teaspoon vanilla extract**
- **250 ml (8 fl oz) milk**
- **Sugar, to taste**
- **4 egg yolks**

Preparation time: 10 minutes
Cooking time: 45 minutes
Serves 6

SLICED PEARS
ÉMINCÉ DE POIRES

- **6 ripe pears**
- **75 g (2½ oz) butter**
- **6 small slices white bread**
- **Caster sugar, to taste**

Preparation time: 10 minutes
Cooking time: 10 minutes
Serves 6

Peel, quarter and core the pears. Melt 50 g (1¾ oz) of the butter in a non-reactive pan and fry the pears for 5 minutes, or until golden and tender, taking care not to burn or break them. Fry the bread slices in the remaining butter for 5 minutes, or until golden, and arrange the pears on them. Sprinkle with sugar. Serve hot.

PEARS WITH CANDIED FRUIT
POIRES AUX FRUITS CONFITS

- **1 brioche ring or loaf**
- **125 g (4¼ oz) caster sugar**
- **6 pears**
- **100 g (3½ oz) glacé cherries, chopped**
- **60 g (2 oz) angelica, chopped**
- **1 quantity crème anglaise (p.694)**
- **Kirsch, to taste**

Preparation time: 30 minutes
Cooking time: 40 minutes
Serves 6

Preheat the oven to 220°C/425°F/Gas Mark 7. Cut the brioche into at least 12 even slices. Place 12 of the slices on a baking sheet and sprinkle with 25 g (1 oz) of the sugar. Bake for 5–10 minutes until crisp and golden. Meanwhile, place 500 ml (18 fl oz) water and the remaining sugar in a pan and bring to the boil. Peel, halve and core the pears. Simmer in the syrup for 10–20 minutes until tender. Put a half-pear on each slice of brioche. Arrange a ring of glacé cherries round half the pears and a ring of angelica round the other half. Flavour the crème anglaise with Kirsch, put it in a serving dish and top with the remaining brioche slices. Serve with the pears.

BAKED APPLES
POMMES AU FOUR

- **6 large eating apples, unblemished and evenly sized**

Preparation time: 5 minutes
Cooking time: 35 minutes
Serves 6

Preheat the oven to 180°C/350°F/Gas Mark 4. Wash the apples and wipe them dry. Arrange in an ovenproof dish and add 1 tablespoon water. Prick each apple with a fork in 2–3 places. This stops them bursting. Bake for 35 minutes, or until tender, depending on the size of the apples. Serve in the same dish without any additions.

APPLES CHÂTELAINE

POMMES CHÂTELAINE

Peel, core and halve the apples. Put the apple halves, cut side up, in a non-reactive pan. Add the sugar, 500 ml (18 fl oz) water and the vanilla and cover the pan with a lid. Place over a medium heat and bring to a simmer. After 8–10 minutes, when the fruit is tender, turn the apples without breaking them. Cook for a further 10 minutes, uncovered. Remove from the pan and arrange the apples on a dish. Reduce the liquid in the pan over a high heat for 7–8 minutes, or until syrupy in consistency, then flavour with lemon juice and pour over the apples. Allow to cool before serving.

- 6 eating apples
- 100 g (3½ oz) caster sugar
- 1 teaspoon vanilla extract
- Juice of 1 lemon

Preparation time: 20 minutes
Cooking time: 30 minutes
Serves 6

STUFFED APPLES

POMMES FARCIES

Peel and core the apples. Preheat the oven to 200°C/400°F/ Gas Mark 6. Widen the apple cavities to 2 cm (¾ inch) in diameter and chop the removed flesh with the candied fruit. Add the rum. Place the apples in an ovenproof dish and fill each one with the stuffing. Pour a little water over. Put a knob of butter and a little sugar on each apple. Bake for 35 minutes, or until tender, depending on size, basting from time to time with the cooking juices.

- 6 large eating apples
- 100 g (3½ oz) candied fruit
- 1 tablespoon rum
- 60 g (2 oz) butter
- 60 g (2 oz) sugar

Preparation time: 20 minutes
Cooking time: 35 minutes
Serves 6

BUTTERED APPLES

POMMES AU BEURRE

Preheat the oven to 180°C/350°F/Gas Mark 4. Peel and core the apples carefully, without damaging them. Butter both sides of the bread slices with most of the butter. Line the base of a large ovenproof dish with a single layer. Place an apple on each slice. Fill the cavity of each apple with small knobs of the remaining butter. Sprinkle the vanilla sugar over the apples and add 2 tablespoons water. Bake for 40 minutes. Serve piping hot in the dish in which the apples were cooked.

- 6 large eating apples, unblemished and evenly sized
- 85 g (3 oz) butter
- 6 slices bread, slightly stale
- 60 g (2 oz) vanilla sugar

Preparation time: 15 minutes
Cooking time: 40 minutes
Serves 6

APPLE PURÉE

PURÉE DE POMMES

- 1 kg (2¼ lb) cooking apples
- 1 pinch of grated lemon zest
- Caster sugar, to taste

Preparation time: 15 minutes
Cooking time: 20 minutes
Serves 6

Cut the apples in quarters, remove the stalks and any damaged parts, but do not peel or core them. Put in a non-reactive pan with 120 ml (4 fl oz) water. Cover and cook over a low heat for 15–20 minutes. Process in a blender until smooth. Pass through a sieve to remove any pips. Stir in the lemon zest and sugar. Transfer to a serving dish and serve cold.

VARIATION

. . . .

APPLE PURÉE WITH CROUTONS

PURÉE AUX CROUTONS

Prepare the apple purée as above. Before it cools, stir in 50 g (1¾ oz) butter. Cut 100 g (3½ oz) white bread into fingers, fry them in butter, and serve hot with the warm purée.

APPLE COMPOTE

COMPOTE DE POMMES

- 1 kg (2¼ lb) eating apples
- Caster sugar, to taste
- Vanilla extract or lemon zest, to taste

Preparation time: 15 minutes
Cooking time: 15 minutes
Serves 6

Peel and core the apples and cut them into quarters. Put in a non-reactive pan with sugar, 250 ml (8 fl oz) water and vanilla or lemon zest. Bring to the boil and cook on a high heat for 15 minutes. Serve warm or cold.

PORTUGAISE

PORTUGAISE

Start 1–2 hours in advance. Peel and core the apples, quarter them and place in a pan with the sugar, lemon zest and 120 ml (4 fl oz) water. Cook gently over a low heat until reduced to a fine purée. Process in a blender if necessary, and allow to cool. Meanwhile, prepare the custard. Put the milk in a pan and mix with the cornflour, vanilla sugar and egg yolks. Place over a gentle heat and stir continuously until thickened. Allow to cool. In a deep serving bowl, put a layer of apple, a few pieces of the candied fruit, a layer of custard, then a layer of apple, and so on, reserving some candied fruit for decoration. Refrigerate for 1–2 hours. When ready to serve, garnish with the reserved candied fruit and, if desired, meringues decorated with cream.

- 1 kg (2¼ lb) cooking apples
- 250 g (9 oz) caster sugar
- Zest of 1 lemon
- 2 level tablespoons cornflour
- 1 tablespoon of vanilla sugar
- 2 egg yolks
- 500 ml (18 fl oz) milk
- 80 g (2¾ oz) candied fruit, chopped

Preparation time: 30 minutes
Cooking time: 50 minutes
Serves 6

APPLE MERINGUE

POMMES MERINGUÉES

Preheat the oven to 180°C/350°F/Gas Mark 4 and grease an ovenproof dish with the butter. Prepare the apple purée and spread it out in the prepared dish. Beat the egg whites and sugar to stiff peaks and cover the apples with them. Sprinkle with a little more sugar. Bake for 15 minutes, or until brown.

- 20 g (¾ oz) butter
- 1 quantity apple purée (p.669)
- 3 egg whites
- 50 g (1¾ oz) caster sugar, plus extra for sprinkling

Preparation time: 20 minutes
Cooking time: 35 minutes
Serves 6

DRIED FRUIT COMPOTE

COMPOTE DE FRUITS SECS

Wash the fruit and soak in cold water for 2 hours. Drain, and place in a pan with the sugar, vanilla and 750 ml (1¾ pints) water. Bring to the boil and simmer over a low heat for 1 hour. Pour into a serving dish and allow to cool. Decorate with almonds, hazelnuts or pistachios.

- 200 g (7 oz) prunes
- 200 g (7 oz) dried figs
- 125 g (4¼ oz) plump raisins
- 125 g (4¼ oz) currants
- 50 g (1¾ oz) caster sugar
- 1 teaspoon vanilla extract
- A few blanched almonds, hazelnuts or pistachios, to decorate

Preparation time: 10 minutes, plus soaking time
Cooking time: 1 hour
Serves 6

APPLE JELLY

ASPIC DE POMMES

- 1 kg (2¼ lb) eating apples
- 350 g (12 oz) caster sugar
- 1 teaspoon vanilla extract
- Juice of 1 lemon
- 25 g (1 oz) butter
- Flavourless oil, for greasing
- Crème anglaise (p.694),
  to serve

Preparation time: 15 minutes,
plus setting time

Cooking time: 3 hours

Serves 6

Prepare the day before. Peel and core the apples and cut them into very thin slices. Place them in a non-reactive pan with the sugar, vanilla and lemon juice. Cover and cook over a very low heat for 3 hours, stirring occasionally and taking care not to allow the mixture to stick and burn. Process to a purée in a blender, adding the butter in small pieces while the motor is running. Oil 1 large or several individual moulds and pour in the apple purée. Leave to set in the refrigerator for 12 hours. Turn out onto a flat serving dish and serve with crème anglaise.

FLAMBÉED APPLES

POMMES FLAMBANTES

- 500 g (1 lb 2 oz) eating apples
- 120 g (4 oz) caster sugar
- 1 teaspoon vanilla extract
- 50 ml (2 fl oz) rum

Preparation time: 10 minutes

Cooking time: 20 minutes

Serves 6

Peel and core the apples without damaging the flesh. Put them in a non-reactive pan with 250 ml (8 fl oz) water, the sugar and vanilla. Cover and cook over a low heat for 15–20 minutes. When the apples are cooked but not falling apart, remove with a slotted spoon, drain, and arrange on an ovenproof dish. Keep warm. Reduce the liquid to a syrupy consistency by boiling it in the pan over a high heat. Add the rum and pour the liquid, piping hot, over the apples. Ensure the dish is well away from anything flammable and, standing well back, carefully touch a lighted match to the edge of the dish to ignite the rum. Serve while flaming.

POACHED APPLES
WITH RICE PUDDING

POMMES AU RIZ

 p.688

- 150 g (5 oz) pudding rice
- 500 ml (18 fl oz) milk
- 120 g (4 oz) sugar
- 1 teaspoon vanilla extract
- 20 g (¾ oz) butter
- 6 eating apples, evenly sized

Preparation time: 10 minutes

Cooking time: 40 minutes

Serves 6

Make a rice pudding (p.711) with the rice, milk, 50 g (1¾ oz) of the sugar and the vanilla. Grease an ovenproof dish with the butter. Peel and core the apples without damaging the flesh. Put the apples in a non-reactive pan with 250 ml (8 fl oz) water and 50 g (1¾ oz) of the sugar. Cover and cook over a low heat for 10–15 minutes. Preheat the oven to 190°C/375°F/Gas Mark 5. When the apples are tender but not falling apart, remove them from the syrup, arrange on the rice pudding in the dish and sprinkle with more sugar. Bake for 15–20 minutes, until brown.

APPLE & RICE CHARLOTTE

CHARLOTTE DE POMMES AU RIZ

Prepare the day before. Make a thick rice pudding and prepare the apple purée, cooking it until very thick. Line a charlotte mould with the sponge fingers, starting at the base; dip the flat sides in the light sugar syrup and arrange evenly in the base with the rounded sides downwards. Arrange the remaining sponge fingers, moistened in the same way, all round the sides of the mould. Cut them level with the top rim if they are too long. Fill the mould with alternating layers of rice pudding and apple purée. Finish with the trimmings from the sponge fingers. Put a saucer and weight on top of the pudding so that it is pressed down. Chill in the refrigerator. The next day, turn out onto a dish. Serve with crème anglaise, redcurrant jelly or apricot compote.

- 500 ml (18 fl oz) rice pudding (p.711)
- 1 quantity apple purée (p.669)
- 150 g (5 oz) sponge fingers
- 5 tablespoons light sugar syrup (p.643)
- Crème anglaise (p.694), redcurrant jelly or apricot compote (p.644), to serve

Preparation time: 10 minutes, plus chilling time
Cooking time: 15 minutes
Serves 6

APPLE TIMBALE

TIMBALE DE POMMES

Preheat the oven to 160°C/325°F/Gas Mark 3. Grease a charlotte mould with some of the butter. Line the base with a layer of bread, then a layer of apples. Sprinkle with some of the sugar, dot with butter and continue in this manner, layering the bread, apples, sugar and butter, until the mould is full. Pour over 100 ml (3½ fl oz) water. Bake for 1 hour. Turn out. Serve on its own or with a crème anglaise.

- 125 g (4¼ oz) butter
- 200 g (7 oz) slightly stale bread, very thinly sliced
- 500 g (1 lb 2 oz) apples, peeled, cored and sliced
- 100 g (3½ oz) caster sugar
- Crème anglaise (p.694), to serve (optional)

Preparation time: 15 minutes
Cooking time: 1 hour
Serves 6

APPLE PUDDING

FLAN AUX POMMES

Preheat the oven to 200°C/400°F/Gas Mark 6. Make the crêpe batter and stir in the sugar, reserving 1 tablespoon. Mix the apples, lemon zest and batter together. Generously butter an ovenproof dish, using half the butter. Pour in the apple mixture. Dot with the remaining butter and sprinkle with the remaining sugar. Bake for 45 minutes–1 hour, until the pudding is puffed and golden, and the batter is cooked.

- 1 quantity crêpe batter (p.721)
- 50 g (1¾ oz) sugar
- 6 apples, peeled, quartered and sliced
- Grated zest of 1 lemon
- 50 g (1¾ oz) butter

Preparation time: 25 minutes
Cooking time: 45 minutes–1 hour
Serves 8

NORMANDY BOURDELOTS

BOURDELOTS NORMANDS

Bourdelots, and the recipe below for preserved apples, come from Normandy in northern France, an area famous for its apple orchards.

Preheat the oven to 180°C/350°F/Gas Mark 4 and butter an ovenproof dish. Roll out the pastry fairly thinly and cover each apple with a layer of pastry. Refrigerate for at least 30 minutes. Place the bourdelots in the prepared dish and bake for 45 minutes.

- Butter, for greasing
- 6 large eating apples, peeled, cored and left whole
- 400 g (14 oz) puff pastry (p.776)

Preparation time: 10 minutes
Cooking time: 45 minutes
Serves 6

PRESERVED APPLES FROM NORMANDY

POMMES NORMANDES

In a large preserving pan, carefully make a syrup with the sugar and 250 ml (8 fl oz) water, cooking it to the hard-crack stage (p.643). Peel the apples and cut into wedges, removing the cores. Gently lower the apples, dried fruit and oranges into the syrup. Cook for 2 hours over a very gentle heat. The apples will become golden and shiny. Stir in the rum. Put in sterilized pots and cover. Turn out when ready to serve.

- 1.5 kg (3¼ lb) caster sugar
- 2 kg (4½ lb) apples
- 65 g (2¼ oz) currants
- 65 g (2¼ oz) sultanas
- 100 g (3½ oz) crystallized oranges, finely chopped
- 25 ml (1 fl oz) rum

Preparation time: 20 minutes
Cooking time: 2½ hours
Makes 3.5 kg (7¾ lb)

PLUM COMPOTE

COMPOTE DE PRUNES

Wash and halve the plums, and remove the stalks and stones. Place in a pan with 100 ml (3½ fl oz) water and the sugar (the amount required depends on the natural sweetness of the plums). Cook over a low heat until tender, about 15–25 minutes. Serve cold.

- 500 g (1 lb 2 oz) plums
- About 100 g (3½ oz) caster sugar, to taste

Preparation time: 10 minutes
Cooking time: 25 minutes
Serves 6

PRUNES
PRUNEAUX

- 350 g (12 oz) mi-cuit or ready-to-eat prunes
- 100 g (3½ oz) caster sugar

Preparation time: 5 minutes, plus soaking time
Cooking time: 1 hour
Serves 6

Wash the prunes and soak them for several hours in 300 ml (½ pint) water. Place the prunes and soaking liquid in a pan with the sugar and bring to the boil. Reduce the heat and simmer gently for 1 hour, stirring occasionally. Serve cold in the cooking liquid.

PRUNES IN TEA
PRUNEAUX AU THÉ

- 350 g (12 oz) large, soft Agen prunes
- 500 ml (18 fl oz) boiling Ceylon tea
- 1 teaspoon vanilla extract
- 80 g (2¾ oz) caster sugar

Preparation time: 10 minutes, plus macerating time
Serves 6

Prepare 4–5 hours in advance. Wash the prunes and soak for 2 hours in cold water. Drain, then place the prunes in a bowl. Pour the tea over the prunes. Stir in the vanilla and sugar. Leave to macerate and cool for 4–5 hours before serving.

FAR
FAR

- 250 g (9 oz) prunes
- 15 g (½ oz) butter
- 250 g (9 oz) flour
- ½ teaspoon salt
- 4 eggs
- 250 g (9 oz) caster sugar
- 1 litre (1¾ pints) milk
- 1 tablespoon rum

Preparation time: 20 minutes, plus soaking time
Cooking time: 40 minutes
Serves 6

This recipe for baked prunes in batter comes from Brittany in northern France.

Start the day before by soaking the prunes in water for 24 hours. The next day, preheat the oven to 220°C/425°F/Gas Mark 7 and grease an ovenproof dish with the butter. Put the flour and salt into a bowl. Break in the eggs one by one, mixing carefully to remove lumps. Beat the batter to make it light. Whisk in the sugar, then the milk, then add the rum. Drain the prunes and add to the batter. Pour the mixture into the prepared dish and place in the oven. After about 20 minutes, when the batter has set, turn down the temperature to 180°C/350°F/Gas Mark 4 and bake for a further 20 minutes.

PRUNES IN WINE

PRUNEAUX AU VIN

Prepare 6–7 hours in advance. Wash the prunes and soak for 2 hours in water. Drain, and place in a bowl. In a pan, bring 500 ml (18 fl oz) water and the wine, cinnamon, lemon slices and sugar to the boil, then pour immediately over the prunes. Leave to macerate and cool for 4–5 hours.

- 350 g (12 oz) large prunes
- 100 ml (3½ fl oz) red Bordeaux wine
- 1 pinch of cinnamon
- 1 lemon, sliced
- 80 g (2¾ oz) sugar

Preparation time: 10 minutes, plus macerating time
Serves 6

PRUNES WITH CUSTARD

PRUNEAUX À LA CRÈME

Cook the prunes (p.675). Drain, reserving the cooking liquid, and allow to cool. Remove the stones and arrange the prunes in a dish. Coat with the crème anglaise. Heat the reserved liquid in a pan over a high heat, then reduce the heat and simmer until the liquid has reduced to a syrupy consistency. Allow to cool, then pour over the prunes and crème anglaise to serve.

- 350 g (12 oz) prunes
- 500 ml (18 fl oz) thick crème anglaise (p.694)

Preparation time: 10 minutes, plus cooling time
Cooking time: 1½ hours
Serves 6

GRAPE TART

FLAN AUX RAISINS

Preheat the oven to 160°C/325°F/Gas Mark 3. Make a short-crust pastry dough (p.784) with the flour and butter. Roll out the pastry and use it to line a tart tin. Fill the pastry with the grapes. In a bowl, mix together the almonds, milk, egg and 50 g (1¾ oz) of the sugar. Pour over the grapes. Sprinkle with the remaining sugar and bake for 45 minutes.

- 150 g (5 oz) flour
- 85 g (3 oz) butter
- 200 g (7 oz) seedless white grapes
- 60 g (2 oz) ground almonds
- 100 ml (3½ fl oz) milk
- 1 egg
- 100 g (3½ oz) caster sugar

Preparation time: 20 minutes
Cooking time: 45 minutes
Serves 6

RHUBARB COMPOTE

COMPOTE DE RHUBARBE

- 1 kg (2¼ lb) rhubarb
- 300 g (11 oz) caster sugar

Preparation time: 10 minutes
Cooking time: 25 minutes
Serves 6

 p.689

- 200 g (7 oz) raspberries
- 150 g (5 oz) redcurrants
- 200 g (7 oz) strawberries
- 150 g (5 oz) cherries
- Juice of 2 oranges
- Juice of 1 lemon
- 250 g (9 oz) caster sugar
- 25 g (1 oz) powdered gelatine
  or 6 leaves
- Grated zest of ½ orange

Preparation time: 25 minutes,
plus setting time
Cooking time: 10 minutes
Serves 6

Wash and trim the rhubarb stems, but do not peel them. Cut into 1-cm (½-inch) lengths. Place in a non-reactive pan with the sugar over a gentle heat. Cook for 25 minutes or until tender, stirring frequently. Serve cold in a dish.

FOUR-BERRY JELLY

ASPIC AUX QUATRE FRUITS

Prepare 4–5 hours in advance. Remove any stalks and stones from the red fruits. Place the fruits in a blender along with the orange and lemon juice and process to a thin purée. Pour into a bowl. In a small pan, gently heat the sugar, 200 ml (7 fl oz) water and the gelatine until the sugar and gelatine dissolve. Do not allow to boil. Add this to the fruit purée and strain the mixture through a chinois (conical sieve) or other fine-meshed sieve. Stir in the orange zest. Pour the mixture into a charlotte or ring mould or a loaf tin and refrigerate for 4–5 hours until set. To serve, dip the mould in warm water and turn out onto a serving dish.

NOTE
Individual jellies can be made in glasses or ramekins. If desired, leave the fruit whole and pour over the fruit juice, syrup and gelatine, then leave to set as described above.

MIXED FRUIT COMPOTE

COMPOTE TOUS FRUITS

- 200 g (7 oz) caster sugar
- 250 g (9 oz) apricots
- 250 g (9 oz) peaches
- 200 g (7 oz) cherries, stoned
- 200 g (7 oz) strawberries,
  hulled, and sliced if large
- 250 g (9 oz) raspberries
- 2 bananas, peeled and sliced

Preparation time: 30 minutes
Cooking time: 15 minutes
Serves 6

In a large pan, bring the sugar and 500 ml (18 fl oz) water to the boil. Stone, peel and quarter the apricots, and stone and slice the peaches. Carefully add the apricots and simmer for 3 minutes. Add the peach slices and simmer for 3 minutes. Add the cherries to the simmering liquid and cook for 1 minute. Remove from the heat and add the other prepared fruit. Allow to cool, transfer to a serving dish and refrigerate to serve very cold.

FRUIT MACÉDOINE

MACÉDOINE DE FRUITS

Prepare 4 hours in advance. Place the cherries, strawberries, grapes and raspberries in a bowl. Peel and dice peaches and pears, or other fruit, and add to the bowl. Peel and slice the bananas and add these. Stir in the lemon juice and sugar. Chill in the refrigerator for 4 hours before serving.

VARIATION

• •

CHILLED FRUIT

FRUITS RAFRAÎCHIS

Proceed as above, but replace the lemon juice with 75 ml (3 fl oz) Kirsch, maraschino or Cognac, or some red or white wine. Chill for 2–3 hours and serve ice cold.

- 200 g (7 oz) cherries, stoned
- 200 g (7 oz) garden or wild strawberries, hulled
- 125 g (4¼ oz) grapes, de-seeded
- 125 g (4¼ oz) raspberries
- Peaches, pears or other fruit, to taste
- 2 bananas
- Juice of 1 lemon
- Caster sugar, to taste

Preparation time: 30 minutes, plus chilling time
Serves 6

WINTER FRUIT SALAD

SALADE DE FRUITS D'HIVER

Peel the oranges, grapefruit and apples, taking care to remove all the pith from the oranges and grapefruit. Core the apples. Cut the fruit into small segments or cubes and remove any pips. Peel the bananas and slice. Combine all the fruit in a bowl, sprinkle with sugar and pour the rum over them. Refrigerate for 1–2 hours.

- 3 oranges
- 1 grapefruit
- 2 apples
- 2 bananas
- Caster sugar, to taste
- 50 ml (2 fl oz) rum

Preparation time: 20 minutes, plus chilling time
Serves 6

MINTED FRUIT SALAD

SALADE DE FRUITS À LA MENTHE

- 125 g (4¼ oz) caster sugar
- 1 small bunch of mint
- 200 g (7 oz) nectarines
- 250 g (9 oz) apricots
- 200 g (7 oz) grapes
- 2 slices pineapple, skin and eyes removed
- 1 large pear
- 1 orange
- ¼ grapefruit
- 500 ml (18 fl oz) lemon or mint sorbet, to serve

Preparation time: 30 minutes
Cooking time: 5 minutes
Serves 6

Place the sugar and 250 ml (8 fl oz) water in a medium pan. Heat gently to dissolve the sugar and then bring to the boil. Reserve a few mint leaves for garnish and shred the remaining leaves. Take the syrup off the heat, add the mint leaves and leave to infuse, with the lid on, while the fruit is prepared. Peel, stone and de-seed the fruit (where appropriate) and cut into a variety of shapes and sizes. Arrange attractively on 6 plates to complement the colours. Half an hour before serving, cover the fruit with a little of the cooled syrup. To serve, place a scoop of lemon or mint sorbet in the centre of each plate. Garnish with the reserved mint leaves and serve immediately.

GINGERED FRUIT SALAD

SALADE DE FRUITS AU GINGEMBRE

- 125 g (4¼ oz) caster sugar
- 50 g (1¾ oz) fresh root ginger, chopped, plus extra grated ginger, to serve (optional)
- 200 g (7 oz) melon
- 250 g (9 oz) peaches
- 200 g (7 oz) nectarines
- 250 g (9 oz) apricots
- ½ grapefruit

Preparation time: 30 minutes, plus macerating time
Cooking time: 5 minutes
Serves 6

Prepare several hours in advance. Place the sugar and 250 ml (8 fl oz) water in a medium pan. Heat gently to dissolve the sugar and then bring to the boil. When the syrup comes to the boil, put in the ginger, cover and leave to infuse off the heat. Peel, stone and de-seed the fruit (where appropriate) and slice into semicircles. Arrange attractively on 6 plates. Strain the ginger syrup over the fruit and leave to macerate for 2 hours before serving. If desired a little fresh ginger may be grated over the fruit at the last moment.

Apricot omelette   (p.646)

Flambéed bananas (p.649)

Strawberries marinated in wine   (p.654)

Raspberry loaf (p.655)

Mont Blanc (p.657)

Chestnut & chocolate terrine (p.659)

Peaches Melba-style (p.664)

Poached apples with rice pudding   (p.671)

Four-berry jelly (p.677)

MILK

&

EGG PUDDINGS

MILK & EGG PUDDINGS

Milk and egg puddings (known as *entremets*) are sweet dishes often served as desserts at the end of the meal. The main ingredients are usually eggs, milk and sugar, but other ingredients such as rice or semolina may be added, along with a variety of flavourings such as coffee, vanilla, lemon, orange, cinnamon, orange-flower water and spirits or liqueurs. They can be served hot, cold or iced. These desserts are both delicious and economical.

CREAMS & CUSTARDS

Creams and custards are made with a combination of milk, sugar and eggs. Their consistency varies according to the quantity of eggs used, and whether the egg whites are included. Great care must be taken when cooking creams and custards with egg yolks. It is important not to overheat the mixture, and it should be heated very gently.

JAPANESE CREAM
CRÈME JAPONAISE

Place the milk in a pan with 100 g (3½ oz) of the sugar and chocolate and gently heat to melt the chocolate. Allow to cool for 5 minutes, then sprinkle the agar-agar over the surface of the chocolate milk. Return the pan to the heat, stir and simmer for 10 minutes, until the agar-agar is dissolved. Make a light caramel with the remaining sugar and 1 tablespoon water (p.643). Line a mould with the caramel by pouring it in and rotating the mould to coat the insides. Pour in the milk mixture and allow to cool and set in the refrigerator. Turn out to serve.

NOTE
Individual Japanese creams can also be made in small moulds or ramekins.

- 1 litre (1¾ pints) milk
- 160 g (5½ oz) sugar
- 150 g (5 oz) chocolate, chopped
- 5 g (⅙ oz) agar-agar

Preparation time: 5 minutes, plus setting time
Cooking time: 20 minutes
Serves 6

MILK JELLY MOULD

GÂTEAU DE CRÈME DOUCE

- 750 ml (1¼ pints) milk
- 160 g (5½ oz) sugar
- Grated lemon zest, vanilla extract or coffee essence, to flavour
- 25 g (1 oz) powdered gelatine or 6 gelatine leaves
- 250 ml (9 fl oz) whipped cream

Preparation time: 10 minutes
Cooking time: 20 minutes
Serves 6

Bring the milk and 100 g (3½ oz) of the sugar to the boil in a pan, and add the chosen flavouring. Soften the gelatine leaves in cold water, if using. Add the gelatine to the hot milk and stir to dissolve. While the mixture is still warm, add the whipped cream. Make a light caramel with the remaining sugar and 1 tablespoon water (p.642). Line a mould with the caramel by pouring it in and rotating the mould to coat the insides. Pour in the milk mixture and allow to cool and set in the refrigerator. Turn out to serve.

 p.730

EGGS IN SNOW

ŒUFS À LA NEIGE

- 1 litre (1¾ pints) milk
- 125 g (4¼ oz) sugar
- 6 eggs, separated
- Flavouring to taste, such as grated lemon zest, vanilla extract or coffee essence

Preparation time: 25 minutes
Cooking time: 40 minutes
Serves 6

Bring the milk and sugar to simmering point in a large pan. Meanwhile, whisk the egg whites until stiff. As soon as the milk starts to boil, add rounded tablespoons of the whisked egg white. As each 'island' comes back to the surface, turn it over and allow it to float to the surface again, then drain. The whites must not cook for more than 1 minute each side. Make a crème anglaise (p.694), with 500 ml (18 fl oz) of the poaching milk and the egg yolks, flavoured to taste. When the custard has cooled, arrange the 'islands' on top. The egg whites can also be poached in boiling water.

 p.731

HEDGEHOGS

HÉRISSONS

- 60 g (2 oz) blanched almonds
- 200 ml (7 fl oz) rum
- 120 g (4 oz) caster sugar
- 12 small madeleines (p.807)
- 500 ml (18 fl oz) milk
- 5 egg yolks

Preparation time: 30 minutes
Cooking time: 25 minutes
Serves 6

Cut the almonds into strips and lightly toast them in the oven or in a non-stick pan, over a medium heat, stirring constantly. Mix the rum with 30 g (1¼ oz) of the sugar and 3 tablespoons of water. Macerate the madeleines in this. Stud the madeleines with pieces of almond so that they resemble hedgehogs. Prepare a crème anglaise (p.694) with the milk, egg yolks and remaining sugar. Pour into a dish and, once cooled, place the madeleines on top and serve.

CRÈME ANGLAISE

CRÈME ANGLAISE

In a large pan, bring the milk and sugar to simmering point over a low heat. Place the egg yolks into a large bowl and, beating with a whisk, add the hot milk a little at a time. Pour back into the pan. Gradually thicken the custard over very low heat, stirring all the time or, alternatively, set the bowl of custard over a pan of simmering water, stirring all the time. The mixture should thicken to coat the back of a spoon. Do not allow it to boil. If the custard does separate and curdle, pour small quantities into a bottle; cover with a clean cloth and shake vigorously for several minutes, after which the custard will thicken. Alternatively, process in a blender. Strain the custard through a fine sieve. Crème anglaise can also be made with whole eggs. Use 4 whole eggs per 500 ml (18 fl oz) milk and take even greater care to thicken over the lowest heat possible.

- 500 ml (18 fl oz) milk
- 60 g (2 oz) sugar
- 6 egg yolks

Preparation time: 5 minutes
Cooking time: 20 minutes
Serves 6

VARIATIONS

. . . .

VANILLA CRÈME ANGLAISE

CRÈME À LA VANILLE

Add a split vanilla pod to the milk and sugar and proceed as above.

. . . .

LEMON OR ORANGE CRÈME ANGLAISE

CRÈME AU CITRON, À L'ORANGE

Add the grated zest of a lemon or orange to the milk and sugar and proceed as above.

. . . .

COFFEE CRÈME ANGLAISE

CRÈME AU CAFÉ

Mix 2 teaspoons coffee extract with the egg yolks and proceed as above.

. . . .

CHOCOLATE CRÈME ANGLAISE

CRÈME AU CHOCOLAT

Replace the sugar with 200 g (7 oz) chopped chocolate and melt it in the hot milk. Use 5 egg yolks instead of 6 and proceed as above.

PINEAPPLE CRÈME ANGLAISE
CRÈME À L'ANANAS

Process 250 g (9 oz) pineapple flesh in a blender as finely as possible. Stir this purée into the crème anglaise and flavour with Kirsch.

STRAWBERRY CRÈME ANGLAISE
CRÈME AUX FRAISES

Blend 500 g (1 lb 2 oz) strawberries to a purée with 80 g (2¾ oz) caster sugar. Stir the purée into the crème anglaise.

PRUNE CRÈME ANGLAISE
CRÈME AUX PRUNEAUX

Cook 250 g (9 oz) prunes (p.675). Stone and mash them, then reduce them in their cooking liquid. Mix this purée thoroughly with the crème anglaise (p.694).

BANANA CRÈME ANGLAISE
CRÈME À LA BANANE

Process 6 bananas in a blender. Stir this purée into warm crème anglaise. Serve cold.

DRIED APRICOT CRÈME ANGLAISE
CRÈME AUX ABRICOTS SECS

Soak 125 g (4¼ oz) dried apricots overnight, then put in a pan with 500 ml (18 fl oz) water and 90 g (3¼ oz) sugar and simmer until soft. Sieve or process the apricots to a purée in a blender. Stir the purée into warm crème anglaise. Serve cold.

CARAMEL CRÈME ANGLAISE

CRÈME AU CARAMEL

Make a dark caramel (p.642) with the sugar and 3 tablespoons water, then remove from the heat and very carefully pour on the hot milk. The mixture will splutter, so stand away from the pan for a few seconds. Stir to melt the caramelized sugar. Strain through a fine strainer or chinois, add the egg yolks and proceed as for crème anglaise (p.694). Cool completely before serving.

- **150 g (5 oz) sugar**
- **500 ml (18 fl oz) hot milk**
- **6 egg yolks**

  Preparation time: 10 minutes
  Cooking time: 30 minutes
  Serves 6

MOCHA CRÈME ANGLAISE

CRÈME PÉRUVIENNE

Place half the milk and the coffee in a pan and slowly bring to simmering point. Set aside to infuse. Make a dark caramel (p.642) with the sugar and 3 tablespoons water and remove from the heat. Very carefully pour the hot, coffee-flavoured milk on to the caramel. The mixture will splutter, so stand away from the pan for a few seconds. Stir to melt the caramelized sugar, and stir in the chocolate until this too has melted. Make a thick crème anglaise (p.694) with the remaining milk and the egg yolks. Stir into the flavoured milk. Cool completely before serving.

- **500 ml (18 fl oz) milk**
- **15 g (½ oz) ground coffee**
- **100 g (3½ oz) sugar**
- **125 g (4¼ oz) chocolate, chopped**
- **6 egg yolks**

  Preparation time: 30 minutes
  Cooking time: 30 minutes
  Serves 6

VENETIAN CRÈME ANGLAISE

CRÈME VÉNITIENNE

Make a crème anglaise with the milk, sugar and egg yolks (p.694), adding one of the flavour variations to taste. Beat the egg whites to stiff peaks. Fold them thoroughly into the thick, hot custard. Serve hot or cold on the same day.

- **1 litre (1¾ pints) milk**
- **100 g (3½ oz) sugar**
- **6 eggs, separated**

  Preparation time: 10 minutes
  Cooking time: 40 minutes
  Serves 6

VANILLA BAVAROIS

CRÈME BAVAROISE À LA VANILLE

- 20 g (¾ oz) powdered gelatine or 5 gelatine leaves
- 1 vanilla pod, split
- 500 ml (18 fl oz) milk
- 100 g (3½ oz) sugar
- 6 egg yolks
- 250 ml (8 fl oz) double cream

Preparation time: 20 minutes, plus setting time
Cooking time: 25 minutes
Serves 6

Prepare at least 3 hours in advance. Soften the gelatine leaves, or dissolve the powdered gelatine, in 3 tablespoons hot water. Scrape the seeds from the vanilla pod and add them to the milk. Make a crème anglaise (p.694) with the milk, sugar, vanilla and egg yolks. Once the crème anglaise has thickened, remove it from the heat. Squeeze out any excess liquid from the gelatine leaves, if using. Add the gelatine into the crème anglaise while it is still hot, stirring to dissolve. Cool to room temperature. Before the mixture starts to set, whip the cream to soft peaks and fold it in. Pour the bavarois into a mould, or 6 individual moulds, and refrigerate for 3 hours or until set. Turn out to serve.

VARIATIONS

. . . .

CHOCOLATE BAVAROIS
CRÈME BAVAROISE AU CHOCOLAT

Make a chocolate crème anglaise (p.694). Stir in 15 g (½ oz) powdered gelatine (or 4 softened gelatine leaves) before the custard thickens and proceed as for vanilla bavarois.

. . . .

COFFEE BAVAROIS
CRÈME BAVAROISE AU CAFÉ

Make a coffee crème anglaise (p.694). Stir in 20 g (¾ oz) powdered gelatine (or 5 softened gelatine leaves) before the custard thickens and proceed as for vanilla bavarois.

. . . .

FRUIT BAVAROIS
CRÈME BAVAROISE AUX FRUITS

Make a vanilla bavarois. Process 500 g (1 lb 2 oz) red berries such as strawberries, raspberries and redcurrants in a blender and pass through a sieve to remove the pips. Serve poured over the bavarois.

p.732

COFFEE CHARLOTTE

CHARLOTTE AU CAFÉ

Prepare 3 days in advance. Infuse the coffee in the milk in the refrigerator for 2 days, covered. Put the egg yolks in a bowl and mix with the sugar. Soak the gelatine leaves (if using) in a little cold water for 3 minutes. Strain the coffee-infused milk and bring to the boil with the vanilla pod. Mix in the egg yolk mixture and cook over a very gentle heat as for crème anglaise (p.694). Remove from the heat and remove the vanilla pod. Squeeze out any excess liquid from the gelatine leaves (if using) and stir the gelatine into the hot egg yolk mixture. Allow to cool. Before the mixture starts to set, whip the cream to soft peaks and fold it in. Divide between 6 individual moulds and chill in the refrigerator for 12 hours. Turn out to serve.

- **40 g (1½ oz) ground coffee**
- **300 ml (½ pint) milk**
- **4 egg yolks**
- **150 g (5 oz) icing sugar**
- **12 g (½ oz) powdered gelatine or 3 gelatine leaves**
- **½ vanilla pod**
- **400 ml (14 fl oz) double cream**

Preparation time: 10 minutes, plus chilling time
Cooking time: 20 minutes
Serves 6

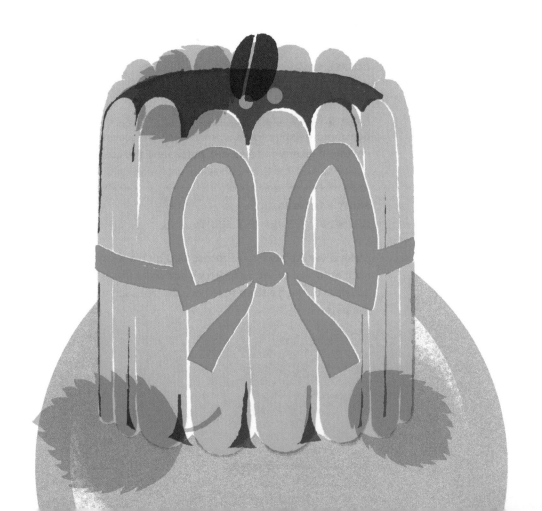

DESSERTS WITH EGG WHITES

Desserts made with egg whites are usually quick to prepare and are best made shortly before serving. Separate the egg white from the yolk carefully, since any stray flecks of yolk in the mix will prevent the whites from achieving their full volume when whisked. Put the egg whites in a very clean bowl, since any grease will also prevent the whites from whipping up effectively, and whisk with a balloon whisk or electric mixer until the whites become thick and stiff. Use the whisked whites immediately, otherwise the mixture will sink.

LIGHT CHOCOLATE MOUSSE
MOUSSE AU CHOCOLAT

- **200 g (7 oz) chocolate**
- **6 egg whites**
- **30 g (1¼ oz) caster sugar**

  Preparation time: 20 minutes, plus chilling time
  Serves 6

Prepare 3 hours in advance. In a heatproof bowl set over a pan of barely simmering water, gently melt the chocolate in 2 tablespoons water, stirring occasionally, to make a thick paste. Whisk the egg whites to soft peaks, add the sugar and continue whisking until very stiff. Fold the chocolate gently into the egg whites. Pour into a bowl and refrigerate for up to 3 hours.

COFFEE MOUSSE
MOUSSE AU CAFÉ

- **6 egg whites**
- **80 g (3 oz) caster sugar**
- **2 teaspoons coffee essence**

  Preparation time: 10 minutes, plus chilling time
  Serves 6

Whisk the egg whites to soft peaks, add the sugar and coffee essence and continue whisking until very stiff. Chill for 30 minutes before serving.

CREAMY COFFEE MOUSSE

CRÈME MOUSSEUSE AU CAFÉ

Prepare several hours in advance. In a large pan, bring the milk to the boil. Mix the egg yolks, vanilla and cornflour to a smooth paste in a large bowl. Pour the hot milk slowly into the egg yolk mixture, stirring continually, and add the coffee. Return to the pan and cook over a gentle heat, stirring constantly, until the custard thickens. Allow to cool. Whisk the egg whites to soft peaks, add the sugar and continue whisking until very stiff. Gently fold the egg whites into the custard. Chill for 1–2 hours before serving.

- 1 litre (1¾ pints) milk
- 5 eggs, separated
- 1 teaspoon vanilla extract
- 15 g (½ oz) cornflour
- 1 tablespoon instant coffee
- 150 g (5 oz) sugar

Preparation time: 20 minutes, plus chilling time
Cooking time: 15 minutes
Serves 6

STRAWBERRY MOUSSE

MOUSSE AUX FRAISES

Crush the strawberries with a fork and pass through a sieve. Whisk the egg whites to soft peaks, add the sugar and continue whisking until very stiff. Fold the strawberries into the beaten egg whites. Pour into a bowl or 6 individual bowls and chill before serving.

- 300 g (11 oz) strawberries
- 4 egg whites
- Sugar, to taste

Preparation time: 15 minutes, plus chilling time
Serves 6

CREAM MOUSSE

MOUSSE À LA CRÈME CHANTILLY

Whip the cream. Whisk the egg whites to soft peaks, add the sugar and continue whisking until very stiff. Fold the whisked egg whites into the cream, along with the chosen flavouring.

- 200 ml (7 fl oz) double cream
- 4 egg whites
- Sugar, to taste
- Vanilla extract, coffee essence or a liqueur, to flavour

Preparation time: 15 minutes
Serves 6

FLOATING ISLAND
ÎLE FLOTTANTE

- **6 eggs, separated**
- **200 g (7 oz) caster sugar**
- **500 ml (18 fl oz) milk**

Preparation time: 20 minutes
Cooking time: 1 hour
Serves 6

Preheat the oven to 150°C/300°F/Gas Mark 2. Whisk the egg whites to stiff peaks with 80 g (2¾ oz) of the sugar. Using 60 g (2 oz) of the sugar, make a light caramel with 1 tablespoon water (p.642) and carefully pour into a mould to coat the insides. Spoon in the egg whites, level the surface and put the dish in a roasting tin half-filled with hot water. Cook in the oven for 45 minutes. Make a crème anglaise (p.694) with the milk, yolks and remaining sugar. Allow the meringue to cool, then turn it out on to a serving dish by dipping the mould in hot water for 30 seconds. Surround with the crème anglaise.

VARIATION

· ·

RICHELIEU CREAM
CRÈME RICHELIEU

Proceed as above, adding 10 crushed pralines and a drop of red food colouring to the whisked egg whites, and adding only 30 g (1¾ oz) sugar to the egg whites.

RUSSIAN MOUSSE
MOUSSE RUSSE

- **6 eggs, separated**
- **240 g (8½ oz) caster sugar**
- **120 g (4 oz) dry meringues**
- **500 ml (18 fl oz) milk**

Preparation time: 20 minutes
Cooking time: 1 hour
Serves 6

Preheat the oven to 150°C/300°F/Gas Mark 2. Whisk the egg whites to soft peaks, add 100 g (3½ oz) of the sugar and continue whisking to stiff peaks. Crush the meringues and fold into the egg whites. Make a light caramel with 60 g (2 oz) of the sugar (p.642) and 1 tablespoon water, and carefully pour into a mould to coat the insides. Spoon in the meringue mixture, level the surface and put the dish in a roasting tin half-filled with hot water. Cook in the oven for 45 minutes. Meanwhile, make a crème anglaise (p.694) with the remaining sugar, and the milk and egg yolks. Turn the mousse out of the mould and serve with the crème anglaise.

MACARONETTE

MACARONETTE

Preheat the oven to 180°C/350°F/Gas Mark 4. Crush the macaroons or amaretti finely. Whisk the egg whites to stiff peaks and fold in the crushed biscuits. Make a light caramel (p.642) with 60 g (2 oz) of the sugar and 1 tablespoon water, and carefully pour into a mould to coat the insides. Spoon in the egg white mixture, level the surface and place in a roasting tin half-filled with hot water. Bake for 45 minutes. Make a crème anglaise (p.694) with the egg yolks, milk and remaining sugar. Turn out the macaronette when cold and serve with the crème anglaise.

- **12 almond macaroons (p.771) or amaretti biscuits**
- **6 eggs, separated**
- **140 g (4½ oz) caster sugar**
- **500 ml (18 fl oz) milk**

Preparation time: 25 minutes
Cooking time: 1 hour
Serves 6

DESSERTS WITH WHOLE EGGS

Many mousses and custards can be made with whole eggs. Custards made with whole eggs are known as *crèmes renversées*, because they are firm enough to be turned out on to a dish for serving. Always use the freshest eggs possible.

LEMON MOUSSE

MOUSSE AU CITRON

In a heatproof bowl set over a pan of barely simmering water, whisk the sugar, lemon juice and zest, egg yolks and 3 table-spoons water until thickened. Remove from the heat and allow to cool. Whisk the egg whites until stiff and gently fold into the cooled lemon mixture. Serve in a one large bowl or 6 individual bowls.

VARIATIONS

- **100 g (3½ oz) caster sugar**
- **Juice of 4 lemons**
- **Grated zest of 2 lemons**
- **6 eggs, separated**

Preparation time: 20 minutes, plus cooling time
Cooking time: 8 minutes
Serves 6

. . . .

ORANGE MOUSSE

MOUSSE À L'ORANGE

Proceed as above, replacing the lemons with the juice of 5 oranges and the grated zest of 3 oranges, and using 80 g (2¾ oz) sugar.

p.733

MARIE-LOUISE MOUSSE
CRÈME MARIE-LOUISE

Melt 250 g (9 oz) dark chocolate in 100 ml (3½ fl oz) very strong coffee over a very low heat and continue as above, omitting the water and sugar.

CHOCOLATE MOUSSE
BALANCÉS

- 250 g (9 oz) dark chocolate
- 6 eggs, separated

Preparation time: 25 minutes, plus chilling time
Serves 6

Melt the chocolate in a heatproof bowl set over a pan of barely simmering water. Meanwhile, whisk the egg whites to stiff peaks. Remove the chocolate from the heat and stir in the egg yolks. Fold in the stiffly beaten whites. Put in 6 small pots or individual ramekins and allow to chill in the refrigerator for several hours.

RUM MOUSSE
CRÈME BACHIQUE

- 6 eggs, separated
- 60 g (2 oz) caster sugar
- 150 ml (¼ pint) rum

Preparation time: 15 minutes
Serves 6

Make immediately before serving. Whisk the egg yolks with the sugar and rum until foamy. Whisk the egg whites until stiff and fold into the egg yolk mixture. The rum may be replaced by the same quantity of Kirsch and 200 ml (7 fl oz) unsweetened whipped cream can be folded in. Serve cold, in 6 small bowls.

EGG CUSTARD
ŒUFS AU LAIT

- 500 ml (18 fl oz) milk
- 125 g (4¼ oz) sugar
- Vanilla extract, coffee essence, liqueur or other flavouring, to taste
- 4 eggs, lightly beaten

Preparation time: 15 minutes
Cooking time: 45 minutes
Serves 6

Preheat the oven to 150°C/300°F/Gas Mark 2. Place the milk, sugar and the chosen flavouring in a medium pan. Bring to the boil over a low heat. Remove from the heat and add the eggs, stirring constantly. Pour into a dish and place in a roasting tin half-filled with hot water, then bake in the oven for 45 minutes.

SMALL CUSTARDS
CRÈME PRISE EN POTS

Preheat the oven to 150°C/300°F/Gas Mark 2. Place the milk, sugar and the chosen flavouring in a medium pan. Bring to the boil over a low heat. Remove from the heat and add the eggs, stirring constantly. Pour the custard into 6 small ovenproof dishes. Place the dishes in a roasting tin half-filled with hot water and bake in the oven for 25 minutes. Take care that the contents of the dishes do not boil.

- 500 ml (18 fl oz) milk
- 125 g (4¼ oz) sugar
- Vanilla extract, coffee essence, liqueur or other flavouring, to taste
- 5 eggs, lightly beaten

Preparation time: 15 minutes
Cooking time: 25 minutes
Serves 6

CRÈME CARAMEL
CRÈME RENVERSÉE

Prepare at least 2 hours in advance. Preheat the oven to 150°C/300°F/Gas Mark 2. Make a dark caramel (p.642) with 70 g (2½ oz) of the sugar and 1 tablespoon water, and carefully pour it into a mould to coat the insides. In a large pan, bring the milk, the remaining sugar and the chosen flavouring to the boil. Remove from the heat and add the eggs, stirring constantly. Pour into the prepared mould and place the mould in a roasting tin half-filled with hot water. Bake in the oven for 45–50 minutes, until set. Allow to cool. When ready to serve, dip the mould in hot water for 30 seconds and turn out.

- 200 g (7 oz) sugar
- 500 ml (18 fl oz) milk
- Vanilla extract, coffee essence, liqueur or other flavouring, to taste
- 6 eggs, lightly beaten

Preparation time: 15 minutes, plus cooling time
Cooking time: 1 hour
Serves 6

CRÈME CARAMEL 'BELLE ET BONNE'
CRÈME BELLE ET BONNE

Make a crème caramel (see above) with 200 g (7 oz) of the sugar and the milk, eggs and vanilla, using a ring mould. Bring the wine and remaining sugar to the boil in a large pan. Dice the small pears and simmer in the wine for 30 minutes. Remove with a slotted spoon and set aside. Peel, core and halve the medium pears and simmer in the wine syrup for 40 minutes, or until tender. When the crème caramel has cooked, allow it to cool and turn it out on to a dish. Arrange the halved pears around the ring and the diced pears in the centre. Whip the cream until thick and use it to decorate the crème caramel.

- 250 g (9 oz) sugar
- 500 ml (18 fl oz) milk
- 6 eggs
- 1 teaspoon vanilla extract
- 400 ml (14 fl oz) red wine
- 4 small pears
- 6 medium pears
- 200 ml (7 fl oz) double cream

Preparation time: 1½ hours
Cooking time: 1¼ hour
Serves 6

VANILLA CRÈME BRÛLÉE

CRÈME BRÛLÉE À LA VANILLE

- 500 ml (18 fl oz) milk
- 500 ml (18 fl oz) single cream
- 4 vanilla pods, split
- 200 g (7 oz) caster sugar
- 10 egg yolks
- 100 g (3½ oz) brown sugar

Preparation time: 20 minutes,
plus chilling time
Cooking time: 1 hour
Serves 6

Prepare in advance. Preheat the oven to 150°C/300°F/Gas Mark 2. Mix together the milk, cream, vanilla pods and 100 g (3½ oz) of the caster sugar. Bring just to the boil over a low heat then remove from the heat and cool. Scrape the seeds out of the vanilla pods into the milk and remove the empty pods for another use. Meanwhile beat the egg yolks in a bowl with the remaining caster sugar until white and creamy. Pour the vanilla-flavoured milk over the eggs and mix well. Pour into an ovenproof dish or 6 individual ramekins. Place the dish or ramekins in a roasting tin half-filled with hot water. Bake for 45–50 minutes, or until just set (the custard must not boil). Cool to room temperature, then refrigerate for 3–4 hours.

Shortly before serving, sprinkle the custard with the brown sugar and put the dish under a very hot grill for just long enough to caramelize. The sugar will form small balls on the surface. Alternatively, use a kitchen blow torch carefully to caramelize the sugar.

FRUIT CUSTARD

CRÈME FRUITÉE

- Butter, for greasing
- 500 ml (18 fl oz) milk
- 100 g (3½ oz) sugar
- 60 g (2 oz) sponge fingers
- 4 eggs
- 50 g (1¾ oz) glacé cherries, chopped
- 50 ml (2 fl oz) rum or Kirsch
- Redcurrant jelly or apricot compote (p.644)

Preparation time: 20 minutes
Cooking time: 1 hour
Serves 6

Preheat the oven to 150°C/300°F/Gas Mark 2 and grease a mould with butter. Put the milk and sugar in a pan and heat to simmering point. Soak the sponge fingers in the sweetened hot milk until very soft. Beat the eggs into the milk and sponge finger mixture and strain through a sieve. Add the cherries and rum or Kirsch. Pour into the prepared mould and put the mould in a roasting tin half-filled with hot water. Bake in the oven for 1 hour or until set. Turn out and serve coated with redcurrant jelly or apricot compote.

ALMOND CUSTARD

CRÈME FRANGIPANE

Bring the milk to the boil in a large pan. In a bowl, mix together the sugar, eggs, egg yolks and flour with 60 g (2 oz) of the butter and the salt. Beat the boiling milk into the egg mixture, then return to the pan and cook over a medium heat, stirring constantly until the mixture thickens. Mix in the remaining butter and the almonds. Stir gently until cool.

NOTE
Almond custard is used as a filling in many tarts and pastries.

- 300 ml (½ pint) milk
- 75 g (2½ oz) caster sugar
- 2 eggs
- 2 egg yolks
- 90 g (3¼ oz) flour
- 90 g (3¼ oz) butter, softened
- 1 teaspoon salt
- 60 g (2 oz) ground almonds

Preparation time: 15 minutes
Cooking time: 20 minutes
Serves 6

CRÈME PÂTISSIÈRE

CRÈME PÂTISSIÈRE

Scrape the seeds out of the vanilla pod, add them and the pod to the milk and bring to the boil in a large pan. Beat the flour, sugar and eggs together in a large bowl. Pour the boiling milk over this mixture, a little at a time, stirring constantly. Pour back into the pan and cook over a gentle heat, stirring constantly. Remove from the heat as soon as the mixture comes to the boil and thickens. Remove the vanilla pod and reserve for another use.

NOTE
Crème pâtissière is used as a filling in many tarts and pastries.

- ½ vanilla pod, split
- 500 ml (18 fl oz) milk
- 50 g (1¾ oz) flour
- 75 g (2½ oz) caster sugar
- 1 egg
- 3 egg yolks

Preparation time: 15 minutes
Cooking time: 10 minutes
Serves 6

PARISIAN CUSTARD PUDDING

FLAN À LA PARISIENNE

Preheat the oven to 180°C/350°F/Gas Mark 4 and grease a mould with butter. Put the flour in a bowl. Make a well and put the sugar, eggs and butter into it, then beat to combine. Stir the vanilla sugar into the milk and add to the flour and egg mixture. Beat the batter until completely smooth. Pour into the prepared mould, place in a roasting tin half-filled with hot water and bake for 45 minutes. Turn out and serve cold.

- 30 g (1¼ oz) butter, melted, plus extra for greasing
- 200 g (7 oz) flour
- 100 g (3½ oz) caster sugar
- 4 eggs
- Vanilla sugar, to taste
- 1 litre (1¾ pints) milk

Preparation time: 10 minutes
Cooking time: 45 minutes
Serves 6

LEMON CUSTARD PUDDING

FLAN AU CITRON

- 160 g (5½ oz) sugar
- 30 g (1¼ oz) potato flour
- 750 ml (1¼ pints) milk
- Grated zest of 1 lemon
- 4 eggs

Preparation time: 15 minutes
Cooking time: 45 minutes
Serves 6

Preheat the oven to 180°C/350°F/Gas Mark 4. Make a light caramel (p.642) with 60 g (2 oz) of the sugar and 1 tablespoon water, and carefully pour it into a mould to coat the insides. In a small bowl, mix the flour with 1 tablespoon of the milk and the lemon zest until smooth. Heat the remaining milk and sugar in a pan. Beat the eggs and mix them into the hot milk, then mix in the flour paste. Stir until smooth, pour into the mould and place in a roasting tin half-filled with hot water. Bake for 45 minutes. Turn out and serve cold.

ORANGE CUSTARD

FLAN À L'ORANGE

- 2 eggs
- 2 egg yolks
- 60 g (2 oz) caster sugar
- 450 ml (16 fl oz) orange juice

Preparation time: 10 minutes,
plus chilling time
Cooking time: 20 minutes
Serves 6

Prepare 2–3 hours in advance. Preheat the oven to 150°C/300°F/Gas Mark 2. Beat the eggs with the sugar. Warm the orange juice and add it a little at a time to the mixture. Pour into 6 individual ramekins and place in a roasting tin half-filled with hot water. Bake in the oven for 15–20 minutes, or until set. Cool and refrigerate for 2–3 hours.

PINEAPPLE CUSTARD PUDDING

FLAN À L'ANANAS

- 185 g (6½ oz) sugar
- 1 x 1-kg (2¼-lb) tin pineapple chunks
- 6 eggs
- 35 g (1½ oz) flour
- Juice of 1 lemon
- 2 tablespoons Kirsch

Preparation time: 15 minutes,
plus chilling time
Cooking time: 1 hour 10 minutes
Serves 6

Prepare the day before. Make a light caramel (p.642) with 85 g (3 oz) of the sugar and 2 tablespoons water, and carefully pour it into a mould to coat the insides. Preheat the oven to 180°C/350°F/Gas Mark 4. Crush three-quarters of the pineapple and place with the juice from the tin and the remaining sugar in a non-reactive pan. Bring to the boil and boil for 5 minutes. Dice the remaining pineapple and add to the pan. Cook for a further 5 minutes. Break the eggs into a bowl and mix with the flour, lemon juice and Kirsch. Add the pineapple. Pour the mixture into the prepared mould, place in a roasting tin half-filled with hot water and bake for 1 hour. Cool and store in the refrigerator. Turn out and serve the next day.

SOUFFLÉS

Soufflés are very light-textured desserts made with flour, butter, milk and eggs. The egg whites are usually whisked separately and gently folded into the mixture, adding air and lightness.

CHOCOLATE SOUFFLÉ

SOUFFLÉ AU CHOCOLAT

Preheat the oven to 160°C/325°F/Gas Mark 3 and grease a soufflé dish with butter. Bring all but 2 tablespoons of the milk to simmering point in a pan over a low heat. Remove from the heat and stir in the chocolate. Mix the remaining milk, flour and sugar to a smooth paste and set aside. Beat the egg yolks in a large bowl and pour on the chocolate milk, stirring. Stir in the flour and sugar paste. Whisk the egg whites to stiff peaks and fold gently into the chocolate mixture. Pour into the prepared dish and gently level the surface. Place in the oven for 10 minutes, then increase the temperature to 200°C/400°F/Gas Mark 6 for a further 20 minutes. Serve immediately.

- Butter, for greasing
- 400 ml (14 fl oz) milk
- 140 g (4¾ oz) chocolate, chopped
- 15 g (½ oz) flour
- 30 g (1¼ oz) caster sugar
- 5 eggs, separated

Preparation time: 10 minutes
Cooking time: 30 minutes
Serves 6

CANDIED FRUIT SOUFFLÉ

SOUFFLÉ AUX FRUITS CONFITS

Preheat the oven to 180°C/350°F/Gas Mark 4. Put the candied fruit in a bowl, pour over the Curaçao and leave to macerate. Proceed as for vanilla soufflé (p.710), using the milk, sugar, flour, butter and eggs, and the macerated candied fruit instead of vanilla. Bake for 10 minutes, then raise the oven temperature to 220°C/425°F/Gas Mark 7 and bake for a further 25 minutes. Serve immediately.

- 125 g (4¼ oz) candied fruit, diced
- 50 ml (2 fl oz) Curaçao
- 300 ml (½ pint) milk
- 60 g (2 oz) caster sugar
- 40 g (1½ oz) flour
- 50 g (1¾ oz) butter, plus extra for greasing
- 4 egg yolks
- 6 egg whites

Preparation time: 20 minutes
Cooking time: 35 minutes
Serves 6

BERRY SOUFFLÉ

SOUFFLÉ AUX FRUITS ROUGES

Remove the stalks from the berries. Put them in a large non-reactive pan with 100 g (3½ oz) of the sugar. Mix 2 teaspoons of the potato flour with a little water, add to the pan and heat gently, stirring until the mixture thickens, and then set aside. Boil the milk in another pan. Meanwhile, mix the egg yolks, 100 g (3½ oz) of the sugar, the remaining potato flour and the flour in a bowl. Stir the hot milk into this mixture. Return to the milk pan and thicken the custard over a gentle heat, whisking by hand or with an electric whisk.

Preheat the oven to 150°C/300°F/Gas Mark 2 and grease 6 individual soufflé dishes with the butter. Sprinkle with half the remaining sugar. Beat the egg whites to stiff peaks with the remaining sugar. Warm the custard and the stewed berries and mix them together. Flavour with the raspberry liqueur. Last of all, fold in the egg whites with a spatula. Fill the prepared dishes and bake for 15 minutes. Serve as soon as the soufflés have risen.

- 250 g (9 oz) strawberries
- 200 g (7 oz) raspberries
- 40–50 g (1½–1¾ oz) redcurrants
- 300 g (11 oz) caster sugar
- 40–50 g (1½–1¾ oz) potato flour
- 750 ml (1¼ pints) milk
- 6 eggs, separated
- 40 g (1½ oz) flour
- 50 g (1¾ oz) butter
- 50 ml (2 fl oz) raspberry liqueur

Preparation time: 30 minutes
Cooking time: 20–30 minutes
Serves 6

VANILLA SOUFFLÉ

SOUFFLÉ À LA VANILLE

 p.734

Preheat the oven to 190°C/375°F/Gas Mark 5 and grease a soufflé dish with butter. Bring the milk, sugar and vanilla pod to boiling point in a pan. In another pan, stir 2 tablespoons of the hot milk into the flour, then gradually add the rest of the hot milk, stirring over a low heat until thickened. Stir in the butter, remove the vanilla pod, scrape out the seeds and add them to the milk mixture. Mix in the egg yolks, and allow to cool. Whisk the egg whites to stiff peaks and fold gently into the mixture. Pour into the prepared dish and gently level the surface. Bake for 30–35 minutes and serve immediately.

- 100 g (3½ oz) butter, plus extra for greasing
- 400 ml (14 fl oz) milk
- 100 g (3½ oz) sugar
- 1 vanilla pod, split
- 50 g (1¾ oz) flour
- 5 eggs, separated

Preparation time: 10 minutes
Cooking time: 30–35 minutes
Serves 6

VARIATION

. . . .

LEMON SOUFFLÉ
SOUFFLÉ AU CITRON

Proceed as above, replacing the vanilla pod with the finely grated zest of 2 lemons.

MILK PUDDINGS

In France, *puddings* are desserts made from milk, eggs and sugar, along with ingredients such as rice, semolina, tapioca, cornflour, sponge fingers or bread. They may be flavoured in the same way as custards, and may be accompanied by a crème anglaise (p.694) or sprinkled with rum and flambéed.

RICE PUDDING

RIZ AU LAIT

- 1 litre (1¾ pints) milk
- ½ vanilla pod, split
- 250 g (9 oz) pudding rice
- 100 g (3½ oz) caster sugar

Preparation time: 5 minutes
Cooking time: 25 minutes
Serves 6

Heat the milk to boiling point in a pan with the vanilla pod, then add the rice. Cover and simmer gently for 20 minutes, or until tender. Remove from the heat, discard the vanilla pod and gently mix in the sugar with a fork. Serve warm or cold.

BAKED RICE PUDDING

RIZ AU FOUR

- 20 g (¾ oz) butter
- 1.25 litres (2 pints) milk
- Vanilla extract or grated lemon zest, to taste
- 175 g (6 oz) sugar
- 250 g (9 oz) pudding rice

Preparation time: 10 minutes
Cooking time: 1 hour 10 minutes
Serves 6

Preheat the oven to 160°C/325°F/Gas Mark 3 and grease an ovenproof dish with the butter. Bring the milk and the vanilla or lemon zest to the boil, then add the sugar. Rinse the rice, drain and place it in the prepared dish. Pour over the boiling sweetened milk. Bake for 1 hour, or until the rice is tender.

BAKED RICE PUDDING WITH CURRANTS

PUDDING AU RIZ

Make a light caramel (p.643) with 60 g (2 oz) of the sugar and 1 tablespoon water, and carefully pour it into a mould to coat the insides. Preheat the oven to 220°C/425°F/Gas Mark 7. Bring the milk and vanilla pod to the boil and stir in the remaining sugar. Rinse the rice and drain. Add it to the boiling milk with the salt and simmer for 15 minutes, or until tender. Remove the vanilla pod. Meanwhile, whisk the egg whites to stiff peaks. When the rice is cooked, fold in the beaten egg yolks, currants and egg whites. Pour into the prepared mould. Bake for 10 minutes. Allow to cool, then turn out to serve.

- 120 g (4 oz) sugar
- 1 litre (1¾ pints) milk
- ½ vanilla pod, split
- 250 g (9 oz) long-grain rice
- 1 teaspoon salt
- 2 eggs, separated
- 100 g (3½ oz) currants

Preparation time: 20 minutes
Cooking time: 30 minutes
Serves 6

RICE À L'IMPÉRATRICE

RIZ À L'IMPÉRATRICE

Put the candied fruit in a bowl with the Kirsch and leave to macerate for 2–3 hours or overnight. Prepare the crème anglaise and keep warm. Place the milk in a pan and bring to the boil. Add the sugar and rice, cover and simmer gently until the rice has absorbed most of the liquid. Put the gelatine in 3 tablespoons warm water and leave to soften for a few minutes, then heat it very gently to melt it. Do not allow it to boil. Add the gelatine to the hot crème anglaise with the rice and candied fruit. Set aside until nearly set. Meanwhile, whip the cream to soft peaks with icing sugar. Grease a mould with butter and pour in the rice mixture. Leave until cool and set, but not chilled. To turn out, dip in hot water and allow to sit for 30 minutes before serving. Serve with the whipped cream.

- 125 g (4¼ oz) candied fruit, chopped
- Kirsch, to taste
- 1 quantity crème anglaise (p.694)
- 750 ml (1¼ pints) milk
- 50 g (1¾ oz) caster sugar
- 150 g (5 oz) pudding rice
- 12 g (½ oz) powdered gelatine or 3 gelatine leaves
- 150 ml (¼ pint) double cream
- Icing sugar, to taste
- Butter, for greasing

Preparation time: 1½ hours, plus macerating and setting time
Cooking time: 35 minutes
Serves 6

NOTE

This pudding can be served with redcurrant jelly or a crème anglaise flavoured with Kirsch instead of whipped cream.

APRICOT RICE RING

COURONNE AUX ABRICOTS

- **250 g (9 oz) dried apricots**
- **1 quantity baked rice pudding with currants (p.712)**

  Preparation time: 30 minutes, plus soaking time

  Cooking time: 20 minutes

  Serves 6

The day before, soak the apricots in water to cover. Make the baked rice pudding with currants. Rinse a ring mould with water and pour the rice pudding into it. In a small pan, cook the apricots with their soaking liquid over a gentle heat until tender, then drain. When ready to serve, turn the rice pudding out and garnish with the apricots. The apricots may be replaced by any tinned fruit such as cherries or plums, or by fresh fruit which has been poached for 5 minutes in boiling water, then coated with a light syrup (p.642).

SEMOLINA PUDDING

PUDDING À LA SEMOULE

- **1 litre (1¾ pints) milk**
- **160 g (5½ oz) sugar**
- **20 g (¾ oz) butter**
- **Zest of 1 lemon**
- **125 g (4¼ oz) semolina**
- **60 g (2 oz) blanched almonds**

  Preparation time: 10 minutes

  Cooking time: 35 minutes

  Serves 6

Preheat the oven to 220°C/425°F/Gas Mark 7. In a large pan, bring the milk, 100 g (3½ oz) of the sugar, and the butter and lemon zest to the boil. Once boiling, pour in the semolina in a steady stream. Simmer gently for 10–15 minutes. Finely chop the almonds and stir into the semolina. Make a light caramel (p.642) with the remaining sugar and 1 tablespoon water, and carefully pour it into a mould to coat the insides. Pour in the mixture and bake for 10 minutes. Allow to cool before turning out and serving.

VARIATION

. . . .

SEMOLINA CROQUETTES

CROQUETTES DE SEMOULE

Cook the semolina as above. Instead of baking it, allow it to cool and thicken, then shape it into small balls and roll in flour. Heat the oil in a deep-fryer to 180°C/350°F or until a cube of bread browns in 30 seconds. Carefully add the croquettes in batches and fry until golden brown.

CREAMED SEMOLINA

SEMOULE À LA CRÈME

Preheat the oven to 220°C/425°F/Gas Mark 7. In a large pan, bring the milk and 60 g (2 oz) of the sugar to the boil. Pour in the semolina in a steady stream and simmer for 10–15 minutes over a low heat. Whisk the egg whites to stiff peaks. Stir the egg yolks and candied fruit into the semolina, then fold in the egg whites. Make a light caramel (p.642) with the remaining sugar and 1 tablespoon water, and carefully pour it into a mould to coat the insides. Pour in the semolina. Bake for 8 minutes. Allow to cool. Turn out and serve coated with the crème anglaise.

- 1 litre (1¾ pints) milk
- 120 g (4 oz) sugar
- 125 g (4¼ oz) semolina
- 2 eggs, separated
- 50 g (1¾ oz) candied fruit
- 1 quantity crème anglaise (p.694), to serve

Preparation time: 10 minutes
Cooking time: 35 minutes
Serves 6

SEMOLINA SQUARES

BOULETTES DE SEMOULE (GRIESKNEPFLES)

This dessert comes from the Alsace region in eastern France.

Place the milk, sugar and vanilla pod in a large pan and heat gently to simmering point. Pour in the semolina a little at a time, stirring frequently, and simmer for 10 minutes, continuing to stir. Remove the vanilla pod and spread the mixture out on a dish using a knife. Cool, then cut in small squares. Melt the butter in a frying pan and fry the squares until golden.

- 500 ml (18 fl oz) milk
- 30 g (1¼ oz) sugar
- 1 vanilla pod, split
- 200 g (7 oz) coarse semolina
- 180 g (6¼ oz) butter

Preparation time: 10 minutes, plus cooling time
Cooking time: 15 minutes
Serves 6

SEMOLINA QUENELLES

QUENELLES DE SEMOULE

Preheat the oven to 200°C/400°F/Gas Mark 6 and grease an ovenproof dish with butter. In a medium pan, bring the milk and sugar to the boil. Pour in the semolina in a steady stream and simmer for 10–15 minutes over a low heat, stirring frequently. Stir in the eggs, butter and currants. Cool, then mould the mixture into small sausage shapes or quenelles. Place in the prepared dish and bake for 20 minutes. Melt the chocolate with 1 tablespoon water in a heatproof bowl set over a pan of barely simmering water and pour it over the quenelles to serve.

- 30 g (1¼ oz) butter, plus extra for greasing
- 600 ml (1 pint) milk
- 60 g (2 oz) sugar
- 125 g (4¼ oz) semolina
- 3 eggs, beaten
- 60 g (2 oz) currants
- 125 g (4¼ oz) chocolate, to serve

Preparation time: 15 minutes
Cooking time: 40 minutes
Serves 6

TAPIOCA PUDDING

PUDDING AU TAPIOCA

- **500 ml (18 fl oz) milk**
- **160 g (5½ oz) sugar**
- **150 g (5 oz) tapioca**
- **6 eggs, separated**
- **40 g (1½ oz) butter**

Preparation time: 8 minutes
Cooking time: 55 minutes
Serves 6

Preheat the oven to 160°C/325°F/Gas Mark 3. In a medium pan, bring the milk and 100 g (3½ oz) of the sugar to the boil. Pour in the tapioca and simmer for 5 minutes. Remove from the heat. Whisk the egg whites to stiff peaks. Stir the egg yolks and butter into the tapioca, then fold in the egg whites. Make a light caramel (p.642) with the remaining sugar and 1 tablespoon water, and carefully pour it into a mould to coat the insides. Pour in the tapioca, place the mould in a roasting tin half-filled with hot water and bake for 40 minutes. Allow to cool, then turn out and serve.

CHARTRAIN CAKE

GÂTEAU CHARTRAIN

- **150 g (5 oz) chocolate, chopped**
- **750 ml (1¼ pints) milk**
- **60 g (2 oz) semolina**
- **25 g (1 oz) tapioca**
- **60 g (2 oz) sugar**

Preparation time: 8 minutes,
plus cooling time
Cooking time: 20 minutes
Serves 6

In a pan, melt the chocolate in the milk over a very low heat. Stirring occasionally, bring the mixture to simmering point and pour in the semolina and tapioca in a steady stream. Simmer gently for 15 minutes. Make a light caramel (p.642) with the sugar and 1 tablespoon water, and carefully pour it into a mould to coat the insides. Leave to cool. Pour the simmering semolina mixture carefully into the cooled mould. Turn out when cold.

CORN PUDDING

PUDDING MAÏZENA

- **1 litre (1¾ pints) milk**
- **60 g (2 oz) sugar**
- **90 g (3¼ oz) cornflour**
- **1 quantity crème anglaise (p.694), to serve**

Preparation time: 5 minutes,
plus cooling time
Cooking time: 15 minutes
Serves 6

In a pan, bring 750 ml (1¼ pints) of the milk and the sugar to the boil. Mix the cornflour with the remaining milk until smooth. When the sweetened milk comes to the boil, pour in the cornflour mixture and simmer for 10 minutes, stirring constantly. Rinse a mould in water, pour in the cornflour mixture and leave to set in the refrigerator. Turn out and serve with the crème anglaise.

CORN PUDDING WITH PEACHES

PUDDING MAÏZENA AUX PÊCHES

Preheat the oven to 180°C/350°F/Gas Mark 4. In a pan, bring 750 ml (1¼ pints) of the milk and 60 g (2 oz) of the sugar to the boil. Mix the cornflour with the remaining milk until smooth. Whisk the egg whites to stiff peaks. Stir the egg yolks into the cornflour mixture, then fold in the egg whites. Pour this mixture into the boiling milk and mix well. Remove from the heat. Make a light caramel (p.642) with the remaining sugar and 1 table-spoon water, and carefully pour it into a charlotte mould to coat the insides. Pour in the cornflour mixture. Bake for 20 minutes then allow to cool. Peel, halve and stone the peaches. Poach for 6 minutes in the sugar syrup. Turn out the corn pudding and decorate with the peaches. The peaches may be replaced with any kind of fresh or tinned fruit.

- 1 litre (1¾ pints) milk
- 120 g (4 oz) sugar
- 75 g (2½ oz) cornflour
- 3 eggs, separated
- 500 g (1 lb 2 oz) peaches
- 1 quantity light sugar syrup (p.642)

Preparation time: 10 minutes, plus cooling time
Cooking time: 35 minutes
Serves 6

CORN PUDDING WITH CANDIED FRUIT

PUDDING MAÏZENA AUX FRUITS CONFITS

Mix the rice flour and cornflour with a few tablespoons of the milk until smooth. In a pan, bring the remaining milk and the sugar to the boil. Pour the cornflour mixture into the hot milk and simmer for 5 minutes, stirring. Chop half the glacé cherries and candied angelica and stir into the cornflour and milk. Grease a mould with the butter and pour in the mixture. Allow to cool. Turn out and garnish with the remaining cherries and angelica.

- 30 g (1¼ oz) rice flour
- 30 g (1¼ oz) cornflour
- 750 ml (1¼ pints) milk
- 60 g (2 oz) sugar
- 125 g (4¼ oz) mixed glacé cherries and candied angelica
- 10 g (¼ oz) butter

Preparation time: 15 minutes, plus cooling time
Cooking time: 10 minutes
Serves 6

BREAD PUDDING

PUDDING AU PAIN

- 500 ml (18 fl oz) milk
- 160 g (5½ oz) sugar
- 3 eggs, beaten
- 500 g (1 lb 2 oz) crustless stale bread, diced
- 125 g (4¼ oz) candied fruit, chopped

Preparation time: 20 minutes
Cooking time: 1 hour
Serves 6

Preheat the oven to 160°C/325°F/Gas Mark 3. In a pan, bring the milk and 100 g (3½ oz) of the sugar to the boil. Remove from the heat and mix the eggs into the hot milk. Stir in the bread and candied fruit and leave to soak until the bread is soft. Make a light caramel (p.642) with the remaining sugar and 1 tablespoon milk, and carefully pour it into a mould to coat the insides. Pour the bread pudding mixture into the mould and bake for 1 hour. Allow to cool and turn out to serve. The fruit may be replaced by a teaspoon of vanilla extract or grated lemon zest or prunes, soaked, drained and stoned.

VERMICELLI PUDDING

PUDDING AU VERMICELLI

- 1 litre (1¾ pints) milk
- 80 g (2¾ oz) sugar
- Grated zest of 1 lemon
- 150 g (5 oz) vermicelli
- 3 eggs, separated
- 60 g (2 oz) ground almonds
- 60 g (2 oz) butter
- 1.5 litres (2½ pints) crème anglaise (p.694) or redcurrant jelly (p.860), to serve

Preparation time: 20 minutes, plus chilling time
Cooking time: 50 minutes
Serves 6

Prepare the day before. Preheat the oven to 180°C/350°F/Gas Mark 4. In a pan, bring the milk, sugar and lemon zest to the boil. Break up the vermicelli and add to the milk. Simmer for 15 minutes. Remove from the heat. Thoroughly mix in the egg yolks, almonds and butter. Whisk the egg whites to stiff peaks and fold them into the mixture. Pour the pudding into a mould rinsed in water. Bake for 30 minutes. Allow to cool and keep in the refrigerator. Serve the next day with the crème anglaise or redcurrant jelly.

APRICOT PUDDING

PUDDING À LA CONFITURE

- 200 ml (7 fl oz) rum
- 250 g (9 oz) sponge fingers
- 250 g (9 oz) apricot jam (p.853)
- 1 quantity crème anglaise (p.694)

Preparation time: 20 minutes, plus chilling time
Serves 6

Prepare the day before. In a shallow dish, mix the rum with 100 ml (3½ fl oz) water and dip in the sponge fingers one by one. Put them very close together round the sides of a charlotte mould, with their flat sides facing outwards. Line the bottom of the mould in the same way. Put in a layer of apricot jam, then a layer of sponge fingers, and so on. Finish with a layer of sponge fingers. Cover the top with a small plate and set a weight on top of it. Chill in the refrigerator for at least 4 hours. Turn out and coat with the crème anglaise.

CHOCOLATE PUDDING

PUDDING AU CHOCOLAT

Prepare the day before. Melt the chocolate with 1 tablespoon water in a heatproof bowl set over a pan of barely simmering water. Whisk the egg whites to stiff peaks. Mix the egg yolks, sugar and butter into the melted chocolate. Fold in the egg whites. Line the bottom and sides of a charlotte mould with the sponge fingers, with their flat sides facing outwards. Pour in the chocolate mixture. Finish with a layer of sponge fingers. Cover the top with a small plate and set a weight on top of it. Chill in the refrigerator until the next day. Turn out and serve with the crème anglaise.

- 160 g (5½ oz) chocolate, chopped
- 4 eggs, separated
- 80 g (2¾ oz) caster sugar
- 60 g (2 oz) butter, softened
- 125 g (4¼ oz) sponge fingers
- 1 quantity crème anglaise (p.694)

Preparation time: 35 minutes, plus chilling time
Serves 6

ROYAL PUDDING

PUDDING ROYAL

Prepare the day before. Preheat the oven to 180°C/350°F/ Gas Mark 4. Chop 30 g (1¼ oz) of the glacé cherries. Bring the milk to the boil and stir in the digestive biscuits, 50 g (1¾ oz) of the butter, the eggs, rum and chopped cherries. Grease a charlotte mould with the remaining butter. Arrange alternating layers of the sponge fingers, milk mixture, macaroons and remaining cherries. Cover and place the mould in a roasting tin half-filled with hot water. Bake for 30 minutes, then uncover and bake for a further 10 minutes. Allow to cool. Turn out the next day and decorate with the crème fraîche sweetened with icing sugar.

- 100 g (3½ oz) glacé cherries
- 500 ml (18 fl oz) milk
- 100 g (3½ oz) digestive biscuits, crushed
- 60 g (2 oz) butter
- 4 eggs, beaten
- 200 ml (7 fl oz) rum
- 100 g (3½ oz) sponge fingers
- 100 g (3½ oz) almond macaroons (p.771)
- 250 ml (8 fl oz) crème fraîche
- Icing sugar, to taste

Preparation time: 35 minutes
Cooking time: 40 minutes
Serves 6

FRIED DESSERTS

SOUFFLÉ OMELETTE
OMELETTE SOUFFLÉE

- **25 g (1 oz) butter**
- **150 g (5 oz) caster sugar**
- **5 eggs, separated**
- **Vanilla extract, or grated orange or lemon zest, to taste**

Preparation time: 10 minutes
Cooking time: 22 minutes
Serves 6

Preheat the oven to 180°C/350°F/Gas Mark 4 and grease a soufflé dish with the butter. In a large bowl, beat 125 g (4¼ oz) of the sugar and the egg yolks with a whisk until smooth. Flavour with vanilla, or lemon or orange zest. Whisk the egg whites to stiff peaks. Add a quarter of them to the yolk mixture and mix well. Fold in the remaining egg whites. Place the mixture into the prepared dish, sprinkle with the remaining sugar and smooth the top with a knife. Make several deep cuts to help the heat penetrate. Bake for 20–22 minutes, or until golden. Serve immediately.

NORMANDY OMELETTE
OMELETTE NORMANDE

- **350 g (12 oz) apples**
- **60 g (2 oz) butter**
- **5 eggs**
- **1 tablespoon milk**
- **1 teaspoon salt**
- **Ground cinnamon, for sprinkling**
- **50 g (1¼ oz) caster sugar**

Preparation time: 10 minutes
Cooking time: 15 minutes
Serves 6

Peel and core the apples and cut them into thin even slices. Melt 30 g (1¼ oz) of the butter in a large frying pan, add the apples and cook over a medium heat for 5 minutes. Remove the apples. Beat the eggs with the milk and salt. Melt the remaining butter in the same pan over a medium heat. Pour half the egg mixture into the hot pan and cook for 2 minutes. Add the apples and cover with the remaining egg mixture. Cook for a further 5 minutes. Flip the omelette over on to a serving dish and sprinkle with cinnamon and the sugar.

NORWEGIAN OMELETTE

OMELETTE NORVÉGIENNE

This dish is composed of 3 different recipes and each component should be prepared well in advance of serving. Make a Savoy cake the day before. Trim it to make a rectangular sponge base 2.5 cm (1 inch) high. Prepare the ice cream and freeze it in a container the same shape as the Savoy cake base to create a long rectangle or cylinder about 5 cm (2 inches) high. Just before serving, make a soufflé omelette mixture, but do not cook it. Put the sponge base on a long serving dish. Preheat the grill and put the ice cream on top of the sponge base. Working quickly, coat with the soufflé omelette mixture, making sure the ice cream is completely covered. Draw patterns with the blade of a knife. Put under the preheated grill just long enough to colour the surface of the omelette, which protects the ice cream and stops it melting. Serve immediately.

- 1 Savoy cake (p.801)
- 1 quantity any ice cream (pp.740–57)
- 1 quantity soufflé omelette (p.719)

Preparation time: 30 minutes, plus freezing time
Cooking time: 3 minutes
Serves 6

FRIED CREAM

CRÈME FRITE

Make a very thick crème pâtissière (p.706) with the milk, egg yolks, sugar and flour. Spread it out on a clean tray to cool and set. Cut into even-sized pieces. In a deep sauté pan, add oil to a depth of around 2 cm (¾ inch) and heat. Dip the pieces in the beaten egg, then in breadcrumbs and fry, in batches if necessary, in the oil for 3 minutes, or until golden. Drain and serve hot.

- 500 ml (18 fl oz) milk
- 6 egg yolks
- 80 g (2¾ oz) sugar
- 40 g (1½ oz) flour
- 1 egg, beaten
- Dried breadcrumbs, for coating
- Oil, for frying

Preparation time: 25 minutes
Cooking time: 10 minutes
Serves 6

PLAIN CRÊPES

CRÊPES ORDINAIRES

- **250 g (9 oz) flour**
- **2 eggs**
- **2 tablespoons vegetable oil**
- **1 teaspoon salt**
- **500 ml (18 fl oz) milk**
- **Rum, Kirsch, orange-flower water or grated lemon zest, to taste**
- **Caster sugar, for sprinkling**

Preparation time: 10 minutes, plus resting time
Cooking time: 3 minutes per crêpe
Serves 6

p.735

Put the flour in a bowl. Make a well in the centre and break in the eggs. Add 1 tablespoon of the oil, and the salt and a little milk. Beat the batter with a whisk to make the mixture light and smooth. Add the remaining milk gradually until the batter falls like a ribbon from the whisk. Add the chosen flavouring. Rest the batter in the refrigerator for a few hours. It will thicken slightly. When ready to cook the crêpes, stir the batter and thin with a little water or milk to return it to its original consistency. Pour very little of the remaining oil into a frying pan and place over a high heat. Pour in a little of the batter, immediately tipping and turning the pan so that it spreads evenly. Turn over as soon as the crêpe is golden brown and can be lifted. Cook on the other side and sprinkle with sugar. Serve piping hot. Repeat with the remaining batter.

NOTE
The oil in the batter can be replaced by 30 g (1¼ oz) melted butter whisked into the batter just before making the crêpes.

VARIATIONS

. . . .

CRÊPES FILLED WITH JAM
CRÊPES FOURRÉES À LA CONFITURE

Proceed as above. Spread 1 tablespoon jam on each crêpe. Roll up and serve.

. . . .

CRÊPES FILLED WITH CREAM
CRÊPES FOURRÉES À LA CRÈME

Proceed as above. Spread 1 tablespoon almond custard (p.706) or crème fraîche on each crêpe. Roll up and serve.

BUCKWHEAT CRÊPES

CRÊPES SARRASIN

This crêpe recipe comes from Brittany in northern France.

Put both kinds of flour and the salt in a bowl. Beat in the egg and a little milk to make a smooth paste, then mix in the remaining milk. Thin down with a little water if the batter is too thick; it should fall easily like a ribbon from the whisk. Brush a frying pan or griddle with oil and set over a medium heat. When it is hot, pour on a small quantity of the batter and spread out to a thin, even layer using a wooden spatula, or by tilting the pan. Cook for 2 minutes on each side. Repeat with the remaining batter. Put a knob of good butter on each crêpe and serve folded into four.

- 200 g (7 oz) buckwheat flour
- 90 g (3¼ oz) flour
- ½ teaspoon salt
- 1 egg
- 500 ml (18 fl oz) milk
- Oil, for frying
- 100 g (3½ oz) butter, to serve

Preparation time: 20 minutes
Cooking time: 4 minutes
per crêpe
Serves 6

LIGHT CRÊPES

CRÊPES LÉGÈRES

- ◆ **250 g (9 oz) flour**
- ◆ **300 ml (½ pint) milk**
- ◆ **200 ml (7 fl oz) warm water**
- ◆ **100 g (3½ oz) butter, softened**
- ◆ **2 pinches of salt**
- ◆ **5 eggs, separated**
- ◆ **Grated zest of 1 lemon**
- ◆ **Caster sugar, to taste**

Preparation time: 10 minutes
Cooking time: 3 minutes per
crêpe
Serves 6

Mix the flour with the milk and warm water in a bowl. Melt 15 g (½ oz) of the butter and stir it into the flour and milk with a pinch of salt. Allow this mixture to rest for at least 1 hour in the refrigerator. Whisk the egg whites with a pinch of salt until stiff. Stir the egg yolks, lemon zest and remaining butter into the flour and milk mixture and fold in the egg whites. The batter must be smooth and light. Cook in the same way as for plain crêpes (p.721). Sprinkle with sugar and serve immediately.

 p.736

FRENCH TOAST

PAIN PERDU

- ◆ **500 ml (18 fl oz) milk**
- ◆ **175 g (6 oz) caster sugar**
- ◆ **2 eggs**
- ◆ **400 g (14 oz) slightly stale bread**
- ◆ **125 g (4¼ oz) butter**
- ◆ **Ground cinnamon or vanilla sugar, to taste**

Preparation time: 10 minutes
Cooking time: 3 minutes per slice
Serves 6

Beat the milk with 150 g (5 oz) of the sugar and the eggs. Cut the bread into even, fairly thin slices and dip into the milk and egg mixture. The bread should not collapse, but merely be wet. Melt a knob of the butter in a frying pan. Fry each slice over a high heat until golden, adding more butter to the pan as necessary. Sprinkle with the remaining sugar and ground cinnamon or vanilla sugar, and serve hot.

SOUFFLÉD FRITTERS

BEIGNETS SOUFFLÉS OU PETS DE NONNE

- ◆ **1 quantity choux pastry dough (p.774)**
- ◆ **Vegetable oil, for deep-frying**
- ◆ **Caster sugar, for sprinkling**
- ◆ **Crème anglaise (p.694), to serve (optional)**

Preparation time: 20 minutes
Cooking time: 5 minutes
per batch
Serves 6

Prepare the choux pastry dough. Heat the oil in a deep-fryer to 180°C/350°F, or until a cube of bread browns in 30 seconds. Carefully drop walnut-sized spoonfuls of the dough into the hot oil in batches. As soon as they expand, increase the heat to 190°C/375°F. Remove when the fritters are golden brown. Drain well, sprinkle with sugar and serve immediately. If desired, the fritters can be served in a bowl with vanilla or other flavoured crème anglaise.

BATTER

PÂTE À FRIRE

Prepare 2 hours in advance. Put the flour in a bowl. Mix the yeast to a paste with the warm water. Make a well in the centre of the flour and put the oil and yeast into the well. Mix in warm water, a little at a time, until the batter falls like a ribbon from the whisk. Beat the egg white for 1 minute with a fork. Stir this into the batter. Allow the batter to stand in the refrigerator for 2 hours before using.

NOTE
Crêpe batter can be used in place of the batter given above, but the result will not be as crisp.

- **250 g (9 oz) flour**
- **1 knob of fresh yeast**
- **1 tablespoon warm water, plus more for mixing**
- **1 tablespoon oil**
- **1 egg white**

  Preparation time: 8 minutes, plus standing time
  Makes 500 ml (18 fl oz)

APPLE FRITTERS

BEIGNETS AUX POMMES

 p.737

Prepare the batter. Heat the oil in a deep-fryer to 180°C/350°F, or until a cube of bread browns in 30 seconds. Peel and core the apples and cut into even slices. Dip the apple slices, one by one, into the batter. Carefully lower the apple slices, in batches, into the hot oil and fry for a few minutes until golden and tender. Drain, sprinkle with sugar and serve immediately.

- **1 quantity batter (see above)**
- **Vegetable oil, for deep-frying**
- **6 eating apples**
- **Sugar, for sprinkling**

  Preparation time: 8 minutes
  Cooking time: 15 minutes
  Serves 6

VARIATIONS

. . . .

STRAWBERRY FRITTERS
BEIGNETS AUX FRAISES

Proceed as above, dipping strawberries into the batter instead of apples.

. . . .

PEACH FRITTERS
BEIGNETS AUX PÊCHES

Cut the peaches in half and remove the stones. Proceed as above, replacing the apples with peaches.

RICE CROQUETTES
CROQUETTES DE RIZ

- 175 g (6 oz) long-grain rice
- 500 ml (18 fl oz) milk
- Grated zest of 1 lemon or ½ vanilla pod, split
- 1 pinch of salt
- 60 g (2 oz) butter, softened
- 2 eggs
- Flour or 1 egg white, beaten, for coating
- Vegetable oil, for deep-frying
- 60 g (2 oz) sugar

Preparation time: 15 minutes, plus cooling time
Cooking time: 30 minutes
Serves 6

Make Indian rice (p.616) with the rice, milk, 500 ml (18 fl oz) water, lemon zest or vanilla pod and salt. Cool slightly, remove the pod if using, and stir in the butter and eggs. When the mixture is completely cold, form into sausage shapes and dip in flour or the egg white. Heat the oil in a deep-fryer to 180°C/350°F, or until a cube of bread browns in 30 seconds. Fry the croquettes in batches until golden brown. Drain well. Sprinkle with the sugar and serve.

OTHER MILK & EGG RECIPES

CHOCOLATE BÉCHAMEL
BÉCHAMEL AU CHOCOLAT

- 750 ml (1¼ pints) milk
- 200 g (7 oz) chocolate, chopped
- 50 g (1¾ oz) butter
- 40 g (1½ oz) flour

Preparation time: 10 minutes
Cooking time: 10 minutes
Serves 6

Heat the milk in a pan until simmering. Stir the chocolate into the milk to melt it. Melt the butter in a separate pan and stir in the flour to make a roux. Pour in the chocolate-flavoured milk a little at a time, constantly stirring. Cook for 10 minutes, stirring until thickened. Serve cold.

A FINE YOUNG MAN

UN BON JEUNE HOMME

Bring the milk to a simmer in a pan. Mix the chocolate and sugar into the milk. Simmer gently for 45 minutes, stirring frequently, to make a very thick paste. After about 30 minutes the chocolate will have the consistency of yoghurt, and should be stirred constantly. Pour into a bowl, and allow to cool. Coat with the crème anglaise and serve very cold.

- 750 ml (1¼ pints) milk
- 175 g (6 oz) chocolate, chopped
- 50 g (1¾ oz) sugar
- 1 quantity crème anglaise (p.694)

Preparation time: 3 minutes
Cooking time: 45 minutes
Serves 6

CHOCOLATE MARQUISE

MARQUISE AU CHOCOLAT

Prepare 4 hours in advance. In a medium pan, melt the chocolate with a little water over a gentle heat until smooth. Remove from the heat and beat in the sugar, egg yolks and butter. Whisk the egg whites to soft peaks. Fold into the chocolate mixture. Pour the marquise into a charlotte mould and chill in the refrigerator until set. To turn out, dip the mould in hot water. Coat with the vanilla crème anglaise and serve.

- 250 g (9 oz) chocolate, chopped
- 60 g (2 oz) caster sugar
- 4 eggs, separated
- 175 g (6 oz) butter, melted
- 500 ml (18 fl oz) vanilla crème anglaise (p.694)

Preparation time: 25 minutes, plus chilling time
Serves 6

CHOCOLATE MAYONNAISE

MAYONNAISE AU CHOCOLAT

Melt the butter and chocolate in a heatproof bowl set over a pan of barely simmering water. Mix the egg yolks one by one into the mixture. Beat the whites to very stiff peaks. Fold into the chocolate mixture and add the rum. Leave for several hours in the refrigerator before serving.

- 30 g (1¼ oz) butter
- 175 g (6 oz) chocolate, chopped
- 4 eggs, separated
- 30 ml (1 fl oz) rum

Preparation time: 25 minutes, plus chilling time
Serves 6

SABAYON

SABAYON

- 200 g (7 oz) caster sugar
- 5 egg yolks
- ½ teaspoon vanilla extract
- Grated zest of 1 lemon
- 200 ml (7 fl oz) fortified wine, such as port, sherry or Madeira

Preparation time: 10 minutes
Cooking time: 5–10 minutes
Serves 6

Whisk the sugar, egg yolks, vanilla and lemon zest in a large bowl until the mixture is thick, white and smooth. Add the wine and put the mixture in a heatproof bowl over a pan of barely simmering water. Heat the sabayon gently for 5–10 minutes, constantly whisking until very thick and foamy. Remove from the heat and serve immediately.

KIRSCH ICING FOR A CAKE

GLACE AU KIRSCH POUR GATEAU

- 120 g (4 oz) icing sugar
- Kirsch

Preparation time: 25 minutes
Serves 6

Put the sugar in a bowl and beat in a little Kirsch, teaspoon by teaspoon, until the mixture forms a thick paste. Use a palette knife dipped in boiling water to spread the icing over the cake.

CHOCOLATE ICING

GLACE AU CHOCOLAT

- 60 g (2 oz) chocolate, chopped
- 60 g (2 oz) butter
- 2 very fresh eggs, separated

Preparation time: 20 minutes
Serves 6

In a small pan, gently melt the chocolate and butter over a low heat. Remove from the heat and mix in the egg yolks. Whisk the egg whites to soft peaks and fold these into the chocolate mixture. Spread the icing over the cake with a palette knife. The icing sets as it cools.

COFFEE FONDANT ICING

FONDANT AU CAFÉ

In a pan over a low heat, dissolve the sugar and glucose in 100 ml (3½ fl oz) water and cook to the long-thread stage (p.643). Carefully pour the syrup on to a marble slab. As soon as it is cold, work it with a wooden or metal spatula until it turns opaque. Add the lemon juice, knead well and form into a ball. Return the icing to the pan and melt over a low heat without boiling. Add the coffee extract and use the icing for a large cake or small choux buns. Ready-prepared fondant icing is also available.

- 300 g (11 oz) sugar
- 1 tablespoon glucose
- 10 drops lemon juice
- 2 teaspoons coffee extract, or to taste

Preparation time: 15 minutes
Cooking time: 10 minutes
Serves 6

SAINT-HONORÉ CREAM

CRÈME SAINT-HONORÉ

In a pan, bring the milk and vanilla pod to boiling point over a low heat. Put the flour, sugar, whole egg and the egg yolks in a large bowl and whisk until smooth. Add the milk a little at a time, continuing to whisk. Return to the pan and cook over a gentle heat, stirring all the time, until the mixture thickens. Remove the vanilla pod. Whisk the egg whites to stiff peaks and fold into the custard. Allow to cool and use immediately as a filling. It will not keep.

- 500 ml (18 fl oz) milk
- 1 vanilla pod, split
- 30 g (1¼ oz) flour
- 125 g (4¼ oz) caster sugar
- 1 egg
- 3 eggs, separated

Preparation time: 15 minutes, plus cooling time
Cooking time: 10 minutes
Serves 6

BUTTER CREAM

CRÈME AU BEURRE

In a large bowl set over a pan of simmering water, whisk the eggs and sugar with an electric whisk until thick and creamy. Remove from the heat and continue whisking until the mixture is almost cold. Whisk in the butter, a little at a time, and continue whisking until the cream is thick, glossy and completely cold. If desired, add the chosen flavouring.

- 3 eggs
- 120 g (4 oz) caster sugar
- 270 g (10 oz) butter, at room temperature
- Grated orange or lemon zest, coffee essence, vanilla extract or crushed praline, to flavour (optional)

Preparation time: 30 minutes
Cooking time: 10 minutes
Serves 6

CHOUX BUN FILLING
CRÈME POUR CHOUX

- 500 ml (18 fl oz) milk
- 50 g (1¾ oz) chocolate, chopped
- 60 g (2 oz) flour
- 100 g (3½ oz) caster sugar
- 1 teaspoon salt
- 3 eggs
- 30 g (1¼ oz) butter

Preparation time: 25 minutes
Cooking time: 10 minutes
Serves 6

In a large pan over a low heat, heat the milk and chocolate, stirring occasionally, until the chocolate has melted. In a large bowl, beat the flour, sugar, salt and eggs until smooth. Whisk in the warm chocolate milk, then return to the pan. Mix in the butter a little at a time. Thicken over a gentle heat, stirring constantly. Cook for 1 minute, then remove from the heat and whisk until completely cold.

CHEESE FILLING FOR SAVOURIES
CRÈME AU FROMAGE POUR PÂTISSERIES SALÉES

- 125 g (4¼ oz) butter
- 30 g (1¼ oz) flour
- 200 ml (7 fl oz) crème fraîche
- 75 g (2½ oz) Gruyère cheese, grated
- 2 eggs, separated
- Salt and pepper

Preparation time: 25 minutes
Cooking time: 15 minutes
Serves 6

Prepare a béchamel sauce (p.50) with 60 g (2 oz) of the butter, and the flour and crème fraiche. Cook over a low heat, stirring, for 15 minutes. Remove from the heat and stir in the cheese and egg yolks, and the remaining the butter in small pieces. Whisk the egg whites to stiff peaks and fold these into the béchamel. Season with salt and pepper and beat well with a wooden spoon before using.

RUM SAUCE
SAUCE AU RHUM

- 125 g (4¼ oz) sugar
- 200 ml (7 fl oz) rum

Preparation time: 5 minutes
Cooking time: 10 minutes
Serves 6

Place 250 ml (8 fl oz) water and the sugar and rum in a pan and bring to the boil over a low heat. Remove from the heat as soon as it starts to boil. Stir well and use immediately, for example poured over a hot rum baba.

Eggs in snow   (p.693)

Hedgehogs (p.693)

Fruit bavarois (p.697)

Chocolate mousse   (p.703)

Vanilla soufflé (p.710)

Crêpes filled with jam   (p.721)

French toast   (p.723)

Apple fritters (p.724)

13

ICES

ICES

Ices are made from a rich mixture of milk or cream (ice creams), or sometimes just fruit, water and sugar (sorbets). The mixture is usually churned steadily and quickly at around −18°C (0°F) in an ice-cream maker fitted with paddles. Once the mixture is frozen but still soft, it can be transferred to a mould or container and kept in the freezer until serving.

If an ice-cream maker is not available, ice creams and sorbets can be made by putting the mixture into a container that is a good conductor of cold (such as metal), placing it in the freezer, and whisking it every 15 minutes to prevent large ice crystals forming. Repeat until it is too stiff to whisk. Too much sugar or alcohol will prevent the mixture freezing, while too much water or milk encourages the formation of ice crystals. Depending on the type of freezer, allow 4–8 hours for the mixture to freeze completely. To turn out, pour cold water – never hot – over the mould for 1–2 minutes, then turn out onto the serving dish.

VANILLA ICE CREAM
GLACE À LA VANILLE

In a large pan, bring the milk and vanilla pod to simmering point, then remove from the heat and leave to infuse. Whisk the egg yolks and sugar in a bowl for at least 10 minutes, until the mixture becomes white and foamy. Pour the milk onto the egg mixture a little at a time, then return to the pan and gradually thicken the custard over a very low heat, stirring all the time, until it coats the back of the spoon. Remove from the heat and continue whisking until creamy and smooth. Allow to cool completely. Pour the custard into an ice-cream maker and freeze following the manufacturer's instructions. For extra creaminess and volume, the whipped cream may be stirred into the ice cream just before it freezes.

- 1 litre (1¾ pints) milk
- 1 vanilla pod, split
- 8 egg yolks
- 150 g (5 oz) sugar
- 500 ml (18 fl oz) sweetened whipped cream (p.121), (optional)

Preparation time: 10 minutes, plus freezing time
Cooking time: 15 minutes
Serves 6

VARIATIONS

. . . .

KIRSCH ICE CREAM
GLACE AU KIRSCH

Proceed as for vanilla ice cream, flavouring the custard with Kirsch to taste before freezing.

. . . .

CHOCOLATE ICE CREAM
GLACE AU CHOCOLAT

Make a chocolate crème anglaise (p.694) using 250 g (9 oz) chocolate, 6 egg yolks, and 60 g (2 oz) sugar. Proceed as for vanilla ice cream.

. . . .

COFFEE ICE CREAM
GLACE AU CAFÉ

Make a coffee crème anglaise (p.694) using 4 teaspoons coffee extract in place of the vanilla pod, and 100 g (3½ oz) sugar. Proceed as for vanilla ice cream.

. . . .

COFFEE ICE CREAM WITH CANDIED COFFEE BEANS
GLACE AU CAFÉ AVEC GRAINS

Proceed as for coffee ice cream, above, and stir in 125 g (4 oz) candied coffee beans before freezing.

FRUIT WATER ICE

GLACE AUX FRUITS

Put the sugar and 400 ml (14 fl oz) water in a pan. Heat to dissolve the sugar, until it starts to boil. Boil for 1 minute, then add the fruit flavouring of your choice from those given below. The syrup should be light in consistency. Freeze as for ices (p.740).

NOTE

500 ml (18 fl oz) crème fraîche may be added to all the fruit water ices. This will make them smoother and less icy.

VARIATIONS

. . . .

STRAWBERRY WATER ICE

GLACE AUX FRAISES

Process 500 g (1lb 2 oz) strawberries and the juice of 2 lemons in a blender until smooth. Mix with the sugar syrup and freeze (p.740).

. . . .

MANDARIN ORANGE WATER ICE

GLACE AUX MANDARINES

Grate the zest from half of 750 g (1 lb 10 oz) mandarin oranges and squeeze the juice from all of them. Mix with the sugar syrup and an additional 200 ml (7 fl oz) water. Freeze (p.740).

. . . .

ORANGE WATER ICE

GLACE AUX ORANGES

Grate the zest from half of 750 g (1 lb 10 oz) oranges and squeeze the juice from all of them. Mix with the sugar syrup and an additional 300 ml (½ pint) water. Freeze (p.740).

- **500 g (1 lb 2 oz) sugar**
- **Fruit (see Variations)**

Preparation time: 20 minutes, plus freezing time

Serves 6

 p.753

FROZEN FRUIT MOUSSE

MOUSSE GLACÉE AUX FRUITS

- **500 ml (18 fl oz) sugar syrup**
- **8 egg yolks**

Preparation time: 30 minutes, plus freezing time

Serves 6

For the mousse base, prepare a sugar syrup to the long-thread stage (p.643). In a large bowl, whisk the egg yolks with an electric whisk until white and creamy and pour in the syrup in a thin, steady stream, without allowing it to touch the whisk. Set the bowl over a pan of simmering water and continue whisking until thick and firm. Remove the bowl from the heat and continue whisking until cool. Add a fruit flavouring from those listed below. Freeze (p.740).

VARIATIONS

. . . .

FROZEN STRAWBERRY MOUSSE

MOUSSE GLACÉE AUX FRAISES

Process 200 g (7 oz) strawberries in a blender until smooth. Stir into the mousse base along with 500 ml (18 fl oz) whipped cream and proceed as above.

. . . .

FROZEN PINEAPPLE MOUSSE

MOUSSE GLACÉE AUX ANANAS

Process 185 g (6½ oz) fresh pineapple, or tinned pineapple in syrup (drained weight), in a blender until smooth. Stir into the mousse base along with 250 ml (8 fl oz) whipped cream and proceed as above.

. . . .

FROZEN MANDARIN OR ORANGE MOUSSE

MOUSSE GLACÉE À LA MANDARINE OU À L'ORANGE

Cook the zest of 6 mandarins or 4 oranges in light sugar syrup (p.643) and continue to make the mousse base as above. Stir in 250 ml (8 fl oz) whipped cream and proceed as above.

COFFEE WATER ICE

CAFÉ GLACÉ

Make strong coffee with 1 litre (1¾ pints) boiling water and the ground coffee. Add the sugar and stir to dissolve. Freeze in an ice-cream maker. When ready to serve, allow to soften slightly while you whip the double cream to soft peaks. Fold the cream into the coffee ice and serve.

- 185 g (6½ oz) ground coffee
- 200 g (7 oz) sugar
- 500 ml (18 fl oz) double cream

Preparation time: 10 minutes, plus freezing time
Serves 6

PEACH MELBA

PÊCHES MELBA

In a large pan, bring 500 ml (18 fl oz) water and the sugar to the boil. Simmer the peaches in the syrup for 15 minutes, or until tender. Allow to cool, then peel them. Serve the whole peaches on the vanilla ice cream in individual serving dishes. Coat with the redcurrant syrup, sprinkle with the almonds and decorate with the cream.

- 100 g (3½ oz) sugar
- 6 large peaches
- 1 litre (1¾ pints) vanilla ice cream (p.740)
- 50 ml (2 fl oz) berry syrup (p.826), made with redcurrants
- 50 g (2 oz) blanched almonds, sliced
- 250 ml (8 fl oz) sweetened whipped cream (p.121), chilled

Preparation time: 5 minutes
Cooking time: 20 minutes
Serves 6

ICED CAFÉ AU LAIT

CAFÉ AU LAIT GLACÉ

Mix the condensed milk and cold milk in a bowl. Add instant coffee, dissolved in 2 tablespoons boiling water, or coffee essence. Taste to ensure the mixture tastes strongly of coffee. Freeze as for ice cream (p.740).

- 1 x 400-g (14-oz) tin sweetened condensed milk
- 400 ml (14 fl oz) milk
- Instant coffee or coffee essence, to taste

Preparation time: 10 minutes, plus freezing time
Serves 6

COFFEE SUNDAE

CAFÉ LIÉGEOIS

 p.754

Prepare several hours in advance. Make the coffee crème anglaise, then freeze it (p.740) to make coffee ice cream. Put 2 tablespoons of the coffee in the bottom of each of 6 chilled sundae glasses. Allow the ice cream to soften slightly and add 2–3 scoops to each sundae glass. Whip the cream with the sugar, arrange on top of the sundaes and decorate with the candied coffee beans.

- 1 litre (1¾ pints) coffee crème anglaise (p.694)
- 175 ml (6 fl oz) black coffee, chilled
- 200 g (7 oz) double cream
- 50 g (1¾ oz) icing sugar
- 60 g (2 oz) candied coffee beans

Preparation time: 20 minutes, plus freezing time
Serves 6

APRICOT ICE CREAM

CRÈME GLACÉE AUX ABRICOTS

 p.755

Stone the apricots and purée in a blender until smooth. Add the sugar and process for a minute more to dissolve the sugar. Freeze until slightly thickened. Whip the cream and stir into the apricot purée. Return to the freezer, and whisk every half hour for 4–6 hours to prevent the formation of ice crystals. Alternatively, churn and freeze in an ice-cream maker.

- 600 g (1 lb 5 oz) ripe apricots
- 90 g (3¼ oz) sugar
- 250 ml (8 fl oz) double cream

Preparation time: 10 minutes, plus freezing time
Serves 6

VARIATION

. . . .

STRAWBERRY OR RASPBERRY ICE CREAM

CRÈME GLACÉE AUX FRAISES OU AUX FRAMBOISES

 p.756

Replace the apricots and sugar with 500 g (1 lb 2 oz) ripe strawberries or raspberries and 100 g (3½ oz) caster sugar and proceed as above.

. . . .

PEACH ICE CREAM

CRÈME GLACÉE AUX PÊCHES

Replace the apricots with peaches, add 1 teaspoon lemon juice to the puréed peaches and proceed as above.

ICED CHOCOLATE SOUFFLÉ

SOUFFLÉ GLACÉ AU CHOCOLAT

- 20 g (¾ oz) butter, melted
- 130 g (4½ oz) caster sugar, plus extra for sprinkling
- 6 egg yolks
- 30 g (1¼ oz) cocoa powder
- 375 ml (13 fl oz) double cream

Preparation time: 25 minutes, plus freezing time
Cooking time: 5 minutes
Serves 6

Prepare the day before. Line the inside of a straight-sided soufflé dish with a strip of greaseproof paper, extending it 10 cm (4 inches) above the rim of the dish. Fold the surplus ends of the paper back over the rim of the dish and secure with string. Brush the inside of the paper with the butter and sprinkle with extra sugar. Add the sugar to 260 ml (9 fl oz) water and prepare a sugar syrup to the long-thread stage (p.643).

In a large heatproof bowl, whisk the egg yolks with an electric whisk until white and creamy, and then, still whisking, pour in the hot syrup in a thin, steady stream, without allowing it to touch the beaters. Set the bowl over a pan of simmering water and continue whisking until thick and firm. Remove the bowl from the heat and continue whisking until cool.

Mix the cocoa with a little warm water in a bowl to make a thick paste. Whisk the cream until it becomes soft and thick, adding 1 tablespoon iced water towards the end, then stir in the cocoa paste. Using a spatula, gently fold the cream and whisked egg yolk mixtures together. Pour the chocolate soufflé mixture into the prepared soufflé dish, filling all air pockets. Smooth the top with a knife blade. Freeze overnight. Remove the paper and string before serving.

SAUTERNES ICE CREAM

CRÈME GLACÉE AU SAUTERNES

- 100 ml (3½ fl oz) Sauternes
- 300 ml (½ pint) crème fraîche
- 200 g (3½ oz) caster sugar

Preparation time: 5 minutes, plus freezing time
Serves 6

Combine the Sauternes, crème fraîche and sugar in a bowl, then pour into an ice-cream maker and churn until almost frozen.

SORBETS

Sorbets are iced desserts made without fat or eggs. They are usually made from sugar and a flavouring such as fruit purée or juice, a herb infusion (such as lemon balm or tarragon), a liqueur (such as Armagnac) or wine (such as port or Champagne). The earliest sorbets were prepared from fruit, honey and snow. Sorbets are served as a light dessert at the end of the meal, or sometimes between courses during a long meal of many courses. Historically, a sorbet served between courses at a celebration meal was called a *trou normand,* or 'Normandy hole', which allowed diners time to pause to help their digestion. Sorbets are best eaten on the day they are made.

BASIC METHOD FOR SORBETS

Heat the suggested quantity of water, sugar, lemon juice and prepared fruit in a pan. Boil for 5 minutes, then process to a purée in a blender. Allow to cool, then pour into an ice-cream maker and freeze as for ice cream. Preserving sugar containing pectin may be used to help the sorbet set. The amounts of water and sugar vary depending on the base ingredient used. Less is needed for alcohol-based sorbets, more for fruit sorbets, and even more for sorbets made with herb teas. Use mineral water for preference.

BLACKCURRANT SORBET
SORBET AU CASSIS

- 1 kg (2¼ lb) blackcurrants
- Juice of 1 lemon
- 350 g (12 oz) sugar

Preparation time: 20 minutes, plus freezing time
Cooking time: 7 minutes
Serves 6

Rinse the blackcurrants and remove the stalks. Place in a pan with 300 ml (½ pint) water and the lemon juice and sugar. Rapidly bring to the boil and boil for 5 minutes. Remove from the heat and allow to cool. Process in a blender, then pass through a chinois (conical sieve) to remove the pips. Pour into an ice-cream maker or container and freeze (p.740). Frozen blackcurrants can be used instead of fresh if necessary. Thaw before using them.

RASPBERRY SORBET
SORBET À LA FRAMBOISE

- 500 g (1 lb 2 oz) raspberries
- Juice of 1 small orange
- Juice of 1 lime
- 200 g (7 oz) sugar

Preparation time: 5 minutes, plus freezing time
Serves 6

Place all the ingredients in a blender and process to a purée. Do not sieve. Pour into an ice-cream maker or container and freeze (p.740).

LEMON BALM SORBET
SORBET À LA CITRONNELLE

Put all the ingredients in a pan with 1 litre (1¾ pints) water. Rapidly bring to the boil. Cover, remove from the heat and leave to infuse for 10 minutes. Allow to cool then strain. Pour into an ice-cream maker or container and freeze (p.740).

NOTE
Use fresh lemon balm if it is available, as the sorbet will have much more flavour.

- **1 tablespoon dried or 1 handful of fresh lemon balm**
- **Juice of 2 oranges**
- **350 g (12 oz) sugar**

Preparation time: 15 minutes, plus freezing time
Serves 6

ARMAGNAC SORBET
SORBET À L'ARMAGNAC

Put all the ingredients in a pan with 350 ml (12 fl oz) water. Heat to just below boiling point. Allow to cool, then pour into an ice-cream maker or container and freeze (p.740).

- **250 ml (8 fl oz) Armagnac**
- **250 g (9 oz) sugar**
- **Juice of 1 lemon**

Preparation time: 5 minutes, plus freezing time
Serves 6

PEAR SORBET
SORBET À LA POIRE

📷 p.757

Peel, quarter and core the pears. Place in a blender with all the other ingredients and 150 ml (¼ pint) water and process until smooth. Pour into an ice-cream maker or container and freeze (p.740).

NOTE
Preserving sugar contains pectin, which helps the sorbet to freeze. Ordinary sugar can also be used.

- **1.5 kg (3¼ lb) ripe pears**
- **250 g (9 oz) preserving sugar**
- **Juice of 1 lemon**
- **100 ml (3½ fl oz) pear brandy**

Preparation time: 10 minutes, plus freezing time
Serves 6

TOMATO SORBET

SORBET À LA TOMATE

Put all the ingredients, except the herbs, in a blender with 100 ml (3½ fl oz) water. Process to a purée for 1–2 minutes. Add the herbs for the last few seconds. Pour into an ice-cream maker or container and freeze (p.740).

- 1 litre (1¾ pints) tomato juice
- Zest and juice of 2 limes
- 1 tablespoon white wine vinegar
- 1 teaspoon salt
- 50 g (1¾ oz) sugar
- 1 pinch of cayenne pepper
- 1 pinch of paprika
- 1 tablespoon tarragon, chopped
- 1 tablespoon chervil, chopped

Preparation time: 5 minutes, plus freezing time
Serves 6

LIME SORBET

SORBET AU CITRON VERT

Strain the lime and lemon juice into a pan. Add 750 ml (1¼ pints) water and the sugar. Rapidly bring to the boil and boil for 5 minutes. Remove from the heat and allow to cool. Pour into an ice-cream maker or container and freeze (p.740).

- Juice of 4 limes
- Juice of 2 lemons
- 400 g (14 oz) sugar

Preparation time: 10 minutes, plus freezing time
Cooking time: 10 minutes
Serves 6

Strawberry water ice (p.742)

Coffee sundae (p.746)

Apricot ice cream   (p.746)

Raspberry ice cream (p.746)

Pear sorbet (p.750)

- 14 -
CAKES
&
PASTRIES

CAKES & PASTRIES

Home-made cakes and pastries turn everyday menus into a celebration. They are generally economical and easy to make, and, made with good ingredients, they can have an incomparable flavour. In addition, minimal equipment is required: a clean work surface and rolling pin, a blender and a few tins of various shapes and sizes are all that is needed. However, the oven temperature and cooking times must be followed carefully for the recipe to succeed.

To check the heat of the oven, leave a piece of white paper in it for a few moments and assess its colour. Variations between ovens are often very marked, so nothing can replace the cook's own experience.

HEAT	TEMPERATURE (°C/°F)	COLOUR OF THE PAPER	GAS MARK	TYPE OF CAKE
Warm	50/120 70/150	Pale straw	¼	Meringues Macaroons
Gentle	90/195	Straw	½	Gingerbread
Medium	120/250 150/300	Pale yellow	1 2	Shortbread Biscuits Fruit cake Sponges
Hot	180/350 200/400	Light brown	4 6	Brioche Soufflés Tarts Choux pastry
Very hot	240/475	Dark brown	8	Puff pastry

BISCUITS

Biscuits come in many types, shapes and sizes. They are made with the same basic ingredients – butter, sugar and flour – in variable proportions, along with many additional flavourings. The way they are prepared and the cooking method give different results. Biscuit dough can be made by hand or with an electric mixer, but in either case, as with pastry, the dough should be worked lightly and quickly, which results in biscuits with a short, melt-in-the-mouth texture. The two main types of biscuit dough are thick doughs, which are rolled out with a rolling pin, and soft doughs, which are placed on the baking tray with a spoon.

SABLÉ BISCUITS
SABLÉS

- 125 g (4¼ oz) caster sugar
- 250 g (9 oz) flour, plus extra for dusting
- 1 pinch of salt
- 125 g (4¼ oz) cold butter, cut into pieces
- 1 egg, lightly beaten
- Grated lemon zest, vanilla extract or ground cinnamon, to taste

Preparation time: 20 minutes
Cooking time: 12 minutes
Serves 6

Preheat the oven to 180°C/350°F/Gas Mark 4. Put the sugar, flour and salt into a bowl and rub the butter in with your fingers until the mixture resembles fine breadcrumbs. Add the egg and the chosen flavouring and turn out onto a floured work surface. Knead lightly to form a dough. Roll out to 5 mm (¼ inch) thick, cut out biscuit shapes with a cookie cutter, and bake on a baking tray for 12 minutes, or until pale golden and crisp.

NORMANDY SABLÉS
SABLÉS NORMANDS

- 250 g (9 oz) flour, plus extra for dusting
- 150 g (5 oz) butter, softened
- 65 g (2¼ oz) caster sugar
- 1 egg yolk
- 1 egg, lightly beaten

Preparation time: 15 minutes
Cooking time: 25 minutes
Serves 6

Preheat the oven to 180°C/350°F/Gas Mark 4. Mix the flour, butter, sugar and egg yolk in a bowl until combined, then turn out onto a lightly floured work surface and briefly knead to make a smooth dough. Roll out to 1 cm (½ inch) thick and cut into triangles. Brush with the beaten egg to glaze. Place on a baking tray and bake for 25 minutes, or until golden brown.

NORWEGIAN BOWS

NŒUDS NORVÉGIENS

 p.808

Hard boil 1 of the eggs in a pan of boiling water. Separate the remaining 2 eggs. Preheat the oven to 180°C / 350°F / Gas Mark 4 and lightly grease a baking tray with butter. Shell the hard-boiled egg and remove the yolk. In a medium bowl, crush the cooked egg yolk and beat with the raw egg yolks to make a smooth paste. Add 100 g (3½ oz) of the sugar and beat for 5 minutes. Beat in half the flour, then the butter. Mix in the remaining flour and knead lightly to form a smooth dough. Divide into small walnut-sized pieces. Roll each piece into a long ribbon and shape into a bow. In a bowl, beat the egg whites with a fork. Dip the bows into the egg whites, then sprinkle with the remaining sugar. Place on the prepared tray and bake for 15 minutes, or until golden brown.

- 3 eggs
- 125 g (4¼ oz) butter, softened, plus extra for greasing
- 150 g (5 oz) caster sugar
- 250 g (9 oz) flour

Preparation time: 25 minutes
Cooking time: 15 minutes
Serves 6

EGGLESS SHORTBREAD

SABLÉS SANS ŒUFS

Preheat the oven to 180°C / 350°F / Gas Mark 4 and lightly grease a baking tray with butter. Beat the sugar, vanilla, milk and bicarbonate of soda in a bowl. In a separate bowl, rub the butter into the flour with your fingers until it resembles breadcrumbs. Combine the 2 mixtures and knead lightly. Roll the dough out on a lightly floured work surface and cut into evenly sized biscuits. Place on the prepared tray and bake for 15–20 minutes, or until golden brown.

- 125 g (4¼ oz) butter, plus extra for greasing
- 125 g (4¼ oz) caster sugar
- 1 teaspoon vanilla extract
- 3 tablespoons milk
- 1 pinch of bicarbonate of soda
- 250 g (9 oz) flour, plus extra for dusting

Preparation time: 15 minutes
Cooking time: 15–20 minutes
Serves 6

WHITE WINE BISCUITS

GÂTEAUX AU VIN BLANC

Preheat the oven to 180°C / 350°F / Gas Mark 4 and lightly grease a baking tray with butter. Combine the flour and sugar in a bowl and turn out onto the work surface. Cut the butter into pieces and rub it into the flour with your fingers until it resembles breadcrumbs. Add the wine and knead lightly, then gather into a ball. If it is difficult to handle, place in the refrigerator for 30 minutes to firm up. Roll out on a floured work surface and cut into shapes. Place on the prepared tray and bake for 15–20 minutes, or until golden brown.

- 150 g (5 oz) butter, plus extra for greasing
- 250 g (9 oz) flour, plus extra for dusting
- 150 g (5 oz) caster sugar
- 1 tablespoon white wine

Preparation time: 10 minutes
Cooking time: 15–20 minutes
Serves 6

ORANGE PEEL BISCUITS

GALETTES D'ORANGE

- 150 g (5 oz) butter, plus extra for greasing
- 300 g (11 oz) flour, plus extra for dusting
- 150 g (5 oz) caster sugar
- 2 eggs
- 50 g (1¾ oz) candied orange peel, chopped

Preparation time: 15 minutes
Cooking time: 15–20 minutes
Serves 6

Preheat the oven to 180°C / 350°F / Gas Mark 4 and lightly grease a baking tray with butter. Combine the flour and sugar in a bowl and turn out onto the work surface. Cut the butter into pieces and rub it into the flour with your fingers until it resembles breadcrumbs. Make a well in the middle, crack in the eggs, add the candied peel and mix to a soft dough. Knead lightly. Roll out thinly on a floured work surface and cut into shapes. Place on the prepared tray and bake for 15–20 minutes, or until golden brown.

ANISEED BISCUITS

GALETTES À L'ANIS

- Butter, for greasing
- 250 g (9 oz) caster sugar
- 2 eggs
- 250 g (9 oz) flour, plus extra for dusting
- 2 teaspoons aniseed
- 1 pinch of bicarbonate of soda

Preparation time: 15 minutes
Cooking time: 15–20 minutes
Serves 6

Preheat the oven to 180°C / 350°F / Gas Mark 4 and lightly grease a baking tray with butter. Beat the sugar and eggs in a bowl. Add the flour, aniseed and bicarbonate of soda. Mix together and knead lightly to form a dough. Roll out thinly on a floured work surface and cut into shapes. Place on the prepared tray and bake for 15–20 minutes, or until golden brown.

MANDARIN BISCUITS

GALETTES À LA MANDARINE

- 15 g (½ oz) butter
- 160 g (5½ oz) blanched almonds, finely chopped
- Grated zest of 2 mandarins
- 100 g (3½ oz) caster sugar
- 70 g (2½ oz) flour
- 2 eggs

Preparation time: 35 minutes
Cooking time: 15–20 minutes
Serves 6

Preheat the oven to 180°C / 350°F / Gas Mark 4 and lightly grease a baking tray with the butter. Combine the almonds and mandarin zest. Mix them into the sugar and flour and add 1 egg yolk and 1 whole egg. Knead lightly to form a dough. Whisk the remaining egg white to soft peaks and fold into the dough. Place small piles of the dough, spaced well apart, on the prepared tray. Bake for 15–20 minutes, or until golden brown.

CHOCOLATE BISCUITS

GALETTES AU CHOCOLAT

Preheat the oven to 180°C/350°F/Gas Mark 4 and lightly grease a baking tray with butter. Stir together the almonds, chocolate, sugar and egg in a bowl, then bring together and knead lightly with your hands to form a smooth dough. Dust your hands with icing sugar and shape the dough into small balls the size of a walnut, keeping the dough as cool as possible. Place on the prepared tray, press lightly on each one and bake for 10–12 minutes, until crisp.

- **Butter, for greasing**
- **125 g (4¼ oz) ground almonds**
- **125 g (4¼ oz) chocolate, grated**
- **125 g (4¼ oz) caster sugar**
- **1 egg**
- **Icing sugar, for dusting**

Preparation time: 25 minutes
Cooking time: 10–12 minutes
Serves 6

NANTES BISCUITS

GALETTES NANTAISES

 p.809

Preheat the oven to 180°C/350°F/Gas Mark 4 and lightly grease a baking tray with butter. Knead together the flour, almonds, butter, salt and sugar. Roll out the dough thinly on a lightly floured work surface and cut out into circles. Put on the prepared tray. Mark the tops with lines with a knife or the tines of a fork. Glaze with the egg yolks. Halve the almonds. Decorate each biscuit with an almond half. Bake for 15–20 minutes, or until golden.

- **60 g (2 oz) butter, softened, plus extra for greasing**
- **125 g (4¼ oz) flour, plus extra for dusting**
- **40 g (1½ oz) ground almonds**
- **1 teaspoon salt**
- **60 g (2 oz) caster sugar**
- **2 egg yolks**
- **50 g (1¾ oz) whole blanched almonds**

Preparation time: 25 minutes
Cooking time: 15–20 minutes
Serves 6

SAVOURY BISCUITS

GALETTES SALÉES

Preheat the oven to 200°C/400°F/Gas Mark 6 and lightly grease a baking tray with butter. Rub the butter into the flour until it resembles breadcrumbs. Make a well and put the baking powder, milk and salt. Mix, then knead to a smooth dough. Roll out to a thickness of 5 mm (¼ inch) on a lightly floured work surface and cut into circles. Place on the prepared tray and bake for 15–20 minutes, or until golden brown.

- **60 g (2 oz) butter, plus extra for greasing**
- **250 g (9 oz) flour, plus extra for dusting**
- **1 teaspoon baking powder**
- **50 ml (2 fl oz) milk**
- **1½ teaspoons salt**

Preparation time: 15 minutes
Cooking time: 15–20 minutes
Serves 6

DUCHESSE PETIT FOURS

PETIT FOURS DUCHESSE

- 110 g (3¾ oz) butter, softened
- 200 g (7 oz) caster sugar
- 2 eggs, separated
- 300 g (11 oz) flour
- 1 teaspoon baking powder
- Almonds or glacé cherries

Preparation time: 10 minutes
Cooking time: 25–30 minutes
Serves 6

Preheat the oven to 180°C/350°F/Gas Mark 4 and grease a baking tray with butter. Beat the remaining butter with 140 g (4¾ oz) of the sugar and the egg yolks. Stir in the flour and baking powder. Knead to form a smooth dough. Divide the dough into balls the size of a walnut. Place on the prepared tray. Brush with the lightly beaten egg whites and sprinkle with the remaining sugar. Decorate each petit four with half an almond or half a glacé cherry and bake for 25–30 minutes, or until golden brown.

SOUVAROFF BISCUITS

SOUVAROFFS

- 210 g (7¼ oz) butter, softened
- 100 g (3½ oz) caster sugar
- 250 g (9 oz) flour, plus extra for dusting
- ½ teaspoon salt
- 1 teaspoon vanilla extract
- Redcurrant or raspberry jelly, to sandwich the biscuits
- Icing sugar, for sprinkling

Preparation time: 10 minutes
Cooking time: 10–12 minutes
Serves 6

Preheat the oven to 180°C/350°F/Gas Mark 4 and grease a baking tray with butter. Mix together the remaining butter, sugar, flour, salt and vanilla to make a soft dough. If the dough is difficult to handle, chill it in the refrigerator for 30 minutes. Roll out on a lightly floured work surface to a thickness of 2 mm (⅛ inch). Cut into circles. Place on the prepared tray and bake for 10–12 minutes. Allow to cool, then stick the biscuits together in pairs using redcurrant or raspberry jelly. Sprinkle with icing sugar.

CURRANT SLICES

GÂTEAUX AUX RAISINS

- 165 g (5½ oz) butter, softened
- 200 g (7 oz) flour, plus extra for dusting
- 150 g (5 oz) caster sugar
- 1 teaspoon salt
- 15 g (½ oz) baking powder
- Milk, to bind (optional)
- 100 g (3½ oz) currants
- Ground cinnamon, to taste

Preparation time: 20 minutes
Cooking time: 20–25 minutes
Serves 6

Preheat the oven to 180°C/350°F/Gas Mark 4. Melt 60 g (2 oz) of the butter and set aside to cool. Mix together the flour, the remaining butter, 60 g (2 oz) of the sugar, the salt and the baking powder. Add a little milk if necessary to bring the dough together, then knead lightly. Roll out the dough on a lightly floured work surface to a rectangle 1 cm (½ inch) thick. Pour the melted butter over the dough. Sprinkle with the currants, cinnamon and remaining sugar. Roll up the dough lengthways. Cut into slices 1 cm (½ inch) thick, place on a baking tray and bake for 20–25 minutes.

HAZELNUT PETIT FOURS
FOURS AUX NOISETTES

Preheat the oven to 180°C / 350°F / Gas Mark 4 and grease a baking tray with butter. Chop the hazelnuts finely. Mix with 125 g (4¼ oz) of the sugar and the unbeaten egg whites. Form the mixture into small balls and roll in the remaining sugar. Place on the prepared tray and bake for 25–30 minutes.

- Butter, for greasing
- 160 g (5½ oz) skinned hazelnuts
- 200 g (7 oz) caster sugar
- 2 egg whites

Preparation time: 15 minutes
Cooking time: 25–30 minutes
Serves 6

ALMOND CRESCENTS
CROISSANTS AUX AMANDES

Preheat the oven to 180°C/350°F/Gas Mark 4 and grease a baking tray with butter. Mix together the flour, butter, almonds and 100 g (3½ oz) of the sugar. Knead the dough lightly into a ball. If it is difficult to handle, place in the refrigerator for 30 minutes to firm up. Shape into small crescents. Place on the prepared tray and bake for 20–25 minutes. Sprinkle the biscuits with the remaining sugar while still hot.

- 200 g (7 oz) butter, plus extra for greasing
- 280 g (10 oz) flour
- 100 g (3½ oz) ground almonds
- 175 g (6 oz) caster sugar

Preparation time: 25 minutes
Cooking time: 25 minutes
Serves 6

ALMOND BUNS
PETITS PAINS AUX AMANDES

Preheat the oven to 180°C / 350°F / Gas Mark 4 and grease a baking tray with butter. Mix the almonds with the sugar. Add the egg, butter, flour and salt and mix to a soft dough. Knead the dough lightly and form into small bun shapes. Place on the prepared tray and bake for 10 minutes, then increase the temperature to 200°C/400°F/Gas Mark 6 and bake for a further 20 minutes.

- 100 g (3½ oz) butter, softened, plus extra for greasing
- 125 g (4¼ oz) ground almonds
- 250 g (9 oz) caster sugar
- 1 egg
- 250 g (9 oz) flour
- 1 teaspoon salt

Preparation time: 20 minutes
Cooking time: 30 minutes
Serves 6

CINNAMON STICKS

BÂTONS DE CANNELLE

Prepare the day before. Chop the almonds. In a large bowl, combine all the ingredients except the egg yolk. Cover and set aside in the refrigerator for 24 hours. Next day, preheat the oven to 200°C/400°F/Gas Mark 6 and grease a baking tray with butter. Shape the dough into sticks and brush with the egg yolk to glaze. Place on the prepared tray and bake for 20 minutes.

- 125 g (4¼ oz) unblanched almond
- 215 g (7½ oz) flour
- 125 g (4¼ oz) sugar
- 1 egg
- 125 g (4¼ oz) butter, softened, plus extra for greasing
- 1 teaspoon ground cinnamon
- 1 egg yolk

Preparation time: 20 minutes, plus resting time
Cooking time: 20 minutes
Serves 6

CROQUIGNOLE BISCUITS

CROQUIGNOLES

Preheat the oven to 180°C/350°F/Gas Mark 4 and grease a baking tray with the butter. Mix all the ingredients together and knead to form a stiff dough. Shape into small biscuits the size of a coin. Place on the prepared tray and bake for 20 minutes.

- Butter, for greasing
- 2 egg whites
- 175 g (6 oz) caster sugar
- 200 g (7 oz) flour

Preparation time: 15 minutes
Cooking time: 20 minutes
Serves 6

RINGS OF SATURN

ANNEAUX DE SATURNE

Stir together the eggs, sugar, salt, crème fraîche, butter, bicarbonate of soda, flour and lemon zest in a large bowl to make a stiff dough. Roll out to 1 cm (½ inch) thick on a lightly floured work surface. Cut into rings using a 9-cm (3½-inch) cutter, and a 5-cm (2-inch) cutter to remove the centres. Heat the oil in a deep-fryer to 190°C/375°F, or until a cube of bread browns in 20 seconds. Fry the rings in batches for 1 minute, or until puffed and brown. Drain on kitchen paper and sprinkle with sugar.

- 3 eggs
- 300 g (11 oz) caster sugar, plus extra for sprinkling
- Pinch of salt
- 175 ml (6 fl oz) crème fraîche
- 75 g (2½ oz) butter, melted
- 1 pinch of bicarbonate of soda
- Grated zest of 1 lemon
- 600 g (1 lb 5 oz) flour, plus extra for dusting
- Vegetable oil, for deep-frying

Preparation time: 20 minutes
Cooking time: 5 minutes
Serves 6

CLOTTED CREAM BISCUITS

GÂTEAUX À LA CRÈME CUITE

- **Butter, for greasing**
- **125 ml (4½ fl oz) clotted cream**
- **125 g (4¼ oz) caster sugar**
- **125 g (4¼ oz) flour**
- **1 teaspoon vanilla extract**

  Preparation time: 5 minutes
  Cooking time: 10 minutes
  Serves 6

Preheat the oven to 180°C/350°F/Gas Mark 4 and grease a baking tray with butter. Mix the cream, sugar, flour and vanilla together. Put small piles of the dough on the prepared tray, well spaced out. Bake for 10 minutes, or until the edges of the biscuits brown. These economical biscuits keep very well.

CRUNCHY SABLÉS

SABLÉS CROQUANTS

- **Butter, for greasing**
- **2 eggs**
- **250 g (9 oz) caster sugar**
- **1 tablespoon rum**
- **250 g (9 oz) flour**

  Preparation time: 10 minutes
  Cooking time: 10 minutes
  Serves 6

Preheat the oven to 200°C/400°F/Gas Mark 6 and grease a baking tray with butter. Mix together the eggs, sugar, rum and flour to make a soft dough. Put small piles of the dough on the prepared tray, well spaced out. Bake for 10 minutes, or until golden brown.

SILLY BISCUITS

BISCUITS RIGOLOS

- **Butter, for greasing**
- **3 eggs**
- **250 g (9 oz) caster sugar**
- **250 g (9 oz) flour**
- **Milk, to bind the dough (optional)**

  Preparation time: 10 minutes
  Cooking time: 10 minutes
  Serves 6

Preheat the oven to 200°C/400°F/Gas Mark 6 and grease a baking tray with butter. Whisk the eggs and sugar together until foamy. Stir in the flour, adding a little milk if necessary to bring the dough together. Knead lightly. Put small piles of the dough on the prepared tray, well spaced out. Bake for 10 minutes, or until golden brown.

LADIES' BISCUITS

PALETS DE DAME

Preheat the oven to 160°C/325°F/Gas Mark 3 and grease a baking tray with butter. Put the currants in a bowl and pour over the rum. Leave to macerate. Cream the sugar and butter. Beat in the eggs, one by one. Mix in all the flour in one go, then the currants and rum. Put small piles of the dough on the prepared tray, well spaced out. Bake for 10 minutes, then increase the temperature to 200°C/400°F/Gas Mark 6 for 15 minutes, or until the edges of the biscuits are golden brown.

- **125 g (4¼ oz) butter, plus extra for greasing**
- **60 g (2 oz) currants**
- **1 liqueur glass of rum**
- **125 g (4¼ oz) sugar**
- **2 eggs**
- **150 g (5 oz) flour**

Preparation time: 15 minutes, plus macerating time
Cooking time: 25 minutes
Serves 6

DOLLAR BISCUITS

DOLLARS

Preheat the oven to 200°C/400°F/Gas Mark 6 and grease a baking tray with butter. Whisk the egg and rum together. Mix in the sugar, butter and flour. Put small piles of the dough on the prepared tray, well spaced out, and bake for 20 minutes, or until golden brown.

- **100 g (3½ oz) butter, softened, plus extra for greasing**
- **1 egg**
- **1½ tablespoons rum**
- **125 g (4¼ oz) caster sugar**
- **150 g (5 oz) flour**

Preparation time: 10 minutes
Cooking time: 20 minutes
Serves 6

CONGOLAIS

CONGOLAIS

Line a baking tray with buttered baking parchment or the rice paper. Preheat the oven to 150°C/300°F/Gas Mark 2. Put the sugar and egg whites in a pan set over the lowest heat possible, and stir to dissolve the sugar. Stir in the coconut and vanilla. Put pyramid-shaped piles of the mixture on the prepared tray. Bake for 30–45 minutes, or until golden brown.

- **Butter, for greasing**
- **Edible rice paper (optional)**
- **300 g (11 oz) caster sugar**
- **5 egg whites**
- **250 g (9 oz) desiccated coconut**
- **1 teaspoon vanilla extract**

Preparation time: 10 minutes
Cooking time: 30–45 minutes
Serves 6

p.810

ALMOND MACAROONS

MACARONS AUX AMANDES

- **Butter, for greasing**
- **250 g (9 oz) ground almonds**
- **3 egg whites**
- **500 g (1 lb 2 oz) caster sugar**

Preparation time: 25 minutes
Cooking time: 20–25 minutes
Serves 6

Preheat the oven to 150°C/300°F/Gas Mark 2 and line a baking tray with buttered baking parchment. Put the almonds in a bowl and mix in the egg whites a little at a time. Stir in the sugar and mix well. Form the dough into slightly flattened balls and place on the prepared tray. Bake for 20–25 minutes, or until lightly browned.

VARIATION

. . . .

HAZELNUT MACAROONS

MACARONS AUX NOISETTES

Replace the almonds with hazelnuts and whisk 2 egg whites to stiff peaks before folding them in. Proceed as above.

SPOON BISCUITS

BISCUITS À LA CUILLÈRE

- **Butter, for greasing**
- **85 g (3 oz) caster sugar**
- **3 eggs, separated**
- **A few drops of orange-flower water**
- **85 g (3 oz) flour**
- **Icing sugar, for sprinkling**

Preparation time: 25 minutes
Cooking time: 15 minutes
Serves 6

Preheat the oven to 160°C/325°F/Gas Mark 3 and grease a baking tray with butter. In a large bowl, whisk the sugar and egg yolks until white and creamy, adding the orange-flower water. Whisk the egg whites to stiff peaks in a separate bowl. Fold the egg and sugar mixture and the egg whites together, along with the flour. Spoon or pipe into fingers on the prepared tray. Sprinkle with icing sugar and bake for 10–15 minutes, without allowing the biscuits to colour.

ALMOND TUILES
TUILES AUX AMANDES

 p.811

Preheat the oven to 200°C / 400°F / Gas Mark 6 and line a baking tray with baking parchment. In a bowl, mix all the ingredients together. Spoon half-tablespoons of the dough, well spaced out, in small piles on the prepared tray. Bake for 8–10 minutes, or until golden and bubbly. Shortly after they come out of the oven, and while they are still hot, drape the biscuits over the lightly oiled neck of a bottle, rolling pin or other cylindrical object. Once cold and set, place the tuiles in an airtight container to keep them crisp.

NOTE
For plain tuiles, omit the almonds.

- 60 g (2 oz) blanched almonds, sliced
- 2 egg whites
- 75 g (2½ oz) vanilla sugar, or caster sugar plus 1 teaspoon vanilla extract
- 50 g (1¾ oz) butter, melted
- 1 pinch of salt
- 75 g (2½ oz) plain flour
- 1 egg, separated

Preparation time: 10 minutes
Cooking time: 10 minutes
Serves 6

SMALL SOUFFLÉ BISCUITS
PETITS SOUFFLÉS   *Merengues?*

Preheat the oven to 140°C / 275°F / Gas Mark 1 and line a baking tray with buttered baking parchment. Place the egg white and sugar in a bowl and whisk until the mixture is fairly stiff and no longer drops like a ribbon from the whisk. Add the chosen flavour. Drop small piles of the mixture onto the prepared tray, well spaced out. Bake for 30 minutes, or until golden.

- Butter, for greasing
- 1 egg white
- 100 g (3½ oz) caster sugar
- Coffee essence, cocoa powder or finely chopped almonds, to taste

Preparation time: 30 minutes
Cooking time: 30 minutes
Serves 6

LANGUES DE CHAT
LANGUES DE CHAT

Preheat the oven to 190°C/375°F/Gas Mark 5 and grease a baking tray with butter. Cream the butter. Beat in the sugar and then the eggs, one by one. Stir in the flour. Spoon or pipe fingers of the mixture onto the prepared tray and bake for 20 minutes. The biscuits should be golden brown on the edges, but pale in the middle.

- 80 g (2¾ oz) butter, plus extra for greasing
- 80 g (2¾ oz) caster sugar
- 2 eggs
- 85 g (3 oz) flour

Preparation time: 20 minutes
Cooking time: 20 minutes
Serves 6

VIEUX GARÇON BISCUITS

VIEUX GARÇONS

- 125 g (4¼ oz) butter, softened, plus extra for greasing
- 250 g (9 oz) flour, plus extra for dusting
- 125 g (4¼ oz) brown sugar
- 1 egg, separated

Preparation time: 20 minutes
Cooking time: 20 minutes
Serves 6

These biscuits from Brittany in northern France are traditionally baked in a wood-fired oven fed with *genêt* (broom) branches to give them a special flavour.

Preheat the oven to 190°C/375°F/Gas Mark 5 and grease a baking tray with butter. Put the flour onto a clean work surface, make a well in the middle and put the butter, sugar and egg white into the well. Incorporate them into the flour to form a soft dough and knead lightly. Flatten the dough on the work surface briefly, then knead again lightly. Sprinkle the work surface and the dough with flour so that it does not stick. Roll out to a thickness of 1 cm (½ inch). Cut out rounds with a cookie cutter. Place on the prepared tray and brush with the egg yolk to glaze. Bake for 20 minutes, or until golden.

MARZIPAN BISCUITS

MASSEPAINS

- 125 g (4¼ oz) blanched almonds
- 200 g (7 oz) caster sugar
- 2 egg whites
- 15 g (½ oz) flour
- Grated zest of 1 lemon

Preparation time: 20 minutes
Cooking time: 30 minutes
Serves 6

Preheat the oven to 180°C / 350°F / Gas Mark 4. Process the almonds with the sugar and egg whites in a food processor, or by hand in a pestle and mortar, to form a semi-liquid paste. Add the flour and lemon zest. Arrange small piles of this mixture on a floured baking tray. Bake for 30 minutes, until golden.

PAIN DE GÊNES

PAIN DE GÊNES

- 120 g (4 oz) butter, softened, plus extra for greasing
- 300 g (11 oz) caster sugar
- 4 eggs
- 250 g (9 oz) ground almonds
- 100 g (3½ oz) flour
- 2 tablespoons Kirsch

Preparation time: 25 minutes
Cooking time: 45 minutes
Serves 6

Preheat the oven to 160°C/325°F/Gas Mark 3 and line a cake tin with buttered baking parchment. In a bowl, beat the butter and sugar. Beat in the eggs, one by one, then stir in the almonds, flour and Kirsch. Put the mixture in the prepared tin. Bake for 45 minutes, covering with foil if it browns too quickly.

SPONGE CAKE
GÉNOISE

Preheat the oven to 180°C/350°F/Gas Mark 4 and grease a round cake tin with butter. Set a heatproof bowl over a pan of barely simmering water. Place the eggs and sugar in the bowl and whisk over a low heat until the mixture is light, creamy and increased in volume. Add the lemon zest or vanilla, then sprinkle over the flour and fold in gently with a spatula. Finally stir in the melted butter. Pour the mixture into the prepared tin. Bake for 30–40 minutes. The cake is cooked when the centre remains firm when pressed lightly.

NOTE
Do not use an aluminium bowl, as the mixture will discolour.

- 125 g (4¼ oz) butter, melted, plus extra for greasing
- 5 eggs
- 150 g (5 oz) caster sugar
- Grated lemon zest or vanilla extract, to taste
- 130 g (4½ oz) flour

Preparation time: 30 minutes
Cooking time: 30–40 minutes
Serves 6

PASTRIES

CHOUX PASTRY
PÂTE À CHOUX

In a large pan, gently heat 120 ml (4 fl oz) water and the sugar, butter and salt until the butter has melted, then bring to the boil. Quickly add the flour all at once, and beat with a wooden spoon. Reduce the heat and continue to beat the dough for about 1 minute until it comes away easily from the sides of the pan. Grease a plate with butter, turn the mixture out onto it and leave to cool to room temperature. Return to the pan and gradually beat in the eggs until the dough is smooth and glossy.

VARIATIONS

. . . .

CHOUX BUNS
CHOUX SOUFFLÉS

Preheat the oven to 220°C/425°F/Gas Mark 7. Pipe or spoon egg-sized pieces of choux pastry dough onto a buttered baking tray. Turn the oven down to 200°C/400°F/Gas Mark 6. Bake for 20 minutes until well risen and golden. Fill as required and serve hot or cold.

- 20 g (¾ oz) caster sugar
- 100 g (3½ oz) butter, plus extra for greasing
- 1 teaspoon salt
- 120 g (4 oz) flour
- 4 eggs, beaten

Preparation time: 20 minutes
Cooking time: 15 minutes
Serves 6

CHEESE CHOUX BUNS

CHOUX AUX FROMAGE

Preheat the oven to 220°C / 425°F / Gas Mark 7. Omit the sugar from the choux pastry dough and instead add 150 g (5 oz) grated Gruyère cheese. Pipe or spoon egg-sized pieces of dough onto a buttered baking sheet. Turn the oven down to 200°C/400°F/Gas Mark 6. Bake for 20 minutes until well risen and golden. Fill as required and serve hot or cold.

CREAM BUNS

CHOUX À LA CRÈME PÂTISSIÈRE

Make some large choux buns. When they have cooled, make a horizontal slit near the top. Fill generously with thick crème pâtissière (p.706), allowing a little to show through the slit.

CHOUX BUNS WITH CREAM

CHOUX À LA CRÈME CHANTILLY

Make some large choux buns. When they have cooled, make a horizontal slit near the top. Fill generously with sweetened whipped cream (p.121).

PASTRIES FOR TEA

GALETTES FEUILLETÉES POUR LE THÉ

- 1 quantity puff pastry (p.776)
- Butter, for greasing
- 1 egg yolk, to glaze
- Caster sugar, for sprinkling (optional)

Preparation time: 45 minutes, plus resting time
Cooking time: 25 minutes
Serves 6

Make the puff pastry. Preheat the oven to 220°C / 425°F / Gas Mark 7 and grease a baking tray with butter. Roll the pastry out to 3 mm (⅛ inch) thick. Cut into circles 3–4 cm (1¼–1½ inches) in diameter. Mix the egg yolk with 2 teaspoons water in a bowl and brush the pastry circles with it. Sprinkle with sugar, if using. Place on the prepared tray and bake for 15–20 minutes, until golden. Serve warm or cold.

PUFF PASTRY

PÂTE FEUILLETÉE

Puff pastry is made with butter and flour, a little water and a pinch of salt. The proportion of butter to flour varies widely, but a good rule of thumb is to use half the weight of butter to that of flour. Puff pastry should be made in a cool place, with all the ingredients kept as cool as possible.

In a bowl, mix the flour, salt and most of the water to make a smooth, elastic dough, adding the rest of the water if necessary. Flour a work surface and roll the dough out to a rectangle 5 mm (¼ inch) thick. Put the butter in the middle of the dough and fold over the 4 corners so that they meet in the middle and the butter is completely enclosed. Allow to rest for 10 minutes in the refrigerator. Turn the dough through a right-angle and roll out again, taking care not to let the butter escape, into a long rectangle 5 mm (¼ inch) thick. Fold both short ends to overlap in the centre to make a smaller rectangle with 3 layers. Rest again for 15 minutes. Roll out the dough again and repeat the folds. Rest for 15 minutes. Do this 6 more times. Each stage is called a 'turn'. After the sixth turn, the pastry is ready, but the more it is worked, the lighter it will be.

NOTE

The butter should be as soft as the dough, or it will tear the carefully constructed layers.

- 200 g (7 oz) flour, sifted, plus extra for dusting
- 1 pinch of salt
- 100 ml (3½ fl oz) ice-cold water
- 100 g (3½ oz) butter, diced and softened

Preparation time: 2 hours, plus resting time
Serves 6

ÉCLAIRS

ÉCLAIRS

Make the choux pastry. Preheat the oven to 200°C/400°F/ Gas Mark 6 and grease a baking tray with butter. Pipe or spoon the dough into fingers on the prepared tray. Bake for 20 minutes and allow to cool. When cooled, slit the éclairs along the side, fill and ice as desired (see below).

VARIATIONS

CHOCOLATE ÉCLAIRS

ÉCLAIRS AU CHOCOLAT

Prepare the éclairs as above. Fill with chocolate crème pâtissière (p.706), and top with chocolate icing (p.727).

- 1 quantity choux pastry (p.774)
- Butter, for greasing

Preparation time: 30 minutes
Cooking time: 20 minutes
Serves 6

COFFEE ÉCLAIRS

ÉCLAIRS AU CAFÉ

Prepare the éclairs. Fill with coffee crème pâtissière (p.706), and top with coffee fondant icing (p.728).

ALMOND ÉCLAIRS

ÉCLAIRS À LA FRANGIPANE

Prepare the éclairs. Fill with almond custard (p.706), and top with Kirsch icing (p.727).

CREAM ÉCLAIRS

ÉCLAIRS À LA CRÈME PÂTISSIÈRE

Prepare the éclairs. Fill with créme pâtissière (p.706), and top with Kirsch icing (p.727).

CHEESE RING

GÂTEAU DE GANNAT

Preheat the oven to 200°C/400°F/Gas Mark 6. Make choux pastry (p.774) with 100 ml (3½ fl oz) water and the butter, salt and flour. Allow to cool, then beat in the eggs and cheese. Season with pepper. Butter and flour a baking tray. Pipe or spoon the dough into a ring on the tray. Place in the oven and increase the temperature to 220°C/425°F/Gas Mark 7. Bake for 30–45 minutes, until risen and golden. Once cooled, cut the ring in half horizontally and fill as desired. Serve as a starter.

- 40 g (1½ oz) butter, plus extra for greasing
- Salt and pepper
- 120 g (4 oz) flour, plus extra for dusting
- 4 eggs, beaten
- 120 g (4 oz) Gruyère cheese, thinly sliced

Preparation time: 20 minutes
Cooking time: 30–45 minutes
Serves 6

VOL-AU-VENT

VOL-AU-VENT

Preheat the oven to 220°C/425°F/Gas Mark 7 and grease a baking tray with butter. Make the puff pastry. On a floured work surface, roll it out to 2.5 cm (1 inch) thick. Using a sharp knife, cut out a circle 12–15 cm (4–6 inches) in diameter. Mix the egg yolk with a little water and glaze the pastry. Make small incisions all round the edge with the point of a knife. Then mark a smaller circle about 3 cm (1¼ inches) in from the edge, taking care not to press too deeply. This will make the lid. Score a criss-cross pattern on the lid. Put the pastry on the prepared tray. Bake for 35 minutes, until deep golden brown. Remove from the oven, carefully remove the lid and reserve. Pull out any uncooked pastry from the middle. Fill the vol-au-vent as desired (see below).

- Butter, for greasing
- 300 g (11 oz) puff pastry (p.776)
- Flour, for dusting
- 1 egg yolk

Preparation time: 45 minutes, plus resting time
Cooking time: 35 minutes
Serves 6

VARIATIONS

• •

VOL-AU-VENT À LA FINANCIÈRE

VOL-AU-VENT À LA FINANCIÈRE

Fill the vol-au-vent with a financière sauce (p.57), made with veal quenelles and mushrooms. Truffles may be added to taste. Replace the pastry lid and serve hot.

. . . .

MUSSEL VOL-AU-VENT
VOL-AU-VENT À LA MARINIÈRE

Fill the vol-au-vent with well-seasoned mussels marinière (p.272). Replace the pastry lid and serve hot.

. . . .

BOUCHÉES À LA REINE
BOUCHÉES À LA REINE

Proceed as above, but cut the circles to no more than 5–6 cm (2–2½ inches) in diameter. Fill with financière sauce (p.57).

MEAT PIE
TOURTE À LA VIANDE

- 300 g (11 oz) puff pastry (p.776)
- 1 egg yolk (optional)

For the filling:
- 200 g (7 oz) cooked meat
- 50 g (1¾ oz) ham
- 50 g (1¾ oz) streaky bacon
- 30 g (1¼ oz) crustless white bread, torn into pieces
- 2 tablespoons milk
- 1 knob of butter
- 100 g (3½ oz) mushrooms, sliced
- 2 eggs, lightly beaten
- Chopped mixed herbs, such as flat-leaf parsley, chives, chervil and tarragon
- Salt and pepper
- Truffles, chopped, to taste

Preparation time: 45 minutes, plus resting time
Cooking time: 35 minutes
Serves 6

First, prepare the filling. Chop all of the meat into small pieces. Soak the bread in the milk. Melt the butter in a frying pan and cook the mushrooms, then remove and allow to cool. In a bowl, combine the chopped meat, bread, eggs and herbs. Season well with salt and pepper, and stir in the truffles and cooled mushrooms. To assemble the meat pie, choose one of the following methods:

METHOD 1
Prepare and cook the pastry in the same way as for vol-au-vent (p.778). Fill the case with the meat mixture. Replace the lid and serve hot.

METHOD 2
Preheat the oven to 220°C/425°F/Gas Mark 7. Roll out two-thirds of the pastry to a 1-cm (½-inch) thick circle. Place on a floured baking tray and fold over the edges to create a small rim. Fill with the meat mixture. Roll out the remaining dough into a circle to form a lid. Place it over the filling and crimp the edges of the pastry to seal. Brush with egg yolk to glaze and bake for 35 minutes.

PÂTÉ IN PASTRY

PÂTÉ EN CROÛTE

Preheat the oven to 200°C / 400°F / Gas Mark 6. First, make the pastry. Place the flour in a bowl, make a well in the centre and add the butter and salt. Add enough ice-cold water to bring the dough together. Turn out onto a floured surface and knead well for 5 minutes, eventually forming a smooth ball. Cover the dough and allow it to rest for half a day in the refrigerator.

Grease a pâté dish or terrine with butter. Roll out two-thirds of the dough and use it to line the dish, leaving 2 cm (¾ inch) of dough above the rim. Place a layer of bacon rashers on the bottom, then a layer of stuffing, a little of the ham, then a layer of the veal, all well seasoned with salt and pepper. Continue making layers using all the ingredients. Roll out the remaining dough to create a lid slightly larger than the dish, and use to cover the filling. Pinch the edges of the dough together to seal. Brush with the egg yolk to glaze, and make a hole in the centre of the lid, keeping it open during cooking with a small funnel made of cardboard. Bake in the oven for 1½ hours, or until deep golden brown.

For the pastry:
- **500 g (1 lb 2 oz) flour, plus extra for dusting**
- **200 g (7 oz) butter, chilled and diced, plus extra for greasing**
- **2 teaspoons salt**
- **Ice-cold water, to bind the dough**

For the stuffing:
- **200 g (7 oz) bacon rashers**
- **250 g (9 oz) stuffing of your choice (pp.79–80)**
- **200 g (7 oz) ham, sliced**
- **200 g (7 oz) veal, cut into strips**
- **Salt and pepper**
- **1 egg yolk, to glaze**

Preparation time: 1½ hours, plus resting time
Cooking time: 1½ hours
Serves 6

SAUSAGE ROLLS

FRIANDS

Make the puff pastry and roll it out to 5 mm (¼ inch) thick. Preheat the oven to 220°C/425°F/Gas Mark 7. Cut rectangles of pastry measuring 4 x 8 cm (1½ x 3 inches). Put chipolatas on half the rectangles, cover with the remaining rectangles and seal the edges with water. Press the edges together with a knife, making a pattern if you like. Bake for 30 minutes, until deep golden brown.

- **250 g (9 oz) puff pastry (p.776)**
- **250 g (9 oz) chipolata sausages**

Preparation time: 1 hour, plus resting time
Cooking time: 30 minutes
Serves 6

VARIATION

. . . .

ANCHOVY ROLLS

FEUILLANTINES AUX ANCHOIS

Proceed as above, but use a preserved anchovy in place of each chipolata and make the pastry rectangles 3 x 10 cm (1¼ x 4 inches).

SMALL MEAT PIES
PETITS PÂTÉS

- **250 g (9 oz) puff pastry (p.776)**
- **1 quantity meat stuffing (p.80)**
- **1 egg yolk**

Preparation time: 1 hour, plus resting time
Cooking time: 25 minutes
Serves 6

Make the puff pastry and prepare the meat stuffing. Preheat the oven to 220°C/425°F/Gas Mark 7. To assemble the meat pies, choose one of the following methods.

METHOD 1
Roll out the pastry to 5 mm (¼ inch) thick. Cut it into circles 5 cm (2 inches) in diameter. Put 1 tablespoon of the meat stuffing on each circle, cover with another circle and seal the edges with water. Glaze the top with the egg yolk. Bake for 25 minutes.

METHOD 2
Make pastry cases in the same way as the vol-au-vent (p.778), but cut the circles to 5–6 cm (2–2½ inches) in diameter. Fill with the meat stuffing and return to the oven for 20 minutes. Other stuffings, such as stuffing for poultry (p.79) or fish (p.80), can also be used.

 p.814

PALMIERS
PALMIERS

- **200 g (7 oz) flour**
- **100 g (3½ oz) butter**
- **1 teaspoon salt**
- **125 g (4¼ oz) caster sugar**

Preparation time: 1 hour, plus resting time
Cooking time: 20 minutes
Serves 6

Make puff pastry with the flour, butter, salt and 2 tablespoons water (p.776). Preheat the oven to 220°C/425°F/Gas Mark 7. Sprinkle a work surface with some of the sugar and roll out the pastry to about 5 mm (¼ inch) thick, in a strip about 10–20 cm (4–8 inches) wide. Fold the short ends of the pastry in so that the 2 edges meet in the middle, then fold again in the same way. Cut the pastry into slices 1 cm (½ inch) thick. Open the slices out slightly to form heart shapes. Sprinkle the baking tray with sugar and put the heart shapes flat on the tray. Bake the palmiers for 15–20 minutes, turning them over once during cooking.

HOUSEHOLD BISCUIT

GALETTE DE MÉNAGE

Make the puff pastry, sprinkling it with the sugar before folding it at every stage. Preheat the oven to 220°C/425°F/Gas Mark 7. Roll the pastry out to a 2-cm (¾-inch) thick circle. Brush the top with the egg to glaze. Mark a criss-cross pattern with the point of a knife. Transfer to a baking tray and bake for 30 minutes, until golden.

- ◆ 350 g (12 oz) puff pastry (p.776)
- ◆ 75 g (2½ oz) caster sugar
- ◆ 1 egg, beaten, to glaze

Preparation time: 45 minutes, plus resting time
Cooking time: 30 minutes
Serves 6

GALETTE DE PLOMB

GALETTE DE PLOMB

Preheat the oven to 180°C/350°F/Gas Mark 4 and grease a tart tin with butter. In a large bowl, combine the flour, butter, crème fraîche, sugar and salt. Transfer to a work surface and knead the dough vigorously. Fill the tin with the dough and brush with the egg to glaze. Bake for 45 minutes, or until golden brown.

- ◆ 165 g (5½ oz) butter, softened, plus extra for greasing
- ◆ 250 g (9 oz) flour
- ◆ 100 ml (3½ fl oz) crème fraîche
- ◆ 1 tablespoon caster sugar
- ◆ 1 pinch of salt
- ◆ 1 egg, beaten

Preparation time: 10 minutes
Cooking time: 45 minutes
Serves 6

SAVOURY CHEESE BISCUITS

GALETTES SALÉES AU FROMAGE

Make the puff pastry. Sprinkle with Gruyère cheese before each of the final 3 folds. Preheat the oven to 220°C/425°F/Gas Mark 7. Roll the pastry out to 1 cm (½ inch) thick. Cut into circles 3–4 cm (1¼–1½ inches) in diameter. Brush with the egg to glaze. Bake for 25 minutes, or until golden.

- ◆ 300 g (11 oz) puff pastry (p.776)
- ◆ 200 g (7 oz) Gruyère cheese, grated
- ◆ 1 egg, beaten

Preparation time: 45 minutes, plus resting time
Cooking time: 25 minutes
Serves 6

CREAM HORNS

CORNETS À LA CRÈME

* **200 g (7 oz) puff pastry (p.776)**
* **Butter, for greasing**
* **1 egg yolk**
* **250 ml (8 fl oz) crème pâtissière (p.706) or sweetened whipped cream (p.121)**

Preparation time: 1 hour, plus resting time
Cooking time: 30 minutes
Makes about 12 cream horns

Make the puff pastry. Preheat the oven to 220°C/425°F/Gas Mark 7 and grease a baking tray with butter. Roll the pastry out very thinly. Cut into long strips 2–3 cm (¾–1¼ inches) wide. Butter some cream horn moulds and wrap a pastry strip in a spiral round the outside of each mould, sealing the edges with a little water as you go. Glaze with the egg yolk mixed with 1 teaspoon warm water. Place on the prepared tray and bake for 30 minutes, or until golden brown. Lift the horns off the moulds, taking care not to break them. Fill with the crème pâtissière or cream.

TARTS

To line a tart tin, roll out the pastry on a floured work surface. Use it to line a pie dish or tart tin. The pastry base must be thin and any excess pastry that comes over the edge of the dish should be trimmed away with a sharp knife. Prick the base with a fork. If the tart is to be filled with cooked fruit, it should first be baked blind (see shortcrust pastry, p.784). Allow it to cool before putting in your chosen filling. Uncooked pastry trimmings may be used to make a lattice of small strips about 5 mm (¼ inch) wide. Form into a lattice on buttered greaseproof paper. Cook separately from the base, then put the cooked lattice over the filling.

Tartlets are made exactly in the same way as tarts. Small round tins are used for large round fruit, such as peaches and apples, and oval tins are used for small fruit, such as cherries and strawberries.

SHORTCRUST PASTRY

PÂTE BRISÉE

Put the flour into a bowl. Make a well in the middle and add the oil, salt and butter. Rub the butter into the flour. Moisten with the water to bring the dough together. Briefly knead the dough by hand; the more quickly this is done, the better the pastry will be. Cover the pastry with clingfilm and leave to rest in the refrigerator for between 30 minutes and 24 hours. Bring it back to room temperature before rolling out. On a lightly floured surface, roll it out to a circle 5 mm (¼ inch) thick and use to line a tart tin, preferably one with a removable base. The pastry may also be used to line small round or boat-shaped tins (barquettes).

To bake the pastry case blind, preheat the oven to 200°C/400°F/Gas Mark 6. Line the pastry case with greaseproof paper and fill with baking beans or uncooked rice. Bake for 10 minutes, then gently remove the greaseproof paper and baking beans or rice and return the pastry case to the oven for a further 10–15 minutes, until it is light golden brown and cooked throughout.

NOTE

Keep the ingredients and utensils as cool as possible. This will help the pastry to retain a short, crumbly texture.

* 250 g (9 oz) flour, plus extra for dusting
* 1 tablespoon flavourless oil, such as sunflower or rapeseed
* ½ teaspoon salt
* 125 g (4¼ oz) butter, chilled and diced
* 1–2 tablespoons ice-cold water

Preparation time: 20 minutes, plus resting time
Serves 6

COOKED FRUIT OR JAM TART

TARTE AUX FRUITS CUITS, À LA CONFITURE

Bake a shortcrust pastry case blind. Fill with cooked fruit or jam of your choice.

VARIATIONS

. . . .

ALMOND TART

TARTE À LA CRÈME FRANGIPANE

Bake a shortcrust pastry case blind. Fill with almond custard (p.706) and bake for a further 15 minutes.

* 1 quantity shortcrust pastry (see above)
* 1 quantity fruit jam or compote of your choice (pp.857–9)

Preparation time: 20 minutes
Cooking time: 25 minutes
Serves 6

RICE PUDDING TART
TARTE AU RIZ

Bake a shortcrust pastry case blind. Pour in some rice pudding (p.711), flavoured to taste with vanilla extract or grated lemon zest. Bake for a further 10 minutes.

CUSTARD TART
TARTE AU FLAN

Bake a shortcrust pastry case blind. Fill with chocolate or vanilla béchamel (p.725), which may be flavoured with grated lemon zest. Bake for a further 10 minutes.

SOFT FRUIT TART
TARTE AUX FRUITS

Bake a shortcrust pastry case blind, ensuring it is fully cooked and nicely browned. Fill with soft fruits such as strawberries, raspberries or redcurrants. Glaze with a syrup (p.642) or redcurrant jelly (p.860).

TART MADE WITH FIRM FRUIT
TARTE AUX FRUITS PEU JUTEUX

Peel and slice firm fruit such as apples or pears and arrange in an uncooked shortcrust pastry case. Add softer fruit such as blackberries if desired. Make a custard by heating 175 ml (6 fl oz) milk and adding 2 tablespoons caster sugar and 1 tablespoon flour. Bring to the boil and stir until thickened. Cover the fruit with the custard and bake in an oven preheated to 200°C/400°F/Gas Mark 6 for 30 minutes.

TARTE TATIN

TARTE TATIN

 p.812

Preheat the oven to 200°C/400°F/Gas Mark 6. Make the shortcrust pastry, cover and allow it to rest. Take a flameproof pie dish with a solid base, preferably made of solid metal, and place in it 100 g (3½ oz) of the sugar and 1–2 tablespoons water. Place the dish over a medium heat and make a fairly dark caramel (p.643). Ensure the base of the dish is coated in caramel and allow to cool.

For the filling, peel, core and thinly slice the apples. Arrange close together in a ring on the caramel in the dish and sprinkle with the remaining sugar. Dot with the butter. Roll out the pastry to a thickness of 5 mm (¼ inch) and place over the apples, tucking the pastry into the tin all round so that the fruit is completely covered. Bake for 30 minutes, then turn out immediately onto a serving dish so that the caramelized apples are on top.

- **1 quantity shortcrust pastry (p.784)**
- **125 g (4¼ oz) caster sugar**

For the filling:
- **500 g (1 lb 2 oz) apples**
- **40 g (1½ oz) butter**

Preparation time: 25 minutes
Cooking time: 30 minutes
Serves 6

ALSACE TART (WITH APPLES)

TARTE À L'ALSACIENNE (AUX POMMES)

Preheat the oven to 200°C / 400°F / Gas Mark 6. Prepare an uncooked shortcrust pastry case. Arrange the apples on the pastry. In a bowl, beat the flour, eggs, sugar and crème fraîche until just smooth. Pour over the apples and bake for 30–40 minutes.

VARIATION

. . . .

RHUBARB TART

TARTE À LA RHUBARBE

Proceed as above, replacing the apples with 500 g (1 lb 2 oz) rhubarb cut into 3-cm (1¼-inch) slices. Coat with the custard mixture and bake for 30–40 minutes. Sprinkle with extra sugar to taste.

- **1 quantity shortcrust pastry (p.784)**

For the filling:
- **500 g (1 lb 2 oz) apples, peeled, cored and sliced**
- **50 g (1¾ oz) flour**
- **2 eggs**
- **100 g (3½ oz) caster sugar**
- **100 ml (3½ fl oz) crème fraîche**

Preparation time: 20 minutes
Cooking time: 30–40 minutes
Serves 6

ORANGE TART

TARTE À L'ORANGE

Preheat the oven to 200°C/400°F/Gas Mark 6. Line a 23-cm (9-inch) loose-bottomed tart tin or 6–8 individual tartlet tins with the shortcrust pastry, reserving a little of the dough. Bake blind (p.784), then brush the pastry base with the egg and return to the oven for 2 minutes. Remove and leave to cool. For the filling, beat together the egg, sugar, orange zest and juice and the butter in a bowl. Pour this mixture onto the cooked pastry. Decorate the tart or tartlets with strips of pastry 5 mm (¼ inch) wide, and brush them with a little more egg. Reduce the oven temperature to 180°C/350°F/Gas Mark 4 and bake for 30–35 minutes, or until golden and risen slightly.

VARIATIONS

. . . .

LEMON TART

TARTE AU CITRON

Proceed as above, substituting a lemon for the orange. The filling will be less sweet.

. . . .

PINEAPPLE TART

TARTE À L'ANANAS

Prepare as above, substituting 2 slices pineapple, 1 crushed and 1 diced, for the orange, and adding an extra 15 g (½ oz) butter and 1 tablespoon Kirsch to the filling.

- **1 quantity shortcrust pastry (p.784)**
- **1 egg, lightly beaten**

For the filling:
- **1 egg**
- **150 g (5 oz) caster sugar**
- **Grated zest and juice of 1 orange**
- **85 g (3 oz) butter, melted**

Preparation time: 20 minutes
Cooking time: 25 minutes
Serves 8

 p.813

SWEET PASTRY

PÂTE À FONCER

- **250 g (9 oz) flour, plus extra for dusting**
- **30 g (1¼ oz) caster sugar**
- **1 egg yolk**
- **150 g (5 oz) butter, softened**
- **1 teaspoon salt**

Preparation time: 20 minutes, plus resting time

Serves 6

This pastry is less absorbent than shortcrust pastry, so it is more suitable for juicy fruits or custards before they are set.

Put the flour in a bowl or on a work surface. Make a well in the centre and add the sugar, egg yolk, butter and salt. Mix together, gradually bringing the flour into the centre. Add just enough water (about 2 tablespoons) to bind the pastry together. Knead lightly and shape into a ball. Cover, and allow to rest for at least 1 hour in the refrigerator before use. Bring back to room temperature before rolling out.

On a lightly floured surface, roll out the pastry to a 5-mm (¼-inch) thick circle and use to line a round tart tin, 25–35 cm (10–14 inches) in diameter, and preferably with a removable base. The dough may also be used to line small round or boat-shaped tins. To bake the pastry case blind, preheat the oven to 190°C/375°F/Gas Mark 5. Line the pastry case with grease-proof paper and fill with baking beans or uncooked rice. Bake for 10 minutes, then gently remove the greaseproof paper and baking beans or rice and return the pastry case to the oven for a further 10–15 minutes until light golden brown in colour and cooked throughout.

APPLE TURNOVERS

CHAUSSONS AUX POMMES

- **250 g (9 oz) puff pastry (p.776)**
- **Butter, for greasing**
- **Flour, for dusting**
- **175 g (6 oz) apple purée (p.669)**
- **1 egg yolk**
- **60 g (2 oz) caster sugar**

Preparation time: 1 hour, plus resting time

Cooking time: 30 minutes

Serves 6

Make the puff pastry. Preheat the oven to 220°C/425°F/Gas Mark 7 and grease a baking tray with butter. Roll the pastry out very thinly on a floured work surface. Cut out even circles 12 cm (5 inches) in diameter using a bowl or pastry cutter. Place a good tablespoon of apple purée on each one. Fold in half, moisten the edges with a little water and press down to seal, forming a crescent shape. Place on the prepared tray. Brush with the egg yolk to glaze and sprinkle with the sugar. Bake for 30 minutes.

NOTE

Jam turnovers can be made by replacing the apple purée with a jam of your choice.

PASTIES

RISSOLES

Make the puff pastry. Preheat the oven to 220°C/425°F/Gas Mark 7 and grease a baking tray with butter. Roll the pastry out very thinly on a floured work surface. Cut out even circles 12 cm (5 inches) in diameter using a glass or pastry cutter. Put some of the filling on each circle, fold in half, moisten the edges with a little water and press down to seal, forming a crescent shape. Brush with the egg to glaze and place on the prepared tray. Bake for 20 minutes, and serve hot. Alternatively, heat the oil in a deep-fryer to 180°C/350°F, or until a cube of bread browns in 30 seconds. Fry the pasties, in batches, until golden brown. Drain well.

* 150 g (5 oz) puff pastry (p.776)
* Butter, for greasing
* Flour, for dusting
* A filling, to taste (see Variations)
* 1 egg, beaten
* Vegetable oil, for deep-frying (optional)

Preparation time: 30 minutes
Cooking time: 20 minutes
Serves 6

VARIATIONS

. . . .

MEAT PASTIES
RISSOLES À LA VIANDE

Chop some cooked meat. Stir in 1 lightly beaten egg, and season with salt and pepper. Proceed as above, filling the pasties with the meat mixture.

. . . .

FISH PASTIES
RISSOLES DE POISSON

Mix some cooked fish with a little white bread soaked in milk and torn into pieces. Season with salt and pepper. Proceed as above, filling the pasties with the fish mixture.

. . . .

VEGETABLE PASTIES
RISSOLES DE LÉGUMES

Use leftover chopped cooked spinach, asparagus tips or mushrooms. Season with salt and pepper and proceed as above, filling the pasties with the vegetable mixture.

. . . .

FRUIT PASTIES
RISSOLES DE FRUITS

Thick stewed fruit may be used to fill the pasties, which can be served sprinkled with caster sugar. Proceed as above.

PITHIVIER

- 250 g (9 oz) puff pastry (p.776)
- 350 g (12 oz) blanched almonds
- 175 g (6 oz) caster sugar
- 1 teaspoon almond extract
- 1 teaspoon grated lemon zest
- 3 eggs
- 175 g (6 oz) butter, softened
- 1 egg yolk

Preparation time: 1 hour, plus
resting time
Cooking time: 30 minutes
Serves 6

Make the puff pastry. Preheat the oven to 220°C/425°F/Gas Mark 7. Pound the almonds in a mortar or process in a blender with the sugar, almond extract and lemon zest. Add the eggs, one by one, and the butter. Knead the mixture. Line a pie dish or tart tin with half the pastry. Fill with the almond mixture. Cover with another pastry circle, moisten the edges with a little water and press to seal. Brush with the egg yolk to glaze. With a sharp knife, starting in the centre, score patterns on the pastry out to the edges, like the spokes of a wheel. Bake for 30 minutes, or until golden brown.

DARTOIS

- 250 g (9 oz) puff pastry (p.776)
- Butter, for greasing

For the almond paste:
- 125 g (4¼ oz) ground almonds
- 60 g (2 oz) butter, softened
- 100 g (3½ oz) caster sugar
- 1 teaspoon vanilla extract
- 2 eggs

Preparation time: 1 hour, plus
resting time
Cooking time: 25 minutes
Serves 6

Make the puff pastry. Prepare the almond paste by mixing the almonds, butter, eggs, sugar and vanilla together and set aside, covered, at room temperature. Preheat the oven to 220°C/425°F/Gas Mark 7 and grease a baking tray with butter. Roll the pastry out to 5 mm (¼ inch) thick.

Prepare 2 strips, one 8–10 cm (3–4 inches) wide, the other 2 cm (¾ inch) wider. Place the larger one on the prepared tray. Spoon the almond paste, which should be quite soft, onto this strip and fold in 1 cm (½ inch) of the edges over the almond paste all round. Put on the second piece of pastry like a lid, seal the edges with water and flute the edges so that they stand upright. Mark with a knife every 4–5 cm (1½–2 inches) to show the individual portions of dartois. Bake for 25 minutes, or until deep golden brown. Immediately after baking, gently cut the dartois in slices at the marked portions.

CAKES MADE WITH RAISING AGENTS

There are many mixtures, doughs and batters where the use of yeast or baking powder increases volume either before or during the baking process. Yeast is always added some time before baking, since the dough must be well risen before being put into the oven. When dissolving yeast in a liquid such as water or milk, ensure the liquid is no more than lukewarm, as anything hotter may kill the yeast. Chemical raising agents such as bicarbonate of soda or baking powder work most effectively when heat is applied.

Finally, stiffly beaten egg whites can play a role in raising a mixture, adding lightness and volume. When cooking a recipe that uses a raising agent, sudden changes in temperature should be avoided, as these will deflate the dish by disrupting the action of the raising agent before it is cooked and stable. For this reason, try to avoid opening the oven door before a cake is cooked.

SAVOURY MEAT BUNS

PETITS PÂTÉS SOUFFLÉS

Preheat the oven to 180°C/350°F/Gas Mark 4. Mix the flour, yeast and salt in a large bowl. Make a well in the centre, then add the butter, eggs and crème fraiche, and mix to a very stiff batter. Leave to rest for 15 minutes. Grease a 12-hole bun or muffin tin with butter and put 1 tablespoon of the batter in each hole. Push a small piece of sausage meat into each one, and cover with some of the remaining batter. Use a wet finger to smooth the batter around the sausage meat to completely seal it in. Leave to rest for 15 minutes, then bake for 20–25 minutes until puffed and golden, and the sausage centre is cooked. Turn out and serve hot as a starter.

- 200 g (7 oz) flour
- ½ x 7-g (¼-oz) sachet fast-action dried yeast
- 1 pinch of salt
- 75 g (2½ oz) butter, melted, plus extra for greasing
- 3 eggs
- 50 ml (2 fl oz) crème fraîche
- 100 g (3½ oz) sausage meat

Preparation time: 20 minutes, plus resting time
Cooking time: 30 minutes
Serves 6

SAVARIN

SAVARIN

- **15 g (½ oz) fresh yeast**
- **50 ml (2 fl oz) lukewarm milk**
- **250 g (9 oz) flour**
- **3 eggs**
- **125 g (4¼ oz) butter, softened, plus extra for greasing**
- **30 g (1¼ oz) caster sugar**
- **1½ teaspoons salt**
- **½ quantity rum sauce (p.729)**

Preparation time: 30 minutes, plus rising time
Cooking time: 30 minutes
Serves 6

 p.815

Prepare 6 hours in advance. Add the yeast to the milk and stir to dissolve. Sieve the flour into a bowl, make a well and pour in the milk. Add the eggs and beat for a few minutes; the dough should come away easily from the hand or beaters. Cover the bowl and leave the dough to rise at room temperature until doubled in volume. Preheat the oven to 200°C/400°F/Gas Mark 6 and grease a ring mould with butter. Mix the butter into the dough along with the sugar and salt. Beat until very smooth. Put the dough in the prepared ring mould, filling it two-thirds full. Bake for 30 minutes. While the savarin is still warm and in the mould, pour over the rum sauce. Leave to soak and cool before turning out.

VARIATION

. . . .

RUM BABA

RUM BABAS

Proceed as above, adding 100 g (3½ oz) currants with the butter. Put the dough into small or large, well-buttered baba moulds. Bake small babas for 15–20 minutes and large ones for 30 minutes. Pour over a rum sauce (p.729) or Kirsch while still warm.

QUICK SAVARIN

SAVARIN RAPIDE

Preheat the oven to 200°C/400°F/Gas Mark 6. Generously grease a 20-cm (8-inch) savarin mould or ring mould with butter. In a bowl, mix the egg yolks, sugar, flour and baking powder. Whisk the egg whites until stiff and mix half of them into the mixture to make a stiff batter. Carefully fold in the remaining whites. Pour the mixture into the prepared mould. Bake for 20 minutes, until golden. Pour the rum sauce over the savarin when it comes out of the oven. Leave to soak and cool before turning out.

VARIATION

. . . .

QUICK RUM BABA

BABA RAPIDE

Proceed as above, adding 50g (1¾ oz) currants with the flour. The centre of the cooled baba may be filled with crème pâtissière (p.706).

- ◆ Butter, for greasing
- ◆ 3 eggs, separated
- ◆ 100 g (3½ oz) caster sugar
- ◆ 100 g (3½ oz) flour
- ◆ ½ teaspoon baking powder
- ◆ ¼ quantity rum sauce (p.729)

Preparation time: 15 minutes
Cooking time: 20 minutes
Serves 6

BRIOCHE

BRIOCHE

- 10 g (¼ oz) fresh yeast, or
  1 x 7-g sachet active dried yeast
- 50 ml (2 fl oz) milk, warm
- 300 g (11 oz) flour, plus extra
  for dusting
- Pinch of salt
- 3 eggs
- 125 g (4¼ oz) butter, softened,
  plus extra for greasing
- 60 g (2 oz) caster sugar
- 1 egg yolk

Preparation time: 40 minutes,
plus resting and rising time
Cooking time: 30 minutes
Serves 6

Prepare the day before. If using fresh yeast, mix it with the milk, stir to dissolve and set aside for 10 minutes. Mix the fresh yeast mixture (or dried yeast, if using), flour and sugar together in a large bowl or in an electric mixer. Mix in the warm milk (if not already added with the fresh yeast) and the eggs to make a very soft, sticky dough. Knead for 5 minutes with the dough-hook attachment of the mixer, or by hand, pulling lumps of the dough upwards, then pushing them back in the bowl with a slapping motion. Cover with oiled clingfilm and leave to rise in a warm place, until doubled in size.

When risen, add the butter, a lump at a time, to the dough, either in the mixer or by hand. To add it by hand, put the dough onto a floured work surface, bury a lump of butter in it, then knead the butter in with the up-and-down motion described above until the dough is silky and smooth, with no visible butter. When all the butter is incorporated, cover again, and leave to rise in the refrigerator until doubled in size (about 4–8 hours). Chill in the refrigerator overnight.

The next day, preheat the oven to 200°C/400°F/Gas Mark 6 and butter and flour a brioche mould or round cake tin. Turn out the dough onto a floured work surface, shape two-thirds of it into a ball and place in the prepared mould or tin to half-fill it. Shape the remaining dough into a small ball and place it on top. Dust the handle of a wooden spoon with flour and push it vertically through the top ball to join it to the bottom one. Brush with the egg yolk to glaze and bake for 30 minutes, or until golden brown.

QUICK BRIOCHE

BRIOCHE RAPIDE

- Butter, for greasing
- 175 ml (6 fl oz) crème fraîche
- 175 g (6 oz) flour
- 3 teaspoons baking powder
- 2 eggs, beaten
- 30 g (1¼ oz) caster sugar
- 1 teaspoon salt

Preparation time: 10 minutes
Cooking time: 45 minutes
Serves 6

Preheat the oven to 180°C/350°F/Gas Mark 4 and grease a brioche tin with butter. In a bowl, mix the crème fraîche into the flour and baking powder. Add half the beaten egg and the sugar and salt. Mix to a soft dough. Put into the prepared tin. Brush with the remaining beaten egg to glaze and bake for 45 minutes, or until golden brown.

WAFFLES

GAUFRES

Prepare 8 hours in advance. Mix the yeast with the milk, stir to dissolve and set aside for 10 minutes. Mix with the flour in a bowl to make a dough and leave to rise in a warm place for 3–6 hours. When the dough has doubled in volume, knead in the eggs, sugar, butter, rum and bicarbonate of soda. Cover and leave to rise again for 2 hours. Turn out onto a floured work surface and roll out to about 2 cm (¾ inch) thick. Cut into pieces. Heat a waffle iron, grease with butter and cook the waffles for 5 minutes, or until golden and cooked through.

- 10 g (¼ oz) fresh yeast
- 150 ml (¼ pint) lukewarm milk
- 250 g (9 oz) flour, plus extra for dusting
- 2 eggs, beaten
- 125 g (4¼ oz) caster sugar
- 125 g (4¼ oz) butter, softened, plus extra for greasing
- 1 tablespoon rum
- 1 small pinch of bicarbonate of soda

Preparation time: 30 minutes, plus rising time
Cooking time: 5 minutes per waffle
Serves 6

HONEY WAFFLES

GAUFRETTES AU MIEL

Combine the flour, honey, eggs and rum in a bowl. Mix to make a soft dough and knead lightly. Roll out the dough on a floured work surface. Cut into pieces. Heat a waffle iron, grease with butter and cook the waffles for 5 minutes, or until golden and cooked through.

- 500 g (1 lb 2 oz) flour, plus extra for dusting
- 250 g (9 oz) honey
- 5 eggs, beaten
- 1 tablespoon rum
- Butter, for greasing

Preparation time: 15 minutes
Cooking time: 5 minutes per waffle
Serves 6

FRUIT CAKE

CAKE

- 40 g (1½ oz) candied fruit
- 2 tablespoons rum
- 175 g (6 oz) butter, softened, plus extra for greasing
- 120 g (4 oz) caster sugar
- 1 teaspoon salt
- 3 eggs
- 250 g (9 oz) flour
- 1½ teaspoons baking powder
- 50 g (1¾ oz) sultanas
- 50 g (1¾ oz) currants

Preparation time: 25 minutes
Cooking time: 50 minutes
Serves 6

Set aside 15 g (½ oz) of attractive-looking candied fruit to decorate the cake. Chop the remainder and put in a bowl with the rum, then leave to macerate. Preheat the oven to 180°C / 350°F / Gas Mark 4. In a bowl, beat the butter, sugar and salt until pale. Beat in the eggs, one by one. Add the flour and baking powder all at once and beat well to lighten the dough. Mix in the candied fruit and rum, sultanas and currants. Grease a loaf tin with butter and pour in the dough. Decorate with the reserved candied fruit. Bake for 5 minutes, then increase the temperature to 200°C/400°F/Gas Mark 6 and cook for a further 45 minutes, covering with foil if the cake browns too quickly.

SWISS ROLL

GÂTEAU À LA CONFITURE

- Butter, for greasing
- 2 eggs
- 110 g (3¾ oz) caster sugar
- 70 g (2½ oz) flour
- 1 teaspoon salt
- 1¼ teaspoons baking powder
- 1 tablespoon milk
- Jam, to taste
- 1 quantity butter cream (p.728), optional

Preparation time: 20 minutes
Cooking time: 15–20 minutes
Serves 6

Preheat the oven to 180°C/350°F/Gas Mark 4 and grease a swiss roll tin with butter. Whisk the eggs and sugar in a bowl for 5 minutes. Still whisking, add the flour a spoonful at a time, and add the salt, baking powder and milk. Place in the prepared tin and level the surface. Bake for 15–20 minutes until golden. Turn out immediately. Cover evenly with a layer of jam and, starting with the long end nearest you, carefully roll into a log shape. The swiss roll may also be filled, once cooled, with butter cream, and then rolled up in the same way.

NOTE
To roll the cake up more easily, turn it out onto a slightly damp tea towel. This helps to prevent it breaking up.

PAIN D'ÉPICE

PAIN D'ÉPICE

Preheat the oven to 150°C/300°F/Gas Mark 2 and grease a loaf tin with butter. Place the sugar, honey and bicarbonate of soda in a large pan with 100 ml (3½ fl oz) water. Melt over a low heat, stirring. Remove from the heat and allow to cool a little before stirring in the flour, orange zest and spices. Half-fill the prepared loaf tin with the mixture. Cover with foil and bake for 1½ hours.

- Butter, for greasing
- 2 teaspoons caster sugar
- 125 g (4¼ oz) dark honey
- 2 teaspoons bicarbonate of soda
- 250 g (9 oz) flour
- Grated zest of 1 orange
- 2 teaspoons ground mixed spices, such as aniseed, cinnamon, cloves, cardamon, ginger, nutmeg and pepper

Preparation time: 10 minutes
Cooking time: 1½ hours
Serves 6

HAZELNUT CAKE

GÂTEAU AUX NOISETTES

Preheat the oven to 180°C/350°F/Gas Mark 4 and grease a cake tin with butter. Mix together the flour, baking powder, butter, sugar and egg yolks. Whisk the egg whites to soft peaks and stir into the flour mixture with the hazelnuts. Pour into the prepared cake tin and bake for 50–60 minutes.

- 225 g (8 oz) butter, softened, plus extra for greasing
- 250 g (9 oz) flour
- 2 teaspoons baking powder
- 240 g (8½ oz) caster sugar
- 4 eggs, separated
- 150 g (5 oz) skinned hazelnuts, chopped

Preparation time: 25 minutes
Cooking time: 50–60 minutes
Serves 6

MARBLE CAKE

GÂTEAU MARBRÉ

- 100 g (3½ oz) butter, plus extra for greasing
- 200 g (7 oz) caster sugar
- 3 eggs, separated
- 200 g (7 oz) flour
- 100 ml (3½ fl oz) milk
- 1 teaspoon baking powder
- 60 g (2 oz) chocolate, grated
- Vanilla extract or grated lemon zest, to taste

Preparation time: 20 minutes
Cooking time: 1 hour
Serves 6

Preheat the oven to 150°C/300°F/Gas Mark 2 and grease a loaf tin with butter. Cream the butter with the sugar until soft and pale. Mix in the egg yolks, flour, milk and baking powder. In another bowl, whisk the egg whites until stiff, then fold into the cake mixture. Divide the mixture into 2 equal parts. Fold the chocolate into one and the vanilla or lemon zest into the other. Put alternating spoonfuls of the white and chocolate mixtures into the prepared tin, filling it two-thirds full. Bake for 1 hour.

AURÉLIA'S CAKE

GÂTEAU D'AURÉLIA

- Butter, for greasing
- 4 eggs
- 250 g (9 oz) caster sugar, plus extra for sprinkling
- 1 teaspoon ground cinnamon
- Grated zest of 1 lemon or orange
- 90 ml (3¼ fl oz) milk
- 105 ml (3¾ fl oz) groundnut oil
- 150 g (5 oz) flour
- 50 g (1¼ oz) cornflour
- 1½ teaspoons baking powder

Preparation time: 20 minutes
Cooking time: 40 minutes
Serves 6

Preheat the oven to 200°C/400°F/Gas Mark 6. Grease a cake tin measuring 15–18 cm (6–7 inches) in diameter and 5 cm (2 inches) high with butter. Break the eggs into a large bowl and beat for 2–3 minutes. Add the sugar, cinnamon, lemon or orange zest, milk and oil. Using a wooden spoon or electric whisk, beat the mixture for about 5 minutes. Gradually stir in the flour, cornflour and baking powder. Pour the cake mixture into the prepared tin. Sprinkle with a little caster sugar and bake for 40 minutes. Halfway through baking, cover with greaseproof paper to prevent the cake browning too much.

KUGELHOPF
KUGELHOPF

Prepare 6 hours in advance. Place the milk in a pan and heat until it is lukewarm. In a small bowl, mix 2 tablespoons of the warmed milk with the yeast. Place the butter in the pan to melt in the remaining warm milk. Place the flour and eggs in a large bowl and mix in the warm milk and butter, yeast mixture and a little salt. Knead the dough until it leaves the bowl clean, and then knead in the raisins. Grease a kugelhopf mould liberally with butter and place an almond at the bottom of each section of the mould. Half-fill the mould with the dough and set aside, covered, in a warm place to rise for 6 hours.

Preheat the oven to 160°C / 325°F / Gas Mark 3. Place the kugelhopf in the oven and bake for 15 minutes, then raise the temperature to 200°C / 400°F / Gas Mark 6 and bake for a further 45 minutes, covering with foil if necessary to prevent it browning too much. Sprinkle with icing sugar before serving.

- ◆ 200 ml (7 fl oz) milk
- ◆ 25 g (1 oz) fresh yeast
- ◆ 100 g (3½ oz) butter, plus extra for greasing
- ◆ 500 g (1 lb 2 oz) flour
- ◆ 2 eggs
- ◆ Salt
- ◆ 125 g (4¼ oz) raisins
- ◆ 12 almonds
- ◆ Icing sugar, for sprinkling

Preparation time: 30 minutes, plus rising time
Cooking time: 1 hour
Serves 6

STEAMED DOUGHNUTS
BEIGNETS À LA VAPEUR

These steamed doughnuts from Alsace are also known as *dampfnoudeln*. The steam created when the water hits the hot fat causes the dough to rise.

Prepare 2 hours in advance. Place the milk in a pan and heat until it is lukewarm. In a small bowl, mix 2 tablespoons of the warmed milk with the yeast. Place the butter in the pan to melt in the remaining warm milk. Put the flour in a large bowl and mix in the milk and butter, yeast mixture, sugar and salt. Knead the dough until it leaves the bowl clean and leave to rise, covered, for 2 hours.

To cook, heat the lard in a heavy-based pan over a medium heat. When the fat is smoking hot, carefully lower in spoonfuls of the dough, in batches of 4 or 5. Almost completely cover the pan with the lid, then pour 50 ml (2 fl oz) water through the gap. Cover immediately with the lid, as the mixture will spit furiously. Once the doughnuts are golden brown, drain and serve immediately, sprinkled with sugar. Serve with stewed fruit, if desired.

- ◆ 500 ml (18 fl oz) milk, plus 2 tablespoons
- ◆ 50 g (1¾ oz) fresh yeast
- ◆ 125 g (4¼ oz) butter, diced
- ◆ 900 g (2 lb) flour
- ◆ 50 g (1¾ oz) caster sugar, plus extra for sprinkling
- ◆ 1 teaspoon salt
- ◆ 75 g (1¾ oz) lard
- ◆ Stewed fruit, to serve (optional)

Preparation time: 30 minutes, plus rising time
Cooking time: 15 minutes
Serves 6

CAKES MADE WITH EGG WHITES

ANGEL CAKE
GÂTEAU MOUSSELINE

- Butter, for greasing
- 5 eggs, separated
- 75 g (2½ oz) caster sugar
- 125 g (4¼ oz) potato flour
- Grated zest of 1 lemon

Preparation time: 15 minutes
Cooking time: 45 minutes
Serves 6

Preheat the oven to 160°C/325°F/Gas Mark 3 and grease a cake tin with butter. Whisk the egg whites to stiff peaks. In a separate bowl, whisk together the sugar and egg yolks until white and foamy. Stir in the flour and lemon zest, and then fold in the egg whites. Pour into the prepared cake tin and bake for 45 minutes, until risen and golden.

SAVOY CAKE
GÂTEAU DE SAVOIE

- Butter, for greasing
- 4 eggs, separated
- 200 g (7 oz) caster sugar
- 40 g (1½ oz) flour
- 60 g (2 oz) potato flour
- Vanilla extract or grated lemon zest, to taste

Preparation time: 20 minutes
Cooking time: 30 minutes
Serves 6

Preheat the oven to 180°C/350°F/Gas Mark 4 and grease a cake tin with butter. Whisk the egg whites to stiff peaks. In a separate bowl, beat the sugar and egg yolks until white and foamy. Add the flour, potato flour and the vanilla or lemon zest. Fold in the egg whites. Fill the prepared cake tin two-thirds full with the mixture. Bake for 10 minutes, then increase the temperature to 200°C/400°F/Gas Mark 6 and cook for a further 15–20 minutes.

ALMOND CAKE
GÂTEAU AUX AMANDES

- 90 g (3¼ oz) butter, melted
- 300 g (11 oz) caster sugar
- 4 eggs, 3 separated
- 50 g (1¾ oz) ground almonds
- 150 g (5 oz) flour
- Orange-flower water, to taste

Preparation time: 20 minutes
Cooking time: 45 minutes
Serves 6

Preheat the oven to 180°C/350°F/Gas Mark 4 and grease a cake tin with a little of the butter. Beat the sugar, 1 egg and the 3 egg yolks with the almonds. Stir in the flour, remaining butter and orange-flower water. In a separate bowl, whisk the egg whites to stiff peaks and fold them carefully into the cake mixture. Fill the prepared cake tin two-thirds full with the mixture. Bake for 45 minutes.

CHERRY GÂTEAU

GÂTEAU DE CERISES

Preheat the oven to 200°C/400°F/Gas Mark 6 and grease a charlotte mould with butter. Wash the cherries and remove the stalks and stones. Place the butter in a heatproof bowl set over a pan of barely simmering water, and beat until it becomes liquid. Add the sugar and almonds and remove from the heat. Mash the brioche into the milk, then add it to the almond mixture. Beat in the eggs one by one, then the cherries. Pour the mixture into the prepared charlotte mould. Bake for 30 minutes. Turn out. Serve cold, sprinkled with the Kirsch.

- **125 g (4¼ oz) butter, plus extra for greasing**
- **600 g (1 lb 5 oz) black cherries**
- **125 g (4¼ oz) caster sugar**
- **125 g (4¼ oz) ground almonds**
- **1 piece of brioche, about 100–150 g (3½–5 oz)**
- **100 ml (3½ fl oz) milk**
- **4 eggs**
- **2 tablespoons Kirsch, to serve**

Preparation time: 15 minutes
Cooking time: 30 minutes
Serves 6

PRALINE CAKE

GÂTEAU AUX PRALINES

 p.817

Preheat the oven to 180°C/350°F/Gas Mark 4. Line two 24-cm (9½-inch) cake tins with baking parchment or grease well with the butter. Mix the sugar and almonds. Stir in 3 of the egg whites and the cornflour and vanilla. Whisk the remaining egg whites to stiff peaks and fold these into the almond mixture. Put the mixture into the prepared cake tins. Bake for 20 minutes, then turn out and allow to cool.

While the cakes are cooking, prepare the crème filling. Beat the egg yolks and sugar for 5 minutes until pale and soft. Beat in the butter. Crush 75 g (2½ oz) praline very finely, and stir into the butter mixture. Spread the mixture over one of the cooled cakes, reserving some for the top if desired. Cover with the second cake. Coarsely crush the remaining praline. Sprinkle the cake with icing sugar and decorate with praline.

- **30 g (1¼ oz) butter**
- **125 g (4¼ oz) caster sugar**
- **100 g (3½ oz) ground almonds**
- **6 egg whites**
- **30 g (1¼ oz) cornflour**
- **1 teaspoon vanilla extract**
- **Icing sugar, for sprinkling**

For the crème filling:
- **4 egg yolks**
- **75 g (2½ oz) caster sugar**
- **150 g (5 oz) butter, softened**
- **100 g (3½ oz) praline**

Preparation time: 50 minutes
Cooking time: 20 minutes
Serves 6

FOUR-QUARTERS CAKE

QUATRE-QUARTS

- Butter, about 150 g (5 oz), plus extra for greasing
- 3 eggs
- Flour, about 150 g (5 oz)
- Caster sugar, about 150 g (5 oz)
- Grated zest of 1 lemon

Preparation time: 20 minutes
Cooking time: 30–40 minutes
Serves 6

Preheat the oven to 160°C/325°F/Gas Mark 3. Grease a round cake tin with butter. Weigh the eggs and measure out their weight in equal quantities of the flour, sugar and butter. Melt the butter and allow to cool. Separate the eggs and beat the yolks with the sugar until the mixture is white and flows like a ribbon from the whisk. Little by little, fold in the flour and butter in alternating spoonfuls. Add the lemon zest. Whisk the egg whites to stiff peaks and fold into the cake mixture. Fill the prepared cake tin two-thirds full. Bake for 30–40 minutes.

ORANGE CAKE

GÂTEAU À L'ORANGE

- Butter, for greasing
- 3 eggs, separated
- 125 g (4¼ oz) caster sugar
- 60 g (2 oz) potato flour
- 125 g (4¼ oz) ground almonds
- Grated zest and juice of 1 orange

Preparation time: 20 minutes
Cooking time: 40 minutes
Serves 6

Preheat the oven to 160°C/325°F/Gas Mark 3. Grease a round cake tin with butter. Beat the egg yolks and mix in the sugar, flour, almonds, and orange zest and juice. Whisk the egg whites to stiff peaks and fold into the cake mixture. Pour into the prepared cake tin and bake for 40 minutes.

ENGLISH CAKE

GÂTEAU ANGLAIS

- 125 g (4¼ oz) butter, softened, plus extra for greasing
- 125 g (4¼ oz) caster sugar
- 125 g (4¼ oz) rice flour
- 3 pieces of candied orange peel, finely chopped
- 2 eggs, separated
- 1 teaspoon vanilla extract
- 1 quantity Kirsch icing (p.727)

Preparation time: 15 minutes
Cooking time: 20 minutes
Serves 6

Preheat the oven to 180°C/350°F/Gas Mark 4. Grease a cake tin with butter. Place the butter in a heatproof bowl set over a pan of simmering water and beat until foamy. Alternately beat in the sugar, flour and orange peel a little at a time. Remove from the heat and stir in the egg yolks and vanilla. Finally, whisk the egg whites to stiff peaks and fold them in. Pour the mixture into the prepared cake tin and bake for 20 minutes. Turn out, allow to cool and coat with the Kirsch icing.

CHOCOLATE CAKE

GÂTEAU AU CHOCOLAT

 p.816

Preheat the oven to 150°C/300°F/Gas Mark 2. Grease a cake tin with butter. In a pan, melt the chocolate with the butter over a very low heat. Remove from the heat and stir in the egg yolks, one by one, followed by the flour and sugar. In a separate bowl, whisk the egg whites and flavouring to stiff peaks. Fold into the chocolate mixture. Pour into the prepared cake tin and bake for 50 minutes. When the cake comes out of the oven, allow to cool, then cover with the chocolate icing and decorate with candied fruit.

- 70 g (2½ oz) butter, plus extra for greasing
- 140 g (4¾ oz) chocolate, chopped
- 4 eggs, separated
- 90 g (3¼ oz) flour
- 140 g (4¾ oz) sugar
- 1 teaspoon flavouring, such as rum, Kirsch or orange-flower water
- 1 quantity chocolate icing (p.727)
- Candied fruit, such as cherries, oranges and angelica, to decorate

Preparation time: 20 minutes
Cooking time: 50 minutes
Serves 6

CHOCOLATE & CREAM CAKE

GÂTEAU AU CHOCOLAT AVEC CRÈME

Preheat the oven to 150°C/300°F/Gas Mark 2. Grease a cake tin with butter. Whisk the eggs and sugar until white and foamy. Fold in the chocolate and flour, and finally gently fold in the crème fraîche. Pour into the prepared cake tin and bake for 30 minutes.

- Butter, for greasing
- 5 eggs
- 250 g (9 oz) caster sugar
- 125 g (4¼ oz) chocolate, grated
- 125 g (4¼ oz) flour
- 100 ml (3½ fl oz) crème fraîche

Preparation time: 20 minutes
Cooking time: 30 minutes
Serves 6

COFFEE & CHOCOLATE CAKE

GÂTEAU SUPRÊME (AU CAFÉ)

Preheat the oven to 160°C/325°F/Gas Mark 3. Grease a cake tin with butter. Place the chocolate in a pan with 1 tablespoon water and melt over a low heat. Remove from the heat and stir in the sugar, cornflour, flour, butter, coffee and egg yolks. Whisk the egg whites in another bowl until they form soft peaks. Fold into the cake mixture. Place in the prepared cake tin and bake for 25 minutes. Serve with plain or coffee crème anglaise.

- 60 g (2 oz) butter, plus extra for greasing
- 240 g (8½ oz) chocolate, chopped
- 60 g (2 oz) caster sugar
- 60 g (2 oz) cornflour
- 30 g (1¼ oz) flour
- 3 teaspoons instant coffee
- 3 eggs, separated
- Crème anglaise or coffee crème anglaise (p.694), to serve

Preparation time: 15 minutes
Cooking time: 25 minutes
Serves 6

CHOCOLATE & RUM CAKE

GÂTEAU DE CHOCOLAT AU RHUM

Make 2 hours in advance. Preheat the oven to 180°C/350°F/Gas Mark 4. Grease a round cake tin with butter. In a medium bowl, mix together the egg, 60 g (2 oz) sugar, baking powder, flour and milk. Pour the mixture into the prepared cake tin and bake for 20 minutes. Turn out and allow to cool. In a small pan, heat the rum and 2 tablespoons sugar with 2 tablespoons water, stirring until the sugar dissolves. Pour it over the cake. Melt the butter and chocolate in a small pan over a very low heat. Cool and spread in a 1-cm (½-inch) layer over the cake. Sprinkle with the cocoa powder and chill for 2 hours before serving.

- 80 g (2¾ oz) butter, plus extra for greasing
- 1 egg
- 60 g (2 oz) caster sugar, plus 2 tablespoons
- 1 teaspoon baking powder
- 50 g (1¾ oz) flour
- 3 tablespoons milk
- 2 tablespoons rum
- 125 g (4¼ oz) chocolate, chopped
- 50 g (1¾ oz) cocoa powder

Preparation time: 20 minutes, plus chilling time
Cooking time: 20 minutes
Serves 6

FINANCIERS

FINANCIERS

- 120 g (4 oz) butter, softened, plus extra for greasing
- 4 egg whites
- 125 g (4¼ oz) caster sugar
- 100 g (3½ oz) flour, sifted

Preparation time: 40 minutes
Cooking time: 20 minutes
Serves 6

Preheat the oven to 180°C/350°F/Gas Mark 4. Grease small financier moulds with butter. Whisk the egg whites and sugar with an electric whisk, until stiff and glossy, then fold in the flour and butter. Half-fill the prepared moulds with the mixture and bake for 20 minutes.

MADELEINES

MADELEINES

- 125 g (4¼ oz) butter, softened, plus extra for greasing
- 2 large eggs
- 150 g (5 oz) caster sugar
- 150 g (5 oz) flour, sifted
- 1 teaspoon vanilla extract, or grated zest of 1 lemon

Preparation time: 20 minutes
Cooking time: 8–10 minutes
Serves 6

Preheat the oven to 200°C / 400°F / Gas Mark 6. Grease madeleine tins with butter. Whisk the eggs and sugar with an electric whisk until the mixture turns white and triples in volume. Slowly fold in the flour and butter, then the vanilla or lemon zest. Pour into the prepared tins and bake for 8–10 minutes.

VISITANDINES

VISITANDINES

- 125 g (4¼ oz) butter, softened, plus extra for greasing
- 5 egg whites
- 125 g (4¼ oz) flour, sifted
- 250 g (9 oz) caster sugar
- 100 g (3½ oz) ground almonds
- Grated zest of ½ lemon

Preparation time: 25 minutes
Cooking time: 30 minutes
Serves 6

Preheat the oven to 160°C / 325°F / Gas Mark 3. Grease small individual cake tins with butter. Whisk the egg whites to soft peaks with an electric whisk, then slowly fold in the flour, sugar, almonds and lemon zest. Finally, add the butter. Pour the mixture into the prepared tins. Bake for 30 minutes.

Norwegian bows (p.762)

Nantes biscuits (p.764)

Almond macaroons (p.771)

Almond tuiles   (p.772)

Tarte tatin (p.786)

Lemon tart   (p.788)

Palmiers (p.781)

Rum babas   (p.793)

Chocolate cake (p.804)

Praline cake   (p.802)

- 15 -
SWEETS,

PRESERVES
&
DRINKS

SWEETS

Home-made sweets have a special flavour and charm and are a treat for adults as well as children. They may be handed round at the end of the meal with the coffee, at tea-time, or given as presents for special occasions. Most are easy to make and need only a small amount of equipment, including a marble slab or a baking sheet, a toffee tray or any rectangular tin, and paper sweet cases for serving.

BARLEY SUGAR
SUCRE D'ORGE

Lightly grease a marble slab or baking tray with oil. Put 100 ml (3½ fl oz) water, the sugar and lemon juice in a large pan. Cook on a high heat, stirring continually, until the sugar turns light brown and reaches the firm-ball stage (p.643). Carefully pour onto the prepared slab or toffee tray and cut up into small squares while warm.

VARIATION

. . . .

SUGAR NOUGAT
NOUGAT DE SUCRE

Toast 300 g (11 oz) mixed almonds, hazelnuts and pistachios in the oven, allow to cool and roughly chop them. Proceed as above, adding the chopped nuts just before pouring the mixture onto the slab or tray.

- **Flavourless oil, for greasing**
- **250 g (9 oz) caster sugar**
- **1 tablespoon lemon juice**

Preparation time: 5 minutes
Cooking time: 10 minutes
Makes 250 g (9 oz)

HONEY NOUGAT

NOUGAT AU MIEL

- Flavourless oil, for greasing (optional)
- Flour, for dusting (optional)
- Rice paper, for lining (optional)
- 400 g (14 oz) almonds, hazelnuts and pistachios
- 150 g (5 oz) honey

Preparation time: 10 minutes, plus cooling time
Cooking time: 20 minutes
Makes 500 g (1 lb 2 oz)

Lightly grease a marble slab or baking tray with oil, or dust it with flour and cover with a sheet of rice paper. Lightly toast the nuts in the oven, allow to cool and roughly chop them. Put the honey in a large pan, bring to the boil and cook for 10 minutes, then add the nuts. Boil, stirring constantly, until the syrup reaches the firm-ball stage (p.643). Remove from the heat. Pour onto the prepared slab or baking tray. Level the surface with a spatula rubbed with lemon. Cover with another leaf of rice paper, if using. Cover with a board and place a weight on top. Cool and cut into squares.

PASTILLES

PASTILLES

- Flavourless oil, for greasing
- 500 g (1 lb 2 oz) caster sugar
- 4–5 drops flavouring, such as mint, lemon or bergamot essence

Preparation time: 5 minutes, plus cooling time
Cooking time: 10 minutes
Makes 500 g (1 lb 2 oz)

Place the sugar and 200 ml (7 fl oz) water in a pan set over very low heat and cook gently, without boiling, to make a thick paste. Lightly oil a marble slab or baking tray. Stir in the flavouring. Pour the mixture in small drops onto the prepared slab or baking tray and leave to set. One hour later, lift off the pastilles.

CHOCOLATE TOFFEES

CARAMELS AU CHOCOLAT

- 75 g (2½ oz) chocolate
- 80 g (2¾ oz) double cream
- 60 g (2 oz) honey
- 100 g (3½ oz) butter
- 100 g (3½ oz) caster sugar
- Flavourless oil, for greasing

Preparation time: 5 minutes
Cooking time: 15 minutes
Makes 40 toffees

Grate the chocolate into a large pan. Add the cream, honey, butter and sugar. Bring to the boil and cook for 12–15 minutes over a gentle heat. Meanwhile, grease a toffee tray or deep baking tray with oil. Pour into the prepared tray and mark into pieces with the sharp knife while still warm.

COFFEE TOFFEES
CARAMELS AU CAFÉ

Put the sugar in a large pan. Add the cream, honey and milk and melt together over low heat. Simmer over very low heat for 15 minutes. Meanwhile, grease a toffee tray or deep baking tray with oil. Add the coffee essence to the pan. Pour into the prepared tray and mark into pieces with a sharp knife while still warm.

- 225 g (8 oz) caster sugar
- 200 g (7 oz) double cream
- 125 g (4¼ oz) honey
- 1 tablespoon milk
- Flavourless oil, for greasing
- 3 tablespoons coffee essence

Preparation time: 5 minutes
Cooking time: 15 minutes
Makes 60 toffees

TOFFEES
TOFFEES

 p.862

Put the black treacle or maple syrup in a pan set over a low heat. Add the brown sugar and butter. Cook, without boiling, for 2 hours, stirring occasionally. Meanwhile, grease a toffee tray or deep baking tray with oil. Increase the heat slightly and cook, stirring constantly, for 15 minutes. Carefully drop a little of the sugar mixture into a glass of cold water. If it hardens immediately, the cooking is complete; if not, continue cooking for a few moments longer. Remove from the heat, pour into the prepared tray and mark into pieces with a sharp knife while still warm. Remove when it has cooled.

- 125 g (4¼ oz) black treacle or maple syrup
- 500 g (1 lb 2 oz) light brown sugar
- 250 g (9 oz) butter
- Flavourless oil, for greasing

Preparation time: 20 minutes, plus cooling time
Cooking time: 2¼ hours
Makes 60 toffees

CHOCOLATE TRUFFLES
TRUFFES AU CHOCOLAT

 p.863

Prepare 4–5 hours in advance. Place the chocolate and milk in a pan over a very low heat and stir until melted. Remove from the heat when it has formed a very smooth paste. Stir in the egg yolks, then the butter. Beat the mixture for 2–3 minutes. Allow to cool for 4–5 hours. Roll small balls the size of a walnut and then roll in cocoa powder. Put in white paper cases and place in a box. Store in the refrigerator and eat within 48 hours.

- 250 g (9 oz) good quality chocolate, chopped
- 2 tablespoons milk
- 2 egg yolks
- 75 g (2½ oz) butter, diced
- 60 g (2 oz) cocoa powder

Preparation time: 25 minutes, plus cooling time
Cooking time: 5–10 minutes
Makes 40 truffles

p.864

QUINCE JELLIES
PÂTE DE COING

- 250 g (9 oz) quinces
- Flavourless oil, for greasing
- 350 g (12 oz) caster sugar

Preparation time: 5 minutes
Cooking time: 30 minutes
Makes 600 g (1 lb 5 oz)

Prepare 5 days in advance. Peel and cut the quinces into quarters, remove the cores and place in a pan. Put the peel, cores and pips in a muslin bag and add them to the pan along with enough cold water to cover the fruit. Bring to a simmer and cook over a medium heat until tender. Lightly grease a marble slab with oil and sprinkle with sugar.

When the quinces are tender, drain them. Process the fruit to a purée with 250 g (9 oz) of the sugar in a blender. Return to the clean pan and cook over very low heat, stirring constantly, until the paste comes away from the sides of the pan. Pour the paste onto the prepared slab. Sprinkle with the remaining sugar. Set aside to dry for 4 days in the refrigerator. Cut into small squares. Stored in an airtight container lined with greaseproof paper, the jellies will keep for months. Other flavours can be made with the same recipe, such as apples, apricots and plums.

CRYSTALLIZED CHESTNUTS
MARRONS GLACÉS

- 1 kg (2¼ lb) large, round chestnuts
- 1 kg (2¼ lb) sugar

Preparation time: 1 hour, plus soaking time
Makes 1 kg (2¼ lb)

Making these luxurious sweets at home is a lengthy procedure spread over several days. However, the results far surpass most shop-bought marrons glacés, and they make superb gifts.

Peel the outer skin from the chestnuts without breaking them. Place in a pan and cover with cold water. Bring to a simmer and cook over low heat at just below boiling point for 3 hours. Discard the water and immediately peel off the inner skins from the chestnuts without breaking them. Make a light syrup with the sugar (p.643) and cool to 20°C/68°F. Put the chestnuts into the syrup and set aside.

After 12 hours, reheat heat gently in a heatproof bowl set over a pan of simmering water. Remove the chestnuts with a slotted spoon and drain on a wire rack with a tray underneath. Heat the syrup to 25°C/77°F. Lower the chestnuts into the syrup and leave for 12 hours. Remove and drain as before, then heat the syrup to 33°C/91°F. Leave the chestnuts in the syrup for 12 hours. Put the chestnuts into a heatproof metal sieve, and cook the syrup to the hard-crack stage (p.643). Carefully lower the chestnuts into the syrup and remove after 1 minute. Dry for several hours in very low oven.

STUFFED WALNUTS

NOIX FARCIES

Put the almonds, icing sugar and chocolate in a bowl and add the egg white. Beat to a paste, then shape into 24 walnut-size balls. Shell the walnuts, taking care not to damage the kernels, and break the kernels gently into halves. Sandwich the almond paste balls with the walnut halves.

- 125 g (4¼ oz) ground almonds
- 100 g (3½ oz) icing sugar
- 50 g (1¾ oz) chocolate, grated
- 1 egg white
- 24 very large walnuts

Preparation time: 40 minutes
Makes 24

STUFFED FIGS

FIGUES FOURRÉES

Using a knife or kitchen scissors, cut the stalks off the figs. Carve a hole in the top of the fruit. In a bowl, beat together the butter, chocolate and almonds to make a paste. Spoon it into the corner of a plastic bag and snip off the tip to make a piping bag. Squeeze the almond paste into each fig through the hole in the top. Place a toasted hazelnut on top of each hole.

- 24 large, moist dried figs
- 80 g (2¾ oz) butter, softened
- 80 g (2¾ oz) chocolate, grated
- 80 g (2¾ oz) ground almonds
- 24 blanched hazelnuts, toasted

Preparation time: 35 minutes
Makes 24

STUFFED DATES

DATTES FARCIES

Grind the pistachios to a powder in a food processor or a blender, transfer to a bowl and stir in the icing sugar and egg white. Beat to make a stiff, smooth paste. Make a slit in one side of each date and remove the stones. Take small balls of the pistachio paste and shape them into cylinders a little smaller than the dates, then stuff the dates with them. Do not close the gap completely, so that the stuffing can be seen.

- 80 g (2¾ oz) shelled pistachios
- 80 g (2¾ oz) icing sugar
- ½ egg white
- 24 large dates

Preparation time: 35 minutes
Makes 24

STUFFED PRUNES

PRUNEAUX FOURRÉS

Select some of the smallest prunes and chop them together with the pistachios, almonds and hazelnuts to make a stuffing. Fill the cavity of the large prunes with this mixture. Close up the opening carefully. Put each prune in a paper case.

- 500 g (1 lb 2 oz) large Agen prunes, stoned
- 60 g (2 oz) pistachios
- 120 g (4 oz) mixed almonds and hazelnuts

Preparation time: 30 minutes
Serves 6

DRINKS

It is recommended that we drink 1.5 litres (2½ pints) of liquid every day, or sometimes more, depending on climate and diet. Water is the only essential liquid and by far the best for health. However, some of the water may be replaced by other drinks, especially those based on fruit or plants.

ALMOND MILK
LAIT D'AMANDE

Soak the almonds for 15 minutes in 1 litre (1¾ pints) warm water. Drain, reserving the water, then pound or purée the almonds with the sugar to form a paste. Add the reserved almond-soaking water a little at a time, stirring to dissolve. Flavour with orange-flower water. Strain through a muslin-lined sieve.

- **30 g (1¼ oz) blanched almonds**
- **1 tablespoon caster sugar**
- **1 tablespoon orange-flower water**

Preparation time: 20 minutes
Serves 6

BERRY SYRUP
SIROP DE FRUITS ROUGES

First, make the fruit juice. Press the chosen fruit through a muslin-lined sieve or chinois (conical sieve) set over a bowl to collect the juice. Chill the juice in the refrigerator for 1 day. Strain it through a muslin-lined sieve. Put the sugar in a large preserving pan and add the juice. Bring to the boil and skim with a large spoon, then remove from the heat. Allow to cool. Pour into sterilized bottles and seal them. To make an excellent drink, dilute 1 litre (1¾ pints) of this syrup with 4 or 5 litres (7–8½ pints) of cold water.

- **500 g (1 lb 2 oz) cherries, redcurrants or raspberries**
- **1 kg (2¼ lb) sugar**

Preparation time: 20 minutes, plus chilling time
Cooking time: 5 minutes
Serves 6

TEA SYRUP
SIROP DE THÉ

In a pan, heat 250 ml (8 fl oz) water to 40°C/105°F and add the tea. Leave to infuse for 3 hours, then add the syrup. Strain, pour into sterilized bottles and seal. To serve, dilute with water to taste for hot or cold drinks.

- **20 g (¾ oz) loose tea leaves**
- **750 ml (1¼ pints) sugar syrup (p.643)**

Preparation time: 5 minutes, plus infusing time
Makes 1 litre (1¾ pints)

p.865

3 large quinces
1 kg (2¼ lb) sugar

Preparation time: 20 minutes, plus chilling time
Cooking time: 45 minutes
Serves 6

QUINCE SYRUP
SIROP DE COING

Prepare 24 hours in advance. Peel, core and grate the quinces and place them in a pan with 750 ml (1¼ pints) water. Bring to the boil and boil for 40 minutes. Strain through a fine-meshed sieve. Chill in the refrigerator for 24 hours. Return to the pan, add the sugar and bring to the boil. Skim with a large spoon, then remove from the heat. Strain through a muslin-lined sieve. Cool. Pour into sterilized bottles and seal. To serve, dilute to taste with water.

NOTE
Pineapple syrup can be made in the same way, substituting 1 peeled and finely chopped pineapple for the quinces.

8 oranges
1 kg (2¼ lb) sugar lumps
Juice of ½ lemon
1 teaspoon citric acid

Preparation time: 15 minutes, plus chilling time
Cooking time: 2–3 minutes
Makes 500 ml (18 fl oz)

ORANGE SYRUP
SIROP D'ORANGE

Prepare 2 or 3 days in advance. Wash and dry the oranges. Rub the sugar lumps over the orange skins one by one, so that they turn orange. Squeeze the juice from the oranges and place them in a bowl with the sugar lumps, lemon juice and citric acid. Bring 500 ml (18 fl oz) water to the boil and pour over the orange and sugar mixture. Cover and chill in the refrigerator for 2 or 3 days, stirring occasionally. Strain through a muslin-lined sieve, pour into sterilized bottles and seal. Dilute the syrup with water to serve. It will keep for several months.

VARIATIONS

. . . .

MANDARIN SYRUP
SIROP DE MANDARINE

Proceed as above, replacing the oranges with 10 mandarins, and using 450 g (1 lb) sugar, 250 ml (8 fl oz) water and ½ teaspoon citric acid.

. . . .

LEMON SYRUP
SIROP DE CITRON

Proceed as above, replacing the oranges with lemons and using 500 g (1 lb 2 oz) sugar and 250 ml (8 fl oz) water.

COFFEE SYRUP

SIROP DE CAFÉ

Roughly chop the coffee beans. Bring 500 ml (18 fl oz) water to the boil and add the coffee beans. Leave to infuse for 3 hours. Place in a pan with the sugar and bring to the boil. Skim, remove from the heat and strain through muslin or a fine-meshed sieve. Pour into sterilized bottles and seal. To serve, dilute with water to taste for hot or cold drinks.

- 300 g (11 oz) roasted coffee beans
- 750 g (1 lb 10 oz) sugar

Preparation time: 5 minutes, plus infusing time
Makes 500 ml (18 fl oz)

VIOLET SYRUP

SIROP DE FLEURS DE VIOLETTE

Bring 500 ml (18 fl oz) water to a boil and pour it over the flowers. Leave to infuse in a sealed container for 24 hours. Add the syrup. Strain through muslin or a fine-meshed sieve. Pour into sterilized bottles and seal. To serve, dilute with water to taste.

- 300 g (11 oz) freshly picked unsprayed violets
- 500 ml (18 fl oz) light syrup (p.643)

Preparation time: 5 minutes, plus infusing time
Makes 500 ml (18 fl oz)

MARSHMALLOW SYRUP

SIROP DE GUIMAUVE

Wash, peel and slice the marshmallow roots. Bring 500 ml (18 fl oz) water to the boil in a pan and add the marshmallow roots. Leave to infuse for 24 hours. Strain and add the sugar. Bring to the boil again, skim and immediately remove from the heat. Strain and leave to cool. Pour into sterilized bottles and seal. To serve, dilute with water to taste.

- 75 g (2½ oz) marshmallow roots
- 1 kg (2¼ lb) sugar

Preparation time: 5 minutes, plus infusing time
Makes 500 ml (18 fl oz)

LEMONADE

CITRONNADE

Squeeze the lemons. Dissolve the sugar in 1.5 litres (2½ pints) boiling water, stirring briskly, then add the lemon juice. Chill and serve very cold. Orangeade can be made the same way, using 6 oranges and 150 g (5 oz) caster sugar. Alternatively, a combination of lemons and oranges can be made into a thirst-quenching drink, using 3 lemons, 4 oranges, 200 g (7 oz) sugar and 2 litres (3½ pints) water.

- 4 lemons
- 180 g (6¼ oz) caster sugar

Preparation time: 20 minutes, plus chilling time
Serves 6

LEMONADE WITH STRAWBERRIES

LIMONADE À LA FRAISE

 p.866

Wash the lemons and rub them with the sugar lumps until they turn yellow. Place the sugar lumps in a heatproof bowl. Squeeze the lemons and process their juice with the strawberries in a blender. Pour the strawberry juice over the sugar lumps. Bring 500 ml (18 fl oz) water to the boil and pour it over the fruit and sugar. Stir and set aside to cool. Strain through muslin or a fine-meshed sieve. Pour into sterilized bottles and seal.

- 2 lemons
- 125 g (4¼ oz) sugar lumps
- 350 g (12 oz) strawberries

Preparation time: 10 minutes, plus cooling time
Makes 600 ml (1 pint)

VARIATIONS

· ·

LEMONADE WITH RASPBERRIES OR BLACKBERRIES

LIMONADE À LA FRAMBOISE, À LA MÛRE

Proceed as above, using 1 lemon, 150 g (5 oz) sugar, 300 g (11 oz) raspberries or blackberries, and 250 ml (8 fl oz) water.

· ·

LEMONADE WITH REDCURRANTS

LIMONADE À LA GROSEILLE

Proceed as above, using 350 g (12 oz) redcurrants, and 750 ml (1¼ pints) water.

RASPBERRY VINEGAR

VINAIGRE DE FRAMBOISE

 p.867

Fill a jar with the raspberries and pour the vinegar over them. Seal the jar and leave to infuse for 40 days. Strain the juice through muslin or a fine-meshed sieve into a pan. Add the sugar to the liquid and bring to the boil. Boil for 5–6 minutes. Skim with a large spoon. Allow to cool. Pour into sterilized bottles and seal.

- 500 g (1 lb 2 oz) raspberries
- 500 ml (18 fl oz) white wine vinegar
- 750 g (1 lb 10 oz) sugar

Preparation time: 5 minutes, plus infusing time
Makes 500 ml (18 fl oz)

NOTE
Sour cherry, strawberry or blackberry vinegar can be made in the same way.

COUNTRY WINES

LINGONBERRY WINE

BOISSON AUX AIRELLES

Gather the berries when they are very fresh, wash them and crush them in an earthenware jar. Add 500 ml (18 fl oz) water. Leave to infuse for 36 hours. Strain through muslin or a fine-meshed sieve. Stir in the sugar and set aside to ferment for several days. Pour into sterilized bottles and seal.

VARIATIONS

· ·

BLACKBERRY WINE

BOISSON À LA MÛRE

Proceed as above, but replace the lingonberries with 300 g (11 oz) blackberries, 300 ml (½ pint) water, ½ teaspoon cream of tartar, and 75 g (2½ oz) sugar.

· ·

CORNELIAN CHERRY WINE

BOISSON À LA CORNOUILLE

Proceed as above, using 300 g (11 oz) cornelian or other wild cherries, and 60 g (2 oz) sugar.

· ·

ELDERBERRY WINE

BOISSON AU SUREAU

Proceed as above, using 300 g (11 oz) elderberries, and 600 ml (1 pint) water.

· ·

BARBERRY COUNTRY WINE

BOISSON À L'ÉPINE-VINETTE

Proceed as above, using 300 g (11 oz) barberries, and 600 ml (1 pint) water.

- **250 g (9 oz) lingonberries**
- **100 g (3½ oz) sugar**

Preparation time: 15 minutes, plus infusing and fermenting time
Makes 500 ml (18 fl oz)

ALCOHOLIC DRINKS

ASH LEAF BEER
BOISSON DE FEUILLES DE FRÊNE

- 30 g (1¼ oz) ash leaves, washed
- 20 g (¾ oz) hops, washed
- 125 g (4¼ oz) wild chicory, washed
- 4 kg (9 lb) sugar
- 80 g (2¾ oz) cream of tartar
- 50 g (1¾ oz) brewer's yeast

Preparation time: 15 minutes, plus fermenting time
Makes 100 litres (20 gallons)

Place the ash leaves, hops and wild chicory in a very large pan with 10 litres (18 pints) of water. Bring to the boil and simmer for 40 minutes. Place the sugar in a large clean bowl or other receptacle and strain the boiling liquid onto the sugar. Stir to dissolve. Add the cream of tartar when the sugar has fully dissolved. Mix the yeast in a small bowl of lukewarm water and set aside for 3–4 hours before adding to the sweetened liquid. Pour into a cask and top up with water to make 100 litres (20 gallons).

MEAD
HYDROMEL

- 5 kg (11 lb) honey
- 125 g (4¼ oz) brewer's yeast
- 1 litre (1¾ pints) white wine

Preparation time: 15 minutes, plus fermenting time
Makes 100 litres (20 gallons)

Mix the honey into 20 litres (4 gallons) warm water. Pour into a cask. Mix the brewer's yeast with 200 ml (7 fl oz) water and add to the cask. Leave to ferment for 8 days, pouring a glass of wine into the cask every day. When the fermentation slows, top the cask up to 100 litres (20 gallons) with water. Fit the bung. Leave for 40–50 days. Decant to draw the clear mead off the sediment. Leave for several months. Decant into sterilized bottles.

MULLED WINE
VIN CHAUD

- 600 ml (1 pint) red wine
- 125 g (4¼ oz) sugar
- 15 g (½ oz) cinnamon sticks
- 1 lemon, sliced

Preparation time: 5 minutes
Cooking time: 1 minute
Makes 900 ml (1½ pints)

Place the wine, 300 ml (½ pint) water, sugar and cinnamon in a pan and bring slowly to the boil. Simmer for 1 minute. Serve piping hot with slices of lemon.

JAM WINE

VIN DE CONFITURE

This is a pleasant recipe for using up the fruit pulp left over from making a jam or compote.

Pour the white wine over the fruit pulp. Leave to macerate in the refrigerator for 24 hours. Strain through a muslin-lined sieve. Add the brandy. Store in sterilized sealed bottles.

- **1 kg (2¼ lb) fruit pulp**
- **1 litre (1¾ pints) white wine**
- **100 ml (3½ fl oz) brandy**

Preparation time: 5 minutes, plus macerating time
Makes 1.25 litres (2 pints)

REDCURRANT WINE

VIN DE GROSEILLE

Bring the redcurrant pulp and a little water to the boil in a large pan. Add enough water to obtain 6 litres (10½ pints) of liquid, then add the vinegar, sugar and yeast mixed with a little warm water. Put everything in a large container (a keg if possible). Uncork the keg so that the liquid is in contact with the air for 4 days. Decant. Strain through a fine-meshed sieve, squeezing the juice from the pulp thoroughly, pour into sterilized bottles and seal. Lay the bottles down for 4 days before drinking.

- **2.5 kg (5½ lb) redcurrant pulp**
- **1 teaspoon vinegar**
- **180 g (6¼ oz) sugar**
- **6 g (1 teaspoon) fresh yeast**

Preparation time: 15 minutes, plus fermenting time
Makes 6 litres (10½ pints)

NOTE

Any leftover pulp from making redcurrant jam or jelly can be used for this recipe.

PUNCH

PUNCH

Put the sugar and tea in a pan and bring to the boil. Zest the lemon and place the zest in a punch bowl. Pour the hot tea onto the zest, juice the lemon and add it to the punch bowl. Heat the rum and pour over the tea very gently so that it stays on the surface. If desired, flambé the rum. To do this, ensure that the bowl is well away from anything flammable, and, standing well back, touch a lighted match to the bowl to ignite. Serve piping hot.

- **175 g (6 oz) sugar**
- **500 ml (18 fl oz) freshly brewed tea**
- **1 lemon**
- **300 ml (½ pint) rum**

Preparation time: 5 minutes
Cooking time: 10 minutes
Makes 800 ml (1½ pints)

GROG

GROG

Preparation time: 5 minutes
Serves 1

Pour 2 teaspoons of Cognac or rum into a glass. Fill with boiling water. Add 3 sugar lumps and 1 slice of lemon. Serve hot.

GREEN WALNUT LIQUEUR

BROU DE NOIX

- **20 kernels from young walnuts with no hard shell**
- **1 litre (1¾ pints) 40% brandy**
- **600 g (1 lb 5 oz) sugar**

Preparation time: 15 minutes, plus infusing time
Makes 1 litre (1¾ pints)

Cut the walnut kernels into thin strips. Pour the brandy over and leave to infuse for 60 days. Strain through a fine sieve. Add the sugar and stir to dissolve. Strain through filter paper. Pour into sterilized bottles and seal. Store for at least 3 months before using.

AMANDINE

AMANDINE

Crack the almonds. Put the shells in a bowl with the spirit and leave to infuse for 3 days. Strain, reserving the spirit and discarding the kernels. Bring 400 ml (14 fl oz) water to the boil and stir in the sugar until dissolved. Strain the two liquids separately. Combine them and pour into sterilized bottles. Seal and store for 5–6 weeks before drinking.

- 200 g (7 oz) almonds in their shells
- 300 ml (½ pint) 90% rectified (distilled) spirit
- 400 g (14 oz) sugar

Preparation time: 15 minutes, plus standing time
Makes 750 ml (1¼ pints)

LEMON BALM WATER

EAU DE MÉLISSE

Chop all the ingredients and put them in a bowl. Pour over the spirit and leave to macerate for 4 days. Strain, pour into sterilized bottles and seal.

- 25 g (1 oz) fresh lemon balm flowers
- 20 g (¾ oz) cinnamon sticks
- 1 lemon
- 40 g (1½ oz) cloves
- 10 g (¼ oz) coriander seeds
- 10 g (¼ oz) angelica root
- 1.25 litres (2 pints) 80% rectified (distilled) spirit

Preparation time: 15 minutes, plus macerating time
Makes 1.25 litres (2 pints)

CHERRY LIQUEUR

LIQUEUR DE CERISE

Stone the cherries. Weigh them and measure the same amount of sugar. Prepare a sugar syrup (p.643) using the same volume of water. When the syrup comes to the boil, carefully add the cherries and simmer for 25 minutes. Strain through a muslin-lined sieve, without pressing. Add the Kirsch, stir well and pour into sterilized bottles. Seal.

- 1.5 kg (3¼ lb) Morello cherries
- Sugar (see method)
- 300 ml (½ pint) Kirsch

Preparation time: 20 minutes
Makes about 1.5 litres (2½ pints)

CHOCOLATE LIQUEUR

CRÈME DE CACAO

- 20 g (¾ oz) cocoa beans
- 300 ml (½ pint) 90% rectified (distilled) spirit
- 350 g (12 oz) sugar

Preparation time: 5 minutes, plus macerating time
Cooking time: 15–20 minutes
Makes 600 ml (1 pint)

Toast the cocoa beans for 10–12 minutes in a frying pan, taking care not to burn them, as this will impair their flavour. Remove from the heat and let cool. Chop roughly. Pour the spirit over them and leave to macerate for 15 days. Strain through a muslin-lined sieve. In a pan, bring 300 ml (½ pint) water and the sugar to the boil and boil for 5–6 minutes. Add the cocoa-infused spirit. Strain through a muslin-lined sieve. Pour into sterilized bottles and seal.

VARIATION

COFFEE LIQUEUR

CRÈME DE CAFÉ

Proceed as above, macerating 50 g (1¾ oz) roasted dark coffee and 5 or 6 bitter almonds in the spirit. Make the sugar syrup with 500 g (1 lb 2 oz) sugar and 250 ml (8 fl oz) water.

BLACKCURRANT LIQUEUR

LIQUEUR DE CASSIS

- 1 kg (2¼ lb) blackcurrants
- 1 litre (1¾ pints) 40% rectified (distilled) spirit
- 375 g (13 oz) sugar

Preparation time: 10 minutes, plus macerating time
Makes 1.5 litres (2½ pints)

Wash the blackcurrants well. Place in a glass jar with a few blackcurrant leaves. Add the spirit to cover the fruit. Cover and leave to macerate for 2–3 months. Strain through a muslin-lined sieve, reserving both spirit and fruit. Make a light sugar syrup (p.643) with the sugar and 500 ml (18 fl oz) water. Add the blackcurrant-infused spirit. Strain through filter paper. Pour into sterilized bottles and seal. The reserved blackcurrants may be rolled in granulated sugar to taste and used as an accompaniment to ice cream and other desserts.

JUNIPER LIQUEUR

LIQUEUR DE GENIÈVRE

Wash the berries and put them in a bowl. Add the sliced lemon, pour the brandy over and leave to infuse for 3 days. Strain. Stir the sugar into 120 ml (4 fl oz) hot water until dissolved, and add to the flavoured brandy. Tie the anise seeds, vanilla and cinnamon in a piece of muslin and drop into the liquid. Leave to macerate for 1 month. Strain through filter paper. Pour into sterilized bottles and seal.

- 1 handful freshly picked green juniper berries
- 750 ml (1¼ pints) 40% brandy
- ½ lemon, sliced
- 300 g (11 oz) sugar
- 10 anise seeds
- 1 vanilla pod, chopped
- 10 g (¼ oz) cinnamon stick

Preparation time: 5 minutes, plus infusing and macerating time
Makes 900 ml (1½ pints)

HOT DRINKS

HOT CHOCOLATE WITH WATER

CHOCOLAT À L'EAU

In a small pan, melt the chocolate in 1 tablespoon of the water. When it has formed a smooth paste, add 175 ml (6 fl oz) water and the vanilla. Simmer over a low heat for 10–15 minutes. Whisk to a foam in a chocolate pot or by hand. Hot chocolate can also be made with milk.

- 25 g (1 oz) dark chocolate, chopped
- Vanilla extract, to taste

Preparation time: 2 minutes
Cooking time: 10–15 minutes
Serves 1

COCOA

CACAO

Mix the cocoa and sugar with 1 tablespoon cold water or milk to a smooth paste. In a small pan, bring the remaining water or milk to the boil and stir into the cocoa mixture, a little at a time, until smooth.

- 25 g (1 oz) cocoa
- 30 g (1¼ oz) caster sugar
- 200 ml (7 fl oz) water or milk

Preparation time: 2 minutes
Cooking time: 5 minutes
Serves 1

SPANISH HOT CHOCOLATE
CHOCOLAT ESPAGNOL

- ◆ **50 g (1¾ oz) chocolate**
- ◆ **½ teaspoon vanilla extract**
- ◆ **½ teaspoon ground cinnamon**

Preparation time: 2 minutes
Cooking time: 8–10 minutes
Serves 1

In a small pan, melt the chocolate in 1 tablespoon water. Add 175 ml (6 fl oz) water. Simmer over a very gentle heat for 8–10 minutes, stirring occasionally. Add the vanilla and cinnamon. Whisk to a foam.

TURKISH COFFEE
CAFÉ À LA TURQUE

- ◆ **Finely ground coffee**
- ◆ **Caster sugar**

Preparation time: 1 minute
Cooking time: 5 minutes

Put 1 teaspoon finely ground coffee per person in a small pan or a copper Turkish coffee pan. Add 1 teaspoon of caster sugar and 200 ml (7 fl oz) boiling water per person, a little at a time. Bring to the boil. When the coffee rises up, remove it from the heat. After 2 minutes, return to the heat and allow it to rise again. Remove. Pour in a teaspoon of cold water to settle the dregs. Serve immediately.

COFFEE ESSENCE
ESSENCE DE CAFÉ

- ◆ **200 g (7 oz) freshly roasted coffee beans**

Preparation time: 5 minutes, plus infusing time
Makes 250 ml (8 fl oz)

Grind the coffee beans. Bring 250 ml (8 fl oz) water to the boil in a pan and add half the ground coffee. Remove from the heat immediately, cover and leave to infuse until completely cold. Strain, then bring back to the boil. Fill a coffee filter or cafetière with the remaining ground coffee and prepare as if for ordinary coffee, but use the re-boiled coffee in place of fresh water. Pour into sterilized bottles and seal tightly.

MINT TEA
THÉ À LA MENTHE

- ◆ **Loose tea leaves, to taste**
- ◆ **Fresh or dried mint leaves, to taste**
- ◆ **Sugar, to taste**

Preparation time: 1 minute, plus infusing time

Pour boiling water into a teapot, leave for a few seconds and then pour it away. Add 1 teaspoon of tea leaves per person to the pot, plus a few leaves of fresh or dried mint, and sugar to taste. Pour on fresh boiling water and leave to infuse for 5 minutes before serving.

HERBAL TEAS

Many delicious drinks can be prepared by infusing plants in hot water. Some of them are believed to have therapeutic properties. There are three methods of preparation: maceration (steeping in cold water), infusion (covering with hot water and leaving to infuse) and decoction (boiling in water).

ANISEED
Pour boiling water over ½ teaspoon of anise seeds.

BARLEY
Pour boiling water over 1 teaspoon of husked barley.

BORAGE
Pour boiling water over a few borage flowers and leaves.

BURDOCK
Pour boiling water over ½ teaspoon burdock root which has been cut into tiny pieces.

CHAMOMILE
Pour boiling water over 3 heads or flowers.

CHERRY STALKS
Pour boiling water over 1 teaspoon of dried cherry stalks.

CHERVIL
Pour boiling water over a few chervil sprigs with leaves.

CHICORY
Pour boiling water over 1–1½ teaspoons of fresh or dried chicory leaves. Thought to stimulate the appetite.

ELDERFLOWER
Pour boiling water over ¼ teaspoon of dried flowers.

HOPS
Pour boiling water over 8–10 g (¼ oz) hop flowers.

HYSSOP
Pour boiling water over a few stems with leaves and flowers.

LEMON, QUINCE OR ORANGE
Pour boiling water over 2–3 slices of unpeeled lemon, orange or quince. This infusion is said to have astringent qualities.

LEMON VERBENA
Pour boiling water over a few stems with leaves and flowers. Lemon verbena infusion is delicious and is thought to be good for the digestion.

LICHEN
Bring 16 g (½ oz) lichen and 1 litre (1¾ pints) of water to the boil and cook for 7–8 minutes. This infusion is believed to prevent coughs.

LIME FLOWERS
Pour boiling water over a few sprigs of fresh or dried lime flowers with their bracts. Lime-flower infusions are believed to have a sedative effect.

LINSEED
Pour 1 tablespoon linseed into ½ glass of water and leave to macerate for 15–30 minutes. Consume the whole glassful. Thought to be beneficial for the digestive system.

LIQUORICE
Pour boiling water over 30 g (1¼ oz) fresh, chopped liquorice root or ½ teaspoon ground root. Liquorice is thought to aid the digestive system.

MINT
Pour boiling water over a few stems of mint with leaves and flowers. Fresh mint tea is delicious after a meal.

ORANGE FLOWERS
Pour boiling water over 3–4 flower buds.

POPPY OR VIOLET FLOWERS
Pour boiling water over a few fresh or dried petals. Along with orange flowers, they are thought to have a calming effect.

QUININE BARK
Chop 10 g (¼ oz) quinine bark roughly, add to 1 litre (1¾ pints) of water and leave to macerate for 2–3 hours.

RICE WATER
Bring 30–50 g (1¼–1¾ oz) rice and 1 litre (1¾ pints) of water to the boil. Boil for 15 minutes.

SARSAPARILLA
Place 50 g (1¾ oz) cut roots in hot water.

YELLOW GENTIAN
Pour boiling water over 1 teaspoon of chopped gentian root.

PRESERVES

Preserving is a very useful technique because it means that a wide variety of ingredients can be available all year round. It is also a good way for owners of a vegetable garden or orchard to make use of fruit and vegetable gluts. However, although home-made preserves often have more flavour than shop-bought ones, they should be prepared with care and bottles and jars should be thoroughly sterilized.

SALTING MEAT

Pork is the meat that is best suited to salting. Cut up the meat into pieces weighing 300–800 g (11 oz–1¾ lb). Rub them carefully with coarse salt. Line the bottom of the receptacle (such as a large earthenware or plastic container) with flavourings such as bay leaf, thyme, juniper or pepper, and put the pieces of meat on top in a single layer. Cover with coarse salt and press down. Make more layers until the container is full. Cover, put a weight on the lid and store in the refrigerator. The brine should rise to the surface after a few days. The meat can be eaten after three weeks.

CONFIT POULTRY, RABBIT & GAME

Pluck, draw and singe the poultry (p.430) and cut into even-sized pieces (keep the head, neck and carcass for another recipe). Place in a large container with coarse salt, pepper, bay leaf, thyme and cloves. Leave to marinate for 4 days in the refrigerator. Rinse the meat under cold water and wipe dry. Remove the fat which has collected in the container and melt it over a very low heat in a large heavy-based pan. Strain it, then replace on the heat. When it comes to the boil, carefully add the pieces of meat and cook for about 3 hours.

To check that it is cooked, insert a knife: the juices that flow out should be clear with no traces of pink. Drain, then put in sterilized jars and cover with 2–3 cm (¾–1 inch) cooking fat. Seal the jars, then sterilize for 1 hour. Wait at least one month before eating the confit meat, which, if properly sterilized, will keep unopened for 2 years. When ready to eat, reheat the pieces of meat in their fat.

VEGETABLES

Vegetables should be preserved as soon as they are picked, and should be ripe, tender, completely unblemished and of good quality. There are many types of preservation. Some vegetables can be dried, although they lose some of their flavour during this process.

PRESERVATION BY STORING & DRYING

CARROTS, BEETROOTS, TURNIPS & CELERIAC
These will keep for months in a cellar, buried under a layer of very dry fine sand.

POTATOES
When thoroughly dry, put in ventilated boxes raised on bricks above the ground. Stored in this way, the potatoes will keep all winter in a cool dark cellar. In spring, they start to sprout and are no longer good to eat. The sprouts should be carefully removed as often as possible.

CABBAGES, CAULIFLOWERS, CARDOONS & SALSIFY
Pull them up with their roots attached, and replant in a cellar leaning against each other in shallow trenches, separated by a narrow strip of earth.

ONIONS, GARLIC & SHALLOTS
Plait in strings and hang from the roof of a very dry place, such as a cellar or barn.

MUSHROOMS
Clean young fresh mushrooms and halve the large ones. Using a needle, thread onto thin string and dry in the sun, or even a very low oven, until completely dry. Store in tins. Morels and chanterelles can be dried very successfully. Soak them for 12 hours in warm water before cooking.

FRENCH BEANS
Choose tender beans and use a needle to thread them on a string. Blanch the strings of beans for 3–4 minutes in boiling salted water. Dry in the shade, then in a moderate oven for 6–8 hours.

PRESERVATION IN SALT

Salting is a very simple process, but the vegetables need to be thoroughly soaked before use.

FRENCH BEANS
Wash, drain, wipe dry and string tender beans. Put them in layers in an earthenware jar, putting coarse salt between each layer. Cover with a cloth, insert a lid that fits inside the jar and put a weight on top to press the beans down. Fill up with more beans 2 days later. Pour enough oil into the jar to completely cover the surface of the beans. Cover in the same way as a jar of jam. The salt should be washed off under running water before use. The beans should be cooked by putting in cold water, and bringing very slowly to the boil. Cook for a further 2 hours.

TOMATOES
Wipe and remove the stalks from the tomatoes. Place them in a jar. Boil some water with salt, allowing 80 g (2¾ oz) per litre (1¾ pints). Pour the cooled liquid over the tomatoes. Pour a little oil on the surface. Seal. Soak in cold water before use.

GREEN OLIVES
Gather very ripe olives. Wash, remove the stalks and prick each fruit with a pin. Put in a container, cover with wood ash and add enough water for the olives to float freely. When the olives have softened, wash them and put in a brine made with 10 g (¼ oz) salt to every 100 ml (3½ fl oz) water, flavoured with a bay leaf, pepper and fennel. Macerate for at least 10 days before eating. The brine should not be removed until about to serve.

PRESERVATION IN VINEGAR

GHERKINS & GREEN TOMATOES
These should be fairly small, unblemished and very fresh. Brush them, cut off the stalks and put in a bowl, well covered with coarse salt. After 24 hours, drain and put in an earthenware jar. Boil some good vinegar for 5 minutes, then pour over the vegetables, covering them completely. Macerate for a further 24 hours. Remove, drain off the vinegar into a pan and boil it again. Put the gherkins or tomatoes in a jar, with tarragon, small onions, chervil, peppercorns, hot peppers and green tomatoes. Pour the boiled cooled vinegar over the vegetables. Seal. Macerate for 2 months before eating.

PICKLED ONIONS

Choose very small onions and peel them. Put them in a jar and cover with good 8% spirit vinegar that has been boiled for 5 minutes with salt, peppercorns and tarragon. Seal and macerate for 2 months.

MUSTARD PICKLE

Clean, trim and wash the vegetables carefully (choosing from the list below) and cut into small pieces. Drain them well, put them in an earthenware jar and pour boiling vinegar over them. Macerate for 24 hours. Remove, drain off the vinegar into a pan and boil it again. Put the vegetables back in the washed jar and pour over the vinegar. Add capers, chopped tarragon and chervil, peppercorns, ground ginger, cloves, garlic and mustard. If the jar is not full, fill it with a little cold vinegar. Macerate for 15 days before serving these pickles as a condiment with cold meat.

- Spring cauliflowers
- Thin French beans
- Small onions
- Gherkins
- Hot peppers
- Small green tomatoes
- New carrots
- Garlic

PRESERVATION IN OIL

BLACK OLIVES

Choose very ripe olives and prick each one with a pin. Macerate for 15 days in a brine made with 10 g (¼ oz) salt to every 100 ml (3½ fl oz) water. Wash. Drain. Wipe dry. Put in jars and cover with good olive oil.

PRESERVATION BY STERILIZATION

To preserve food in sterilized jars, the same method should always be followed. Choose young, unblemished, very fresh vegetables. Peel and wash them. Sort according to size. Blanch for a few minutes in boiling salted water in a covered pan. Plunge into cold water to keep them firm. Pack into jars and cover with boiled and cooled salted water, allowing 30 g (1¼ oz) salt per litre (1¾ pints). Seal and sterilize according to the jar manufacturer's instructions. To use vegetables preserved in tins or jars, drain off the water in which the vegetables are pre-served (keep it for soup). Re-heat the vegetables and use in any recipe. Preserved vegetables are already cooked – they just need reheating for a few minutes before serving.

FRENCH BEANS
Wash, sort and de-string the beans. Blanch for 6–7 minutes. Plunge into cold water. Drain. Fill the jar. Pour in the brine until it reaches 2 cm (¾ inch) short of the edge. Sterilize for 2 hours.

PEAS
Shell, wash and sort. If the peas are very small, there is no need to blanch them. Pack into a jar, top up with brine and add 1 teaspoon of sugar per litre (1¾ pints). Seal and sterilize for 2 hours. For larger peas, blanch for 5 minutes. Plunge in cold water to stop the cooking, then continue as for smaller peas. Sterilize for 2 hours.

ARTICHOKE HEARTS
Snip the tips off the leaves with scissors and wash them. Cook for 30 minutes in salted water. Plunge in cold water. Remove the leaves and the hairy choke, working under acidulated water to prevent them discolouring. Ensure that any remaining stalk is removed. Put in jars. Fill with brine to within 2 cm (¾ inch) of the top. Seal and sterilize for 1½ hours.

TOMATO COULIS
Wash, de-stalk, and cut the tomatoes into pieces. Put in a pan with onion, garlic, thyme, bay leaf, parsley, salt and pepper. Cook over a gentle heat for 40 minutes, stirring. Sieve very thoroughly. Reduce the coulis for 5–6 minutes over a high heat, stirring. Fill small bottles, seal and sterilize for 45 minutes.

MIXED VEGETABLES

Peel, wash, and dice an assortment of vegetables. Blanch the vegetables according to type, the hardest (beans, carrots, turnips) for 10 minutes, the tender ones (asparagus tips, peas) for 5 minutes only. Plunge into cold water, then drain. Pack into the jars, add brine to cover, seal and sterilize for 1½ hours.

ASPARAGUS

Sort carefully, cut into equal lengths, trim and wash. Blanch by covering the stalks in the boiling water for 6 minutes, then the tips for 1 minute. Plunge in cold water. Arrange upright in bottles. Add brine to cover, seal and sterilize for 1½ hours.

HERBS

THYME

Pick the thyme in hot, dry weather. Remove the leaves over paper to catch any that fall. Put the leaves in a tin with a tightly fitting lid. To use, do not add the leaves directly to sauces, but put a pinch in a muslin bag and put this into the pan.

PARSLEY

Pick the parsley in hot, dry weather, and leave the stems long. Dry in the shade in a well ventilated place, then store in well-sealed brown paper bags. Before use, soak for 15–20 minutes in warm water. Chervil can be dried in the same way, although it loses much of its flavour.

BAY LEAVES

Pick long branches with lots of leaves, tie in a bunch and leave to dry in the shade. Store in brown paper or cloth bags.

TARRAGON

Blanch the leaves for 2 minutes in boiling salted water, then drain. Rinse in cold water. Put the leaves into small bottles. Fill the bottles with a brine made with 5 g (⅛ oz) salt. Seal and sterilize for 5 minutes.

FRESH FRUIT

NATURAL PRESERVATION

Some fruits can stay fresh for weeks or months, thus extending pleasant autumn desserts into the heart of winter. They must be completely unblemished, slightly under-ripe, and of the correct variety. They should be prepared for preservation as soon as possible after gathering. Ideally, fruit should be stored on wooden racks in a cool, dark, dry and well ventilated place. The fruit should be inspected often and turned. Any fruit that is spoiling should be removed immediately.

APPLES, PEARS & QUINCES
These are easy to store and need no special treatment.

GRAPES & NUTS
Grapes will keep on racks, but the fruit will wither. Although the flavour remains excellent, they have an unpleasant appearance. To make them look fresh again, soak the whole bunch for 30 minutes in a bowl of lukewarm water. Grapes will also retain a very attractive appearance if the bunches are picked with long stalks, and rehydrated by immersing in bowls of water and kept topped up. Almonds, walnuts and hazelnuts should be shelled and dried in the sun, without any other treatment apart from keeping them dry. To restore a fresh appearance, soak for 24 hours in water.

MEDLARS
These should be picked at the first frost and stored on wooden racks or on straw, where they will continue to ripen.

APPLES TO TASTE LIKE PINEAPPLE
This is an old way of storing apples and giving them a very marked flavour of pineapple. Choose unblemished eating apples. Wipe them. Line the bottom of a white wooden box with elderflowers dried in the shade. Put in a layer of apples, making sure they do not touch, then a thick layer of flowers and so on until the box is full. Close the box and stick strips of paper over any gaps to stop air penetrating. After 1 to 2 months, the fruit will have acquired a very strong taste of pineapple.

PRESERVATION BY DRYING

Many fruits cannot be stored fresh and must lose most of their water if they are to keep for a long time. This drying can be done in the sun, in regions where the sun is strong and can be relied upon. Otherwise, dry them in a warm oven.

FIGS

This Mediterranean fruit is dried in the sun, on reed racks which are brought in each night to protect them from the dew. The figs are turned frequently so that they become wrinkled and dry out. After 7–8 days, or more, they are flattened and stored in white wooden boxes.

APRICOTS & PEACHES

Once cut in half and stoned, these fruits are treated in the same way as figs, in the sun, or like plums, in the oven.

PLUMS

Once dried, plums are called prunes. Whole, very ripe fruit is left in the strong sun, then placed in a cool oven (35°C/95°F) overnight. They are taken out of the oven and left to cool the following day, then put back in a hotter oven (60°C/140°F) for the following night. They are left to cool for one more day and finally put in a hot oven (90°C/195°F) for 1 hour, with the door open. Sliced apples and pears can be dried in the same way.

PRESERVATION IN ALCOHOL

CHERRIES, PLUMS, APRICOTS, PEACHES & PEARS

Blanch the fruit in boiling water, allowing 1 minute for cherries and plums, 2 minutes for apricots, and 5 minutes for peeled pears. Prick the fruits through to the centre with a pin. Arrange in a glass jar, sprinkling each layer of fruit with granulated sugar. The proportion of sugar is 250 g (9 oz) per 1 kg (2¼ lb) of prepared fruit. Fill the jar with 40% brandy. Seal the jar. Macerate for at least 7–8 weeks before eating.

PRESERVATION IN VINEGAR

CHERRIES, PEARS & PRUNES

Pack the washed and drained whole fruit into an earthenware jar. Simmer some white wine vinegar for 5 minutes and pour it over the fruit. Leave to macerate for 24 hours. Drain the vinegar into a pan, return the fruit to the jar. Bring the vinegar to the boil and pour it over the fruit. Add tarragon, white pepper and a little salt. Cool, then seal the jars. Leave to macerate for at least 15–18 days before serving as a condiment with cold meats.

BOTTLING

Fruit can be bottled with or without liquid in glass preserving jars with a lid and rubber seal (or gasket) held in place by a metal spring clip. To bottle without liquid, place washed, dried or peeled fruit, with or without stones, in the jars. Fill them three-quarters full. Cover, placing the rubber seal between the jar and the lid. Secure the lid with the spring clip, which should be very tight. Follow the jar manufacturer's sterilizing instructions. The fruit should be sterilized for the following amounts of time:

* Strawberries & raspberries: 15 minutes
* Redcurrants: 20 minutes
* Cherries: 30 minutes
* Plums & mirabelle plums: 30–40 minutes
* Apricots: 40 minutes
* Peaches: 40 minutes
* Pears: 30–40 minutes

BOTTLING IN SYRUP

Follow the same procedure as for fruit bottled without liquid. Before closing the jar, pour over a sugar syrup (see below), which has been boiled for 2 minutes, strained and cooled.

STRAWBERRIES

Place the hulled fruit in glass preserving jars, filling them three-quarters full. Make a syrup (p.643) with 600 g (1 lb 5 oz) sugar per litre (1¾ pints) of water. Boil for 2 minutes, then cover the fruit. Place the rubber seal between the jar and the lid. Secure the lid with the spring clip, which should be very tight. Sterilize for 20 minutes.

CHERRIES

Proceed as for strawberries. Make the syrup with 800 g (1¾ lb) sugar per litre (1¾ pints) of water. Sterilize for 25 minutes.

RASPBERRIES

Proceed as for strawberries. Make the syrup with 600 g (1 lb 5 oz) sugar per litre (1¾ pints) of water. Sterilize for 20 minutes.

REDCURRANTS

Proceed as for strawberries. Make the syrup with 800 g (1¾ lb) sugar per litre (1¾ pints) of water. Sterilize for 20 minutes.

APRICOTS

Scald the fruit by pouring boiling water over it, then peel, cut in half and remove the stones. Continue as for strawberries, making the syrup with 350 g (12 oz) sugar per litre (1¾ pints) of water. Sterilize for 30 minutes.

PEACHES

Scald the fruit by pouring boiling water over it, then peel, cut in half and remove the stones. Continue as for strawberries, making the syrup with 500 g (1 lb 2 oz) sugar per litre (1¾ pints) of water. Sterilize for 30 minutes.

PLUMS

Do not remove the stones. Prick each fruit with a needle. Blanch in boiling water. Plunge into cold water. Continue as for strawberries, making the syrup with 500 g (1 lb 2 oz) sugar per litre (1¾ pints) of water. Sterilize for 30 minutes.

RED PLUMS

Cut open the fruits. Remove the stones. Continue as for strawberries, making the syrup with 400 g (14 oz) sugar per litre (1¾ pints) of water. Sterilize for 45 minutes.

PEARS

Peel and blanch for 30 seconds in boiling water. Plunge in cold water for 1 minute. Drain. Continue as for strawberries, making the syrup with 350 g (12 oz) sugar per litre (1¾ pints) of water. Sterilize for 40 minutes.

ORANGES

Soak the fruit in cold water for 24 hours. Bring to the boil in fresh water and cook for 5 minutes. Rinse in cold water. Soak for 24 hours in cold water, then drain. Make the syrup with 1.5 kg (3¼ lb) of sugar per 1 litre (1¾ pints) of water, and cook to the firm-ball stage (p.643). Cut the oranges into slices and remove the pips. Fill the jars with the syrup. Sterilize for 50 minutes.

JAMS

Jams are preserves based on fruit and sugar cooked together. The sugar acts as an anti-bacterial, while cooking boils off some of the water. The fruit and sugar mixture achieves a concentration that stops the fruit fermenting and prevents the sugar from crystallizing. Using unblemished, fully ripe fruit, many types of delicious and original jams can be made. However, the method should be carefully followed. Fruit may be treated in three different ways: as a jam, in which the fruit is preserved whole or cut in segments; as a compote or marmalade, in which the fruit gradually falls apart during cooking; or as a jelly, in which only the fruit juice is used.

MAKING JAM

SUGAR
Do not use brown sugar, as this changes the flavour and colour of the jam and may cause it to ferment. Choose caster sugar, or preserving sugar with added pectin for fruit without enough pectin of its own to set properly.

COOKING
Make jam in a large heavy-based pan or preserving pan with a thick base (copper if possible) to ensure that the heat is evenly distributed. The jam must be cooked quickly and skimmed so that it remains translucent. Check whether the jam has set by dropping a spoonful onto a cold plate. It must just set as it cools. Boiling jam is dangerously hot and can boil over quickly, so use a large pan and do not fill it more than one-third full.

POTTING
Pour the jam into pots that have previously been washed, scalded and left to dry in their own heat. Jars can also be sterilized in a moderate oven. Fill the jars carefully, preferably using a jam funnel to ensure the rims remain clean.

COVERING
Wait until the jam is cold. Pour 1 cm (½ inch) of melted edible wax over the jam and cover with a piece of cellophane moistened on the outside, and held in place with a rubber band. It is easier to use pots with screw-on lids: fill the pots, put on the lids, then immediately turn them upside-down until completely cold.

APRICOT JAM

CONFITURE D'ABRICOTS

Preparation time: 20 minutes
Cooking time: 45 minutes

Cut the apricots in half lengthways and remove the kernels. Weigh the raw fruit. Prepare a sugar syrup using the same weight of sugar as fruit and add the appropriate amount of water (p.643). When the syrup reaches the feather stage, add the fruit. Remove the fruit as soon as it comes to the boil, drain and boil the syrup until it reaches the feather stage again. Return the apricots to the pan. Bring to the boil, and add a few kernels. Remove from the heat and put into sterilized jars.

NOTE
The above recipe also works for cherry jam, strawberry jam, mirabelle plum jam and greengage jam.

DRIED APRICOT & PUMPKIN JAM

CONFITURE D'ABRICOTS SECS ET DE POTIRON

 p.868

- **1 kg (2¼ lb) dried apricots**
- **3 kg (6½ lb) pumpkin, peeled and chopped**
- **3 kg (6½ lb) caster sugar**

Preparation time: 1 hour, plus soaking time
Cooking time: 1½ hours

Prepare the day before. Wash the apricots and cut into strips. Soak in 2 litres (3½ pints) water for 24 hours. Drain, reserving the water. Place the reserved soaking water in a large pan and bring to the boil. Boil the pumpkin in the soaking water for 30 minutes. Sieve to make a smooth paste, then return to the pan with the sugar and cook the pumpkin purée over low heat, stirring, for 30 minutes. Add the soaked apricots and cook for a further 30 minutes. Pour into sterilized jars.

CHESTNUT JAM

CONFITURE DE CHÂTAIGNES OU DE MARRONS

Preparation time: 1 hour
Cooking time: 1 hour

Remove the outer shell from the chestnuts (p.558) and cook in boiling water for 30 minutes. Peel the chestnuts while hot and immediately pound or process them to a purée using a mortar and pestle or a food processor. Using an equal weight of sugar to that of the chestnut purée, prepare a syrup to the feather stage (p.643). Carefully stir the syrup and purée together to make a smooth paste and cook gently for 30 minutes, stirring regularly. Pour into sterilized jars.

FIG JAM

CONFITURE DE FIGUES

Peel the figs and weigh them. Using an equal weight of sugar, make a syrup, cooking it to the soft-ball stage (p.643). Carefully add the fruit to the syrup along with the juice of 1 lemon and 1 split vanilla pod per 1 kg (2¼ lb) of fruit. Cook for 5 minutes. Remove the figs and drain them, reserving the liquid. Boil the syrup in the pan, adding any syrup drained from the figs, over a high heat for 10 minutes. Return the figs to the pan for the last time and cook gently for a further 30 minutes. Cool before pouring into sterilized jars.

Preparation time: 20 minutes, plus cooling time
Cooking time: 45 minutes

ORANGE JAM

CONFITURE D'ORANGES

Prepare the day before. Cut 10 of the oranges into thin slices. Squeeze the juice from the remaining 2 oranges. Put the orange slices in a preserving pan with 2 litres (3½ pints) water, lemon and orange juice and macerate for 24 hours. Add the sugar. Bring gently to the boil and simmer for 2 hours. Skim. Pour into sterilized jars.

- **12 oranges, washed**
- **Juice of 2 lemons**
- **3 kg (6½ lb) caster sugar**

Preparation time: 15 minutes, plus macerating time
Cooking time: 2 hours

APPLE JAM

CONFITURE DE POMMES

Peel the apples. Cut into small slices and cover with water. Cook them until tender, drain and then weigh the fruit. Using an equal weight of sugar, prepare a sugar syrup to the feather stage (p.643). Return the apples to the pan along with the grated zest of 1 lemon per 1 kg (2¼ lb) of apples and cook gently over a low heat for 1 hour, stirring from time to time. Pour into sterilized jars.

Preparation time: 20 minutes
Cooking time: 1 hour

FOUR-FRUIT JAM

CONFITURE DE QUATRE FRUITS

- 500 g (1 lb 2 oz) sour cherries
- 500 g (1 lb 2 oz) strawberries
- 500 g (1 lb 2 oz) raspberries
- 500 g (1 lb 2 oz) redcurrants
- 3 kg (6½ lb) caster sugar

Preparation time: 30 minutes
Cooking time: 40 minutes

Stone the cherries and hull the remaining fruit. Make a syrup with the sugar, cooking it to the firm-ball stage (p.643). Carefully add the cherries to the boiling syrup and cook for 15 minutes. Add the strawberries, cooking for a further 15 minutes. Finally, add the redcurrants and raspberries and cook for a further 10 minutes. Skim and pour into sterilized jars.

GRAPE JAM

CONFITURE DE RAISINS

Preparation time: 15 minutes
Cooking time: 10 minutes

Remove the grapes from the stalks without damaging them. Remove the pips by swiftly pulling out the stalks (or use seedless grapes). Using an equal weight of sugar to fruit, make a syrup, cooking it to the firm-ball stage (p.643). Carefully add the grapes to the boiling syrup and boil for 10 minutes. Skim and pour into sterilized pots.

MARMALADES

APRICOT MARMALADE

MARMELADE D'ABRICOTS

Preparation time: 20 minutes,
plus macerating time
Cooking time: 20 minutes

Prepare the day before. Split the apricots in half lengthways and remove the stones. Reserve a few of the stones. Put the fruit in a preserving pan with the same weight of sugar. Macerate for 12 hours. Bring to the boil and cook for 20 minutes, along with the kernels from the reserved stones. Skim and pour into sterilized pots.

NOTE
For other flavours, proceed as above, using strawberries, redcurrants, mirabelle or red plums, blackberries or greengages.

CHERRY MARMALADE

MARMELADE DE CERISES

Prepare the day before. Choose Morello or other sour cherries. Remove the stones. Put the fruit in a bowl with three-quarters of their weight in sugar. Leave to macerate for 12 hours. Place in a pan, bring to the boil and cook for 20 minutes. Remove all the fruit with a slotted spoon and use to half-fill sterilized jars. Continue simmering the juice left in the pan over a low heat for 1 hour to reduce. Top up the pots with the juice.

Preparation time: 30 minutes, plus macerating time
Cooking time: 1 hour 20 minutes

CARROT MARMALADE

MARMELADE DE CAROTTES

- **500 g (1 lb 2 oz) carrots**
- **500 g (1 lb 2 oz) sugar**
- **Zest and juice of 4 lemons**

Preparation time: 20 minutes
Cooking time: 4 hours

Peel the carrots and cut them into thin slices. Layer them in a preserving pan with the sugar and the lemon zest. Pour over the lemon juice and add enough water just to cover. Cook over very gentle heat for 4 hours. Transfer to sterilized jars.

MELON MARMALADE

MARMELADE DE MELON

- **2 melons**
- **800 g (1¾ lb) sugar per 1 kg (2¼ lb) pulp**
- **Zest and juice of 2 lemons**

Preparation time: 30 minutes, plus macerating time
Cooking time: 4 hours

 p.869

Prepare the day before. Cut the melons in half, remove the seeds and peel them. Cut the flesh into 2-cm (¾-inch) cubes, weigh them, and place in a preserving pan with the lemon zest and juice. Cover with 800 g (1¾ lb) of sugar per 1 kg (2¼ lb) of melon. Leave to macerate for 12 hours. Set the pan over a very gentle heat and cook until the syrup thickens and turns the colour of amber. Transfer to sterilized jars.

RED TOMATO JAM

CONFITURE DE TOMATES ROUGES

Preparation time: 30 minutes
Cooking time: 3 hours

Cut the tomatoes into pieces. Force the pulp through a sieve, or process in a blender and then sieve. Weigh the pulp. Put the tomato pulp in a preserving pan with sugar, allowing 300 g (11 oz) sugar per 500 g (1 lb 2 oz) tomatoes. Set over a gentle heat and cook for 2 hours. Flavour with 100 ml (3½ fl oz) rum per 500 g (1 lb 2 oz) of tomatoes and cook for a further hour. Transfer to sterilized jars.

GREEN TOMATO JAM

CONFITURE DE TOMATES VERTES

Preparation time: 30 minutes, plus macerating time
Cooking time: 2½ hours

Prepare the day before. Weigh the tomatoes and cut them into thin slices. Put alternating layers of tomatoes and sugar in a bowl, allowing 300 g (11 oz) of sugar per 500 g (1 lb 2 oz) of tomatoes. Leave to macerate for 24 hours. Put everything in a preserving pan with the juice and chopped zest of 1 lemon per 500 g (1 lb 2 oz) of fruit. Cook gently for 2½ hours. Transfer to sterilized jars.

PUMPKIN JAM

CONFITURE DE POTIRON

Prepare the day before. Cut the pumpkin and lemons into small dice. Put in a bowl with the sugar and leave to macerate for 24 hours. The next day, transfer to a pan and cook gently for 1 hour, stirring regularly. Transfer to sterilized jars.

- 1 kg (2¼ lb) pumpkin, peeled and seeded
- 2 lemons
- 500 g (1 lb 2 oz) caster sugar

Preparation time: 20 minutes, plus macerating time
Cooking time: 1 hour

JELLIES

Jellies are traditionally made with fruit that is high in pectin, as it is the pectin that makes them set as they cool. High-pectin fruits include quinces, apples, redcurrants, blackcurrants and blackberries. It is now possible to make jellies with most fruits, by using preserving sugar, which contains added pectin.

BLACKCURRANT JELLY

GELÉE DE CASSIS

Weigh the blackcurrants and place them in a preserving pan with 120 ml (4 fl oz) water per 500 g (1 lb 2 oz) of fruit. Heat until the fruit bursts, then transfer the mixture to a sieve lined with muslin and set over a bowl to collect the juice. (Do not press it through, otherwise the jelly will not be clear.) Weigh the juice and add the same weight of sugar. Bring slowly to the boil and simmer for 25 minutes. Skim and put in sterilized jars. Blackberry jelly can be made in the same way.

Preparation time: 15 minutes, plus hanging time
Cooking time: 30 minutes

GRAPE JELLY

GELÉE DE RAISIN

Preparation time: 15 minutes,
plus hanging time
Cooking time: 25–30 minutes

Wash and remove the grapes from the stalks. Put the grapes in a preserving pan, with no water, and cook over low heat until tender, then burst the fruit with a pestle or potato masher. Strain through a muslin-lined sieve and collect the juice. Weigh the juice. Weigh out half its weight in preserving sugar. Place the sugar in the preserving pan, then add the juice. Bring to the boil and cook for 25–30 minutes. Stir and skim off any scum. Put in sterilized jars. Leave to set in the refrigerator and cover.

QUINCE JELLY

GELÉE DE COING

Preparation time: 15 minutes
Cooking time: 1 hour

Cut the quinces into quarters, remove the cores and pips and put them in a muslin bag. In a preserving pan, cover the quinces with cold water. Add the muslin bag. Cook gently until the quinces have softened (about 40 minutes). Place in a sieve and collect the juice that drains from it. Weigh the quince juice and add the same weight of sugar. Bring slowly to the boil and then boil for 10 minutes. Skim and put in sterilized jars.

NOTE
Apple jelly can be made in the same way, and can be flavoured with the juice of 1 lemon or 1 orange per 1 kg (2¼ lb) of apples.

REDCURRANT JELLY

GELÉE DE GROSEILLE

METHOD 1

Follow the method for blackcurrant jelly (p.858). Redcurrants and whitecurrants may be combined.

Preparation time: 15 minutes, plus hanging time
Cooking time: 15–30 minutes

METHOD 2

Strip the currants from their stalks and put them in a preserving pan with 120 ml (4 fl oz) of water per 500 g (1 lb 2 oz) fruit. Heat the currants until they burst and cook for about 8 minutes, stirring constantly. Put the fruit into a sieve lined with muslin and collect the juice in a bowl. (Do not press it, otherwise the jelly will not be clear.) Weigh the juice and add the same weight of sugar. Put over a gentle heat, stirring constantly, to ensure that the heat is evenly distributed. As soon as it comes to the boil (small waves will move from the centre to the edges), stop stirring. Skim and cook for 3 minutes more. This is the time needed for the pectin in the redcurrants to combine with the sugar and set quickly as a jelly. If you cook it for too long by accident, continue cooking it for about another 30 minutes, but this will cause it to lose some of its flavour.

METHOD 3

Put the currants, a few at a time, in a preserving pan, stirring with a slotted spoon. Heat, without water, until they burst, then place in a fine-meshed sieve. Drain over a bowl for 2 hours, without pressing. Add 1.05 kg (2 lb 5 oz) caster sugar per 1 kg (2¼ lb) of fruit juice. Allow to dissolve, stirring frequently. When the sugar has completely dissolved, put immediately in sterilized jars and leave the jelly to set in the refrigerator.

UNUSUAL JAMS

ROSE HIP JAM
CONFITURE DE BAIES D'ÉGLANTIER

Preparation time: 15 minutes
Cooking time: 45 minutes

Only use rose hips that are fully ripe (usually around mid October or after the first frosts). Split the rose hips lengthways and remove the hairs that are inside. Put them in a preserving pan, and cover with water. Bring to the boil and simmer. When they are tender, drain and reserve the cooking liquid. Process the rose hips in a blender to make a purée. Weigh the purée, and add the same weight of cooking juices. Add the weight of the fruit and cooking juices combined in sugar. Bring to the boil. Boil for 15–20 minutes, then pour into sterilized jars.

MEDLAR JELLY
GELÉE DE NÈFLE

Preparation time: 5 minutes
Cooking time: 30–45 minutes

Wash the medlars. Put them, unpeeled, into a preserving pan and cover with cold water. Bring to the boil and cook without stirring. Scrape out the contents of the preserving pan into a sieve placed over a bowl. Allow to drain well. Put the juice in a bowl and weigh it, then add an equal weight of sugar. Pour into a preserving pan and boil for 30–45 minutes, skimming to remove any scum. Transfer to sterilized jars when the syrup has reached setting point.

ELDERBERRY JELLY
GELÉE DE SUREAU

Preparation time: 15 minutes
Cooking time: 45 minutes

Put bunches of rinsed elderberries in a preserving pan. Cover with cold water. Heat very gently until it comes to the boil: this should take at least 30 minutes. When the berries are cooked, extract the juice, either in a blender, or pressing through a sieve set over a bowl. Weigh the juice. Add 1 kg (2¼ lb) of sugar per litre (1¾ pints) of juice. Cook the juice and sugar over a moderate heat for at least 45 minutes, until the juice has reached setting point. Put in sterilized jars.

Toffees (p.822)

Chocolate truffles (p.822)

Quince jellies   (p.823)

Quince syrup   (p.827)

Lemonade with strawberries (p.830)

Raspberry vinegar (p.830)

Dried apricot & pumpkin jam   (p.853)

Red tomato jam (p.857)

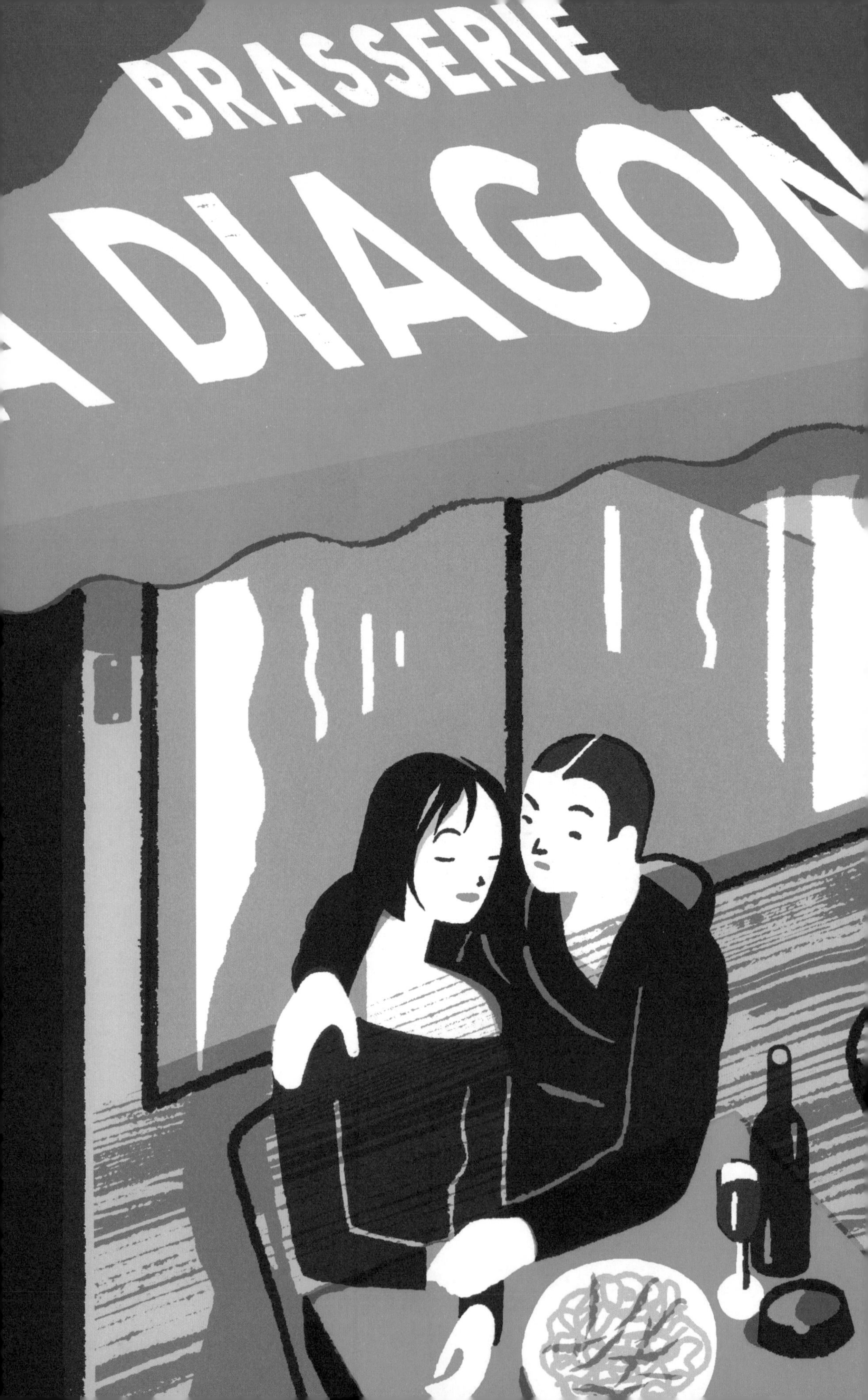
BRASSERIE
A DIAGON

MENUS BY CELEBRATED CHEFS

The following pages contain menus from some of the world's best chefs cooking French bistro-style food. As these chefs show, traditional French dishes do not have to involve the rarefied complexity of haute cuisine. Authentic French cooking is delicious, flavoursome and can be the ultimate in comfort food. It seeks to bring the best out of humble ingredients through care and attention, and it is no wonder that traditional French cooking is growing hugely in popularity around the world.

I KNOW HOW TO COOK GUEST CHEFS

PASCAL AUSSIGNAC, LONDON, UK
- Stuffed baby squid, black escabèche
- Terrine of foie gras & fennel
- Roast rib of veal, Savora mash & olivade

GUILLAUME BRAHIMI, SYDNEY, AUSTRALIA
- Seared scallops with cauliflower purée, shiitake mushrooms & veal jus
- Steak frites with bordelaise sauce
- Poires Belle-Hélène with vanilla ice cream

THIERRY BRETON, PARIS, FRANCE
- Red mullet fillets with black radish rémoulade
- Coucou de Rennes with morels & vin jaune
- Paris-Brest

DANIEL BOULUD, NEW YORK, NY, USA
- Grilled Moroccan spiced tuna with carrots & mint oil
- Boeuf en gelée with foie gras, root vegetables & horseradish cream
- Tomato tart tatin

ANTHONY DEMETRE, LONDON, UK
- Pigs' cheek, ear & trotter salad with crisp barley
- Slow-cooked breast of lamb, sweetbreads & golden sultanas
- Roast yellow-fleshed peaches with lemon thyme & vanilla

HENRY HARRIS, LONDON, UK
- Crab Florentine
- Poached leg of mutton with caper cream sauce
- Colonel

RIAD NASR & LEE HANSON, NEW YORK, NY, USA
- Onion soup
- Salad Niçoise
- Crêpes suzette

FRANÇOIS PAYARD, NEW YORK, NY, USA
- Gougères
- Bouillabaisse
- Lemon tart

DAVID & MEREDITH POIRIER, SYDNEY, AUSTRALIA
- Poached oysters with ham hock & kipfler potatoes
- Pork tenderloin with celeriac crème & Puy lentils
- Rhubarb crème brûlée

FRANCK RAYMOND, LONDON, UK
- Scallops cooked in their shells with hazelnut butter
- Baked sea bass with tomato confit & black olives
- Pan-fried calves' liver with fresh herbs & vinegar
- Roast peaches with basil & lemon

PIERRE SCHAEDELIN, NEW YORK, NY, USA
- Pigs' cheeks, frisée & lentil salad, mustard
  & cumin vinaigrette
- Skate wing meunière, broccoli rabe, lemon, capers,
  brown butter
- Tarte tatin with crème fraîche

STEPHANE SCHERMULY, PARIS, FRANCE
- Tartare of sea bream & mixed green salad with
  wholegrain mustard sauce
- Shoulder of lamb cooked slowly with rosemary,
  crushed potatoes with olive oil & chives
- Trio of egg custards (vanilla, coffee & chocolate)

MARTIN SCHMIED, LYON, FRANCE
- Marbled sea bass with mixed vegetables & wasabi cream
- Roast pigeon, legs cooked with green Chartreuse
- Apple strudel

SYLVAIN SENDRA, PARIS, FRANCE
- Carpaccio of Paris mushrooms, clams & citron cream
- Grilled cod & vegetables cooked with preserved lemon
- Carpaccio of chocolate, pineapple, cucumber & basil

PASCAL AUSSIGNAC

. . . .

CLUB GASCON, LONDON, UK
CELLAR GASCON, LONDON, UK
LE COMPTOIR GASCON, LONDON, UK
LE CERCLE, LONDON, UK

Toulouse-born chef Pascal Aussignac worked under several renowned French chefs in Paris before opening Club Gascon in Smithfields, London, ten years ago. Delicious dishes inspired by south-western France have won Aussignac many awards including a Michelin star. A more informal wine bar, Cellar Gascon, and a bistro-deli, Le Comptoir Gascon, followed. At these more informal restaurants smaller dishes of Aussignac's regional French specialities can be tasted.

STUFFED BABY SQUID, BLACK ESCABÈCHE

Separate the heads from the bodies of the squid and reserve them. Rinse and clean the squid bodies and dry them. Heat the olive oil in a frying pan and sear them in the hot pan for a few seconds. Leave to cool. Bring a pan of water to the boil, add the quinoa, and cook, covered, for 15 minutes. Slice the gherkins and cocktail onions and crush the capers and parsley. Add them to the cooked quinoa with the lemon juice and season with salt and piment d'espelette. Stuff the cleaned bodies of the squid with the quinoa mixture.

To make the sauce, heat the oil in a pan and sear the squid heads. Add the flour and 200 ml (7 fl oz) water. Simmer for 15 minutes. Add the white wine, vinegar, sugar and garlic and cook for a further 15 minutes. Process in a blender until smooth and pass through a sieve. Return to the pan, add the ink paste and bring to the boil. Simmer to reduce to the colour and consistency of a shiny glaze. To finish the dish, melt the butter in a large pan, add the stuffed squids and cook until golden. Transfer to a plate and cover with the sauce.

NOTE
Piment d'espelette is a variety of hot red pepper from the Basque region. Black pepper can be substituted.

For the squid:
- 30 whole baby squid
- Olive oil, for searing
- 40 g (1½ oz) butter
- 500 g (1 lb 2 oz) quinoa
- Gherkins, to taste
- Small cocktail onions, to taste
- Capers, to taste
- Flat-leaf parsley, to taste
- Juice of ½ lemon
- Salt and piment d'espelette

For the escabèche:
- Olive oil, for searing
- 100 ml (3½ fl oz) white wine
- 30 g (1¼ oz) sugar
- 1 pinch of flour
- 4 garlic cloves
- 60 g (2 oz) squid ink paste
- 10 g (¼ oz) white wine vinegar
- Salt

Serves 6

TERRINE OF DUCK
FOIE GRAS & FENNEL

For the foie gras:
- 1 x 500–600-g (1 lb 2-oz) raw lobe of duck foie gras
- 4 g (⅛ oz) salt
- Generous pinch black pepper

For the fennel:
- 1 fennel bulb
- 50 ml (2 fl oz) olive oil
- 50 g (1¾ oz) sugar
- 5 g (⅛ oz) salt
- 5 g (⅛ oz) pepper
- 400 ml (14 fl oz) water

For the fennel caramel:
- ½ fennel bulb
- 50 g (1¾ oz) icing sugar
- 1 soup spoon honey
- 50 ml (2 fl oz) sherry vinegar
- 50 ml (2 fl oz) balsamic vinegar

Serves 6

Clean the foie gras, removing any nerves and sinews and season with salt and pepper. Slice the fennel into 1-cm (½-inch) slices and place in a pan. Add the olive oil, sugar and salt and 400 ml (14 fl oz) water, then cook gently until very soft. Allow to cool. Preheat the oven to 80°C/175°F/Gas Mark ½. In a small terrine, layer the fennel and the foie gras on top of each other until they almost reach the top of the dish. Cover the terrine with aluminium foil and half-fill a roasting tin with boiling water. Put the terrine in the tin and cook in the oven for 45 minutes. Once cooked, allow to cool and refrigerate for at least 24 hours with weights on top of it.

To make the caramel, slice the fennel finely and cook slowly in a pan over a gentle heat, without allowing it to colour. Add the honey and sugar and continue to cook until the sugar starts to caramelize and turns brown. Add both types of vinegars, cook for 1 minute more, stirring to dissolve any sediment, and pass through a sieve. Using a very hot knife, slice the foie gras terrine and serve with the very finely sliced fennel salad and the fennel caramel.

ROAST RIB OF VEAL,
SAVORA MASH & OLIVADE

Preheat the oven to 180°C / 350°F / Gas Mark 4. Heat the oil in a heavy ovenproof pan. Season the veal with salt, add it to the pan and brown on all sides. Add the butter, and when it has melted and become frothy, transfer the pan to the oven and roast for 45 minutes. Check the veal is cooked by inserting a knife into the centre of the meat. The tip of the knife should feel warm when it comes out. Once cooked, leave to rest for 10 minutes.

While the veal is cooking, prepare the mash. Bring a pan of salted water to the boil and cook the potatoes until tender. Drain and put in the oven for 2 minutes to dry them out. Warm the milk and mash the potatoes in a tall container with the milk, adding the butter and the mustard. The mash should be soft, almost runny. Season with salt and pepper. Do not allow the potatoes to cool down too much while preparing the mash.

For the olivade sauce, bring a pan of water to the boil and blanch the watercress for 6 minutes. Drain, and while it is still warm, process it in a blender with the olives, garlic, basil and lemon juice. Season with salt and pepper and strain through a sieve. To serve, slice the veal, which should be pink in the middle, and serve with the mash and olivade.

For the rack of veal:
- 1 x 4-rib rack of veal
- 1 tablespoon olive oil
- 10 sprigs of lemon thyme
- 30 g (1¼ oz) butter
- 10 g (¼ oz) coarse salt

For the mash:
- 1 kg (2¼ lb) potatoes
- 400 ml (14 fl oz) milk
- 100 g (3½ oz) cold butter, cut into pieces
- 100 g (3½ oz) Savora (sweet) mustard

For the olivade:
- 1 bunch watercress
- 150 g (5 oz) green olives, stoned
- 50 g (1¾ oz) garlic
- 1 bunch basil
- Juice of 1 lemon
- Salt and pepper
- 1 pinch piment d'espelette

Serves 4

GUILLAUME BRAHIMI

BISTRO GUILLAUME, MELBOURNE, AUSTRALIA
GUILLAUME AT BENNELONG, SYDNEY, AUSTRALIA

Guillaume Brahimi was born in France and was invited to train under Joël Robuchon at Jamin, the three-Michelin-star Paris restaurant, at the age of 19. He later began a distinguished career in Australia, opening Guillaume at Bennelong in Sydney to great success. His most recent venture is Bistro Guillaume, where the irresistible authentic French bistro cuisine has gained several awards.

SEARED SCALLOPS WITH CAULIFLOWER PURÉE, SHIITAKE MUSHROOMS & VEAL JUS

- 500 g (1 lb 2 oz) veal shin
- Mirepoix (p.44)
- 2 tomatoes
- ½ garlic bulb
- Peppercorns, crushed
- 1.35 litres (2¼ pints) chicken stock
- 2 kg (4½ lb) cauliflower, cut into small florets
- 170 ml (6 fl oz) whipping cream
- 40 g (1½ oz) butter
- 100 g (3½ oz) shiitake mushrooms, quartered and stalks removed
- 12 large scallops
- Sea salt and pepper
- Chopped flat-leaf parsley, to taste

Serves 4

First, make the veal jus. Place a pan over a high heat. Add the veal bones, mirepoix, tomatoes, garlic and peppercorns, and cook quickly until golden. Transfer to a large pan and cover with cold water. Bring the pan to the boil, then lower the heat and cook for 4–6 hours, skimming any scum from the surface regularly. Strain the liquid into another pan and simmer the liquid to reduce to 250 ml (8 fl oz) and reach a sauce-like consistency. Set aside and keep warm.

In another pan, heat the stock and season with salt and pepper. Add the cauliflower to the pan, cover and simmer for about 15 minutes, or until tender. Drain the pan, transfer the cauliflower to a food processor and blend to a purée, then return to the pan. Whip the cream and add it gradually to the puréed cauliflower. Set aside and keep warm.

Melt the butter in a frying pan over a high heat and add the mushrooms. Fry until golden brown, then season with salt and pepper and set aside, keeping them warm. Add the scallops to the pan, reduce the heat slightly and sear them by cooking for 45 seconds on one side, then turning them and cooking for another 10 seconds. Serve the cauliflower purée topped with the mushrooms and scallops, with 2 tablespoons of veal jus poured over the scallops and sprinkled with parsley.

STEAK FRITES
WITH SAUCE BORDELAISE

For the red wine reduction, cook the beef trimmings, carrot, celery, tomato, onion and garlic over a medium-high heat. Cook until the vegetables are soft and translucent, then add the thyme, bay leaves, peppercorns and juniper berries. Remove the pan from the heat and add the red wine. Leave to infuse overnight. The following day, simmer for 6 hours, until at least half the liquid has evaporated. Set aside.

To finish the bordelaise sauce, put the shallots, 140 ml (5¼ fl oz) of the red wine reduction and the veal stock in a pan and cook until one-third of the liquid has evaporated. Add the puréed carrot and the bone marrow, stirring gently until combined. Finally, stir the crème fraîche and lemon juice into the sauce, and set aside.

Heat the olive oil in a heavy-based frying pan and add the steaks, cooking each for 4 minutes on one side. Heat the oil in a deep-fryer to 140°C/285°F and add the potatoes to the hot oil, cooking until soft. Meanwhile, turn the steaks, cook for a further 2 minutes, then add the butter to the pan. Cook for a final 2 minutes, basting the steaks with the melted butter. Set the steaks aside to rest for 4 minutes. Once the potatoes are soft but not coloured, remove them from the deep-fryer and increase the heat of the oil to 180°C/350°F. Return the potatoes to the fryer for a final 2–3 minutes, or until crisp and browned, then remove and drain. Serve the steak and potatoes topped with the sauce bordelaise.

For the red wine reduction:
- 1.5 kg (3¼ lb) beef trimmings
- 1 carrot, chopped
- 1 celery stick, chopped
- 1 tomato, chopped
- 1 small onion, chopped
- 2 garlic cloves, crushed
- 4 sprigs of thyme
- 6 bay leaves
- 30 g (1¼ oz) white peppercorns, roughly crushed
- 15 g (½ oz) juniper berries
- 2 litres (3½ pints) red wine

For the bordelaise sauce:
- 115 g (3¾ oz) sliced shallots
- 60 ml (2½ fl oz) veal stock
- 1 large carrot, puréed
- 2–3 slices bone marrow
- ½ tablespoon crème fraîche
- 1 teaspoon lemon juice

For the steak frites:
- 50 ml (2 fl oz) extra-virgin olive oil
- 4 x 200-g (7-oz) beef fillets
- 4 large Desirée potatoes, peeled and cut into 1-cm (½-inch) thick strips
- 50 g (1¾ oz) unsalted butter
- Salt and pepper
- Oil, plus extra for deep-frying

Serves 4

POIRES BELLE-HÉLÈNE
WITH VANILLA ICE CREAM

- 550 ml (1 pint) double cream
- 650 ml (1 pint 3 fl oz) milk
- 2 vanilla pods
- 200 g (7 oz) egg yolks
- 550 g (1 lb 3 oz) caster sugar
- 4 perfect Williams pears, peeled and cored
- 1 tablespoon honey
- 200 g (7 oz) couverture chocolate, chopped
- 30 g (1¼ oz) butter

Serves 4

To make the ice cream, place a pan over a medium heat and add 500 ml (18 fl oz) cream and 500 ml (18 fl oz) milk. Bring to the boil, adding the seeds of one of the vanilla pods. In a bowl, whisk the egg yolks with 200 g (7 oz) of the sugar, until well combined. Gradually add one-third of the cream and milk to the egg mixture, stirring slowly. Add the egg and sugar mixture to the pan, then stir over a medium heat until the custard reaches 80–85°C/175–185°F, or until it is thick enough to coat the back of a spoon. Strain the mixture through a sieve and refrigerate. The next day, churn in an ice-cream machine.

To poach the pears, place a pan over a high heat, add 670 ml (1 pint 3 fl oz) water, the remaining sugar and the second vanilla pod. Bring the mixture to the boil, then reduce the heat and add the pears. Simmer for 10 minutes, then allow to cool in the syrup and refrigerate. For the sauce, put the honey and the remaining milk and cream in a pan and bring the mixture to the boil, then add the chocolate and whisk until smooth over a gentle heat. Finally, whisk in the butter. Serve the chilled pears with the ice cream and warm sauce.

NOTE
Couverture chocolate has a high percentage of cocoa butter, which means it melts well, but any other good quality dark chocolate can also be used.

THIERRY BRETON

CHEZ MICHEL, PARIS, FRANCE

Thierry Breton was born in Rennes and spent his childhood in Brittany, France. He was one of the first chefs to raise bistro food to a high gastronomic level, serving stylish country food from a modestly priced menu. At Chez Michel he has remained true to his Breton roots.

RED MULLET FILLETS WITH BLACK RADISH RÉMOULADE

Preheat the grill. Rinse the red mullet fillets and wipe them dry, then remove any pin bones, put the fillets in a dish and sprinkle with olive oil. To make the mayonnaise, put the egg yolk in a bowl with the mustard, salt and a little pepper. Add the oil very gradually, whisking constantly to obtain a smooth, thick sauce. Finally, add the vinegar. Mix the mayonnaise with the grated black radish and the chives, spread it on the bottom of a serving dish and set aside.

Season the red mullet fillets with salt and put them skin-side up on a baking tray and grill for 5–7 minutes. Remove the red mullets from the grill, put them on top of the black radish rémoulade and serve immediately.

- 4 red mullets, filleted (reserve the bones to make fish soup)
- 1 black radish, peeled and grated
- 1 tablespoon chives, washed thoroughly and finely chopped
- Olive oil, for sprinkling
- Salt and pepper

For the mayonnaise:
- 1 egg yolk
- ½ tablespoon wholegrain mustard
- ½ teaspoon salt
- Pepper
- 200 ml (7 fl oz) olive oil
- 1 tablespoon white wine vinegar

Serves 4

COUCOU DE RENNES WITH MORELS & VIN JAUNE

- A bird (see note), about 2.5 kg (5½ lb), plucked and cleaned, with the fat, offal, wings and neck
- 125 g (4¼ oz) semi-salted butter
- Guérande fleur de sel
- Pepper
- 1 bulb of garlic, cut in two widthways
- 1 bunch of thyme
- 4 bay leaves
- 200 g (7 oz) chopped hazelnuts
- 200 g (7 oz) shallots, finely chopped
- 5 tablespoons walnut oil
- 600 g (1 lb 5 oz) morels or 300 g (11 oz) black truffle
- 200 ml (7 fl oz) vin jaune
- 500 ml (18 fl oz) thick crème fraîche
- 1 tablespoon sherry vinegar
- 2 bunches watercress, leaves removed from the stalks
- ½ bunch tarragon, chopped
- ½ bunch flat-leaf parsley, chopped

Serves 6

Preheat the oven to 220°C/425°F/Gas Mark 7. Melt the poultry fat in a small frying pan. Add the offal (the comb, liver, gizzards, heart, neck and wings) and cook, covered, over a gentle heat for 30 minutes; drain and set aside. Coat the whole of the outside of the bird with semi-salted butter. Sprinkle the inside and the outside with fleur de sel and coarse ground black pepper. Put the halved bulb of garlic, thyme, bay leaves and the bird in an ovenproof dish and roast for 1½ hours, basting regularly and adding some water if necessary. Add the hazelnuts 15 minutes before the end of the cooking time.

In a large frying pan, fry the shallots in 2 tablespoons walnut oil over a high heat. Add the morels or truffle and season with salt and pepper. Add the vin jaune and continue to cook, scraping the bottom of the pan to release any sediment. Add the crème fraîche and simmer over a gentle heat for 15 minutes. Joint the cooked bird into pieces. Put the pieces in the frying pan on top of the morels and cook for 10 minutes over a gentle heat.

Meanwhile, prepare the watercress and offal salad. In a large bowl, mix 1 tablespoon of sherry vinegar, 3 tablespoons of walnut oil, and salt and pepper. Add the watercress and the cooked offal, and stir to combine. Sprinkle the bird with tarragon and parsley immediately before serving. Take the bird to table in the frying pan and serve the watercress and offal salad separately. Drink Breton cider with it.

NOTE

The *coucou de Rennes,* raised in the traditional way in Brittany, is an old breed of chicken that is now protected and has been given officially approved status. It is a muscular, hardy bird with barred plumage like a cuckoo. It has firm flesh that tastes of hazelnuts. Here, it is accompanied by a watercress salad from Nantes, mixed with its offal braised in its own fat.

VARIATION

. . . .

Add 1 kg (2¼ lb) potatoes instead of, or as well as, the morels. They should be cooked in slightly salted water for 30 minutes in their skins, then cut in half and fried in 200 g (7 oz) slightly browned semi-salted butter. When it has coloured, add 1 bunch each of chopped flat-leaf parsley and tarragon.

PARIS-BREST

The day before, make the choux pastry. Bring 125 ml (4½ fl oz) water and the butter to the boil in a pan. Remove from the heat, pour in the flour and stir quickly with a wooden spoon to make a smooth paste. Put the pan back over a gentle heat and stir for ten minutes to dry out the batter. Remove from the heat, beat in the 2 whole eggs one at a time, and mix well. Allow to cool in the refrigerator overnight.

Next, make the crème pâtissière. Beat the sugar and egg yolks in a large bowl until the mixture turns thick and white. Add the flour and stir continuously, pouring in the hot milk a little at a time. Put the mixture back into the milk pan and cook for 5–6 minutes over a gentle heat. Chill in the refrigerator. Next, make the praline filling. Beat the softened butter and both chocolate spreads together. Mix in the well-chilled crème pâtissière and beat together. Store the praline filling in the refrigerator for 12 hours.

On the day it is to be served, preheat the oven to 250°C/500°F/Gas Mark 9. Pipe the choux paste into 6 circles 8 cm (3¼ inches) in diameter, like bicycle wheels. Put in the oven and cook until the pastry is well risen and golden brown. Turn the oven off and leave the pastry to dry for 3–4 minutes with the oven door open. Remove from the oven and allow to cool to room temperature. Put the chilled praline filling in a piping bag with a fluted nozzle. Once the pastry is completely cold, carefully split it in half with a sharp knife and cover the base with praline filling, using the piping bag to make swirls. Toast the almonds in a pan over a high heat, allow to cool slightly and sprinkle the praline filling with the toasted almonds. Cover with the choux pastry lid and sprinkle the Paris-Brest with icing sugar. Make all 6 Paris-Brests in the same way and arrange them attractively on a serving plate.

NOTE

Created in 1938 in the shape of a bicycle wheel to commemorate the first bicycle race from Paris to Brest, this great classic of French pastry-making is easier to make than you might think. In any case, it is less challenging than this famous race. To guarantee success, the choux pastry and the praline filling should be made the day before serving.

For the choux pastry:
- 40 g (1½ oz) semi-salted butter
- 65 g (2¼ oz) flour
- 2 whole eggs

For the crème pâtissière:
- 150 g (5 oz) caster sugar
- 5 egg yolks
- 100 g (3½ oz) flour
- 750 ml (1¼ pints) hot full-cream milk

For the praline filling:
- 200 g (7 oz) softened unsalted butter
- 150 g (5 oz) Valrhona almond and hazelnut chocolate spread (50% nuts)
- 50 g (1¾ oz) Valrhona almond and hazelnut chocolate spread à l'ancienne
- 400 g (14 oz) crème pâtissière (see above)

To finish:
- 200 g (7 oz) shredded almonds
- Icing sugar, for sprinkling

Serves 6

DANIEL BOULUD

DANIEL, NEW YORK, NY, USA
CAFÉ BOULUD, NEW YORK, NY, USA
DB BISTRO MODERNE, NEW YORK, NY, USA
BAR BOULUD, NEW YORK, NY, USA
DBGB KITCHEN AND BAR, NEW YORK, NY, USA

Originally from Lyon in France, Daniel Boulud has spent the last two decades in America creating a series of successful restaurants serving the very best of French food. His cooking has won many accolades and he is one of the foremost culinary authorities on French cooking in America.

GRILLED MOROCCAN-SPICED TUNA WITH CARROTS & MINT OIL

- 1 bunch mint, leaves only
- 250 ml (8 fl oz) plus 2 tablespoons extra-virgin olive or grapeseed oil
- 3 spring onions
- 5 carrots, cut on the diagonal into very thin slices
- 10 cumin seeds
- 175 ml (6 fl oz) freshly squeezed orange juice
- 1 teaspoon thinly sliced lemon confit
- Salt and pepper
- 5 sprigs coriander

For the tuna:
- 2 teaspoons zaatar
- ¾ teaspoon coriander seeds
- ¾ teaspoon fennel seeds
- ¾ teaspoon cumin seeds
- ¼ teaspoon paprika
- ¼ teaspoon black peppercorns
- ¼ teaspoon cayenne pepper
- 2 pounds tuna loin
- Salt
- 2 tablespoons extra-virgin olive oil
- Vegetable oil, for brushing

Serves 4

For the mint oil, fill a bowl with iced water. Bring a pan of salted water to the boil and blanch the mint for 1–2 minutes, then plunge into the iced water. Once cooled, squeeze out any liquid. In a blender, purée the mint and olive or grapeseed oil until the emulsion is bright green. Strain through a muslin-lined sieve.

For the vegetables, heat 2 tablespoons olive oil in a large sauté pan over a medium-high heat. Cut the onions into 8 wedges and cook, stirring, for 7–8 minutes. until tender and translucent. Add the carrots, cumin seeds and orange juice, reduce the heat to medium-low and cook until the liquid has evaporated. Add the lemon confit and season with salt and pepper. Set aside and keep warm. Just before serving, add the coriander sprigs.

For the tuna, finely grind the zaatar, paprika, coriander, fennel and cumin seeds, peppercorns and cayenne pepper in a spice grinder or pestle and mortar. Cut the tuna into 2.5-cm (1-inch) slices. Season with salt and the ground spices. Drizzle the olive oil over the tuna on both sides. Preheat the griddle and brush with vegetable oil, add the tuna and cook for 2 minutes on each side for medium-rare, then rest the tuna for 1 minute. To serve, place a mound of the vegetables in the centre of each warmed plate. Top with a tuna fillet and drizzle the mint oil around it.

NOTE
Zaatar is a blend of spices including dried thyme or savory, toasted sesame seeds, salt, and sometimes cumin and sumac.

BOEUF EN GELÉE
WITH FOIE GRAS, ROOT VEGETABLES
& HORSERADISH CREAM

Heat a griddle or heavy-based pan until very hot, add the onions cut-side down and cook until blackened. In a deep, tall stock pot, combine the blackened onions, shank bones, garlic, bay leaves, thyme, coriander seeds, parsley, black peppercorns, the green sections of the leeks, sea salt and enough water to cover the beef by at least 12.5 cm (5 inches). Bring to the boil, then lower the heat and simmer for 3 hours, regularly skimming off the foam and any solids that rise to the surface.

Remove the beef from the pot and set aside. Discard the vegetables, herbs, spices and bones. Strain the poaching liquid through a fine-meshed sieve. Wash the pot and add the beef, carrots, celery, turnips, remaining white sections of the leeks and tomato. Pour the reserved poaching liquid back in. Bring back to the boil, reduce the heat and simmer for 1 hour, regularly skimming off the foam and any solids that rise to the surface. Discard the tomato and carefully remove the beef and vegetables from the liquid. Set them aside and leave to cool, then cut the beef and vegetables into 5-mm (¼-inch) dice.

Meanwhile, soften the gelatine leaves in a small bowl of cold water, then squeeze them gently to remove the excess liquid. Strain the hot poaching liquid through a fine-meshed sieve into a bowl. Add the softened gelatin leaves to the hot broth and stir until dissolved. Taste and season with salt, if necessary. Set the bowl over a dish of iced water and stir until the liquid becomes syrupy. Season with salt and pepper, if necessary. Place a thin layer of the jelly in the bottom of a 350-ml (12-fl oz) glass or shallow soup bowl. Top with 1–2 tablespoons of the diced vegetables. Add another thin layer of jelly to cover the vegetables and place a few pieces of foie gras and beef on top. Repeat, making layers until the glass is three-quarters full. Finish with a thin layer of jelly to smooth out the top. Refrigerate for 1 hour to set.

To make the horseradish cream, bring the cream and horseradish to the boil in a small pan. Reduce the heat and simmer until the cream has reduced by half, about 10–15 minutes. Strain the cream through a fine-meshed sieve. Season with salt and pepper. Refrigerate until cool. To serve, spoon the horseradish cream on top of the jelly and spread the cream with the back of a spoon to cover the entire surface. Serve immediately.

- 2 large onions, peeled and cut in half
- 1 beef shank (ask your butcher to de-bone the shank, give you the bones, cut the shank lengthways into 4 x 675–900-g/1½–2-lb pieces and trim off all the fat)
- 1 head garlic, cut in half horizontally)
- 2 bay leaves
- 3 sprigs thyme
- ½ tablespoon coriander seeds
- 10 sprigs of flat-leaf parsley
- 1 teaspoon black peppercorns
- 4 medium leeks, green and white parts separated and trimmed
- 2 tablespoons coarse sea salt
- 4 medium carrots, trimmed
- 4 stalks celery, trimmed and cut into 15-cm (6-inch) segments
- 4 turnips, trimmed
- 1 large beefsteak tomato, cut in half and de-seeded
- Salt and white pepper
- 8 x 2-g (⅛-inch) gelatine leaves
- 120 g (4 oz) foie gras terrine, cut into 5-mm (¼-inch) dice

For the horseradish cream:
- 250 ml (8 fl oz) double cream
- 30 g (1¼ oz) finely grated fresh horseradish
- Salt and pepper

Serves 6

TOMATO TART TATIN

- 450 g (1 lb) frozen puff pastry
- 1 egg whisked with 1 teaspoon water
- 10 large plum tomatoes, cut horizontally into 2-mm (⅛-inch) slices
- Salt and pepper
- 2 tablespoons extra-virgin olive oil
- 2 tablespoons unsalted butter
- 2 medium yellow onions, about 200 g (7 oz) each, peeled and thinly sliced
- 4 sprigs thyme, leaves only
- Salt and pepper
- 120 g (4 oz) fresh goat's milk cheese, softened
- 2 teaspoons mascarpone cheese
- 2 teaspoons double cream
- 2 tablespoons pesto sauce, plus extra for drizzling
- 4 tablespoons finely chopped shallots
- 2 tablespoons finely chopped chives
- 1 teaspoon finely chopped garlic
- 2 small heads frisée lettuce, white and light yellow parts only, trimmed, washed and dried, or 120 g (4 oz) mesclun
- 16 kalamata olives, pitted and halved
- 16 cherry tomatoes, cut in half
- 8 chives, cut into 1-cm (½-inch) batons
- 60 ml (2½ fl oz) extra-virgin olive oil
- 1 tablespoon freshly squeezed lemon juice

Serves 8

Preheat the oven to 200°C/400°F/Gas Mark 6 and put one of the shelves in the middle of the oven. Line a baking tray with parchment paper. Roll the puff pastry out on a lightly floured surface to a thickness of 3 mm (⅛ inch). Cut the dough into 4 x 10-cm (4-inch) diameter circles. Place the circles on the prepared baking tray and refrigerate for 15 minutes. Brush the circles with egg wash and prick the surface with a fork. Bake until golden brown (10–12 minutes). Transfer to a wire rack to cool.

Place the tomato slices in an even layer on baking trays lined with several layers of kitchen paper. Season with salt and allow the sliced tomatoes to drain in the refrigerator for 2–3 hours. Preheat the oven to 180°C/350°F/Gas Mark 4. Brush ½ tablespoon olive oil in the bottoms of 4 x 10-cm (4-inch) non-stick round tart tins. Arrange the tomato slices in an overlapping circle in the bottom of each tart tin. Season with salt and pepper. Bake until the tomatoes are soft (about 10 minutes). Using the back of a spoon, press tomatoes flat into their tins. In a large sauté pan, melt the butter over a medium-low heat. Add the onions and thyme and season with salt and pepper. Cook until the onions start to caramelize (10–15 minutes). When brown, remove and set aside.

In a small bowl, mix together the goat's milk cheese, mascarpone, double cream, pesto sauce, shallots, chives and garlic. Season with salt and pepper. To serve, place a scoop of the goat's milk cheese mixture in the centre of the warm tomatoes. Divide the warm caramelized onions evenly over the goat's milk cheese and top with a puff pastry circle. Invert each tomato tart onto the centre of each plate and remove the moulds. If necessary, use a spoon to gently tap the bottom of the moulds to release the tarts. In a bowl, toss together the frisée or mesclun, olives, tomatoes, chives, olive oil and lemon juice. Season with salt and pepper. Place a small mound of the salad on top of each tart. Drizzle some pesto sauce around each plate.

ANTHONY DEMETRE

. . . .

ARBUTUS, LONDON, UK
WILD HONEY, LONDON, UK

Anthony Demetre opened Arbutus and Wild Honey in London 2007 and 2008, where his exquisite but affordable and relaxed style of French cooking has been hugely successful. His refined but traditional French food has won him many fans, as well as Michelin stars.

PIGS' CHEEK, EAR & TROTTER SALAD WITH CRISP BARLEY

Preheat the oven to 160°C / 325°F / Gas Mark 3. Heat 1 tablespoon oil in a heavy ovenproof pan, add the pork and sauté until golden. Remove the pan from the heat, add 1 litre (1¾ pints) water and the sherry, cover and bake in the oven for about 3 hours. When the meat is tender, drain the liquid from the pan, reserve the liquid and allow to cool. Chop the pork coarsely, season with salt and pepper and mix with the sage, shallots and parsley. Using clingfilm, shape the mixture into cylinders, tie at both ends and refrigerate for about 4 hours.

Meanwhile, heat the butter in a pan, and add the apple, kohlrabi and a splash of water. Cover the pan and simmer until the apple and kohlrabi are tender. Blend the mixture to a purée in a food processor. Heat the remaining oil in a pan (rapeseed oil has a great nutty flavour) add the cooked barley, if using, and sauté until crisp. Assemble the ingredients and serve.

- 2 tablespoons rapeseed or olive oil
- 2 pig's ears
- 1 pig's trotter, split
- 12 pigs' cheeks, split
- 200 ml (7 fl oz) dry sherry
- Salt
- Pepper
- 1 teaspoon chopped sage
- 2 shallots, diced
- 3 tablespoons chopped flat-leaf parsley
- 1 knob of butter
- 1 Granny Smith apple, cut into pieces
- 2 kohlrabi, cut into pieces
- 4 tablespoons pearl barley, cooked and dried on kitchen paper (optional)

Serves 6

SLOW-COOKED BREAST OF LAMB, SWEETBREADS & GOLDEN SULTANAS

- 2 breasts of lamb, bones removed and reserved
- 8 garlic cloves, puréed
- 2 sprigs of rosemary, finely chopped
- Salt
- Pepper
- 100 g (3½ oz) butter
- Olive oil, for frying
- 2 onions, finely sliced
- 1 teaspoon fennel seeds
- 1 teaspoon herbes de provence (mixed dried herbs such as thyme, rosemary and savory)
- 200 ml (7 fl oz) white wine
- 200 g (7 oz) lamb sweetbreads, blanched and peeled (p.363)
- 1 teaspoon honey
- 1 tablespoon balsamic vinegar
- 1 handful golden sultanas
- Vegetable purée, to serve

Serves 6

Preheat the oven to 150°C/300°F/Gas Mark 2. Rub the inner side of the lamb with the garlic, rosemary, salt and pepper. Roll each breast and tie with kitchen string, the skin side outward. Melt half the butter with a little olive oil in a pan just larger than the lamb breasts. Add the lamb and cook for about 15 minutes, or until golden in colour, turning frequently. Remove the lamb and add the onions, fennel seeds and herbes de provence to the pan. Cook for about 15 minutes, until the onions are very soft. Return the lamb to the pan, also adding the wine and reserved bones. Add water to half-cover the lamb, season with salt and pepper and cover the pan with a tightly fitting lid, place in the oven and bake for at least 2 hours, until tender.

When the lamb is tender, remove from the pan and keep warm. Simmer the cooking liquid over a gentle heat until reduced to about 200 ml (7 fl oz). Strain the liquid through a fine sieve. Melt half the butter with a little olive oil in a non-stick pan, increase the heat and sauté the sweetbreads until golden. Add the honey and allow the sweetbreads to caramelize a little. Add the vinegar, sultanas and a quarter of the strained stock and mix thoroughly, then season with salt and pepper. Serve the sweetbreads with the lamb, accompanied by a vegetable purée.

ROAST YELLOW-FLESHED PEACHES WITH LEMON THYME & VANILLA

- 6 large yellow, just-ripe peaches
- 100 g (3½ oz) butter
- 1 vanilla pod, split
- 40 g (1½ oz) caster sugar
- 4 sprigs lemon thyme
- Splash of any stone fruit liqueur

Serves 6

Preheat the oven to 150°C/300°F/Gas Mark 2. Bring a large pan of water to the boil. Score the peaches, cutting crosses in the top and bottom of each one. Place in the pan for about 20–30 seconds, remove and place immediately in cold water. Once cooled, skin the peaches. In a small pan, melt the butter until it begins to foam, then add the vanilla, caster sugar, thyme and liqueur, stirring well. Place the peaches in a large ovenproof dish and pour the butter mixture over them. Sprinkle with 3 tablespoons of water, place in the oven and roast, basting the peaches frequently. Once the peaches are tender, remove from the oven and serve cool.

HENRY HARRIS

. . . .

RACINE, LONDON, UK

Henry Harris trained under Simon Hopkinson at Hilaire restaurant, and later helped set a new standard for French cuisine in the UK at the renowned Bibendum restaurant in London. In 2002 he opened Racine, which has since attracted widespread acclaim and a sheaf of awards for its unpretentious, flavoursome French food and faultless service.

CRAB FLORENTINE

Wash the spinach 3 times in plenty of clean water. Bring a large pan of salted water to the boil, add the spinach for 30 seconds and drain, squeezing out any excess liquid. Return it to the pan with the garlic and crème fraîche and cook for 3 minutes. Blend the mixture to a smooth purée in a food processor, transfer to a small pan and set aside. Place the egg yolks and lemon juice in heatproof bowl set over a pan of barely simmering water, and whisk until the mixture becomes light, moussey and pale. Melt 200 g (7 oz) of the butter, then whisk it gradually into the egg mixture. If it begins to curdle, beat in a splash of hot water. Season with salt and pepper and keep warm.

Preheat the grill. Melt a little butter in a pan and add the crab and Tabasco sauce. Season with salt and cook, stirring frequently. Stir in 1 tablespoon of the chives. Cut the brioche into circles using a cookie cutter. Toast the brioche circles on both sides under the grill, then place them on a baking tray. Spread each slice with spinach purée, top with the crab and spoon over the hollandaise sauce. Grill to a pale brown glaze. To serve, garnish with the remaining chives.

- 125 g (4¼ oz) spinach leaves, with stalks removed
- ¼ garlic clove, crushed
- 1 tablespoon crème fraîche
- 2 egg yolks
- Juice of ½ lemon
- 200 g (7 oz) unsalted butter, melted, plus extra for frying
- Salt and pepper
- 300 g (11 oz) white crab meat
- Tabasco sauce, to taste
- 3 tablespoons chives, finely chopped
- 4 slices brioche

Serves 4

POACHED LEG OF MUTTON
WITH CAPER CREAM SAUCE

- 1 leg of mutton, 80% of the exterior fat removed (it is important to keep on some fat to enrich the poaching liquid)
- 12 large Spanish onions, sliced
- 2 teaspoons Maldon sea salt
- 6 bay leaves
- 1 teaspoon whole black peppercorns
- ¼ stick of cinnamon
- Zest of 1 orange
- 750 ml (1¼ pints) white wine
- About 3 litres (5¼ pints) very light chicken stock
- 300 g (11 oz) unsalted butter
- 4 tablespoons shallot, finely chopped
- 4 tablespoons capers
- 500 ml (18 fl oz) double cream

Serves 6

Put the mutton into a pan and cover with the sliced onions and salt. Tie the bay leaves, peppercorns, cinnamon and orange zest into a piece of muslin and add this to the pan with half the white wine. Cover with the stock and simmer over a gentle heat for about 3 hours, or until tender, skimming off any residue that forms on the surface.

After 1½ hours, melt 150 g (5 oz) of the butter in a small pan, add the shallots and capers and cook gently until softened. Increase the heat and cook a little longer to colour the shallots lightly. Add the remaining white wine and simmer until half the liquid has evaporated. Drain about 1 litre of the stock from the mutton pan into the shallots and capers, and continue to simmer this mixture until half the liquid has evaporated. Add the cream, simmering until the mixture has the consistency of a glossy cream gravy. Season with salt and pepper and keep warm.

Transfer the cooked mutton to a serving dish and keep warm. Strain the contents of the mutton pan, reserving the onions. Melt the remaining butter in a frying pan, add the onions and cook until the mixture is softened and deep golden. Serve the mutton in thin slices with the caper cream sauce, and garnished with the onions.

NOTE
The mutton stock can be retained and used for making soup.

COLONEL

- 700 g (1 lb 8½ oz) sugar
- 300 g (11 oz) glucose
- Zest of 5 lemons
- 1 litre (1¾ pints) fresh lemon juice
- 400 ml (14 fl oz) milk
- 400 ml (14 fl oz) crème fraîche
- Russian vodka, frozen, to serve

Serves 6

Put 1 litre (1¾ pints) water, the sugar, glucose and lemon zest in a pan and simmer for 5 minutes. Strain the infusion through a fine-meshed sieve, discard the zest and add the liquid to the lemon juice. In a separate bowl, mix the crème fraîche and milk. Churn one-third of the lemon infusion in an ice-cream maker. When it is nearly frozen, add one-third of the milk mixture. Do not over-churn the mixture once the crème fraîche and milk are added, as it may separate. Transfer to the freezer and churn the remaining batches. To serve, carefully scoop 3 quenelles of lemon sorbet into a chilled ice cream glass. Serve with a shot of frozen Russian vodka.

RIAD NASR
& LEE HANSON

. . . .

BALTHAZAR, NEW YORK, NY, USA

Lee Hanson and Riad Nasr met as sous-chefs at Daniel restaurant. In France, Nasr worked at the three Michelin-starred restaurant Michel Bras. Hanson trained at Aureole, Von and Le Cirque. Working together at Daniel, the duo discovered that their cooking styles uniquely complemented one another. They have been joint head chefs at iconic French bistro Balthazar since its opening in 1997.

ONION SOUP GRATINÉE

Cut the onions in half through the stem end, and cut each half into 5-mm (¼-inch) slices. Heat the olive oil in a 5¼-litre (9¼-pint) cast-iron ovenproof pan over a medium heat. Add the onions and sauté for 30 minutes or until golden, stirring frequently. Add the butter, garlic, thyme, bay leaf, salt, and pepper and cook for 10 minutes more. Increase the heat to high, add the white wine, bring to the boil and reduce the liquid by half. Add the chicken stock and simmer for 45 minutes.

Remove the thyme sprigs and add the port to the finished soup. Preheat the grill. Ladle the soup into 6 flameproof bowls. Place the toasted bread into the bowls, sprinkle the grated Gruyère cheese onto the bread and place under the hot grill for 3 minutes, or until the cheese melts to a crispy golden brown.

- 4 medium yellow onions
- 75 ml (3 fl oz) olive oil
- 1 tablespoon butter
- 1 clove garlic, peeled and thinly sliced
- 4 sprigs of thyme
- 1 bay leaf
- 1 tablespoon salt
- ¼ teaspoon freshly ground white pepper
- 200 ml (7 fl oz) dry white wine
- 2¼ litres (4 pints) chicken stock
- 125 ml (4½ fl oz) port
- 6 slices country bread, about 2.5 cm (1 inch) thick, toasted
- 225 g (8 oz) coarsely grated Gruyère cheese

Serves 6

SALAD NIÇOISE

Place the eggs in a medium pan and cover with water. Bring to the boil, remove the pan from the heat and leave to stand, covered, for 8 minutes. Remove the eggs with a slotted spoon and set aside. (This can be done ahead of time). Peel and cut into quarters just before serving.

In another pan, cover the potatoes with cold salted water and bring to the boil. Cook for 40 minutes, or until tender enough to cut with a fork. While the potatoes are cooking, bring another medium pan of salted water to the boil, add the French beans and cook for about 6 minutes, until tender. Drain and plunge the beans into ice-cold water. Drain, dry on kitchen paper and set aside. Drain the potatoes, and when cool enough to handle, cut into eighths and toss with 60 ml (2½ fl oz) of the balsamic vinaigrette. Set aside.

Season the tuna on both sides with salt and pepper. Heat the olive oil in a large non-stick frying pan over a high heat until quite hot. Sear the tuna for 2 minutes on each side (for rare) or 4 minutes on each side (for well done). Slice across the grain into 1-cm (½-inch) slices. In a large bowl, toss the rocket, peppers, red onion, radishes, tomatoes, French beans and cucumbers with the remaining dressing, so that everything is well coated. Add the potatoes, and season with salt and pepper to taste. Divide the salad among 6 individual bowls. Garnish the top of each salad with a few slices of tuna, 4 hard-boiled egg quarters, 4 olives, and 2 anchovy fillets. Serve immediately.

- 6 eggs
- 4 Yukon Gold or other waxy potatoes
- 175 g (6 oz) French beans, trimmed
- 1 quantity vinaigrette (p.66) made with balsamic vinegar
- 450 g (1 lb) tuna, cut into 5-cm (2-inch) thick slices
- Salt and pepper
- 3 tablespoons olive oil
- 1 bunch rocket, stems removed
- 1 red pepper, cut into thin strips
- 1 yellow pepper, cut into thin strips
- 1 red onion, cut in half and into 2-mm (⅛-inch) slices
- 6 radishes, thinly sliced
- 9 red cherry tomatoes, halved
- 9 yellow cherry tomatoes, halved
- 1 cucumber, peeled, halved lengthways and de-seeded
- 24 Niçoise olives
- 12 anchovy fillets

Serves 6

CRÊPES SUZETTE

- 4 eggs
- 330 ml (11 fl oz) milk
- 125 ml (4½ fl oz) double cream
- 60 g (2 oz) butter, melted, plus extra for frying
- 1 teaspoon grated orange zest
- 120 g (4 oz) flour
- 2 tablespoons sugar
- ¼ teaspoon salt

To serve:
- 4 tablespoons butter
- 1 tablespoon sugar
- 1 tablespoon grated orange zest
- 2 tablespoons Grand Marnier
- Vanilla ice cream

Serves 4

Mix the wet ingredients in a bowl. Mix the dry ingredients in another bowl. Add the wet ingredients to the dry. Leave to rest for at least 2 hours or overnight in the refrigerator. The batter will become thicker, so add a touch of milk to return it to the consistency of double cream.

Heat a 25-cm (10-inch) non-stick or crêpe pan over a medium heat. Brush the pan with a little melted butter. When the pan is hot, add 60 ml (2½ fl oz) of the batter and swirl it around the pan so that it covers the pan evenly. Cook until golden brown, flip it over, count to 10 and remove. Consider the first 2 crêpes as testers and discard them; after this, the pan is ready to go. Crêpes can be cooked the day before using.

To serve, fold the crêpes into quarters. Heat a large frying pan over a medium-high heat. Add the butter and sugar to the pan. When the butter is hot, add the orange zest, toss for a few seconds and add the crêpes. Cook for 1 minute and turn the crêpes over for another minute. Add the Grand Marnier and, standing well back and ensuring the pan is positioned away from anything flammable, carefully tilt the pan towards the flame to ignite the alcohol. When the flame goes out, divide the crêpes onto 4 plates and pour a little of the butter sauce over them. Top with a scoop of vanilla ice cream.

FRANÇOIS PAYARD

· ·

PAYARD PÂTISSERIE & BISTRO, NEW YORK, NY, USA

Born in Nice, François Payard inherited a love of classic French pastry dishes from his parents and grandparents. In 1997, he opened his first restaurant, Payard Pâtisserie & Bistro, on Manhattan's Upper East Side, where executive chef Philippe Bertineau serves exquisite food in the classic French tradition.

GOUGÈRES

Preheat the oven to 200°C/400°F/Gas Mark 6. Line a baking tray with parchment paper. Place 250 ml (8 fl oz) water and the butter in a medium pan over a medium-high heat and bring to the boil. Reduce the heat to low and add the flour, salt, cayenne, and nutmeg. Cook the mixture for 15–20 seconds, stirring constantly, until it turns into a thick paste and comes away from the sides of the pan. Transfer the mixture to the bowl of an electric mixer fitted with a paddle. Mix at low speed, incorporating the eggs, one at a time. Do not add an egg until the previous one is completely incorporated. Add the cream to the mixture while the mixer is running. Then stop the mixer and gently fold in the grated Gruyère with a spatula, taking care not to knock the air out of the dough.

Fit a piping bag with a 1-cm (½-inch) star-shaped nozzle, and fill it with the dough. Pipe 2.5-cm (1-inch) circles of the dough onto the prepared baking tray. Wet a finger and smooth out the top of the gougères. Bake for 10–15 minutes, until golden brown. Remove from the oven and sprinkle grated Gruyère on top if desired. Arrange on a serving dish, and serve warm.

NOTE
Gougères are best served warm, so pipe them at the last minute and bake them just before your guests arrive. Freeze any leftover baked gougères in a tightly sealed plastic bag for up to a month. Warm them up before serving by placing them in a 180°C/350°F/Gas Mark 4 oven for 3–4 minutes.

- 6 tablespoons unsalted butter
- 250 g (9 oz) flour, sifted
- 1 pinch salt
- 1 pinch cayenne pepper
- 1 pinch freshly ground nutmeg
- 5 large eggs
- 150 ml (5 fl oz) double cream
- 420 g (15 oz) grated Gruyère cheese, plus more for garnish if desired

Makes 40

TWICE-BAKED UPSIDE-DOWN CHEESE SOUFFLÉ WITH PARMESAN CREAM SAUCE

For the Parmesan cream:
- **400 ml (14 fl oz) cream**
- **100 ml (3½ fl oz) milk**
- **100 g (3½ oz) Parmesan, grated**
- **Salt and white pepper**

For the soufflé:
- **420 ml (15 fl oz) milk**
- **1 garlic clove, lightly crushed**
- **Salt and white pepper**
- **1 pinch of freshly grated nutmeg**
- **180 g (6¼ oz) butter**
- **100 g (3½ oz) flour**
- **100 g (3½ oz) Parmesan cheese, grated**
- **50 g (1¾ oz) Gruyère cheese, coarsely grated**
- **6 eggs**
- **White truffle oil (optional)**

Serves 12

First, make the Parmesan cream. Bring the cream and milk to the boil and carefully pour into a blender along with the grated Parmesan. Blend until smooth and season with salt and pepper. Set aside. (The Parmesan cream can be made ahead of time and refrigerated for up to 3 days.)

For the soufflé, put the milk and the garlic in a pan, season with salt, pepper and nutmeg and bring to the boil. In a separate pan, melt the butter and stir in the flour to make a roux, then cook for 3–4 minutes. Strain the garlic-infused milk into the pan with the roux and bring back to a simmer, whisking continuously. Place the milk mixture in a mixer fitted with a paddle, mix on low speed and add the Parmesan and Gruyère cheeses. Once the cheeses are incorporated, add the egg yolks. Meanwhile, whisk the egg whites to stiff peaks. Using a large spoon, fold the whipped egg whites into the mixture.

Preheat the oven to 180°C/350°F/Gas Mark 4. Grease some ovenproof ramekins or aluminium timbale moulds generously with oil and place them about 2.5 cm (1 inch) apart in a roasting tin with high sides. Fill the moulds with the cheese mixture using a spoon or a piping bag. Place in the oven and fill the tin with hot water so that it comes three-quarters of the way up the moulds. Bake in the oven for 8–10 minutes.

When cooked, the cheese soufflé should be firm on the outside but very soft and springy to the touch on the inside. Carefully turn the cheese soufflés upside-down into 6 soup bowls and gently remove the moulds. Place the soufflés under a grill for 1–2 minutes, until brown on top. Pour the warm Parmesan cream around the sides of each soufflé. Place a drop of white truffle oil on each soufflé, and serve hot.

BOUILLABAISSE

First, rinse the fish bones under cold running water for a few hours. Heat the olive oil in a large pan, add the onion, celery, leek, garlic, bouquet garni and fennel, and cook gently for 20 minutes. Add the fish bones and cook for 10 minutes more. Add the tomato purée and cook for 5 minutes, then add the Pernod and white wine and simmer to reduce almost completely. Add water to cover the fish bones and bring to the boil, then lower the heat to a simmer. Add the fresh tomatoes, saffron and star anise and cook slowly for 30 minutes, skimming to remove any scum. Grind everything in a food mill or mouli, then strain through a chinois (conical sieve), pressing the bones to extract the liquid. Set the liquid aside and discard the bones.

To make the aioli, cook the potato in salted boiling water with 1 pinch of saffron until tender, then mash it. In a bowl, mix the mashed potato, chopped garlic, egg yolk, salt and white ground pepper to taste, and mix well. Pour in the olive oil in a slow stream, whisking to create an emulsion. Soak the remaining saffron in 1 tablespoon hot water and add to the sauce. Serve the aioli in a ramekin on the side. To make the garnish, slice the baguette in quarters. Sprinkle with olive oil, grill until golden brown and rub with the garlic clove. Place around the ramekin. To serve, transfer the broth to a clean pan and bring to the boil. Add the clams, mussels, fish and vegetables and cover. Ladle into bowls and garnish with chopped parsley.

NOTE
This recipe is by Payard Pâtisserie & Bistro executive chef Philippe Bertineau.

For the broth:
- 4.5 kg (10 lb) fish bones, cut into small pieces
- 60 ml (2½ fl oz) olive oil
- 2 onions, chopped
- 2 stalks celery, chopped
- 1 leek, chopped
- 1 bulb of garlic
- 1 bouquet garni with 2 sprigs of basil, parsley, thyme, rosemary and bay leaf
- 2 bulbs of fennel
- 1 tablespoon tomato purée
- 250 ml (8 fl oz) Pernod
- 250 ml (8 fl oz) white wine
- 10 red plum tomatoes, halved
- 2 pinches saffron threads
- 4 pieces star anise

For the aioli:
- 1 Idaho or other baking potato
- 1 pinch of saffron, plus 1 pinch dissolved in hot water
- 4 cloves garlic, chopped
- 1 egg yolk
- Salt and white ground pepper
- 250 ml (8 fl oz) extra-virgin olive oil

For the garnish:
- 1 French baguette
- 1 garlic clove
- Chopped flat-leaf parsley, to taste

Serves 4

LEMON TART

- **4 unwaxed lemons,**
  zested and juiced
- **3 large eggs**
- **110 g (3¾ oz) sugar**
- **40 g (1½ oz) butter, cut into**
  1-cm (½-inch) pieces
- **1 x 23-cm (9½-inch) sweet**
  pastry case (p.789),
  baked blind

For the garnish:
- **1 lemon**
- **60 g (2 oz) apricot jam, sieved**
  and mixed with 1 tablespoon
  water
- **Mint leaves**

Serves 6

Preheat the oven to 160°C/325°F/Gas Mark 3. Fill a medium pan one-third full of water and bring to a simmer. Put the lemon zest and juice in a medium heatproof bowl and whisk in the eggs. Add the sugar and butter and place the bowl over the simmering water; the water must not touch the bottom of the bowl. Cook, whisking constantly, until the butter is completely melted and the mixture is smooth. Remove the bowl from the pan of hot water and allow the mixture to cool for 15 minutes. Place the sweet pastry case on a baking tray. Pour the filling into the shell and bake the tart for 8–10 minutes, or until the centre is just set. Cool the tart completely on a wire rack.

Next, make the garnish. Using a canelle knife or small sharp knife, cut 6 lengthways grooves in the lemon, removing 6 thin strips of rind. Cut a slice horizontally from the centre of the lemon and place it in the centre of the tart. Slice the remaining lemon halves lengthways in half and then cut the sections into thin half-moon slices. Arrange the slices around the edge of the tart with the cut sides facing out. If necessary, reheat the apricot glaze over a low heat. Using a pastry brush, lightly brush the top of the tart with the warm apricot glaze. Garnish with a few mint leaves.

NOTE

Pastry chefs sometimes make things too complex, but this perfectly simple lemon tart proves that complexity is unnecessary. Some chefs are afraid of tartness, but when people want lemon, they don't want to eat a bowl of sugar. With this tart, you taste the lemon. The pastry case can be made the day before, and so can the filling, but they should be stored separately.

DAVID & MEREDITH POIRIER

LA GRAND BOUFFE, SYDNEY, AUSTRALIA

The menu at Sydney's La Grande Bouffe attests to the experience of restaurateurs David and Meredith Poirier, and the traditional French-influenced menu has created some of the most acclaimed French bistro dining in Australia. Chef Robert Hodgson has explored French cuisine with great energy across a career that has taken him all over the world.

POACHED OYSTERS WITH HAM HOCK & KIPFLER POTATOES

Bring a large pan of water to the boil, add the ham hock and cook for about 2½ hours, or until tender. Meanwhile, cook the potatoes in salted boiling water and break them roughly with a fork. Allow to cool, then and drain, reserving the cooking liquid. Shred 100 g (3½ oz) of the ham, and set the rest of the meat aside for use in other dishes. Melt the butter in a pan, add the ham, potatoes and 400 ml (14 fl oz) of the cooking liquid and 75 ml (3 fl oz) of the vinaigrette. Simmer for 2 minutes.

In another pan, poach the oysters gently for 2–3 minutes in salted boiling water. Add the poached oysters with their juice, the cucumber balls, chives and dill to the vinaigrette. Serve immediately, garnished with the watercress leaves and remaining vinaigrette.

- 1 ham hock
- 15 g (½ oz) butter
- 4 Kipfler or other small waxy potatoes such as Anya
- 100 ml (3½ fl oz) vinaigrette (p.66)
- 12 oysters, freshly shucked and juice reserved
- ½ cucumber, peeled and cut into balls with a small melon baller
- ¼ bunch of dill, divided into small sprigs
- ½ bunch of chives, finely chopped
- 1 bunch watercress

Serves 4

PORK TENDERLOIN WITH CELERIAC CRÈME & PUY LENTILS

- 2 pork tenderloins, cut into 2 pieces and trimmed of sinew
- 1 teaspoon fennel seeds, ground
- 200 g (7 oz) pancetta strips
- 200 g (7 oz) caul, cut into 4 pieces
- 1 celeriac
- 200 ml (7 fl oz) cream
- 100 ml (3½ fl oz) milk
- Salt and white pepper
- 15 g (½ oz) butter
- 100 g (3½ oz) cooked Puy lentils
- 1 garlic bulb, puréed
- 1 teaspoon hazelnut oil
- 100 ml (3½ fl oz) veal jus
- ½ teaspoon sherry vinegar
- ½ bunch flat-leaf parsley, roughly chopped

Serves 4

Preheat the oven to 250°C/500°F/Gas Mark 9. Dust the pieces of pork with ground fennel, roll each in pancetta, then wrap in the caul. Cut half the celeriac into 1-cm (½-inch) dice, bring a pan of salted water to the boil and cook the dice until tender, then drain and reserve. Roughly chop the other half of the celeriac. Heat the cream and milk in a pan and add the raw celeriac. Simmer until the celeriac is very tender and half the milk mixture has evaporated. Transfer the contents of the pan to a food processor and blend to a smooth purée. Season with salt and white pepper.

Heat a griddle, add the pork pieces and cook them quickly on each side until golden brown. Transfer to a baking tray and roast for 6–7 minutes, then allow to rest. Melt the butter in a pan and add the lentils, garlic purée, cooked diced celeriac, hazelnut oil, veal jus and vinegar. Stir well, simmer for 3 minutes and add the parsley. To serve, slice each roasted pork tenderloin and rest for a further minute. Place the slices over a layer of celeriac purée, and spoon the lentil mixture over the pork.

RHUBARB CRÈME BRÛLÉE

- 1 bunch rhubarb, roughly chopped
- 200 g (7 oz) caster sugar
- 10 egg yolks
- 1 litre (1¾ pints) double cream
- 1 vanilla pod, split
- 100 g (3½ oz) soft brown sugar

Serves 8

Preheat the oven to 150°C/300°F/Gas Mark 2. Place the rhubarb in a heavy-based pan and add a quarter of the caster sugar. Cook over a gentle heat until the rhubarb breaks down. In a large bowl, whisk the egg yolks with the remaining sugar until pale and thick. Pour the cream in a pan, add the vanilla pod and place over a high heat. Bring to the boil. Add the cream to the beaten yolks, then strain the mixture through a sieve. Skim any bubbles from the surface. Place a layer of rhubarb in 8 brûlée pots or small ovenproof ramekins and bake for 5 minutes to dry out the rhubarb and prevent it from splitting the brûlée mixture.

Remove the rhubarb from the oven and pour the brûlée mixture carefully into each pot or ramekin. Place the pots in a roasting tin half-filled with hot water and return to the oven for around 40 minutes, until just set. Allow to cool. To serve, top each brûlée with the brown sugar, then caramelize with a blow torch or place under a hot grill until the sugar melts.

FRANCK RAYMOND

MON PLAISIR, LONDON, UK

Franck Raymond achieved two Michelin stars at Le Marignac restaurant in Geneva, opened Le Cheval Blanc in Evian and, on moving to England, worked under Marco Pierre White. As head chef at Mon Plaisir in London, his understanding of French cuisine shines through in the breadth and finesse of his menu.

SCALLOPS COOKED IN THEIR SHELLS WITH HAZELNUT BUTTER

Preheat the oven to 180°C/350°F/Gas Mark 4. Mix the butter with the chives, hazelnuts, breadcrumbs and lemon juice. Season with pepper. Using clingfilm, shape the butter into a roll and refrigerate. Shuck and clean the scallops, and scrub and blanch the shells in boiling water for 5 minutes. Return the scallop meat to the shells and divide the hazelnut butter between them, then roast in the oven for 5 minutes, or until just cooked through.

Meanwhile, divide the rock salt between 4 serving plates to form a bed of salt, which will stabilize the shells. Remove the scallops from the oven, and place the shells on the beds of salt. Season with sea salt and pepper and serve.

For the hazelnut butter:
- 100 g (3½ oz) slightly salted butter, softened
- 30 g (1¼ oz) chives, finely chopped
- 50 g (1¾ oz) hazelnuts, chopped
- 30 g (1¼ oz) fine breadcrumbs
- Juice of ½ lemon
- Pepper

For the scallops:
- 12 scallops in their shells
- 1 kg (2¼ lb) rock salt, to serve
- Sea salt and pepper

Serves 4

BAKED SEA BASS WITH TOMATO CONFIT & BLACK OLIVES

- **1 garlic clove**
- **1 sea bass, about 800 g (1¾ lb), gutted and cleaned**
- **100 ml (3½ fl oz) olive oil, plus extra to serve**
- **50 ml (2 fl oz) lemon juice**
- **50 g (1¾ oz) butter**
- **12 sun-dried tomatoes**
- **12 black olives, stoned**
- **Pepper**
- **Salt**
- **12 basil leaves, chopped**

Serves 2

Preheat the oven to 160°C/325°F/Gas Mark 3. Rub an oven-proof dish with the garlic clove, and place the sea bass in the dish. Pour in the olive oil, lemon juice and 100 ml (3½ fl oz) water over the fish, and dot with the butter. Bake for about 16 minutes, basting frequently. To check whether the fish is cooked, insert a wooden toothpick: it should pass easily through the thickest part of the fish. If it does not, cook for a further 5 minutes before checking again. Just before the fish is cooked, add the tomatoes and olives to the dish and return to the oven.

When the fish is cooked, drain the cooking juices into a small pan, place on a high heat and simmer until half the liquid has evaporated. Add a splash of olive oil and season with salt and pepper. To serve, return the reduced sauce to the ovenproof dish with the sea bass, and garnish with the basil.

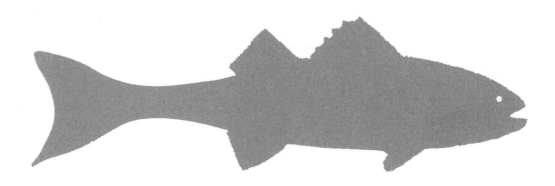

PAN-FRIED CALVES' LIVER
WITH FRESH HERBS & VINEGAR

Season the calves liver with salt and pepper on one side only.
Heat the oil in a non-stick pan. Fry the calves' liver on the seasoned side over a gentle heat for 2 minutes. Season the other
side and turn it over. Add a knob of butter to the pan and cook
for another 2 minutes, basting constantly with the melted butter. When the liver is cooked, place on a warmed serving plate.
Rub the garlic clove over the pan, then discard the clove. Add
half the herbs, the vinegar, crushed back pepper and the stock,
and simmer gently, stirring and scraping the bottom of the pan
to release any sediment. Finally, add the rest of the herbs and
pour the contents of the pan over each slice of liver.

- 4 slices of calves' liver,
  about 180 g (6¼ oz) each
- Salt and pepper
- 50 ml (2 fl oz) peanut oil
- 40 g (1½ oz) butter
- 1 garlic clove
- 50 g (1¾ oz) chopped herbs,
  such as flat-leaf parsley,
  tarragon and chervil
- 50 ml (2 fl oz) red wine vinegar
- 5 g (⅛ oz) crushed black
  pepper
- 150 ml (¼ pint) chicken
  or beef stock

Serves 4

ROAST PEACHES
WITH BASIL & LEMON

Preheat the oven to 240°C/475°F/Gas Mark 8. Cut a cross in
the top of each peach. Place the peaches in an ovenproof dish,
then place a knob of butter on each one, sprinkle with the sugar
and the basil, reserving 3 or 4 leaves. Mix half the lemon juice
with the oil, lemon zest and 100 ml (3½ fl oz) water. Pour the
mixture over the peaches and place the dish in the oven for 25
minutes, basting every 5 minutes.

Once the peaches are cooked, remove them from the dish and
keep them warm. Add the remaining lemon juice to the dish,
place it over a high heat and reduce the liquid to a syrup. Add
2–3 grinds of pepper, the remaining basil and 1 tablespoon oil.
Process the syrup with a hand blender and pour it over the
peaches to serve.

- 8 peaches
- 16 basil leaves, torn
- 30 g (1¼ oz) caster sugar
- 40 g (1½ oz) butter
- Juice of 4 lemons, and zest of
  1 lemon
- 10 ml (½ fl oz) olive oil,
  plus 1 tablespoon
- Pepper

Serves 4

PIERRE SCHAEDELIN

. . . .

BENOIT BISTROT, NEW YORK, NY, USA

Born in Alsace, eastern France, Pierre Schaedelin has worked in many of France's finest kitchens, including the Auberge d'Ill and Le Louis XV. He moved to the USA in 1999 and now heads up Benoit, Alain Ducasse's French bistro in New York, serving authentic fare which reflects his love of French cuisine and its simple flavours.

PIGS' CHEEKS, FRISÉE & LENTIL SALAD, MUSTARD & CUMIN VINAIGRETTE

For the pigs' cheeks:
- 900 g (2 lb) pigs' cheeks
- 1 carrot
- 1 celery stalk, cut in half
- 1 onion, cut in half
- 1 bulb garlic, cut in half
- 4 slices bacon, cut into pieces

For the mustard & cumin dressing:
- 2 tablespoons Dijon mustard
- 3 teaspoons ground cumin
- 330 ml (11 fl oz) vegetable oil

For the vegetables:
- 225 g (8 oz) green lentils
- ½ white onion, chopped
- Salt and pepper
- 1 carrot
- ½ head celeriac
- 225 g (8 oz) frisée

Serves 4

In a large pan, cover the pigs' cheeks with water. Bring to the boil and skim to remove any scum. Add the carrot, celery, onion, garlic and bacon. Bring to a simmer and cook for 2 hours. Remove the pigs' cheeks and set aside. Remove the vegetables and reserve the cooking liquid. To make the cumin and mustard vinaigrette, mix together 125 ml (4 fl oz) of the cooking liquid, the mustard, ground cumin and vegetable oil. Process with a hand blender and season with salt and pepper.

While the pigs' cheeks are cooking, place the lentils in a small pan over a medium heat and add 500 ml (18 fl oz) of the reserved cooking liquid. Simmer until the lentils are tender, then drain and add 2 tablespoons of the vinaigrette and the onion, and season with salt and pepper. Bring a separate pan of salted water to the boil over a high heat, add the carrot and celeriac and cook until tender. Set aside and keep warm. To assemble, season the frisée with the remaining vinaigrette dressing, add the lentils and vegetables and top with the pigs' cheeks.

SKATE WING MEUNIÈRE, BROCCOLI RABE, LEMON, CAPERS, BROWN BUTTER

To prepare the sauce, cut the rind off the lemon and segment it, removing all the pith. Remove the seeds and cut the flesh into small pieces, then set aside. Bring a small pan of water to the boil. Cut a cross in the bottom of each tomato and place in the boiling water for 10 seconds. Remove with a slotted spoon and transfer to a bowl of cold water. Leave for 2 minutes, then peel off the skins. Cut into quarters and remove the seeds, then cut into small pieces and set aside.

To make the croutons, cut the crusts off the bread and cut it into cubes. Melt 4 tablespoons butter in a small frying pan, add the bread cubes and cook, stirring, until golden on all sides. Sprinkle with salt and drain on paper towels. Set aside.

Trim the broccoli until each stem is about 7.5 cm (3 inches) long. Bring a pan of salted water to the boil and cook the broccoli until tender. Keep warm. Put the potatoes in a pan, cover with cold water and add a bay leaf, a pinch of salt and the garlic. Bring the water to a simmer and cook the potatoes gently until tender. Allow to cool slightly, then peel and keep warm.

Pour the milk into a large dish, and add the flour to another large dish. Season the skate on both sides with salt and pepper. Dip each fillet one by one into the milk and flour. Heat the olive oil in a 30-cm (12-inch) frying pan over a high heat. Add the skate fillets one at a time and cook, turning once, until brown on both sides. Repeat for the remaining skate. Set aside. In the same pan, add the remaining butter and cook until it turns brown and smells nutty. Add the capers, diced tomatoes, diced lemon, parsley and croutons. Pour over the cooked skate and serve with the warm broccoli rabe and potatoes.

- 1 lemon
- 2 plum tomatoes
- 1 tablespoon capers, rinsed
- 4 slices day-old white bread
- 225 g (8 oz) butter
- Salt
- 1 bunch broccoli rabe or sprouting broccoli
- 450 g (1 lb) fingerling (long waxy) potatoes, unpeeled
- 1 bulb garlic, halved widthways
- 1 bay leaf
- 120 ml (4 fl oz) milk
- 120 g (4 oz) flour
- 4 skate fillets
- 1 tablespoon extra-virgin olive oil
- 1 tablespoon flat-leaf parsley, chopped

Serves 4

TARTE TATIN WITH CRÈME FRAÎCHE

For the pastry:
- 80 g (2¾ oz) flour
- ¼ teaspoon baking powder
- 50 g (1¾ oz) cold butter
- ½ teaspoon salt
- 1 egg yolk
- 1 tablespoon milk
- 1⅓ tablespoons sugar

For the apples:
- 100 g (3½ oz) sugar
- 1¾ tablespoons butter, plus extra for greasing
- 10 Golden Delicious apples
- 80 g (2¾ oz) butter
- 2 tablespoons sugar
- 225 g (8 oz) crème fraîche

Serves 4–6

To make the dough, preheat the oven to 180°C/350°F/Gas Mark 4. Mix the flour, baking powder, butter and salt in a mixer with a paddle attachment, or by hand in a bowl. Add the egg yolk, milk and sugar to make a dough and mix until it comes together. Rest in the refrigerator for at least 1 hour, and then roll it out to 2 mm (⅛ inch) thick. Cut out circles 20 cm (7¾ inches) in diameter. Bake on a flat baking tray for 15 minutes, then remove and increase the oven temperature to 200°C/400°F/Gas Mark 6.

Peel, core and cut the apples into quarters. Place on a baking tray, brush with melted butter and dust with sugar. Cook in the oven for 20 minutes, then leave to cool. Turn the oven down to 140°C/275°F/Gas Mark 1. Place ovenproof tart tatin moulds or cake tins the same size as the pastry circles on a baking tray. Make the caramel by melting the sugar in a pan over a low heat until it turns brown, then add the butter and whisk carefully to make a smooth mixture. Pour the caramel in the bottom of the tins while it is still hot. Fan out the apples in a circular pattern inside the tins, and cook in the oven for about 1½ hours.

Leave to cool for 1 hour, then place the cooked pastry bases on top of the moulds and flip them over so that the apples are inverted onto the pastry. Serve with crème fraîche.

STEPHANE SCHERMULY

· ·

CHEZ GEORGES, PARIS, FRANCE

Stéphane Schermuly learned about food in the French restaurant run by his family for five generations. His cooking style is simple, traditional and influenced by the Provençal food of his childhood. He is head chef at Chez Georges restaurant in Porte Maillot, Paris, a typically Parisian bistro dating back to 1930, whose regulars enjoy classic, perfectly executed French bistro dishes.

TARTARE OF SEA BREAM & MIXED GREEN SALAD WITH WHOLEGRAIN MUSTARD SAUCE

To make the tartare, cut the sea bream fillets into small dice and refrigerate. Cut the tomato into quarters, de-seed and dice it, and add it to the sea bream along with the shallots, chives and tarragon. Mix the tartare with 1 tablespoon wholegrain mustard, the lemon juice, 1 tablespoon of sunflower oil, and season with salt and pepper. Whisk together 1 tablespoon wholegrain mustard, the sherry vinegar and 3 tablespoons sunflower oil to make a vinaigrette.

To make the sauce, mix 1 tablespoon wholegrain mustard with the single cream and season with salt and pepper. Fill an 8-cm (3¼-inch) cooking ring or cookie cutter with the sea bream tartare, smooth the top and then carefully lift off the ring. Toss the salad leaves with the vinaigrette, then make a mound of them on top of the tartare and spoon the sauce around the tartare. Serve well chilled.

- 3 fresh sea bream, about 600–800 g (1 lb 5 oz–1¾ lb) each, filleted and pin-boned
- 1 large tomato
- 2 shallots, finely chopped
- 1 bunch of chives, chopped
- 1 bunch of tarragon, chopped
- 3 tablespoons wholegrain mustard
- 1 tablespoon sherry vinegar
- 4 tablespoons sunflower oil
- 200 g (7 oz) mixed green salad leaves
- 100 ml (3½ fl oz) single cream
- Juice of ½ lemon

Serves 6

SHOULDER OF LAMB COOKED SLOWLY WITH ROSEMARY, CRUSHED POTATOES WITH OLIVE OIL & CHIVES

- 1 shoulder of lamb, about 2.8–3 kg (6¼–6¾ lb)
- Oil, for drizzling
- 1 onion, diced
- 2 carrots, diced
- 2 tomatoes, de-seeded and diced
- 250 ml (8 fl oz) white wine
- 1 large sprig rosemary
- 150 g (5 oz) butter
- 300 ml (½ pint) olive oil
- 1 kg (2¼ lb) Charlotte potatoes
- 3 garlic cloves
- 2 shallots, finely chopped
- 1 bunch of chives, finely chopped

Serves 6

Remove and reserve the bones from the shoulder of lamb (or ask your butcher to do this for you, keeping the bones) and cut the meat into 50-g (1¾-oz) pieces. Drizzle the meat with the oil, season with salt and pepper then fry it over a medium heat in a cast-iron heavy-based pan with the bones until brown. Remove the meat, add the onion, carrots and 2 cloves of garlic and cook until golden. Add the tomatoes and the white wine, stirring to release any sediment from the base of the pan. Bring to a rapid boil and return the meat with the rosemary. Add enough water to cover the meat, cover and simmer for 2 hours over a gentle heat.

Bring a pan of salted water to the boil, add the potatoes with the remaining garlic and cook for 15–18 minutes. The potatoes should be tender but remain whole. Drain and return to the pan. Add the butter and olive oil, then crush the potatoes using a whisk, and add the shallot and the chives. Keep warm. When the lamb is tender, remove the meat from the sauce and vegetables and remove and discard the rosemary. Purée the sauce in a blender and strain it, then mix with the meat. Arrange the crushed potato on each plate to form a hollowed-out mound and put the meat and sauce in the middle. Decorate with a sprig of rosemary.

TRIO OF EGG CUSTARDS (VANILLA, COFFEE & CHOCOLATE)

- 1 litre (1¾ pints) double cream
- 3 vanilla pods, split
- 10 egg yolks
- 180 g (6¼ oz) caster sugar
- 6 g (1 teaspoon) instant coffee
- 25 g (1 oz) cocoa powder

Serves 6

Preheat the oven to 100°C/200°F/Gas Mark ½. In a pan over a gentle heat, bring the cream to the boil with the vanilla pods. Put the egg yolks in a large bowl. Add the sugar and beat until white and thick. Strain in the boiled cream and stir well. Divide the mixture into 3 bowls and add the cocoa powder to one, the coffee to another and leave the third one plain. Fill 18 heatproof ceramic coffee cups with the mixtures, then bake in the oven. Remove the chocolate pots after 30 minutes and the coffee and vanilla after 50 minutes. Allow to cool, then refrigerate for 4 hours.

MARTIN SCHMIED

. . . .

MAGALI ET MARTIN, LYON, FRANCE

Martin Schmied worked at the Ledoyen, Chez Taillevent and at the Plaza-Athénée restaurants in Paris before opening gourmet bistro Magali et Martin in 2006. His cooking shows a personal style that is still steeped in French tradition. Only three years after opening, Magali et Martin is already a huge success and sets the standard for French bistros throughout the Lyon region.

MARBLED SEA BASS WITH MIXED VEGETABLES & WASABI CREAM

To make the stock, heat the white wine, shallot, soy sauce and garlic in a pan and simmer gently for a few minutes. Add the Hamburg parsley, swede and celery to the pan and cook gently under tender, then lift out with a slotted spoon. Add the sea bass fillets and poach in the stock until just cooked through. Soften the gelatine leaves in a bowl of cold water, then squeeze out the excess liquid. Remove the fillets from the stock and add the gelatine, stirring to dissolve. Season with salt and pepper. Allow to cool to room temperature.

In 2 large teacups or glasses, place a spoonful of the jelly, then a spoonful of vegetables, then a spoonful of fish. Repeat until all the ingredients are used up. Put the cream in a small pan, bring to the boil and simmer until reduced by half. Mix with enough wasabi paste to achieve the strength you like. Allow to cool and pour a small amount on top of the jellies.

NOTE
Hamburg parsley is a root vegetable which resembles parsnip, and tastes like celeriac and parsley.

- 750 ml (1¾ pints) white wine
- 1 shallot, chopped
- Soy sauce, to taste
- 1 garlic clove
- 20 g (¾ oz) Hamburg parsley (see note), cut into strips
- 20 g (¾ oz) swede, cut into strips
- 1 stick celery, cut into strips
- 150 g (5 oz) sea bass fillet, skinned and boned
- 5 gelatine leaves
- Salt and pepper
- 200 ml (7 fl oz) double cream
- Wasabi paste, to taste

Serves 2

ROAST PIGEON, LEGS COOKED WITH GREEN CHARTREUSE

- 1 whole pigeon
- 1 garlic clove
- 1 sprig of thyme
- Oil, for sautéing
- 10 g (¼ oz) raw foie gras
- 1 tablespoon Green Chartreuse
- 1 slice white bread, toasted

Serves 1

Preheat the oven to 220°C/425°F/Gas Mark 7. Clean the pigeon (pp.430–1) and reserve the liver. Place the pigeon in a heavy-based ovenproof pan with the garlic and thyme and roast in the oven for about 15–20 minutes (the meat should be rare). Keep warm for 10 minutes.

Remove the breasts and legs and sauté them in a little oil in a frying pan with the carcass over a gentle heat. Add the Chartreuse, and, ensuring the pan is positioned well away from anything flammable and standing well back, touch a lighted match to the edge of the pan to ignite the alcohol. In a separate pan, fry the liver and the foie gras until just cooked, then process to a purée in a blender. Spread on the toasted bread. Arrange the breasts and legs on the toast on a plate. Strain the cooking juices through a fine-meshed sieve, season with salt and pepper and pour over the meat.

APPLE STRUDEL

For the pastry:
- 250g (9 oz) flour
- ½ teaspoon salt
- 20 ml (1 fl oz) olive oil
- 50 ml (2 fl oz) egg, lightly beaten (approximately 2 eggs)

For the filling:
- 40 g (1½ oz) butter, softened
- 1.5 kg (3¼ lb) apples, peeled, cored and cut into small pieces
- 100 g (3½ oz) sugar
- Ground cinnamon, to taste
- 80 g (2¾ oz) of breadcrumbs
- 80 g (2¾ oz) melted butter

Serves 4

To make the pastry, put the flour and salt in a bowl, add the oil, eggs and 125 ml (4½ fl oz) warm water and mix together to form a dough. Allow to rest for 20 minutes. Preheat the oven to 180°C/350°F/Gas Mark 4. Roll out the pastry very thinly into a rectangular shape on a clean cloth and spread the butter on it with a pastry brush. Sprinkle the apples, sugar, cinnamon and breadcrumbs on top of the pastry. Roll it up from the long end to create a long, flat cylinder, brush with melted butter and bake in the oven until golden.

SYLVAIN SENDRA

ITINÉRAIRES, PARIS, FRANCE

Sylvain and Sarah Sendra opened their first restaurant in Rue Paul Bert, Paris, four years ago. At their hugely popular Itinéraires restaurant, opened in 2008, Sendra cooks inventive and contemporary French bistro food based on fresh ingredients inspired by the local markets.

CARPACCIO OF PARIS MUSHROOMS, CLAMS & CITRON CREAM

Remove the pith and zest from the citron, bring a small pan of water to the boil and blanch it 3 times, changing the water between each blanching. Drain, reserving the final cooking liquid, and process in a blender with the sugar and a little of the liquid to make a purée. Peel the mushrooms, rub them with lemon and slice into very thin strips. Prepare the fennel in the same way. Cook the clams for a few minutes in a hot oven or griddle until the shells open. Discard any that do not open.

To serve, arrange 4 dots of the citron cream on a plate, place the clams on top, and arrange the fennel and mushrooms in a rosette around them. Season with salt and pepper and drizzle on a little olive oil.

- 1 citron
- 10 g (¼ oz) sugar
- 6 large Paris (white) mushrooms
- 1 lemon, cut in half
- 1 fennel bulb
- 20 palourde clams, cleaned
- Salt and pepper
- Olive oil, to serve

Serves 4

GRILLED COD & VEGETABLES COOKED WITH LEMON CONFIT

- 4 thick fillets of cod
- 3 spears green asparagus
- 3 spears white asparagus
- 1 courgette
- 1 sweet red pepper
- 1 yellow carrot
- ½ confit lemon or preserved lemon
- 200 ml (7 fl oz) fish stock
- Salt and pepper

Serves 4

Grill the cod over a barbecue or other open flame until just cooked through. Slice the asparagus, courgette, pepper, carrot and lemon diagonally and thinly. In a heavy-based pan, brown the vegetables for 1–2 minutes, then add the fish stock and simmer, stirring and scraping the bottom to release any sediment. Season with salt and pepper. Arrange the vegetables on the plate, add a little of the fish stock, and place the cod on top. Serve with spoons for the broth.

CARPACCIO OF CHOCOLATE, PINEAPPLE, CUCUMBER & BASIL

- 160 ml (5½ fl oz) double cream
- 200 g (7 oz) plain chocolate, chopped
- 10 small cubes of bread
- 1 tablespoon olive oil
- 50 g (1¾ oz) pineapple, diced
- 1 avocado, diced
- ½ cucumber, diced
- 2 mint leaves
- 2 basil leaves
- Mint granita, to serve (optional)

Serves 4

In a small pan, bring the cream to the boil over a gentle heat and add the chocolate, stirring until melted. Line a baking tray with 2 sheets of greaseproof paper and pour the chocolate mixture onto it. Chill in the refrigerator for 4 hours, until set. Meanwhile, heat 1 tablespoon olive oil in a pan and fry the bread cubes until golden on all sides. Cut out circles of the chocolate mixture 15–20 cm (6–8 inches) in diameter.

Place a chocolate circle on each plate and arrange the vegetables and fruit in the middle of it. Add the mint and basil leaves and sprinkle with the mint granita and croutons sparingly.

GINETTE'S KITCHEN ADVICE

COOKING TIPS

BRAISING BEEF

If the beef is still tough after 2½ hours of cooking, add 2 teaspoons of warmed brandy. This will help tenderize it.

CAKES

Place cooked cakes in their tins on a clean cloth folded into four, and place on a cold stone for 5 minutes. The cake will then turn out more easily.

CLARIFIED BUTTER

To clarify butter, melt it in a pan over a gentle heat. Scum will appear on the surface, but it will disappear and the sediment will remain at the bottom of the pan. Pour off the clear liquid, leaving the sediment behind.

CRÈME ANGLAISE

To rescue a curdled crème anglaise, shake it vigorously in a sealed container or process in a blender.

GRUYÈRE CHEESE

Gruyère cheese can be preserved for longer by wrapping it in a slightly damp cloth that has been soaked in water with a little vinegar. To store it in the refrigerator, put the Gruyère in a box with a lid. Add one or two sugar lumps and replace them when they start to melt. The Gruyère will not dry out.

HOLLANDAISE

To rescue a curdled hollandaise, put 1 teaspoon of hot water into a clean bowl and gradually mix in the curdled sauce.

MAYONNAISE

If the mayonnaise seems to be about to curdle, add a little salt or a drop of vinegar. To rescue a curdled mayonnaise, try one of the following remedies:

- Put 1 teaspoon of mustard in a large bowl and beat in the curdled mixture a little at a time.

- Put a drop of vinegar in a clean bowl and beat in the curdled mixture a little at a time.

- Put ¼ teaspoon of cold water in a clean bowl. Add the curdled mayonnaise a little at a time, stirring constantly.

- Put an egg yolk in a clean bowl, beat well and beat in the curdled mixture.

MILK

If you burn the milk when heating it, keep it warm and immerse a clean damp cloth into it. Remove, rinse and squeeze it out, and repeat until the burnt flavour disappears.

MUSTARD

To prepare mustard at home, put 1 tablespoon of mustard powder in a bowl; trickle in white wine vinegar, stirring briskly, to make a smooth paste. Add 1 teaspoon of olive oil and a pinch of white pepper; finish by mixing well. Allow to rest for 2 days. Transfer to a sealed container. To add flavour to the mustard, macerate chives, tarragon, parsley, peppercorns, coriander or cloves in the vinegar before adding it to the mustard.

RED CABBAGE

Peel and slice an eating apple and add to the red cabbage during cooking. This will give it a delicious flavour.

ROASTING

When roasting meat, sprinkle the bottom of the roasting tin with a little salt. This prevents the fat from burning.

SALT

Add salt at the end of the cooking, as it can sometimes curdle dairy products. To prevent salt from becoming damp in the salt cellar, add a few grains of rice to the cellar. To remove excess salt from an over-seasoned dish, add a sugar lump (remove after 2 seconds) or some sliced raw potato (remove before serving). When soaking a salted meat or fish product, put it in a colander inside the container of water so that it does not touch the bottom. The salt will settle on the bottom of the container. Change the water two or three times.

SANDWICHES

To keep sandwiches fresh, pile them together and wrap in a clean damp cloth.

TOMATOES

Tomatoes can sometimes be watery. If so, cut them in half, sprinkle each half with salt and leave to stand for 30 minutes. Discard the liquid, then cook as usual.

VANILLA SUGAR

To make vanilla sugar, pound 60 g (2 oz) caster sugar with a vanilla pod cut into small pieces with a pestle and mortar. Store in an airtight container.

VINEGAR

To prepare vinegar at home, all that is needed is a small wooden cask holding 10–15 litres. It must be very clean and pierced with two holes: one should be fairly large, a little above the centre, to allow air to enter; the second should be set higher, through which to pour the wine. The cask should be fitted with a tap. Boil 3 litres (5 pints) of good wine vinegar for 10–15 minutes. Pour into the cask and allow to cool. Add a vinegar culture, taken from a cask in the process of fermentation, or bought as 'vinegar mother'. Place a film on the surface, taking care not to submerge it.

Leave for 10 days. Then add 250 ml (8 fl oz) good quality wine every 10 days, and draw off an equal quantity of vinegar.

PLANNING MENUS

We have to eat to live, but it is not enough to consume whatever food comes your way, simply to satisfy hunger. Food should be chosen intelligently, based on what is most nutritious, and the cook must be a good judge of both the quantity and the quality of ingredients. To create a good menu, you must also take into account the needs and tastes of the people you are cooking for.

When planning a menu, use nutritious food at a reasonable price. With expensive food, we are often paying for rarity, appearance or flavouring, or a brand or packaging. Some cheaper ingredients, such as beef skirt, are just as nourishing as expensive ones, such as sirloin, and can be just as tasty if skilfully prepared and elegantly presented. Food is expensive when it provides little nutritional value relative to its cost, rather than due to its high price alone.

Whenever possible, create menus using seasonal ingredients. Out-of-season ingredients are usually expensive, and they will not have as much flavour as when they are in season. Serve a light dish to start the meal to take the edge off hunger. For the starter, offer raw vegetables, mixed salads or hors-d'œuvres. Serve each person only with the amount they need. For less active adults, the evening meal should be light to balance the midday meal. The menus on pp.918–19 give examples of seasonal, balanced meals.

There are many occasions on which it is important to select the menu carefully. For the family, the dishes should be simple but not monotonous. For friends, serve simple but thoughtfully composed meals, each course of which should be cooked with care. Celebrations may be a pretext for forgetting about the need to economize, but one should not forget the principles of nutrition. It is possible to devise a delicious, plentiful meal which is still very nutritious.

When eating out, trust the specialities that are recommended. The restaurant wants to ensure that its clients are satisfied and remain loyal. In all cases, wines should be carefully chosen so that they harmonize with the dishes. If the wine's bouquet clashes with the flavour of a dish, both will be spoiled.

SOUPS AND HORS-D'ŒUVRES

These are important components in creating menus. They help to create an appetite for the rest of the meal, contribute to the balance of the meal and give a good impression of what is to follow.

MAIN COURSES

Usually meat or fish with vegetable accompaniments. The vegetables must be in perfect keeping with the main item in terms of flavour, colour, presentation and culinary style. They must enhance the main item and the sauce without dominating or masking it.

SALADS

Salads are very healthy and support main courses very well. They also aid digestion.

CHEESE

Cheese is high in calcium and is a good addition to a balanced meal. If the starter includes cheese, it is not needed at the end of the meal. Cheese aids digestion and is also much appreciated by gourmets.

DESSERTS

Desserts should supplement the meal and conclude it with a final good impression.

SPRING

- Potato gnocchi   (p.571)
- Pan-roasted turkey breasts   (p.438)
- Braised lettuce   (p.556)
- Yoghurt   (p.121)

• • • • • • • • • • • • • • • • • •

- Pollack or hake mould   (p.245)
- Duchesse potatoes   (p.570)
- Seasonal salad   (p.97)
- Cream cheese   (p.122)

• • • • • • • • • • • • • • • • • •

- Asparagus with mousseline mayonnaise   (pp.71, 145)
- Roast leg of lamb   (p.378)
- Mashed potatoes   (p.568)
- Lemon crème anglaise   (p.694)

• • • • • • • • • • • • • • • • • •

- Raw mushroom salad   (p.527)
- Chicken Marengo with pasta   (pp.453, 625)
- Chocolate mousse   (p.703)

• • • • • • • • • • • • • • • • • •

- Sautéed scallops on lettuce salad   (pp.279, 583)
- Steak   (p.316)
- Creole rice   (p.617)
- Orange salad   (p.661)

• • • • • • • • • • • • • • • • • •

- Radishes   (p.94)
- Flaked skate with herbs   (p.259)
- Steamed potatoes   (p.567)
- Lemon tart   (p.788)

• • • • • • • • • • • • • • • • • •

- Snails with Chablis   (p.111)
- Macaroni loaf   (p.630)
- Mixed salad leaves   (p.97)
- Cheese   (p.122)

• • • • • • • • • • • • • • • • • •

- Artichokes with vinaigrette   (p.92)
- Fillets of sole with tomato and pasta   (pp.264, 625)
- Iced chocolate soufflé   (p.747)

• • • • • • • • • • • • • • • • • •

- Grated carrots
- Rabbit in white wine with sauté potatoes   (pp.480, 574)
- Cherry compote   (p.652)

• • • • • • • • • • • • • • • • • •

- Cucumber à l'antiboise   (p.541)
- Stuffed shoulder of lamb   (p.381)
- Dauphinois potatoes   (p.570)
- Vanilla crème brûlée   (p.705)

SUMMER

- Tomatoes à l'antiboise   (p.579)
- Fried calves' sweetbreads and kidneys with mustard sauce   (pp. 68, 363, 370)
- Potatoes boiled in their skins   (p.566)
- Fruit salad with mint   (p.679)

• • • • • • • • • • • • • • • • • •

- Fresh radishes
- Veal paupiettes   (p.352)
- French beans à l'anglaise   (p.551)
- Plum tart   (p.785)

• • • • • • • • • • • • • • • • • •

- Fresh melon
- Red mullet with tomatoes   (p.260)
- Courgette & tomato gâteau   (p.544)
- Raspberry sorbet   (p.749)

• • • • • • • • • • • • • • • • • •

- Tomatoes with vinaigrette   (pp.66, 578)
- Roast pigeon with peas   (pp.498, 563)
- Peaches Melba-style   (p.664)

• • • • • • • • • • • • • • • • • •

- Asparagus tips in puff pastry   (p.514)
- Steak   (p.316)
- Chips   (p.575)
- Strawberry tart   (p.785)

• • • • • • • • • • • • • • • • • •

- Fresh melon
- Tournedos   (p.320)
- Braised lettuce   (p.556)
- Strawberry or raspberry ice cream   (p.746)

• • • • • • • • • • • • • • • • • •

- Cauliflower loaf   (p.539)
- Red mullet with tomatoes   (p.260)
- Fruit fritters   (p.724)

• • • • • • • • • • • • • • • • • •

- Mixed salad leaves   (p.97)
- Beef with parsley sauce   (p.328)
- Dauphine potatoes   (p.570)
- Raspberries

AUTUMN

- Tomato salad   (p.94)
- Fried beef   (p.329)
- Chips   (p.575)
- Plum compote   (p.674)

• • • • • • • • • • • • • • • • • •

- Cep cassolettes   (p.529)
- Roast pheasant   (p.496)
- Coffee charlotte   (p.698)

• • • • • • • • • • • • • • • • • •

- Mushrooms à la grecque
  (p.95)
- Braised pork with cabbage
  (p.393)
- Pear compote (p.666)
- Langoustine salad (p.287)
- Beef à la mode (p.322)
- Tarte tatin (p.786)

- Fresh melon
- Chicken fricassée (p.448)
- Fresh haricot beans
  à la provençale (p.553)
- Apple fritters (p.724)

- Raw mushroom salad (p.527)
- Chicken terrine (p.455)
- Macédoine (p.96)
- Plum compote (p.674)

- Red cabbage salad (p.95)
- Duckling with tarragon
  (p.435)
- Pear condé (p.651)

- Faubonne soup (p.198)
- Warm pheasant salad (p.497)
- Steamed potatoes (p.567)
- Crêpes filled with jam (p.721)

- Mixed salad leaves (p.97)
- Rabbit with prunes (p.482)
- Mashed potatoes (p.568)
- Richelieu cream (p.701)

- Snails with Chablis (p.111)
- Rabbit stew with pasta
  (pp.482, 625)
- Gingered fruit salad (p.679)

WINTER

- Celeriac salad (p.524)
- Venison chasseur (p.476)
- Apple fritters (p.724)

- Kipper salad (p.250)
- Shoulder of lamb provençale
  (p.382)
- Vichy carrots (p.521)
- Apples châtelaine (p.668)

- Mixed salad leaves (p.97)
- Fillets of sole with tomato and
  pasta (pp. 264, 625)
- Dried apricot compote
  (p.644)

- Spinach soup (p.187)
- Cod steaks (p.243)
- Steamed potatoes (p.567)
- Orange salad (p.661)

- Mussels marinières (p.272)
- Stuffed cabbage (p.536)
- Floating island (p.701)

- Eggs in cocottes (p.152)
- Flaked skate with herbs
  (p.259)
- Diplomat pudding (p.646)

- Red cabbage salad (p.95)
- Haddock in ramekins (p.248)
- Creole rice (p.617)
- Fresh apples

- Marine soup (p.207)
- Potato stew (p.574)
- Lime sorbet (p.752)

CHRISTMAS
& NEW YEAR

COLD MEAL
- Consommé (p.178)
- Oysters (p.275)
- Grey mullet on a macédoine
  (p.258, 96)
- Foie gras in aspic (p.442)
- Christmas log (p.658)
- Fresh fruit
- Duchesse petit fours (p.765)

HOT MEAL
- Bouchées à la reine (p.779)
- Turkey with chestnut stuffing
  (p.439)
- Braised lettuce (p.556)
- Cheese (p.122)
- Christmas log (p.658)
- Duchesse petit fours (p.765)

PICNICS

It is often difficult to think of dishes to prepare for a picnic that can be easily transported. Here are a few ideas.

PASTA SALAD WITH MAYONNAISE

Cook 250 g (9 oz) pasta in boiling salted water. Drain and allow to cool. Flake 1 tin of crabmeat, mix with mayonnaise (p.70) and stir into the cold pasta.

VEGETABLE MACÉDOINE

Prepare a Russian salad (p.588) dressed with a well seasoned mayonnaise (p.70). Take a large long or round loaf. Cut off the top crust. Use a knife to remove the interior crumb and replace it with the Russian salad. Cover with the crust and tie it to make it easier to transport.

STUFFED HARD-BOILED EGGS

Hard boil some eggs (p.134). Leave the shell on and cut in half lengthways. Remove the yolk from each half and pound it, mixing in chopped herbs and a vinaigrette (p.66). Put a small ball of this mixture into each half egg. Put the egg back together and wrap each egg in a square of aluminium foil.

GREEN SALADS

Green salads may be prepared and wrapped in a damp cloth to be transported. Prepare the vinaigrette in advance and pour it into a well-sealed bottle.

ROAST MEAT

All roast meat and poultry can be eaten cold at picnics.

FOIE GRAS MOUSSE

Mix together equal quantities of goose foie gras and very cold butter. Add a little stiffly beaten egg white, or whipped cream.

SANDWICHES

Sandwiches can be prepared with farmhouse bread, fine white bread, brown bread (wholemeal or rye), rolls or very small milk rolls. Sandwiches may be cut into any shape, such as rectangular, square or triangular, and any size. Suitable fillings include olives, cheese, mustard, prawn butter (p.99), anchovy butter (p.100), roast beef, cooked chicken, cured or cooked smoked ham, sausage, mortadella, tongue, foie gras, liver pâté, sardines in oil, tuna in oil, herring or anchovy fillets, smoked salmon, spiny lobster, lobster, prawns, crayfish, tomatoes, radishes, macédoine or green salad. Or, try chopping 1 hard-boiled egg and mixing it with 1 roughly chopped lettuce heart and 4 tablespoons mayonnaise (p.70).

DESSERTS

Rice (p.711) or semolina (p.713) puddings can be easily transported in their mould. Any large or small biscuits are also suitable as desserts for picnics.

MELON SURPRISE

This very refreshing dessert can be tied with string to make it easily transportable, and is very pleasant in summer. Cut a lid from the top of the melon. Scoop out the pips. Scoop out the flesh from the inside and cut it into small pieces. Dice some fruit, such as pineapple, peaches, apricots, pears, apples, banana, strawberries or cherries. Put the fruit and chopped melon back in the melon and cover with caster sugar. Replace the lid. Tie with kitchen string.

THE KITCHEN

Cooking can be time-consuming and painstaking, but a well-designed kitchen can save time and effort. In a well thought-out kitchen you can work methodically and practically. You may not have the perfect kitchen, but you can always organize to make it more efficient, even one with many flaws.

The walls should have a washable painted surface in a light colour and should be tiled to a height of around 2 metres (6½ feet). The floor should have a durable, easy-to-clean covering. Open shelves and cupboards should be kept to a minimum, as it is better to have everything enclosed. Surfaces should be smooth with rounded corners, avoiding mouldings which can be difficult to clean, and all the shelves covered in light-coloured plastic. Avoid displays of innumerable spice jars: their aesthetic appeal is debatable, and they can be time-consuming to clean.

A kitchen should be generously lit, but the lighting can be difficult to adjust. However, opaque glass can be replaced with transparent window panes, and glass panels can be inserted into a solid door. Electric fittings should be placed in the centre of the room and over the various work tops, and good diffusers will make the lighting more pleasant.

The furniture and appliances should be arranged in a logical way so that work can be performed continuously in the right order and the same ground does not have to be covered twice. This saves time and is more convenient, and can be achieved by grouping together the furniture used for different operations, such as food preparation, washing up and eating. A kitchen clock is very useful, particularly if it also functions as a timer. Tea towels also deserve special attention: they must be kept very clean so that any crockery that has just been washed is not contaminated. A good supply of kitchen paper is extremely useful, especially when preparing food, cleaning fish, draining vegetables, and so on.

PUBLISHER'S NOTE
Ginette Mathiot's notes on kitchen design and dining etiquette have appeared in various guises throughout the history of *Je sais cuisiner*. Although some of her suggestions may seem to belong to a bygone era of French home-makers, much of her advice is still relevant for modern cooks today.

To maintain the refrigerator in good working order, ensure the cold air can circulate. Do not cover the plastic racks or over-fill the shelves. It should be defrosted and cleaned once a week. Store the foods logically, taking account of the fact that the coldest part is often at the top, and therefore suitable for meat or fish, and it is less cold at the bottom, and therefore good for storing fruit and vegetables. Wrap food, or put it in boxes with lids, before storing in the refrigerator. In the refrigerator and the freezer, food should be rotated and use-by dates should be checked frequently.

A vegetable rack is a useful way to store potatoes, onions, shallots and garlic. Racks can be fixed under a shelf to save space.

DINING ETIQUETTE

The way a meal is organized is very important: guests should be able to say that the dinner was good and properly served, and everyone feel that special attention has been paid to them. The hosts have the responsibility for all the practical organization. The hosts should lead the conversation, and the liveliness and good manners that will be maintained at the table. This is an important but delicate task; as the eighteenth-century French gastronome Brillat-Savarin said, inviting people to share your table amounts to taking responsibility for their happiness during the whole time that they are under your roof.

A perfect dinner party depends on a well-devised menu, an elegant table, appropriate lighting (perhaps candelabras with candles), a sensible seating plan and efficient service.

Guests must be given a warm welcome. The hosts should be ready to greet guests as soon as they arrive and go to meet them to take them into the living or drawing room. A few friendly words will suffice to introduce the guests to each other.

SETTING THE TABLE

Whatever the occasion, it is important to make the table look welcoming and attractive. Mealtimes symbolize family life, and bring the family closer together. Isn't it sad to sit down at a place laid any-old-how at the corner of the table! But how restful and relaxing to come home after a tiring day to a table that has been laid beautifully. It isn't difficult, it doesn't take long, and the small effort it takes is amply rewarded by the family's pleasure and enjoyment.

It is a good idea to put a woollen or cotton under-felt on the dining table, as it prevents the wood being marked by hot dishes and protects tableware, and it also reduces the clatter of cutlery. The tablecloth goes on top. To avoid a bare table and reduce the amount of laundry, try using individual place-mats, which create a warm, decorative effect more economically.

FOR DINNER PARTIES

PLACE SETTINGS

Each person must have enough space to feel part of things without inconvenience. Allow at least 60–70 cm (24–28 inches) per person. Plates should be laid symmetrically around the table.

CUTLERY

Cutlery is always laid with the fork's tines and the hollow part of the spoon pointing upwards, unless the cutlery is engraved with a monogram or a coat of arms. The fork goes to the left of the plate, the spoon to the right alongside the knife, with its end resting on a knife-rest. Cutlery for later courses, left ready on a side table, is laid onto a clean plate. For dessert, the plates should contain the cutlery for puddings and the cutlery for fruit. For cheese, small plates with a knife and fork should be provided.

GLASSES

A set of glasses should consist of a water glass, a red wine glass and a white wine glass. The glasses are laid in front of the plate; their order varies according to personal taste. As a general rule, three glasses are laid on the table: the water glass in the centre, then, slightly to the right, the glass for red wine and the glass for white wine. This is logical, since the white wine is usually served first, then the white wine glass is taken away when the red wine is served. The champagne flute is laid to the left of the water glass if the champagne is served at the end of the meal, or to the right of the white wine glass if it is served at the beginning of the meal.

SALT CELLARS

Depending on the size of the table, a salt cellar is laid at each end, or two in the middle, with a small spoon, unless each guest has their own salt cellar.

NAPKINS

Depending on whether soup is served, napkins are placed on the plate or at the side. Complicated folds should not be used. Keeping it simple and pretty is much better.

BREAD

Rolls are placed in a fold of the napkin. Sliced bread should be placed in a metal or wicker basket. It may also be placed on a small plate placed on the left of the guest.

MENUS

In front of each guest should be placed a small card, which can be decorated and should show the guest's name and the menu, if desired.

DRINKS

Water should be served in carafes that match the glasses, unless commercial mineral water has been chosen. The table wine is poured into smaller carafes. AOC wines remain in their bottles, except for old wines, which may be decanted.

TABLE DECORATIONS

If the tablecloth is simple, a table runner can decorate the centre. Give full rein to your imagination for your table decorations, as long as they remain unobtrusive and in good taste.

FLOWER ARRANGEMENTS

The use of very large or highly scented flowers should be avoided, as well as tall arrangements that can obstruct the view across the table. A simple straight or curved bouquet of flowers and light foliage, placed directly on the tablecloth, makes an elegant decoration that is simple to create, without being expensive. A floral centrepiece with arrangements at each end of the table requires more flowers and must remain very low. The flowers should be placed in florist's foam (oasis), as this makes arranging them easier and keeps them fresh. A nice basket of fruit may replace the flowers.

TABLE ETIQUETTE

The guests should be seated at the dining table as soon as everyone has arrived. If the dinner is for twelve or more, a small box with the name of the guest may be put at each place. The back of the menu may also be used. The hosts of the house are seated in the middle of the table, facing each other. To the right of each of them are seated the lady and gentleman who command the most respect because of their social position or age. The seating of the other guests demands great tact; ladies and gentlemen should alternate as far as possible. Do not seat together guests who do not know each other, so that conversation does not flag. No-one should sit down before the lady of the house; everyone rises from the table when she does, so she must be careful not to let the meal drag on, while ensuring that she does not give the signal to leave the table before everyone has finished.

ORDER OF SERVING FOOD

The dishes are brought in succession, following the order of the menu decided in advance: soup or hot or cold hors-d'œuvres, depending on the season and circumstances; starters; main dish (fish or meat with accompaniments); vegetables; salad; cheese; dessert; fruit (if the dessert does not include it). The dish of food, placed on a napkin, is offered from the left for guests to help themselves, first to the ladies in order of rank, although a quicker modern practice is now to serve distinguished persons first, then the other guests in turn, without taking their status into account. When the dish has been offered to all the guests, it is taken back to the kitchen and kept hot, while it waits to be offered again. The bread, water and wine are served by the hosts. Drinks are served from the right of the guest if someone is employed to do it.

Between courses, the cutlery should be changed. The host takes from the right of the guest the used plate, on which the fork and knife are placed, and serves the clean plate from the left, with the clean cutlery. Before the dessert, crumbs should be removed from the tablecloth using a special dustpan and small brush, an automatic crumb-sweeper, or a napkin. After oysters or fruit, finger bowls containing warm water and a slice of lemon may be offered, with each bowl placed on a plate. Coffee may be served either at the table, or away from the table in a comfortable group. Cups, small spoons and sugar lumps should be placed ready on a tray and coffee should be served very hot. There should also be liqueurs with their special glasses waiting on a tray for those who want them.

FOR FAMILY MEALS

THE TABLE

Family meals are always simple and require less preparation. The table setting should be less complicated, while remaining welcoming and neat. The table is laid in the same way as for big occasions, but wine glasses are not used. A wine glass may be put beside the water glass. Napkins are placed on the left of the plate; they should be kept strictly for each person and, at the end of the meal, they are placed in a marked ring, or in a cloth envelope, which gives more effective protection. Even the simplest of tables should have a breadboard, a basket to hold the pieces of bread and a bread knife. The salt cellar and oil and vinegar should always be on the table so that the seasoning can be adjusted if necessary.

The dish of food is placed in the middle of the table on a table mat, and everyone serves themselves without standing on ceremony. It is a good idea to prepare as much as possible in advance, if this can be done without affecting the quality. A meal where the cook has to get up several times is badly organized. Where they have to be changed, cutlery and clean plates can be placed on a trolley, but it is better to use as few as possible.

CLEARING AWAY

Once the meal is over, everyone can go about their business happy and well fed, although the table still needs to be cleared by one member of the family, although more people will do it in less time. In the dining room, the table must be cleared and aired, the tablecloth shaken, folded and put away, along with the napkins, in its own place, such as a drawer in the sideboard or cupboard, but always protected from dust. Then the room should be vacuumed, as the dining room is very often also the room where the family spend most of their time. In the kitchen, the leftovers are put in sealed boxes and placed in the refrigerator. They should be eaten as soon as possible, preferably the same evening.

Stacking the crockery makes things easier if it is to be washed up immediately, or makes it ready to be done later: it is not always necessary to wash up after every meal, especially if there is a dish-washer. Plates should be scraped clean and stacked with the cutlery. Or they can be placed together on a cupboard shelf. Pans should be filled with water and left to soak to make cleaning easier. This keeps the kitchen clean, and dirty crockery is out of sight. In this way, washing up can be done only once a day.

RECIPE NOTES

Unless otherwise specified, use a light olive oil, or a flavourless oil such as sunflower or groundnut.

All pepper is freshly ground black pepper, unless otherwise specified.

All herbs are fresh, unless otherwise specified.

All crème fraîche is full-fat; if you cook with half-fat crème fraîche it may split. Double cream can always be substituted for crème fraîche.

All flour is plain white flour, unless otherwise specified.

Eggs are medium size, unless otherwise specified.

Cooking times and temperatures are for guidance only, as individual ovens vary. If using a fan oven, follow the manufacturer's instructions to adjust the oven temperatures as necessary.

Exercise caution when deep-frying: add the food carefully to avoid splashing, wear long sleeves, and never leave the pan unattended.

Exercise caution when flambéing. Ensure that the pan is positioned well away from anything flammable, stand well back and keep the lid of the pan close by.

Some recipes include raw or very lightly cooked eggs, fish or meat. These should be avoided by the elderly, infants, pregnant women, convalescents and anyone with an impaired immune system.

Metric and imperial measurements have been used throughout. Stick to one system consistently to ensure good results.

All spoon measurements are level. 1 teaspoon = 5 ml; 1 tablespoon = 15 ml. Australian standard tablespoons are 20 ml; Australian readers are advised to 3 teaspoons in place of 1 tablespoon when measuring small quantities.

LIST OF RECIPES

SWEETS, PRESERVES & DRINKS

SWEETS

DRINKS

COUNTRY WINES

ALCOHOLIC DRINKS

HOT DRINKS

MAKING JAM

MARMALADES

JELLIES

MENUS BY CELEBRATED CHEFS

PASCAL AUSSIGNAC

GUILLAUME BRAHIMI

THIERRY BRETON

INDEX

Q

marbled sea bass with mixed
vegetables & wasabi cream
908
sea bass in a seaweed
court-bouillon 241
sea bream 246
sea bream à la Monaco 247
sea bream with herbs 246,
297
sea bream with seaweed 246
tartare of sea bream & mixed
green salad with wholegrain
mustard sauce 906
seafood omelette 158
sea urchins 279
seared scallops with cauliflower
purée, shiitake mushrooms
& veal jus 877
seaweed
sea bass in a seaweed
court-bouillon 241
sea bream with seaweed 246
semi-cured saddle of young
rabbit 479
semolina croquettes 713
semolina pudding 713
semolina quenelles 714
semolina squares 714
semoule à la crème 714
shad 223
shad à la chartreuse 224
shad à la portugaise 224
shad montagnarde 225
stuffed shad 223
shallots 28
preserving 843
sheep's trotter rémoulade 387
shelled soft-boiled eggs 132
shellfish à la mornay 288
shellfish debelleyme 288
shepherd's pie 330
shortcrust pastry 784
shoulder of lamb cooked slowly
with rosemary, crushed
potatoes with olive oil &
chives 907
shoulder of lamb provençale
382, *421*
silly biscuits 769

simple croque-monsieur 125
simple rice soup 201
sirop de café 828
sirop de citron 827
sirop de coing 827, *865*
sirop de fleurs de violette 828
sirop de fruits rouges 826
sirop de guimauve 828
sirop de mandarine 827
sirop de sucre 642–3
sirop de thé 826
sirop d'orange 827
skate 259
flaked skate with herbs 259
sautéed skate 260, *300*
skate wing meunière, broccoli
rabe, lemon, capers, brown
butter 904
sliced pears 667
sliced rabbit 484
slow cooked breast of lamb,
sweetbreads & golden
sultanas 887
small custards 704
small meat pies 781
small soufflé biscuits 772
snails 111
snails with Chablis 111, *117*
stuffing for snails 111, *112*
snipe 489
snipe à la grassoise 491
soft-boiled eggs in the shell 132
soft cheese balls 124
soft fruit tart 785
sole 262
Dover sole 262
fillets of sole with tomato 264
fillets of sole Orly 265
fricassée of sole with
asparagus 265
lemon sole 262
sole à la basquaise 264
sole à la normande 263
sole meunière 263, *302*
timbale of sole 266
sole à la meunière 263, *302*
sole à la normande 263
sorbet à l'armagnac 750
sorbet à la citronelle 750

sorbet à la framboise 749
sorbet à la poire 750, *757*
sorbet à la tomate 752
sorbet au cassis 749
sorbet au citron vert 752
sorrel 562
red kidney bean & sorrel soup
199
sorrel omelette 158
sorrel soup 180
soubise sauce 52
soufflé à l'orange 662
soufflé à la vanille 710, *734*
soufflé au chocolat 708
soufflé au citron 710
soufflé de bananes 651
soufflé de langouste 282
soufflé de poisson 291
souffléd fritters 723
soufflé au fromage 128, *165*
soufflé au fruit confits 708
soufflé au fruit rouges 710
soufflé glacé au chocolat 747
soufflé au jambon 398
soufflé aux marrons 659
soufflé aux nouilles 627
soufflé omelette 719
soup à l'aurore 179
soup à l'oignon 191
soupe à l'ail 196
soupe à l'oignon 214
soupe aux choux 187
soupe aux choux de bruxelles
186
soupe de poissons 205, 209
soupe écconomique 195
soupe aux épinards 187
soupe gratinée 191, *214*
soupe au pistou 181, *211*
soupe aux poireaux 195
souvaroff biscuits 765
souvaroffs 765
spaghettis sauce aux noix 634
spaghetti with walnut sauce
634
Spanish hot chocolate 839
spinach 548
eggs vert-pré 147
green spinach purée 43

Phaidon Press Limited
Regent's Wharf
All Saints Street
London N1 9PA

www.phaidon.com

First published in 2009
© 2009 Phaidon Press Limited

ISBN 978 0 7148 4804 4
(UK edition)

Original edition: *Je sais cuisiner*
© Éditions Albin Michel S.A.,
1932, 1959, 1965, 1984, 1990,
2002, 2003

A CIP catalogue for this book
is available from the British
Library.

Translated by Imogen Forster
Illustrated by Blexbolex
Photographs by Andy Sewell
Designed by Sonya Dyakova
Printed in Italy

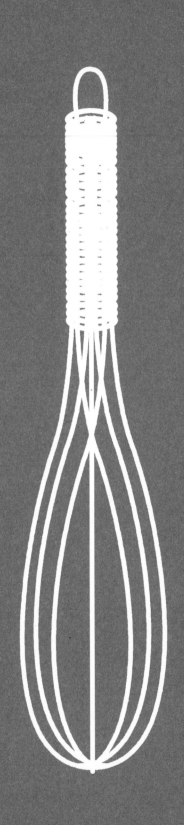